A 21ST CENTURY

ETHICAL TOOLBOX

A 21ST CENTURY

ETHICAL TOOLBOX

SECOND EDITION

ANTHONY WESTON

New York   Oxford
OXFORD UNIVERSITY PRESS
2008

Oxford University Press, Inc., publishes works that further Oxford University's
objective of excellence in research, scholarship, and education.

Oxford   New York
Auckland   Cape Town   Dar es Salaam   Hong Kong   Karachi
Kuala Lumpur   Madrid   Melbourne   Mexico City   Nairobi
New Delhi   Shanghai   Taipei   Toronto

With offices in
Argentina   Austria   Brazil   Chile   Czech Republic   France   Greece
Guatemala   Hungary   Italy   Japan   Poland   Portugal   Singapore
South Korea   Switzerland   Thailand   Turkey   Ukraine   Vietnam

Copyright © 2001, 2008 by Oxford University Press, Inc.

Published by Oxford University Press, Inc.
198 Madison Avenue, New York, New York 10016
http://www.oup.com

Oxford is a registered trademark of Oxford University Press

Library of Congress Cataloging-in-Publication Data

Weston, Anthony, 1954–
   A 21st century ethical toolbox / Anthony Weston. — 2nd ed.
       p. cm.
   Includes bibliographical references and index.
   ISBN 978-0-19-530967-6 (pbk.)
   1. Ethics.   2. Applied ethics.   I. Title: Twenty-first century ethical
toolbox.   II. Title.
   BJ1012.W447 2008
   170—dc22   2007039010

Printing number: 9 8 7 6 5 4 3 2 1

Printed in the United States of America
on acid-free paper

CONTENTS

PREFACE

A 21st Century Ethical Toolbox is a textbook for a first college ethics or applied ethics course, with applications in any course that ventures into practical ethical issues. Its aim is to enable its users to make a more constructive difference, in both word and deed, in problematic ethical situations. In service of that aim, you will find here a wide range of topics, from a careful survey of moral values to tools for critical thinking and creative problem-solving, and finally a set of chapters on putting ethics into action. You will also encounter a wide range of writers, from ancient Greek and Chinese philosophers and the recent pope to contemporary college students, famous novelists, Nobel Peace Prize winners, unsung community activists, and many others too. Good company. I hope you find this book a rewarding, inspiring, and consistently useful resource—a good toolbox indeed.

Dozens of introductory ethics textbooks are available. Mostly they distinguish themselves in subtle ways: a slightly different selection of theories here, a little more history or a more multicultural perspective there. Each approach is important and useful. For better or worse, though, this text differs from the others in bigger and bolder ways.

First, every theme introduced here is directly in service of an engaged and enabled kind of moral citizenship, an improved ethical intelligence. Other skills often lovingly inculcated in ethics courses, such as theory-building and exegetical skills, do come up, but only in the way that music theory might come up in a piano course. We're really here, as it were, to make music.

Second, a far wider range of skills are offered than in traditional ethics texts. Problem-solving creativity may be as crucial to ethical intelligence as responsiveness to values and the analytical and critical skills usually featured in ethics texts. Finding the facts, taking care with the shape of our very speech itself, moral vision and imagination, learning how to "break out of the box" that reduces so many ethical problems to dilemmas between two sharply opposed and supposedly exhaustive options—all have their place here.

Contentious issues are likewise approached with a reconstructive intent. The familiar controversies are here—abortion, animals, sex, environment, social justice—as well as some that may be less familiar. But the familiar arguments pro and con are not the main focus—certainly not the *only* focus—of attention. Moral theories are not deployed as argumentative frameworks, and issuing definitive moral judgments is not the aim. About the various contending arguments we instead shift the questions we ask. Rather than trying to figure out which side is right, we ask what *each* side is right *about*. Then we may be able to find some common ground, or at least some creative ways to shift the problem toward matters that we can do something about—together.

Finally, the working hypothesis of this book is that it is actually possible to make progress on the ethical issues of the day. Thinking clearly about those issues is a good start, for sure, but we can ask for much more than that. We can also make progress on a deeper level: devising new, mutually agreeable ways forward, while strengthening and enlivening the ethical community that enables us to take up any issue constructively together in the first place. The closing section of this second edition—unique, as far as I know, in any ethics textbook—is an extended exploration of how to make real ethical change, built around examples of people and communities who *have*.

TEACHING WITH THIS BOOK

Ethics so conceived readily lends itself to interactive teaching. In fact it *requires* interactive teaching. It requires constant in-class practice. There is no other way to learn it. This book therefore differs from many other ethics texts in pedagogical terms too. It insistently invites, and consistently supports, an active and engaged pedagogy.

Toolbox had its start in ever-growing sets of readings designed to free up my own classes' time for practice. My aim was to collect most of the necessary introductions and discussions and put them in material that could be assigned prior to class and for the most part could be understood by students on their own. At the same time, my focus on teaching constructive ethical skills pushed me into regions and topics not usually visited by ethical philosophers: creative problem-solving in ethics, for example, which recently resulted in a little book by that very title, published by Oxford in 2007, and, more recently, moral vision and imagination. Throughout, my aim is to do the usual work of lecture outside of the classroom, leaving actual class meetings for the class to *work*.

This text therefore invites a wide range of experiential and "applied" activities for an ethics class. Some of these are in-class activities: structured dialogues and workshops, simulations, surveys, idea-generating challenges. Exercises at the end of each chapter introduce some of these activities. My Appendix, "Notes for Teachers," offers follow-up and more suggestions. A second Appendix, by Sharon Hartline of Radford University, frames the pedagogical possibilities in terms of emerging paradigms of experiential education.

Many of these activities in turn aim beyond the classroom. My classes have sponsored workshops on conflict mediation and creativity, staffed local shelters for the homeless, conducted a "Council of All Beings" for the college community to conclude our discussion of environmental ethics, created websites to help local teens think and act responsibly in sexual explorations, and launched an initiative to partner with a local high school to overcome socioeconomic isolation on both sides. Lately I have been structuring my entire course around student-designed ethical change projects, using this book as a conceptual and practical support structure and scaffolding for the process. All of this flows naturally from the *Toolbox*. More, again, in "Notes for Teachers."

CHANGES IN THE SECOND EDITION

This book has been systematically reworked in the course of preparing a second edition. The spirit of the original edition is emphatically preserved—in fact, enhanced. But there are also major changes.

First, the structure is simplified. The book has gone from seven main sections to four, with the third and largest part devoted to a full range of ethical tools. Second, the "applied" sections that concluded the first edition have been replaced. Judging from the reviews, many users used them sparingly if at all. Their themes remain, mostly, but they are framed differently and worked into other places in the text. In their place are three completely new chapters on "Making a Difference": how to put ethics and ethical tools into action.

Part I is now a broad introduction to ethics, conceived as a call to careful and creative thinking, dialogue, and action. The first edition's theme of "Ethics as a Learning Experience" has expanded into an introduction to the possibilities for ethics in this skill-based key. Chapters on ethical dialogue and on service-learning have been moved from the middle of the book to Part I, together with the first edition's chapters on ethics and religion, somewhat revised, and on pitfalls in ethics (now polemically called "Ethics-Avoidance Disorders").

In Part II, "Moral Values," the center of gravity has shifted from the articulation of values, more or less on the lines of traditional ethical theories, to a survey of families of values from a much wider range of sources, including some of the usual philosophical theories of ethics but also religious ethics and Eastern philosophy, and with more attention to multicultural representation as well. The families themselves are now four: the ethics of care and community is disentangled from virtue ethics and gets a family of its own. Here and in Part III there is also less felt need to mediate or "resolve" the conflicts of values that this diversity of sources might create. This too is a preoccupation of the tradition that I am learning to rethink. In the first place, actual conflict is less pervasive than we often suppose, or so I will suggest. Moreover, and most importantly, there are liveable and in fact inspiring ways forward together, despite and sometimes even because of our conflicts—a theme throughout.

Part III combines the first edition's Parts III, IV, and V. Each chapter offers practical tools and skills, some much more fully developed than in the first edition, others scaled back a bit. They also overlap and flow into each other, more than the divided structure of the first edition suggests. All of the old themes are here, though, from critical thinking to creative problem-solving, and there are new ones too, such as moral vision (Chapter 17). "Mindful Speech," by Professor Spoma Jovanovic, is a much better developed replacement for the first edition's chapter on "Watching Words."

Part IV replaces the final two parts in the first edition, which surveyed a range of "applied" ethical issues. Much of this material has been worked into the rest of the new edition as illustrations, exercises, and examples. The all-new Part IV, meanwhile, addresses change-making: how to carry the ethical tools into action that makes a difference. We can change our own lives, and we can change the world, acting individually and also together. Here are tools and stories to open some paths.

This edition has more readings than the first, including a number of quite short pieces, and nearly all of them are new. There were some much-beloved pieces in the first edition, I know—and a few remain—but times and themes have changed, not to mention reprint costs, and others, also truly wonderful, have edged their way in. Many of the authors and/or their representatives were very generous in sharing their writing.

RETURN OF THANKS

More than twenty-five years of teaching ethics in a wide variety of settings leave me with many debts both large and small. First among these is my debt to my students, who have always taught me much and who lately, especially, have answered the challenge to take ethics into action with a range of projects I could never have anticipated but that open up novel and inspiring prospects. Their feedback on the text has also been invaluable. Carry on!

Among colleagues, I am continuously grateful to my collaborators in the Elon University Department of Philosophy—Nim Batchelor, Ann Cahill, Martin Fowler, Yoram Lubling, Stephen Schulman, and John Sullivan—where for some years we have been moving, each in our own interlacing ways, toward a practical ethics in something like the sense laid out here. Other colleagues, far and near and recent and past, have inspired various commissions and omissions: Amy Halberstadt, Peter Williams, Elsebet Jegstrup, Tom Birch,

Betty Morgan, J. Christian Wilson, Bob Jickling, Eva Feder Kittay, Joe Cole, Mike Simon, Richard McBride, and Patrick Hill, as well as a host of others, including my children, Anna Ruth and Molly. A deep bow to you all.

One of the lovely features of the second edition is that some of the users of the first edition have become treasured colleagues and contributors to the second. Among my colleagues, Professors Fowler and Sullivan contribute writing here. Professor Hartline, long ago my student, has authored an energetic and useful Appendix. Professor Vance Ricks of Guilford College has contributed a discussion to Chapter 11, based on a running dialogue we have had for years about the places that critical thinking intersects with and informs ethics. Professor Spoma Jovanovic of the University of North Carolina at Greensboro was a publisher's reviewer between the first edition and the second, and I am indebted to her not only for a detailed and thoughtful review but for showing me how much further the book could go in the direction of communicative ethics. The result is Chapter 13, "Mindful Speech," which she authored.

I am also enormously grateful to many other users of the first edition of this book, along with my little book *A Practical Companion to Ethics* (Oxford University Press, 3rd edition, 2006), whose enthusiasm and encouragement have emboldened me to undertake this second edition. People across the United States and Canada are using this book to approach ethics in a new key, and increasingly in institution-wide general studies programs concerned with moral citizenship and "ethics across the curriculum" as well. I have heard from many and even met some of you. I am honored, and I hope this second edition, tailored with some of your needs in mind, will be even more helpful.

At Oxford University Press, Robert B. Miller patiently nurtured the first incarnation of this project through its slow coalescence and allowed it to come to completion in its own good time. For the second edition he repeated the feat, generally under conditions of more alarm from my end. I could not ask for a more supportive and politic editor. Publisher's reviewers for the first edition were David Boersema, Richard L. Lipke, Verna Gehring, Patricia Murphy, and Jack Green Musselman. Reviewers for the second edition, along with Professor Jovanovic, included Ralph Acampora, Greta Bauer, Deborah Hawkins, and Stevens Wandmacher. Among my colleagues, Professors Sullivan and Cahill read significant parts of the second edition and offered helpful feedback and encouragement. Needless to say, the commissions and omissions that remain—some of them even repeated—are to be charged to me alone.

Finally, I could not have even begun to shoulder the immense practical project of a second edition, let alone actually carry it through, without the utterly reliable and savvy assistance of Beth G. Raps. Brainstorming and inspiring me with ideas about what a second edition could be, casting wide nets for possible new readings, translating pieces when needed, editing and re-editing when called upon, and managing the entire permissions process with unmatchable finesse and the patience and persistence of a saint—Beth's fellow-traveling was invaluable to the whole process. A deep bow of thanks and appreciation to you too.

As always, feedback of all sorts is very welcome. May the circle continue to widen!

Anthony Weston
Durham, North Carolina
January 2007

I

GETTING STARTED

CHAPTER 1

Ethics as a Learning Experience

STEPS INTO ETHICS

On her thirteenth birthday a young friend of mine stood up in her congregation and began to speak about human slavery and "fair trade" products. She'd been reading in Deuteronomy about the treatment of slaves in the ancient world. Her first reaction to this, she told us, was that it is no longer relevant in the modern world, since slavery is dead and gone. But she soon learned otherwise. She had discovered that up to thirty million people live in some form of slavery right now, from sex slaves in Southeast Asia to harvesters of chocolate in western Africa. And she wanted to tell the world—starting with us.

She also took action and invited us to join her. She announced her commitment to buying only products that are certified "fair trade"—produced by workers who are paid a free and fair wage. And indeed, in the celebration of her rite of passage that followed, the only chocolate to be found was fair trade chocolate. Moreover, her choice to bring this cause to her community also informed and inspired others. Even my telling *you* about it, in this book, is another of the widening circles that began with her public commitment.

Of course she had a sense of ethics before this. Something new, though, happened on this day. She claimed ethics for herself. It was no longer a matter of following rules that others posed to her or imposed on her. Now she herself was bringing certain values to the fore and committing herself to act on them. Perhaps she even saw herself in some of those pictures or stories of modern slaves that you can find on the Web. What changed with her "step into ethics" is that ethical rules were now understood from the *inside*...as hers too.

IN THE MIDST OF THE GENERATIONS

You've heard of the Native American idea that we must consider the consequences of our acts for seven generations into the future. We must not consume or despoil the Earth, they say, in ways that will dispossess our descendants.

The "seven generations" idea also can mean seeing yourself in the *midst* of the generations. In a lifetime, if you are lucky, you will actually experience your great-grandparents, as a very young person, and your great-grandchildren, at the other end of life as an elder yourself. This adds up to seven generations, counting yourself in the middle. When you think about what you can or must do, then, you must think as the great-grandchild of particular known people, and likewise as the great-grandparent of particular though not-yet-known people who will inherit this earth after your stewardship.

Again, it changes your view. The world seems deeper and richer and, yes, also harder. It carries with it both love and responsibility. Your ancestors and descendants bear you up, and you also bear them up. That responsibility is now, once again, yours. You claim it from the inside. One of the most powerful imperatives in Native culture is to "Remember who you are!" Responsibility and awareness are one.

AND YOU?

This same kind of shift happens, again and again, with young people in a variety of ways. Some take up the plight of other animals and work in animal shelters or stop eating meat or refuse to do dissection. Others—increasingly, by school requirement, at least at first—take up community service. Some step up to military service; others step up to antiwar activism.

Of course it is not easy to decide what to do or which way to go. Here too the study of ethics can help, but that is not our concern quite yet. The first step is just the awakening itself: a new way of *paying attention*. Certain concerns emerge that were not present at all before or were present only "externally," imposed on you. Now you make them your own. You see a need to act to repair a breach, to make the world better, to involve yourself more deeply in care for others and for the world in its unfolding—and you choose to step into that breach, into action.

It's not just young people, of course. Any of us at any time may awaken or reawaken to the need for ethical attention and care, maybe in directions we hadn't imagined before. High-powered lawyers, jailed for tax fraud, have turned into crusaders for social justice after helping inmates with appeals, all of their ideas about criminals and criminal justice (and lawyers) turned on their heads. Peter Benchley, the author of *Jaws*, was so chagrined by the hysteria his book created that he devoted his life and fortune to shark conservation and ocean protection to try to repair the damage.

Ethical awakening can also be less dramatic and life-changing: it can mean beginning to realize that *what we're already doing* is profoundly ethical. Parenting, for example: the day-to-day care of children, feeding and nurturing and "being there" and eventually learning also to let go. Farming, maybe: nurturing a certain special part of the Earth. Ministering, doctoring, teaching, and indeed probably just about any profession, approached in the right ways.

Keeping a community going. Recognizing and affirming the care and depth in our ongoing work is also a step into ethics.

DEFINITIONS

Ethics invites us, I've said, to attend to the world in new ways. But we need a more formal and focused definition as well. What *is* ethics, exactly?

The basic answer is that *ethics is a concern with the basic needs and legitimate expectations of others as well as our own.* Ending human slavery, passing on the precious gift of the Earth from past generations to our descendants, "being there" for a child or community—these are ways of responding to human and more-than-human needs, trying to reduce or end certain kinds of suffering, stepping up to the needs and expectations of a community or a people. Ethics asks us to look at the "ripple effects" of who we are and what we do, to see ourselves as "one among others."

Basic needs include things like food, clothing, shelter—more broadly, sustenance. Health. Education. Community and a chance to participate. Freedom. A voice. These are goods that all of us need to survive and to have some chance to flourish. I don't mean that people are obliged to simply give these things to anyone in need—that is one possible ethics, yes, but not the only one. Ethics in general, though, requires us to at least pay attention to them—not to live as an island, unaware or unconcerned.

We all have *legitimate expectations* to be treated with respect and as equals. Some legitimate expectations are *rights:* to "life, liberty, and the pursuit of happiness"; to speak your mind or worship as you please; and so on. We also legitimately expect each other (and ourselves!) to act responsibly, keep promises, and so on. There are a variety of views within ethics about how to think about legitimate expectations (what makes some expectations "legitimate"? what is a right? ... and so on)—we come to them in due time.

One more term needs comment: *others.* Ethics, we are saying, is concerned with the basic needs and legitimate expectations of *others* as well as our own. "Others" includes other people, obviously, but may also include (some?) other animals and the natural world too. Exactly what other "others" ethics may include is itself an ethical question.

Finally, note that our own selves are included too. Ethics is concerned with the basic needs and legitimate expectations of others *as well as our own.* Ethics on this definition is not opposed to the self. It does not exclude our own needs and expectations. Quite the contrary: our own needs and expectations are built into the definition. Others' needs get a voice *as well as* our own. The essential thing, though, is that our own needs cannot be the whole story. Ethics connects us to a larger world. The self doesn't vanish—it gets company.

WHY STUDY ETHICS?

Of course it's not as though once you "step into ethics" there's nowhere further to go. Change and growth do not stop. On the contrary, ethics itself requires and provokes constant change and growth.

I ask my students what they've learned about moral values in the last few years. A few say that very little has changed for them. More say that not so much has changed yet, but they're looking forward to it. Most say that they *have* changed, ethically, sometimes in ways they could never have predicted. They travel, for fun maybe, but come back with whole new ideas about life. They learn about some new subject and have to change their ways. They have a friend or a family member who has an accident or a challenged child, and suddenly they have both more sympathy for others and more passion for the moment. Some learn the hard way to see people beyond labels and categories: race categories, sexual orientation, politics. The phrase, "They're people just like me" keeps coming up—something we know (we know the *words,* anyway) and yet, often, don't quite "know" well enough. This too must actually be learned, perhaps again and again.

The story of ethics itself is continuously unfolding. The idea of rights, for example, which most of us take for granted, is a piece of ethical theory that was literally revolutionary in the 18th century. On July 4 we shoot off fireworks and celebrate the Declaration of Independence as if it were the most natural and obvious thing. But it was a radical document in its time—after all, it started a revolution—and even now we struggle to realize the full promise of "all [people] are created equal."

Now instead of Declarations of Independence we are beginning to see Declarations of *Inter*dependence: the insistence that humans are deeply dependent on the rest of the biosphere for health, wealth, and indeed our very survival—and that it would therefore be a good idea to treat nature with more respect. "Environmental ethics" itself is a coming field. So we continue to learn and change. Thirty years ago whales were being slaughtered all over the high seas and no one recycled anything. Now we listen to whale songs on CD, whale hunting is banned (though some still goes on), and recycling bins are everywhere. And we have much further to go.

More of the same is coming down the road. Revolutionary issues will come up, such as an entire range of thorny and unprecedented questions about cloning and genetic engineering. Old issues will come up in new forms, such as questions about privacy rights in an age preoccupied with security. In personal and professional life, "just getting by" by current standards is soon likely to be nowhere near enough. Ethical norms for managers and CEOs are changing so fast that some of yesterday's accepted behavior is already becoming grounds for dismissal, or even jail. Stop learning and the world will pass you by.

CRITICAL AND SYSTEMATIC THINKING

One part of change and growth in turn is critical investigation. The study of ethics requires us to *look into* the issues and possibilities that come up as ethical questions. We need to do more than simply assert what we think is obvious or seek out a few facts that seem to support what we already think. The real challenge is to find out more, to understand better, even if we have to change what we think as a result.

Do children raised by gay couples grow up any more sexually confused than the average adolescent? Is "restorative justice"—reconciliation rather than retribution—possible? How much do animals suffer in laboratories and slaughterhouses? Who actually is on welfare? Do homeless people tend to be drug addicts—or is it that drug addicts tend to be homeless? All of these questions are primarily factual. That is, actual evidence is available, though it can be complex and uncertain at times. Many of these questions have been the subjects of thorough study. You can find some answers—but it takes looking.

Later chapters will explore some of the necessary tools in detail. We will discuss how to discern (all) the values at stake in difficult matters. We'll look at how to "find the facts" when issues turn, as they usually do, on specific facts, and opinion is not enough. We'll explore the uses of language in ethics, and even such seemingly obvious topics as how to have a useful and productive conversation—for it is a remarkable (though melancholy) fact that our collective conversations about ethical matters are very often not conducted in anything like an ethical way themselves. We need to *learn* how to talk things through together.

Learning about other cultures' practices may provoke critical thinking. In Australia many couples live together in so-called "de facto" marriages—a legally-recognized category. They do about as well as the more official kind. You can get marijuana legally in the Netherlands and the result is not disaster. There are some societies that will not tolerate leaving even a single person homeless. Abortion, one of America's most divisive and painful and seemingly fundamental social conflicts over the past thirty years, is barely an issue in many other countries (though now we're exporting it), and historically was not much of an issue even here. Can't we learn anything from all this? Well, sure...

Critical thinking also requires us to generalize our reasons. For example, if you support gay marriage on the general grounds that people ought to be able to choose whatever life partners they wish, then shouldn't you also be willing to affirm marriages of, say, more than two people? Contrariwise, if you oppose gay marriage on the grounds that gay couples can't have their own biological children, then why do we allow infertile people to marry, or people who choose to remain childless? Why do we even allow straight people to have sex when the woman is not fertile? It seems that both positions need to be more carefully thought out. And: what if *most* ethical positions are like that?

Finally, beyond questions of generalizability in turn, there are questions about how our ethical values as a whole hang together. Do they have some common wellspring, some single source? (Does it seem like they might, to you?) If so, what is it? If not, how can we make any practical decisions? All of these questions are part of ethics as well.

CREATIVE PROBLEM-SOLVING IN ETHICS

Putting values into practice also calls for inventiveness—for practical creativity.

> A child in second grade underwent chemotherapy for leukemia. When she returned to school, she wore a scarf to hide the fact that she had lost all her hair. But some of the children pulled it off, and in their nervousness laughed and made fun of her. The child was mortified and that afternoon begged her parents not to make her go back to school. Her parents tried to encourage her, saying, "The other children will get used to it, and anyway your hair will soon grow in again."

Suppose you are the teacher. This is your class. Rights and wrongs are pretty clear in this case, don't you think? You need to defend the afflicted child. You can defend her with more or less skill—maybe by angrily lecturing the class about not hurting her feelings, maybe by telling a parable that makes the point more deftly—but the fact is (so it seems) that you need to read the riot act. This is a time when even young children must take some responsibility to avoid causing hurt. Even second grade is not too early to learn the lesson.

Still, you can predict what the effects will be. A few children will get it, maybe. More are just going to "really feel sorry" for the poor kid, making both her and themselves terribly self-conscious. Others will retreat into sullenness. A few will put on a show of care but keep on taunting her behind your back, maybe even with sharper (because hidden) twists of the knife. And she herself will be even more embarrassed and hurt.

Is there any other way? Are there alternative ways to approach the whole situation so that the class begins to learn the right kind of sensitivity and care but does not end up feeling strained or stuck? Think about it. Really, what would *you* do?

The story continues:

> The next morning, when their teacher walked into class, all the children were sitting in their seats, some still tittering about the girl who had no hair, while she shrank into her chair. "Good morning, children," the teacher said, smiling warmly in her familiar way of greeting them. She took off her coat and scarf. Her head was completely bald.
>
> After that, a rash of children begged their parents to let them cut their hair. And whenever a child came to class with short hair, newly bobbed, all

the children laughed merrily, not out of fear but out of the joy of the game. And everybody's hair grew back at the same time.

This teacher did not lecture or moralize. Indeed, she did not say anything about "the problem" at all. Maybe she even carried on all day as if nothing unusual had happened. Yet in one stroke she did something dramatic and memorable, and morally far more powerful than a lecture ever could be.

We could say it like this: by shaving her own head, she invited the children into a new way of relating to the child with no hair. She showed them that there is something to do besides gape at her or feel sorry for her. The bald child was no longer a problem or an object of pity, but became a playmate with options, just like she was before. Maybe even better.

So we begin to glimpse the possibilities for ethics a little beyond—maybe *more* than a little beyond—what we're usually shown. And notice that this teacher's inventiveness was not just in getting the class to leave the bald kid alone. It was not just a matter of solving the specific practical problem before her. She did much more than that: she created a whole new kind of ethical solidarity in the class, for all the students. This is the key moral lesson: we are all in this together. But the lesson is not taught with any heaviness. Quite the contrary, the teacher's genius was to make it fun—and to show the class a way that everyone can join in.

Last year I had a student who shaved his head, along with all of his family members, in solidarity with his mother who had lost her hair from chemotherapy. Whole city blocks have done it for a stricken neighbor. Fighting cancer is partly a lonely battle, but there is still a great deal that the rest of us can offer. We can all practice more solidarity—and surely there are equally unsuspected and creative ways to do so. This too is ethics!

"Made by Us: Young Women, Sweatshops, and the Ethics of Globalization"

SARAH STILLMAN

Sarah Stillman was an anthropology student at Yale University when she wrote the paper excerpted here, which won first place in the Elie Wiesel Foundation Prize in Ethics Essay Contest for 2005. Today a Marshall Scholar at Oxford, she is writing her Ph.D. thesis on race and gender within mass media coverage of violence against young women and intends to pursue a career in human rights

Reprinted by permission of the Elie Wiesel Foundation for Humanity.

journalism. She is active in the international global justice movement and is author of *Soul Searching: A Girl's Guide to Finding Herself.*

Close your eyes, stick out your finger, and spin the globe. Chances are, you'll land on one of the countless nations where goods destined for the U.S. are being produced with the help of young women's sweatshop labor. In an era when most American manufacturers have discovered the profit-boosting miracle of low-wage off-shore production, teenage girls are increasingly bearing the burdens of globalization while reaping relatively few of its tremendous rewards. Tragedies like Li Chunmei's* no longer read like horror stories from a parallel universe; instead, they seem part and parcel of the ethical crisis plaguing our international corporate economy. Herein lies one of my generation's greatest dilemmas: as global trade opens up new opportunities for society's economic and social advancement, how can we ensure that its path is charted by ethical as well as financial imperatives?

If the developing world's toy industry is any indication, globalization's moral compass is in desperate need of repair. This December, as U.S. college students like me trek home for the holidays, three million toy workers in China alone—the vast majority of whom are young women like Li Chunmei—will be locked inside some 2,800 factories to produce the season's hot new toys in time for Hanukah, Christmas, and Kwanzaa. They will work 15 hours a day, 7 days a week, 30 days a month, while earning wages as abysmal as 12 cents an hour. Many will be required to handle toxic chemicals with their bare hands; some will be physically or sexually abused in the process.

Although China scrapes the very bottom of the sweatshop barrel, exploitative factory work marks a right of passage for young women across the developing world. In Bangladesh, girls as young as 13 stitch caps for American universities like Cornell, Columbia, and Georgetown. In Nicaragua, young women sewing garments for Sears and J.C. Penney recently lost their jobs for demanding the right to unionize. In American Samoa, teenage girls producing clothes for Wal-Mart, Target, and other U.S. retailers were held as indentured servants in the Daewoosa factory—cheated of their wages, beaten, starved, and molested until the factory owner was detained for human trafficking. The depressing inventory of abuses goes on like Satan's wish list to Santa.

Given all this, I am stunned by the mounting gulf between my daily reality and that of the average teenage girl in other corners of the world—places as distant as China and as close as Central America. Has globalization—touted as the great homogenizer—in fact rendered our

---

* The death of a 19-year-old Chinese factory worker from overwork, described in the introduction to this essay (omitted here).

lives unrecognizable to each other? Perhaps the only way to know is to ask, which is why I quickly embrace the chance to visit with Lydda Gonzalez.

When hip-hop superstar P. Diddy launched a new clothing line with the slogan "It's not just a label, it's a lifestyle," I somehow doubt he had Lydda Gonzalez in mind. Lydda, a 19-year-old from Honduras, once sewed shirts for P. Diddy's posh "Sean John" label for the paltry wage of fifteen cents apiece. Like Li Chunmei, she figured that sweatshop labor was her only hope of pulling her family out of poverty.

In 2002, while I was packing my bags for my freshman year of college, Lydda was starting her job with Southeast Textiles—a Honduran factory producing for Sean John, Old Navy, Polo Sport, and other popular name brands. While I was busy attending history lectures and poetry seminars, she was enduring compulsory pregnancy tests, twelve-hour shifts six days a week, and mandatory unpaid overtime. While I was catching up on sleep over summer vacation, Lydda was staring at a pink slip; she and fourteen co-workers were fired from Southeast Textiles after lobbying for better working conditions.

Now, Lydda Gonzalez and I are fighting the wind on a harsh November evening in New Haven, carrying bags of grated cheese and pinto beans to a dinner lecture at Yale's Latino Cultural Center. Lydda shouldn't be toting groceries tonight, I know; she is one of the guests of honor. But, as she jokes in Spanish, *No es nada nuevo:* hard work, for her, is nothing new. Besides, there's a whole lot of food to transport; a big crowd of students and community members will soon gather to eat tostadas and listen as Lydda imparts her striking but sadly quotidian account of working in a maquiladora factory.

This blustery walk is my first moment alone with Lydda since she arrived at Yale in the afternoon with two other Honduran sweatshop workers and Charles Kernaghan, director of the National Labor Committee, a human rights group. The team of four has been traveling the U.S. in a gray van, visiting high school and college campuses in hopes of rekindling the student anti-sweatshop movement. Last week, Lydda and her cohorts Fabia Gutierrez and Martha Iris Lorenzo spoke at a crowded press conference in front of P. Diddy's soon-to-be boutique on New York City's Fifth Avenue, denouncing the appalling working conditions in Sean John factories. Tomorrow, they will share their testimonies before the U.S. Senate. But right now, in the wind that is blowing us sideways and making us huddle close with elbows intertwined, Lydda is mine for a brief flash; the others have scurried ahead. There is so much to be asked.

What does she think of America? It is like *la luna, las peliculas, un sueño:* the moon, the movies, a dream. Is she scared to go home now that right-wing Honduran newspapers have labeled her a terrorist? She refuses to give in to fear; two hundred union members have promised to greet her at the Tegucigalpa airport. What do most girls our age do for fun in Honduras? See movies, go to the *discoteca*, hang out in the street. Does she have a boyfriend? Oh. Do *I* have a boyfriend? We blush.

I already know the more formal details of Lydda's biography. She recited them to a crowd of 70 attentive Yalies earlier this afternoon, and I'd read the *New York Times* and *Washington Post* profiles. I am aware that Lydda began her first job at age 11, working in a bakery. I know that she moved to Honduras's San Miguel Free Trade Zone when she was 17, hoping to find employment inside the maquiladora factories surrounded by tall metal gates and armed guards.

I understand that she was quickly hired by Southeast Textiles. That she sewed 190 Sean John shirts a day. That the only drinking water inside the factory often contained fecal matter. That her supervisor urged her to work faster with shouts of "Donkey," "Bitch," and worse. And the grand finale: that when she finally spoke up and asked to be treated with dignity, she was fired and blacklisted from the Honduran maquiladora industry.

But there is so much more to be known—things that newspaper articles and public testimonies can't divulge about years of sweat and quietly preserved dreams in a world with horizons half the size of my own. I notice it when we stop by my dorm room to pick up the bags of groceries and rest for an instant between the afternoon lecture and the evening dinner event. Lydda and I begin chatting about our dream jobs, and she remarks with a sheepish smile, "I would have liked to be a writer." "Me, too!" I respond, eager for common ground, not realizing until later the vast difference between her "I would have liked to be" and my "I hope to be." I ask if she keeps a journal. "No, when I come home from work at night, my bed is my diary," she replies somewhat cryptically. I want to ask more, but I realize we're late for the dinner. We grab the groceries and run.

Charles Kernaghan, director of the National Labor Committee, has the first indignant words before the crowd at the Latino Cultural Center. His booming voice knows how to command attention; each sentence catapults from his lips like an exclamation point on steroids. He emphatically waves a gray Sean John shirt in the air as he hollers at wide-eyed Yalies: "These women started working when they were eleven years old!…Lydda made 15 cents for this $40 shirt! That's an enormous mark-up: DO THE MATH!"

Once Kernaghan has purged his fireball homily, Lydda walks slowly to the front of the room. "Mi nombre es Lydda Eli Gonzalez, y soy de Honduras…My name is Lydda Eli Gonzalez, and I am from Honduras." The room falls silent. "I am 19 years old."

Lydda, too, has learned the art of working a crowd. But her style takes the audience for a spin: if Kernaghan was thunderous, she's as hushed and concentrated as lightning; if he flung his words like boomerangs, she places each sentence calmly before you in all its naked, unpretentious dreadfulness.

"My job is to attach sleeves to the shirts," she explains. "There is a lot of dust in the air.... You breathe it in, and you go into the factory with black hair and come out with hair that is white or red or whatever the color of the shirts we are working on." She tells of being forbidden to talk to her co-workers, of being sexually harassed by supervisors, and of being searched by random male guards on the rare occasions when she was allowed to use the bathroom. Like any good organizer, Lydda finishes her testimony with an entreaty: "There is too much injustice in the Sean John factory, and that is why I came here.... We sew your clothing. Please demand that the companies treat us with respect. Thank you."...

...When it comes time for Q & A, hands spring up with inquiries about how students can take up arms. "First of all," Charles Kernaghan commands, "realize that there are 15.6 million college students in the U.S. today, and that you have $268 billion dollars a year of purchasing power." In other words, aim and fire with your pocketbooks. "We're not pansies," Kernaghan says, drawing a few laughs. "This is guerrilla warfare."

But Lydda soon chimes in. Her quiet words remind us that the military analogy is more than a cute rhetorical flourish. When she returns to Honduras next week, she explains, she will likely face intimidation and even death threats. Who knows what the Honduran newspapers will call her next; they've already tagged her a "terrorist of the maquila," a liar, and a traitor to her country. But Lydda won't be turning back. Next week, she'll ask to be reinstated at the Sean John factory.

It's clear that we, too, are needed on our home turf: to write letters to Sean John and other companies, to raise consciousness, and—perhaps most significantly—to throw a wrench in the upcoming Miami negotiations of the FTAA and other trade deals negotiated without young women like Lydda or Li Chunmei in mind.

With that rally cry, their talk is suddenly done. People rise in a standing ovation. Some jot down notes on their hands or loose scraps of paper. The room echoes with that strained sense of the in-between: should we cry or should we cheer? Maybe both? As I begin folding chairs, I finding myself wondering how long Lydda's words will fill our heads and hearts.

Soon, we've reached departure time. Lydda grabs my hand. "Continue your struggle," she says, stealing the words from my mouth. I'm not quite ready for her to go. I had promised to play her P. Diddy's latest album; she'd mentioned that, until she came to the U.S., she had no idea whom she was sewing shirts for (that is, until Mr. Kernaghan described P. Diddy as "the ex-boyfriend of J-Lo"). I had meant to ask her about her family and her friends, and maybe to tell her about mine. Instead, we hug. She descends the steps of the Latino Cultural Center into the unfamiliar cold, turning back to wave.

When I return to my dorm that evening, the women's stories weave in and out of my mind. I sit on the couch with my roommate, and we talk about the otherworldliness of having Lydda, Martha, and Fabia in our room just five hours ago, drinking milk and chatting. We feel like fish in dirty water as we use a National Labor Committee report to take an inventory of our suite:

- 1 Nike T-shirt: Made by company that employed Martha for five cents a shirt.
- 1 Adidas soccer ball: Made by company notorious for anti-unionism, low wages, and abuse of young women workers.
- 1 Barbie doll, legs missing: Made in China by Mattel, in factory much like Li Chunmei's, average worker age = 14.
- 2 pairs New Balance sneakers: Chinese workers there are paid 18 cents an hour and forced to live in crammed 12-person dorm rooms.

At some point the list-making gets old. The message is clear. Somehow we've become submerged in a system that genuinely repulses our ethical sensibilities. The 1990's may have been the decade of the depressing sweatshop exposé, but I finally see why the past few years have rendered talk of sweatshops blasé. If we can't untangle ourselves from the corporate icons we depend upon, then the only way to maintain our sanity, too often, is to close our eyes.

My roommate reminds me that Lydda didn't come here to stir up guilt. She came with a mission and finished her talk with a plea: "We need people in the streets." I get online and book an $89 Jetblue flight.

It's settled. I am going to protest the free trade negotiations in Miami.

Three police helicopters hover above our heads like giant, genetically modified mosquitoes. Bright spotlights slice through the dark as throngs of activists hustle in and out of the abandoned warehouse that's been reclaimed as the "Convergence Center"—a headquarters in downtown Miami where people from around the country can gather to plan direct actions against tomorrow's Free Trade Area of the Americas meeting.

This is a motley crew. Some are here because they believe the FTAA will wreak havoc on the environment—ushering the destruction of rainforests, the patenting of biodiversity, and the production of genetically engineered crops. Others are here because they fear the FTAA will enshrine investors' rights at the expense of American workers, causing massive job losses as more manufacturing plants are shipped south of the border.

Still others have come out of anger that the treaty is being negotiated in secrecy, by undemocratic institutions that all but ignore the voices of civil society.

I am here because the moral battle over sweatshops is here. In its current incarnation, the FTAA is structured to drastically accelerate corporate globalization across the Americas—largely at the expense of young women my age. An epic free trade treaty that threatens to repeat the bloopers of past trade agreements on a larger scale, the FTAA will invite U.S. industries to set up factories in Latin America that have virtually no accountability to labor and human rights standards.

Many neoliberal economists rationalize this system of exploitation, arguing that "Sweatshops are better than no shops, right?" They might even point out that Lydda Gonzalez's earnings at Southeastern Textiles surpassed Honduras's prevailing minimum wage of 55 cents an hour by more than ten cents.

Yet relativism doesn't erase the fact that 65 cents an hour is still not a salary of survival. It doesn't mitigate the degradation Lydda and many other young women confront daily: needing special permission to use the bathroom; being sexually harassed by supervisors, and facing anti-union intimidation from managers. Nor does it exonerate U.S. consumers from our duty to demand more of the multinational corporations whose products fill our closets and deck our bodies, as well as from the trade negotiators who purport to represent our will.

I have good company in which to raise my voice against the FTAA. Hundreds of activists are already funneling into the Convergence Center to meet fellow protesters and to brainstorm creative acts of civil disobedience. Thousands more are expected to fill the streets tomorrow.

As the evening goes on, the whine of the helicopters reminds us that whatever we are planning for tomorrow, the police are busy preparing for it. Clearly, the stakes are high in this fight over the future of globalization. Tomorrow, the goal of more than 2,500 riot cops will be to create the illusion, contrived as it may be, of business as usual. The goal of the direct action protesters, on the other hand, will be to create crisis—a loud, media-savvy, in-your-face state of emergency. As well-known labor activist Lisa Fithian puts it, "I create crisis, because crisis is that edge where change is possible."

After hearing Li Chunmei's chilling story and listening to Lydda Gonzalez's testimony less than one week ago, I have a slightly different take on things. My goal is not to *create* crisis—it already exists in abundance, as Lydda can attest. My hope is that the thousands of us marching together will be able to *unveil* it, to *make it visible* as a first step toward rendering global sweatshops untenable. The moment globalization enabled so many of the wealthy and powerful to detach from the realities of exploitation—shipping the abuses thousands of miles away—was also the moment that sweatshops became, to them, morally tolerable. My belief is that the reverse will also prove true: the moment that the sad fact of sweatshops explodes in the streets—half carnival, half apocalypse—could be the moment that young women like Li and Lydda are finally recognized as fully human.

The next day starts pure circus. I can understand why the media might overlook the serious motivations driving many of the protestors; it's easy to get lost in the whirl of drums, chants, songs, and even a conga line. I begin to explore, weaving in and out of speeches, heated political conversations, and guerrilla theater performances under the hot sun.

Suddenly, the spirit of carnival disappears and everyone is frantically running, though we're not quite sure why or where. We come face-to-face with a line of riot cops in front of the massive wire fence separating protesters from trade ministers. I'm brought back to Earth, back to the enormous moral issues that are on the line today. I begin to feel claustrophobic. It looks as if a few people are getting arrested thirty feet in front of me. *What am I doing here?* I find myself asking.

An answer comes zipping back almost reflexively as I hear someone shout, "Corporate greed kills!" Several years ago, such a cry might have struck me as an over-zealous cliché, but today it does not. I think of how Lydda's supervisor once screamed, "Hurry up! Do you know how many girls are lined up in China who would die for this work?" I remember Li Chunmei, who proved him right.

And, for a moment, I grasp the bigger picture. Lydda now has returned to the Southeast Textiles factory in Honduras to sew and fold as I chant and march. She has plans to start a union and believes that the other workers will join her. But she also knows that the battle for young women's rights in the sweatshops cannot be won in a single locale—especially in an age of transnational capital. She has challenged people like me who sit within the belly of the corporate beast, and I am here to answer.

This is not a movement that will be stamped "Made in the USA." The tag won't read "Made in Honduras" or "Made in China." Instead, the profound battle over the ethical future of globalization will be assembled by young women everywhere—those fighting the sexual harassment of their supervisors, those refusing to handle toxic chemicals with their bare hands, those leading the struggle for unionization, and those rallying against unfair trade deals. It's a movement that will feature girls bent over sewing machines *and* university computer screens. It will harness our sweat and sorrow for the sake of human rights and social progress.

And, if we do it right, our struggle will raise the ghost of Li Chunmei and the dreams of Lydda Gonzalez into the same blue sky our daughters will inherit.

SOURCES

Interviews with Lydda Gonzalez, Charles Kernaghan, Martha Iris Lorenzo, Fabia Gutierrez, and Barbara Briggs, 11/13/03.

Interviews with anti-FTAA activists, 11/19/03 and 11/20/03.

www.nlcnet.org.

Pan, Philip. "Few Protections for China's New Laborers." *The Washington Post.* May 13, 2003. Page A01.

Garcia, Michelle, and Powell, Michael. "P. Diddy Feels the Heat Over Sweatshop Charge." *The Washington Post.* October 29, 2003. Page C03.

FOR REVIEW

1. What is ethics?
2. What are "basic needs"?
3. What are "legitimate expectations"?
4. "Remember who you are!" Explain the text's interpretation of this Native American idea and its relevance to ethics.
5. Give an example of ethical growth in an individual.
6. Give an example of ethical growth in our society.
7. How can critical thinking serve ethics?
8. How can creative thinking serve ethics?
9. Why does Sarah Stillman say that her goal is not to create moral crisis but to *unveil* it?
10. Does she succeed? (Explain.)

EXERCISES AND NOTES

QUESTIONS

What experiences and expectations do you bring to the study of ethics? What did you expect when you signed up for this course or first cracked the covers of this book? Are you going to find ethics challenging and inviting in ways you didn't expect? What hopes and fears do you bring to this new study?

What events in your life were occasions for ethical learning? What did you learn? What made that learning possible? How specifically do you think you have changed, morally speaking? How do you expect to change in the future?

"Fair Trade" issues challenge us to focus on the effects of certain purchasing decisions on workers elsewhere. What other effects (environmental? social? …) are also caused by our purchasing (or other) decisions? What's at stake, for example, with what we eat? How about driving habits? Vacation choices?

One person on reading a draft of this chapter, wrote "Ethics is the development of solidarity." What do you think?

Look for biographies or autobiographies of people you admire (and maybe some of people you don't) and pay attention to the ways in which *they* learned and changed—to what made learning and change possible for them. Or interview some people you know or could contact, asking the same questions: What have been major ethical changes in your life? Why did those changes happen? Were they hard? Why? How do you feel about them now that you look back at them? What advice do you have for younger people looking ahead to such changes in their own lives?

LIMBERING UP

Here are some provocative questions—just to think about, for now, as we begin a broad and open-ended engagement with ethics, and also specifically to open class discussion or for reflective writing projects. Take them in an open-ended way: to explore, not to judge.

- Imagine that people lived forever. Would that be wonderful? Awful? How would we adjust? Totally switch identities every few hundred years? (Would you want to be the same person forever?) Would some people want out? What about you? What might be some of the effects on ethics as we know it?

- What if men got pregnant rather than (or in addition to) women? Would we think about sexual relations differently? What about abortion? What do you think Gloria Steinem meant when she said "If men got pregnant, abortion would be a sacrament"? (Is this an uneasy subject? Why?)

- Could a computer have moral rights? What kind of computer would it take? What kind of rights?

- Take some painful and "stuck" contemporary moral issues—abortion is one but certainly not the only possible example—and deliberately and creatively look for some alternative possible approaches, off the scale of "pro" or "con." Look for alternative approaches *now*: are there organizations, say, working on reconciliation, or alternative ways of framing the problem so that it doesn't come up in so destructive a way? How is abortion, for example, dealt with in societies that do not have the polarized kind of abortion debate we have?

- What if there were a cheap, legal, "up" hallucinogenic drug with no side effects? What moral objections would remain?

- Try designing a company (or if you're really ambitious, a whole economic or political system) without knowing what your own status will be within it. If you don't know whether you'll be a janitor or a CEO, a movie star or a bag lady, how will you set up your company's decision-making processes, or your society's way of taking care of the needy?

- What if the world developed an international reconstruction and peace-keeping force? What kinds of skills would such a "force" call for? Who would join? (Think afresh here: it wouldn't have to be, perhaps should not be, the young and able-bodied.) How would it work? How would the peace-makers and peace-keepers be trained?

- If you could use genetic engineering to totally remake human beings, how would you do it? Don't stop with everyday stylistic improvements, like adding gills so we can breathe underwater and such. How about creating people without the capacity, say, for certain kinds of violence or fanaticism? How would you do that? Would there be losses as well as gains?

- Think about whatever you know about the effects of global warming. Now try thinking of those effects as positive things. How could we as a planet make the most use of them—as opportunities? Would there be different ways you would want different nations to consider using global warming as an opportunity? How? Would there be things that richer countries (who also have contributed most of the greenhouse gases) could do to help poorer countries (who in some cases are going to suffer the most)?

NOTES

Shifra Starr Erez highlighted the human slavery issue at her bat mitzvah service at Congregation Or Hadash, Atlanta, Georgia, in September 2006. For more information, start with Kevin Bales, *Disposable People: New Slavery in the Global Economy* (revised ed., University of California Press, 2004), and Kevin Bales (ed.), *Understanding Global Slavery Today. A Reader* (University of California Press, 2005).

For a first sense of the range of ethics and an introduction to some philosophical resources in ethics, check out the "Ethics Updates" website at http://ethics.sandiego.edu/.

The Elie Wiesel Foundation Prize in Ethics Essay Contest is offered by the Elie Wiesel Foundation for Humanity. Go to http://www.eliewieselfoundation.org/EthicsPrize/index.html to find the full text of Sarah Stillman's 2005 first-prize-winning essay, to read other prize-winning essays back to 1990, and to learn how you can submit an essay of your own.

CHAPTER 2

Ethics-Avoidance Disorders

Ethics can be inviting, intriguing, and expansive. For just the same reasons, though, it can also be challenging, difficult, even painful. Sometimes we may even have to change our minds!

For these reasons, there is always also the temptation to avoid and resist ethics too. In fact, some people regularly invest huge amounts of energy in avoiding and resisting it. Others stumble into the common pitfalls without meaning to, so common and familiar are some of those traps. Before moving full-scale into ethics, in any case, we need to survey some of the common pitfalls in ethics and equip ourselves with a few good counter-measures.

FLYING BY INSTINCT

The easiest way to avoid ethical thinking is simply not to think at all. Go with the flow, fly by instinct, follow your feelings. It may mean taking the path of least resistance, or simply doing what's easy or familiar or popular or profitable without a second thought.

Feeling is part of the story—of course. Care, concern, and passion are part of what make ethics so engaging and so compelling. Even instinct plays a role. Sometimes feelings and instincts alert us to moral problems that we might otherwise paper over with excuses. Feelings like these can even start moral revolutions. The arguments come later.

Still, we must also examine and temper our feelings, even the strongest feelings. Take prejudice. To be prejudiced may be to have a strong negative feeling about someone because they are of a different ethnicity or gender or age or social class (or...) from yourself. If ethics were just a matter of feelings, then there would be nothing to say against such prejudices. It would be perfectly moral to discriminate against people you don't like.

Feeling may say yes. Ethics says no. Ethics instead asks us to challenge these very feelings. "Prejudice" literally means "prejudgment": it is one way of not really paying attention. But we *need* to pay attention. We need to ask why we feel as we do, whether our beliefs and feelings are true or fair, how we would feel in the other person's shoes, and so on. In short, we need to ask whether our feelings are *justified*—and, when not, what alternative feelings might be.

Instincts and feelings may also oversimplify complex situations. We want things to feel clear-cut even when they are not, and so we may persuade ourselves that they really are. Mindful thinking, by contrast, is more patient. Where things are really unclear, in particular, feeling may even have to wait. Premature clarity is worse than confusion. We may have to live with some questions a long time before we can decide how we ought to feel about them.

Our feelings are also easily manipulated. For instance, it is easy to be swayed either way by "loaded language," language that plays upon our emotional reactions. Define abortion as "baby-killing" and you create a negative feeling that closes the case against abortion before it really can even be opened. But fetuses are not babies (look the words up). On the other hand, if you describe abortion as no more than "minor surgery," you suggest that it is both unintrusive and even healthy. Either way, we are led into a prepackaged emotional commitment without ever thinking it through. Habit and conformity take over.

Mindful thinking, by contrast, is more complex and open-ended. It is in this spirit that ethics approaches controversial issues of the day, like abortion or professional ethics or assisted suicide. We do want to honor life, for instance. But we don't necessarily think that life should be prolonged under all circumstances, either. Should people be allowed to request medical help in dying, then? Or would this violate the spirit of medicine itself? Could assisted suicide be allowed sometimes and not others? Why? How do you decide? Questions like these cannot be adequately answered by consulting your preexisting feelings. There are too many different possibilities, too many different opinions and prejudices (on all sides) that need to be sorted out carefully. Think, think, think!

OFFHAND SELF-JUSTIFICATION

Apart from not thinking at all, the next easiest ethics-avoidance strategy is to think as little as possible. Imagine, for example, that I offer some view in a moral discussion. I endorse assisted suicide, maybe. Someone challenges me. My natural first reaction may be to defend whatever it was I just said—even if the challenge is exactly on target. It's a kind of ethical laziness, an automatic excuse-making or defensiveness, or what we sometimes call "rationalizing." I will call it *offhand self-justification*.

I may not even get to the point of asking if the challenge actually is on target or not. Indeed, that's the idea. I'd rather not. Self-defense is all that counts. I try to paper over my uncertainties (or insecurities, or half-knowledge, or wishful thinking) by grabbing for some excuse—and any excuse will do. "It's OK to cheat the phone company, because... because, well, everyone else does it too... because the phone company cheats *you*... because... "

Asked for your reasons, you should give them. There is nothing wrong with trying to defend yourself. The problem lies with the offhand or automatic spirit (or, more accurately, spiritlessness) of the defense. Once again, it becomes an excuse for not really *thinking*.

S: Of course the death penalty deters murders. It's a proven fact that murder rates are lower in states with the death penalty.

A: I'm not so sure about that. My understanding is that most states with the death penalty have higher murder rates.

S: Well, you can prove anything with numbers.

S initially appeals to "numbers"—comparative murder rates—to support her position. Challenged, though, she does not reconsider her position or explore other possibilities. She just dismisses any studies that disagree with what she believes—and in the process manages to dismiss the very "numbers" she herself just cited. But she doesn't even notice. You can tell that in the next discussion she'll be right back citing the same "proven fact" again.

RESISTING OFFHAND SELF-JUSTIFICATION

There are no surefire ways to avoid rationalizing. It takes a kind of self-confidence, honesty, and maturity that develop slowly, and even then we seldom escape the temptation entirely. Sometimes it's hard even to recognize an offhand self-justification when it is right in front of our eyes. Yet there are some useful strategies for overcoming the urge.

Remind yourself how self-defeating it is. Making excuses only allows us to go on with some questionable behavior until we get into even worse trouble. It may even be worse than merely hanging on to one unintelligent opinion. When we rationalize, we saddle ourselves with more and more unintelligent opinions—new ones invented, off the top of the head, to patch up the holes in the old ones. But the new ones are likely to be full (or fuller) of holes too. It's not a winning game.

Watch yourself. Step a little more slowly the next time you find yourself casting about for some excuse to put questions to rest. Ask instead whether you really are justified in the first place.

Watch for that telltale anger or irritation at being challenged. We often find ourselves becoming irritated or angry when our especially precious excuses are too persistently or effectively challenged by someone else. But of course, we get angry at the person challenging us, rather than considering that we might be at fault for offering an offhand excuse in the first place. Anger at someone else keeps us from having to be angry at ourselves. Better take the irritation as a warning sign.

Avoid the automatic counterattack. Again, watch yourself. Listening to someone else, are you trying to understand, or just waiting for them to stop so that you can give your comeback? Are you trying to win, or to learn? Watch your voice tone: are you conveying ridicule, irritation? Take a time-out if you need it. Give yourself some space to think.

"EVERYONE IS SELFISH"

Here is an especially tempting kind of offhand self-justification that needs a special look of its own. It is the assertion that "everyone is selfish"—sometimes even taken to the point of arguing that there is no other way anyone could possibly be, a view usually called "psychological egoism." It's certainly an easy way out of ethics: if everyone is really selfish anyway, you have no reason not to be selfish yourself, right? Indeed, you can't help it!

We Are Social Animals

Actually, though, very few people past infancy are *that* wrapped up in themselves. We're social animals—and in almost any life with others there's also awareness and responsiveness to others. An athlete sets a new record and all of us, watching, are thrilled too. A kid gets lost in the airport and right away a dozen strangers are ready to help. Think of parents' love for children. Teachers, scientists, soldiers, artists—our lives become compelling and meaningful only when we give them over to something greater than our selves.

Not that the self doesn't count at all. We do not have to go so far as self-sacrifice—although very often people do: think again of parents or teachers or soldiers. For basic ethics it's enough that others' needs register as well as our own. Of course most people are *somewhat* self-concerned—it's just that the self is nowhere near the whole story.

"Sure," says the egoist, "but if I give myself to science or art, or feel compelled to help the lost kid in the airport, it's because I *want* to. And doing what I want is certainly following my self-interest."

But it all depends on how you want it. If you want to discover a cure for cancer just because it would make you famous, then maybe it's just a selfish want. Most people, though, would actually want to discover a cure for cancer at least in part because it would alleviate a lot of suffering. And that's enough to get us well beyond egoism. Same for the kid in the airport. You want to help the kid because the kid needs help. It's only a kind of extremism to try to reduce everything to some variety of self-interest. We are actually much more interesting creatures than that.

Egoism as a Self-Fulfilling Prophecy

Egoism can sometimes drive others *into* a cynical kind of selfishness. If everyone around you is acting selfishly, you may feel driven to do the same out of discouragement, hurt, or sheer self-protection. If all of your soccer teammates hog the ball, so will you, probably. If all of your business competitors are solely driven by the bottom line (you think), you will be tempted too.

Here, as in offhand self-justification, egoism is made an *excuse*—in this case, for convenient kinds of selfishness. It allows people to justify their own egoism to themselves as well as to others. It is an invitation to mutual mistrust and cynicism. Selfishness becomes a sort of self-fulfilling prophecy, but not because it is somehow "natural." Rather, normal ethical relations have failed.

The point is that this is not how things usually go. In soccer, for example, no team of ball-hogs is going very far. Some basic lessons about teamwork have been forgotten. In business too, most of the time, businesses answer to other values too: some community responsibility, some care for employees and customers. (It's just that we tend to hear about the flagrant violations.)

Anthropologists do offer (a few) examples of whole societies of seemingly totally selfish people. If you look at those societies closely, though, you will see that they are on the brink of extinction, living in desperate straits. The lesson here too is *not* that "Deep down, everyone is really selfish," but very much the opposite: that it takes almost total social collapse to bring us to actual, full-scale egoism. And oftentimes not even that is enough.

The Truth in Egoism

Any view as persistent as egoism must have something going for it. So we also need to ask: what's the *truth* in egoism? I think there are several.

There are times in your life when you are naturally and appropriately more self-oriented than at other times. Young people going to college, for one example, may find themselves with fairly few attachments and somewhat unsure of their direction. At such times, a turn inward—a preoccupation for awhile with your self—is natural and probably healthy. It's dramatically limited (I've been suggesting) as a full-time way of life, but it can be sensible in the short run.

Besides, selves are often fragile. Sometimes we are *too* tuned to the needs and expectations of others. Sometimes we need to give ourselves the support and attention we need to recover a sense of who we are and what we want. This is probably much more common than the opposite—the self that claims too much and needs to be put in its place. Here too a little bit of self-preoccupation is again a good idea.

More common than any kind of egoism, I think, are other reasons we fail to take account of the needs and expectations of others. The real concern of moralists should be *inattention*. Habit, for one thing, and the inability to listen. Or maybe the unwillingness to listen, as in offhand self-justification. Or the unwillingness to acknowledge sheer *difference*—this would be "self-centeredness," not in the sense of pursuing only one's own interests but in the sense of taking one's self to be the only kind of self there can be. You can't even begin to cross the gap between self and other if you don't think there is a gap in the first place.

So of course ethics sometimes has an uphill fight. There are parts of ourselves that resist. It just may not be so useful to think of those parts as "selfish." To say it again: we're more complex and interesting than that!

DOGMATISM

We all know people who are so committed to their moral beliefs that they cannot see any other side and cannot defend their own beliefs beyond simply asserting and reasserting them. This is dogmatism. They may appear to listen (or not), but they *will not* change their minds. Name "their" issue (or perhaps *any* issue), and they know the answer already.

To be clear: being committed to a certain set of values—living up to them, or trying to, and sticking up for them when we can—is a fine thing. And there are certain basic moral values to which we are and *should be* deeply and unshakably committed. Dogmatism is a problem because some people go much further. They make no distinction between the basic "givens" of our moral life and everyday moral opinions that are not at all so clear-cut. Every one of their value judgments, to them, has the same status as the Ten Commandments.

Dogmatists tend to disagree about the actual issues—which in fact is a bit ironic. Dogmatists do agree, though, that careful and open-ended thinking about moral issues is not necessary. After all, if you already know the answer, there is no need to think about it. If you need to argue for your position, you admit that it needs defending, which is to say that people can legitimately have doubts. But that can't be true: you already know that your position is the only right one. Therefore, any reasoned argument for your position is unnecessary. And any reasoned argument *against* your position is obviously absurd. So, why listen?

Dogmatism, then, is a form of ethics-avoidance too. No more thinking is going on here than when we offhandedly justify ourselves with whatever reasons come along. Dogmatists may have their reasons better organized, and may happily debate them with you all afternoon, but they are not really *thinking* about those reasons only repeating them—more and more loudly, probably.

AVOIDING DOGMATISM

Ethics, once again, paints a different picture. Despite the stereotypes, the point of ethics is generally not to moralize or to dictate what is to be done. The real point of ethics is to offer some tools, and some possible directions, for thinking about difficult matters, recognizing from the start—as the very rationale for ethics, in fact—that the world is seldom so simple or clear-cut. Struggle and uncertainty *are* part of ethics, as they are part of life.

So we need to think carefully if we are to act ethically. In fact, thinking carefully about moral issues—avoiding dogmatism—is *itself* a moral act. Thinking carefully *is* (part of) acting morally. Philosopher Joshua Halberstam puts it well:

> We need an "ethics of belief" that places value on the way we arrive at our opinions. A healthy ethics of belief requires that our judgments be based on sound evidence. Opinionated people have a weak ethics of belief. They make no distinction between a legitimate opinion and an arbitrary opinion; all that matters is that they have an opinion. The problem with opinionated people is that they don't take their own views seriously enough! When we do take our opinions seriously, humility follows.

Or, as the bumpersticker says:

> DON'T BELIEVE EVERYTHING YOU THINK!

Here are some strategies for avoiding dogmatism.

Whenever you find yourself insisting too strongly on some view of your own, try to stop yourself and really listen to the "other side." Imagine that you're an anthropologist or psychologist studying other people's views. Just consider what they're saying without immediately thinking of your responses to it. What sort of world do these people live in? How does it hang together? How can it seem like the simple and obvious truth to them, just as yours does to you? Later on you can kick in your own views and compare them. First just give yourself a little space to listen.

Another useful strategy is to seek out *arguments* for the other side(s). One way that dogmatic views ensure themselves long lives is by systematically avoiding the other side's arguments. Only the other side's *conclusions* are registered. This person is for (or against) capital punishment, let's say, and that's all a dogmatist needs to know. He doesn't ask *why:* he's not interested. Looking at the *reasons* for other and opposed positions both helps you understand the positions better and may begin to introduce some more complex thinking. It's amazing but true: people don't just disagree with us out of sheer perversity or ignorance! Again this is an "obvious" thing that sometimes we don't really quite know well enough.

It pays to adjust our language as well. Instead of categorical statements of dogmatic opinions, especially bumpersticker–style slogans ("Meat Is Murder"; "It's Adam and Eve, Not Adam and Steve," etc.), try to speak in a way that is less categorical and final. Very few reasonable moral positions can be shoehorned into a bumpersticker or slogan, clever as they might be—in fact, you might avoid any view that *could* be shoehorned into a bumpersticker for just that reason—and besides, this way of putting things polarizes views and makes the other side seem stupid and misled. Don't call names either ("You animal-rights fanatics..."; "You Bible-thumpers..."). Avoid the easy labels ("liberal," "right-wing," etc.).

Sometimes language leads the mind. Speaking in an open-ended way may help you begin to *think* in an open-ended way way as well. Certainly it will create quite different conversations. Typically one dogmatic statement just provokes an equal and opposite dogmatic statement. Speak differently and not only your mind but your discussions may open up differently, and more constructively too! (This book will have a lot more to say about language in Chapters 4 and 13.)

Halberstam again:

> Don't elevate your every whim into a conviction. Having an opinion is one thing, delivering the Ten Commandments is something else. Intellectual honesty demands that unless you're a bona fide expert in the field, a hint of tentativeness should accompany all your views and decisions. Indeed, a hint of uncertainty is appropriate even if you *are* an authority. Here's a simple device to ensure that you have the proper humility when offering your opinion: When you speak, imagine that an expert is sitting right across from you. Now offer that opinion.

RELATIVISM

"It's all relative," we sometimes say. What's right for you may not be right for me. Mind your own business. Don't criticize. Any moral opinion is as good as the next. This attitude is a form of *relativism.*

Relativism begins with the simple observation that different individuals and societies sometimes have different moral values. Maybe I think speeding is OK. You think speeders ought to have their licenses revoked. Some societies actually execute them! Or again, some societies tolerate homeless populations running into the millions, while in others the very idea of allowing even one person to be homeless, whatever the cause, would be shameful, unthinkable. Some societies condemn sex between unmarried young people; others approve and even encourage it.

Relativists go on to wonder if any single standard can be "right." And we should acknowledge right away that this can be a good question. At the very least, it's mind-opening to look at other points of view, and moral matters are complex enough that no one point of view is likely to have a monopoly on the truth anyway. Besides, sometimes we need to assert our right to do as we please, even if others think we are making a big mistake. This is one of relativism's chief uses in practice: making a space for us to figure things out for ourselves.

OFFHAND SELF-JUSTIFICATION AGAIN

But relativists typically go much further—and here relativism becomes a "disorder." From our differences about moral values they may conclude that there is no legitimate basis for arguing about them at all. It's all just opinion, they say, and one opinion is as good as another. But here, though relativism may appear to be the very model of open-mindedness, it actually has just the opposite effect. It begins to close our minds instead.

U: I support the death penalty. I believe that it saves lives because it makes murderers think twice before killing someone. As the Bible says, "An eye for an eye, a tooth for a tooth."

V: I don't agree.

U: Why?

V: I just don't. That's my opinion and it's as good as yours!

Maybe that's a little blatant, but you get the idea. Here relativism slides right into offhand self-justification. V treats it like a magic key to escape any kind of thinking whatsoever. She cannot even be bothered to offer any reasons, let alone engage U's.

In fact, all opinions on this and most moral subjects require further thinking. Are U's arguments good ones? What values stand on the other side? What are V's reasons *against* the death penalty? Is the death penalty really a deterrent? Doesn't the Bible also tell us not to kill?

The key point here may be a bit surprising to people who have grown used to using "relativism" as another form, in effect, of offhand self-justification (and to their teachers too, maybe). To say it again: *even if moral values vary all over the map, there is no way out of some good hard thinking.*

The very contrast of values is a great occasion for thinking, for one thing. When we look at other societies' or people's values, we may find ourselves asking if our own moral values are really the best ones: usually a useful question, even if we end up deciding that they are the best, at least for us.

MINDING OUR OWN BUSINESS

There is another practical problem with relativism—again, *even if* values really do differ, maybe even fundamentally.

Ethics often concerns matters that affect us all. Take pollution. If the air is polluted, it doesn't merely affect the polluters. If we spend money on pollution cleanup and prevention, on the other hand, we can't spend that money on other things, perhaps better things, maybe again for all of us. For some people it could be a life-or-death matter however we decide. The same goes for issues like fair trade, professional ethics, other animals, and many others. None of these are just our "own" business. Other people's lives and health and possibilities are at stake too. These matters—basic moral issues—are *everyone's* business.

The relativist's stock phrase, "Mind your own business," is therefore an antisocial response. It not only avoids thinking on the relativist's part, it also refuses to acknowledge that on issues like these, however much we differ, we still need to work out some way of going on together.

D: I oppose legal abortion.

E: Why don't you just mind your own business? Like the slogan says, if you're against abortion, then don't have one!

But there is more to it than this. If some of us practice abortion and some do not, the result is a society in which abortion is practiced. The rest of us have to stand for it, at least insofar as we have to stand aside. Likewise, if some of us pollute and some don't, the result is pollution for everyone. In such matters, we cannot act as though everyone can simply do as they please without anyone else being affected.

Some philosophers argue that this is the very *point* of ethics: to help us arrive at certain standards that we all are to live by when all of us are affected by each other's behavior. Some philosophers even start from this point to build a theory of ethics. On this view, ethics is precisely for those cases where "Mind your own business!" doesn't work as an approach to a problem. Instead, we need to work things out together. Keep an open mind; stay in touch and keep talking.

Relativism actually isn't a bad beginning: it does remind us that there are others, probably with different views, with whom we have to work things out. But then we need to go and do it!

RELATIVISM: PHILOSOPHICAL QUESTIONS

This chapter concentrates on practical objections to moral relativism. Even if most of relativism's claims are true, I argue, we can and must actually *think*, long and hard, about moral issues. The tools in your ethical toolbox are no less vital.

Relativism is also much argued over among philosophers. In this box I want to explore some of these further objections and arguments over moral relativism—briefly—to give you a sense both of how philosophers argue and of how complex some seemingly obvious things really are. Here are a number of loosely linked questions and challenges to think about.

Is the Diversity of Values Overrated?

Moral relativism is based upon the claim that moral values differ in fundamental ways between different people and cultures. This is called *descriptive* relativism: it is an empirical claim about the world.

Empirical claims need testing. So what's the evidence? How much *real* disagreement is there about moral values? That is, do we really disagree "all the way down," so to speak, or might apparently different moral values flow instead from different factual beliefs about the world?

Eskimo (Inuit) bands were discovered by early European explorers to sometimes leave their old people out in the cold of winter to die. This was contrasted to the European attitude, which was supposed to be one of respect and care for the old (though in fact it was a fair bit spottier than that). The explorers, anyway, were scandalized. It looked like a clear difference of values.

Later explorers, however, discovered several more things. One was that these bands often lived at the margins between survival and starvation during the winter and had to move quickly in the spring to find food. Very old people could not keep up. Leaving them behind was a matter of social survival—a choice that we too might make in the same circumstances.

Another discovery was that the Eskimo believe in an afterlife—and believe that people enter the afterlife in the same condition they leave this one. So allowing or even encouraging the old to die once their usefulness was past was not evidence of heartlessness or disrespect for life—quite the opposite. Again, if we (really, truly) shared their belief, we presumably would do the same.

In this case, then, what seemed to be a disagreement about moral values turned out to be a disagreement about certain facts. So how real are other alleged disagreements about moral values? Do we really differ that much? Is descriptive relativism true? Can you think of contemporary moral disagreements that might dissolve under scrutiny, like the Eskimo case might? Can you think of some that wouldn't?

Why Should Diversity Be the Last Word?

No doubt there are at least *some* serious disagreements about moral values themselves. But what exactly does this prove? Is disagreement the last word?

After all, we could take our disagreements as *starting points*—something to think about and learn from—rather than end points. The fact that some people are racists, for example, doesn't prove that racism is only wrong *for us*. It only proves that people have some learning to do. Now people are disagreeing about global warming. Perhaps the same thing can be said: if and when we really look at the evidence, will we really conclude that we have no moral obligation to take global warming seriously?

So perhaps the real question is: how much disagreement about moral values would remain after all of this thinking and learning? Is it so obvious that we would still disagree in such fundamental ways, about values themselves? Again, a little humility and investigation—and indeed, some real moral argument—would be a much better idea.

What Does the Diversity of Values Imply?

Now suppose that descriptive relativism *is* true. That is, suppose we really do differ, and differ sharply, about values, and would continue to differ even after careful criticism and argument. What then? What follows, if anything, about moral values or moral arguments? That is, what follows about relativism in what philosophers call the *prescriptive* sense?

Does it follow, in particular, that there is no single "right" answer to moral questions? Not necessarily. Sheer difference, by itself, does not prove that no one single standard is "right." Maybe all sides but one are *wrong*. People disagree about all kinds of facts (Is the Earth flat? Does vitamin C prevent colds?), but we don't suppose there is no truth of the matter in those cases. Is there something special about value judgments that makes them different from "facts" in this way? Maybe, but if you think so, see if you can explain what it is. Spell out the argument.

One note of caution. It may actually be true that there is no one single "right" answer to (many) moral questions—but not for relativistic reasons. Maybe there is no one single "right" answer because most moral situations are so *complex* that a variety of different but equally good responses are possible. This would not mean that any answer is as good as the next (there are still plenty of *wrong* answers) or that critical thinking is somehow pointless in ethics. Quite the opposite: once again, it would call for more flexible and subtle thinking still.

Does the Diversity of Values Make a Practical Difference?

Now suppose that prescriptive moral relativism *is* true. That is, suppose there is no arguably "right" answer to moral questions, and maybe even that any answer is in some sense as good as the next. What exactly would this imply?

Suppose the "cultural" relativist is right that you and I cannot argue with, say, cannibals about cannibalism. Well, how often do you argue with cannibals? Mostly we argue with people who share our terms. I have never argued with a cannibal, not even once, but I argue constantly with my own children, whose eating habits also leave something to be desired. And I *can* argue with them—they are growing into *our* culture and have some learning to do.

On the other hand, sometimes we *are* asked to make moral judgments across cultural lines, as when American corporations were pressured to (and mostly did) pull out of South Africa to protest apartheid. Was that a valid action, in your view? What would the relativist say about it? What do you think of the relativist's response?

The Truth in Relativism

Finally, for those who reject relativism, what do you think relativism is nonetheless *right* about? The complexity of many situations, making it hard to say that there is one single right answer? That's a useful reminder: it encourages some moral humility.

The need for some moral space, even to make our own mistakes? A good point also: moral demands can sometimes be very confining, especially when dogmatic moralists get going on them. Relativism is a way of at least winning a little space to think for yourself. Just don't think that you therefore have to defend "relativism" in the sense we have been exploring. Again, it may not be relativism at all, really: more like the *complexity* of real moral issues. "Relativism" here just stands for a freer spirit, more flexibility in ethics, a reminder that the truth is not so easy to come by.

Relativism also can amount to an insistence that we need to look at things from others' points of view. Our own view is *not* the only view around; we have much to learn from others, as they may from us, and in any case we have to work out some way of going on together. Again relativism tempers dogmatism...but still, we'd be better off without either.

FOR REVIEW

1. What is an "ethics-avoidance disorder"?

2. Why not fly by instinct?

3. Illustrate "offhand self-justification."

4. What is wrong with offhand self-justification?

5. "Everyone is really just out for themselves." How is this true? How is it not true?

6. Illustrate dogmatism, using yourself if you can.

7. What are some concrete strategies for avoiding dogmatism?

8. When does relativism "slide into offhand self-justification"?

9. Why does the text accuse relativism of being antisocial?

10. What are some philosophical difficulties with relativism?

EXERCISES AND NOTES

SELF-REFLECTIONS

We have noted some of the ways in which people avoid ethical thinking—often without even noticing or admitting that that is what is happening. So now consider yourself. About what do you get dogmatic? About what do you rationalize? About what do you get defensive? What do you have trouble hearing? Why? (Explore that *why* question—understanding yourself better is often the key to change.)

Give yourself some credit too. What are you *good* at hearing? On what topics are you truly open-minded? Where do you *embrace* ethical thinking? And why is this?

Admitting to a degree of ethics-avoidance does not mean that you instantly have to change. Perhaps you will never be able to change completely. The point is instead to mark out the areas that need special attention—places where you need to watch yourself and others need to be both more sensitive and maybe more insistent.

HEARING THE "OTHER SIDE"

Name some ethical positions that you find especially hard to take seriously. Do this before reading on.

Now, as an exercise in opening the mind a little, your task is to write or state these positions in as neutral a way as possible. You don't have to be effusive, and don't try to be extremely positive—usually it is easier to be overly positive than to state a view carefully. Just try to state each position in a reasonable way, not loaded or satirical but simply straight. You may have to do a little research to get them right. In class, ask a classmate who holds those moral views to help you out.

Consider also the *reasons* that are typically used to support these views. What are those reasons? What are the best reasons according to *you*—the reasons that would persuade you if any reasons could? Again, don't argue with the positions. Just look for the strongest defense of each position you can find.

You don't have to *agree* with these positions, of course—after all, you picked them because you not only disagree with them but also find them hard to take seriously. The point is to try to understand them, and in general to try to get a little distance from your own reactions: to create a little more space for open-mindedness.

This exercise works best if you avoid the hottest issues that we have all heard debated too many times already, such as abortion. People seem to have heard the two main positions on abortion enough that it is too easy to rattle them off. On other issues, it takes more care and work—and that is really the point.

A DIALOGUE

Ethics-avoidance disorders are partly conversational or argumentative moves: they occur in dialogue, in the back-and-forth of conversation or argument. Sometimes they are also subtle!

Carefully consider the following extended dialogue (based on a class dialogue about the reading in Chapter 1). Consider where (and why) you think ethics-avoidance strategies are being used. You might also try rewriting the dialogue, or writing your own, to avoid the pitfalls you point out.

F: It's true that conditions in some third-world factories are horrible. On the other hand, those workers wouldn't have jobs at all if the factories weren't there, and even Sarah Stillman acknowledges that the factories pay better than the prevailing wages. Maybe it feels like a great liberation to them.

G: It didn't sound like a great liberation to Lydda Gonzalez.

F: Then she should just go back to her village or wherever. Why should she think she's entitled to decide for everyone else?

G: Nobody should have to put up with how those women are treated.

J: I thought some companies were responding—pulling out of really exploitative situations and forcing better working conditions when they deal with suppliers. Haven't there been improvements?

G: Maybe they pay a dollar instead of fifty cents an hour, but they still work people to death.

J: Aren't some companies at least better than others? If we are going to buy products made overseas at all, we could at least buy them from the more responsible companies.

K: Sure, but how do you find out who's responsible and who's not? We're talking about factory conditions halfway around the world, and the companies are not exactly going to publicize it.

J: If you dig deep enough, you can find out. There are websites and books that rate them.

K: They're biased, too.

L: You guys are complaining about the mistreatment of foreign workers, but you profit from it as well. We all do. You, me, everybody. Not even Sarah Stillman wants to pay four times as much for the same shirt. Cheap foreign oil, tropical fruits…you'd better start rethinking it all.

M: Yeah, I wonder what Lydda Gonzalez was wearing. I mean, who made *her* clothes?

L: I'll listen to these activists when they practice what they preach. Wear clothes you've made yourself. Only use gas or plastics or other products made from American oil. As if !

N: I'd buy a shirt made by Honduran women if they ran the factory themselves and set their own prices. Get the corporate middlemen out of the way and go right to the craftspeople.

L: Pie in the sky.

P: You can't be saying that because the world isn't perfect, we don't have to do anything at all?

NOTES

It's not entirely fair to label dogmatism, relativism, and so on as "disorders," at least on the model of "attention deficit disorder" and other cognitive disorders that can be long-standing physiological conditions. Ethics-avoidance is a matter of habit and choice. But the label also makes a point. These are actually *disorders,* patterns of behavior that are not good for you or anyone else and that can be identified and corrected. I've tried to show how.

Joshua Halberstam's book *Everyday Ethics* (Penguin, 1993) is an interesting and opinionated complement to this one. He is cited here from pages 155 and 156.

Rationalizing may be one of the deepest of all pitfalls in ethics (and probably in life generally). For some psychological background, including some fascinating and unsettling experiments, see David Myers, *Social Psychology*

(McGraw-Hill, 8th edition, 2004), Chapters 2–4. For a useful overview of self-deception, see Chapter 6 of Mike Martin's *Everyday Morality* (Wadsworth Publishing Company, 2006).

For a more traditional discussion of relativism, see James Rachels, *The Elements of Moral Philosophy* (McGraw-Hill, 5th edition, 2006), Chapter 2. I deal with relativism from a different angle in my *Toward Better Problems* (Temple University Press, 1992), Chapter 7. Ethical thinkers who have tried to derive a substantive ethics precisely from the need to go on together in the face of diverse values include John Rawls, in *A Theory of Justice* (Harvard University Press, 1971), sections 3 and 20–26, and David Gauthier, in *Morals by Agreement* (Clarendon Press, 1986).

For a discussion of pluralism and relativism in ethics, ethical egoism, and related questions, go to the Ethics Updates website at http://ethics.sandiego.edu and look under "Ethical Theory."

CHAPTER 3

Ethics and Religion

We look next to those large regions where ethics and religion overlap. Despite how it may sometimes seem when we are in the midst of certain heated public debates, religious ethics fits readily into the picture that the last two chapters have been painting. All ethics, whether it be divinely inspired or empirically based, is in more or less the same boat when it comes to real-life practice: serious and constant thinking is required. And serious and constant thinking is in fact the *norm,* even at the very heart of religious ethics.

AN APPROACH TO RELIGIOUS ETHICS

RELIGIOUS ETHICS AS A LEARNING EXPERIENCE

Most religions take moral values very seriously. Religious texts advance explicit statements of values, such as the Ten Commandments for Jews and Christians and the Eightfold Path for Buddhists. Religions also provide moral training—for many people the only formal moral training we ever get. And they offer moral support communities, backed by long and honored histories of ethical thinking and moral engagement. Think of again my young friend who spoke out against human slavery—it was no accident that she spoke in a religious context. That was the natural place for it.

Religions also understand moral values as *complex.* Christianity developed elaborate schools of casuistry. Muslim ethical thinking has the additional complication of politics, since Islam does not separate church and state. Judaism offers volume upon volume of intricate rabbinical discussion of all kinds of moral issues in light of Torah.

All of these religions also are changing and adapting. Of course they work from their existing bodies of doctrine, interpretation, and experience. But experience keeps changing. In America in the 1960s, the big challenge was civil rights. Most established religions entered the decade with a poor record of speaking up against segregation. They rose to the challenge to do better. Then came the Vietnam War; then the rise of multiculturalism; now, among other things, global environmental issues.

Most religious texts say little or nothing about ecology or climate change either, but now religions are working out their own forms of environmentalism. Evangelicals are getting on board too, speaking now of "Creation Care" as a frontline, high-priority moral issue. Broad-based religious covenants are forming around global warming. A coalition cheekily called Interfaith Power and Light, for instance, includes Catholics and Baptists and Sufi (Islamic mystics) and other Muslim groups, fundamentalist Christian churches, African Methodist Episcopalians (AME), and Jewish, Unitarian, Buddhist, and Independent congregations. They all seek "to be faithful stewards of Creation by responding to global warming through the promotion of energy conservation, energy efficiency, and renewable energy. This ministry intends to protect the earth's ecosystems, safeguard public health, and ensure sufficient, sustainable energy for all…" Neither Jesus nor Buddha nor Mohammed talked about sustainable energy or "Creation Care"—yet this is what their legacy now seems to ask of us. As the Quakers say, truth is continually revealed.

DIVERSITY IN RELIGIOUS ETHICS

Just like nonreligious ethical and philosophical systems, religious views of ethics also vary—often fundamentally. And variation goes all the way down. The world's great religions vary, in fact dramatically, and so do their denominations, and so do specific congregations within denominations. Even individual religious persons may find themselves, in their own thinking, pulled in different directions.

Despite how people sometimes talk, then, there is really no such thing as "the" Christian view of gay marriage or capitalism or preemptive war, any more than there is any one Jewish or Buddhist (or atheist) view either. There are *many* Christian views, as there are many views in general. Meanwhile Christians are also in dialogue with a variety of other religions—which are just as varied and diverse within themselves—and with a variety of secular points of view as well. Episcopalians and Methodists and Jews contend with each other over gay marriage. Some affirm it, some condemn it, some are trying to find a middle way. Some radicals hold that the Koran sanctions terror; most Muslim religious authorities hold the opposite.

Once again, all of this thinking and rethinking, this challenging and moral back-and-forth, is the *norm*. In fact, we should *welcome* it as part of the interest and depth of ethics. In any case, welcome or not, the key response to any religious dogmatist, as against any other kind of dogmatist, is that there are people with at least as much intelligence and good faith who hold opposite views, based as thoroughly and conscientiously on *their* experience and training as our own dogmatists' views are on theirs. The only option is open-ended discussion.

Regardless of whether or not you are Catholic or agree with the pope, for example, it isn't a bad thing for the Catholic Church to speak so insistently in favor of "life"—and remember that in this they not only oppose abortion and contraception but also question multinational capitalism and try to defend local communities and "good livelihood." It's a challenge to just about everyone. Defending "life," they say, also means defending the poor, resisting wars, and speaking for the larger living Earth. We may not agree about these issues, but (again) it is essential to *think* about them, and indeed also to "defend life" in some form—however much we disagree about how.

FINDING SHAREABLE TERMS

How do we proceed when religion seems to divide us on moral matters? The answer is more or less the same as when we are morally divided for any other reason. As Chapter 2 suggested, part of the very point of ethics is to help us find ways to go on together when we do have basic disagreements but must still work out some shared values to live by, even while we may still choose to keep the contention alive. The main way we do so is by *finding shareable terms and arguments.*

You or your group may be totally persuaded already. Still, when the task is to persuade others—*all* of us, in the broader and more diverse moral community that includes differently religious people as well as nonreligious people—then the appeal must be to mutually agreeable starting points. You need to give reasons that address listeners in their own terms, and to acknowledge counterarguments.

Obviously, appeals to a specific Bible, or specific interpretation of a Bible, only work for those who share that Bible or that interpretation. Beyond that, no side can simply insist on its way without careful and open-ended dialogue. What's required are not pronouncements but *arguments:* giving reasons that actually address the listener and acknowledge counterarguments.

While many non-Catholics admire the pope, for example, we are unlikely to take his word on family planning or the economy just because it is his word. (Many Catholics don't either.) Just like the rest of us, he has to *persuade.* In fact, the late Pope John Paul II was so effective for just this reason: he could reach across many differences not by appealing to his official religious authority but by thoughtful argument and by example. In communist countries he spoke for freedom and individual dignity—hardly just Catholic ideas, or just Christian ideas, or just religious ideas. In the West, he spoke of respect for life and against our obsessions with material things: again, *common* values, even if we don't always live up to them. Some of his proclamations are controversial even among Catholics, but he was still in certain ways "the world's conscience." His biographer called him "a pope for the world, not just the Church."

This book should help. We will learn to identify the values at stake in ethical issues, both shared and not shared, and will develop a variety of tools to help us address those values and issues more clear-headedly, collaboratively, and creatively. You will see, I hope, that there are ways to enter the ethical discussion not so much as Catholics or Muslims, agnostics or atheists, but instead as people united by certain basic values we are aiming to understand and put into practice together, meanwhile valuing our disagreements as invitations to more learning.

On the other hand, if you *can't* make an argument work in common terms, maybe it is not so strong an argument after all. Here some caution is wise. As Chapter 2 put it, not every moral matter has the status of the Ten Commandments. The commandments themselves really do lay out common values—values that others might come to or express in other ways, but common values nonetheless—but again, even in religious terms, not every value or value judgment is like them.

NELSON MANDELA AND DESMOND TUTU

Nelson Mandela's remarkable life carried him from his birth into one of the leading families of the Xhosa people to the resistance movement against South African apartheid as one of the founders of the African National Congress (ANC); twenty-seven years imprisonment, some of it in solitary confinement; and then release and election as the first president of post-apartheid South Africa. Through it all he carried himself with a kind of saintliness that made him one of the most striking moral exemplars of recent times. Without rancor, without racial hatred, he and South African Anglican Archbishop Desmond Tutu were able to guide a hatefully divided society into majority rule without the massive bloodshed everyone expected and feared. His own life story showed a whole nation how to transcend the bitterness of past oppression.

Mandela is also a resolutely secular person. His values were shaped by a wide mix of factors, starting with Xhosa heritage and coming in time to encompass moral traditions from around the world. The ANC was influenced by the revolutionary ideas of English nonconformists and Jewish immigrants and by South Africa's Indian community (both Hindu and Muslim) with its Gandhian traditions (Gandhi himself lived and worked in South Africa for twenty years). Over a quarter-century of imprisonment, Mandela and his fellow prisoners, from all over the religious and revolutionary spectrum, debated politics in the mineshafts, staged Sophocles and Shakespeare, read Xhosa poets and the atheist and pacifist Bertrand Russell, and on and on.

You begin to see why in the end no single religious or ethical orientation was enough for them, and thus what forged the ANC's distinctive vision of a multicultural and multireligious society, bound together by a common goal and based on that "common ground" that Mandela describes as "greater and more enduring than the differences that divide."

The South African regime, throughout those long years, smeared the ANC as "godless" while appealing to the Bible to justify apartheid. Yet Mandela, characteristically, continues to speak appreciatively of religion. Religious schools educated him, for one thing—the apartheid regime had no interest in educating blacks. And more:

> In a South African jail under apartheid, you can see a cruelty of human beings to others in a naked form. But it was religious institutions, Hindus, Moslems, leaders of the Jewish faith, Christians, it was them who gave us the hope that one day, we would come out, we would return. And in prison, the religious institutions raised funds for our children, who were arrested in thousands and thrown into jail, and many of them one day left prison at a high level of education, because of this support we got from religious institutions. And that is why we so respect religious institutions. And we try as much as we can to read the literature, which outlines the fundamental principles of human behaviour...like the [Bhagavad Gita], the Qur'an, the Bible, and other important religious documents.

Notice again: Mandela is not embracing any one of these religions. He appreciates them all. "Hope" is not sectarian. At times he himself uses religious language—for sometimes, surely, only the language of the sacred will do—but he does not feel the need to take it literally.

Yet here alongside him stands his great colleague Desmond Tutu, who does. Tutu's lifelong struggle against apartheid was from his pulpits, and the result is a stunning "Truth and Reconciliation" movement both in South Africa—facing apartheid in order to move ahead together—and in the wider world.

Two very different life paths, then, but common values still: one direction and one heart. Mandela and Tutu *together* moved people of all stripes—religious and secular, Anglican and Buddhist and Catholic, political leaders and CEOs as well as ordinary folks—to action. An example both inspiring and instructive!

LET THE STORIES BE STORIES

All of the world's great religious traditions offer a rich bounty of stories. Many of them are moral stories, and naturally we look to them for moral guidance—which is why we so often speak of "the moral of the story." Those stories that are part of a religion's Bible often claim a special authority that makes their interpretation both essential and, well, contentious.

The stories are often fascinating and deep. Whole generations of devout people have devoted themselves to them. But again: precisely because our religious stories are so often rich, poetic, and complex, they seldom yield clear, specific guidance in specific situations—certainly not in the problematic situations that really concern us. They are contentious because they are ambiguous, and thus they invite (surprise!) more *thinking*.

Consider this parable from the Sufi master Yusuf of Andalusia:

> Nuri Bey was a respected and reflective Albanian, who had married a wife much younger than himself. One evening when he had returned home earlier than usual, a faithful servant came to him and said: "Your wife, our mistress, is acting suspiciously. She is in her apartments with a huge chest, large enough to hold a man, which belonged to your grandmother. It should contain only a few ancient embroideries. I believe that there may now be much more in it. She will not allow me, your oldest retainer, to look inside."
>
> Nuri went to his wife's room, and found her sitting disconsolately beside the massive wooden box. "Will you show me what is in the chest?" he asked.
>
> "Because of the suspicion of a servant, or because you do not trust me?"
>
> "Would it not be easier just to open it, without thinking about the undertones?" asked Nuri.
>
> "I do not think it possible."
>
> "Where is the key?"
>
> She held it up. "Dismiss the servant and I will give it to you."
>
> The servant was dismissed. The woman handed over the key and herself withdrew, obviously troubled in mind.
>
> Nuri Bey thought for a long time. Then he called four gardeners from his estate. Together they carried the chest by night unopened to a distant part of the grounds, and buried it. The matter was never referred to again.

Sufis have been teaching with this story for eight hundred years. But exactly what lesson does it teach? You might take some time to figure out how *you* would interpret it—and see how your interpretation compares with others.

Is Nuri Bey's act a wise one? Does the story mean to suggest that it is? He doesn't push the point—he doesn't open the chest—but he apparently doesn't entirely trust his wife either. Or in burying the chest is his idea to also bury mistrust—is he still trying to avoid the "undertones"? Would his wife agree that he succeeded at this? Is the "moral" therefore that certain matters between husband and wife shouldn't be pushed?

And—after all—what was in the box? Is it obvious that his wife is hiding a lover? This is probably what we think at first, but could it be something else—a present, maybe, that she is not prepared to give him yet? Some other kind of magical possibility that his jealousy "buries" for them? Notice that for *her* the issue is trust. "Because of the suspicion of a servant," she asks, "or because you do not trust me?" She "herself withdrew, obviously troubled in mind"—but not in denial or defiance.

The Sufis themselves, by the way, value such stories precisely because they *are* complex and unclear in this way. To insist that they mean one and only one thing misses the very point—so they would say. How many other stories are like that?

THE SIN OF SODOM?

Here's another religious story—this one a little closer to home. When some Christians insist that the Bible condemns homosexuality, a common scriptural reference is to the story of the destruction of Sodom.

> The two angels came to Sodom in the evening; and Lot was sitting in the gate of Sodom. When Lot saw them, he rose to meet them . . . and said, "My lords, turn aside, I pray you, to your servant's house, and spend the night, and wash your feet; then you may rise up early and go on your way." . . . He urged them strongly; so they turned aside to him and entered his house; and he made them a feast, and baked unleavened bread, and they ate.
>
> But before they lay down, the men of the city, the men of Sodom, both young and old, all the people to the last man, surrounded the house, and they called to Lot, "Where are the men who came to you tonight? Bring them out to us, that we may know [i.e, rape] them." Lot went out of the door to the men, shut the door after him, and said, "I beg you, my brothers, do not act so wickedly. . . . Do nothing to these men, for they have come under the shelter of my roof. Behold, I have two daughters who have not known man; let me bring them out to you, and do to them as you please; only do nothing to these men, for they have come under the shelter of my roof." But [the crowd] said, "Stand back!" . . . Then they pressed hard against Lot, and drew near to break the door. But [the angels] put forth their hands and drew Lot into the house to them, and shut the door. And they struck with blindness the men who were at the door of the house, so that they wearied themselves groping for the door. (Genesis 19:1–11)

God destroys the city the next day, after helping Lot and his family to flee.

So what *is* the true sin of Sodom? Some insist that it is homosexuality. And it's true that homosexual acts (of a sort) are in the story. Other verses can be cited in support of this reading as well. Nonetheless, the insistence that *the* sin *must* be homosexuality—that no other reading is even possible, and no other possible sin matters—misses the depth of the story itself.

An ancient reading is that the true crimes of Sodom are its shocking level of violence and its extreme disrespect for strangers. That's certainly in the story too—in fact, one might have thought, a lot more central to it. Ezekiel had another interpretation: "Behold, this was the guilt of…Sodom: she and her daughters had pride, surfeit of food, and prosperous ease, but did not aid the poor and needy" (Ezekiel 16:49). On this view, the story is really a call to social justice!

Moderns might suppose that if anything is specifically condemned in this story, it is rape. After all, rape is what the crowd had on their minds. It turns out that gang rape was a common practice of the times for humiliating enemies. So maybe *that* is the true sin of Sodom—the readiness to sexualize humiliation?

But we can't stop there either. Lot, who is presented as the only decent man in Sodom, actually offers the crowd his own daughters in the place of his guests. The angels prevent these rapes too from happening. But God still saves Lot from the destruction of the rest of the city. Does not Lot's treatment of his own daughters offend God? Is the shelter of his roof for strangers more important than the shelter of his home for his own children? We are reminded that this story was written at a time when some values were very different than they are now: when, for one thing, women were regarded only as a father's or husband's property, for him to dispose of as he saw fit. And it therefore becomes hard to take the story, whatever exactly it condemns or doesn't condemn, as the moral last word.

In any case, again, the main point can hardly be said to be *clear*. You begin to see why, for some religious traditions, exploring the interpretation of such stories is the core of the worship service itself. Christians inherit long traditions of debate and disagreement about Scripture, and Judaism's second most sacred text, the Talmud, is essentially a history of (loving!) disputation about the Torah.

Reading the stories in this way is, once again, a shareable approach—a kind of common ground. It's the opposite of trying to squeeze a single moral out of them, which barely is to read them as *stories* at all. Let us approach them, together, as the complex, many-layered narratives that they are.

THINKING FOR YOURSELF

The Bible is not all stories, of course. Sometimes God explicitly commands certain acts and condemns others. Here too, though, for better or worse, it turns out that things are complicated. Here too is a large element of interpretation and choice. Ethical thinking remains essential!

THE NEED FOR INTERPRETATION

"Thou shalt not kill" seems the clearest of the Ten Commandments. But almost all Christians and Jews eat other animals, which requires killing on a massive scale. Many Christians and Jews support capital punishment. Most fight in wars. Some also believe that suicide (self-killing) may be permissible too.

The Torah reads, "Thou shalt not *murder*." This seems a little more reasonable: It is at least arguable that killing in war or in the electric chair is not murder (though it is also arguable that it is) and the notion of murder is implicitly limited to other humans (though it is arguable that it shouldn't be). Once we get into alternative translations, however, we return quickly to the question of alternative interpretations. After all, the word in the Christian Bible is *kill*—so if you take it literally—anyway in English—that should be the end of the matter.

Also, to say "Thou shalt not murder" is not helpful as a practical guide. In effect it says: "Don't kill unjustly." But when is killing unjust? Is capital punishment, for example, "murder"? You may have views about the answers to these questions, but they aren't given in the commandment "Thou shalt not murder." One way or the other we are back to, well, interpretation.

Or again: we are commanded to honor the Sabbath. But when is the Sabbath? Even this simplest of questions is unclear. Jews celebrate Sabbath from Friday sunset until Saturday sunset. Early Christians followed Jewish practice, only gradually shifting the observance to Sundays. Some Christians still celebrate Sabbath on Saturdays (the "Seventh-Day Adventists"). Is there a "right" answer? Not, it seems, in the text...

WE STILL DECIDE

There are also a large number of explicit commandments that almost no one takes seriously and almost all of us feel free to ignore. Not too many people even "Honor the Sabbath" any more, come to think of it—whenever we think it is. Here are a few more dramatic examples from Leviticus:

> 11:7: "You shall not eat the swine; it is unclean to you."
>
> 11:11–12: "Everything in the waters that has not fins and scales is an abomination to you. Of their flesh you shall not eat, and their carcasses you shall have in abomination."
>
> 19:9–10: "When you reap the harvest of your land, you shall not reap your field to its very border...and you shall not strip your vineland bare, neither shall you gather the fallen grapes of your vineyard; you shall leave them for the poor and the sojourner."
>
> 19:19: "There shall not come upon you a garment of cloth made of two kinds of stuff."
>
> 19:27: "You shall not round off the hair on your temples or mar the edges of your beard."

A few people actually do follow (some of) these commandments: some Orthodox Jews, some Amish orders. But almost all other Christians feel free to disregard them entirely. Even confronted with explicit commandments, then, and commandments put in the strongest terms too (Leviticus's punishment for "abomination" is usually stoning), we still feel entirely free to go our own way—if for example we think that some of these commands are just "historical relics," as I hear many people say, like dietary restrictions that once made sense but no longer are necessary.

The point is not that we are hypocritical. The point is that *we can and must decide for ourselves*—understanding, for example, that regardless of what the text literally says, it comes from a historical place very unlike our own, and is also the product of contentious translations and interpretations, and therefore may apply differently to our time, or not apply at all. Even if we decide to follow its commands, that is still a *decision*—our decision.

This is not just an abstract point. Here is another passage from the same part of Leviticus:

> 20:13: "If a man lies with a man as with a woman, it is an abomination."

This commandment is regularly cited by people who claim (as they put it) that "God hates homosexuality." But these very same people, like most of the rest of us, disregard most of the rest of Leviticus. Down where I live, certain churches even hold pig roasts at rallies where speakers rail against homosexuality and other modern sins. If you take the text literally, though, it seems that God hates pig-eating just as much as He hates (male) homosexuality. And if you *don't* take the text literally, as seems plausible enough in the case of pig-eating, you can hardly claim that you have no choice but to take it literally in cases where it happens to accord with your preexisting convictions. In neither case, really, is even an explicit commandment the end of the story.

People who continue reading Exodus after the Ten Commandments are often disturbed to discover that in the very next chapter the Bible seems to condone slavery:

> When you buy a Hebrew slave, he shall serve six years, and in the seventh he shall go out free, for nothing. If he comes in single, he shall go out single; if he comes in married, his wife shall go out with him. . . . [But] when a man sells his daughter as a slave, she shall not go out as the male slaves do. . . . When a man strikes his slave, male or female, with a rod and the slave dies under his hand, he shall be punished. But if the slave survives a day or two, he is not to be punished; for the slave is his money. (Exodus 21:2–3, 7, 20–21)

These passages were used by American slaveholders during the struggle over abolition to show that God approved of slavery. Now, with slavery gone and its evil recognized, the rationalization is transparent. Yet the words are there. Literally, the text does not say that slavery is wrong. Literally, it condones slavery under pretty broad conditions.

We can appreciate the writers of Exodus for what they tried to do: adapt a living ethical tradition to the needs of the time. No doubt these rules promised at least some small improvement over slavery as it had been practiced. They began to give (some) slaves (some) rights. But now of course times have changed—drastically. We still have a living tradition (again, *many* living traditions) but the needs of three thousand years ago are no longer our needs. We need to rethink and adapt the tradition just as the prophets and lawgivers of biblical times did. And that may mean—as clearly it does mean in the case of these words about slavery—that we need to go beyond their words to the *spirit* of their acts and of our shared tradition, as full of ambiguity and uncertainty as that is too. Again there is no refuge in the text—no alternative but to decide for ourselves.

A BIBLICAL IDEAL

On the angels' way to Sodom, they visit the patriarch Abraham in his desert tent. As they leave, they declare God's intention to destroy Sodom if the rumors about it are true. Abraham is troubled by this. He cannot see the justice of killing the innocent along with the wicked. So Abraham, says the Bible, "went before the Lord." He actually took it upon himself to question God!

> Abraham drew near and said: "Wilt thou indeed destroy the righteous with the wicked? Suppose there are fifty righteous within the city; wilt thou then destroy the place and not spare it for the fifty righteous who are in it? Far be it from thee to do such a thing, to slay the righteous with the wicked, so that the righteous fare as the wicked! Far be that from thee! Shall not the Judge of all the Earth do right?"
>
> And the Lord said, "If I find at Sodom fifty righteous in the city, I will spare the whole place for their sake." Abraham answered, "Behold, I have taken upon myself to speak to the Lord, I who am but dust and ashes. Suppose five of the fifty righteous are lacking. Wilt thou destroy the whole city for lack of five?" And He said, "I will not destroy it if I find forty-five there." Again he spoke to him, and said, "Suppose forty are found there." He answered, "For the sake of forty I will not do it." Then he said, "Oh let not the Lord be angry, and I will speak. Suppose thirty are found there." He answered, "I will not do it, if I find thirty there." He said, "Behold, I have taken upon myself to speak to the Lord. Suppose twenty are found there." He answered, "For the sake of twenty I will not destroy it."
>
> Then [Abraham] said, "Oh let not the Lord be angry, and I will speak again but this once. Suppose ten are found there." The Lord answered, "For the sake of ten I will not destroy it." And the Lord went his way, when he had finished speaking to Abraham; and Abraham returned to his place. (Genesis 18: 23–33)

What is the Bible telling us here? Surely not that we should simply do what we're told and accept whatever authority—even the highest religious authority of all—decides to do. Quite the contrary. Abraham, the revered fore-father, did not simply obey. He would not accept injustice even when God Himself proposed to do it. Abraham went to God—Abraham who is "but dust and ashes"—and complained. He questioned, he challenged. "Shall not the Judge of all the Earth do right?"

Abraham thought for himself. Moreover, he was honored for doing so. God listened and answered. Indeed Lot himself was saved, the Bible says later, because God was "mindful of Abraham."

Mustn't we do the same? Of course I don't mean that we must never listen to others. Listening to good advice and thinking about new perspectives are crucial. Religious texts too have long been sources of great inspiration and stimulation. Use them. Speak the shared language; retell the stories. Still, in the end, it is up to *us* to interpret, ponder, and decide what they mean. So the next time someone acts as though it is yours only to obey the commands of God (according to their interpretation), or yours only to obey some other authority—remember Abraham!

A LAST WORD FROM THE WISE

Some people may find it hard to reconcile such a message with the experience of tight-knit religious communities in which the leaders fervently believe that they speak for God Himself and therefore *do* expect obedience. Critical thinking may be explicitly forbidden, and even when it is tolerated it is seldom understood or encouraged. Not only is it hard to buck such insistent and accepted authority—it can also be hard to question leaders whom you rightly respect and may even love.

Still, though—one last time—there is a deep wisdom in what ethics asks. We can see this best by looking to the wisest of the wise. We have spoken of Nelson Mandela and Archbishop Tutu; I also think of Gandhi, the Sufi poet Rumi, the original philosopher Socrates, just to name a few. Many others will be cited and discussed in later chapters. These are great people. And they don't avoid moral issues—often they wade right in. They may *advise* us. They may attempt to *persuade* us, as may any respected and loved moral leader.

But here is the crucial thing: none of these people would claim to speak for God or demand that you put their judgment in place of your own. On the contrary, they are acutely aware of their own limits as well as the limits of others. They recognize that even with the best of intentions, they are still creatures of their time and place, and therefore that *even they* will hear the voice of God (or however they might describe their moral perceptions) through the filters of partial understanding or the residues of local prejudice or the lack of the full range of human experience. So they lead by inspiring *more* thinking—not less.

God came to Elijah alone in the cave at Mt. Horeb. There, the Bible says, God spoke in a "still small voice" (1 Kings 19:12)—a phrase that can also be translated as "gentle breeze," "soft whisper," "hardly a sound." A hiss, a rustle. There is a vital caution here. Hearing that voice can be a very tricky thing—and in any case it comes to each of us, very quietly, on our own. You begin to see why Quakers and many others, both religious and secular, have put their livelihoods and even their lives on the line for freedom of conscience. Protestant Christianity itself began with the insistence that everyone should be able to read and interpret the Scriptures for themselves. Thinking for yourself is not somehow irreligious—it is at the very core of the religious experience.

CAN GOD DEFINE THE GOOD?

Here's an old philosophical paradox for you—something to think about. Are good things good because God says they are, or does God say they are good because they are good?

One view is: what's good is good because God says so. God's commanding something *defines* it as good. This view is called the *Divine Command Theory*.

The Divine Command Theory seems simple, straightforward, and—if you believe in God—pretty natural. That it doesn't work for atheists may be a problem—after all, atheists have values too—and there certainly will be problems when the commands of God are unclear or the commands of one religion's God conflict with those of another's. But there is also an intriguing problem with this theory first pointed out nearly 2500 years ago by the Greek philosopher Socrates.

If God's commands alone define the good, then God's commands begin to seem arbitrary. Suppose that instead of commanding us not to kill, God had commanded us to kill. *Thou shalt kill.* According to the Divine Command Theory, then, killing would be good and refraining from killing would be bad.

But this can't be right. Killing really is wrong whether God says so or not. And in fact we do have reservations and second thoughts at some of the points in the Bible where God's own ethics actually seem a little questionable. If the Divine Command Theory were true, Abraham's question—"Shall not the Judge of all the Earth do right?"—could not even be asked.

There's a related problem too. If the Divine Command Theory is true, it makes no sense to say "God is good." Whatever He commands is—well, whatever He commands. If His commands *define* the good, then there is no point admiring Him for His goodness. (This is also why we can't respond by arguing that God never *would* command killing. Why not? *Whatever* He commanded, whatever He did, would be good—by definition.) But this seems, in a sense, to cheapen God. It ought to mean something (and God ought to want it to mean something) to say "God is good."

We could conclude that God says certain things are good because they *are* good. Then, however, we consider the good to be independent of God. To say "God is good" *is* in a certain sense to judge God. God's commands are not the end of the story: we must still decide whether or not God (or rather, God's many and varied interpreters) is right. In the abstract this may sound like some kind of heresy, but as I've just been arguing, we actually do it all the time, for example, when we disregard commandments that we consider outdated. Once again, it appears that there is no alternative to thinking for ourselves.

FOR REVIEW

1. What are some examples of change and growth in religious ethics?
2. How does the text argue that there is no such thing as "the" Christian view on controversial moral matters?
3. What are "shareable terms"?
4. How might Pope John Paul II's broad appeal illustrate the possibilities of shareable terms?
5. What might we learn from Nelson Mandela's and Desmond Tutu's collaboration?
6. What are two interpretations of the story of Nuri Bey?
7. What are two interpretations of the story of the destruction of Sodom?
8. How does the text argue that "we still decide" even when explicit commandments tell us what to do?
9. How does Abraham argue with God, and what might be the moral of that story?
10. What is one difficulty with the Divine Command Theory?

EXERCISES AND NOTES

CARRY ON

Is there a distinctive way that you approach moral questions that traces back to your religious background? If so, what is it? If you are religious, explore the ethics of your religion more fully. Ask your priest, minister, rabbi, or other leader for some guidance—and ask to explore a variety of views within your own tradition.

Next, explore moral and religious frameworks other than your own (see some references in the Notes). Talk to people from other traditions. Take a course in comparative religions. And read. Learn how other people see things. Is there a distinctive way that *they* approach moral questions that traces back to *their* religious background? If so, what is it? You don't have to give up your own beliefs to do so, of course, but you will certainly come back to them with greater understanding.

READ THE BIBLE!

All of the great figures of the Old Testament are morally complex—and fascinating. Abraham, the chosen forefather of the forefathers, raises the knife over one son and exiles the other, mirroring the immensely painful divide of closely related Semitic peoples to this day. Jacob cheats his own brother out of his birthright and is in turn roundly cheated, misled, manipulated, and exploited by his own family for the rest of his life. Rachel steals her own father's household idols and lies about it all around. Yet she is the beloved wife and matriarch.

Ask some questions. For one thing, since Abraham is so willing to argue with God over the fate of Sodom, why will he not, only a decade or so later, argue with God over the fate of his very own son? And why would God ask him to kill Isaac in the first place? (Don't just say "to put Abraham to the test." There is more depth in the story. Why would God need or *want* to put Abraham to the test? And why this particular test?) Were these (and others) good acts? Did God think so? How could we tell?

Consider the Cain and Abel story in Genesis 4:1–16: the story of the first murder in history, mythologically speaking. Why does God reject Cain's offering and accept Abel's, thus setting off Cain's anger and the murder—not an entirely unforeseeable result? What does Cain mean when he asks, "Am I my brother's keeper?" Is the moral of the story that he *is* (that we *are*) his/our brothers' (each other's) keepers? If so, or in any case, why doesn't God say so—why doesn't God answer him? Isn't Cain partly suggesting that *God* ought to be Abel's "keeper"—that God also bears some responsibility for what happened? Does God dodge the question?

In the New Testament, Jesus' disciples constantly complain that his parables are confusing and ambiguous. (And don't you think it's interesting that the Bible reports this?) Each has been interpreted in many ways—put to many uses. Might they be more than a little like the story of Nuri Bey?

Could it be—could it just possibly be—that what Jesus meant to teach us with these stories is not an exact moral lesson or rule, but something more like a sense for the subtlety of things, maybe the mysterious ways of God Himself?

Some intriguing parables and sayings of Jesus can be found in Matthew 6:25–33, Matthew 20:1–16, Luke 19:12–26, and Luke 9:23–27—just for a few of many examples.

A variant: Look carefully at the ethical arguments of religious leaders. For example, why do the popes oppose birth control? Read Pope Paul VI's *Humanae Vitae* and other relevant papal encyclicals (most papal encyclicals are available directly from the United States Catholic Conference Publishing Service at www.nccbuscc.org) and find out. It's *not* because the embryo or fetus is a human being—in many cases, there's no fertilization at all. So why *is* it? Once you figure out the argument (it *is* an argument, not a mere pronouncement) ask yourself whether the values to which Pope Paul appeals are specific to Catholicism or more general. You may not necessarily agree, but there's often a lot to be learned anyway.

Another remarkable encyclical is John Paul II's "Laborem Exercens" (1981). John Paul's marriage of Christian humanism and Marxist influences here produces a widely applicable and eloquent plea for work and workplaces that befit human beings, and therefore a sharp critique of what John Paul calls the "economism" of both capitalism and communism. John Paul II also made himself an eloquent and persistent advocate of third-world debt relief and income redistribution. Here too a pope entered the contemporary discussion in a way that was far broader and more powerful than a merely sectarian pronouncement.

Finally, consider moral stories from other religions and their sacred texts. Read the Koran. Read Zen stories in collections such as *Zen Flesh, Zen Bones*, compiled by Paul Reps and Nyogen Senzaki (Shambhala, 1994), and explore African stories, such as Mohammed Naseehu Ali, *The Prophet of Zongo Street* (Amistad, 2006), and Sufi stories, in lovely collections such as Idries Shah's *Tales of the Dervishes* (Penguin, 1993), and others.

ABORTION AND THE BIBLE

Nowhere does the Bible discuss abortion explicitly, but related themes do come up, and Christian pro-life advocates regularly cite certain passages that suggest that a fetus has human standing in the eyes of God. For example, there is a stirring passage in Psalms 139:

> For thou didst form my inward parts; thou didst knit me together in my mother's womb. . . . My frame was not hidden from Thee, when I was being made in secret, intricately wrought in the depths of the earth. Thy eyes beheld my unformed substance, in thy book were written, every one of them, the days that were formed for me.

If God cares for us even in the womb, then—pro-life advocates conclude—there must be an "us" to care for: we must already exist as persons in His eyes.

However, others have questioned this reading of the passage, pointing out that it is more poetic than anything else (the Psalms are hardly meant literally) and is more concerned with creation in general than with the point at which life begins (indeed the last two lines seem to suggest that God knows and cares for us even before we are in the womb, but it's hardly plausible that we are fully human even *before* conception).

Christian pro-*choice* advocates, meanwhile, cite other passages that seem to suggest that abortion might be acceptable. One is in Exodus 21:

> When men strive together, and hurt a woman with child, so that there is a miscarriage, and yet no harm follows, the one who hurt her shall be fined, according as the woman's husband lays upon him; and he shall pay as the judges determine.

The penalty for murder is death (e.g., in verse 12 of the same chapter: "Who strikes a man so that he dies shall be put to death"), so pro-choice Christians argue that the Bible can hardly consider causing the death of a fetus (miscarriage) to be murder if only a fine is specified as punishment.

On the other hand, the phrase "and no harm follows" is puzzling. Isn't there necessarily harm to the fetus? From this pro-life advocates have taken heart, arguing that the passage is, well, ambiguous. The Hebrew phrase translated in the Revised Standard Version (given here) as "so that there is a miscarriage" *might* also be translated as "so that her child comes out" (apparently there is no ancient Hebrew word specifically for miscarriage), which *might* be read as meaning that birth occurs prematurely but with no (other?) harm to the baby—in which case the passage could have just the opposite meaning. The Greek version has still other ambiguities.

It seems that neither passage is really very clear!

Here are some other places where the Christian Bible touches (or has been interpreted as touching) on the question of the status of fetal human life: Job 3 and 10, Ecclesiastes 4 and 6, Jeremiah 1, Luke 1. Read them (all), and read them in context (that is, read the whole chapters, even when only a few verses are relevant; also, read all of Psalm 139 and Exodus 21, cited earlier). Then ask what you can conclude about what the Bible thinks of the status of fetal human life. Does a clear picture emerge from these chapters taken together? Does a clear picture emerge from any of them taken separately? Explain your answers. (Good luck!)

NOTES

A synoptic and constructive exploration of many of the themes of this chapter —starting with common values—is Joseph Runzo and Nancy Martin, editors, *Ethics in the World Religions* (Oneworld Publications, 2001).

Interfaith Power and Light's mission statement is cited from http://www .interfaithpower.org, accessed 1/23/07. On Mandela and Tutu, see Mandela's autobiography, *Long Walk to Freedom* (Back Bay Books, 1995) and Michael Battle's *Reconciliation: The Ubuntu Theology of Desmond Tutu* (Pilgrim Press, 1997). For Mandela's multicultural and secular formation, along with his words cited here (part of a 1999 speech to the Parliament of the World's Religions in Capetown), see Anders Hallengren, "Nelson Mandela and the Rainbow of Culture,"   http://nobelprize.org/nobel_prizes/peace/articles/mandela/index .html, accessed 12/29/06.

"The Ancient Coffer of Nuri Bey" comes from Idries Shah, *Tales of the Dervishes* (Penguin, 1970). Citations from the Christian Bible (Revised Standard Version) are given in the text. On the Genesis passage cited in the text, remember that in Biblical Hebrew, "to know" means to have sexual intercourse. Compare Genesis 4:1: "And Adam knew Eve his wife, and she conceived and bore Cain." A short but pointed treatment of the ambiguities and complexities of the Lot story and the biblical treatment of homosexuality (in Torah and the Koran as well) is Arthur Ide, *The City of Sodom* (Dallas: Monument Press, 1985). On arguing with God, see also Exodus 32:1–15, where Moses dissuades God from destroying Israel after the incident of the Golden Calf. Here Moses argues with God almost as with an equal. And the Bible explicitly says that, as a result, God "repented of the evil which He thought to do to His people." I am grateful to my colleague J. Christian Wilson for help with biblical references and translation issues.

For the original of the argument cited in the box "Can God Define the Good?" see Plato's *Euthyphro*, available in many editions, in complete editions of Plato's work and in collections such as Penguin's *The Last Days of Socrates*.

CHAPTER 4

Ethical Talk
Ground Rules

As we begin to explore ethical issues with others, much of our actual day-to-day or class-to-class practice is *talking*. Judging by the usual ethical debates, though, our ways of talking about ethics could use some improvement. How can we talk more constructively with each other about ethical issues?

HOW TO HAVE A FRUITLESS DEBATE

A meets B in the cafeteria line, one thing leads to another, and a familiar kind of verbal fistfight begins.

A: Eating meat is natural! Humans have always done it. I wish all you vegetarians would get off my back. You want to go against nature.

B: Oh right, I suppose people have always lined up at McDonald's for their quarter-pounder with shake and fries.

A: Well, what do you want, to line up at some juice bar for your little organic carrot with spring water? Give me a break! Besides, you animal rights fanatics want to stop all medical research. What about the cures for so many diseases, found through experiments on animals? If it weren't for those experiments, you wouldn't even be here to bad-mouth them.

B: Why do we need all those new cosmetics and toilet bowl cleaners? That's what 99% of animal testing is about! You're just rationalizing torture.

A: I bet you don't even like pets. You're telling me I don't love my dog?

B: You think that your dog wants to live stuck in some tiny little apartment all day? You call it "love" when you pen up a dog? Talk about unnatural!!

And so it goes—a fruitless debate, but sure loud enough. This one is only slightly exaggerated from the kinds of real-life debates we have all the time.

Each side aims primarily to shut the other side up, to put them down in their own eyes and the eyes of anyone who may be listening. Potentially helpful points come up, but they are immediately dropped like hot potatoes. The actual arguments don't connect.

If put-downs and "winning" are your goals, you may deliberately try to create such debates. We could even spell out some of the "rules" both sides seem to be following. One is:

- **Take All the Room You Can.** Talk *loud* and talk a lot. Fill all the space you can with *your* thoughts and opinions. Worry about your *comeback*. Restate your opinion. Use a lot of "I think that..." statements. After the other person is done, come right back with "Yeah, but..."

Neither person really listens or tries to understand what the other person is saying. They're angry; they have a lot to say on the subject; they cannot wait to jump back in with some new peeve or assertion. If one side raises a good point, the other one would not think of acknowledging it or trying to respond. Neither is willing to give an inch. Apparently the best defense instead is just to change the subject. Having a comeback is everything.

Second:

- **Separate and Polarize.** *Polarize:* that is, exaggerate differences. Emphasize what you and the other side disagree about. Define their view as simply the opposite of yours. Always *assume the worst. Stereotype* the other side ("You're just a..."). Use *black/white labels* ("pro-life," "pro-death"). Try to define the other side before they can define themselves. Make your stereotyped labels stick.

Either all medical research or none; either a quarter-pounder or carrot sticks for lunch. No space for possible agreement is explored, no shared values are acknowledged or sought. Polarizing in this way reinforces the put-downs generally: the other side is made to look silly and stupid by constant exaggeration, as if they could not be in favor of anything sensible or balanced. Again there is no attempt to understand what the other person might actually mean. Instead the worst is assumed, and then attacked and mocked.

Finally, two related further "rules":

- **Exploit All Weaknesses or Openings.** Take *potshots.* Follow "red herrings." Pounce on any small discrepancies or other difficulties; don't engage the main point. *Run down partial solutions.* If an idea is not a perfect solution, attack it as no solution at all. Protect yourself by avoiding constructive thinking or making suggestions. Always be *against* something rather than *for* something.

- **Go for the Quick Kill.** Talk in *slogans* and *soundbites.* You'll infuriate the other side and everyone will remember your brilliant pithiness. Use facts only as *weapons.* Only seek out the ones that support your side; deny and suppress any others. *Disengage quickly* once you have secured an advantage. Demand closure; expect "final" answers; pull out as soon as you can claim you're "right."

Slogans and labels abound (like "you animal rights fanatics"), and all sorts of assumptions are made with no thought of checking them out to see whether they're true or not. Does B really know that A's dog is penned up all day? Does A really know what B thinks about medical research? No—they just make an assumption and blast away.

The whole debate is a series of potshots and changes of subject. Often the comeback is on a subject different from the one just being discussed. They start out talking about meat-eating, then about medical research, then about pets. A's opening claim is mostly about whether eating meat is natural. B responds in a sarcastic way, though she does have an argument of sorts. Not surprisingly, A in turn responds chiefly to the sarcasm, derides what he *assumes* to be B's alternative—and then changes the subject to medical research…

WELL, WHAT'S WRONG WITH THAT?

Debaters know these "rules" and use them often. For some purposes they may even be useful. For other purposes it is at least useful to know about them: they may help you fight back or avoid getting caught in such a debate in the first place.

But—obviously—these "rules" do *not* work well when we are trying to think constructively about a problem. For one thing, they are ineffective, at least at persuasion. They don't really persuade—they only dominate and silence. The "loser" in such debates goes away angry, frustrated, maybe self-blaming—and certainly not feeling understood.

Second, they don't expand or develop ideas. They give us no way of cooperatively improving an idea. Quite the contrary: since the whole aim is to gain some personal advantage from criticizing any weakness in the other side's ideas, putting forward any kind of proposal is the last thing these rules encourage. Tentativeness, hope, enough trust to take up a rough idea and brainstorm together: this is just what these "rules" *prevent.*

In short, debate in this key drives people apart; it does not promote understanding; and at bottom *it is not ethical itself.* It is not committed to listening, open-mindedness, cooperation, and careful and responsible attention to values or arguments or concepts. We need to find another way.

HOW TO HAVE A USEFUL DISCUSSION

Now imagine a dialogue on the same subject in exactly the opposite key: listening carefully, respecting the other side, hoping to learn something and perhaps even to change your own ways as a result. Not mere acceptance ("Well, whatever…"), which leads to no dialogue and no learning at all. No: a real discussion, even disagreement, but in a constructive key. How would the discussion go then?

Rewind the tape. A meets B in the cafeteria line, and the debate begins again.

A: Eating meat is natural! Humans have always done it. I wish all you vegetarians would get off my back. You want to go against nature.

In the very first place, a good listener would notice the defensiveness in this statement. "I wish all you vegetarians would get off my back." It seems that more is at stake for A than just a disagreement about the facts. You might guess that A has felt put on the spot, or put down, for eating meat. You could easily predict, too, that A will therefore find it hard to hear and acknowledge even the best arguments against meat-eating. So although B's first impulse seems to be to mock A's argument and put her down even more cleverly, this is exactly the wrong strategy. Better to deal with the anger before taking up any arguments at all.

B: So someone's been on your case, eh? Sorry about that. For my part, I'm really not interested in playing guilt games, though I know it happens with subjects like this…

B's response in the original dialogue does raise an important point. But B should raise this point in a way that is clearer and (obviously) not sarcastic. In the original, remember, after A says that eating meat is natural, that humans have always done it, B responds:

B: Oh right, I suppose people have always lined up at McDonald's for their quarter-pounder with shake and fries.

B may be thinking that humans may *not* always have eaten meat, at least in the way we do now. Generalizations about what has "always happened" are often made in a pretty offhand way, more as a rationalization than anything else. Is this what B suspects? If so, B could make his point a lot more effectively: by asking a question, for example.

B: I'm not so sure that people have always eaten meat. We're not built for it, biologically: Our teeth are the munching sort, not the tearing teeth of real carnivores. At least, I doubt that humans ate so much meat as we do now. What kind of diet do you think humans evolved with?

Now consider the next exchange. In the original, A mocks B's point in turn, and then goes on to something else. Remember:

A: Well, what do you want, to line up at some juice bar for your little organic carrot with spring water? Give me a break! Besides, you animal rights fanatics want to stop all medical research. What about the cures for so many diseases, found through experiments on animals? If it weren't for those experiments, you wouldn't even be here to bad-mouth them.

My students, analyzing this exchange, point out: (1) it would be more useful for A to ask B what kind of diet he actually proposes, rather than respond to the sarcasm with more of the same; (2) A should stay on the subject (the naturalness of meat-eating) rather than shift to something else; and (3) A should *ask* B what he thinks about medical research rather than assuming he's against all of it. Suppose A said:

A: I'm pretty sure our ancestors ate meat when they could get it, though you might be right that it wasn't very often. But I'm interested in what you propose instead. Eating no meat at all, ever? What about people who need to eat meat to survive in their environments, like the Eskimo? This also makes me think of the debate about using animals in medical research. Are you also opposed to that? Always?

These are good questions, and once again have the effect of opening up a thoughtful discussion rather than closing the talk down into "comebacks." Notice also that A no longer assumes that B must hold the most extreme possible position. Instead, she *asks* B what he thinks—and raises the question for B himself of just how far he will go.

B in turn can respond in a more constructive way.

B: Probably many people did eat meat when they could get it. And yes, maybe some people have to. But *we* don't have to. My real point is that it's not exactly natural to eat meat like we eat meat, anyway. Not meat at every meal, and the fattiest meat at that!

A has helped B to get to his *real* point—now we are getting somewhere!

Notice that in his original response, B never answers the question about medical research: he talks only about product testing.

B: Why do we need all those new cosmetics and toilet bowl cleaners? That's what 99% of animal testing is about! You're just rationalizing torture.

He might now be able to answer that part of A's question more thoughtfully too:

B: I'm troubled by how much pain animals are put through for even the most minimal human gain. What right do we have to do that to animals even if there is a gain for us? This relates to the question of product testing too. If some new kind of shampoo or cosmetic or cleaner can only be brought out if it is tested on animals, then maybe it just shouldn't be brought out. We shouldn't be causing so much suffering when we don't have to.

This last discussion is in place of B's passing remark in the original debate about "torture." No longer is it merely a passing remark. Now it opens up new aspects of the issue to explore.

Notice how shared values begin to come into view. For example, A is un-likely to think that unnecessary suffering is morally acceptable. She does not want to be responsible for imposing needless suffering on animals. This is why many people have stopped eating veal, even though they may eat other animals and use animal products. A would probably argue that in other cases the suffering isn't needless—that in some way it is necessary—or that the animals don't really suffer so much. In any case, this is now a constructive discussion, and it is beginning to sound like ethics in a more familiar sense: trying to spell out and apply shared values. It's a mutual exploration, no longer a fight.

RULES FOR CONSTRUCTIVE TALKING

Ethical dialogue *could* be like this. All it takes is some skills that are not even so difficult. No part of the discussion in the last few pages, I trust, has been some shocking new revelation. All of the skills, and the possibilities they open up, are familiar. We just need to learn how to put them into practice at the right times.

Earlier we spelled out "rules" for fruitless debates. We can now spell out four corresponding rules for constructive talking—your ground rules for ethical discussions.

- **Slow Down and Listen.** Speak *calmly* and listen a lot. *Avoid the automatic comeback.* If you find yourself too ready with the "Yeah, but...", stop and take a deep breath. Then say, "Let me see if I understand you..." Watch the surprise (and appreciation). And work for better *understanding*. Ask questions, and mean them. Restate others' views to make sure you "get it"—later you can ask for the same consideration back. Expect that you have as much to learn as they do.

In the revised dialogue, instead of taking all the room they can, A and B actually show some interest in each other's views and take the time to try to understand each other. They try to put their points carefully, admit uncertainty, and identify conflict without escalating it.

- **Connect.** Seek *common ground*. Approach differences against a background of probable agreement. (Differences may emerge as interesting against this background. They certainly emerge as *bridgeable*.) Recognize complexity on the other side (and yours). Don't polarize. There are no simple "yes" and "no" positions. Keep the focus on the *main points*. You might even help other people clarify and develop their thoughts and avoid distraction.

In the revised version, A and B are not preoccupied with their differences, but explore them carefully while also identifying key points of agreement. They try to "integrate values," recognizing that each side speaks for something important. It's up to us to figure out what it is.

Finally, two more related rules:

- **Welcome Openings and Opportunities.** *Look for first steps and partial measures.* No problem is going to be resolved all at once. Think constructively; make suggestions. Always be *for* something and not just *against* something.

- **Stay Engaged.** Think of discussion as a collaboration in search of better understanding and creative ideas. Try to speak in a careful, open-ended, and helpful way. Avoid slogans or soundbites. Treat facts as *tools*. They're probably also more ambiguous than either side makes it seem. Keep exploring and looking for them. Expect the key questions to remain *open*. There is always more learning to do; the discussion will continue.

Instead of taking potshots and seeking to disengage the moment they have an advantage, A and B now take a much more exploratory approach, and don't imagine that they are going to settle things once and for all. And therefore, oddly enough, they actually get much further than the debators for whom finding a final and "right" position, right now, is everything. Debaters lock themselves into their positions and cannot budge. Collaborators, interested in a constructive discussion and making at least *some* difference, can *move*.

And notice finally, as I have been insisting throughout, that these are *moral* rules too. Unlike the first set of rules, these rules reflect a commitment to listening, cooperation, and careful attention to values or arguments or concepts. They offer a way to talk about moral issues that is itself moral.

DIALOGUE UNDER DURESS

Dialogue sounds wonderful in theory. But what if you are talking with someone who is not interested in dialogue? Or someone who does not know how to have one, or does not trust you or the situation enough to listen or believe they will be listened to?

Don't Give Up Too Soon

Sometimes ethical discussions reduce to fruitless debates because some of the participants have no idea that there is any other way to talk—or, even if they do, they don't trust anyone else to try it.

In that case, clearly the thing to do is to try it. Create an alternative. Set alternative ground rules for discussion, such as the Common Ground Rules in the reading to follow. Anyone who thinks that debate is the only way will be pleasantly surprised—and so will you, when people who appeared to be interested only in debate turn out to prefer something else, once given a real choice. The point is that *you* may have to be the one who creates that choice— *you* may have to set the alternative ground rules, formally or explicitly or gently by example. You do not simply have to accept whatever kind of discussion you find yourself stuck in.

Even habitual complainers can be lured onto more constructive ground. To the people whose main mode of discussion seems to be constant criticism and complaining, ask: "So, what's *your* idea?" Show some interest. Carping is usually a safe strategy because carpers can avoid sticking their necks out by making positive suggestions. So make positive suggestions safer. Create a setting in which creativity and openness are rewarded and carping is not.

Resisters

Some people just *love* to argue—so much so that they do not even notice, and certainly do not respond to, invitations to dialogue. They automatically turn any discussion into a debate.

You can leave this kind of discussion. You are not obliged to keep trying dialogue forever. Usually you can pull out in a way that isn't "losing," but just refusing to play the game.

You might also challenge the debate rules. Point out what is happening, and ask your partner or the group if this is really how they want to proceed. This is uncomfortable, of course, and not subtle at all. But it may sometimes work. At least it keeps people from falling into debate as if it were the only possible way to discuss things.

Some people enter dialogue in bad faith. People may use dialogue as a means of stalling. The idea might be to talk an issue to death so that nothing really changes—an appealing option for those who like things the way they are. So you need to be sure that all parties to the dialogue enter it with some good faith. If they don't, you are again entitled to pull out.

Or stay but refuse to play along. You might still make some progress. Stallers may find it hard to keep up polarizing values and grandstanding when you are speaking carefully and in general refusing to "play debate." Try it: it can actually be fun. If you have low expectations at least you won't be disappointed.

Some people may join a dialogue (or may have to, for example in a classroom) but be unwilling to speak honestly and openly in it. I have seen students in discussions of homophobia or racism or other kinds of prejudice unwilling to express views they actually hold, especially if they fear seeming prejudiced. But then many useful questions never get asked, stereotypes never get addressed, and some people leave feeling oppressed by a general atmosphere of "correctness."

This can be a way of resisting dialogue too, though often well-intentioned. Some indirection might help. *You* name the stereotypes, so at least they're out on the table. Find a story or movie whose characters bring them up, so the class or group can discuss them in the third person. Encourage others to bring up views in the third person too, as in: "Someone might say that..." or "It's not my view, but..."

Silencing

Some people go into dialogue easily and feel welcomed and rewarded. Others come into the same space disadvantaged and with well-established habits of deference and silence. The results are very uneven patterns of participation and influence.

Usually the advantaged ones, though, are blissfully unaware of this imbalance—it's just "the way things are," to them—and if it is brought up by the disadvantaged (who are generally *quite* aware of it) the reaction is typically denial and anger. So, naturally, it is seldom brought up. Things just go on as before.

Still, dialogue fails when only some members of a group do all the talking: only men in gender-mixed groups, only whites in racially mixed groups, only teachers when teachers and students are together. Phyllis Beck Kritek, a nurse-administrator experienced at "negotiating at an uneven table," gives another example:

> I once served on a statewide committee looking at maldistribution of health care services.... There were several Native American reservations in this state. Health care needs on these reservations were profound. Historically, these needs had been easily rendered invisible.... An honest effort was made to change this pattern, to invite representatives from the tribal councils to the table. They attended the first organizational meeting.
>
> The tribal councils, of course, had a well-developed model for deliberating on conflicts: requesting all parties to speak their minds on the issue one by one and uninterrupted, in a deliberative fashion; consulting the elders; seeking guidance from spirits...; reflection. The approach to conflict offered by the statewide committee was open discussion and political posturing,

a tug of war between competing agendas. The tribal representatives sat silently watching, saying nothing. Later one participant commented to me privately that the American Indians were sure not going to get their fair share if they didn't participate better. No one asked them to speak their mind during this time. They would only have had the opportunity to speak if they had chosen to participate in the competition for airtime. At the second meeting, they were absent.

If You Feel Silenced

When you find yourself silenced or disadvantaged, here are some suggestions.

For one thing, again, don't assume that you must play the game by the prevailing rules. Maybe the prevailing rules are the *problem*. You might try to bring up this problem directly, or you might try to subvert the rules in a less direct way. For example, if the advantage of others is sustained partly by a distinctive language or jargon, request translations. Use your own language sometimes and translate for others. As Kritek says, this at least "highlights the inequity structured into the negotiation that requires you to sit at an uneven table speaking someone else's language." Make things more complicated—you can do it.

Democratic talk needn't be the kind of "free-for-all" that Kritek describes. There are many other traditions and styles of dialogue. Native Americans often used a "talking stick," giving the holder an uninterrupted "floor," passed around to everyone in turn so that each voice could be heard and each voice had its "space." Try it. At least, if debate is not a style that you can even enter, ask for a different kind of hearing from your group. If they care to hear you out, they will agree (or at least discuss it). If they don't, then at least you know where you stand—and they will have to admit where *they* stand.

Classroom settings can be changed too. Talk to your instructor; find a way to raise the issue for the class. In a class that uses this book, call on this chapter.

When You Are Advantaged

Suppose you are one of the advantaged. Others may be feeling silenced, but not you: you might even be feeling quite expansive.

Your job first of all is to recognize the problem. Advantage is usually invisible to the advantaged because the space of dialogue does not seem constrained to *them*. It is easy to enter when you know you will be listened to and taken seriously. It is hard to imagine that others could feel any differently. "Well, why don't they just *talk?*"

But of course it is not so simple from the other side. It may help to remember those times that *you* felt intimidated from saying anything, or that no one would really listen or care anyway. Recognize now that others may feel the same way in a discussion that feels entirely open and natural to you.

Second, raise the problem with your group as a whole. Point out the unequal pattern of participation. State as directly and honestly as you can *your* interest in hearing from those who have been silent. Ask on behalf of the group (step up to leadership here) in what ways the group can change so as to lessen the barriers to participation that others may be feeling. Maybe you need a talking stick? Maybe...?

Once again, the challenge may be to *you* to move yourself—and to move *first.* You may have to disrupt and challenge familiar and comfortable ways (to you, anyway) and make things more difficult. There may even be dialogues that you conclude aren't possible right now. Trust must first be built in other ways, maybe; or some other kind of institutional or personal change is necessary first. Things don't get easier! But they might, slowly, get better.

"Common Ground Rules"

MARY JACKSTEIT AND ADRIENNE KAUFMANN, THE COMMON GROUND NETWORK FOR LIFE AND CHOICE

The Common Ground Network for Life and Choice worked from 1993 to 2000 to bring together activists from opposing sides in the abortion conflict in the hopes of creating real dialogue, understanding each other better, and finding common ground that the two sides could build upon together, rather than frustrating each other's every move. The reading that follows comes from the group's manual *Finding Common Ground in the Abortion Conflict,* by Mary Jacksteit and Adrienne Kaufmann, published by the Common Ground Network (1601 Connecticut Avenue NW, Washington, DC, 20009) in January 1995. The "spirit of common ground," they say, is dialogue—a good in its own right as well as a precondition for actually working together to promote shared goals.

The organization that sponsored the Network in turn, and produced this manual, is called Search for Common Ground (SFCG). The Common Ground Network for Life and Choice was SFCG's first project in the United States. Six projects in the

United States have now been completed, with four others ongoing, as well as an impressive number of international projects, all using the same basic approach. For more information on all of these projects, as well as a downloadable version of the manual excerpted here, see www.sfcg.org/programmes.

WHAT IS THE COMMON GROUND APPROACH?

For many people the idea of searching for common ground in the abortion conflict is strange and unbelievable—even unthinkable. Some people can only imagine that you are inviting them to engage in an activity in which they will have to "compromise" their values and beliefs. Viewing the conflict as a black or white contest to see which "side" will "win," the only alternative they can envision is the creation of some shade of gray in which their values and concerns are diluted and diminished. For some, the idea of any conversation with "Them" is dismissed as an act of betrayal.

Because the very idea of "common ground" in the abortion conflict is foreign and radical to many people in this society, we are offering a variety of approaches to answering the frequently asked questions "what do you mean by common ground?" and "what is the common ground approach?"

THE SPIRIT OF COMMON GROUND IS THE SPIRIT OF DIALOGUE

The practice of dialogue lies at the heart of the common ground approach. Dialogue is different from debate. Debate is about persuading others that your views are "right" and that the views of others are "wrong." Debate tends to create winners and losers and often leads to pain and divisiveness when the subject is sensitive and people's views are as heart-felt as they tend to be on the issue of abortion.

Dialogue is a gentler, more respectful process than debate. The spirit of dialogue is to acknowledge and honor the humanity of *all* persons present regardless of their points of view. The goals of dialogue center around increasing understanding and being understood rather than persuading others and being "right."

When dialogue is attempted in a sustained and polarized conflict, a primary goal is to change the relationship between those who see each other as demonized adversaries. When an issue is explosive and relationships are already highly strained, dialogue is more likely than debate to lead to understanding and trust. A carefully constructed dialogue process can enable hard issues to be addressed without leading to bad feelings.

THE COMMON GROUND APPROACH IS A SEARCH
FOR WHAT IS GENUINELY SHARED

The idea of common ground can be illustrated by two interlocking circles. Each circle represents a point of view about abortion (one circle, pro-life: the other, pro-choice). A common ground process recognizes the integrity of each circle as a complete set of concerns, beliefs, and values around this issue. A common ground process primarily focuses attention on and explores the *area of intersection*. Through the search for concerns, beliefs, and values that are *shared,* a platform of understanding is built.

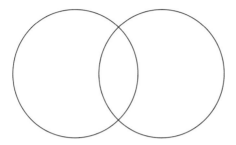

When participants stand together in the area of genuine intersection, they can also look at their *differences* with fresh eyes. The differences remain the same as before, but the perspective on these differences has changed. The angle of vision is from the common space looking out, instead of from the areas of difference where adversaries glare at one another across the submerged and unseen area of what is shared.

COMMON GROUND IS NOT COMPROMISE

Searching for common ground is not about compromising to reach a middle position but about focusing on areas of *genuinely* shared values and concerns. People are not asked to change their views on abortion or sacrifice their integrity. Participants in a common ground process seek to understand one another, not to force or pretend agreement where it does not exist.

A COMMON GROUND APPROACH ENCOURAGES LOOKING BEYOND THE LABELS AND THE STEREOTYPES

A common ground approach assumes that even in a polarized conflict, people's views fall on a continuum.

Pro-life _____|_____ *Pro-choice*

When people identify themselves as "pro-choice" or "pro-life," they are only placing themselves *somewhere* on the continuum other than the exact center.

The idea of a continuum encourages awareness of how little we can assume about another person's set of beliefs if all we know about them is that they choose one label over the other. It opens us to look for diversity on both sides, and to imagine that two given people with different labels may be as similar as two other people with the same label. It fosters curiosity about the views of the particular individuals on the "other side" encountered within a common ground approach.

A COMMON GROUND APPROACH ENCOURAGES CONNECTIVE THINKING

Debates tend to focus attention on the weaknesses of a speaker and to encourage a search for the flaws in what is said. Dialogue encourages *connective thinking* that focuses attention on the *strengths* of the speaker and encourages a search for the gems of wisdom, or pieces of truth, in what is said. Over time, the practice of connective thinking in a group can lead to the creation of a web of shared knowledge woven from the threads of truth contributed by its members. Connective thinking fosters the building of constructive relationships and the development of community because it ties together the best wisdom of each member of the group. It is an important practice in the search for common ground.

A COMMON GROUND DIALOGUE ENCOURAGES THE SHARING OF PERSONAL EXPERIENCE

A common ground dialogue usually begins with the sharing of personal experiences. Life has been experience by each person in a unique way. Personal experiences cannot be argued about nor agreed or disagreed with. They *are*. Sharing life stories invites understanding responses from those who hear them. They are a constructive place to begin.

A COMMON GROUND DIALOGUE ENCOURAGES GENUINE QUESTIONS

Genuine questions are questions asked in a spirit of real curiosity and a sincere interest in hearing the answers. Rhetorical or leading questions are **not** genuine questions. They are questions for which we already know the answers. We usually ask them not to learn but to test or trap someone whom we view as an opponent. The posing of genuine questions and the omission of all other kinds is a trademark of common ground dialogue.

THE SEARCH FOR COMMON GROUND ACKNOWLEDGES OUR SHARED MEMBERSHIP IN THIS SOCIETY

Common ground involves acknowledging the connections that exist between people related to one another by shared community, faith, and/or citizenship. This approach can allow us to see how we are all affected by stressful and troubling circumstances in the larger social environment. It can enable participants to relate to one another as "all of us against the problems we face" rather than "part of us against the rest of us."

ANSWERS TO FREQUENTLY ASKED QUESTIONS

In this section we offer ingredients for answers to questions that are frequently asked of us or members of the Network.

WHY DO PEOPLE GET INVOLVED IN COMMON GROUND?

People have become involved in common ground activities for a variety of reasons. Prominent among those reasons are desires to promote a civil democratic society, effective problem-solving on important social issues, and peace. More specific motives frequently offered include:

- A belief that the level of confrontation over abortion is "out of hand" and destructive.
- A perception that the conflict is getting in the way of needed social change and is not helping the powerless and disadvantaged.
- The sense that the tone of the conflict is uncomfortably "out of sync" with personal systems of beliefs.
- A painful experience of division—division between people of faith, between women, between family members, between community members—and a belief in reconciliation, reconnection, and the need for people to learn to live in community despite serious differences.

WHAT FRAME OF MIND DOES IT TAKE TO "SEARCH FOR COMMON GROUND"?

Not everyone is willing or able to join in the search for common ground at the moment they are invited to do so. Ideally, a person participation in common ground brings:

- A willingness to respect a human being who disagrees with you on the abortion issue and pledges to respect you in turn.
- An ability to listen to statements and views with which you strongly disagree without trying to convert those on the "other side" to your way of thinking and without feeling compromised by the act of listening.
- A belief in the importance of finding out what each person knows and understands about an issue.

- A desire to meet the human beings behind the stereotypes and media images.
- An openness to the unexpected, to the potential of "connecting" with an "adversary."
- A belief that conflict can be a positive opportunity for growth and understanding.
- An ability to handle skepticism and criticism from people on one's "own side" who view common ground as compromise and a dangerous way of conferring legitimacy on the "enemy."

Few people have all these qualities fully or equally developed when they enter into a common ground process. What is essential is that participants be committed to respecting the ground rules that govern the dialogue process.

WHAT SORT OF PEOPLE ARE INTERESTED IN COMMON GROUND?

- Women and men, of different ages and different backgrounds, in widely separate parts of the country.
- Catholic and Protestant Christians, Jews, people of all faiths and those who have no religious orientation.
- Committed and active advocates on the abortion issue.
- People who have a position on abortion but are not activists, and people who feel "in the middle" on this issue.

WHAT ARE PEOPLE ACTUALLY DOING?

Around the country, pro-life and pro-choice people in local communities are coming together in a number of different ways—in small informal groups, in workshops, in structured dialogues with facilitators, in retreats, in joint endeavors to solve real problems. To date, efforts to find common ground on abortion have been happening primarily at the grassroots level where people are trying to create community at a face-to-face level. This is a "bottom-up" change in the dynamics of the conflict.

HOW DO PEOPLE SEARCH FOR COMMON GROUND ON ABORTION?

- They set aside generalities and rhetoric.
- They meet and talk within a framework of ground rules based on a willingness to listen, to speak with respect, and to keep what is said confidential.
- They speak as individuals, not as representatives of advocacy organizations.

- They share personal experiences and beliefs about abortion.
- They explore areas of common concern as well as difference.
- They confront the stereotypes, perceptions, and misperceptions that people on each side hold about those on the other.
- They may organize to work on a specific project or issue of mutual concern.

FOR REVIEW

1. What are two good ways to "take all the room that you can" in a debate?
2. What is the opposite of taking all the room you can? (Be concrete.)
3. What are some specific ways to separate and polarize people and arguments?
4. What are some specific ways to "connect" instead?
5. What is the opposite of exploiting weaknesses and openings? (Be concrete.)
6. What is the opposite of going for the quick kill? (Be concrete.)
7. Why is dialogue an ethical task as well as a practical one?
8. How does the text recommend responding when dialogue is under duress?
9. What is the Common Ground approach to dialogue?
10. Why do Jacksteit and Kaufmann say that the Common Ground approach is not the same as compromise?

EXERCISES AND NOTES

REWORKING DYSFUNCTIONAL DIALOGUES

This section gives a number of "dysfunctional dialogues"—short exchanges that never rise above the level of fruitless debates. Each of them also presents some opportunities for new directions, for more constructive conversations. Each could be taken in many different constructive directions.

Read each dialogue aloud together. Then identify the places where the dialogue goes bad. What are its failures? Why does it so quickly turn fruitless?

Next, identify its missed opportunities. What are some of the places where this dialogue could have taken a more constructive turn? Are there interesting ideas that the opposed sides could explore together? Do points of possible agreement come into view? Are questions asked that could be understood as genuine questions and answered without more rhetoric?

Finally, rewrite the dialogue in a more constructive key, and read the new dialogue aloud for the whole group. Comment on the methods of dialogue you are trying to use.

Business Ethics

R: "Business ethics" is a contradiction in terms. The business of business is to make money, not to be nice to people.

P: Besides, business is pretty ethical. I know a lot of business people, they're not out there breaking laws and screwing people just to make an extra buck.

Q: Oh yeah? Think of all the scandals. The military contractors that overcharge a thousand percent for screwdrivers and deliver faulty equipment that endangers servicepeople's lives. Oil companies that ravage the rainforests. Companies like Wal-Mart that deliberately destroy whole downtowns while pretending to be such patriotic American citizens. It makes me sick.

P: Well, like I always say, the exceptions prove the rule.

Q: Then there are all the scandals that we don't even know about. I bet we've only scratched the surface.

R: The real problem are all the self-proclaimed whistleblowers who keep accusing businesses of scandals just so they can get some attention. I think they're damn troublemakers. Should keep their heads down and their mouths shut.

Q: Yeah, it's a cushy life getting thrown out of your job, blacklisted in the industry, having snoops dragging up everything they can to discredit you...

Homelessness

M: I just saw a homeless guy holding his sign out at the intersection.

N: It's disgusting how people like that come and put themselves on display and play on your sympathies and tie up traffic too.

M: I guess he should just go off into the woods and die quietly.

N: He should get a job! I'm tired of these welfare bums eating up my tax dollars.

M: If he's homeless I doubt he's on welfare. He's probably one of the ones that you and your Bible-thumping right-wing friends threw off welfare to fend for themselves. Now look what you've done. Now he has absolutely nothing. You call that Christian?!

N: There's plenty of work in this country if people just got out and did it.

M: Oh right, the way corporations are downsizing jobs around here, you should be glad *you've* got a job. Maybe that will be you out there in the intersection in a couple of years. You think I'll toss you a coin?

Wasteful Ways

A: The amount of waste around here is just incredible. Every time the college has a party, look at all the plastic forks and spoons and styrofoam cups—thousands and thousands of the things, and they last forever. We just throw them out. Then people go back to their muscle cars and drive two blocks that it would be healthier to walk, wasting gas too. Not to mention that the stupid cars themselves are deliberately designed to go out of style and even stop working after a few years. Then we have to buy a new one. And already there are more cars than people in America.

B: Oh, lighten up. People choose to buy these things. It's their right—that's what America is all about. They know it will be out of style in four years. They choose to change it.

A: Then why is advertising the biggest industry in this whole country? They're spending millions of dollars to make you want this stuff. You don't object to that, you think that's just fine. . . . If I happen to have an opinion, though, but not a million dollars to spend promoting it, you get mad!

B: People choose to watch the ads, don't they? Besides, what do you want? Ban them all? OK, let's make a law: no ads, no new models, everyone has to buy the same boring old car, keep it ten years at least. . . . Give me a break!

Rich and Poor

T: I can't believe the insensitivity of some people. Everywhere there is hunger and need. Twenty thousand children in this world die every day of starvation or diseases that are easy to prevent. Yet we waste and waste and waste.

M: Yeah, but the poor will always be with us. You're ranting and raving about how terrible we are, but if you think about it, the poor in America are rich compared to even the rich in other countries. Whole families in Africa may get less money in a year than one welfare mother in Chicago gets in a month.

T: Oh, right, I'd like to see you try to live on it, even for a week.

M: I certainly wouldn't sit around all day feeling sorry for myself. I believe in work—that's how to get ahead in America. As my grandfather used to say, if you need a hand, look at the end of your arm. God helps those who help themselves.

T: What a crazy idea of God! It seems to me that a really sensible God would help those who need help.

Sexual Violence

Q: Women who get raped are asking for it!

R: I don't see how you can say that. Men have all the power, including greater physical strength than women.

Q: Women are adults and can say "no," can't they?

R: If men would listen!

Q: A lot of men listen but a lot of women say "yes" when they mean "no."

R: That's not women's fault, it's the way we were brought up.

Q: Well, a lot of men are brought up to hear what people actually say, not what they don't say.

R: Are you blaming women for men's actions, then? Don't you think men should be able to tell when they are forcing women to do something they don't want to do? If a man gets into a fight with another man, he doesn't think they're playing around—he knows when they're fighting!

Youth Curfews

Y: It stinks that young people have special curfews, special times they have to be indoors. It's not fair.

Z: Young people are responsible for more thefts in neighborhoods. If we keep them off the streets after dark, burglaries will go down.

Y: How can you prove that? You only think it because you have a stereotyped view of young people.

Z: It's obvious: look at all the young offenders either in prison or in the courts trying to stay out of prison.

Y: You can't just point to those people. You have to look at all the young people who aren't doing anything wrong but want to do something fun after dark. It's not fair to keep us all off the streets because your generation is afraid of us!

Z: We have every reason to be afraid of your loud noisy gangs roaming the streets, forcing us off the sidewalks sometimes, hanging around the malls, making so much noise...

Y: If your generation would provide us with more fun places to be and go, maybe we'd go there! But you think we're just a bunch of hoodlums. You are waiting around for us to grow up and be just like you. We don't wanna be just like you!

Here are two more steps you might consider taking with this exercise. One is to listen in everyday life for similar dialogues—interchanges on moral subjects, or indeed any subjects—that, let's just say, could go more productively than they may be going. Talk radio will give you extreme cases, but listen in the same way to family discussions, political debates, religious dialogues, and so on. Think about why they take unconstructive turns. Again, as with the exercises here, be *specific:* that is, exactly at what point in these interchanges do you see people getting stuck or provoked and things starting to turn bad? How could you help head them in a different direction?

A next step is to try to join in those discussions at the time they are happening in the hopes of making a constructive difference. What strategies will you use? What can you achieve when you do?

NOTES

Two helpful practical book on ethics and dialogue are Roger Fisher and William Ury's *Getting to Yes* (Penguin, 1983)—more on this in Chapter 14—and Tom Rusk, *The Power of Ethical Persuasion* (Penguin, 1994). Rusk "applies the ethical principles of respect, understanding, caring, and fairness...to high-stakes conversations often threatened by strong emotions and defensive reactions." Many of Rusk's themes parallel this chapter's, though his focus is chiefly on one-on-one conversations about professional or personal matters, rather than larger conversations about moral issues.

For a practical introduction to the emerging field of "invitational rhetoric" —an explicitly ethical and constructive approach to public argumentation— see Sonja K. Foss and Karen A. Foss's text *Inviting Transformation* (Waveland Press, multiple editions). I am grateful to Linda Powers of Wofford College for alerting me to this new area.

The box on dialogue under duress draws upon an intriguing book by Phyllis Beck Kritek, *Negotiating at an Uneven Table: Developing Moral Courage in Resolving Our Conflicts* (Jossey-Bass, 2nd ed., 2002). The story about Native Americans comes from her page 36, the advice about "using your own language" from page 279. There is much other useful advice.

Chapter 13, "Mindful Speech," returns to deepen the dialogue theme and to broaden ethical attention to all aspects of speech.

CHAPTER 5

Service and Service-Learning

CALLS TO SERVICE

A lost child at the store or the airport needs reassurance and aid. A struggling child at school needs tutoring. There is an accident on the highway. In situations like these there is no puzzle at all what to do. The point is just to do it. This is "walking the talk." Your grandmother has stories to tell but no one to listen to them—and thirty years from now your own children will want to know. After a storm, trees are down on people's houses all over the neighborhood—and you have a chain saw. Hungry people are everywhere, and the rainforests are still burning in the Amazon—don't you have a little money to spare? No puzzles here.

Even about controversial and unclear matters, there is usually a lot to do that isn't controversial or unclear at all. Don't use the debate as an excuse for staying away. Welfare programs may be controversial, for example, but it's clear that there are many poor people who need help. No one disagrees about that. And many are not getting that help now. Your church may run a soup kitchen or provide meals to a homeless shelter. You can join in. Or maybe you are hiring people—why not someone in special need?

"SERVICE-LEARNING"

Service can also be a kind of *learning*—so much so that many high schools and colleges now speak of "service-learning" not just as a combination of two separate things but as *one* kind of thing, where the learning is integral to the helping and the helping is integral to the learning. In fact, many schools are beginning to require it. More than a few of my students have spoken of Habitat for Humanity house-building trips or working at the homeless shelters as among the richest experiences of their college years. Think of it: all of that struggling through classes, and all of that work to pay for it all, and yet the best parts are free...

You learn about life from very different perspectives. You get to know people quite different from yourself. Work in a soup kitchen, tutor underprivileged children, answer a suicide prevention hotline, and you begin to understand what life is like for some other people. Situations and needs that might have been easy to dismiss—that may never have been more real than a quick glimpse in a TV news report or stereotypes in some politician's speech—now are right before you, real people. Your learn what *their* struggles involve. The world begins to look a little different.

You learn what is possible for people past the usual labels and assumptions. Only by meeting different people and working with them can you crack those stereotypes, can you begin to see them as actual *people:* individuals just like ourselves, with their own distinctive struggles and needs, humor and depth.

The Special Olympics World Games came to town a few years back. Mentally handicapped people from all around the world came to compete and be honored—so many that it took three hours just for all the teams to march into the stadium. Thirty years ago the mentally handicapped were kept out of sight, not believed capable of physical skill or speed or grace. Now there are Special Olympics marathoners and swimming teams and horseback riders and soccer and volleyball teams, many of whom also compete with non-handicapped athletes in open competitions. It seemed like every store in the state was sponsoring a team or highlighting its own mentally handicapped employee-participants. They were visible, and proud. Thousands of volunteers did the behind-the-scenes work, met the athletes, and found themselves looking at the mentally handicapped in a new way.

You learn to remember what really matters. Volunteer in a hospital or deliver meals to the sick or old, and you remember again how precious is just the ability to walk down the street. Work at a homeless shelter, and every time you get into your car or open your front door you will remember what an amazing freedom you have. Make a child laugh, and life's little frustrations go back to the corners where they belong.

PERSONAL CHALLENGES

But helping is not necessarily easy. Especially when it is face-to-face, service can be upsetting and unsettling, an uneasy experience. Collecting money for "charity" feels pretty safe, but serving meals to the homeless or showing a mentally retarded South African the town may be a real stretch.

Yet it is precisely when we "stretch" the most that we learn the most—especially about ourselves. Say Ram Dass and Paul Gorman:

> Often we reach out to help one another and succeed. Natural compassion
> comes easily and we're equal to the challenge. But…deep questions of

identity and relationship are going to arise much of the time we are caring for one another. The more wrenching the situation, the more likely such issues will be central. Who *are* we to ourselves and each other?—it will all come down to that. *Will we look within?* Can we see that to be of most service to others we must face our own doubts, needs, and resistances? We've never grown without having done so. This wouldn't be the first time we've fought the inertia of conditioning.

"Doubts, needs, and resistances"—yes. First there are the little nagging things. Maybe we think that it's not our job to help. Don't we pay taxes to hire other people to do this? Or: how will we know what to do? Or maybe we're too used to holding aloof even from family and friends. Sharing life stories with a stranger is asking a lot! Or maybe we're afraid of being rejected. What do we really have to offer?

Worries like these don't last long once you begin helping. There's certainly enough to do, taxes or no, and often it's the simplest things—sometimes just being with someone or pulling fallen branches off a lawn or serving up supper. And rejection is very rare if you respond to a clear call for help and remember your basic courtesies. Anyway, asking ourselves what we really have to offer is probably a useful thing from time to time: it is a way of taking stock of our own lives.

The deeper worries are the harder ones. Maybe we fear our *own* weakness and suffering, seeing in others' suffering what may await us in turn. In that case helping is a hard thing indeed, but it can also be a path back to a kind of ethical recognition: acknowledging and accepting suffering, our own included, as part of life. There is no way around the pain; the only way is through. One of Dass and Gorman's many stories makes this point well:

> I have a friend, a chemotherapy nurse in a children's cancer ward, whose job it is to pry for any available vein in an often emaciated arm to give infusions of chemicals that sometimes last as long as twelve hours and which are often quite discomforting to the child. He is probably the greatest pain-giver the children meet in their stay in the hospital. Because he has worked so much with his own pain, his heart is very open. He works with his responsibilities in the hospital as a "laying on of hands with love and acceptance." There is little in him that causes him to withdraw, that reinforces the painfulness of the experience for the children. He is a warm, open space which encourages them to trust whatever they feel. And it is he whom the children most ask for at the time they are dying. Although he is the main pain-giver, he is also the main love-giver.

Maybe the deepest worry is that once we open to suffering and needs like these, they may eat us alive. We can come face to face with suffering on a scale so unexpected and enormous that we do not know what to do. It may even be that there *is* nothing that anyone can do. We want to run away, to retreat into a safe world where there is hope and laughter and love.

But here even we can help. There may be nothing else to do, but we can almost always just *listen*. Often that is what people really want above all—just a chance to tell their story, to be heard. And as a listener you can accept the story as a kind of gift, not as an added burden. It is not as though the weight somehow shifts to you. No—but it does lighten for the other person. Funny thing about us: sharing actually helps.

HOW MUCH IS ENOUGH ?

There are people who give their lives, in one way or another, to service. Think of Mother Theresa, who dedicated her whole life to helping the outcast of India. Or "St. John of the Trees," a man who devoted decades to reforesting parts of the Alps, each day and every day, one seedling at a time. Or the ordinary and unnamed heroes of some catastrophe, like the unidentified passenger in a Washington, DC, plane crash a few years back who, as his plane was sinking into the ice-filled Potomac, pulled passenger after passenger out of the cracked fuselage and into a helicopter lift until the plane went down for good and took him with it. Or the countless parents and teachers and many, many others in all walks of life who keep life going by daily small acts of self-sacrifice and spunk.

Examples like these may inspire us—and they may also make us feel guilty. Is such selflessness really morally required of us all? Once we acknowledge the need for service, doesn't it sometimes seem that we are being asked to hand over our lives as a kind of moral blank check? Is there any legitimate and honest way to draw a line?

Yes there is. Christian moral tradition, for one, draws such a line. We are obliged, naturally, to do our duty by others—to respect others, keep our promises, follow the law, and so on. We are *not* obliged, however—or rather, not *obliged*—to go further than that. Great acts of generosity or sacrifice are certainly good things to do, but they are not *required*. You do not have to make such sacrifices to be a moral person. These are the acts of "saints": what moral tradition calls "supererogatory" acts—above and beyond the call of duty.

In short, it's not required that we take the whole burden of the world on our shoulders. It's not required that we do absolutely everything we can, whatever the cost to ourselves, to help others. Ordinary ethics calls for something more like a balancing act.

In Part II you'll also see that each family of values both urges us toward service and also suggests certain limits. There is, for instance, the imperative to serve the greatest good of the greatest number. But we must include ourselves and those close to us—our families, friends, co-workers, communities—among that "number." Likewise, we are asked to seek justice and fairness for both others and the self. Besides, even purely for the sake of better serving others, some kind of space for the self is also necessary—some kind of breathing room, some sense of a center.

Morality, then, is not infinitely demanding. The real story is more complicated—and more humanly realistic. We need at least to *pay attention* to the needs and legitimate expectations of others as well as ourselves—remember, that is our very definition of ethics—and we need to *respond* to those needs and expectations at least to some extent. But the best way to respond, and how far we should respond, may vary with each of us and with each of our situations.

As a broad and rough general guide, Christian moral tradition challenges us to consider "tithing": that is, to give 10 percent of our income—and by extension, perhaps, 10 percent of our time and energy—to others beyond self, family, and friends. It's interesting to note that American volunteerism runs at just about this level. About half of all Americans over age 13 volunteer an average of 3.5 hours a week—which is about 10 percent of the average work week.

The most important point, though, is that "helping" and "self" are not necessarily at odds. So it's not quite as though the tradition tells us that we can morally have 90 percent of our time and energy to ourselves, as long as we give 10 percent "away" to others. No: the tithing idea is instead a reminder that among the many forms of giving and receiving in our lives there needs to be a level of conscious giving beyond one's immediate self, family, and friends. And we also "receive" in the same way. Making the extra phone call, coaching a kids' soccer team, welcoming the new neighbors with a surprise dinner—these can sometimes open up whole new possibilities, new dimensions of life for us. They serve the self as well—as long as the "self" is not narrowly defined in opposition to "others."

VISITS TO A HOMELESS SHELTER

Ten minutes from my semi-rural oasis of a college campus is a small city's shelter for the homeless. Half an hour on the freeway takes us to a large urban shelter. My students and I go to both places to help—and to learn.

Today we are standing in the lobby of Weaver House, a shelter run by Greensboro Urban Ministries in Greensboro, North Carolina. We have already run a kind of gauntlet to get in here—a gauntlet, at least, of our stereotypes: inner city, people hanging around the door, "The Homeless." We're uneasy, glad to be here in numbers. Yet there is something else here too: a sense of reality, and of need, need so palpable as to hang in the air. After all, this place is the last thing standing between most of these people and sleeping on the streets, hungry. We begin to see the world a bit through their eyes. Are *we* the gauntlet that the homeless all too often have to run?

"The primary objective of Weaver House," says the shelter's mission statement,

> is to provide Greensboro's homeless with the necessities for basic human survival on a temporary basis, including: food, refuge, clothing, medical and spiritual counseling. In addition to the above, Weaver House seeks to empower those homeless persons who wish to be empowered by providing them with the programs, the linkage to service agencies, and the advocacy that is needed to generate a new start.

This statement is part of a Volunteer Information Sheet written by Paul Davis, the shelter's director and our guide today. In it Davis spells out certain values in an extraordinarily precise way—and not in the way we probably expected.

You might expect an appeal to pity. Certainly that is how the homeless are often presented—as pitiable—and how charity often goes. But Davis is talking about *respect*—respect and fairness, equality and rights. To speak of "basic human survival" is a plea for the most fundamental equality, and the words themselves have weight and an echo: Basic. Human. Survival. These are the most minimal but essential things, he says. How could they be too expensive for the richest society on earth?

GUESTS

"All people who come are guests," the statement goes on, "sojourners for whom God demands hospitality." The overriding message of this way of putting things is not the religion. (This place calls itself a *ministry*, after all, where religious language comes naturally, but it is not the only language one could use.) No: the point is that at bottom we are not so different. We are *all* "sojourners" along the way. To say that "God demands hospitality" might for some invoke the image of a stern, commanding figure. It might also simply remind us that just as each of us is sometimes vulnerable and in need, so too each of us has a certain right to be here, to walk the Earth and know something of the joys this life can bring—sojourners all.

> We seldom ask why a person has come. All people who come are guests....
> Most of our guests are wonderful. Some cannot follow our rules and must leave. Some cannot follow our rules and we will bend them to be hospitable. Our guests, in short, are just like us, only they are more poor, under stress, and are forced to make more difficult choices than most of us face.

For this reason, people who stay in the shelter are never labeled as homeless (or even as "clients"—that's how social service agencies talk)—just, always, as "guests." They are not made into objects of pity by our very language.

Seventy-five to eighty percent of Weaver House's guests have jobs, Paul tells us. More have two jobs than have none. Some are highly trained. An aerospace worker, displaced when his company abruptly left town. One of the masons who built the latest classroom building on our own campus. Most have a college education: sometimes we meet guests who were graduates of our own college. (One night, hearing where my students are from, one guest pulls out his old college ID card for them. Wide eyes all around.) Some will only stay until they get enough money together to move into a place of their own.

People are shocked. This is not what the stereotypes tell us. We wonder how a person working two jobs still can't manage to make it. Paul's answer is that the pay is low and the conditions are bad, and even people who move into their own apartments are one disaster away from the shelter again. Kid gets sick, car breaks down, and they're destitute again.

Others can never seem to do it, he says. They can't handle money, never learned how to keep a checking account, can't seem to understand that it might be better to take a job that pays more money less often rather than daily work that pays little but right now. A whole range of people.

And, yes, some are no longer interested. Think of it as another culture, Paul says. Many of the homeless want just what these students want: a good job, money, a house, a nice comfortable middle-class life. But not all do. In much of the rest of the world there are cultures in which these things might be nice but are not worth working for and worrying about all the time. Homeless culture, or part of it, Paul says, can be like that too. Besides, if you have worked hard for twenty years and still have nothing, why would you still want to work? Why indeed.

LISTENING

"Talking with the guests," says the Volunteer Information Sheet,

> is probably the most important thing you can do at Weaver House. Just listen and be polite. You may feel the need to "fix" some problem, and indeed fixing is very important. But, listening is even more important. Our guests are rarely listened to, and it is our privilege (and sometimes our burden) to listen to another person's story.

It is hard to welcome or deal with those who remind us of vulnerability, those whose needs are too great or too unfamiliar. My students sometimes wonder how they can really help out here, what difference they can really make in these people's lives, not realizing yet that simply being here, willing to help and to listen, is already the biggest step they can take. And that they too will learn in the process.

"My experience at Weaver House," wrote one student,

> was not what I expected...I went in with a narrow mind. I thought I was going to see a bunch of drugs and drunken men in horrible dirty and ripped clothes. Now I cannot believe I went in with an attitude like that....

I was afraid to go up to someone to start a conversation, but I did anyway. I ate dinner with a woman while we talked. She was an interesting lady. You could tell she was very lonely and had no friends or family. She talked about when she was younger. She seemed to be very happy then.... I do not know what happened to her. It is probably better that I don't know, but I am broken up to hear how someone who seemed to have such a "normal" life could end up like her. Maybe she got into drugs or whatever, but she appeared to have a very good heart.

"I did not know what to think," she concludes, "because if my grandmother was in a situation like that I would cry my heart out." She goes home and cries her heart out anyway. Then she goes back.

"Our guests," says Paul, "are just like us..." We know that too, but usually only in the abstract. Here in the shelter it gets more real.

All of my insecurities were running through my head as I approached the door and had to be let in by one of the guests. Some people were gathered by the TV and it's funny to me now, but the first thing I thought was "Hey, I watch that show too!" It's embarrassing to look back now at how nervous I was because then it hit me that homeless people are just the same as me.... Right away I was so glad I had come.

Again and again the students encounter people their own age—and see themselves.

Just before the doors closed at eight o'clock a young girl walked in. She handed me her card and walked into the dining hall. I could not help noticing how young she looked—like me. I looked her up in the book. She and I are only two months apart by birth. I could not imagine being in her situation.

When dinner was over and it was time for a smoke break, she walked out the door with the others for a cigarette. I don't smoke but I really wanted to talk to her so I got a cigarette and followed them out the door. I sat down next to her and asked her if she had a light. Then we started talking. She told me that she was born in Texas, then her family moved to Greensboro. She attended NC State for the first month of school but had to drop out for medical reasons. She and her mother did not get along and that was why she had come to the shelter. I asked her if the people at the shelter ever intimidated her. She answered without hesitation "yes." I then questioned why she didn't go home...if the shelter scared her and her mother wanted her to go home. She responded that she wanted time on her own. Later she got up and called her mom.

I'm not sure what she will end up doing—whether or not she will go home or return to school. What I do know is that I saw myself in her...

LEARNING

Other things happen—puzzling, provocative, scary, painful. In one shelter there are small children. Thinking of their lives is very hard for some students. "Why do we allow children to live on the streets?"

Sometimes the reality is more complicated. One pair of kids is in daycare while their mother works—and daycare costs enough that she can't afford an apartment. So, in effect, homelessness is the price of working. In the evenings one of my students finds herself rocking the little ones to sleep while their mother studies for her GED. It is certainly not an easy life, but it is not a dead end, and they are not "living on the streets" either. They live at the shelter. One child has so many friends at her shelter that it is really, for her, an extended family. Let in early, on a cold night, she cries until all her friends get in too. ("Home is where the heart is," one student wrote after a night like this.)

People at Weaver House often have only one bag of things to their name. Volunteers have to check their bags when they come in. They discover to their amazement that many bags are filled with *books*. "The very things students like us take for granted," writes one, "are the prize possessions of people who have nothing." Another writes:

> Up in the laundry room they have a shelf of books...B. [a guest] came in and began looking through them and asked if I had ever read any of them...not these in particular but just any at all. It felt awkward to answer "no," but that was my answer. He then replied, "These are good, you should read them sometime. Right now these are pretty much all I got and when I read them, in my mind I do have opportunity, and that is what keeps me going.

This student concludes: "It took me a few seconds to realize that a 22-year-old, just like me, who has fallen upon hard times had basically made me feel like I have pretty much cheated myself out of a semester of top-quality education."

Some students are brought up short when they assume that a well-dressed person in the shelter must be another volunteer—only to find that he or she is a guest. "At that moment," says one, "I realized that *I too* could be here." It also happens in reverse: "A young black man came in and stood at the counter talking with some of the guests. I felt completely embarrassed after I had asked him his name to check him in and he told me he was not a guest." He was, in fact, the manager.

Sports-minded students go for the ballgames. They could stay at home and watch by themselves in their dorm rooms or a bar, but they go to the shelter, help out, and then sit and watch the game with the guests.

> All of the guests' eyes were glued to the TV. One man was even decked out in Duke accessories....He and K. [another student volunteer] had a bet for the evening that the person whose team lost would have to fall to their knees after the game and admit that the other was the best. I sat in the room the entire game,

talking to the guests sitting in chairs next to me. The scene was one I will never forget: a group of about 15 homeless men and K. and I sitting around and watching basketball. We would get excited and disappointed together.

"When I signed up for this course," writes another,

> I didn't really think that the highlight of the term would be spending Monday night watching football with a bunch of homeless people in a shelter in Greensboro. I mean, what would my parents think? "Bunch of lazy bums," my dad always says. I don't know, though—I actually think he'd have a good time here. He sits around just like this too. Maybe his mind wouldn't snap shut so fast. The world looks so different from here…

Of course there are hard times too. Some guests are rude or angry; people are turned away if drunk or stoned; there are fights and hard words. Most of my students do not think they themselves would survive the guests' situation, emotionally or even physically. They are amazed at the guests' relative good humor. Some remark that the guests are better mannered than, for example, patrons at the country club where some students also work.

We may or may not conclude from our experiences at the shelters that governmental welfare programs as we know them are necessarily a good idea. For one thing, these are private shelters, supported by local churches and synagogues, and they are sometimes pretty tough on the guests too. Students are often motivated to come back on their own time, or bring their friends. They talk their parents into sending boxes of food or clothes to help out. Those opposed to governmental welfare programs often favor just such actions. Yet one is left wondering if private and local initiatives can be enough. The realities can be overwhelming, and what shelters can offer is very partial. We carry away questions and uncertainty too. Ethical learning doesn't stop!

SERVICE AND CHANGE-MAKING

This chapter looks mostly at direct person-to-person acts of kindness and concern, at what we usually call *ethical service*. Personal growth and personal learning are corresponding results for the one serving: hence what we now call service-*learning*.

For now let it be enough just to note that, alongside service, there are also a multitude of *other* ways of taking ethics into action. Individual acts of kindness and comfort are at one end of the continuum. On the community level, you might promote better facilities for homeless people—and explore what they themselves might want, rather than designing facilities for them according to what social work professionals or architects think they should want. Another and farther-sighted community project would be to create or sustain better jobs for people who might otherwise be jobless. Surely there are many worthwhile things the community needs!

On the state or national level, meanwhile, we might find ourselves working to end homelessness itself, by addressing its root causes, such as companies relocating their factories to foreign countries and the lack of a social and economic "safety net" here at home. Here ethics merges into politics. A line from Martin Luther King, Jr: "True compassion is more than flinging a coin to a beggar; it comes to see that an edifice which produces beggars needs restructuring."

The politics is more controversial, of course, which is one reason why people talking about ethical service, and school-based service-learning programs in particular, sometimes restrict their attention to individual acts of kindness and concern. Later chapters of this book will suggest that the politics is crucial too, all the same—and also that a much more constructive politics is possible. It does not have to reduce to endless and fruitless ideological debates.

In any case, for now, remember that there are many different kinds of ethical engagement. Of course no one can do them all—but everyone can do *something*!

"Living Ideals"

DANUSHA VERONICA GOSKA

Danusha V. Goska is a writer living in New Jersey.

It was September 1998, in Bloomington, Indiana. As part of the conference on Spirituality and Ecology: No Separation, a group of concerned citizens was gathered in the basement of St. Paul Catholic Center. They were thinking and talking about living their ideals. Some had planted trees in Africa. Some described ways that they honor the indigenous spirit of a place, and their own ancestors. Elderly nuns and young feminists recounted their part in women's struggle. One frustrated woman voiced the nagging worry of many. "I want to do something, but what can I do? I'm just one person, an average person. *I* can't have an impact. I live with the despair of my own powerlessness. I can't bring myself to do anything. The world is so screwed up, and I have so little power. I feel so *paralyzed*."

I practically exploded.

Years before I had been stricken by a debilitating illness. Perilymph fistula's symptoms are like those of multiple sclerosis. On some days I was functional. On others, and I could never predict when these days would strike, I was literally, not metaphorically, paralyzed. I couldn't leave the house; I could barely stand up. I had moved to Bloomington for grad school. I knew no one in town. I couldn't get health care because I hadn't enough money, and the Social Security administration, against the advice of its own physician and vocational advisors, denied my claim.

That's why I imitated Mount Vesuvius when the conference participant claimed that just one person, one average person, can't do anything significant to make the world a better place; that the only logical option was passivity, surrender, and despair.

I raised my hand and spoke. "I have an illness that causes intermittent bouts of paralysis," I explained. "And that paralysis has taught me something. It has taught me that my protestations of my own powerlessness are bogus. Yes, some days I can't move or see. But you know what? Some days I can move. Some days I can see. And the difference between being able to walk across the room and not being able to walk across the room is epic.

"I commute to campus by foot along a railroad track. In spring, I come across turtles who have gotten stuck. The track is littered with the hollowing shells of turtles that couldn't escape the rails. So, I bend over and I pick up the still living trapped turtles that I do find. I carry them to a wooded area and let them go. For those turtles, that much power that I have is enough.

"I'm just like those turtles. When I have been sick and housebound for days, I wish someone—anyone—would talk to me. To hear a human voice say my name; to be touched: that would mean the world to me.

"One day an attack hit me while I was walking home from campus. It was a snowy day. There was snow on the ground, and more snow was falling from the sky. I struggled with each step; wobbled and wove across the road. I must have looked like a drunk. One of my neighbors, whom I had never met, stopped and asked if I was okay. He drove me home.

"He didn't hand me the thousands of dollars I needed for surgery. He didn't take me in and empty my puke bucket. He just gave me one ride, one day. I am still grateful to him and touched by his gesture.

"I'd lived in the neighborhood for years, and so far he has been the only one to stop. The problem is not that we have so little power. The problem is that we don't use the power that we have."

Why do we deny that power? Why do we not honor what we can do?

Part of the reason is that "virtue" is often defined as the ultimate commodity, something exclusive, like a Porsche or a perfect figure, that only the rich and famous have access to. "Virtue" is defined as so outside of normal human experience or ability that you'd think, if you were doing it right, you'd know; because camera crews and an awards committee would appear on your lawn.

Thus the defining of virtue is surrendered to a Madison Avenue mentality. I remember when the Dalai Lama came to Bloomington in 1999. The words "virtue" and "celebrity" were confused until they became synonymous. The Dalai Lama's visit was the most glamorous event Bloomington had seen in years. Suddenly even our barbershop scuttlebutt featured more movie stars than an article from *People* magazine. "Did you see Steven Segal on Kirkwood Avenue? Richard Gere gets in tomorrow." Virtue becomes something farther and farther out of the reach of the common person.

I was once a Peace Corps volunteer. I also volunteered for the Sisters of Charity, the order begun by Mother Teresa. When people learn of these things, they sometimes act impressed. I am understood to be a virtuous person.

I did go far away, and I did wear a foreign costume. But I don't know that I was virtuous. I tried to be, but I was an immature, inadequately trained girl in foreign countries with obscenely unjust regimes and little to no avenues for progress. My impact was limited.

To put myself through college, I worked as a nurse's aid. I earned minimum wage. I wore a pink polyester uniform and I dealt with the elderly and the dying, ignored people who went years without seeing a loved one, who died alone. When I speak of this job, I never impress anyone. I am not understood to be a virtuous person. Rather, I am understood to be working class.

I loved this difficult, low-paid work not out of any masochistic sense of personal elevation through suffering. I loved it because I physically and emotionally touched people every day, all day long; I made them comfortable; I made them laugh; I challenged them; they rose to meet the challenges. In return, patients shared with me the most precious commodity in the universes: their humanity.

I go to a food bank every two weeks to get my food. I have no car. I can't carry two weeks worth of food the three miles back to my house. Every week, I get a ride home from other food bank patrons. These folks don't pause for a second to sigh, "Oh, problems are so big, I'm so powerless; will it really help anything if I give you this ride?" They don't look around to make sure someone is watching. They just, invisibly, do the right thing. I get rides in old, old cars. In one car I could see the road beneath whiz past under broken-down flooring; in another, I shared space with a large, lapping dog. I once got a ride from a man who told me he'd just gotten out of jail. Another time, my chauffeur's tattoos ran up and down his naked chest and back. When I was sick, I went from agency to agency, begging people with glamorous title, and impressive virtue résumés for help. Most did nothing.

The *Lamed Vov Tzaddikim* are the thirty-six hidden saints of Jewish folklore. Unlettered and insignificant, they work at humble trades and pass unnoticed. Because of these anonymous saints, the world continues to exist. Without their insignificant, unnoticed virtue—Poof!—God loses divine patience, and the world goes up in smoke.

Sometimes we convince ourselves that the "unnoticed" gestures of "insignificant" people mean nothing. It's not enough to recycle our soda cans; we must Stop Global Warming Now. Since we can't Stop Global Warming Now, we may as well not recycle our soda cans. It's not enough to be our best selves; we have to be Gandhi. And yet when we study the biographies of our heroes, we learn that they spent years in preparation doing tiny, decent things before one historical moment propelled them to center stage.

Moments, as if animate, use the prepared to tilt empires. Ironically, saints we worship today, heroes we admire, were often ridiculed, tortured, or, most punishingly, ignored in their own lifetimes. St. John of the Cross gave the world the spiritual classic, *The Dark Night of the Soul*. It was inspired by his own experience of being imprisoned by the members of his own religious order. Before Solidarity, Lech Walesa, the Nobel Peace Prize winner who helped bring down communism, was a nonentity; a blue-collar worker in an oft-ridiculed Eastern European backwater. He was always active; one moment changed this small man's otherwise small-time, invisible activism into the kind of wedge that can topple a giant. Now, that moment past, Walesa has returned to relative obscurity.

While working or traveling in Africa, Asia, and Eastern Europe, I occasionally met people who really did have next to nothing, but who stunned me with their insistence on the abundance of their own humanity. One afternoon, as I trekked to my teaching post in the Himalayas, a monsoon storm turned day into night and a landslide wiped out my trail. I got terribly lost; coming to a strange village, exhausted, I sat on the porch of a peasant home. Inside, the family was eating roasted cow-corn kernels for dinner. Roasted cow-corn kernels were to be their entire dinner; there was nothing else on their menu.

A man inside saw that a human form was sitting on his porch. He couldn't have seen that I was American, or anything else for that matter. It was dark night by then, in a village without electricity. In any case, I was wearing a sari. He whispered to his wife, "Someone is sitting on our porch. We have to cook rice." Rice is the highest status food in that economy. And, by "rice," they meant, for them, an elaborate meal consisting of rice, lentils, and vegetables.

This feeling of being seen, this conviction that every act one performs matters to a supremely consequential audience, can come from a belief in God. Psalm 139 articulates how thoroughly and consequentially *witnessed* the theist feels.

> O lord, You have searched me
> and You know me.
> …Before a word is on my tongue
> You know it completely, O Lord.
> Where can I go from Your Spirit?
> Where can I flee from Your presence?
> If I go up to the heavens, You are there;
> If I make my bed in the depths, You are there.

The very marrow of the believer's bones is impregnated with the conviction that everything he does is avidly witnessed by God, and that everything he does matters to God. Whether or not one's fellow incarnate beings see is secondary.

Non-theists, including atheists, can also have this feeling that one is witnessed, that everything one does matters, Not just a personalized God sees and tallies human action. Disembodied forces that can never be tampered with also weigh our deeds. For some, karma plays witness. You may be able to fool your fellow humans, but, ultimately, you can't cheat karma.

In many cultures, there is a disembodied force that demands that every action be ethical: honor. "*Bog, Honor, Ojczyzna*" or "God, Honor, Country," is the Polish national motto. My stays in Poland introduced me to otherwise empty-handed activists who faced off against Nazis, Communists, and now, capitalism, with relentless personal power. "Burnout" and "apathy" were not in their vocabulary. Even when serving time in prisons that appeared on no map, they felt visible. Honor recorded their every deed, and ensured that it mattered.

I suspect that we all have our three-in-the-morning moments, when all of life seems one no-exit film noir, where any effort is pointless, where any hope seems to be born only to be dashed, like a fallen nestling on a summer sidewalk. When I have those moments, if I do nothing else, I remind myself: the ride in the snow; the volunteers at the food bank; the Nepali peasants who fed me. Activists like the Pole Wladyslaw Bartoszewski who, decades before he would earn any fame, got out of Auschwitz only to go on to even more resistance against the Nazis, and then the Soviets. Invisible, silent people who, day by day, choice by choice, unseen by me, unknown to me, force me to witness myself, invite me to keep making my own best choices, and keep me living my ideals.

"The Ethics of Transformation"

COURTNEY MARTIN

Courtney E. Martin was a student of political science and sociology at Barnard College when she wrote this essay, which won the Elie Wiesel Prize in Ethics for 2002. She later studied at the Gallatin School at New York University. She has published *Perfect Girls, Starving Daughters,* a book about "The Frightening New Normalcy of Hating Your Body"; was codirector/producer of two short documentaries; and performs poetry at bookstores, cafés, schools, and benefits as well as on radio. She's now an adjunct professor of women's studies at Hunter College.

An aggressive hand shot up on the right side of the classroom. It belonged to Vuyiseka, a slender young woman with a perfectly oval face and an almost completely shaven head. There was a fire in her eyes.

"Yes Vuyiseka?" I asked.

"I want to read my poem today." She was adamant.

The class miraculously quieted down, shifting back into their wooden seats and putting their bags into their laps. It was the very first day of the poetry workshop that I had initiated and no one, thus far, had volunteered to read any of their work out loud. Vuyiseka was born brave.

She read. She read a piece about regrets, about God's forgiveness, and about hope. She read standing up at her desk, delicate hand shaking against the stiffness of the paper, lips curling around each word laboriously. She approached the last line: "I wish I had never…that is in the past. The new me promised that never again to say 'I wish I had never.'" As she reached the end her face grew swollen and tense. She burst into tears. The class went wild with applause.

Vuyiseka was yearning to express herself, to name something that had grown up inside of her. It was not until someone asked her to put a pen to paper and purge some kind of inside epiphany, however, that she realized what she was capable of. The simple combination of a pen, a piece of paper, and the bravery to assign words to her emotions created Vuyiseka anew. She became a poet.

And I, this American exchange student with a head full of ideas and a heart full of good intention, became a better person. I learned so much from my experience there, not only about a nation with a nascent sense of justice and that often used and rarely understood word—diversity— but about myself. I, like all of South Africa, had felt in the dark for some time when it came to understanding the complexities of difference and

Reprinted by permission of the Elie Wiesel Foundation for Humanity.

the ethical implications of celebrating and cultivating these differences. My months living in South Africa and the week I spent teaching a poetry workshop to high school students there illuminated a very important truth for me. It is the kind of truth that dwells in the deepest part of who you are, the kind that doesn't necessarily have a name, but if it did, it would be something like...hope.

You see there is hope. There is hope all over South Africa. You can see it in the faces of the young; hope there, of course, is not surprising. The huge eyes and naked laughter of the children who lived in the same neighborhood as me—I lived for four months in the all-black township of Langa—were saturated in the kind of light that only hope can radiate. They were full of dreams. My little sister, the long-legged and angel-voiced Nodidi, used to tell me about her future: "I will be either a doctor or a teacher I think. The doctor thing because I would love to save lives, but the teacher...well I think I could be much better than the teacher I have." Over card games of an African version of Go-Fish or Spoons we would all collapse in fits of laughter when my Xhosa could not get me where I needed to go; a dozen five-year olds would reach over to my hand and point at the right card to play next, deliberate and generous in their assistance.

I too, wanted to be of assistance. Like most young Americans, especially white and middle-class, who make their way over to a country like South Africa, I was full of a sense of duty. I wanted, not only to study there, but to leave having helped. I wanted to contribute something to this teeter-totter country, at once third world and first. I wanted to come back to my Midwestern American home with stories of empowerment, with stories of transformation. These children with their hope and dirty palms reminded me of the urgency, reminded me of all there was to make right.

So when the program I studied with introduced the month of independent study option, I immediately jumped at the opportunity. I searched the dark eyes of my playmates for the perfect thing. I started making lists of injustices in my head. There was just too much to be mended in a country so torn and tattered by violence, a violence, it must be understood, that was completely inclusive. Every citizen of South Africa is a soldier in one way or another; psychologically or physically, spiritually or reluctantly, racial war makes militants out of us all.

And I, in my idealist and well-intentioned American disposition, was going to bring some small moment of peace. In some small way, I was going to make things better.

I decided to teach a poetry workshop in a township high school. I had become very involved in the spoken word poetry scene in New York City ever since I began to go to school here; the immediacy and the political backbone of the art thrilled me. I had spent years pecking away on keyboards that didn't talk back to me and, through spoken word, I found a genre and a venue that turned poetry into something very active, something very real. In my experiences in three short years I found people were always connected by the orality of words. It coaxed them into a climate of association and liberation.

I wanted the same for these students. In my short time in South Africa I had quickly learned that very few South African students are taught to express themselves. Instead, the rigid curriculum introduced there—with good intention—to equalize the job market has become very vocational in its focus. Students are searching for right answers most of the time, not searching for themselves.

I spent many nights staying up late in my little bedroom on Mshumpela Road thinking of a design for my workshop. I would talk about identity, because surely if anything was plaguing the post-apartheid nation it was that. I couldn't talk about identity, I realized, unless I first talked about history. Most of these students had never read a poem before, much less one written by a South African poet. Their history, rich with protest poetry and the ancient tradition of the imbongi—a poet designated by the Xhosa chief who was in charge of reciting explicitly political poetry—was mostly lost to them, getting mixed up with a past that their parents would rather forget altogether. Yes, I would talk about history and identity, and finally, all twisted up and shiny with hope, I would talk about future. I decided I had to show them how to be visionary.

At the last moment I convinced a young man I had met, 19 years old and brimming with enthusiasm about spoken word poetry and hip hop, to co-teach the workshop with me. Melisizwe had, in fact, grown up in Langa and he was eager to give something back; he had just never had the organizational fortitude to do so. When we headed into town the first day, smashed together in a packed mini-bus, I passed over some mimeographed sheets about the structure of the workshop. "These are great," he said, smiling at me with a surprised smirk.

"Do you think it is too much planning?" I questioned, suddenly very self-conscious of my own ambition and glowing white skin (mini-buses are far too dangerous for white South Africans to ride.)

"No, no. It's good. We'll just have to explain it a lot."

When we entered the classroom, a few students looked up at me, confused by my presence in the regular school day, but most were unfazed. They grouped in corners, completely separated by gender, laughing and shouting at one another playfully. Their English teacher, a bald-headed man with a joyous disposition...though perhaps just joyous not to have to teach his class for a week, introduced Melisizwe and I. "They are going to teach you about poetry!"

The students were clearly skeptical. They reluctantly shifted in their seats, scratchy polyester school uniform skirts and flesh dragged across the unforgiving wood of the desks, and all of the sudden I was met with 40 eyes. I was instantly terrified. "Introduction," I thought numbly, "introduce the design of the workshop." Melisizwe looked up at me as if pushing me along with his eyes.

"Molo. Like Zolani said, I am Courtney and I want to spend time with you this week, talk about poetry, and hopefully, if you feel comfortable, have you write some of your own. We are going to start out talking about poetry in terms of history, like, you know, read some South African poets that you may or may not have seen before, talk about their intention, that kind of stuff. Then we are going to talk about poetry in terms of identity…"

One of the brazen young men in the back, dressed in a striped tie and a perfectly pressed blazer, interrupted, "What do you mean by identity miss?"

"Well, you don't have to call me miss at all. I'm just 21 and studying here for a bit of time. I'm from America…"

Again I was interrupted. This time by his friend, another straight-backed, long-legged teenage boy, "Are you married?"

"No, actually I'm not at all." I was trying so hard to remember the outline I had designed, the sense it had all made at the time, the logic. "But you know I really want to talk about poetry. I want to talk about identity because I think so much of South Africa's population has been silenced…you know, very few people have been able to write about what their lives are like."

Melisizwe got out of his chair, baggy jeans unfolding, and cleared his throat. "When you wake up in the morning, the sun is so bright, yebo, because your tatomcici keeps spending the money for the drapes on beer at the shebeen. And you are so tired and then you smell your mama's cooking, yebo, and you know it is samp and beans and that's what you've been wishing for, yebo?"

Forty heads nodded in unison, 80 eyes were transfixed on Melisizwe as he swayed and spoke.

"So that's what you are. You can write about that and you will be doing something revolutionary because no one wanted you to write about that before. The government, especially, didn't want you to write about that. But now you could, yebo? You could write about your mama's samp and beans and no one could ever take that away from you, yebo?"

And the whole world changed forever…for me. Certainly for the students, whose hands began to be very busy with pencils and words they didn't know they owned, the world was different after that moment, but also—quite unexpectedly—for me.

I learned that my voice was courageous and that my intention was noble, but that if I did not possess the wisdom necessary to recognize my own limitations, my work would be nothing short of unethical. It was in the sudden recognition of myself in relation to the students that I stumbled upon the truth about helping people. The best way to change people's lives is to trust in their ability to change their own.

Langa Township was Melisizwe's home. He knew the smell of morning in that sun-filled, dusty place like I never could. And this, I have come to respect, was profound for those students in a way that three years of a first-class college education and a big liberal bleeding heart was not. What does post-colonial mean when instead Melisizwe could say, "the way your tata keeps talking about slow change, yebo?" It was as if I had the terms and Melisizwe had the manifestations.

This is not to say, of course, that I learned that I didn't have a place in that classroom, or that my help was futile in a country I didn't grow up in. In fact, my epiphany was the opposite. Instead I learned that the most ethical and effective kind of assistance that I could give was to act as a facilitator, an organizer. I had the vision to recognize that those kids would benefit from the liberating power of poetry and the enthusiasm of Melisizwe, so I put them in the same room on a Monday morning in April. This was my profound role; I possessed a precious foresight for transformation, an aching need to help, and a knack for organization. It is as if I was my most effective when I was not writing the script, but putting the pen and the paper in deserving people's hands.

At a time when so much heated debate is ensuing about foreign policy, I think that my ethical epiphany is painfully clear and certainly applicable on a larger scale. As Americans we will never truly know what it is like to be South African, French, or Haitian. As Melisizwe put it, we will never know what morning smells like in a childhood home in these places. But we may visit them and we may recognize needs. This is our vision. This is our power. To become part of a community, to care about it deeply, and then to encourage that it heal itself...that is where our capacity to change the world dwells. We are effective only as far as we are facilitators. We are ethical only as far as we are humble....

Americans are a big-hearted, ambitious people, but I wonder if we sometimes just move too fast to see our own effect. It is in a little stillness—in that moment of silence that followed Melisizwe's speech—that we may learn something about our own choices, about our own capacities. As Melisizwe's explanation came to a close, the nodding heads of the eager students signified the success of my project. My vision was only realized through the eyes of the local community. It was their sight, not my own, that was the most sharp. Just as it is local communities, not the big brother of policy and capital that our country has become, that can see what is best. Americans must learn to trust other people; we must learn to give, but then step back, facilitate, but not teach. We must learn to learn.

And when we have, a glorious connection will be made, a glorious transformation will take place...as it did in that classroom that April morning in South Africa.

On the last day of our workshop, Melisizwe and I entered the classroom like old friends. I immediately sat down in a desk next to Nobuhle,

Monellisa, and Busiswe. We were all bubbling over with excitement for our final celebration: an open mic where each student was encouraged to stand up in front of the class and share one of the pieces they had written over the course of the week.

Monellisa began, "I believe that we, the teenagers, we are the future of this country. It can happen if we can all fall in love with this beautiful country..."

Then Lindelwa, "I wish that I could collect the street kids/Give them a shelter/Give them clothes/Give them education/I wish that I could be a helping hand finding a cure for AIDS and HIV/I'm praying for a transformation in my country."

Luvuyo had us all close to tears: "I wish I had never seen/the way my friend died, but/god disagreed with me/that he made me to see/everything that has happened/to my friend that made him die/he dies on my hands./fortunately,/I was not alone with him/but to me it seemed like I was alone."

And Wendy: "...he thought as we are black/our brains are also black/so we won't be able to get light in our education/I feel so painful about that/because apartheid is still remain in our society/although we say we are in new freedom."

And on and on, the students approached the front of the room with new courage and spoke their minds. They were loud and they were soft, they were big-headed and they were insecure, but most of all, they were expressing themselves for the first time; for some of them, it was like speaking for the first time all over again. Finally Vuyiseka, again, marched in front of the class, this tiny soldier with huge bravery and said, "We would like to say thanks to Courtney and Melisizwe for coming here at our school. Your being here did a first for us. It awoke that part of life that no one likes to talk about. Before you came we thought poetry was nothing but words, words written by white people, but we were wrong and you helped us to realize that. Now poetry is our new best friend. We gained a first from you guys. As they say, the pen is mightier than the sword. We actually know what it means. Because of poetry we can conquer a lot."

FOR REVIEW

1. When is service-learning *one* kind of thing, not a combination of two separate things?

2. What are some of the ways that service work can be unsettling?

3. What are some ethical ways to deal with these challenges?

4. Why does Weaver House's Mission Statement take special care *not* to appeal to pity?

5. Why are the residents of Weaver House called "guests"?

6. What are some of the ethical lessons my students learned in their work at the homeless shelters?

7. What are some of the reasons, according to Danusha Goska, that "we don't use the [ethical] power we have"?

8. Who are two of the people who have shown her what powers we *do* have?

9. What does Courtney Martin conclude is the best way to help change people's lives?

10. Why do her students conclude that poetry "can conquer a lot"?

 EXERCISES AND NOTES

FOR DISCUSSION

How *can* we help—really, deeply, ethically? How can we help in ways that genuinely empower people, for instance, rather than putting ourselves in a subtle or not so subtle position of power over them? We don't want to patronize people by pretending that there are no differences in social power or need, but it's equally patronizing to treat others as pure objects of pity, as if all the help goes one way or as if because *we* have the power we also know what *they* need. Aren't we all needy in some ways? And don't we all have some power to answer others' needs? How then can we all connect in a more reciprocal and respectful place?

You probably noticed some tension between the essays by Danusha Goska and Courtney Martin. Martin finds her work in South Africa difficult and surprising in many ways, but finds it transformative both for her and her students. Goska also worked abroad, but thinks her impact was problematic and limited. In her view it would be better to work on making a difference right at home. On the other hand, both Goska and Martin are concerned with the same thing—hope—and both find many sources of personal power to make change.

What do you conclude from these contrasts? What might Goska and Martin say to each other if they met? What do you think Martin means by "transformation"? How is it that poetry, of all things, turned out to be transformative for her students? Are there implications back home? What do you think Goska would have us do—say, *you*, specifically, right where you are?

Revisit the narratives of students working at local homeless shelters. How do you view them against the background of Goska's and Martin's essays?

How do they relate to your own experiences? One of my students speaks with an older woman at Weaver House who reminds her of her grandmother. What if it *was* her grandmother? What if it was you?

What would your ideal service-learning project look like? Why? What would you want to learn from it? Where and how could you learn that now, in service?

GET OUT THERE AND DO SOMETHING

In the end there is no substitute for actually going out and helping. Pick some way to help that is genuinely face-to-face. Tutor a struggling child. Volunteer at a local homeless shelter or soup kitchen. Work with retarded citizens. Read to children at an inner-city childcare. Teach a class at a community center or a nursing home. Help build a house with Habitat for Humanity.

The mechanics are usually easy. Making the arrangements only takes a phone call. Most homeless shelters, for example, are desperate for volunteer help and have staff coordinators to arrange volunteers' dates and times. Many consider public education part of their mission: they regularly run orientation and training sessions. When floods or storms strike, many cities or counties set up volunteer hotlines to match willing volunteers with people in need of help. Community newspapers often run appeals for help. School offices schedule community volunteers and tutors.

Most colleges and universities have offices that match community organizations' needs and student volunteers. Find yours and use it. My school even has a volunteer fair at which community organizations in need set up information tables and sign up people.

For better or worse, it's not hard to find the opportunities. Start with the readily available ones; then be on the lookout for the less visible opportunities that may arise only after you are actively involved.

NOTES

The quotations under "Personal Challenges" are from Ram Dass and Tom Gorman's excellent book *How Can I Help? Stories and Reflections on Service* (Knopf, 1994), pages 14–15 and 86–87.

Greensboro Urban Ministry's Weaver House, whose Volunteer Information Statement is cited here, is in downtown Greensboro, North Carolina. My students also work at the Alamance County Allied Churches Emergency Night Shelter in Burlington, North Carolina. Students quoted in this chapter include Tracy Cournoyer, Lee Hawley, Andrew Hendryx, Becky Rosso, Christine Sanlorenzo, Jennette Schorsch, and Emily Tucker.

Danusha Veronica Goska's essay appears along with a number of other inspiring pieces in Paul Rogat Loeb's collection, *The Impossible Will Take a Little*

While: A Citizen's Guide to Hope in a Time of Fear (Basic Books, 2004), where it is titled "Political Paralysis."

The Elie Wiesel Foundation Prize in Ethics Essay Contest is offered by the Elie Wiesel Foundation for Humanity. See http://www.eliewieselfoundation .org/EthicsPrize/index.html to read other prize-winning essays like Courtney Martin's and for application guidelines.

II

MORAL VALUES

CHAPTER 6

Taking Values Seriously

Let us begin our survey of moral values with a clearer sense of what sorts of things values are, and how to be more attentive to them when they arise, in all their concreteness and diversity, in real situations.

VARIETIES OF VALUES

We hold many values. There is fairness, trustworthiness, the well-being of others and the world. We also value good neighbors, good music, good humor, daily exercise, children and parents, old friends and new, and many other things that are not ethical or moral values (not *im*moral values, simply *non*-moral or *non*ethical values). Truth, cleanliness, good sportsmanship, wilderness; life, liberty, and the pursuit of happiness; random kindness and senseless acts of beauty; the thrill of victory and maybe even the agony of defeat—all of these are "values" in the broad sense.

Or rather: all of these are *examples* of values in a broad sense. They are all things that we value. But they do not tell us what values themselves *are*. A philosopher will ask: What do they all have in common that makes them all examples of "values"? We need a working definition of "value" in general.

Try this: our values are *those things we care about, that matter to us; those goals and ideals we aspire to and measure ourselves or others or our society by.* When I say that I value playing fair or staying healthy, then, I mean (at least) that I am interested in these things, that I care about them, and probably that I do specific things to promote or safeguard them—certainly that I *would* under the right circumstances.

Notice that this definition does not say anything about where values ultimately come from or how they might be prioritized or justified or theorized. All of that comes later. Right now we just need a standard for classification. Notice also that nearly anything could be included. "Bad" or questionable or conflicting values count too. We value having a lot of stuff, driving fast, and lording it over others too. Maybe we shouldn't, but sometimes we do. Pirates value their loot; addicts value their drugs; misers obsess over their money. Without all of this confusion and conflict, life would be a lot less interesting.

We may classify values-in-general into a variety of types. *Aesthetic* values have to do with art, beauty, and attractiveness. *Scientific* values and others have to do with knowledge, truth, experiment, and so on. *Economic* values have to do with production, efficiency, and market prices. *Instrumental* values have to do with the means to our ends: the effectiveness of technologies, the usefulness of our tools. There are other types too.

Ethical values, then, are a kind of value distinct from those just listed, a subset of values generally. You know the examples: fairness, equality, respect, and responsibility; reducing pain and suffering; "life, liberty, and the pursuit of happiness"; humility, benevolence, keeping your promises. From Chapter 1 you also have a definition: ethical values are *those values that give voice to the basic needs and legitimate expectations of others as well as our own.* Ethical values connect us to a larger world ("the needs of others as well as ourselves") and introduce the ethical question of what others are entitled to ask from us and what we are entitled to ask from ourselves ("legitimate expectations").

When you turn to specific ethical questions and debates, then, keep this definition in mind. To spell out the values involved, ask: what needs and legitimate expectations—both your own and others'—are at stake here? For what needs and legitimate expectations are the parties to this debate trying to speak?

Some ethical debates will be new to you, and answering these questions will take some research or exploration—listening carefully to the different sides, asking around. For other debates we can fill in the blanks more easily—we've heard the contending positions already, or can easily figure them out. The point of our definition of ethical values, in any case, is to give us the right blanks to fill in. It gives us the right questions to ask.

"ETHICAL" AND "MORAL"

You may be wondering how "ethics" in the sense defined here relates to "morality." The same? Different in some subtle way?

Often the terms are used interchangeably. Look up dictionary definitions and "ethics" and "morality" are sometimes even defined in terms of each other. Still, the terms have some useful differences. When we speak of the "moral" or "morality" we are more likely to be thinking of the values involved as fixed, not in question. A "moral" person sounds like a person who almost reflexively does what's right, while an "ethical" person is likely to be less sure, or more concerned about issues where values are more in flux or at odds. Moral matters invite readier judgment, while ethical questions are really *questions*. The answers aren't so clear.

In the same vein, philosophers sometimes use the word "moral" to describe the values we actually hold—remembering that the word "moral" itself traces back to the Latin "mores," meaning manners or customs. "Ethics" is then defined as the *study* of morals: more broadly, the deliberate process of thinking them through, of systematizing and criticizing and possibly even revising our moral values, as well as more consciously embracing them.

In this book, from now on, I will try to use the word "moral" to describe a direct concern with basic needs and legitimate expectations of others as well as our own. Correspondingly, I will use the words "ethical" and "ethics" to describe the *exploration* of moral values so understood: an exploration of their grounding, interrelations, and even conflicts, enabling in turn a more conscious and critical embrace of those values.

FAMILIES OF MORAL VALUES

Within the category of moral values itself are further distinctions. Certain types of moral values are linked together, sometimes loosely and sometimes tightly, around certain key ideas or central values. They form, we may say, certain *families*.

Much of the rest of Part II of this book will be a guide to these families of moral values. They will grow on you! Right now I just want to outline them by way of introduction. On the next two pages you will find four families of moral values, each identified by its moral focus or center.

UNDERSTANDING MORAL DEBATES

Most moral values have a family. A few don't—and there is no reason they must. A few, on the other hand, have several. Justice, for example, shows up in two—under the values of the person and as a virtue—though in somewhat different senses. You could argue that virtues like loyalty and sensitivity also fit in the relationship family. And so on. Still, on the whole, these four families of values give us a useful way to begin to organize the field of moral values and to sort out ethical issues and debates.

Let us look briefly at the different families of moral values in action. North Carolina has just instituted a state lottery—a bitterly fought-over measure, brought up again and again, finally to pass the State Senate by one vote. The

PERSONS

Central to ethics is the insistence that *persons* are special, precious, and have a dignity that demands respect. No one is to be treated as a mere means to others' ends. Social relations require fairness, justice, and equality. Human and civil rights are essential too: they secure the space in which each person, you and I and everyone else, is recognized and can flourish. We explore these values of persons in Chapter 7.

HAPPINESS

What is our final goal in this life? Many thinkers have answered: *happiness.* Well-being, satisfaction, pleasure, the relief of pain and suffering—or rather, more precisely, the best balance that we can achieve of happiness over suffering. Add in not just ourselves but the needs of others as well, and we have a famous ethical formula: "Seek the greatest happiness of the greatest number." Moral thinking with this family of values is quantitative and economic, concerned with trade-offs and the distribution of goods, maximizing tangible social benefits. We explore this family of values in Chapter 8.

chief argument for the lottery is that the state can raise more money for essential services, especially the schools. Tax funds are limited by people's unwillingness to support the taxes, but more money is needed from somewhere. So we have here an argument from social benefits, our second family of values. A lottery will enhance the schools, it's argued, and in the long run make society better off.

Critics aren't so sure. For one thing, the social benefits may be questionable. Poorer communities, whose schools will benefit the most from state-distributed lottery money, are also the communities that in fact spend the most on lottery tickets. It would be much more efficient simply to give the money to the schools rather than gambling it away and having the schools get only a fraction back.

Social benefits are the theme of this disagreement, then, but the critics argue that the lottery's social benefits are minimal, or maybe even that it is a net detriment. It's a question that must be settled, too, with careful looks at the facts and the actual benefits, or lack of benefits, of lotteries elsewhere.

Another counterargument steps entirely outside of the debate over social benefits. A different family of values comes into play: the third family, the virtues. A lottery is, after all, a form of gambling. But gambling is a *vice,* isn't

VIRTUE

Ethics is also concerned with *character*: with traits like self-discipline, responsibility, honesty, charity, loyalty, devotion. Christendom's great virtues are faith, hope, charity, prudence, justice, temperance, and fortitude. In the Eastern traditions other virtues come to the fore: tranquillity, nonattachment, compassion, truthful speech and thought, "right livelihood," and nonviolence. We explore these and many other virtues in Chapter 9.

RELATIONSHIP

We are social beings as well as individuals. We are born to other humans, grow up in families, and take on traditions and heritages and communities. And we all live, in turn, in deep interrelation with the larger-than-human natural world. Values central to relationship are caring, participation, and community. Recognizing how much our communities make us who we are also calls forth not only gratefulness but also a responsibility to protect, sustain, and attend to them. We explore these values in Chapter 10.

it? What's more, it associates all too easily with other vices, such as laziness, greed, and a weak sense of the value of work. It suits us better to work for an honest living. Quite apart from its financial benefits, then, we need to worry about what sort of people the lottery will make us, what kind of character the lottery will build, and some critics find the answer unappealing.

You begin to see how these four families of moral values can help us map out a moral debate that may otherwise seem just a hodgepodge of values. We can also use the families of moral values to inquire after values that may not emerge or be recognized right away in moral discussions. That is, you can always ask, of whatever is under discussion, how we might think about it from the point of view of a family of values not yet heard from.

For example, in regard to the lottery, we've heard a little from the second and third families of values, but we might ask after the first. What might *justice* say about a state lottery?

Maybe it approves: some argue that taxes should be kept minimal because it is unjust, or a violation of rights, to take away people's money to spend on purposes they might not choose themselves. People have the right to gamble their money away, this argument goes, but the state has no right to tax away any more money than absolutely necessary for purposes of its own choosing. On the other side, a subtle but striking argument is that the lottery is *un*just because it encourages false hopes in 99.99 percent of the ticket buyers. The state should be giving people *real* hope, say the critics, not misleading them with false hopes.

Is one family of values somehow more basic, more comprehensive, or even more *right* than the others? Many moralists and philosophers have thought so. Certainly some types of values apply better in some situations than others, and some may matter more to some people than others. Maybe certain values even matter more than the others in general. Respecting persons, some people say, is more important—if it comes to a pinch—than achieving the greatest good of the greatest number. Some philosophers, on the other hand, try to show that all moral values can really be reduced to (or, they might say, fitted into) one system. For example, some argue that respecting persons, properly understood, really *reduces* to achieving the greatest good of the greatest number.

We will consider these kinds of claims in due course. For now, however, let us stick to values as they actually show up in our lives. It's no disgrace, to them or to us, if they come in more than one flavor or type of family. Even the theorists and moralists who ultimately want to simplify or theorize them need to start with values as they actually show up in our experience. Let us start there too!

ATTENDING TO VALUES

Suppose now that you are looking at a specific moral issue and trying to discern the moral values involved. You want to figure out the main values, not overlooking anything big, and to articulate each of them at least a little. You want to *understand* the moral discussion of this issue, in short, as a prelude perhaps to trying to make a constructive contribution. Here are some guidelines.

WELCOME DIVERSITY

We hold a lot of moral values, and they aren't shy about showing up all the time. In the first place, then, *welcome diversity.*

You've seen some of the diversity already, just considering the four families of moral values and beginning to look at one case in point. You can do the same at every turn. Just read the newspaper, for example. A photo today shows a line of Amish buggies stretching along a country road—a funeral procession for a buggy driver killed by a drunk driver in a car. An all too familiar story, made more poignant still because the accident we imagine is also a collision—literally—of two radically different cultures. A life of <u>sobriety</u> and <u>devotion</u> (I will underline some of the values involved) cut short too soon.

We also remember how much <u>trust</u> we place in each other on the roads: how can people better live up to it?

We learn from another article, meanwhile, that the Texas State Senate is about to approve a bill that "would make people under age 21 who climb behind a wheel after drinking subject to losing their licenses for four to six months—even if there is only a trace of alcohol on their breaths." "Zero tolerance," the sponsor calls it. If we expect <u>responsibility</u> in drivers, he says, we have to get (very) tough.

The federal minimum wage is being raised for the first time in many years. It's a matter of basic <u>fairness</u>, advocates say. Incomes at the top end have gone off into the stratosphere: How can we justify leaving behind other people, at the low end of the wage scale, who are also working hard, supporting themselves and their families and contributing to society? They should be able at least to get by, to be able to raise their children in <u>dignity</u>. Many of those struggling to get by on minimum-wage jobs are single mothers whose only fallback is welfare or homelessness. Meeting even their basic needs—<u>survival</u> and some degree of <u>independence</u>—requires action.

Opponents worry about losing the <u>social benefits</u> of lower wages, such as more jobs, and about <u>fairness</u> again, this time to employers at the margins. Would raising the minimum wage push some of them out of business? Might it therefore actually reduce the number of jobs available?

Global warming is all over the news. Climate is changing: we are worried about the future of the earth and the <u>well-being of our children</u> as well as <u>justice to future generations</u>. We are beginning to rethink our practices and to consider new questions about <u>sustainability</u>: how can we live so as to pass on an Earth in as good (or better) shape as we found it? As we begin to comprehend the fact that we may have altered the very Earth, seemingly so immense and for so long taken for granted, we find that ethics now reaches into the biosphere. What does good "<u>biospheric citizenship</u>" require?

So: There are three issues, broadly speaking—and already a baker's dozen or so values, across all four families, including some overlaps (fairness comes up more than once, for instance). Many more could be found in each issue too. And that's just a start. Each debate also has its own context—from political and environmental issues to personal responsibility and the nature of the "simple life"—or sometimes several at once. Doing the best by the most people, for instance (as in: what are the overall social effects of raising the minimum wage?). Old ways versus new ways. The place of the Earth, as the setting for all of our other values, in ethics itself. And others as well.

LOOK IN DEPTH

Many different values also come up *within* each issue, quite apart from other issues. Call this *depth*.

That Amish funeral again. Most obviously, what's at stake is drunk driving: once again, a severe form of social irresponsibility. Think of what it means to take the wheel of a machine that can maim and kill when you are not fully aware and capable. Even worse is when you are just a beginning driver: hence the Texas response.

The Texas response, however, raises questions too. Other concerns come up. If a "trace of alcohol" is enough to revoke someone's license, how small is a "trace"? If an officer smells anything, is that enough? Is a blip on a Breathalyzer enough? What about people whose prescription drugs might have a trace of alcohol? My students, barely 21 themselves, worry that the proposed law gives police officers an unsettling amount of discretion.

Fairness comes up. Is it fair only to target minors in this way? Isn't drunk driving an irresponsible act regardless of the driver's age? Or is the idea that minors are more dangerous at the wheel with *any* alcohol because they are inexperienced drivers? Or is the idea that if minors have been drinking at all, they've already violated the law, and therefore deserve even stricter strict punishment? The article doesn't say. In that case, is a four- to six-month revocation strict *enough*?

There is still more. This photo would not have appeared in the paper had the victim not been Amish. The Amish won the legal right to drive buggies on the roads only after a hard-fought struggle in many states and over many years. Why? They don't care for the conveniences that the rest of us take for granted. Why not? Modern "conveniences," they say, corrupt the simplicity of our relation to each other, the Earth, and God. Without them, the Amish have created and sustained tight-knit, mutually supportive communities and farms that are the finest in their areas. Lately some environmentalists have begun to champion Amish methods on ecological grounds. A world of Amish people, for one thing, would certainly not have created global warming!

So there is much to think about here. Can we reclaim some of the virtues the Amish represent without giving up on the 21st century? If not, what does that say about how things are with us? If so, why aren't we doing it?

Notice again: all of this complexity arises from thinking about just one photograph—and still we have just scratched the surface. Moral issues like these have histories, and they represent the intersection or manifestation of many different concerns and struggles, many of them still unfolding. When you are exploring a moral issue, then, don't just mention one or two main concerns and move on. Take some time with them—and give yourself some time to take. Look in depth.

BE FAIR

Spelling out some of the moral values at stake in these cases may be hard, especially when you disagree with them. Buggy drivers, or drunk drivers, may make you impatient, and you may not want to consider the dangers of "zero tolerance." People who always complain about helping the poor, or tobacco company representatives who still won't admit that smoking causes cancer, may just annoy you. And maybe you've already heard too much about global warming.

But your first job is not to decide what *you* think. Suspend judgment until later. Here is another place that we often turn more dogmatic than we should. It's wiser to remind ourselves again that we don't know everything there is to know. In particular, if we dismiss some moral values without any kind of exploration or careful attention, we might never know what kinds of depth we missed. To look at a buggy driver as a mere curiosity, or as a hazard that ought to keep out of your way, misses a lot that is intriguing and maybe even enriching. So *be fair* to those who come at ethical issues from other angles and places. Don't rush to judge. Ask what these people are about instead. What are their goals and ideals? What matters to them? What are their needs and expectations? How do they invite us to rethink our own?

At least try to see matters from others' points of view. You're not being asked to decide who is "right" and who is "wrong," or which way we ought finally to choose. The task here is just to figure out the values involved. And that means on all sides. Not just filtered through a moral position you've already taken. Put your own position aside for a moment. Listen first; decide later.

CLARIFY!

Moral values often show up in forms that are not fully spelled out or clear. Part of our job in unpacking moral issues, then, is to do some of the explaining and clarifying ourselves. We may need to make some distinctions.

Molly [4 years old]: Ruthie got to use the big markers and I only got to use the plain ones.

Me: Yup. [to myself: Uh-oh.]

Molly: That's not fair!

Me: Why not?

Molly: Because I should get to use the big ones if Ruthie does!

Me: But the big markers are not washable and you're not quite old enough to remember to keep them off your clothes and the table. As soon as you can keep them just on the paper, you can use them too.

Molly: I can! I can! [sniffle]

Me: Oh, Molly, that's what you said yesterday, and I let you use them, but you ended up with a big orange splot on your shirt. A nonwashable splot!

Is it fair that Molly cannot use the big markers? If so, it is because fairness is not as simple as it looks on its face—because fairness cannot necessarily be measured by immediate equality of results. It's complicated. Fairness asks us to allow each child all that he or she is capable of, consistent with other needs and limits, including fairness to the parents who have to try to wash markers off clothes or tables, or buy new ones.

It's not so easy to spell out in a way that a 4-year-old can understand. In fact, just for that reason, some other approach to the problem sometimes may be needed—may even be more fair. Getting bigger washable markers, for example. The point is that this is how it goes, in real-life practice. Pay attention and take seriously the demand for clarification and distinctions.

In fact, fairness is a passion with all of us. Is it fair, for example, to set up a system of preferences for one group over another, even if it only comes into play when qualifications are otherwise equal and/or does not compel any particular choice? Some people argue that it is; others argue that it cannot be. It's the same sort of issue. Would some distinctions help? Can you know until you've tried?

GIVE EMOTION ITS DUE

One last clip from the newspaper. Developers and environmentalists clash over new building along a river that serves as many downstream communities' water supply and feeds major shellfish banks in the sounds off the coast. The river is already stressed by runoff from farms and lawn fertilizers, sewage treatment plants and so on, though for just that reason the impact of any single new development by itself is not that great.

The civil engineer who works for the developer and presented the case to the City Planning Commission has this to say about his environmentalist counterparts: "We're doing this from a fact standpoint and they [the environmentalists] are doing this from an emotional standpoint." *We* have facts, he says; *they're* just "emotional." His suggestion, of course, is that they should not be taken seriously. Emotion is supposed to be inappropriate when ethical or political matters come up.

It's not. Being emotional can be entirely appropriate. In fact, it's necessary. Remember: values themselves are things we *care* about. "Care" is an emotion. It's not *only* an emotion—it rests on "facts," perspectives on the world, histories and personal choices, and many other things—but the emotional side, the caring side, is essential as well.

The developers "care" too, of course. They too have values. They want to build houses and roads and malls and make money. They're a little annoyed in this case too, if you read between the lines, because they have to work under many more restrictions than they used to, and still are being criticized for not doing enough. The suggestion is that this isn't quite fair—and that is a feeling, in part, too.

What *would* be inappropriate is "pure" emotion: having no facts at all, *just* a "feeling." But clearly this is not true of either side in this debate. The environmentalists in this case have at least as many "facts" as the developers: facts about the overall state of the river, about alternative uses of the site in question, and so on. Perhaps the developers, sensing they have the Planning Commission on their side, can afford to speak with the appearance of dispassion, while the environmentalists sound more upset or desperate. But this has nothing to do with who has "facts" and who doesn't—it has to do with who is being heard.

In short: moral values are partly emotional, just as they are partly fact-based. All moral values, on both (all) sides. Moral emotions are parts of our thinking, parts of our very selves, and by including them we keep ourselves more intact, less fragmented, better able to integrate our selves as well as our values. How many unethical results of ethical deliberation come because we disconnect from our decision-making emotionally, because we unhook deliberation from caring? Do not therefore become maudlin or hysterical; but also do not pretend to be dispassionate and accuse the other side of being uninformed or "emotional." Both are unhelpful extremes. Just speak carefully, listen sympathetically, and try to give all of the relevant values a voice that is measured but strong.

"Am I Blue?"

ALICE WALKER

I now invite you to practice paying attention to values by reading and thinking about a well-known short essay by the celebrated novelist and activist Alice Walker. Walker is best known as the author of the novel *The Color Purple,* but she has penned other fine novels too as well as numerous books of reflective and autobiographical essays.

Read the essay first, then think about the moral values it invokes before going on to the discussion that follows.

*"Ain't these tears in these eyes tellin' you?"**

For about three years my companion and I rented a small house in the country that stood on the edge of a large meadow that appeared to run from the end of our deck straight into the mountains. The mountains, however, were quite far away, and between us and them there was, in fact, a town. It was one of the many pleasant aspects of the house that you never really were aware of this.

It was a house of many windows, low, wide, nearly floor to ceiling in the living room, which faced the meadow, and it was from one of these that I first saw our closest neighbor, a large white horse, cropping grass, flipping its mane, and ambling about—not over the entire meadow, which stretched well out of sight of the house, but over the five or so fenced-in acres that were next to the twenty-odd that we had rented. I soon learned that the horse, whose name was Blue, belonged to a man who lived in another town, but was boarded by our neighbors next door. Occasionally, one of the children, usually a stocky teen-ager, but sometimes a much younger girl or boy, could be seen riding Blue. They would appear in the meadow, climb up on his back, ride furiously for ten or fifteen minutes, then get off, slap Blue on the flanks, and not be seen again for a month or more.

There were many apple trees in our yard, and one by the fence that Blue could almost reach. We were soon in the habit of feeding him apples, which he relished, especially because by the middle of summer the meadow grasses—so green and succulent since January—had dried out from lack of rain, and Blue stumbled about munching the dried stalks half-heartedly. Sometimes he would stand very still just by the apple tree, and when one of us came out he would whinny, snort loudly, or stamp the ground. This meant, of course: I want an apple.

It was quite wonderful to pick a few apples, or collect those that had fallen to the ground overnight, and patiently hold them, one by one, up to his large, toothy mouth. I remained as thrilled as a child by his flexible dark lips, huge, cubelike teeth that crunched the apples, core and all, with such finality, and his high, broad-breasted *enormity*; beside which, I felt small indeed. When I was a child, I used to ride horses, and was especially friendly with one named Nan until the day I was riding and my brother deliberately spooked her and I was thrown, head first, against the trunk of a tree. When I came to, I was in bed and my mother was bending worriedly over me; we silently agreed that perhaps horseback riding was not the safest sport for me. Since then I have walked, and prefer walking to horseback riding—but I had forgotten the depth of feeling one could see in horses' eyes.

I was therefore unprepared for the expression in Blue's. Blue was lonely. Blue was horribly lonely and bored. I was not shocked that this should be the case; five acres to tramp by yourself, endlessly, even in the most beautiful of meadows—and his was—cannot provide many interesting events, and once rainy season turned to dry that was about it. No, I was shocked that I had forgotten that human animals and nonhuman animals can communicate quite well; if we are brought up around animals as children we take this for granted. By the time we are adults we no longer remember. However, the animals have not changed. They are in fact *completed* creations (at least they seem to be, so much more than we) who are not likely *to* change; it is their nature to express themselves. What else are they going to express? And they do. And, generally speaking, they are ignored.

After giving Blue the apples, I would wander back to the house, aware that he was observing me. Were more apples not forthcoming then? Was that to be his sole entertainment for the day? My partner's small son had decided he wanted to learn how to piece a quilt; we worked in silence on our respective squares as I thought...

Well, about slavery: about white children, who were raised by black people, who knew their first all-accepting love from black women, and then, when they were twelve or so, were told they must "forget" the deep levels of communication between themselves and "mammy" that they knew. Later they would be able to relate quite calmly, "My old mammy was sold to another good family." "My old mammy was ———— ————." Fill in the blank. Many more years later a white woman would say: "I can't understand these Negroes, these blacks. What do they want? They're so different from us."

And about the Indians, considered to be "like animals" by the "settlers" (a very benign euphemism for what they actually were), who did not understand their description as a compliment.

And about the thousands of American men who marry Japanese, Korean, Filipina, and other non-English-speaking women and of how happy they report they are, *"blissfully,"* until their brides learn to speak English, at which point the marriages tend to fall apart. What then did the men see, when they looked into the eyes of the women they married, before they could speak English? Apparently only their own reflections.

I thought of society's impatience with the young. "Why are they playing the music so loud?" Perhaps the children have listened to much of the music of oppressed people their parents danced to before they were born, with its passionate but soft cries for acceptance and love, and they have wondered why their parents failed to hear.

I do not know how long Blue had inhabited his five beautiful, boring acres before we moved into our house; a year after we had arrived—and had also traveled to other valleys, other cities, other worlds—he was still there.

But then, in our second year at the house, something happened in Blue's life. One morning, looking out the window at the fog they lay like a ribbon over the meadow, I saw another horse, a brown one, at the other end of Blue's field. Blue appeared to be afraid of it, and for several days made no attempt to go near. We went away for a week. When we returned, Blue had decided to make friends and the two horses ambled or galloped along together, and Blue did not come nearly as often to the fence underneath the apple tree.

When he did, bringing his new friend with him, there was a different look in his eyes. A look of independence, of self-possession, of inalienable *horse*ness. His friend eventually became pregnant. For months and months there was, it seemed to me, a mutual feeling between me and the horses of justice, of peace. I fed apples to them both. The look in Blue's eyes was one of unabashed "this is *it*ness."

It did not, however, last forever. One day, after a visit to the city, I went out to give Blue some apples. He stood waiting, or so I thought, though not beneath the tree. When I shook the tree and jumped back from the shower of apples, he made no move. I carried some over to him. He managed to half-crunch one. The rest he let fall to the ground. I dreaded looking into his eyes—because I had of course noticed that Brown, his partner, had gone—but I did look. If I had been born into slavery, and my partner had been sold or killed, my eyes would have looked like that. The children next door explained that Blue's partner had been "put with him" (the same expression that old people used, I had noticed, when speaking of an ancestor during slavery who had been impregnated by her owner) so that they could mate and she conceive. Since that was accomplished, she had been taken back by her owner, who lived somewhere else.

Will she be back? I asked.

They didn't know.

Blue was like a crazed person. Blue *was*, to me, a crazed person. He galloped furiously, as if he were being ridden, around and around his five beautiful acres. He whinnied until he couldn't. He tore at the ground with his hooves. He butted himself against his single shade tree. He looked always and always toward the road down which his partner had gone. And then, occasionally, when he came up for apples, or I took apples to him, he looked at me. It was a look so piercing, so full of grief, a look so *human*, I almost laughed (I felt too sad to cry) to think there are people who do not know that animals suffer. People like me who have forgotten, and daily forget, all that animals try to tell us. "Everything you do to us will happen to you; we are your teachers, as you are ours. We are one lesson" is essentially it, I think. There are those who never once have even considered animals' rights: those who have been taught that animals actually want to be used and abused by us, as small children "love" to be frightened, or women "love" to be mutilated and raped.... They are the great-grandchildren of those who honestly thought, because someone taught them this: "Women can't think," and "niggers can't faint." But most disturbing of all, in Blue's large brown eyes was a new look, more painful than the look of despair: the look of disgust with human beings, with life; the look of hatred. And it was odd what the look of hatred did. It gave him, for the first time, the look of a beast. And what that meant was that he had put up a barrier within to protect himself from further violence; all the apples in the world wouldn't change that fact.

And so Blue remained, a beautiful part of our landscape, very peaceful to look at from the window, white against the grass. Once a friend came to visit and said, looking out on the soothing view: "And it *would* have to be a *white* horse; the very image of freedom." And I thought, yes, the animals are forced to become for us merely "images" of what they once so beautifully expressed. And we are used to drinking milk from containers showing "contented" cows, whose real lives we want to hear nothing about, eating eggs and drumsticks from "happy" hens, and munching hamburgers advertised by bulls of integrity who seem to command their fate.

As we talked of freedom and justice one day for all, we sat down to steaks. I am eating misery, I thought, as I took the first bite. And spit it out.

EXPLORING MORAL VALUES IN "AM I BLUE?"

What are the chief moral values that Alice Walker invokes in this essay? Remember, we are not analyzing it as a piece of writing—though it is a beautifully done and instructive piece, to be sure—and we are not looking at it in relation to her other work or asking for the kinds of analysis you might do in a literature or writing class. We are also not asking whether we agree with her claims or with her decision to stop eating animals. No: our goal is simply to understand her essay as a moral expression. Here is a person struggling with the fate of a horse who has become a distant sort of friend, with her commitment to fighting oppression of all sorts, and ultimately—in the very last lines—with diet as a moral issue. So what moral values come up?

We might begin with the most explicit ones; some are named in the essay. Justice, in particular, is invoked explicitly: "There was a different look in his eyes. A look of independence, of self-possession, of inalienable *horseness*. . . . For months and months . . . there was a feeling of justice, of peace." Peace is named here too. But it's justice that brings peace. Like any creature, Blue has basic needs and expectations, and for these few months, they are met. "Justice" is that sense of things being right, the world being rightly ordered. He's able to truly *be* what he is.

But Blue is a horse, of course, not a human, and so we may wonder whether morality, strictly speaking, even applies. Some people think that only human needs and expectations are relevant to ethics. Walker is out to show the opposite. All the way through the essay she draws parallels between the suffering of animals and the suffering of oppressed humans. We're invited to see the owners' treatment of Blue—and, by extension, it seems, much human treatment of all animals—as another kind of oppression. And overcoming oppression and reducing suffering are understood to be key moral values, though not stated explicitly.

Walker also draws parallels between our *denials* of the suffering of animals and our *denials* of the suffering of oppressed humans. And so something else is going on beneath her explicit appeal to justice and the implicit appeal to reduce suffering: it's an appeal to all of us to pay attention to the sufferings of others, especially those others whose suffering we have learned to deny (or perhaps, worse, *need* to deny in order to go on living as we do, eating meat, for example).

The moral value here, then, is something like sympathy—real, compassionate attention, especially to those so oppressed and stereotyped that we usually give ourselves excuses not to notice. We need to commit ourselves to no longer "ignore" what animals, or any suffering beings, really express. You could also call it honesty—with ourselves—about what is really happening. Walker puts it very personally. Chilled by the sense that Blue has retreated from her, that he has taken on a "disgust" with human beings, we sense that she pulls away too, but still with the hope that we may find ways of being able to look into animals' eyes (if not Blue's, then some animals, sometime) without shame, without a sense of having failed them. *With* a kind of sympathy that has made a difference. The ideal is that someday we may be able to come into the larger-than-human world with a sense of mutuality and, again, peace.

Sympathizing can be tricky. Sometimes we respond to the sufferings of others by imagining how *we* would feel if we were them—which is laudable as far as it goes, but also has the danger of imagining that the other (person *or* creature) is really just like us. It doesn't allow for *difference*. That disturbing story about American men who marry non-English-speaking wives, for instance: "The very possibility that they might have something of their own to communicate is often denied. Too often we see only our own reflections in those we subordinate and oppress." I think this is why Walker is careful to acknowledge Blue in what she calls his "inalienable *horse*ness" and "his high, broad-breasted enormity." He's a horse, not a human, but that does not somehow disqualify him from moral considerations: rather, it qualifies him *in his own way*.

And so Walker ends with the decision not to eat meat. Indeed she has made herself a major advocate for animal-rights causes and animal-free diets. It is interesting to compare her approach with the usual arguments for vegetarianism. The usual arguments against raising and killing animals for food are appeals to animals' suffering—the key values fit into, and aim to extend, the happiness-centered family of values—and "animal rights," which would be an extension of the person-centered family of values, arguing that at least some other animals are "persons" too. But Walker does not appeal to anything so general or formal as "animal rights," and even suffering is approached on a more personal and sympathetic level. Although values from all four families are present, I would say that the overall tone of Walker's essay places her main values in the relationship-centered family. Ultimately, for her, it is a question of how we can live *with* other animals and other humans, rather than in exploitation and denial: so truly a question of mutuality and community.

It's important to add, finally, that you or I might have responded differently. After all, there's no direct connection between how Blue was treated and the production of steaks. But Walker's essay follows a much bigger track. By compelling us to see Blue as a real, feeling being, she raises both the question of animals in general and the question of our own moral defensiveness, as we could put it, in an unforgettable way. It is now, unavoidably, one of the ethical questions of the times. If this brief exploration of "Am I Blue?" has done its work, you can begin to see why.

From Bloodties

TED KERASOTE

Naturalist and author Ted Kerasote is another writer struggling with the question of the human relation to animals. Kerasote wrote *Bloodties* (subtitled *Nature, Culture, and the Hunt*) to explore hunting in many varied forms, from aboriginal hunters in Greenland to globe-trotting trophy hunters, but he ends back at home, with his own hunting practice. He's as reflectively autobiographical, and seriously ethical, as Walker. He even holds many of the same values—but he ends up in a very different place.

Read Kerasote's thoughts in the same spirit that you read Walker's. (You're on your own for the analysis.) What specific moral values does Kerasote invoke? How do they compare with Walker's? Certain values he makes explicit: reducing pain, for instance; responsibility (in hunting, specifically, but also in thinking through our impacts on the Earth in general); respect for life. Ask yourself how he *shows* these valves, but ask yourself too if there isn't something still deeper in his commitment to hunting, harder to express but vital to his practice. Notice how lovingly he speaks of his high Wyoming home country, "still singing of glaciers and big mammals." Like Walker, he too ends by writing of sympathy, but does he mean the same thing by it?

Slowly, she angles away from me. In a few more steps she will be gone from sight and down the steep north slope. In the many miles walked this fall, among all the elk I've seen, she has become the possible elk—the elk approached with care, the elk close to home, the elk seen far enough into the season so that soon the season will be over...the elk whom the morn-

---

From Ted Kerasote, *Bloodties* (Kodansha International, 1994), pages 232–236, 240, 245–247.

ing, the snow, and the elk themselves have allowed me to approach. Only the asking remains.

"Mother elk," I say. "Please stop." I speak the words in my mind, sending them through the trees and into her sleek brown head. She crosses an opening in the forest, and there, for no reason I can understand, she pauses, her shoulder and flank visible.

It is a clear shot, though not a perfect one—I have to stand at full height to make it. But I know I can make it and I say, "Thank-you. I am sorry." Still I hesitate, for though I can lose myself in the hunting, I have never been able to stop thinking about its results—that I forget it's *this* elk rather than *that* elk who is about to die; that it's *this* creature whom I'm about to take from the world rather than some number in an equation proving the merits of wild-food harvesting over being a supermarket vegetarian; that this being before me—who sees, who smells, who *knows*—will no longer be among us, so that I may go on living. And I don't know how to escape this incongruous pain out of which we grow, this unresolvable unfairness, other than saying that I would rather be caught in this lovely tragedy with those whom I love, whom the ground beneath my feet has created alongside me, than with those far away, whose deaths I cannot own. Not that I think all this. I know it in my hesitation.

Still she stands, strangely immobile. I raise the rifle, and still she stands, and still I wait, for there have been times that I have come to this final moment, and through the air the animal's spirit has flown into my heart, sending me its pride and defiance, or its beseeching, frightened voice, saying, "I am not for you." And I have watched them walk away. She sweeps her eye across the forest and begins to graze down the north slope, exposing her flank for one more instant, and allowing me to decide. I listen, hearing the air thrum with the ambivalence of our joining, about which I can only say, once again, "I am sorry." As she disappears from sight, I fire behind her left shoulder, the sound of the shot muffled by the forest.

Then she's gone, and the woods are alive with the sound of hooves and branches crashing. I run forward, seeing a dozen cows and an enormous six-point bull stream from the pines and climb into the upper meadow, full of aspen. They pause and look back at me, but I can't see the elk I fired at. For one instant I think of shooting another cow as they stand and stare—the easiest shot imaginable. But I know I hit the animal I shot at.

As I start forward, the elk wheel and run up through the white trees, their tan rumps bobbing. Then they disappear into the next stand of conifers. In a few more steps I see an elk lying in the swale below me, her legs tucked under her, her head erect. She jumps up and moves off at an ungainly trot. I fire, and miss, and she disappears behind a small knob of pines that juts into the aspen.

I climb over several fallen trees and find her lying not thirty feet away, her head turned over her left shoulder, great brown eyes utterly calm. My heart tears apart....

She kicks several more times, gasps once, and lies still, a great, reddish-brown creature, her rear legs straight, her front ones tucked under her. There isn't a speck of blood anywhere....

It takes about an hour to skin her, and as she passes under my hands I note what she is as food—the layer of white fat on her hips, which is good for frying pancakes and for mixing into pemmican; the steaks decreasing in tenderness from the loins to her rump; the burger, jerky, kabob, and sausage. I smile because I can feel saliva lubricating my mouth. Going in the other direction, I smell what she has been—her hair smells of pine, her meat of grass, her fat like the undersides of rocks.

Then I saw her into quarters, the hardest job, and warmest. I'm down to my shirt as the sun begins to shine into our snowy north-facing dell, and the temperature feels as if it finally goes above zero. I hang her two hindquarters in a nearby aspen that has been tilted over by the wind. I also hang her shoulders there, and put each side of her rib cage on a downed aspen. Then I fold the hide and place it alongside the rib cage. The liver and heart I bury in the snow so the Canadian jays, already pecking at the fat around her intestines, will leave them alone.

I wash my hands with snow, have another cup of tea, then I take her hooves and place them on a nearby rise that looks north across the valley. I place her head on top of her legs. Her eyes have sunken a bit forward and are no longer wide and glistening. Sometimes I have used the head, boiling off its meat and eating the tongue. Today I don't. Kneeling by her hooves and head, I stroke her long brown hair and say a few more words....

Bullfighting, cockfighting, dogfighting...shooting live pigeons and prairie dogs for "sport" and money...dropping cosmetics into rabbits' eyes so humans can have nonirritating and frivolous products...keeping calves in stalls for tender veal, and chickens in crowded, filthy boxes to increase production...wounding elk through carelessness—all of these examples, and thousands of others whose common denominator is disrespect, seemed to me to be gratuitous forms of pain that are best removed from the world. Different from them is the instrumental pain caused by the honest biological clamor of our guts' wanting to be fed and which seems irreducible.

Once, in an attempt to outwit this pain, I became a vegetarian, and stayed one for quite a while. But when I inquired about the lives lost on a mechanized farm, I realized what costs we pay at the supermarket. One Oregon farmer told me that half the cottontail rabbits went into his combine when he cut a wheat field, that virtually all of the small mammals, ground birds, and reptiles were killed when he harvested windrow crops like rye and sugar beets, and that when the leaves were stripped from bush beans all the mice and the snakes who were living among them were destroyed as well. Perhaps he exaggerated; certainly he hadn't taken a census of his fields' small-animal populations. Nonetheless, from boyhood, he had seen many animals being killed as he made America's food. Because most of these animals have been seen as expendable, or not seen at all, few scientific studies have been done measuring agriculture's effects on their populations. Those that have been done demonstrate that agricultural lands often act as "ecological traps," attracting birds, for instance, who begin their nesting only to have machinery pass over the land, destroying their nests and often the birds themselves. This is particularly true in the case of alfalfa, grown to feed livestock, but it also happens in corn, soybean, and spring wheat fields. When one factors in the lives lost to pesticides, the toll is enormous....

...And as one biologist told me, when you find dead birds, you're only finding what's been "hit over the head with a baseball bat." You don't see, except after several years, the decline in reproduction among these bird populations, which these pesticides also cause. Raised on a farm in Iowa, he went on to say that current agricultural practices, particularly combining, left the earth a "biological desert." Our fields might be brimming over with wheat and corn and soybeans, but unless we began to leave habitat for wildlife—stubble, hedgerows, and ditches—we were going to find ourselves in an austerely quiet world, as silent as the silent spring about which Rachel Carson warned...unless one counted the growl of tractors as song.

Such data, scanty as it is, addresses only the lives lost on the farm itself. When our produce is transported along the interstate highway system, birds...deer...skunks...raccoons all get flattened. Who hasn't witnessed the carnage? And this doesn't even begin to count the animals lost to the development of the oil fields themselves, the transportation of petroleum across tundra, mountain ranges, and the oceans, and in the wars fought over that oil. In short, being a supermarket vegetarian didn't take me out of the web in which animals are constantly dying to feed humans, it merely put their deaths over the horizon, making them, in the bloodless jargon of cost-accounting, externalities.

When I looked into that web, so full of pain, I came to see that my killing an elk each year did less harm, expressed in animal lives who I believe count equally, than importing the same amount of vegetable food to my bioregion. That didn't ease my conscience; but it did make the choices clearer....

...I'm attached to these cold places, still singing of glaciers and big mammals, and in my bones I know that farming has abandoned a connection to them, a relationship of provision by uncultivated land, and concern for that land by its inhabitants, that seems clearest while hunting well. I decided to go back to hunting because it attaches me to this place and the animals I love, asking me to own what each of us ought to own in some personal way—the pain that runs the world. And hunting elk in particular because they are the loved totem of my home...because this home makes them and leaves them free...and because eating them does nothing to increase the aggregate pain of the world. In fact, by attaching me lovingly here, the relationship between elk and me decreases it.

All of this I have known most keenly walking in this forest, with the wind in my face, and pine in my nostrils, and snow under my boots. None of which means that someone else, trying the same experiment, would have reached a similar conclusion about how to treat animals. In the end, I think you have to *listen,* and if you can't *listen* to the quiet sadness of this world, a lifetime of roaming the outdoors, or thinking in libraries, is not going to tell you that the country is you and you are it, and when you cause it to suffer needlessly then you have broken a cord of sympathy, which is a much more demanding tie to nature than any system of ethics.

FOR REVIEW

1. What are values?
2. How are moral values different from other kinds of values?
3. What are the four families of moral values?
4. How (roughly) are the four families distinct?
5. What are this chapter's general guidelines for drawing out the moral values at stake in an issue?
6. Explain: "Give emotion its due."
7. What are two moral values invoked by Alice Walker in "Am I Blue?"
8. Why, in the end, does Walker give up meat?
9. What are two moral values invoked by Ted Kerasote in the selection from *Bloodties*?
10. Why, in the end, does Kerasote hunt?

EXERCISES AND NOTES

FOR REFLECTION

What values are most important to you? Not just moral values, first of all, but *any* values. What is it that you most deeply care about? Love? Money?

Satisfying and productive work? One or two things, or a great many? Things easily described in a few words, or things that take a long story or two to explain?

Now turn to *moral* values. What moral values are most important to you? Respect? The greatest happiness (your own *and* others')? Keeping your word? Care and community? Fairness? Are there one or two things, or a great many? Things easily described in a few words, or things that take a long story or two to explain? Are most of your key values in one specific family? Which one, and why?

Think of a time when you felt proud of yourself. What were you proud of having done (or not done) or of being (or not being)? Then think of some time when you felt angry at yourself. What were you angry about? Why? What values are called upon when you make these judgments? How many of these are moral values?

WALKER AND KERASOTE

What is most painful to you about Alice Walker's "Am I Blue?" Write a short list or paragraph. Be sure to give emotion its due. Now consider the moral values you felt the story expressed. (The ones you thought about before reading the discussion following the story.) What connections do you see between what was most painful for you about the story and the moral values you see in the story?

Imagine a dialogue between Walker and Ted Kerasote—what would they say to each other? What would *you* say if you were a third voice? Do you think Kerasote is less morally demanding (or more?), or just differently morally demanding, than Walker? Explain.

Are there other values also involved in the question of eating animals? What values? (Make a start here: the exercises in the next several chapters return to the animal question.)

ISSUES

Here are some issues to explore with an eye for the values in play—and other relevant values that perhaps *ought* to be in play!

- What moral values (if any) are involved in driving (besides not driving drunk)? Does ethics have anything to say about following speed limits, keeping your insurance up to date, keeping the car well-maintained, and so on? (Clearly there *are* values involved; the question is whether you consider them *moral* values, and why or why not.) What about radar detectors? Moral, nonmoral, immoral? Why? What families of values are involved?

- What moral obligations do you have toward your parents? Why? Are they (and if so *why* are they) different from the moral obligations your parents have toward you? If there is a difference, is the difference fair? Or does the value of fairness just not apply here?

- Ease of life today may impose immense costs on the future. When we waste scarce natural resources and litter the earth with nonbiodegradable but cheap items, our descendants bear the burdens of compensation and cleanup. When we alter the climate, we impose unknown but possibly immense costs on the future too. William McDonough calls this "intergenerational remote tyranny." What kinds of moral values is he invoking? What others are relevant?

- Population policy. What kinds of moral values are at stake as we think about having children and about religious or political policies that affect family choices and reproduction rates, at home or abroad?

- Many businesses now have codes of ethics. What kinds of moral values would, or should, such a code include? Also: could there be a debate about this? That is, might it be that a business code of ethics should only concern certain kinds of moral values and not others? Must business serve the social good, for example, or should businesspeople be judged only by their personal virtuousness?

- Rights of accused (and convicted) criminals (to fair trials, against cruel and unusual punishments, etc.) versus the social good (*what* good(s), exactly?) that might be achieved by rapid trials, limited appeals, and cheap jails. What families of moral values are most directly invoked here? Are there other moral values also in play?

- Some of us expect that U.S. presidents will be sterling personal role models. Others ask: Isn't it enough if they do what they can to improve the quality of life, the economy, world politics, and so on? What values, again, are invoked here? Do the same expectations apply to other leaders, for example, corporate CEOs, movie stars, athletes? Why or why not? What moral values shape these expectations?

- Should academic honor codes require students to turn in fellow students who cheated on an exam? What kinds of values have something to say about this?

- How should the government respond to the demands of dispossessed Indian tribes for some kind of compensation or return of ancient ancestral lands? Is this a *moral* issue? What kinds of options can be morally considered? How does this issue relate to the question of reparations for slavery?

READING VALUES STATEMENTS AND STORIES

Look at the mission statements of a variety of organizations: local business, big corporations, nonprofit organizations, groups like Amnesty International or the Sierra Club or the National Rifle Association (NRA) or the American

Civil Liberties Union (ACLU). Nearly all of these can be found on the Web: the research is easy.

Once again, spell out the moral values involved. What kinds of values tend to show up? Typically in what families? Many of these organizations we only know through a few media stereotypes, or perhaps because they are very visible on one or two controversial issues. Don't assume that you already know who and what they are and that you don't need to look carefully at what they themselves say they are. Every organization on this list will surprise you if you look closely enough.

Look at your own college or university catalog. The first pages usually offer some larger sense of the institution's mission, often in moral terms. Again, what kinds of values tend to show up? Typically in what families? Would it be the same for educational institutions of other sorts—like military academies, Zen monasteries, museums, auto-mechanic training? Check them out.

Political speeches and party platforms are a good place to look as well. (Full texts can sometimes be found in newspapers like the *New York Times,* or on the Web.) Don't forget the United Nations—look at its founding documents, like the UN Declaration of Human Rights. Look at the speeches of ambassadors from places you don't like. For those with an historical bent, look to the great documents and speeches of American history. Look again at the encyclicals of the popes.

If your interests run in a more literary direction, look at popular stories in the same way. Children's stories, for example. They often clearly promote moral values, and in fact invite us to spell them out as we interpret the story—as we find the "moral." Useful collections are William Bennett's *The Book of Virtues* (Simon and Schuster, 1993) and his follow-up *The Moral Compass* (Simon and Schuster, 1995).

NOTES

Many disciplines study values. The aim may be to classify them, to relate them to each other and to other factors, or sometimes to begin to systematically evaluate them as well. For a useful survey of social-scientific approaches to the question of the nature of values, as well as a survey of typologies and developmental theories of value, see Richard Kilby, *The Study of Human Values* (University Press of America, 1993). A stimulating and accessible look at values that goes back to the very beginning (how do we know values are even *real?*) is Howard Richards, *Life on a Small Planet: A Philosophy of Value* (Philosophical Library, 1966). For the classic introduction to the philosophical theory of values, see Risieri Frondizi, *What Is Value?* (Open Court Library of Philosophy, 1963). Classic but more difficult sources are John Dewey, *Theory of Valuation* (University of Chicago Press, 1939) and G. H. von Wright, *The Varieties of Goodness* (Humanities Press, 1963).

The Ethics of the Person

In the last chapter we outlined the family of person-centered values like this:

P E R S O N S

Central to ethics is the insistence that *persons* are special, precious, and have a dignity that demands respect. No one is to be treated as a mere means to others' ends. Social relations require fairness, justice, and equality. Human and civil rights are essential too: they secure the space in which each person, you and I and everyone else, is recognized and can flourish.

Let us now explore the ethics of persons in more detail.

PERSONS FACE TO FACE

I am sure that there have been times in your life when some other person suddenly has emerged out of the background of friends or co-workers or even strangers on the street, out of routine everyday experience, and you were brought up short with a realization: here is a unique spark, another soul. Falling in love can be like that, sometimes. It can also happen with people you don't know and will never see again. Even a brief encounter with another person can be complete in itself, and it may change the way we experience not just him or her but people in general.

One of my students wrote about meeting a homeless woman in New York's Pennsylvania Station.

> I was waiting for a friend, but she was late and I was all alone and scared. A woman who was selling spin tops outside the station saw me and came over to me. She asked my name and I told her and she said her name was

> Mona Lisa. We ended up talking for an hour and a half....She told me all
> about her life and how she ended up in the streets of New York. All for
> love...

A country kid, alone and frightened on a first visit to New York, approached by a kind of person she had never known face to face, who she
knew only as a stereotype—the Homeless—repeated a thousand times over
on television and in the papers: still this student found herself able to see her
and respond to her as a person, as "Mona Lisa" did in return.

Notice that responding in this way was not at all the same as just being
nice. To be "nice" would have been to buy a spin top and back away: to stay
on the level of habit and stereotyped response. This student did something
entirely different. She responded to something unique and unexpected in
this stranger, and some very basic recognition and affirmation then passed
between them.

We also know what it's like when others do *not* treat us as "persons" in
this sense. Cheery salespeople greet you on the phone like an old friend but
hang up in midsentence when they realize that they are not going to make a
sale. Sexual exploitation—realizing that you are only a body for someone else,
only a means to someone else's momentary pleasure—is far more deeply
chilling. We say: "You're just treating me like an object." And cases in which
people are completely reduced to "things" are among the greatest of evils.
The Nazi concentration camps were meant to dehumanize: it is no surprise
that they were the first step to mass slaughter.

The key ethical recognition is that none of us are really just "objects" that
can be related to as if we are just things, easily reduced to someone else's
stereotype or "use." Philosophers put it like this: we are *subjects* (as opposed
to "objects"), centers of our own experience and thinking, our own hopes and
fears and dreams, choices large and small. And, crucially, we recognize also
that others are just like us in the same way.

BUBER'S *I AND THOU*

Martin Buber (1898–1965) was a philosopher and theologian especially concerned to highlight the special recognition of others in a time when he saw
depersonalization increasing dramatically. His entire project was ethical from
beginning to end. But his is not an ethics of rules and theories and principles.
In his famous book *I and Thou*, Buber tried to go back to absolute basics and
to carefully describe the encounter with persons in this sense: as unique and
self-determining beings.

Too often, Buber says, we "go over the surface of the world" and just "pile
up information" without really going to the depths of anything. When we
confront a "Thou" or a "You," however, we are pulled up short. The person
we are encountering "is no longer He or She, limited by other Hes or Shes,

a dot in the world grid of space and time, nor…a loose bundle of named qualities. Neighborless and seamless, he fills the firmament. Not as if there were nothing else but he, but everything lives in *his* light." Buber writes of this kind of encounter as if it strikes us with a "flash," like lightning. The "You" or "Thou" is unpredictable, spontaneous, deep. Our "I" (the other half of the "I/Thou" relationship) is transformed too: we no longer stand apart but are wholly engaged with the other person. "Relation is reciprocity."

And it is, naturally, deeply ethical. To see others in this way is to treasure them—certainly not to stand in their way or impose anything upon them, but much more too: to recognize a profound kind of value, both in the other person and in the encounter itself. We stand in awe and respond with respect. Buber goes on to conceive our relation to God in very similar relational terms.

True, it's not really as though the *only* way to experience persons is in this electrifying, one-on-one kind of way, totally distinct from everyday habitual experience. Most of the time, as Buber admits, we relate to other people both as subjects *and* objects, and in other ways besides (as parts of "We's," for example). Still, by returning to basics and exalting one compelling way in which the world of persons opens up to us, Buber reminds us of *a* core ethical experience, even if not the only one. In fact we have an "innate longing for relation," he says, traceable even in the attentions of babies and in animistic worldviews. We want the whole world to be alive to the I/Thou relation.

LEVINAS AND "THE FACE"

Another thinker to probe deeply into the experience of others was Emmanuel Levinas (1906–1995), a French philosopher whose ethical thinking was shaped both by Buber's work and by his experiences in the brutal environments of war and as a captured Jewish French soldier in a Nazi prisoner-of-war camp.

Levinas looks specifically at the experience of another's *face*. Like Buber, Levinas is concerned that we not glance over the face—the other, the subject—too fast, as if everything there is to know about the person were somehow on the surface, just pieces of "objective information" (that is, having to do with the self as *object*), to be defined or pinned down. Instead, Levinas stresses the "infinity" or unplumbable depth of a person, which may be seen *through* the face but not, as it were, *on* the face. When we really see the person as a person, Levinas says that we don't even notice the person's features, like their eye color. What we do "see" is their spontaneity, their "inexhaustibility"—that is, precisely that they *can't* be pinned down or objectified.

And then, Levinas concludes, we also can't do violence to them. The face—the other, the person—demands infinite respect. Of course Levinas could hardly deny that people actually do violence to each other, in fact all the time. His suggestion is that when we do, though, we either have not really seen the other's face at all (which is often literally true: think of how readily we can do things to people at a distance that we could never do if they were right in front of us and looking us in the eye) or do it in "uneasy awareness" of what an evil it is. We see their faces but deny our own response.

Dialogue is another way that others' "infinity" opens up to us. Here too, as in the face literally, there is spontaneity, something more and unknown, always just now emerging. Indeed, Levinas says that the "face" names both the actual face and also the tendency for the other, in whatever way, to "exceed the idea of him in me." "The face refuses to be contained." "The other overflows absolutely every idea I can have of him."

Levinas, in fact, insists that ethics always comes first. We don't "pile up information," as Buber puts it, about the world or about others, and then, later, somewhere down the road, get an ethics. No: ethics shapes how we relate to the world from the very start. Knowledge is only possible through love, he says. "Knowledge of love" works before "love of knowledge." The only way we can really know anything about the other person is to see them in this "infinite" way.

"Ethics and the Face"

EMMANUEL LEVINAS

Interviews with Philippe Nemo in a new translation by Beth Raps

The following is, you might say, a dialogue on dialogue. It is a translation of part of a radio talk between Emmanuel Levinas and a philosopher-interviewer (Nemo) on French radio, published in French in 1982. It's one of the most accessible pieces ever written conveying Levinas's thinking—with perhaps the exception of a word that crops up right away in the interview, "phenomenology." Phenomenology is a kind of philosophy, more common in French-speaking countries, that starts from our lived experience—in this case, our analysis of the lived experience of truly looking into someone else's face.

NEMO: *You talk about the face at length in [your earlier book]* Totality and Infinity. *It's one of your common themes. This phenomenology of the face—that is, this analysis of what happens when I look into another person's face—what does it consist of and what is it for?*

LEVINAS: ...When you see a nose, eyes, a forehead, a chin, and you can describe them, you are turning toward the other person as toward an

From "The Face" and "The Responsibility for Others," originally prepared for Radio France's show "France-Culture" by Philippe Nemo (the interviewer) and published as *Ethique et Infini: Dialogues avec Philippe Nemo,* by Emmanuel Levinas (Librairie Artheme Fayard et Radio-France, 1982). Translation copyright © 2007 by Beth Raps.

object. [But] the best way to truly see others is not even to notice the color of their eyes! When we observe their eye color, we are not in a social relationship with them. Our relation to another person's face can indeed be dominated by perception, but what is specific to that face is what cannot be reduced to perception.

First of all, there is the way the head is held up, its naked, defenseless exposure. Facial skin stays the nakedest, the most stripped—the nakedest, although not indecent. The most stripped as well: in a face lies an essential poverty; we prove this by trying to hide its poverty by posing, with looks and attitudes. The face is exposed, threatened, as if inviting us to commit an act of violence. And yet at the same time, the face is what enjoins us from killing.

NEMO: It's true, war stories say that it is hard to kill someone looking you in the face.

LEVINAS: The face is meaningful and its meaning has no context. I'm saying that the other person, in upholding her or his face, is not a character in a context. Ordinarily, we are characters: we are on the faculty of a prestigious university, hold a high-ranking government post, are the son or daughter of so-and-so—all the things it says on our passports[*]; the way we dress or look. And every meaning, as we usually use the word, is relative to some context: something's meaning comes from its relationship to something else.

Here, it's the opposite: a face has meaning all on its own....This is how the face's meaning goes beyond being, if we think of being as correlated with what's known. Quite the contrary: seeing is always a way of trying to grasp what is seen: it is what, more than anything else, absorbs being.

But our relationship to a face is an ethical question. A face is what we cannot kill, or at least, that is its very meaning: "Thou shalt not kill." Although it is true that murder is an ordinary occurrence: we can kill others—the ethical obligation is not an ontological necessity. The commandment not to kill does not make murder impossible, although the power of the commandment endures in the uneasy awareness of the evil which has taken place—the malignancy of malice....

NEMO: The other person is a face, but we also speak to each other. Isn't human speech also a way of breaking what you call "totality"?

LEVINAS: Sure it is. Face and speech are connected. Faces speak. They speak, and this is what makes all speaking possible, begins it. Earlier, I rejected the idea of sight as a way of describing authentic relationships; it is speech, and more precisely, responding or responsibility, which is this authentic relationship.

---

[*] Translator's note: French passports contain a brief listing of the holder's employment.

NEMO: But because ethical relationship goes beyond knowing, and is taken on in an authentic way by speech, are you saying that speaking itself is not a kind of knowing?

LEVINAS: Within speech, I've always drawn a distinction between *speaking* and what is *said*. *Speaking* must include *something said*—this is a requirement of the sort society imposes on us, with its laws, its institutions, its social relationships. But *speaking* is the fact that in front of a face I do not simply sit there and contemplate it, I respond to it. Speaking is a way of greeting the other person, but to greet someone is already to respond on that person's behalf.

It is difficult to keep quiet in someone else's presence; the difficulty is ultimately based in the meaning of speaking unto itself, no matter what is being said. We have to speak about something, about the weather or the price of tea in China, it doesn't matter—but speak, respond to the other person, and respond on his behalf.

NEMO: In the other person's face there is, you say "an uplifting," a "high-ness." The other is higher than I am. What do you mean by that?

LEVINAS: "Thou shalt not kill" is the face's first Word. And it's an order. There is, in the face's appearance, a commandment, as if a master were speaking to me. Yet, at the same time, the other's face is stripped, it's the poverty-stricken person for whom I can do anything and to whom I owe everything. And I, whoever I am, but in the "first person," am the one who finds the resources to respond to the call.

NEMO: I want to say to you, yes, in some cases...but in others, no, my encounter with the other is violent, hateful, disdainful.

LEVINAS: Of course. But I think that whatever motivation can explain this reversal, analyzing a face as I've just done, seeing the other's mastery and poverty, and my submissiveness and wealth, comes first. It is the primary assumption of all human relationships. If it weren't there, we wouldn't even say, when we stood before an open door, "After you!" What I'm trying to describe here is the very first "After you!"

NEMO: ...What do you mean by responsibility?

LEVINAS: ...I am talking about responsibility as an essential structure, a primary, a fundamental structure of subjectivity. I describe subjectivity in ethical terms. Here, ethics is no add-on to some pre-existing existential base. The knot of subjectivity is tied right into ethics, understood as responsibility.

I understand responsibility to mean responsibility for others, that is, responsibility for what is not my doing, or may not even be in my purview—or precisely what is in my view, is approached by me, like a face.

NEMO: How, having discovered another person's face, do we discover that person as someone for whom we are responsible?

LEVINAS: By describing the face as what it is, and not simply as what it is not. You'll remember what we were saying: approaching a face is not just simple perception.... When we talk about what a face *is,* we can say that the moment the other looks at me, I am responsible for that person. I do not have to *take* responsibility, responsibility is *incumbent* on me. This is responsibility that goes beyond what I do. Usually, we are responsible for what we ourselves do. I say, in [my book] *Other Than Being,* that responsibility is first of all *a thing in and for others.* It means that I am responsible for the other's very responsibility....

My link to the other is tied only using responsibility, and this is so whether the responsibility be accepted or refused, whether we know or don't know how to take it on, whether we are able to do something concrete for the other person or not. It is to say, "I'm here." To do something for the other person. To give. To be a human spirit, that's what it is.

What guarantees the spirituality of human subjectivity is its embodiedness. I can't see what angels would be able to give each other, or how they could help each other.... It is as if what lies in the other's nearness—beyond the image I have of the other person—the face, whatever is expressive in the other person (and the whole human body is, in this sense, a face, more or less)—were what *ordered* me to serve that person.

I use an extreme word. The face asks me, and orders me. Its meaning means an order. When I say that the face means an order I've been given, it does not do so in the same way anything means what it means; this order is the face's very meaning.

NEMO: But isn't the other also responsible for me?

LEVINAS: Maybe, but that is not *your* concern.... [R]elations between people are not symmetrical. This is how I can be responsible for someone else without waiting for the other person to reciprocate, even if it costs me my life. Reciprocating is the *other* person's concern. It's precisely insofar as the relationship between the other person and myself is not reciprocal that I am subject to the other, and I am essentially "subject" in this sense. It is I on whom it all rests

MADE IN THE IMAGE OF GOD

Buber and Levinas suggest that our experience of persons immediately points the way toward person-centered values. And indeed, historically, it has. Let us follow the path a little further along and consider some of the forms that person-based ethics has taken.

In the Judeo-Christian view, Creation is an act of free and gracious love that produces a world that at its heart must be beautiful and good, like God himself. Persons too must partake of this sort of innocent and original goodness. But humans are usually also pictured as a *distinctive* part of Creation. Jews and Christians make much of the passage at Genesis 1:26–27 where God declares that He has made humans "in his own image": "Then God said, 'Let us make man in our image, in our likeness...' So God created man in his own image, in the image of God he created him; male and female he created them."

Human persons are therefore pictured as uniquely and directly partaking in God's own nature. We too—by God's grace—can comprehend the world rationally and with full self-consciousness; we too are free beings, able to deliberate and choose for ourselves; we too can create worlds and re-create even ourselves; and as a result we too can act morally and think ethically, consciously identifying values and bringing them into reality. In Psalms 8:4–5, the Psalmist writes:

> What is man, that you think of him?
> What is the son of man, that you care for him?
> For you have made him a little lower than God,
> and crowned him with glory and honor.

The moral upshot is that in loving God we are also called to love other humans—and ourselves—as *reflections* of God. Again, the traits that make us persons—self-consciousness, creative freedom, morality itself—are the ways in which we mirror God, and consequently are of supreme value. They define an ethic both of self-actualization and of a profound respect for other humans. Not that it's easy: the very freedom that makes us Godlike persons also gives us the possibility of deliberately falling away, turning from God and also from the reflection of God in each other and even ourselves. Correspondingly, though, striving to live in accord with the "image of God" in one's life can be seen as a quest for one's essential self.

Of course there are differences. Jews and Christians often picture God as a Father and speak of persons as all being equal and precious as "children of God." Muslims understand God (Allah) as more distinct and unique—though Allah nonetheless has seemingly human characteristics, such as compassion, mercy, wisdom, and goodness. Muslims also do not think of Allah as having children: instead we're related to God as his creatures and as servants (in an affirmative sense, that is, not as slaves but as free service-givers).

Yet the idea that persons are special, sacred, morally central "subjects," even of infinite value, is emphatically shared. Commenting on the killing of Abel by his brother Cain, the Koran (Qur'an) tells us that "Anyone who saves one life, it is as if he has saved the whole of mankind, and anyone who has killed another person (except in lieu of murder or mischief on earth) it is as if he has killed the whole of mankind (Book 5:32)." So somehow a single self can be the moral equivalent of all selves, a microcosm of the whole world. Levinas's theme of the "infinity" of persons reemerges here. Even one life somehow has the same value as the whole. There is an identical teaching in the Jewish *Mishnah:* "Anyone who destroys a single person, the Torah accounts it to him as if he has destroyed a whole world. And anyone who maintains a single person, the Torah accounts it to him as if he maintained a whole world." (*Sanhedrin* 4:5)

A whole ethics then follows—in parallel ways across the great traditions. There is a shared prohibition against murder: "Thou shalt not kill." The preciousness of persons must be maintained in all things: so there are shared prohibitions of theft, dishonesty, unprovoked war, callousness to the sufferings of others as well. We are enjoined to help reduce suffering, to care for those who need help. "Love your neighbor as yourself"—for you are equally beloved creatures of God.

All of this is idealistic, of course. In practice, as we also know, people in all the great traditions (and not just the religious ones) are capable of huge moral blind spots, selective and self-serving interpretations, and even ongoing hatefulness. Christianity has been harsh in its treatments of heretics and unbelievers and has been deeply mistrusted in the Muslim world since the Crusades. The historical parts of the Old Testament are all too often records of wars and slaughters. The quote from the Koran above comes, ironically enough, in the midst of a violent harangue against Jews and Christians. In modern times too, as we know all too well, mistrust and hatred continue. Yet it is at least somewhat reassuring that at the hearts of all of these religions— the point toward which all but the harshest feel the pull and which many of the most intent never leave—is still the message of love and respect for each other, premised, once again, on the profound value of the person. We are left with the ongoing challenge to better live up to it.

From *"Evangelium Vitae"*

POPE JOHN PAUL II

Pope John Paul II issued his encyclical "Evangelium Vitae" ("The Gospel of Life") on March 25, 1995. His aim is to restate Catholic doctrine on what he calls "the incomparable value of every human person" in an age when, he fears, there is an "extraordinary increase and gravity of threats to the life of individuals and peoples.... In addition to the ancient scourges of poverty, hunger, endemic diseases,

From Pope John Paul II, "Evangelium Vitae." Online at http://www.vatican.va/ holy_father/john_paul_ii/encyclicals/documents/hf_jp-ii_enc_25031995_evangelium- vitae_en.html.

violence and war, new threats are emerging on an alarmingly vast scale," such as, among others,

> any type of murder, genocide, abortion, euthanasia, or wilful self-destruc-
> tion, whatever violates the integrity of the human person, such as mutilation,
> torments inflicted on body or mind, attempts to coerce the will itself; what-
> ever insults human dignity, such as subhuman living conditions, arbitrary
> imprisonment, deportation, slavery, prostitution, the selling of women and
> children; as well as disgraceful working conditions, where people are treated
> as mere instruments of gain rather than as free and responsible persons.

Note the extensive list! All these things and others like them, he declares, "are infamies indeed. They poison human society, and they do more harm to those who practise them than to those who suffer from the injury. Moreover, they are a supreme dishonour to the Creator."

Here are a few sections of the encyclical in which he summarizes his argument. Notice in particular the vision of the *person* that the pope advances here.

Man is called to a fullness of life which far exceeds the dimensions of his earthly existence, because it consists in sharing the very life of God. The loftiness of this supernatural vocation reveals the greatness and the in-estimable value of human life even in its temporal phase. Life in time, in fact, is the fundamental condition, the initial stage and an integral part of the entire unified process of human existence. It is a process which, unex-pectedly and undeservedly, is enlightened by the promise and renewed by the gift of divine life, which will reach its full realization in eternity (cf. 1 John 3:1–2). At the same time, it is precisely this supernatural calling which highlights the relative character of each individual's earthly life. After all, life on earth is not an "ultimate" but a "penultimate" reality; even so, it remains a sacred reality entrusted to us, to be preserved with a sense of responsibility and brought to perfection in love and in the gift of our-selves to God and to our brothers and sisters.

The Church knows that this Gospel of life, which she has received from her Lord, has a profound and persuasive echo in the heart of every person—believer and non-believer alike—because it marvellously fulfils all the heart's expectations while infinitely surpassing them. Even in the midst of difficulties and uncertainties, every person sincerely open to truth and goodness can, by the light of reason and the hidden action of grace, come to recognize in the natural law written in the heart (cf. Romans 2:14–15) the sacred value of human life from its very beginning until its end, and can affirm the right of every human being to have this primary good respected to the highest degree. Upon the recognition of this right, every human community and the political community itself are founded.

In a special way, believers in Christ must defend and promote this right, aware as they are of the wonderful truth recalled by the Second Vati-can Council: "By his incarnation the Son of God has united himself in some fashion with every human being." This saving event reveals to humanity not only the boundless love of God who "so loved the world that he gave his only Son" (John 3:16), but also the incomparable value of every human person. . . .

A stranger is no longer a stranger for the person who must become a neighbour to someone in need, to the point of accepting responsibility for his life, as the parable of the Good Samaritan shows so clearly (cf. Luke 10:25–37). Even an enemy ceases to be an enemy for the person who is obliged to love him (cf. Matthew 5:38–48; Luke 6:27–35), to "do good" to him (cf. Luke 6:27, 33, 35) and to respond to his immediate needs promptly and with no expectation of repayment (cf. Luke 6:34–35). The height of this love is to pray for one's enemy. By so doing we achieve harmony with the providential love of God: "But I say to you, love your enemies and pray for those who persecute you, so that you may be children of your Father who is in heaven; for he makes his sun rise on the evil and on the good and sends rain on the just and on the unjust" (Matthew 5:44–45; cf. Luke 6:28, 35)

Thus the deepest element of God's commandment to protect human life is the requirement to show reverence and love for every person and the life of every person. This is the teaching which the Apostle Paul, echoing the words of Jesus, addresses to the Christians in Rome: "The commandments, 'You shall not commit adultery, You shall not kill, You shall not steal, You shall not covet,' and any other commandment, are summed up in this sentence, 'You shall love your neighbour as yourself.'" (Romans 13:9–10).

KANT'S CATEGORICAL IMPERATIVE

Philosopher Immanuel Kant (1724–1804) advanced the claim that persons are not just means but "ends in themselves."

You know the language of "means." A means is a way of getting something: a car is a means of getting around, money is a means of buying what we want or need to live. An "end," by contrast, is valued at least in part for its own sake—it is not just one more link in a chain of means, but a place where the chain comes to an end.

To some degree, unavoidably, we inevitably are "means" to each other. A waiter is partly our means of getting food; a parent is partly a means of support. But the claim is that we get the world itself wrong—we mistake reality itself—if we begin to take other people (or ourselves) *just* as means in this sense. Another person is not just a way to get something for ourselves, whether it be something trivial or something vital, such as ongoing pleasure or company. We are all *also* centers of our own experience and thinking and choice. We are also ends in ourselves!

THE CATEGORICAL IMPERATIVE

Means-thinking is situational and dependent. It recommends things to us "hypothetically": *if* we want such-and-such, *then* we should choose something else which is a means to it. But ethics, says Kant, applies "categorically." It is not dependent on something else, but calls to us simply by virtue of our ability to think of it in the first place. No *ifs*. Thus Kant seeks what he calls the "Categorical Imperative": a basic obligation that applies to us regardless of our other goals or situation.

Kant proposes four forms of what he thinks is one basic Categorical Imperative. The most approachable form he puts explicitly in terms of ends and means:

> *Always act so as to treat humanity, whether in yourself or in another, as an end and never merely as a means.*

Kant is careful here. He is not saying that we should never treat others as means at all. Again, the truth is that we must. Even Buber, the apostle of I/Thou relations, allows that sometimes and in some ways we do have to treat other people at least in part as "Its" or objects. The point for both Kant and Buber is that we must *also* always keep alive a fuller and more complete sense of others as more-than-Its, more-than-means.

SELF AS ONE AMONG OTHERS

So how do we justify placing this kind of value on persons? Levinas and Buber appeal to direct experience. The pope bases his appeal on revelation. By contrast, most philosophy is committed to making *arguments*. The aim is to *show*—that is, by a chain of reasoning—that persons have the sort of ultimate value being claimed for them. It is here that Kant makes his distinctive contribution.

The essence of morality, according to Kant, is to live according to the moral law. It is not merely to act in accord with "inclination" (to be ethical because it pleases us, even if it does in fact deeply please us) or even to act in opposition to inclination (because we would still be in the orbit of inclination, still obsessed with desire though now for the purpose of putting it down). No: to be moral is to do what is right just because it is right. It is of the essence of ethics to be impersonal, impartial—not to depend on passing, personal feeling.

But it is no merely political or legal "law" that Kant has in mind. "Law" for Kant means a universal principle that all rational minds could hold themselves to in the situation in question. That is, the idea of "law" leads us to the ideal of universality, and thus to the recognition that, even though I may be deciding for myself, to decide *morally* means to decide as one rational mind among others, as if setting the law for all. Anyone else in the same situation should do the same thing.

Another form of Kant's Categorical Imperative therefore reads:

Act only according to that maxim whereby you can at the same time will that it become a universal law.

By "maxim" he means, roughly, the rule you propose to yourself when trying to decide what to do. This form of the Categorical Imperative thus is a test to see whether the rule you have in mind can be moral: the test is whether you could consistently will it to be a rule that everyone follows.

Should I lie, for example, to get myself out of an embarrassing or sticky situation? No, says Kant. I could not will it to be a universal law that *everyone* should lie to get out of a sticky situation, for then no such lie would work. On the contrary: by wanting my lie to work, I am implicitly willing that others *not* lie in the same situation, so that the general expectation of truthfulness will be maintained, that is, so that my lie will succeed. I am only making an exception for myself.

And there's the crucial thing: making an exception for myself. That is the place at which everything goes wrong. For there is no basis for taking myself to be somehow different or more special than other people in a way that could justify my flaunting a rule that I expect everyone else to follow. No: again, others are centers of experience and choice as real as we know ourselves to be. Others are persons too! Recognize that, says Kant, and a recognition of equal dignity and equal standing necessarily follows—thus the second form of the Imperative.

A profound sense of equality follows—and also, in a way, a sense of wonder. The first impulse is one of standing aside, of letting the other person *be*—in the sense of "letting them alone," and also, more fundamentally perhaps, in the sense of pure appreciation. Let them *be*! The essence of personhood again shines through.

From Grounding for the Metaphysics of Morals

IMMANUEL KANT

Now I say: man and generally any rational being exists as an end in himself, not merely as a means to be arbitrarily used by this or that will, but in all his actions, whether they concern himself or other rational beings, must be always regarded at the same time as an end.

From Immanuel Kant, *Grounding for the Metaphysics of Morals*, translated by T. K. Abbott. Online at http://www.gutenberg.org/catalog/world/readfile?fk_files= 10995, accessed 1/5/07, pp. 26–31.

...Beings whose existence depends not on our will but on nature's, have nevertheless, if they are irrational beings, only a relative value as means, and are therefore called things. Rational beings, on the contrary, are called persons, because their very nature points them out as ends in themselves, that is as something which must not be used merely as means, and so far therefore restricts freedom of action (and is an object of respect). These, therefore, are not merely subjective ends whose existence has a worth for us as an effect of our action, but objective ends, that is, things whose existence is an end in itself; an end moreover for which no other can be substituted, which they should subserve merely as means, for otherwise nothing whatever would possess absolute worth; but if all worth were conditioned and therefore contingent, then there would be no supreme practical principle of reason whatever.

If then there is a supreme practical principle or, in respect of the human will, a categorical imperative, it must be one which, being drawn from the conception of that which is necessarily an end for everyone because it is an end in itself, constitutes an objective principle of will, and can therefore serve as a universal practical law. The foundation of this principle is: rational nature exists as an end in itself. Man necessarily conceives his own existence as being so; so far then this is a subjective principle of human actions. But every other rational being regards its existence similarly, just on the same rational principle that holds for me: so that it is at the same time an objective principle, from which as a supreme practical law all laws of the will must be capable of being deduced. Accordingly the practical imperative will be as follows: So act as to treat humanity, whether in thine own person or in that of any other, in every case as an end withal, never as means only.

[Declaring that we must now see whether such a "practical imperative" can be put into action, Kant considers a range of examples. One of these is the case of the lie in the sticky situation, discussed in the text. Kant considers it in terms of both forms of the Categorical Imperative. Here it is in terms of the "end in itself" form.]

He who is thinking of making a lying promise to others will see at once that he would be using another man merely as a means, without the latter containing at the same time the end in himself. For he whom I propose by such a promise to use for my own purposes cannot possibly assent to my mode of acting towards him and, therefore, cannot himself contain the end of this action. This violation of the principle of humanity in other men is more obvious if we take in examples of attacks on the freedom and property of others. For then it is clear that he who transgresses the rights of men intends to use the person of others merely as a means, without considering that as rational beings they ought always to be esteemed also as ends, that is, as beings who must be capable of containing in themselves the end of the very same action.

[Here is the same case considered in terms of the "universal law" form of the Categorical Imperative.]

A [person] finds himself forced by necessity to borrow money. He knows that he will not be able to repay it, but sees also that nothing will be lent to him unless he promises stoutly to repay it in a definite time. He desires to make this promise, but he has still so much conscience as to ask himself: "Is it not unlawful and inconsistent with duty to get out of a difficulty in this way?" Suppose however that he resolves to do so: then the maxim of his action would be expressed thus: "When I think myself in want of money, I will borrow money and promise to repay it, although I know that I never can do so." Now this principle of self-love or of one's own advantage may perhaps be consistent with my whole future welfare; but the question now is, "Is it right?" I change then the suggestion of self-love into a universal law, and state the question thus: "How would it be if my maxim were a universal law?" Then I see at once that it could never hold as a universal law of nature, but would necessarily contradict itself. For supposing it to be a universal law that everyone when he thinks himself in a difficulty should be able to promise whatever he pleases, with the purpose of not keeping his promise, the promise itself would become impossible, as well as the end that one might have in view in it, since no one would consider that anything was promised to him, but would ridicule all such statements as vain pretences....

If now we attend to ourselves on occasion of any transgression of duty, we shall find that we in fact do not will that our maxim should be a universal law, for that is impossible for us; on the contrary, we will that the opposite should remain a universal law, only we assume the liberty of making an exception in our own favour or (just for this time only) in favour of our inclination. Consequently if we considered all cases from one and the same point of view, namely, that of reason, we should find a contradiction in our own will, namely, that a certain principle should be objectively necessary as a universal law, and yet subjectively should not be universal, but admit of exceptions.... Now, although this cannot be justified in our own impartial judgement, yet it proves that we do really recognise the validity of the categorical imperative and (with all respect for it) only allow ourselves a few exceptions, which we think unimportant and forced from us

RIGHTS, EQUALITY, JUSTICE

RIGHTS AND PERSONS

Jefferson's "Declaration of Independence" famously announces that:

We hold these truths to be self-evident, that all men are created equal, that they are endowed by their Creator with certain unalienable Rights, that among these are Life, Liberty and the pursuit of Happiness.—That to secure these rights, Governments are instituted among Men, deriving their just powers from the consent of the governed...

On this view, human beings have certain moral claims—rights—so basic they can't be taken away (hence, "unalienable"). And they are rooted, once again, in personhood.

Rights create the necessary space for persons to become what they are. The first section of this chapter, remember, concluded that "in truth we are *subjects* (as opposed to 'objects'), centers of our own experience and thinking, hopes and fears and dreams, choices large and small." Jewish and Christian traditions, again, picture the person as a model of God: rational, self-aware, creative, and free. The term "person" itself originates in Greek drama, where the *personae* were individual parts in the drama, as opposed to the impersonal, non-individual characters who spoke together in the Chorus. But without life and liberty, obviously, it is pretty hard to act rationally or creatively or to take your own individual path.

Of course there are many different interpretations of rights. Human life is sacred, the pope says, and taking life is therefore wrong: a right to life immediately follows. Catholic moral theology would go on to say that the right to life implies the moral requirement to protect and support those whose life is endangered—especially the poor and dispossessed and disempowered (notice again that this goes a lot further than fetuses). Others more concerned with liberty would argue that even basic rights like the right to life are only "negative" rights: that is, they only prohibit people doing certain things, but do not demand that they do other things. The right to life, on this view, only prohibits killing. We're not required to feed and shelter the needy too. Likewise, libertarians are fond of pointing out that Jefferson does not speak of a right to happiness: he only speaks of the right to *pursue* happiness. Success is not guaranteed—and presumably could not be, without constraining a lot of other people's liberty.

EQUALITY

We are all equally persons. Therefore, it seems to follow that all persons are, in some basic sense, morally equal. "All men are created equal" is the very first of Jefferson's "self-evident truths." Of course we know that he wasn't thinking quite as broadly as we would today about who counts as "men." Still, there was a built-in widening tendency in this "self-evident truth," and it continues to inspire many groups' struggles for moral and political recognition.

What does equality require? Not that every person should be treated exactly the same or have exactly the same things or life prospects—that is only a caricature. "Equality" in the civil rights struggle, for example, meant certain very specific and very basic things: the right to vote, the equal protection of the law, an end to second-rate schools and segregated facilities. In employment and education it might mean equal *opportunity*—not being closed out because of some prejudice or irrelevant factor. It's not as though everyone should have the same job, but everyone should have a fair chance, based on qualifications alone, at the good ones.

Economic equality gets trickier. Certainly it could require taking some corrective actions when economic disparities get too great. Economists track the ratios between the highest-paid members of corporations and the average worker: in America, currently the best-paid get about 100 times what the average (note: by no means the *worst*-paid) get—and the ratio is increasing. It's a fair question whether any person's contribution is really 100 times more than another's, when both are giving their best energies to the enterprise. We need to ask (and can debate about, of course, but surely need to *ask*) how this kind of arrangement could truly respect persons—all individuals who are after all equally precious from a moral point of view.

JUSTICE

Justice may be a more complex idea than equality. For one thing, it is a little less tempting to think that justice necessarily requires literally equal outcomes. Again, maybe it's more that everyone have an equal *chance*, an equal opportunity. Or that, however things end up, our way of getting there was at least *fair*.

This last idea—that a just arrangement is one that is the outcome of a fair process—emerged into philosophical attention in the late 20th century with the work of the philosopher John Rawls. Rawls asks us to imagine a group of people gathered to choose the principles under which they will live together. These people are a little unusual, however, because they don't yet know who they are, so to speak. Rawls argues that a fair set of principles would be principles that people would choose prior to knowing how the principles would affect them—when they have to imagine possibly being *anyone* in the society that will eventually result. After all, if being an "end in yourself" has nothing to do with your particular accomplishments (or lack thereof) or family or willpower or anything else—that is, with "who we are" in the usual sense—then it would be helpful to put these things aside, at least in imagination, while trying to think about basic moral principles. At the most basic moral level, we are all just persons!

If you see some shades of Kant here, you're right. Rawls agrees with Kant that ethics asks us to take a sort of universal point of view. Rawls's innovation was to give us a specific and decidable way to visualize such a point of view.

You might think in such a situation that people would opt for complete equality. Rawls agrees that this would indeed be so when one person's having more of something—say, political liberty—would mean an equivalent loss for someone else. Equality is the best we can do. Thus one principle of justice is what he calls the *Equal Liberty Principle*.

However, there are some goods—chiefly economic goods—that work in a different way. Here, one person's gain does not necessarily mean someone else's loss. Sometimes everyone can have more—although not necessarily equally. In this case, still under what Rawls calls the "veil of ignorance" (that is, not yet knowing who we are), we will aim, Rawls says, to make sure that any inequalities that arise bring the least well-off persons as far up as any arrangement can. This is what Rawls calls the *Difference Principle*. It is a second and far more subtle principle of justice.

Careful argument and evidence may be required to decide. One could argue, for example, that large ratios between the best-paid and the average-paid in corporations serve the good of everyone because large benefits at the top serve as incentives to attract the most talented executives, ultimately making everyone in the enterprise better off. But it's an empirical question. How much incentive is really necessary? The top-to-average ratio is only about 15 to 1 in Japan, for example, and no one could argue that Japan isn't competitive.

Also, by Rawls's principles, it's not enough that inequalities merely improve the lot of the least well-off: they have to improve it more than any other workable arrangement. We may have to get quite creative!

You see once again that vital and intriguing questions arise—and questions we will not settle here. They are, however, the natural and logical questions once we enter the discussion of what the ethical value of *persons* actually implies—and that, as you now see, is a discussion for all of us.

 **FOR REVIEW**

1. Why is treating someone as a person not the same as being nice to them?
2. What is Martin Buber's view of persons?
3. What is Emmanuel Levinas's view of persons?
4. Why are persons so precious, on the modern religious view?
5. How does Pope John Paul II ground the specifically Christian view of the sacredness of human life?
6. What are Immanuel Kant's Categorical Imperatives?
7. Why shouldn't we lie to get ourselves out of sticky situations, according to Kant?

8. How do rights relate to personhood?

9. How does equality relate to personhood?

10. How does justice relate to personhood?

EXERCISES AND NOTES

FOR DISCUSSION

Can you identify times in your own experience when other persons emerged in the radical, stop-everything kind of way that Buber and Levinas describe? Correspondingly, when do you live mostly in the "I/It" world? What do you think of the balance between the two in your own life?

Or put it in Kantian terms. Where and how do we tend to treat others as "ends"—and where mainly (or entirely?) as "means"? How about how you yourself are treated? When and by whom are you treated in each way?

Why do you think it is sometimes so hard to see other people as persons? Is it something inherent in us, selfishness for example? Is it our language—all too often reducing people to objects to be derided or exploited? Is it our stereotypes? Notice also that when people are reduced to objects in one way or another, the reductions can easily become self-fulfilling prophecies. One of the chief excuses for the enslavement of blacks in America, for example, was that black people were naturally "ignorant and depraved." But one of the prime effects of slavery was that the slaves were often *made* ignorant and depraved. Slavery wore down and degraded the slave; then this very degradation was blamed on the slaves themselves (it was said to be "their nature"), thus justifying more slavery and still more degradation.

Call this *self-validating reduction*. Can you see similar processes at work today?

THE QUESTION OF ANIMALS

We speak easily of "human rights," thinking that in so doing we are being liberal, inclusive, and even radical (in places where human rights are not recognized, at least in the ways we think they should be). Maybe so. But in so doing we also emphatically close off moral consideration at the species boundary. Humans have rights, nonhumans don't. And this may not really be liberal or inclusive at all.

At the very least, it looks arbitrary to limit personhood or rights to humans simply on the basis of species. That biological category must be connected with *morally relevant traits* in order to make an argument: it cannot be just a matter of how we are pleased to talk about ourselves. On the one hand, then, we may at least wonder whether a biological human couldn't lose human rights, or indeed personhood itself, under certain conditions. What do we mean when we say of a person in an irreversible coma that they have become (not to mince words here) a "vegetable"? A vegetable is a living form, but not capable of the self-awareness and choice essential to personhood. If such people continue to have rights anyway, what rights might they be (life, for example, or maybe more like the right to die with dignity)? Is this because once they were persons, rather than because in some way they still are?

Parallel questions arise at the other end of life. Fetuses have few of the capacities we have been identifying as essential to personhood. They are human, we might say, but not yet human *beings.* Do they have human rights because they are *potential* persons, then? Or perhaps do they not yet have such rights, after all, or have them only partially?

Such line-drawing questions become especially pointed when we ask the same about other animals. Surely some other animals are as self-aware and free as many humans (say, humans in reduced states; but then again, apparently some animals are perceptually much sharper than nearly any humans). So if those humans are persons and have rights, why not those animals?

Animal rights advocates have at least succeeded in showing that a system of rights that includes animal rights is not impossible or incoherent or even that cumbersome. Even partial rights for animals, or subordinate-but-still-serious rights, are entirely imaginable. We might not even want to think that personhood is all-or-nothing. Maybe the question of "marginal" humans and other animals should make us think seriously about partial persons, or a variety of ways to be *somewhat* a person.

Animal rights theories have their critics, including people who want to defend animals but mainly from the point of view of other families of values. Meanwhile, note that the same sorts of questions arise for views like Buber's or Levinas's too. It's not just a question of rights. Here's a bumpersticker slogan you may have seen:

| I DON'T EAT ANYTHING WITH A FACE |

Animals have faces too, don't they? Couldn't we have "I/Thou" relations, then, beyond the human sphere? Don't we in fact already have them? In *I and Thou,* in fact, Buber's first example of an I/Thou relation is in fact a relation to a *tree*—relations to other humans only come later. Mightn't Buber's or Levinas's ways of thinking about the experience of persons be far more powerfully inclusive than even they themselves thought?

NOTES

Martin Buber's *I and Thou,* translated by Walter Kaufmann (Scribner's, 1970), is cited from pages 69–72 and 59. Emmanuel Levinas's *Totality and Infinity* (Duquesne University Press, 1969) is cited from page 50. A good introduction to Levinas's philosophy is *Ethics and Infinity,* translated by Richard Cohen and published in 1985 by Duquesne University Press. See also Alphonso Lingis, *The Community of Those Who Have Nothing in Common* (Indiana University Press, 1994).

   For a systematic look at respect for persons more or less in its own terms, see R. S. Downie and Elizabeth Telfer, *Respect for Persons* (Schocken, 1970). A classic theory of the right, much less formal than Kant's, is W. D. Ross's *The Foundations of Ethics* (Oxford University Press, 1939). For background reading on Kantian ethics, start with Onora O'Neill, "A Simplified Account of Kant's Ethics," in Tom Regan, ed., *Matters of Life and Death* (McGraw-Hill, 1986). For a vigorous introduction to contemporary theories about rights, see Lawrence Becker, "Individual Rights," and Hugo Bedeau's essay, "International Human Rights," both in Tom Regan and Don Vandeveer, eds., *And Justice for All: New Introductory Essays in Philosophy and Public Policy* (Rowman and Allenheld, 1982).

   John Rawls's classic work on Justice is *A Theory of Justice* (Belknap Press, Harvard, 1971). Michael Walzer, in *Spheres of Justice: A Defense of Pluralism and Equality* (Basic Books, 1990), argues that there is no single criterion for the just distribution of all goods: each has its own meaning and appropriate criteria, and a "fair" society is simply one that keeps inequalities in one "sphere" from spilling over into others. Robert Nozick, in *Anarchy, State, and Utopia* (Basic Books, 1977), argues for a libertarian, lasseiz-faire view of justice based on strong individual rights. For a useful survey of this very large discussion and literature, see the "Ethics Updates" website at http://ethics.acusd.edu/theories/Justice/index.asp. There is also a detailed and helpful page under "Animal Rights."

CHAPTER 8

The Ethics of Happiness

Chapter 6 outlined the family of happiness-centered values like this:

HAPPINESS

What is our final goal in this life? Many thinkers have answered: *happiness*. Well-being, satisfaction, pleasure, the relief of pain and suffering—or rather, more precisely, the best balance that we can achieve of happiness over suffering. Add in not just ourselves but the needs of others as well, and we have a famous ethical formula: "Seek the greatest happiness of the greatest number." Moral thinking with this family of values is quantitative and economic, concerned with trade-offs and the distribution of goods, maximizing tangible social benefits.

Let us now explore the ethics of happiness in more detail.

HEDONISM

A great deal of what we do is obviously not for its own sake but is on the way somewhere else. We go to the dentist, even though it's no one's idea of a fun afternoon, to keep our teeth in shape. We fight the rush hour traffic to get to work or the pool or some store.

Even these goals don't seem "final," though. We don't really keep our teeth in shape for its own sake (come on, *flossing*?!). And getting to work or pool or store—what's the point?

Well, we know why: we want good jobs, healthy teeth and bodies, some level of physical comfort and ease. But again, why? These may not exactly be final goals either. But then, what is?

The natural answer is unsurprising, everyday, even "obvious" to many people. Our ultimate goal, we say, is to be happy. Happiness is the "final end" of human action. That is why we want everything else that we seek.

Or perhaps it is better to say that our final goal is "pleasure" or "satisfaction" or even "welfare." These terms have different connotations. "Pleasure" suggests something immediate and related to the senses; "welfare" suggests a longer-term and deeper happiness. Still, however we put it, we are picturing a certain positive kind of experience as a basic, ultimately good thing, and the goal for which we seek most other things along the way. Of course!

This is a strong claim—stronger than it might seem at first. It is actually a rough psychological theory: a systematic account of human motivation. More than anything else, we are saying, people seek happiness—and, correspondingly, in the end, what we try to avoid is *un*happiness: pain and suffering. In terms of values: we *value* happiness as a basic and inclusive goal, and everything (?) else is valued insofar as it serves happiness. What we *dis*value, we disvalue in the end because it impedes or counteracts happiness.

Classically this sort of theory is called *hedonism*. But we must add right away that "hedonism" in the classical, philosophical sense does not necessarily have the modern or popular connotations of the term. Popularly, "hedonist" tends to suggest a self-seeking and shallow person, probably preoccupied with sex and maybe a few other sensual gratifications, liquor maybe. This is not what (most of!) the ancients had in mind. Early hedonists, such as the Epicureans—a Greek school of philosophy of the third century BCE, not a kind of gourmet—actually recommended only the most modest pleasures. Epicurus himself, the founder and namesake, virtually advocated asceticism. The best way to be happy, they said, was to live a simple life and reduce pains as far as possible. We're not built to take too much intensity. For a sustainable life of pleasures—not blazing out too quickly and spending the rest of our lives unhappily regretting it—something quieter is best.

We moderns are sometimes more active in the pursuit of happiness. Even when intense pleasure is sought and celebrated, though, there is not necessarily anything crude or shallow about it. We get crude when we reduce sex, say, to nothing but the immediate pleasure or release of tension. But you can only get "crude" in this way by missing most of the pleasure itself. Sex involves the many pleasures of companionship and mutual appreciation; of touching and simple physical togetherness; of gracefulness and humor and spiritual connection too. The needs it can fulfill are not just passing and physical but go to the very core of our beings. That's the source of its deepest pleasures, and there is nothing crude or shallow about that.

We might say much the same about other supposedly crude pleasures: that there is much more there than the stereotypical hedonist sees. The problem with the stereotypical hedonist, then, is not really with pleasure-seeking as such, but, ironically enough, with too shallow a view of pleasure itself.

From Flow: The Psychology of Optimal Experience

MIHALY CSIKSZENTMIHALYI

What exactly *is* happiness, anyway? The temptation is to think of it as a static state of mind. The senses are being agreeably stimulated, no pain or distraction intrudes...we're feeling good. Psychological understandings, though, suggest that this is far too simple a picture. In fact, people can have all sorts of agreeable sense stimulation and still be desperately unhappy. Conversely, we can be in a great deal of pain or under stress and still be having the time of our lives. Happiness is not so simple.

Lionel Barrymore, of all people, once said that "Happiness is not a station you arrive at—it is the train you are riding on." There is a clue here. In his well-known work *Flow: The Psychology of Optimal Experience,* the American psychologist Mihaly Csikszentmihalyi argues that Barrymore is exactly right. Happiness lies in the flow of experience itself.

Indeed, Csikszentmihalyi uses the very term *flow* for "the state in which people are so involved in an activity that nothing else seems to matter; the experience itself is so enjoyable that people will do it...for the sheer sake of doing it." We must be confronting a task, he says, that we have a chance of completing and that has clear goals and immediate feedback. We concentrate on it with "an effortless involvement that removes from awareness the worries and frustrations of everyday life." Concern for the self disappears, and even our sense of time is altered: "hours can seem like minutes," yet at other times mere minutes seem endless. "The combination of all of these elements causes a sense of deep enjoyment that is so rewarding people feel that expending a great deal of energy is worthwhile simply to be able to feel it." *That's* happiness!

Twenty-three hundred years ago Aristotle concluded that, more than anything else, men and women seek happiness. While happiness itself is sought for its own sake, every other goal—health, beauty, money, or power—is valued only because we expect that it will make us happy. Much has changed since Aristotle's time. Our understanding of the worlds of stars and of atoms has expanded beyond belief. The gods of the Greeks were like helpless children compared to humankind today and the powers we now wield. And yet on this most important issue very little has changed in the intervening centuries. We do not understand what happiness is any better than Aristotle did, and as for learning how to attain that blessed condition, one could argue that we have made no progress at all.

Despite the fact that we are now healthier and grow to be older, despite the fact that even the least affluent among us are surrounded by material luxuries undreamed of even a few decades ago (there were few bathrooms in the palace of the Sun King, chairs were rare even in the richest medieval houses, and no Roman emperor could turn on a TV set when he was bored), and regardless of all the stupendous scientific knowledge we can summon at will, people often end up feeling that their lives have been wasted, that instead of being filled with happiness their years were spent in anxiety and boredom.

Is this because it is the destiny of mankind to remain unfulfilled, each person always wanting more than he or she can have? Or is the pervasive malaise that often sours even our most precious moments the result of our seeking happiness in the wrong places? The intent of this book is to use some of the tools of modern psychology to explore this very ancient question: When do people feel most happy? If we can begin to find an answer to it, perhaps we shall eventually be able to order life so that happiness will play a larger part in it.

Twenty-five years before I began to write these lines, I made a discovery that took all the intervening time for me to realize I had made. To call it a "discovery" is perhaps misleading, for people have been aware of it since the dawn of time. Yet the word is appropriate, because even though my finding itself was well known, it had not been described or theoretically explained by the relevant branch of scholarship, which in this case happens to be psychology. So I spent the next quarter-century investigating this elusive phenomenon.

What I "discovered" was that happiness is not something that happens. It is not the result of good fortune or random chance. It is not something that money can buy or power command. It does not depend on outside events, but, rather, on how we interpret them. Happiness, in fact, is a condition that must be prepared for, cultivated, and defended privately by each person. People who learn to control *inner experience* will be able to determine the quality of their lives, which is as close as any of us can come to being happy.

Yet we cannot reach happiness by consciously searching for it. "Ask yourself whether you are happy," said J. S. Mill, "and you cease to be so." It is by being fully involved with every detail of our lives, whether good or bad, that we find happiness, not by trying to look for it directly. Viktor Frankl, the Austrian psychologist, summarized it beautifully in the preface to his book *Man's Search for Meaning:* "Don't aim at success—the more you aim at it and make it a target, the more you are going to miss it. For success, like happiness, cannot be pursued; it must ensue...as the unintended side-effect of one's personal dedication to a course greater than oneself."

So how can we reach this elusive goal that cannot be attained by a direct route? My studies of the past quarter-century have convinced me that there is a way. It is a circuitous path that begins with achieving control over the contents of our consciousness.

Our perceptions about our lives are the outcome of many forces that shape experience, each having an impact on whether we feel good or bad. Most of these forces are outside our control. There is not much we can do about our looks, our temperament, or our constitution. We cannot decide—at least so far—how tall we will grow, how smart we will get. We can choose neither parents nor time of birth, and it is not in your power or mine to decide whether there will be a war or a depression. The instructions contained in our genes, the pull of gravity, the pollen in the air, the historical period into which we are born—these and innumerable other conditions determine what we see, how we feel, what we do. It is not surprising that we should believe that our fate is primarily ordained by outside agencies.

Yet we have all experienced times when, instead of being buffeted by anonymous forces, we do feel in control of our actions, masters of our own fate. On the rare occasions that it happens, we feel a sense of exhilaration, a deep sense of enjoyment that is long cherished and that becomes a landmark in memory for what life should be like.

This is what we mean by *optimal experience*. It is what the sailor holding a tight course feels when the wind whips through her hair, when the boat lunges through the waves like a colt—sails, hull, wind, and sea humming a harmony that vibrates in the sailor's veins. It is what a painter feels when the colors on the canvas begin to set up a magnetic tension with each other, and a new *thing*, a living form, takes shape in front of the astonished creator. Or it is the feeling a father has when his child for the first time responds to his smile. Such events do not occur only when the external conditions are favorable, however: people who have survived concentration camps or who have lived through near-fatal physical dangers often recall that in the midst of their ordeal they experienced extraordinarily rich epiphanies in response to such simple events as hearing the song of a bird in the forest, completing a hard task, or sharing a crust of bread with a friend.

Contrary to what we usually believe, moments like these, the best moments in our lives, are not the passive, receptive, relaxing times—although such experiences can also be enjoyable, if we have worked hard to attain them. The best moments usually occur when a person's body or mind is stretched to its limits in a voluntary effort to accomplish something difficult and worthwhile. Optimal experience is thus something that we *make* happen. For a child, it could be placing with trembling fingers the last block on a tower she has built, higher than any she has built so far; for a swimmer, it could be trying to beat his own record; for a violinist, mastering an intricate musical passage. For each person there are thousands of opportunities, challenges to expand ourselves.

Such experiences are not necessarily pleasant at the time they occur. The swimmer's muscles might have ached during his most memorable race, his lungs might have felt like exploding, and he might have been dizzy with fatigue—yet these could have been the best moments of his life. Getting control of life is never easy, and sometimes it can be definitely painful. But in the long run optimal experiences add up to a sense of mastery—or perhaps better, a sense of *participation* in determining the content of life—that comes as close to what is usually meant by happiness as anything else we can conceivably imagine.

UTILITARIANISM

The great strength of hedonism is that it affirms that we are indeed, in part, creatures of the senses, creatures who experience physical vulnerabilities and joys, and indeed we are, simply, "creatures"—for the dynamics of pleasures and pains don't stop at the species border. Other living beings revel in life and suffer its cruelties as well, and may enter our moral thinking for just that reason.

We could stop here. It might be best simply to recognize happiness as essential to our values without pushing its claim to be the only ultimate value. For this much is certainly true: happiness is *one* of our basic values. An entire family of values does begin and end with pleasure, satisfaction, welfare, the relief of pain and suffering. These are good and worthy goals, as long as they don't turn too shallow or self-centered. What we have here, so far, is an appealingly relaxed and inclusive family of values, like going home to a soft chair after spending a little too long in church with the person-centered in-laws.

But modern philosophical hedonists go further. They up the ante. In their hands, the rather relaxed and unsystematic hedonism we have so far been sketching becomes something much more far-reaching: a *theory* of ethics. Indeed it can become so systematic that the result, the theory or family of theories known as "utilitarian," pretty much defines what an ethical theory as such is now expected to look like and the questions it is expected to answer.

THREE STEPS

Three basic steps, each of them arguably very plausible, lead us straight from hedonism to utilitarianism.

One step we have practically made already. We have said that happiness is one of the main ultimate aims of human action. In truth, though, isn't it *the* ultimate aim of human action? Don't we want *everything* else, in the end, for the sake of the happiness it brings or the suffering it avoids?

Remember that we are not defining "pleasure" or "happiness" in any crude or narrow sense. We are speaking generally of positive experiences, positive states of mind, flow. What else could we want but that? Happiness in this sense, then, we are urged to take as *the* "final end" of human action.

A second step also seems natural. If something is a good thing, more of it is pretty clearly better. If the fundamental good of our lives is happiness, then, best of all must surely be the *most* happiness. Thus, in general, we should act in such a way as to produce the most happiness. Maximize happiness; minimize pain and suffering.

The claim is that this is just what any rational person already does. You may have to do some careful thinking, and even restrain yourself at times— giving up some short-term pleasure, for example, for longer-term gains. Maximizing happiness over a *life* does not mean that we will be happy every moment of that life. Hedonism, in short, must be calculating. Even suffering can sometimes actually be a good thing in the long run. It may be painful to work hard, for instance, but we do it for the extra-pleasurable rewards the status or more money bring. You sweat in the sauna, uncomfortably, for the unmatchable rush of pleasure that comes when you leap into the cold water afterward. The trick is to work in just enough adversity to maximize flow, or at least pleasure later, without overdoing the pain. No point in sweating too long or working too hard or flossing more than you have to. But when a little pain now increases your net happiness in the long run, it's worth it.

One step remains. This one may also seem hardly more than a clarification of what we've been saying already, a more careful look at the nature of pleasure—but it turns out to make a dramatic claim.

Happiness is *social*. Our concern with happiness hardly stops at the boundaries of our own selves. For one thing, quite simply, it is hard to be happy all alone. Our lives take on their emotional tone from the people around us. Moreover, we naturally seek the well-being of others close to us—spouses, children, parents, friends, lovers, students and teachers, those we work for and those who work for us. Anyone who knows love knows this simple fact. Often we also care for those who are distant, those whose plight or whose successes engage our sympathies or inspire us.

These are psychological, empirical points: our own happiness is in fact bound up with the happiness of others. Beside them, some philosophers propose a more conceptual argument as well. When we say that happiness is a *morally* good thing, remember that by definition we are speaking of the needs—and by extension, goals or ultimate aims—of others as well as ourselves. Thus, when we recognize happiness as the ultimate good thing, we say nothing about *whose* happiness. I cannot say that someone else's happiness is of no concern to me simply because I'm me, so to speak, and they're them. (Notice there's a shade or two of Kant here.) The conclusion is that happiness *as such* is a morally good thing, wherever it occurs—and it is good in the same way and to the same extent.

We are left, in short, with a moral commitment to the happiness of *all*, to the good of the whole. And if happiness alone is the good, and if more of it is better and the most the best, then we have a moral commitment to the "greatest good of the greatest number." We have arrived at utilitarianism.

FOUNDERS

Two English thinkers advanced utilitarianism as a modern theory of ethics: Jeremy Bentham (1748–1832) and John Stuart Mill (1806–1873.)

Bentham started out as a social critic, concerned for more enlightened legislation, and was a lifelong opponent of the severe British penal codes of his time. It was Bentham who popularized the familiar utilitarian first principle just cited: *seek the greatest good of the greatest number.* He called it the "Principle of Utility" in ethics—the formula that economists put as "Maximize Utility"—from which the term "utilitarianism" comes.

"Good" for Bentham emphatically meant *pleasure.* Moreover, he thought pleasures could readily be quantified, and he tried to devise criteria for weighing pleasures directly against each other. Bentham actually imagined that we could one day solve moral problems by sitting down with a calculator, figuring up the amounts of pleasure on either side!

Mill inherited the utilitarian project from Bentham and from his own father, James Mill. He gave it his own characteristic twists and developments, but on the key points he is one with them:

> Pleasure, and freedom from pain, are the only things desirable as ends; all desirable things…are desirable either for the pleasure inherent in themselves, or as means to the promotion of pleasure and the prevention of pain….Actions are right in proportion as they tend to promote happiness; wrong as they tend to produce the reverse of happiness.

And Mill insists that such an ethic appeals directly to our social nature.

> The deeply rooted conception which every individual even now has of himself as a social being, tends to make him feel it one of his natural wants that there should be harmony between his feelings and those of his fellow creatures….This feeling in most individuals is much inferior in strength to their selfish feelings, and is often wanting altogether. But to those who have it, it possesses all the characters of a natural feeling. It does not present itself to their minds as a superstition of education, or a law despotically imposed by the power of society….This conviction is the ultimate sanction of the greatest happiness morality.

UTILITARIANISM IN PRACTICE: ECONOMIC THINKING

Solving moral problems by quantifying pleasures turns out to be trickier than Bentham thought. For one thing, pleasure seems to be too subjective to measure in that way, even when we are comparing our own pleasures with each other, certainly when we are trying to compare different people's. Utilitarianism in practice has therefore moved toward a more economic way of thinking. In place of a calculus of pleasures and pains, we are invited instead to look at a more external calculus of costs and benefits, and the more neutral and seemingly objective language of "utilities."

The logic, though, stays the same. When there are multiple choices with different utilities, or when utilities conflict, we should always pick the greatest one. Should you finish your degree now, say, even under financial and emotional hardship, or let it go and make things easier? Each choice has its specific benefits and its costs, and many can be at least partly quantified. In theory, the utilitarian answer is clear: choose a way that achieves the greatest net benefit—the highest total benefits over costs.

Social questions are to be decided the same way. We debate about assisted suicide, for example: about whether doctors should be allowed or expected to help people die if they so choose. Utilitarians would decide the question by looking at the effects on society as a whole. If assisted suicide would promote social utility, all told, then it should be allowed. If it doesn't, it shouldn't. What else (they would ask) could be relevant?

This looks like an empirical question. Maybe we can actually resolve it. The benefits of assisted suicide seem very concrete: relief of suffering—for dying people, who are often in great physical pain and sometimes emotional pain too, unable to secure relief by themselves, and also for their families, who may suffer greatly too, emotionally and financially, when dying is prolonged and hard. The costs are much more indefinite, by contrast, and do not necessarily have any effect on happiness. Some people may feel pressured into choosing assisted suicide, for example, and we might come somehow to "devalue life." Put in the balance with the clear benefits, though, many utilitarians tend to think that these sorts of costs—such as they are—will be outweighed.

Sometimes utilitarians call on economics quite directly. Suppose that the question is whether to build a dam that will generate electricity and provide irrigation and recreation but will also cost money, displace families or towns, and flood valuable land. How do we decide? Naturally, say utilitarians, we try to quantify the various benefits and costs. How much social utility will be gained from the dam? How much will be lost?

As far as possible, economists calculate the answers in dollars. What will the dam cost? How much money will it take to compensate people who have to move? What is the monetary value of the land that will be lost? All of these costs must be weighed against the monetary value of the electricity produced, the dollar gain in food production due to irrigation, added income from recreation, and so on—as well as the net benefits that could be gained from doing something else with the same resources. More sophisticated calculations factor in the long-run probability of these benefits continuing (maybe high but less than 100 percent) and consider the costs when the dam's useful life is over (dams eventually silt up and become useless). In the end, though, once again, the aim is still to answer a simple question: which choice has the highest net benefits?

Utilitarianism, then, draws attention squarely back to what is actually good or bad for people—to specific consequences for utilities, and behind it for what we suppose to be happiness—rather than to the sometimes abstract rules that too often (say utilitarians) are supposed to define what's moral. In this utilitarianism regards itself as no more than systematized common sense. *Do what has the best effects*—surely no one could disagree with so obvious a maxim! All utilitarianism thinks it does is to clarify and systematize it.

From Utilitarianism

JOHN STUART MILL

The creed which accepts as the foundation of morals, Utility, or the Greatest Happiness Principle, holds that actions are right in proportion as they tend to promote happiness, wrong as they tend to produce the reverse of happiness. By happiness is intended pleasure, and the absence of pain; by unhappiness, pain, and the privation of pleasure. To give a clear view of the moral standard set up by the theory, much more requires to be said; in particular, what things it includes in the ideas of pain and pleasure; and to what extent this is left an open question. But these supplementary explanations do not affect the theory of life on which this theory of morality is grounded—namely, that pleasure, and freedom from pain, are the only things desirable as ends; and that all desirable things (which are as numerous in the utilitarian as in any other scheme) are desirable either for the pleasure inherent in themselves, or as means to the promotion of pleasure and the prevention of pain...

The ultimate end, with reference to and for the sake of which all other things are desirable (whether we are considering our own good or that of other people), is an existence exempt as far as possible from pain, and as rich as possible in enjoyments, both in point of quantity and quality; the test of quality, and the rule for measuring it against quantity, being the preference felt by those who in their opportunities of experience, to which must be added their habits of self-consciousness and self-observation, are best furnished with the means of comparison. This, being, according to the utilitarian opinion, the end of human action, is necessarily also the

---

From John Stuart Mill, *Utilitarianism,* Chapter 2 (available in many editions, including online; I draw on http://etext.library.adelaide.edu.au/m/mill/john_stuart/m645u/).

standard of morality; which may accordingly be defined, the rules and precepts for human conduct, by the observance of which an existence such as
has been described might be, to the greatest extent possible, secured to all
mankind; and not to them only, but, so far as the nature of things admits,
to the whole sentient creation.

...When it is positively asserted to be impossible that human life
should be happy, the assertion, if not something like a verbal quibble, is
at least an exaggeration. If by happiness be meant a continuity of highly
pleasurable excitement, it is evident enough that this is impossible. A state
of exalted pleasure lasts only moments, or in some cases, and with some
intermissions, hours or days, and is the occasional brilliant flash of enjoyment, not its permanent and steady flame. Of this the philosophers who
have taught that happiness is the end [goal] of life were as fully aware as
those who taunt them. The happiness which they meant was not a life of
rapture; but moments of such, in an existence made up of few and transi-
tory pains, many and various pleasures, with a decided predominance of the
active over the passive, and having as the foundation of the whole, not to expect more from life than it is capable of bestowing. A life thus composed,
to those who have been fortunate enough to obtain it, has always appeared
worthy of the name of happiness. And such an existence is even now the
lot of many, during some considerable portion of their lives. The present
wretched education, and wretched social arrangements, are the only real
hindrance to its being attainable by almost all.

The objectors perhaps may doubt whether human beings, if taught
to consider happiness as the end of life, would be satisfied with such a
moderate share of it. But great numbers of mankind have been satisfied
with much less. The main constituents of a satisfied life appear to be
two, either of which by itself is often found sufficient for the purpose:
tranquillity, and excitement. With much tranquillity, many find that they
can be content with very little pleasure: with much excitement, many can
reconcile themselves to a considerable quantity of pain. There is assur-
edly no inherent impossibility in enabling even the mass of mankind to
unite both; since the two are so far from being incompatible that they
are in natural alliance, the prolongation of either being a preparation
for, and exciting a wish for, the other...When people who are tolerably
fortunate in their outward lot do not find in life sufficient enjoyment to
make it valuable to them, the cause generally is, caring for nobody but
themselves. To those who have neither public nor private affections, the
excitements of life are much curtailed, and in any case dwindle in value
as the time approaches when all selfish interests must be terminated by
death: while those who leave after them objects of personal affection, and
especially those who have also cultivated a fellow-feeling with the collective interests of mankind, retain as lively an interest in life on the eve
of death as in the vigour of youth and health. Next to selfishness, the

principal cause which makes life unsatisfactory is want of mental culti-vation. A cultivated mind—I do not mean that of a philosopher, but any mind to which the fountains of knowledge have been opened, and which has been taught, in any tolerable degree, to exercise its faculties—finds sources of inexhaustible interest in all that surrounds it; in the objects of nature, the achievements of art, the imaginations of poetry, the incidents of history, the ways of mankind, past and present, and their prospects in the future...

The deeply rooted conception which every individual even now has of himself as a social being, tends to make him feel it one of his natural wants that there should be harmony between his feelings and aims and those of his fellow creatures. If differences of opinion and of mental cul-ture make it impossible for him to share many of their actual feelings—perhaps make him denounce and defy those feelings—he still needs to be conscious that his real aim and theirs do not conflict; that he is not opposing himself to what they really wish for, namely their own good, but is, on the contrary, promoting it. This feeling in most individuals is much inferior in strength to their selfish feelings, and is often wanting altogether. But to those who have it, it possesses all the characters of a natural feeling. It does not present itself to their minds as a superstition of education, or a law despotically imposed by the power of society, but as an attribute which it would not be well for them to be without. This con-viction is the ultimate sanction of the greatest happiness morality. This it is which makes any mind, of well-developed feelings, work with, and not against, the outward motives to care for others, afforded by what I have called the external sanctions; and when those sanctions are wanting, or act in an opposite direction, constitutes in itself a powerful internal binding force, in proportion to the sensitiveness and thoughtfulness of the charac-ter; since few but those whose mind is a moral blank, could bear to lay out their course of life on the plan of paying no regard to others except so far as their own private interest compels.

"The Harm That Good Men Do"

BERTRAND RUSSELL

Bertrand Russell (1872–1970) was a famous 20th-century philosopher who made his philosophical name working in logic and mathematics but who contributed to nearly every area of philosophy, including ethics, over his long life. He also was famous—or infamous—for regularly changing his mind. This essay, written during his utilitarian period, nicely counterpoints Mill's earnestness by setting out utilitarianism in an ironic and rhetorical fashion.

A hundred years ago there lived a philosopher named Jeremy Bentham, who was universally recognized to be a very wicked man. I remember to this day the first time that I came across his name when I was a boy. It was in a statement by the Rev. Sydney Smith to the effect that Bentham thought people ought to make soup of their dead grandmothers. This practice appeared to me as undesirable from a culinary as from a moral point of view, and I therefore conceived a bad opinion of Bentham. Long afterwards, I discovered that the statement was one of those reckless lies in which respectable people are wont to indulge in the interests of virtue. I also discovered what was the really serious charge against him. It was no less than this: that he defined a "good" man as a man who does good. This definition, as the reader will perceive at once if he is right-minded, is subversive of all true morality. How much more exalted is the attitude of Kant, who lays it down that a kind action is not virtuous if it springs from affection for the beneficiary, but only if it is inspired by the moral law, which is, of course, just as likely to inspire unkind actions. We know that the exercise of virtue should be its own reward, and it seems to follow that the enduring of it on the part of the patient should be its own punishment. Kant, therefore, is a more sublime moralist than Bentham, and has the suffrages of all those who tell us that they love virtue for its own sake.

It is true that Bentham fulfilled his own definition of a good man: he did much good. The forty middle years of the nineteenth century in England were years of incredibly rapid progress, materially, intellectually, and morally. At the beginning of the period comes the Reform Act, which made Parliament representative of the middle-class, not, as before, of the aristocracy. This Act was the most difficult of the steps towards democracy in England, and was quickly followed by other important reforms, such as the abolition of slavery in Jamaica. At the beginning of the period the penalty for petty theft was death by hanging; very soon the death penalty was confined to those who were guilty of murder or high treason. The Corn Laws, which made food so dear as to cause atrocious proverty, were abolished in 1846. Compulsory education was introduced in 1870. It is the fashion to decry the Victorians, but I wish our age had half as good a record as theirs. This, however, is beside the point. My point is that a very large proportion of the progress during those years must be attributed to the influence of Bentham. There can be no doubt that nine-tenths of the people living in England in the latter part of last century were happier than they would have been if he had never lived. So shallow was his philosophy that he would have regarded this as a vindication of his activities. We, in our more enlightened age, can see that such a view is preposterous; but it may fortify us to review the grounds for rejecting a grovelling utilitarianism such as that of Bentham.

We all know what we mean by a "good" man. The ideally good man does not drink or smoke, avoids bad language, converses in the presence of men only exactly as he would if there were ladies present, attends church regularly, and holds the correct opinions on all subjects. He has a wholesome horror of wrongdoing, and realizes that it is our painful duty to castigate Sin. He has a still greater horror of wrong thinking, and considers it the business of the authorities to safeguard the young against those who question the wisdom of the views generally accepted by middle-aged successful citizens. Apart from his professional duties, at which he is assiduous, he spends much time in good works: he may encourage patriotism and military training; he may promote industry, sobriety, and virtue among wage-earners and their children by seeing to it that failures in these respects receive due punishment; he may be a trustee of a university and prevent an ill-judged respect for learning from allowing the employment of professors with subversive ideas. Above all, of course, his "morals," in the narrow sense, must be irreproachable.

It may be doubted whether a "good" man, in the above sense, does, on the average, any more good than a "bad" man. I mean by a "bad" man the contrary of what we have been describing. A "bad" man is one who is known to smoke and to drink occasionally, and even to say a bad word when someone treads on his toe. His conversation is not always such as could be printed, and he sometimes spends fine Sundays out-of-doors instead of at church. Some of his opinions are subversive; for instance, he may think that if you desire peace you should prepare for peace, not for war. Toward wrongdoing he takes a scientific attitude such as he would take towards his motor-car if it misbehaved; he argues that sermons and prison will no more cure vice than mend a broken tire. In the matter of wrong thinking he is even more perverse. He maintains that what is called "wrong thinking" is simply thinking, and what is called "right thinking" is repeating words like a parrot; this gives him a sympathy with all sorts of undesirable cranks. His activities outside his working hours may consist merely in enjoyment, or, worse still, in stirring up discontent with preventable evils which do not interfere with the comfort of the men in power. And it is even possible that in the matter of "morals" he may not conceal his lapses as carefully as a truly virtuous man would do, defending himself by the perverse contention that it is better to be honest than to pretend to set a good example. A man who fails in any or several of these respects will be thought ill of by the average respectable citizen, and will not be allowed to hold any position conferring authority, such as that of a judge, a magistrate, or a schoolmaster. Such positions are open only to "good" men....

Consider, again, such a matter as venereal disease: it is known that this can be almost entirely prevented by suitable precautions taken in advance, but owing to the activities of good men this knowledge is disseminated as little as possible, and all kinds of obstacles are placed in the way of its utilization. Consequently sin still secures its "natural" punishment, and the children are still punished for the sins of the fathers, in accordance with Biblical precept. How dreadful it would be if this were otherwise, for, if sin were no longer punished, there might be people so abandoned as to pretend that it was no longer sin, and if the punishment did not fall also upon the innocent, it would not seem so dreadful. How grateful we ought to be, therefore, to those good men who ensure that the stern laws of retribution decreed by Nature during our days of ignorance can still be made to operate in spite of the impious knowledge rashly acquired by scientists. All right-thinking people know that a bad act is bad quite regardless of the question whether it causes any suffering or not, but since men are not all capable of being guided by the pure moral law, it is highly desirable that suffering should follow from sin in order to secure virtue. Men must be kept in ignorance of all ways of escaping the penalties which were incurred by sinful actions in pre-scientific ages. I shudder when I think how much we should all know about the preservation of mental and physical health if it were not for the protection against this dangerous knowledge which our good men so kindly provide.

To speak seriously: the standards of "goodness" which are generally recognized by public opinion are not those which are calculated to make the world a happier place. This is due to a variety of causes, of which the chief is tradition, and the next most powerful is the unjust power of dominant classes. Primitive morality seems to have developed out of the notion of taboo; that is to say, it was originally purely superstitious, and forbade certain perfectly harmless acts (such as eating out of the chief's dish) on the supposed ground that they produced disaster by magical means. In this way there came to be prohibitions, which continued to have authority over people's feelings when the supposed reasons for them were forgotten. A considerable part of current morals is still of this sort: certain kinds of conduct produce emotions of horror, quite regardless of the question whether they have bad effects or not. In many cases the conduct which inspires horror is in fact harmful; if this were not the case, the need for a revision of our moral standards would be more generally recognized. Murder, for example, can obviously not be tolerated in a civilized society; yet the origin of the prohibition of murder is purely superstitious. It was thought that the murdered man's blood (or, later, his ghost) demanded vengeance, and might punish not only the guilty man, but any one who showed him kindness. The superstitious character of the prohibition of murder is shown by the fact that it was possible to be purified from blood-guiltiness by certain ritual ceremonies, which were apparently designed, originally, to disguise the murderer so that the ghost would not recognize him. This, at least, is the theory of Sir J. G. Frazer. When we speak of repentance as "washing out" guilt we are using a metaphor derived from the fact that long ago actual washing was used to remove blood-stains. Such notions as "guilt" and "sin" have an emotional background connected with this source in remote antiquity. Even in the case of murder a rational ethic will view the matter differently: it will be concerned with prevention and cure, as in the case of illness, rather than with guilt, punishment, and expiation.

Our current ethic is a curious mixture of superstition and rationalism. Murder is an ancient crime, and we view it through a mist of age-long horror. Forgery is a modern crime, and we view it rationally. We punish forgers, but we do not feel them strange beings set apart, as we do murderers. And we still think in social practice, whatever we may hold in theory, that virtue consists in not doing rather than in doing. The man who abstains from certain acts labelled "sin" is a good man, even though he never does anything to further the welfare of others. This, of course, is not the attitude inculcated in the Gospels: "Love thy neighbour as thyself" is a positive precept. But in all Christian communities the man who obeys this precept is persecuted, suffering at least poverty, usually imprisonment, and sometimes death. The world is full of injustice, and those who profit by injustice are in a position to administer rewards and punishments. The rewards go to those who invent ingenious justifications for inequality, the punishments to those who try to remedy it. I do not know of any country where a man who has a genuine love for his neighbour can long avoid obloquy.

Those who defend traditional morality will sometimes admit that it is not perfect, but contend that any criticism will make all morality crumble. This will not be the case if the criticism is based upon something positive and constructive, but only if it is conducted with a view to nothing more than momentary pleasure. To return to Bentham: he advocated, as the basis of morals, "the greatest happiness of the greatest number." A man who acts upon this principle will have a much more arduous life than a man who merely obeys conventional precepts. He will necessarily make himself the champion of the oppressed, and so incur the enmity of the great. He will proclaim facts which the powers that be wish to conceal; he will deny falsehoods designed to alienate sympathy from those who need it. Such a mode of life does not lead to a collapse of genuine morality. Official morality has always been oppressive and negative: it has said "thou shalt not," and has not troubled to investigate the effect of activities not forbidden by the code. Against this kind of morality all the great mystics and religious teachers have protested in vain: their followers ignored their most explicit pronouncements. It seems unlikely, therefore, that any large-scale improvements will come through their methods.

More is to be hoped, I think, from the progress of reason and science. Gradually men will come to realize that a world whose institutions are based upon hatred and injustice is not the one most likely to produce happiness....We need a morality based upon love of life, upon pleasure in growth and positive achievement, not upon repression and prohibition. A man should be regarded as "good" if he is happy, expansive, generous, and glad when others are happy; if so, a few peccadilloes should be regarded as of little importance.

CAN UTILITY BE THE SINGLE MEASURE OF VALUES?

The utilitarian idea of ethics is compelling in its way and surely must find *some* place in our moral thinking. However we theorize it, happiness and the means to happiness are among our prime values. Sometimes at least, we must calculate and weigh different benefits and costs, and different benefits and costs to different people, under conditions of scarcity. Hard choices are necessary, but there are rational ways to make them.

But there are also questions and problems, and some serious objections, once utilitarianism pushes beyond these modest claims. We must enter, at least a little, the debate over utilitarianism as an ethical theory.

UTILITY AS THE SINGLE MEASURE OF VALUES

One of the main motives for ethical theory is simplification: finding some sort of order and unity in what might seem to be a hodgepodge of different values, both for intellectual elegance and to make it easier to decide what to do in the end. From this point of view, even four families of values are three too many. Ideally—so theorists say—we need just one.

Utilitarians argue that ultimately all values reduce to benefits and costs. All moral thinking, and all moral conflict, they say, is really about one thing— what will truly achieve the greatest happiness of all, all things considered and in the long run. And so, utilitarians say, we are justified in *translating* all other values into benefit-and-cost terms—"cashing them out," so to speak. Happiness becomes utilitarianism's single measure for all moral thinking.

Think of assisted suicide again, or the dam-building example. In the last section we discussed these issues briefly from a utilitarian point of view. On the face of it, though, there are also nonutilitarian values involved. Issues of justice and rights, for example: justice to people whose land the dams might flood, say—maybe long-time owners who have cherished this one place on Earth—or people's rights to choose to die, even if it doesn't serve the "greatest good."

But: couldn't these values be understood in terms of happiness, a calculus of benefits and costs? Certainly justice, say, promotes happiness much of the time. Indirectly, it also promotes social stability, which in turn leads to happiness. An unjust social order—unfair, unequal, arbitrary—would make a lot of people unhappy much of the time, and it would also be prone to resistance and overthrow, leading to even more uncertainty and unrest: not a picture that looks too satisfying.

Mill explicitly grounded justice on utility:

> Justice is a name for certain classes of moral rules which concern the essentials of human well-being more nearly, and are therefore of moral absolute obligation, than any other rules for the guidance of life.... [T]hey are the main element in determining the social feelings of mankind. It is their observance which alone preserves peace among human beings.

We should indeed promote justice, then, but not ultimately for its own sake. We should promote it because it helps maximize utility. It serves the social good.

Utilitarians would go on to argue that while justice is *usually* a good thing, it is not *always* a good thing. In fact, it is not a good thing if it irremovably conflicts with social utility. In an emergency, for example, we sometimes cut corners—even violate some people's rights—for the sake of saving greater social goods. Mill again:

> [C]ases may occur in which some other social duty is so important as to overrule...the general maxims of justice. Thus, to save a life, it may not only be allowable, but a duty, to steal or take by force the necessary food or medicine, or to kidnap and compel to officiate the only qualified medical practitioner.

So even stealing or kidnapping doctors might be morally acceptable, or even a duty, in a pinch! Strong stuff—but not necessarily implausible, and perfectly natural if you are a utilitarian. In a system where utility rules, every other value must eventually pass utility's muster.

Utilitarians would say the same of the virtues. No character trait, they argue, is simply good by itself. Rather, good traits are good because they promote utility. Take honesty for example. It might seem that dishonesty often has major benefits. Little (or not so little) deceptions can keep you ahead of the crowd and out of trouble. But deception also has costs and dangers. It takes a lot of work. It's emotionally draining to have your guard up all the time. Besides, when the deceptions fail, as they often will, you may lose your friends. Thus, arguably, dishonesty is a bad idea, even on utilitarian grounds. It is not a matter of benefits to you being trumped by some more abstract kind of value, but simply of thinking more carefully about the tangible costs in the long run.

Some people think that no deception can ever be ethical, and propose to tell the truth even to criminals who threaten you and to children too young to understand. But it is not at all clear that this kind of "hyper-truthfulness" has positive overall effects. Surely, at least in this case, most of us will say that here is where the value of honesty ends: when it really does have bad consequences, all things considered. Here, in short, the utilitarian "single measure" becomes the *judge* of other values. Those moral values that don't "cash out" in terms of utility are not really moral values after all.

DOES UTILITARIANISM GO TOO FAR?

As you might imagine, though, these utilitarian moves are controversial. Critics argue that while utility and utilitarian considerations are indeed important, they cannot be the whole story.

First of all, is it really true that justice, say, is only good so far as it serves social utility? Certainly our legal system doesn't think so. Everyone is entitled to a fair trial and to be presumed innocent, even though they may turn out to be guilty. It might be much more satisfying, not to mention cheaper, simply to put away a whole class of criminal suspects without any trial at all. Yet we will not stand for it. It is not *right*—not just, not fair, not respectful of persons.

Utilitarians do try to defend many important rights. Rights to free speech, liberty, and all the rest serve social utility. They maximize the general happiness—usually. When they don't, though, utilitarians can only conclude that there are just no such rights. Mill, again, even endorses kidnapping doctors under some (extreme) circumstances. But what good is a utilitarian kind of "right," critics say, if the moment social needs conflict with them, utilitarianism no longer stands behind them? The whole point of rights is to stop this kind of thinking—taking a person as a mere means to some social good—dead in its tracks.

We may be no happier with utilitarianism's treatment of the virtues. Can pleasure (or "utility" in *any* guise) really be the ethical bottom line? Aren't some pleasures just wrong, however pleasurable they may be? And not wrong because they lead to greater displeasure somewhere down the line, but just plain *wrong*—wrong because they are inappropriate for beings of the sort we are.

Mill vacillated on this point, actually, speaking at times of "higher" and "lower" pleasures. "Higher" pleasures are supposed to be better—worthier of human beings. "It is better to be a human being dissatisfied than a pig satisfied; better to be Socrates dissatisfied than a fool satisfied." But it is not at all clear why. If pleasure alone is the good, how can one of two equally pleasurable pleasures still be "better"? It appears that Mill himself wants to introduce some nonutilitarian factors into the mix—a sensible move, for sure, but no credit to utilitarianism.

THE PROBLEM OF MEASUREMENT

If utility is to be the single measure of values it must also, obviously, be a *measure* of values. It must offer a usable and concretely applicable way to think. Some critics of utilitarianism argue, however, that "happiness" and "utility" are such vague terms that we cannot really "measure" or "weigh" the relative utilities of different courses of action. Seldom am I even sure about what would make *me* happiest, for instance, let alone other people—or how to compare my happiness to theirs, or even my own specific happinesses to each other. Meanwhile, the ripple effects of even the simplest act are almost incalculable, all the more so if it affects large numbers of people.

Should I spend my vacation at the beach or helping build houses with Habitat for Humanity? I would probably enjoy the beach more—though I do like to build and to help out too. Building houses would help make the future occupants happier—though the houses will get built anyway, just about as well whether I am there or not. Is there any precise way to weigh a sharp and immediate pleasure for me—one person—against the smaller and less definite contribution I might make to the quite different and longer-term happiness of others? And even this is just the beginning. If I go on the Habitat trip, someone else will not go: perhaps the trip would be better for them than for me? Or maybe *they* would up the total happiness more by going to the beach? (Or somewhere else?) Who are they, anyway? And how do I weigh in the possible benefits to others (my students, say) from my being somewhat better rested after the beach? What about my long-run contribution to beach erosion and the commercial overdevelopment of fragile coast ecologies?

Despite its appearance of hardheaded practicality, then, utilitarianism may actually be useless, or worse, as a practical way to make decisions. What really happens in such cases, critics worry, is that utilitarian language lends itself to offhand self-justification. Whatever I do, I can justify myself by pointing to the happiness I (might) produce or costs I (might) avoid. Just this accusation has been leveled against the monetary calculation of "costs" and "benefits," for example, as in the dam project. All the numbers look very rational and impartial and responsible, but underneath it's all really guesswork, say the critics, dressed up to justify whatever the decision-maker is inclined to do anyway.

CONCLUSIONS

You can see that these are controversial matters. My proposed conclusion (itself debatable, of course!) is that utilitarianism is a limited tool. It systematizes *some* of our moral values and can help resolve *some* conflicts of moral values, especially conflicts between fairly specific utilities. These are genuine and important uses.

Utilitarianism also has some edgy implications very much worth exploring, such as serious moral consideration for other animals, whose pains and sufferings are sometimes as great or greater than ours but who have traditionally been ignored in moral thinking entirely. Some modern utilitarians campaign strongly for "animal liberation." Other implications may also be radical. Jeremy Bentham, as I've mentioned, was best known as a prison and criminal law reformer, and one could argue, as Russell does, that we have still not learned his lessons. From a utilitarian point of view, the point of punishment is not to somehow exact revenge or retribution, but to serve the social good, which surely argues for a more restorative and less punitive approach to crime than we continue to practice today.

Still, arguably, utilitarianism is not the whole story, or even close. There are many other moral values that need to be understood in their own rights, as we have tried to do with the values of the person and will continue in the next two chapters. Much as we might want everything simple and neat, the moral world may not cooperate. We'd do better to celebrate its complexity than to try to reduce it to a single measure—at least in my view—and we'd do best to seek the skills that allow us to deal with it *in* its complexity and depth, as this book as a whole proposes to do.

FOR REVIEW

1. How could it be argued that pleasure or happiness is our ultimate goal?
2. What is hedonism?
3. What is "flow"? How does it relate to happiness?
4. How could hedonism morph into utilitarianism?
5. Who was John Stuart Mill?
6. What is "the harm that good men do"?
7. How do utilitarians argue that utility is the single measure of all values?
8. Why do critics argue that there is no single measure of all values?
9. What are some important uses of utilitarian thinking, according to the text?
10. What are some important limits of utilitarian thinking, according to the text?

EXERCISES AND NOTES

WHO'S REALLY A HEDONIST?

Hedonists believe that pleasure or happiness is the chief and indeed only ultimate human end. How might they deal with people who pretty clearly seek something other than happiness, or even seek things that are guaranteed to produce *un*happiness: people who give their lives in battle, say, or willingly undergo great suffering in order to achieve something magnificent or uncertain? You could stretch and say that in some metaphysical or unusual sense they're "happy," but this is not true, really, if they're in great pain or never see the fruits of their labors or die in the pursuit. Yet these may still be morally admirable things to do.

Even without a moral mission we sometimes seek things that are guaranteed to produce unhappiness. Indeed, if you look around the world today you do not find that people in general are very happy. Rich countries seem to be even less happy than poor ones. We are now spectacularly richer and more technologically accomplished than anyone could even have dreamed for most of human history, but at the same time suicide and depression are epidemic and massive numbers of people need medication just to get through their day.

How can this be? Why do we reliably produce our own unhappiness? Is the answer that we really don't understand happiness? Or that we don't understand what we are doing? But how could *that* be? Happiness is supposed to be our prime concern . . .

UTILITARIAN NIRVANA?

Imagine that it becomes possible to set up a grand virtual-reality computer that creates for you any kind of experience you choose. For the rest of your life you could be plugged into a fantasy world, tailor-made to make you absolutely delirious with pleasure, riding the biggest surf in the world, or heroically saving the galaxy from evil invaders, or playing Mozart piano concertos while conducting the New York Philharmonic from the keyboard, or whatever else your fantasy might be (filling in the blanks is always a fun part). You'd never know that really you are just lying on a bed somewhere, kept alive by IV and a few doctors, your head wired to a monitor. But what's the difference, if happiness is the only thing that counts?

This is a famous philosophical thought-experiment meant to challenge hedonistic utilitarianism. Like the questions just raised about unhappiness and the modern world, it is not merely hypothetical, either. Americans currently watch 250 billion hours of TV a year. The average elementary-school child watches four hours a day. (And you?) Is this so very different? If this kind of experience-machine makes you uneasy, why not TV? If you say in either case that we ought not to be settling for such paltry substitutes for the real world, what kinds of moral values are you appealing to?

MORE QUESTIONS

Can utilitarianism take better account of justice and fairness? How? Should it try? What do you think of Mill's endorsement of kidnapping doctors? Are there any real-world analogues to this? How about torturing someone in order to extract information that might save a lot of lives—as U.S. law now allows the military and CIA to do under certain not-very-restrictive conditions, as part of the "war on terror"?

On the utilitarian view, the pleasures of a sadist are not bad in themselves. *No* pleasure can be bad in itself, remember, since pleasure just *is* the good. Rather, as with everything else on the utilitarian view, the pleasures of the sadist are supposed to be bad because of their effects: more unhappiness for other people than the sadist gains for himself or herself. So could sadistic pleasure be OK (in fact, be *good*) if no one else were harmed by it (for example, if it were only "virtual," with no likelihood of spilling over into actual harm to others)? Or: what if a sadist had an enormous capacity for pleasure, so that his or her pleasures actually exceeded the suffering of those who were harmed? Would sadism be a good thing *then*? Is this what utilitarianism implies? Ought we be able to criticize some pleasures or happinesses themselves?

Chapter 7's last exercise raised the question of animals in the context of the ethics of persons. How do you think utilitarianism might address the same question? Some hints: first, consider the question of who or what kind of beings utilitarian ethics applies to, and why. Then consider the question of animal pain and suffering, which of course is front and center in utilitarian ethics. (There is a relevant discussion of moral vegetarianism at the end of Chapter 18, by the way.) Finally, consider some implications and complications. If animals count, or some animals count, under utilitarianism, must they or should they count in the same way as humans? To the same extent? Why or why not?

NOTES

Bertrand Russell's essay "The Harm That Good Men Do" is excerpted from a longer piece of the same title in his book *Sceptical Essays* (Unwin Paperbacks, 1977), pages 84–92. One note: Russell's remark about "good" men "preventing an ill-judged respect for learning from allowing the employment of professors with subversive ideas" is not just ironic: it refers to an incident in his own life. A world-renowned scholar by 1940, Russell was offered a professorship by the City College of New York only to have the offer rescinded after a massive, politically orchestrated outcry against him because he was something of a sexual free-thinker for his time—supporting trial marriage, for example.

A readable and provocative application of utilitarianism to a range of contemporary issues is Peter Singer's *Practical Ethics* (Cambridge University Press, 1979). Dan Brock's essay "Utilitarianism" in Tom Regan and Don Vandeveer, eds., *And Justice for All: New Introductory Essays in Philosophy and Public Policy* (Rowman and Allenheld, 1982), is a useful though dense survey of contemporary philosophical utilitarianism. Also see J. J. C. Smart's classic "Outline of a System of Utilitarian Ethics," in J. J. C. Smart and Bernard Williams, *Utilitarianism: For and Against* (Cambridge University Press, 1983.) On utilitarianism and animals, start with Peter Singer's *Animal Liberation* (many editions).

CHAPTER 9

The Ethics of Virtue

Chapter 6 outlined the family of virtue-centered values like this:

VIRTUE

Ethics is also concerned with *character*: with traits like self-discipline, re-sponsibility, open-heartedness, loyalty, devotion. Christendom's great virtues are faith, hope, charity, prudence, justice, temperance, and fortitude. In the Eastern traditions, other virtues are highlighted: tranquillity, nonat-tachment, compassion, truthful speech and thought, "right livelihood," and nonviolence.

Let us now explore the ethics of virtue in more detail.

AN ABUNDANCE OF VIRTUES

Character traits are specific and varied. The usual lists of moral virtues therefore tend to be long and lovingly detailed. For starters, here are eighty (!) or so:

acceptance, altruism, appreciation, autonomy, awareness, charity, chastity, cleanliness, compassion, continence (i.e., sexual self-discipline), cooperation, courage, courtesy, creativity, dependability, diligence, discipline, empathy, en-durance, enthusiasm, fairness, faith, fidelity, foresight, forgiveness, fortitude, freedom, friendship, generosity, helpfulness, honesty, honor, hope, hospital-ity, humility, humor, idealism, imagination, independence, innocence, integ-rity, kindness, knowledge, love, loyalty, mercy, moderation, manners, modesty, nonviolence, nurturance, obedience, openness, optimism, patience, peaceful-ness, perseverance, piety, prudence, purpose, respect, social responsibility, restraint, sacrifice, self-awareness, self-discipline, self-esteem, self-reliance, sensitivity, sharing, sincerity, spirituality, sympathy, tact, temperance, tolerance, trustworthiness, truthfulness, understanding, wisdom...

Even this list is far from complete. On other lists you find lightheartedness, neighborliness, valor, liberality. My mother would insist that I add politeness. The familiar "work ethic" is primarily a system of virtues: hard work, frugality, persistence, self-reliance, thrift, industriousness, dependability. Eastern moralists stress tranquillity, nonattachment, compassion. People speak of still other virtues in specific contexts, in business or sports, for example. And the list changes over time, as societies evolve and understandings shift.

Any particular item on these lists may also be contested. Not every society affirms every single one of them as moral virtues—not even everyone in our own society does. You yourself may have doubts about some of them. Still, they are all at least recognizable. Even when specific virtues conflict, as they sometimes do—obedience versus independence, empathy versus fairness, humor versus sensitivity—we do not feel the need to reject one or the other. It's just that another virtue is *balance*: finding a good ways to keep them all in play.

CLASSIFICATIONS

Are some virtues more basic than others? The classical Greeks emphasized four basic virtues: temperance, prudence, courage, and justice. When Greek philosophy was Christianized, three "theological" virtues were added: faith, hope, and charity, getting us to medieval Catholicism's key seven: faith, hope, charity, prudence, justice, temperance, and fortitude.

Among moderns, Joseph Pieper categorizes Western virtues into three general categories: virtues of *self-control*, such as temperance and other forms of self-restraint and self-redirection; virtues of *self-efficacy*, such as persistence and courage; and virtues of *regard*, such as justice and fairness. William Bennett, former U.S. Secretary of Education and advocate of character education, lists ten key virtues, under which he argues many others fall: self-discipline, compassion, responsibility, friendship, work, courage, perseverance, honesty, loyalty, and faith.

Opposite the virtues, meanwhile, stand the vices. Medieval Catholicism's Seven Deadly Sins are pride, wrath, envy, lust, gluttony, avarice, and sloth. Note these are not the exact reverses of the key virtues, though there are lists that emphasize parallels: temperance opposite gluttony, humility opposite pride, service opposite avarice. I have seen yet other traits listed as vices, more modern and secular: gracelessness, insensitivity, discontent, insatiability, willful ignorance or denial, crudeness, bad temper, and even discouragement.

Christian moral tradition distinguishes two basic kinds of vice: those we owe to the body, such as lust, and those that are spiritual perversities, like blasphemy or pride, which are seen as false idolatries. False idolatries are supposed to be much worse than merely perverse instincts—although they too are sinful. Pride was supposed to be the worst of all. Essentially a kind of idolatry of the self, pride was thought to bring the worst evils into being.

DO WE NEED A THEORY OF THE VIRTUES?

Notice that we have moved from lists of virtues to questions about their interrelationships and classifications. There are still other such questions, leading us to look for something like—yes—a *theory* of virtue.

One question is: Is everything considered a virtue really so? After all, we have been looking not only at long lists of possible virtues, but at a conglomeration of virtues from many different historical times and social contexts. All manner of outdated customs, prejudices, even accidents, are probably implicated. Etymologically the term "virtue" itself comes from the Latin *vir*, meaning "man" and suggesting, originally, the supposedly manly warlike virtues like courage and martial valor. By the Middle Ages it most often referred to a woman's chastity: that is, sexual self-restraint. Especially on sexual and gender matters, the traditional Western virtue framework seems to be rife with double standards and dubious valuations. At least a little critical reconsideration would be a good idea.

This leads to a deeper question: What *makes* something a virtue? In practice, we seem to be tempted simply to declare that certain things are virtues and then enthusiastically start listing them. There seems to be much less reflection on *why* some character trait is a virtue in the first place, that is, about what makes a virtue a virtue (and a vice a vice). How do we really tell which are which?

You know how utilitarians would answer. A character trait is a virtue, they'd say, if it makes people happier on the whole and in the long run—if it serves the greatest good of the greatest number.

There is surely something to this. It might even be true that, on the whole, virtue does promote happiness and vice causes misery. On the other hand, even if the virtues do make us happier and vices unhappier, that may not be the *reason* that they are virtues or vices. The virtues' advocates would say that the virtues are the kinds of character traits that we *ought* to seek and to sustain, maybe because they flow from something very deep in human nature, or about the world. If so, then the real relation between virtue and happiness may be the other way around: maybe the virtues make us happy because they are virtues, rather than being virtues because they make us happy.

Something more may be going on. We have a genuinely different set of values here. There may be more of a story to tell.

A GREEK VIEW OF VIRTUE

The most influential Western theory of the virtues comes from the Greek philosopher Aristotle (384–322 BCE).

Everything in the world, according to Aristotle, has a distinctive and essential function or activity. Trees grow in certain ways depending on their kinds; buildings are made for certain purposes; human artisans have their particular arts. And in Aristotle's view, this function or activity in turn determines admirable or "excellent" characteristics or traits—that is, virtues.

"For all things that have a function or activity," Aristotle writes, "the good and the 'well' [as in: doing a job well] is thought to reside in the function." Good carpenters, for example, are those who build sturdy and beautiful things. Therefore virtue in carpenters is an eye for proportion, skill with saw and plane, a feel for what a piece of wood can and cannot do, and so on.

Similarly, there must be a characteristic or set of characteristics that defines *our* essence—the human "function," as Aristotle also puts it:

> For just as for a flute player, a sculptor, or any artist, and, in general, for all things that have a function or activity, the good and the "well" is thought to reside in the function, so it would seem to be for man, if he has a function.

According to Aristotle, rational self-regulation is the characteristic activity and therefore "function" of humans. We are, in his famous definition, *rational animals*. What Aristotle means by "rational," though, is quite different from what Kant means by the same word. For Aristotle, reason means the ability—the habits and the wisdom and the judgment—that enables us to bring a complex self into order as it unfolds. This vision of balanced self-actualization Aristotle even calls "happiness"—but notice that it is a rather different conception than the utilitarians'.

This essentially human function and activity in turn therefore determine morally admirable or "excellent" characteristics or traits for us—in short, moral virtues. For example, one key activity of practical reason is to find the "mean"—the appropriate middle—between extremes of emotion or action. In responding to danger we may feel either fear or confidence, leading to two opposite failings: either cowardice (too much fear, too little confidence) or foolhardiness (too much confidence, too little fear). We need to find the appropriate, rational middle—and this is the virtue, says Aristotle, of courage. The vices, on this view, are the *excesses* (too much) or the *defects* (too little): that is, going to the extreme, either extreme, rather than following the middle path of moderation.

Likewise, between excessive self-indulgence or profligacy on the one hand and self-denial on the other lies the mean of temperance. Between the defect of miserliness and the excess of prodigality lies the mean or virtue Aristotle calls "liberality." Between vanity on the one hand and undue humility on the other lies the virtue he calls "high-mindness." Even a sense of humor is a virtue on this view—the mean between being foolish and being a bore.

From Nicomachean Ethics

ARISTOTLE

If, then, there is some end of the things we do, which we desire for its own sake (everything else being desired for the sake of this), and if we do not choose everything for the sake of something else (for at that rate the process would go on to infinity, so that our desire would be empty and vain), clearly this must be the good and the chief good. Will not the knowledge of it, then, have a great influence on life? Shall we not, like archers who have a mark to aim at, be more likely to hit upon what is right? If so, we must try in outline at least to determine what it is, and of which of the sciences or capacities it is the object.... Verbally there is very general agreement, for both the general run of men and people of superior refinement say that it is happiness, and identify living well and doing well with being happy, but with regard to what happiness is they differ, and the many do not give the same account as the wise. For the former think it is some plain and obvious thing, like pleasure, wealth, or honor; they differ, however, from one another—and often even the same man identifies it with different things, with health when he is ill, and wealth when he is poor, but, conscious of their ignorance, they admire those who proclaim some great ideal that is above their comprehension....

Presumably, however, to say that happiness is the chief good seems a platitude, and a clearer account of what it is is still desired. This might perhaps be given, if we could first ascertain the function of man. For just as for a flute player, a sculptor, or any artist, and, in general, for all things that have a function or activity, the good and the "well" is thought to reside in the function, so would it seem to be for man, if he has a function. Have the carpenter, then, and the tanner certain functions or activities, and has man none? Is he born without a function? Or as eye, hand, foot, and in general each of the parts evidently has a function, may one lay it down that man similarly has a function apart from all these? What then can this be? Life seems to be common even to plants, but we are seeking what is peculiar to man. Let us exclude, therefore, the life of nutrition and growth. Next there would be a life of perception, but it also seems to be common even to the horse, the ox, and every animal. There remains, then, an active life of the element that has a rational principle; of this, one part has such a principle in the sense of being obedient to one, the other in the sense of possessing one and exercising thought. And, as "life of the rational element" also has two meanings, we must state that life in the sense of activity is what we mean; for this seems to be the more proper sense of the term. Now if the function of man is an activity of soul which follows or implies a rational principle, and if we say "a so-and-so" and "a good so-and-so"

From Aristotle, *Nicomachean Ethics*, translated by W. D. Ross, Book I, 1097b23–1098a19.

have a function which is the same in kind, for example, a lyre player and a good lyre player, and so without qualification in all cases, eminence in respect of goodness being added to the name of the function (for the function of a lyre player is to play the lyre, and that of a good lyre player is to do so well): if this is the case, [and we state the function of man to be a certain kind of life, and this to be an activity or actions of the soul implying a rational principle, and the function of a good man to be the good and noble performance of these, and if any action is well performed when it is performed in accordance with the appropriate excellence: if this is the case,] human good turns out to be activity of soul in accordance with virtue, and if there are more than one virtue, in accordance with the best and most complete.

But we must add "in a complete life." For one swallow does not make a summer, nor does one day; and so too one day, or a short time, does not make a man blessed and happy....

We must...not only describe [moral] virtue as a state of character, but also say what sort of state it is. We may remark, then, that every virtue or excellence both brings into good condition the thing of which it is the excellence and makes the work of that thing be done well; e.g., the excellence of the eye makes both the eye and its work good; for it is by the excellence of the eye that we see well. Similarly the excellence of the horse makes a horse both good in itself and good at running and at carrying its rider and at awaiting the attack of the enemy. Therefore, if this is true in every case, the virtue of man also will be the state of character which makes a man good and which makes him do his own work well.... If reason is divine, then, in comparison with man, the life according to it is divine in comparison with human life. But we must not follow those who advise us, being men, to think of human things, and, being mortal, of mortal things, but must, so far as we can, make ourselves immortal, and strain every nerve to live in accordance with the best thing in us; for even if it be small in bulk, much more does it in power and worth surpass everything. This would seem, too, to be each man himself, since it is the authoritative and better part of him. It would be strange, then, if he were to choose not the life of his self but that of something else. And what we said before will apply now; that which is proper to each thing is by nature best and most pleasant for each thing; for man, therefore, the life according to reason is best and pleasantest, since reason more than anything else *is* man. This life therefore is also the happiest.

AQUINAS ON THE VIRTUES

Aristotle deeply influenced medieval Christian thinkers such as Saint Thomas Aquinas (1224–1274). Aquinas borrowed Aristotle's "logic of virtue," so to speak—deriving virtue from our essential activity or function—but understood our essential activity or function in very different terms. In particular, reason is not an end in itself, for Aquinas, but instead a means to better knowing ourselves and God. Our ultimate purpose he supposes to be communion with God, as far as we can achieve it in this life.

Here we begin to see the underlying rationale for the Christian systems of virtue so prominent in the lists like the key or "Cardinal" Virtues given earlier. It was Aquinas who added the "theological" virtues of faith, hope, and charity to the older Greek or "natural" virtues like justice and temperance. Those Greek virtues were also expanded. Temperance, for example, came to include humility, patience, and chastity. All of them are now conceived as character traits essential to drawing and staying as close to God as we can in this life.

The Seven Deadly Sins, meanwhile, were those traits considered fatal to that same spiritual quest. Pride, lust, avarice, and all the rest: to fall into these pits was a sure way of allowing yourself to be pulled away from God, and thus to fail not only to meet God's dictates but also as a human being: to fall away from our own deepest and most essential possibilities and nature.

PROFESSIONAL ETHICS: ARISTOTELIAN VIRTUE ETHICS IN PRACTICE

Aristotle speaks of carpenters and tanners, whose work defines their goals and therefore their virtues *as* carpenters or tanners. Likewise for teachers and doctors and athletes and (why not?) car mechanics and computer programmers and even fund-raisers. Each of these professions or activities we entrust with important things; each of them therefore has a moral dimension; and for each of them, just as by now you'd expect, their moral dimension is determined by their specific function or goal—just as Aristotle proposes. Teachers enable and inform; doctors heal; athletes must "play fair"; and so on.

Here virtue is determined by what contemporary philosopher Alasdair MacIntyre calls "practices." Medicine, teaching, and so on are practices, like many other organized, cooperative activities—politics, child-raising, even games. Each of these activities or disciplines has its own "internal goods"— goals that define the practice itself, such as health and life for medicine, justice for the law, and so on. Thus, technically, on MacIntyre's view, a virtue is

> an acquired human quality the possession and exercise of which tends to enable us to achieve those goods which are internal to practices and the lack of which effectively prevents us from achieving any such goods.

Devotion to the truth, for example, enables lawyers to seek justice. Cool-headedness enables chess masters to concentrate. Liveliness and imagination make a good teacher.

Consider medicine in a little more detail. Doctors' famous oath traces back to Hippocrates, a Greek physician of the fifth century BCE. The core of the Hippocratic Oath reads:

> I will apply dietetic measures for the benefit of the sick according to my ability and judgement; I will keep them from harm and injustice.

I will neither give a deadly drug to anybody if asked for it, nor will I make a suggestion to this effect....In purity and holiness I will guard my life and my art.
Whatever houses I may visit, I will come for the benefit of the sick....
What I may see or hear in the course of the treatment...which on no account one must spread abroad, I will keep to myself....

There are more modern medical codes of ethics too. The Hippocratic Oath does not deal with questions of truthfulness, for example, but the American Medical Association (AMA) Principles of Medical Ethics (last revised, 2001) requires that "A physician shall uphold the standards of professionalism, be honest in all professional interactions" and even "strive to report physicians deficient in character or competence." The International Council of Nurses Ethical Code as well as the Constitution of the World Health Organization require "respect for life...unrestricted by considerations of nationality, race, creed, age, sex, politics, or social status." Many codes also oblige the medical professional to try to improve the profession, including "establish[ing] and maintain[ing] equitable social and economic working conditions" (International Council of Nurses), as well as contributing to the community at large. The AMA again: "A physician shall recognize a responsibility to participate in activities contributing to the improvement of the community and the betterment of public health."

These codes make explicit the *virtues* of a good doctor or nurse—and they begin to show us how these virtues flow from what MacIntyre would call the "internal goods" of medicine considered as a "practice." Medicine serves health—it is practiced "for the benefit of the sick"—therefore, medical professionals must put their patients' health above all other goals, including the professional's own enjoyments or income and even, sometimes, personal safety. The doctor must above all "do no harm." A doctor also enters a person's life at moments of great vulnerability—sickness and death—and is therefore bound to utmost respect for the patient and all of his family and household, including confidentiality. "What I may see or hear in the course of the treatment...I will keep to myself."

The Hippocratic Oath also has some clearly outdated parts. Would-be Hippocratic doctors also promised not to do surgery (in Greek times, that was another profession's work) or have sex with household slaves. Other parts are currently in contest: Hippocratic doctors also swear not to give "abortive remedies" or, as we just saw, "deadly drugs." Still, the oath remains in use—it still speaks to us—because it identifies the key virtues of medicine against the background of medicine's *function* or medicine as a *practice*. Aristotle's and MacIntyre's logic is still at work.

Once you understand professional codes of ethics in this way, you can begin to outline the virtues for almost any profession. Teachers nurture the young, open minds, inform and enable: hence teachers must be supportive, must not indoctrinate, should be accurate and clear, and so on. Airline pilots must remain alert at all times and keep themselves well-trained and ready.

Same for truck drivers. Accountants must be objective, avoid conflicts of interest, and report clearly and accurately.

Or consider journalism. The aim of journalism is to inform people and by so doing to help promote democratic decision-making. Therefore, telling the truth is crucial. Some attempt to present both (all) sides of a dispute is crucial too, especially when most of the established powers stand on one side. Careful distinction between news and "advocacy" allows people to make up their own minds.

> Members of the Society of Professional Journalists believe that public enlightenment is the forerunner of justice and the foundation of democracy. The duty of the journalist is to further those ends by seeking truth and providing a fair and comprehensive account of events and issues....
>
> Journalists should be honest, fair, and courageous in gathering, reporting, and interpreting information....

Again all of these are quite literally *virtues;* and again the proposed list of virtues is inferred directly from the "internal goods" of the profession.

CHINESE VIEWS OF VIRTUE

On the other side of Eurasia from ancient Greece, at about the same time, three great philosophical and ethical systems were taking shape. All of these systems concentrate on the virtues as well.

CONFUCIAN VIRTUE: PROPRIETY AND PIETY

For the Chinese sage Confucius (551–479 BCE) the greatest virtue is humanity (*jen* or *ren,* variously translated as humaneness, kindheartedness, or benevolence). Associated virtues are just or appropriate action, ritual propriety (and not just going through the motions: truly seeing to the heart of the ritual), wisdom, loyalty, faithfulness, trustworthiness, courtesy, magnanimity, good faith, diligence, and piety.

On the Confucian view, these virtues derive from *relationship*. Our task is not so much to live up to our own inner nature, as Aristotle thought, as to live up to the requirements of the relationships within which we find ourselves. We stand among the generations, for example: we are children to our parents and at the same time parents to our own children. More generally, we find ourselves among a variety of relationships, all with their histories and rituals and depth and therefore associated virtues. We are citizen and ruler: here the prime virtue is righteousness. We are sibling among siblings: here the prime virtue is order. We are friend among friends: the prime virtue here is faithfulness. These virtues make possible a harmonious society—very unlike the constantly warring and fractured Chinese society of Confucius's time—and likewise a harmonious society allows us to cultivate the virtues.

Confucius spent his middle life traveling throughout China trying to persuade various rulers to put his ideas into effect. Unsuccessful in his lifetime (he eventually gave up and went home), he nevertheless would have been happy to know that a version of his ideas eventually became the official Chinese system, literally for millennia. Virtue was the essential—and only—requirement for serving the Chinese state. It was Confucius's radical idea that heredity is not enough: even a high-born man can be but a "small man" without virtue. Contrariwise, any person who cultivates virtue or "humaneness" can become truly noble and worthy to lead.

BUDDHISM AND TAOISM

Buddhism was founded in India by Siddhartha Gautama (fifth century BCE?), also called "the Buddha," meaning "the Enlightened One." Buddhism flourished in India, spread to China and Japan, and reached the ancient Western world—Greece—as well.

What we call "self," the Buddha taught, is an imagined entity, not any kind of permanence but only a flux. We are different today than we were yesterday and will be tomorrow. In fact, to be attached to a supposedly permanent "I" only leads to suffering because change and eventually death are inevitable. Really we are just a part of the ceaseless becoming of the whole universe—a beautiful thing, too, but a fact that calls for awareness, acceptance, and adjustment, not resistance or dramatic gestures.

Here we begin to glimpse a very different view of the virtues—different both from the self-actualizing virtues of Aristotle and the society-centered virtues of Confucius. In a Buddhist view, the key virtues are traits like tranquillity, nonattachment, compassion, truthful speech and thought; "right livelihood," which means finding a way to live that does not increase your own or others' suffering; and nonviolence. These are all ways of living in appropriate relationship with the world as it really is, and of freeing ourselves from "craving." Desire in the Buddhist view is not so much the having of desires as it is the desire having *us*. We are invited instead to try not only to free ourselves from craving but also to free others as well.

Free from craving, Buddhists say, we can rejoin the world on its own terms. "To forget the Self is to be enlightened by all things," the Japanese Zen master Dogen wrote, and "To be enlightened by all things is to remove the barrier between the Self and Other." But how do we know what the world's terms actually are? The answer, especially for Taoism, is to look at the workings of *nature*—not the human world, which is usually a distraction and often a hyperstimulation of craving, but the workings of winds and streams, mountains and forests.

A prominent analogy in the *Tao Te Ching* is the working of water. To be virtuous, in fact, is to be very much like water: to be infinitely flexible and responsive, "going with the flow," a life based on spontaneity, simplicity, tranquillity, unselfishness, and humility. It is not, however, *weak*. The *Tao Te*

Ching notes that though nothing in the world is as soft and yielding as water, "yet nothing can better overcome the hard and the strong."

> According to the book of Chuang-tzu, an old man is seen by some followers of Confucius swimming in a raging torrent; suddenly, he disappears. The pupils of Confucius rush to save him, but the man reaches the bank entirely unaided. Asked how he had pulled off this remarkable feat of survival, the man replied that he had simply let himself go with the descending and ascending currents in the water. The true Taoist, in other words, moulds his senses, body and mind until they are at one with the currents of the world without.

Notice the "letting go" as well. We don't have to resist the world. In fact, we can't. Resistance will only get us drowned, actually or metaphorically. Even fighting is not really a matter of meeting blow for blow, irresistible force meeting immoveable object. The wisdom of the martial arts: if someone is rushing at you to fight, don't rush back at them. Step aside and let them rush past, but maybe just change their direction a little as you do. "Tao abides in non-action. Yet nothing is left undone"

And the Tao itself? The *Tao Te Ching* opens with these words:

> The Tao that can be told
> is not the eternal Tao
> The name that can be named
> is not the eternal Name...

We sense, in short, a vast and all-encompassing reality, which at some level just is the whole world considered all together, but nothing that can be pinned down, labeled and dissected and analyzed. The Tao is not God; it is not personal, or even unchanging; and it is not to be worshiped. It is not graspable in language yet can be clear enough when we sit with a clear mind by a peaceful stream—or, just as well, entering a raging current. May the Flow be with you!

From the Tao Te Ching

LAO TSU

Translated by Stephen Mitchell

The *Tao Te Ching* is the founding expression of Taoism and the second most translated book in the world. It was written, officially, by Lao Tsu in third or fourth

Numbers 8, 10, 13, 16, 22, 23, 24, 49, 59, 67 from *Tao Te Ching by Lao Tsu*. A new English Version, with foreword and notes by Stephen Mitchell. Translation copyright © 1988 by Stephen Mitchell. Reprinted by permission of HarperCollins Publishers.

century BCE China. But little is known about who Lao Tsu was or even whether such a person actually existed. One story is that a bridgekeeper asked the wanderer Lao Tsu to write a book containing his thoughts and beliefs, which he did—and then disappeared forever. Other stories, perhaps not inconsistent with this one, consider the author of the *Tao* a divine being.

Tao literally means "way" or "path." *Te* means "virtue," both in the sense of "personal character" and in the sense of "inner potency," as when we speak of the "healing virtue" of a drug. *Ching* originally meant "norm" but expanded to mean "scripture," "canon," or "classic." Thus, *Tao Te Ching* means something like: "The Scripture/Classic/Canon of the Way/Path and the Power/Virtue."

8

The supreme good is like water,
which nourishes all things without trying to.
It is content with the low places that people disdain.
Thus it is like the Tao.

In dwelling, live close to the ground.
In thinking, keep to the simple.
In conflict, be fair and generous.
In governing, don't try to control.
In work, do what you enjoy.
In family life, be completely present.

When you are content to be simply yourself
and don't compare or compete,
everybody will respect you.

10

Can you coax your mind from its wandering
and keep to the original oneness?
Can you let your body become
supple as a newborn child's?
Can you cleanse your inner vision
until you see nothing but the light?
Can you love people and lead them
without imposing your will?
Can you deal with the most vital matters
by letting events take their course?
Can you step back from your own mind
and thus understand all things?

Giving birth and nourishing,
having without possessing,

acting with no expectations,
leading and not trying to control:
this is the supreme virtue.

16

Empty your mind of all thoughts.
Let your heart be at peace.
Watch the turmoil of beings,
but contemplate their return.

Each separate being in the universe
returns to the common source.
Returning to the source is serenity.

If you don't realize the source,
you stumble in confusion and sorrow.
When you realize where you come from,
you naturally become tolerant,
disinterested, amused,
kindhearted as a grandmother,
dignified as a king.
Immersed in the wonder of the Tao,
you can deal with whatever life brings you,
and when death comes, you are ready.

22

If you want to become whole,
let yourself be partial.
If you want to become straight,
let yourself be crooked.
If you want to become full,
let yourself be empty.
If you want to be reborn,
let yourself die.
If you want to be given everything,
give everything up.

The Master, by residing in the Tao,
sets an example for all beings.
Because he doesn't display himself,
people can see his light.
Because he has nothing to prove,
people can trust his words.
Because he doesn't know who he is,

people recognize themselves in him.
Because he has no goal in mind,
everything he does succeeds.

When the ancient Masters said,
"If you want to be given everything,
give everything up,"
they weren't using empty phrases.
Only in being lived by the Tao can you be truly yourself.

23

Express yourself completely,
then keep quiet.
Be like the forces of nature:
when it blows, there is only wind;
when it rains, there is only rain;
when the clouds pass, the sun shines through.

If you open yourself to the Tao,
you are at one with the Tao
and you can embody it completely.
If you open yourself to insight,
you are at one with insight
and you can use it completely.
If you open yourself to loss,
you are at one with loss
and you can accept it completely.

Open yourself to the Tao,
then trust your natural responses;
and everything will fall into place.

24

He who stands on tiptoe
doesn't stand firm.
He who rushes ahead
doesn't go far.
He who tries to shine
dims his own light.
He who defines himself
can't know who he really is.
He who has power over others
can't empower himself.

He who clings to his work
will create nothing that endures.

If you want to accord with the Tao,
just do your job, then let go.

49

The Master...is good to people who are good.
She is also good to people who aren't good.
This is true goodness.

She trusts people who are trustworthy.
She also trusts people who aren't trustworthy.
This is true trust...

67

Some say that my teaching is nonsense.
Others call it lofty but impractical.
But to those who have looked inside themselves,
this nonsense makes perfect sense.
And to those who put it into practice,
this loftiness has roots that go deep.

I have just three things to teach:
simplicity, patience, compassion.
These three are your greatest treasures.
Simple in actions and in thoughts,
you return to the source of being.
Patient with both friends and enemies,
you accord with the way things are.
Compassionate toward yourself,
you reconcile all beings in the world.

CULTIVATING VIRTUE

The ethics of virtue is concerned with character traits. But character traits do not just happen. They need to be consciously developed and sustained, both by the people whose character traits they are and by others around them: parents, teachers, role models, and the community at large. A little like plants, they need seeding and nurturing and regular attention in order to prosper. This is what is called the *cultivation* of the virtues.

HOW VIRTUE IS TAUGHT

To some extent the virtues can be taught directly. They can be identified, praised, and rewarded early on, by parents and later by schools and society. Discipline is a good example. Originally imposed from outside, it is gradually internalized to become, later, *self-*discipline. Not that this kind of parenting or teaching is easy—and obviously I am not talking about the kind of harshness that really serves the discipli*ner* and not the learner—but surely it is also crucial.

Stories play an essential role too. William Bennett, former U.S. Secretary of Education and compiler of several very large books of virtue stories, writes in the preface of one of them that

> what we choose to read to our children matters a great deal. Legends, folktales, sacred stories, biographies, and poems can introduce the youngest children to the virtues; they can clarify notions of right and wrong for young people; and they can serve as powerful reminders of [humanity's] best ideals all the way through adulthood. More than one great man or woman at a critical instant has recalled a simple fable, a familiar verse, a childhood hero.

Other virtues must come from the heart, of course—empathy, generosity, hospitality—but even here, early experience of these virtues in others may be a critical part of the learning. Or perhaps they are "innate," but even so, it's clear that people can *lose* them without the proper development and support.

For Confucius too, cultivating the virtues is a social project. Virtuous rulers and other role models, in particular, are crucial. Virtue is not something we discover for ourselves; it is *shown* to us, daily, in the actions of those most visible and most admired. Classic texts reinforce virtues, art and story celebrate them. In China, ultimately the entire society came to be built around the virtues of its officials. By 165 BCE, candidates for high public office began to be called for examination of their moral excellence by the emperor. More and more were examined until finally almost anyone who wished to become an official had to pass written examinations, and thus it went for centuries. In fact this Confucian system inspired the modern European civil service.

"It takes a village," then—maybe even a whole society. Aristotle would invoke the city or *polis*. Remember that "cities" for the Greeks were self-sufficient political entities, city-*states,* not parts of any larger nation. Governance was face-to-face, and everyone in the ruling class (landowning, free, male citizens, often also those who fought the city's wars) knew each other intimately. When you grow up and fight and decide alongside others in this way, visibly interdependent though distinctive personalities, everyone's virtues and vices are well known to all, and a man's training of his sons (and, sometimes, protégés) clearly reflects his own virtue—or lack of it. Conversely, some observers have argued that the decline of such face-to-face communities in modern societies underlies our (perceived) decline in virtue as well.

PRACTICE IS ESSENTIAL

In the individual moral life especially, *practice* is crucial to cultivating virtue. Think psychologically for a moment here. A character trait is (at least) a reliable disposition to act in certain ways in certain specific circumstances. Another term we could use is "habit." But habits need practicing. The simplest principle of psychology is that habits are established and grow stronger with repetition. So, to promote and engrain virtue in oneself, repetition is key. Honesty, hospitality, temperance, and all the rest—we don't come by these settled character traits simply by choice or commitment. We have to *be* honest, *be* hospitable, *practice* temperance—again and again and again.

Sometimes we are inclined to excuse our moral lapses by arguing that we couldn't help ourselves. "Circumstances made me do it!" And it may well be true that, faced with specific temptations with no settled habits of resistance or redirection, temptations are hard to resist. Too much liquor, the white lie or worse, the habit of denigrating others behind their backs, or much worse: all of these can come out all too easily. But here is the key point: the contrary power does not necessarily lie in a pure act of will at the moment of choice, as if each time we must "just say no" all over again. *The power lies with the reconstruction of our habits.* Make it a *habit* never to say something behind someone's back that you wouldn't say to their face, and each time it becomes easier. Moral character is an ongoing project.

From Living Large

JOHN SULLIVAN

John Sullivan is emeritus professor of philosophy at Elon University and a mentor and inspiration to me and many others. He works, as he puts it, "at the place where philosophy, psychology and spirituality—East and West—intersect and mutually enhance one another."

Sullivan's question in this selection is this: how to win ourselves some freedom of mind. Awareness is crucial. What Sullivan calls *response-ability* arises when we come to recognize that our ways of understanding and responding to events and experiences are themselves choices—and then *practice* making different and more conscious ones. Response-ability is both a key virtue in itself and also the means by which other virtues can be cultivated and deepened.

Confucius (Master K'ung) would say we have a *small-minded person-in-us* and a noble or *large-minded person-in-us*—both possibilities existing at any moment.[1] He would encourage us to remember our nobility and to live in large mind. He would remind us that this takes daily practice.

What is "practice" on this model? It is *to recognize when we are in small mind and to shift to large mind....* In small mind, we tend to be partial in the double sense of being biased and of seeing less than the whole. In small mind, we are asleep in our life, on automatic pilot, "going through the motions" according to cultural scripts. In small mind, we are enslaved and reactive in the sense that someone or something triggers us and we react immediately—with no space and no time between the incoming stimulus and the automatic response.

In large mind, we see more of the whole and live in a larger world. In large mind, we are more mindful, more wakeful, opening the senses and opening the heart. In large mind, we are freer, acting from a place beneath surface disturbance. In large mind, we are *response-able*—able to choose our response in a way that benefits the whole.

RECOGNIZING TWO LEVELS

Practice begins with recognizing when we are in small mind. To do this, we must distinguish two levels—a WHAT and a HOW. Call this the fundamental distinction for all inner work: the distinction between (a) *what is going on* and (b) *how I am relating to what is going on.*

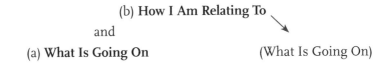

Always there are two levels. Yet often we merge the two. "How we are relating" disappears from our awareness, as if how we are relating is the only possible way we could relate.

Victor Frankl was an Austrian psychiatrist and a Jew. During the time of the Holocaust, the Nazis sent him to the camps. While he was a prisoner under unimaginable conditions, Frankl discovered this fundamental distinction. His way of phrasing it was to distinguish "liberty" (on the first level) and "freedom" (on the second level). In the camps, Frankl had no liberty—he could not go and come as he wished. Yet Frankl discovered that he did have a bit of freedom—the freedom to choose how he would relate to his situation. This he came to call "the last human freedom." It was something his Nazi captors could not take from him.[2]

Consider liberty and freedom in our own lives. We may or may not have the power to change what is occurring. Hurricanes and floods, sicknesses and accidents may restrict our liberty. Yet we still have an important freedom—the capacity to recognize, and possibly alter, how we relate to what is occurring in our life.

Leadership consultant Stephen Covey uses the Frankl example to emphasize the first of his seven habits of highly successful people.[3] "Be proactive," Covey says. "Develop the capacity to choose your response."

Covey speaks not of small and large mind but of reactivity and pro-activity. The stimulus happens—someone makes a cutting remark. The response follows immediately—an angry retort. *Reactivity.* No freedom, no ability to choose your response. *Proactivity,* on the contrary, is another name for "response-ability." Proactivity is the ability to choose one's re-sponse. Being proactive is often confused with being nice. This misses the key distinction. At times, hard truths must be faced. Proactivity, in this instance, is the ability to choose what you will say, and when, and how. It may or may not be "nice."

Several years ago, my wife, Gregg, discovered she had breast cancer. At that moment, she had no choice about having cancer. Cancer was already present. But she did have a second level choice: how to relate to the cancer. First, she could choose her treatment. Second, during and after treatment, she could choose how she would live with this illness. She chose not to let cancer be her identity (not to be "Miss Cancer of the Year," she would say). And she chose not to die before she died. By cultivating *awareness,* she realized that she was at least *free to choose* **how** she would understand and respond to this event in her life....

We humans are "meaning-creating, value-generating" beings. The odd thing is that generally we forget that *we* are labeling situations. We for-get that *we* are generating the emotions we feel. It's as if we are wearing glasses and forgetting we are wearing them. We "see through" our stories and emotions. We do not see that the stories and emotions are produced by us.

Without awareness, I take my interpretation as the truth of the matter. I defend it as such. I am unaware that I have any choice about the story I am telling. I think: "That is just the way it is!"

Without awareness, I fail to see that, in the wake of the story, I am the one putting an emotional charge on the situation. It is as if situations arrived already wrapped in language and already charged with strong emotion. I simply think: "That's the way it is." Aren't I justified to be angry about it?

When the stakes are high or emotions are high, reactivity increases. Yet, even in these situations, with awareness, I can notice the key distinction: what is happening is one thing; how I interpret and respond is another. Victor Frankl could distinguish liberty and freedom even under horrendous conditions. My wife could distinguish between having cancer (no liberty here) and how she would relate to having cancer (some freedom here). To notice this fundamental distinction does not come easily. We need practice.

TEACHING STORY 1: FIGHT OR KEY?

When my daughter Heather was very little, she thought that I existed solely to play with her. In order to get my work done, I decide one Sunday afternoon to go over to my office in Carlton Building on the Elon campus. When I arrive, I find that the locks have been changed and I cannot get to my office. Immediately the soap opera of my mind scoops up the whole situation and I launch into high drama. "That's just the way THEY are (THEY being the nasty, unfeeling administration and WE being the hard-working, noble faculty). Just the way they are—never thinking of faculty, acting without any consultation, so insensitive as to not even bother telling us!"

I start to fume and get into a state. I try to call campus security, with no results. Anger mounts. Finally, I spy the Vice President for Academic Affairs coming out of a campus luncheon. I jump him like a hungry lion. He produces a key and I get into the building.

Yet the soap opera of oppression continues to pop up when I'm working, when I'm driving home, when I'm lying in bed. And of course, I tell the tale on Monday. This, I am now ashamed to say, continues for several days.

Finally, after days pass, I become conscious of a small voice that cuts through the tattered tale of imagined abuse. The voice says: "*John, do you want a fight or do you want a key?*"

Now part of me wants a fight. After all I am Irish. I share the heritage of the Irish man who saw a fight and inquired: "Is this a private fight or can anyone join in?" Yet the better part of me answers: "Well—[*long pause*]—I guess I really want a key." I dial Physical Plant and ask: "May I have a key to Carlton Building?" "Sure," comes the reply, "it'll be ready in an hour." . . .

My emotions would have been very different that Sunday, if the meaning I attached to my frustration had been different. Suppose, for instance, I had thought, "Oh, they've changed the locks. The locksmiths must have worked overtime to do it when the fewest people would be around to be inconvenienced—too bad I'm one of the few!" From that understanding, my response might have been a hearty laugh—and then I could have sought a key in a completely different spirit. Or I could have worked under a tree. Or I could have taken the whole event as a sign from the gods to go home and take a nap, or take my family for a picnic. Any such response flowing from a larger understanding would have caused a good deal less suffering, both for me and for other people. My ranting was far from harmless!

That's not what I did, though. In the grip of my small-minded self, my understanding was small, my language followed. On the basis of my quick judgment, my response was anger, resentment, and condemnation. And I locked onto those feelings, I froze my interpretation and valuation together by saying, in effect, "That's just the way it is!"

"That's just the way it is!" or "That's just the way I am" is a hallmark of a small mind. Labels, emotions, stereotypes—these are part of the dynamic. Also, in small, ego-centered mind, I move very quickly to EITHER-OR (dualistic understanding and response—us vs. them; right vs. wrong, win vs. lose). In such a mindspace, true partnership cannot even be thought or spoken, let alone achieved. Alternatively, Confucius, by pointing out the large-minded-person-in-us, was laying the groundwork for partnership, for community.

TEACHING STORY 2: HARRIET'S CHILDHOOD

Some years ago, I was participating in a group. One of the other participants—I'll call her Harriet—was in her mid-sixties at the time. Her mother had been dead for some years. Here is Harriet's story:

"When I was a little girl, I lived in Texas with my mother. I never knew who my father was. My mother would be in and out of work. She kept sending me to my grandmother whenever she was 'laid off' from work. My grandmother would care for me. Then back to my mother and the same cycle."

On the basis of what she perceived was going on, Harriet installed a "story" about her mother. The story centered on Harriet's mother sending her away. Harriet came to believe that her mother did not want her, never loved her. Harriet's evidence? The fact that her mother kept sending her away—to stay with her grandmother. When did Harriet install this story? At age four or five perhaps. At any rate, quite early on.

Suppose that you were Harriet, the little girl, and you interpreted the situation as a sign that your mother never loved you. What thoughts and emotions might arise? Perhaps confusion, anger, resentment—all directed outward. Perhaps feelings of being unworthy, worthless, alone, unloved—all directed inward.

The interpretation and consequent emotional charge arose early and lasted long. Harriet and her mother were estranged for all of her mother's life. Even after her mother's death, Harriet's alienation continued.

In the group, people listened to Harriet, hearing the pain and suffering this story had caused and was causing still. Then the group members began to explore what life must have been like for Harriet's mother—a "single mother" before there was such a term. How was it in Texas at that time for a young woman with a young child—the woman poorly educated and without many skills? A woman who had to pick up what work she could. A woman working in situations where she was easily laid off. Harriet's mother did send Harriet away. And she also asked for her back. Again and again and again. Was Harriet's interpretation the only way of understanding the situation? Would an alternative interpretation open up alternate emotional responses? We who have an observer present can see how Harriet "languaged her life." We who have an observer present can understand the emotional charge that followed her interpretation. Harriet had no observer for this story. For her it was the truth of the matter—that was exactly how it was!

Through the group work we were doing, Harriet awoke to notice that this was not the only way to interpret and respond to the events. The events were in the past—"frozen in amber" as it were.[4] Harriet had no liberty to change the past but, with awareness, she did have the freedom to observe her story and the emotions arising with the story. She did, with awareness, have the freedom to shift her story. This she did. She came to see that perhaps her mother did love her after all. That her mother did the best she could for Harriet in difficult circumstances. Tears and grieving. Then regret: why did I not see this possibility while my mother was still alive? Regret and finally closure. To tell her mother certain things—even now. We do not quite have the words. Some kind of forgiveness—of Harriet for herself, for her mother, for the human condition we all share. How easy to see in others, how difficult to see in our own lives!

Being asleep in our lives can cause great unnecessary suffering. Great pain. Waking up can bring the capacity for compassion, forgiveness, and renewed hope.

NOTES

1. I am rendering the Confucian term "hsiao jen" as the small-minded person-in-us. I am rendering the Confucian term "chün-tzu" as the noble or large-minded person-in-us. This distinction can be seen in the Image section of the commentary on each hexagram in the *I Ching*, where Wilhelm translates the terms as "the superior man" and "the inferior man." See the *I Ching or Book of Changes*, trans. Richard Wilhelm, 3rd ed. (Princeton, N.J.: Princeton University Press, 1967). It is also a key distinction used by Confucius. See *The Analects* (Lun Yu), trans. D.C. Lau (New York: Viking Penguin, 1979) where the distinction appears more than 50 times.

2. See Victor Frankl, *Man's Search for Meaning*, 3rd ed. (New York: Simon & Schuster, 1984).

3. See Stephen Covey, *The Seven Habits of Highly Effective People* (New York: Simon & Schuster Fireside Book, 1990), pp. 66–93. Covey acknowledges that the

first habit must be joined to the second—"Begin with the End in View," and, in fact, that all the habits interlock.

4. The phrase is from Kurt Vonnegut.

FOR REVIEW

1. What (kind of thing) is a virtue?
2. What is a vice?
3. Why would anyone want a *theory* of the virtues?
4. What is Aristotle's theory of virtue?
5. How do professional codes of ethics determine what traits to put forward as virtues?
6. What is the Confucian view of virtue?
7. What is the Taoist view of virtue?
8. How does the *Tao Te Ching* invite us to live?
9. What are some ways that virtue can be taught?
10. What is "response-ability"? How can we cultivate it?

EXERCISES AND NOTES

INTERCONNECTIONS

In the Greek view, the virtues connect. Plato and Aristotle argued that the key virtues each depend on the others—to have one, you need all—and Plato in particular argued that virtue is a kind of knowledge, so that the lack of any virtue suggests the lack of the knowledge of virtue as such.

What do you think? Is it really true that the virtues are something of a package deal? If a person has one, are they more likely to have others? Why or why not? Use some examples to help your investigation along.

Are the vices connected in the same way? Does every vice require the others to some extent? Do most? Could we then infer the presence of other vices in a person who has one? For example, take a mild vice like littering. Are litterers more likely to have other vices too? To be pushy drivers or white liars or . . . ? Can you get any evidence to help answer this question?

Is it best to cultivate all the virtues? Though tradition would say so, not everyone agrees. The philosopher Friedrich Nietzsche thought that we could and should develop only a few, indeed maybe a few vices too: it makes us more interesting and possibly fertile personalities...

VIRTUES IN FLUX

Some virtues remain constant over time, even between us and the ancients and/or between East and West. Others shift. The Greeks of the Golden Age found themselves in the middle of a shift from the old Homeric warrior virtues to the new and very different virtues of the democratic citizen of a city-state. The tension between them is part of what provoked the rise of philosophy itself. Or consider the work ethic. The work ethic was itself a relatively new set of virtues a few hundred years ago. It dominated the stage for a while. But now we are (perhaps!) moving beyond it to something new. Fifty or a hundred years ago, for example, no one would have used a term like "workaholic." Those character traits that we now think are a little obsessive would then have been widely admired. It's arguable that we are still obsessively overworked, and overwork ourselves, anyway, but—maybe partly for just this reason—the question of the work ethic is at least on the table.

Which virtues, in general, do you think stay constant, and which change? Why? And specifically, how do you think we will look back on the work ethic in yet another fifty or a hundred years? What will take its place? What in your view *should* take its place?

In November 1987, *Harper's* magazine commissioned seven major advertising firms to write ads promoting the Seven Deadly Sins: gluttony, envy, wrath, and all the rest. The results were disturbing—not so different, in some ways, from the ads we see every day. Have we turned even deadly sins into virtues? Is this a good idea?

THEORIZING VIRTUE

We've looked at several theories of the virtues. Would one of these theories be yours? Which—and why? Or perhaps you'd suggest some other and better theory?

MacIntyre argues that virtue theory is most plausible with regard to specific practices with clear "internal goods." Assuming this is true, how far do you think virtue theory can be generalized? Does human life as a whole have a clear and specific "internal good"? What is it? How can you establish this?

Utilitarians sometimes argue that virtue theory is radically incomplete if taken as an overall theory of ethics. We can say, with MacIntyre, that the "internal goods" of certain "practices" elevate those character traits that serve those goods. The utilitarians' question, though, would be: what makes those practices themselves good? We would not consider an effective concentration-camp guard to be a virtuous person, even though he or she served ably and well the "internal goods" of the concentration camp. No—we need some external standard, they conclude, by which to judge social practices as well. Utilitarians would argue that this standard can only be social utility. What do you think?

When roles with different "internal goods" conflict, how do we decide which takes priority? How I respond to a student's needs as a *teacher* may be very different than how I'd respond as a *friend*. If I can only respond in one way or the other, which should it be? Often the question of which role takes priority lies at the very core of the ethical issue in the first place. Can you make such a decision without sliding back into utilitarianism? How?

PRACTICING LARGE MIND

John Sullivan speaks of "small mind" and "large mind" as contrasting "ways of understanding and reacting to things" and calls our attention to two modes in which they can be seen at work: in the *language* we tend to use and in the *emotional charge* we experience.

Small-mindedness arises in speech when we say things like "I'm bad at X"— whatever X is. To shift to larger mind, we might rephrase the same description as something more like "I am a beginner at X." Notice how the second phrasing gives you a space, a possibility, that is decisively closed out in the first.

Small-mindedness arises in "emotional charge" when we find ourselves blaming others, complaining about the state of things, and excusing and justifying ourselves and perhaps our inaction. We separate ourselves from the situation, interpret it in a fixed and often narrowly self-serving way, and contribute nothing to resolving it. A shift to larger mind would be to ask instead how the same events or behavior might be interpreted in a more expansive way, what could be done about them, and where there might be room to move in the situation.

For practice, notice your own ways of understanding and relating to things as they arise in these two ways. Once you begin to see patterns, try to shift them toward larger mind. Can you tell a different story in a troubling but open-ended situation, as Harriet learned to do in Sullivan's example? When you are tempted by complaint or self-justification, try instead to express a sense of joint purpose and mutual appreciation. In general, Sullivan advises, try to "recognize 'story as story'—recognize when you take one point of view as the only point of view and get stuck there. Shift to another wider way of seeing and being, of speaking and emotionally responding."

It may be that your practice will first consist mostly of noticing what Sullivan calls "reactivity"—our tendency to fasten on to one story about things as if that is the one and only story that can be told. Later on, you might become more proactive: try out some new attitudes in advance, rather than waiting to see what daily forms of small-mindedness need expanding. Can you make a practice of greeting everyone in a fresh way? How about decisively viewing problems as something to work out together, separate from the people involved, rather than the other people *being* the problem?

NOTES

The opening list of virtues is selected from a still more extensive list at http://en.wikipedia.org/wiki/Virtue, accessed 11/19/06. One striking feature of this list is that every single virtue listed has its own linked page. Follow up some of these links, or search around a little, and all manner of intriguing websites come up (check it out!). It is not always clear who is putting up these sites or what their agenda is. Some of them seem to be designed mainly to sell certain books or services. But the very diversity and appeal of this material is telling.

Joseph Pieper's book is *The Four Cardinal Virtues* (University of Notre Dame Press, 1990). Interesting reading on changes in virtues is Maria Ossowska's book *Social Determinants of Moral Ideas* (University of Pennsylvania Press, 1970). On the work ethic, see Juliet Schor's now-classic book *The Overworked American* (Basic Books, 1993).

On Aristotle's ethics, a classic and accessible treatment is Henry Veatch, *Rational Man* (Indiana University Press, 1966). Aristotle's cited work is the *Nicomachean Ethics* (sometimes just titled *Ethics*). I use the W. D. Ross translation published by the Clarendon Press, 1908.

For Aquinas, see Anton Pegis, ed., *Introduction to St Thomas Aquinas* (Modern Library, 1948). Alasdair MacIntyre is quoted from *After Virtue* (University of Notre Dame Press, 1981), pages 178 and 204. Full texts of the Hippocratic Oath and the AMA Principles of Medical Ethics can found online, as can the Society of Professional Journalists' code at http://www.spj.org/ethics. For general resources and a detailed guide to the extensive (Western) philosophical literature on the virtues, see "Aristotle and Virtue Ethics" at the Ethics Updates site, http://ethics.sandiego.edu/.

On Confucianism and the virtues, see Philip Ivanhoe, *Confucian Moral Self-Cultivation* (Hackett, 2000). For Taoism, start with the *Tao Te Ching* itself. Zen master Dogen is cited from Hee-jin Kim, *Eihei Dogen, Mystical Realist* (Wisdom Publications, 2004), page 25. The story of the old man and the current shows up in many discussions of Taoism: this one I have from http://www.meaningoflife.i12.com/flow.htm, accessed 11/27/06. The selections from the *Tao* reprinted here are from Stephen Mitchell's fine translation, online at http://academic.brooklyn.cuny.edu/core9/phalsall/texts/taote-v3.html. For the translation of the title "Tao Te Ching," I draw on Alan Chan's entry "Laozi" in the Stanford Encyclopedia of Philosophy, online at http://plato.stanford.edu/entries/laozi/ and accessed 5/26/07.

William Bennett is cited from the preface to his collection *The Moral Compass* (Simon and Schuster, 1995), pages 12–13.

CHAPTER 10

The Ethics of Relationship

Chapter 6 outlined the family of relationship-centered values like this:

RELATIONSHIP

We are social beings as well as individuals. We are born to other humans, grow up in families, and take on traditions and heritages and communities. And we all live, in turn, in deep interrelation with the larger-than-human natural world. Values central to relationship are caring, participation, and community. Recognizing how much our communities make us who we are also calls forth not only gratefulness but also a responsibility to protect, sustain, and attend to them.

We can now explore the ethics of relationship in more detail.

CARE ETHICS

At the very beginning someone bore us into this world. We will never again be so intimately connected to anyone as we are to our own mothers for the nine months of pregnancy. There's a song by Stan Rogers in which he sings of birth as the time "when communion is lost forever, when a heart first beats alone." It's a sad song. His larger point is that even though we later may become very invested in separateness, on some deep level we still remember and yearn for that primal "communion."

Mothers and others cared for us through all those years of babyhood and childhood. Without that care in our time of utter dependence, we simply wouldn't be here. Later, when we start becoming conscious of ourselves and our social relations and much of that early care for us is mostly lost to our memory, we also feel an urge to be separate. That's the developmental project of late childhood. Our culture also stresses independence—indeed we learn to practically identify it with personhood itself—and the result is that some people never recover a sense of how deeply we are bound up with others. Still, for most people, separateness is only a phase that doesn't last long. Friends come and go but soon some grow close and stick around. You fall in love. Teammates claim your care and concern. Co-workers do the same. Causes arise, and there are others with you in religious groups or building houses or fighting wars. You have children, maybe, yourself.

There is a dual point here. First, we are deeply, inescapably, and permanently in relationship with particular other people, and in a way that goes far beyond the relatively distant sort of relationships that seem to be the main models for the other types of moral values. Sure, we have moral and legal obligations to our children (and parents!) as well as to co-workers and fellow soldiers and so on. But these obligations do not truly get to the core of the values at stake.

Second, relationships like these evoke deep *feelings,* and it is these feelings that ground the deepest values in turn. Sometimes it is the helpless love of a parent for a child. (A line from the writer Elizabeth Stone: "Having a child is to decide forever to have your heart go walking outside your body.") Sometimes it is the chosen love of a life partner; sometimes love of friends or care for long-time fellow workers—but in any case feeling is key.

You'll remember that Martin Buber and Emmanuel Levinas lay out "philosophies of encounter." People can certainly emerge in certain extraordinary experiences as unique and precious others. Yet the suggestion here is that this is only one aspect of our relation to others. There is also an earthier way in which we come to care for and love some of those people close to us. It's extraordinary in its own way but at the same time totally ordinary too. Care does grow for those who care for us and for those with whom we work and act together. Everyday love is crucial to ethics too.

AN ETHICS THAT HONORS FEELINGS

The formal tradition in ethics, as so far sketched, does not speak much of love, or indeed of feeling in general. Kant even argued that feelings distort ethics. We need to act morally toward others out of a sense of duty and obligation, he argued, and not on the basis of feelings. After all, feelings can vary between people and for ourselves from moment to moment as well, but morality claims us "categorically," as Kant says: all of us and all the time. We should tell the truth, comfort the sick, speak up for downtrodden, even if we don't especially feel care, let alone love, for them.

These are not the best arguments. For one thing, in terms of constancy, feelings often greatly outdo the intellectual convictions to which Kant appeals. Feelings certainly motivate a great deal of moral action.

It might be better to conclude that care and connection need development and cultivation, just like the virtues. Indeed, they *are* virtues. Certainly the practice of sustaining relationship has "internal goods," to use Alasdair MacIntyre's term. The virtues, in this view, will be those traits that sustain and deepen relationship, enable us to raise children well, keep love strong, and build comradeship and solidarity. Thus the psychologist Carol Gilligan describes an "Ethics of Care," rooted once again in a specific view of the (or *a*) world, this time "a world of relationships and psychological truths where an awareness of the connection between people gives rise to a recognition of a responsibility for one another, a perception of the need for response. Seen in this light, morality arises from a recognition of relationship." Believing in "the restorative activity of care," as Gilligan puts it, we come to

> see the actors in [moral] dilemma[s] arrayed not as opponents in a contest of rights but as members of a network of relationships on whose continuation they all depend. Consequently [the] solution to the dilemma[s] lies in activating the network by communication, . . . strengthening rather than severing connections.

Key virtues thus include perceptiveness, imagination, and sensitivity; skill in responding and nurturing; patience and creativity; and acceptance. Morality itself emerges, in the philosopher Margaret Walker's lovely words, as (in part) "a collection of perceptive, imaginative, appreciative, and expressive skills and capacities which put us and keep us in contact with the realities of ourselves and specific others."

CARE ETHICS AND MORAL DEVELOPMENT

Gilligan began her work with the moral development research of the psychologist Lawrence Kohlberg. Kohlberg had concluded that most children go through several markedly different stages of moral reasoning. They start, he thought, with obedience to authority figures such as parents or teachers. Self-interest then begins operating. At its middle stages, moral thinking becomes "conventional," meaning that children are oriented toward social approval, and later toward the law and responding to the obligations of duty. Kohlberg's final stages of moral thinking are initially a kind of utilitarianism, an eye for the good of society as a whole. Those few who reach the height of ethical maturity then move to an ethics of universal principles.

Gilligan noticed some striking omissions in this research. For one thing, Kohlberg's interviewers initially talked only to boys—but he generalized his results to girls as well. When they did look at girls, the girls were judged by the boys' standards and tended to score lower in moral development. But what if they were actually developing *in a different way?* When Gilligan began using the same dilemmas with girls, she got very different results. As Eve Browning Cole puts it,

> Gilligan's results... showed a pattern of moral reasoning among the women studied which diverged from [Kohlberg's] paradigm in several distinct ways. First, women reasoning their way through a moral dilemma tended to focus on the specific personal relationships within which the principal agents find themselves situated. They pondered... the nature and character of these relationships, tending to derive relevant ethical considerations from specific connectedness among persons. Second, they reasoned that relationships generate responsibilities and that these responsibilities might be quite specific within the relationship.... [T]here was thus an emphasis on... the concrete details of a moral situation, as opposed to its universalizable or general features, which figure so prominently in mainstream ethical discourse.

Gilligan pointed out that this approach—working within particular relationships and attending to the feelings that constitute them—is every bit as appropriate an ethics as the more familiar "male" model. Many times, surely, it is more appropriate. To construct a seemingly empirical theory of ethics built from the first on devaluing this "different voice" is, for one thing, sexist. It is also just plain bad science. We need a more inclusive view.

Gilligan produced her own stage theory of moral development. On Gilligan's model too, moral thinking begins with selfishness. The "conventional" middle stage, however, is the opposite of selfishness: self-sacrifice. The more mature final stages find a balance between self and other, including the growing sense that self and other are intertwined—an ethics, once again, of relationship.

From Caring

NEL NODDINGS

Since Gilligan's groundbreaking book *In a Different Voice* (Harvard University Press, 1982), Care Ethics has become a major project of feminist philosophers and other thinkers intent on recovering ethics in a relational key. Nel Noddings is prominent among them. A teacher and philosopher of education now retired from Stanford University after a long and varied career—also the mother of ten children!—she is author, most influentially, of *Caring: A Feminine Approach to Ethics and Moral Education,* along with other books. This essay is a selection from the introduction.

From Nel Noddings, *Caring* (University of California Press, 1984), pp. 1–6.

Ethics, the philosophical study of morality, has concentrated for the most part on moral reasoning. Much current work, for example, focuses on the status of moral predicates and, in education, the dominant model presents a hierarchical picture of moral reasoning. This emphasis gives ethics a contemporary, mathematical appearance, but it also moves discussion beyond the sphere of actual human activity and the feeling that pervades such activity. Even though careful philosophers have recognized the difference between "pure" or logical reason and "practical" or moral reason, ethical argumentation has frequently proceeded as if it were governed by the logical necessity characteristic of geometry. It has concentrated on the establishment of principles and that which can be logically derived from them. One might say that ethics has been discussed largely in the language of the father: in principles and propositions, in terms such as justification, fairness, justice. The mother's voice has been silent. Human caring and the memory of caring and being cared for, which I shall argue form the foundation of ethical response, have not received attention except as outcomes of ethical behavior....

The view to be expressed here is a feminine view. This does not imply that all women will accept it or that men will reject it; indeed, there is no reason why men should not embrace it. It is feminine in the deep classical sense—rooted in receptivity, relatedness, and responsiveness. It does not imply either that logic is to be discarded or that logic is alien to women. It represents an alternative to present views, one that begins with the moral attitude or longing for goodness and not with moral reasoning. It may indeed be the case that such an approach is more typical of women than of men, but this is an empirical question I shall not attempt to answer.

Women...enter the practical domain of moral action through a different door, so to speak. It is not the case, certainly, that women cannot arrange principles hierarchically and derive conclusions logically. It is more likely that we see this process as peripheral to, or even alien to, many problems of moral action. Faced with a hypothetical moral dilemma, women often ask for more information. We want to know more, I think, in order to form a picture more nearly resembling real moral situations. Ideally, we need to talk to the participants, to see their eyes and facial expressions, to receive what they are feeling. Moral decisions are, after all, made in real situations; they are qualitatively different from the solution of geometry problems. Women can and do give reasons for their acts, but the reasons often point to feelings, needs, impressions, and a sense of personal ideal rather than to universal principles and their application. We shall see that, as a result of this "odd" approach, women have often been judged inferior to men in the moral domain.

...[P]ractical ethics from the feminine view is very different from the utilitarian practical ethics of, say, Peter Singer. While both of us would treat animals kindly and sensitively, for example, we give very different reasons for our consideration. I must resist his charge that we are guilty of "speciesism" in our failure to accord rights to animals, because I shall locate the very wellspring of ethical behavior in human affective response. Throughout our discussion of ethicality we shall remain in touch with the affect that gives rise to it. This does not mean that our discussion will bog down in sentiment, but it is necessary to give appropriate attention and credit to the affective foundation of existence. Indeed, one who attempts to ignore or to climb above the human affect at the heart of ethicality may well be guilty of romantic rationalism. What is recommended in such a framework simply cannot be broadly applied in the actual world.

I shall begin with a discussion of caring. What does it mean to care and to be cared for? The analysis will occupy us at length, since relation will be taken as ontologically basic and the caring relation as ethically basic. For our purposes, "relation" may be thought of as a set of ordered pairs generated by some rule that describes the affect—or subjective experience—of the members.

Taking *relation* as ontologically basic simply means that we recognize human encounter and affective response as a basic fact of human existence. As we examine what it means to care and to be cared for, we shall see that both parties contribute to the relation; my caring must be somehow completed in the other if the relation is to be described as caring.

The focus of our attention will be upon how to meet the other morally. Ethical caring, the relation in which we do meet the other morally, will be described as arising out of natural caring—that relation in which we respond as one-caring out of love or natural inclination. The relation of natural caring will be identified as the human condition that we, consciously or unconsciously, perceive as "good." It is that condition toward which we long and strive, and it is our longing for caring—to be in that special relation—that provides the motivation for us to be moral. We want to be *moral* in order to remain in the caring relation and to enhance the ideal of ourselves as one-caring.

It is this ethical ideal, this realistic picture of ourselves as one-caring, that guides us as we strive to meet the other morally. Everything depends upon the nature and strength of this ideal, for we shall not have absolute principles to guide us. Indeed, I shall reject ethics of principle as ambiguous and unstable. Wherever there is a principle, there is implied its exception and, too often, principles function to separate us from each other. We may become dangerously self-righteous when we perceive ourselves as holding a precious principle not held by the other. The other may then be devalued and treated "differently." Our ethic of caring will not permit this to happen. We recognize that in fear, anger, or hatred we will treat the other differently, but this treatment is never conducted ethically. Hence, when we must use violence or strategies on the other, we are already diminished ethically. Our efforts must, then, be directed to the maintenance of conditions that will permit caring to flourish. Along with the rejection of principles and rules as the major guide to ethical behavior, I shall also reject the notion of universalizability. Many of those writing and thinking about ethics insist that any ethical judgment—by virtue of its *being* an ethical judgment—must be universalizable; that is, it must be the case that, if under conditions X you are required to do A, then under sufficiently similar conditions, I too am required to do A. I shall reject this emphatically. First, my attention is not on judgment and not on the particular acts we perform but on how we meet the other morally. Second, in recognition of the feminine approach to meeting the other morally—our insistence on caring for the other—I shall want to preserve the uniqueness of human encounters. Since so much depends on the subjective experience of those involved in ethical encounters, conditions are rarely "sufficiently similar" for me to declare that you must do what I must do. There is, however, a fundamental universality in our ethic, as there must be to escape relativism. The caring attitude, that attitude which expresses our earliest memories of being cared for and our growing store of memories of both caring and being cared for, is universally accessible. Since caring and the commitment to sustain it form the universal heart of the ethic, we must establish a convincing and comprehensive picture of caring at the outset.

Another outcome of our dependence on an ethical ideal is the emphasis upon moral education. Since we are dependent upon the strength and sensitivity of the ethical ideal—both our own and that of others—we must nurture that ideal in all of our educational encounters. I shall claim that we are dependent on each other even in the quest for personal goodness. How good *I* can be is partly a function of how *you*—the other—receive and respond to me. Whatever virtue I exercise is completed, fulfilled, in you. The primary aim of all education must be nurturance of the ethical ideal.

To accomplish the purposes set out above, I shall strike many contrasts between masculine and feminine approaches to ethics and education and, indeed, to living. These are not intended to divide men and women into opposing camps. They are meant, rather, to show how great the chasm is that already divides the masculine and feminine in each of us and to suggest that we enter a dialogue of genuine dialectical nature in order to achieve an ultimate transcendence of the masculine and feminine in moral matters.

An important difference between an ethic of caring and other ethics that give subjectivity its proper place is its foundation in relation. The philosopher who begins with a supremely free consciousness—an aloneness and emptiness at the heart of existence—identifies *anguish* as the basic human affect. But our view, rooted as it is in relation, identifies *joy* as a basic human affect. When I look at my child—even one of my grown children—and recognize the fundamental relation in which we are each defined, I often experience a deep and overwhelming joy.

> It is the recognition of and longing for relatedness that form the founda-
> tion of our ethic, and the joy that accompanies fulfillment of our caring
> enhances our commitment to the ethical ideal that sustains us as one-
> caring.

ETHICS AND COMMUNITY

A community is some linked set of others with whom we have some compelling commonality. Maybe we share interests or work; maybe we share political convictions; maybe we live in the same neighborhood or country. There
are faith communities, sports communities, online communities, and all
sorts of others. Each of us, in fact, belongs to many such communities. All of
us belong to at least the largest and most inclusive ones.

Here, then, ethical relationship is with a *group* of others: and with the associated institutions, like churches or professions or organizations or forms
of governance, all the way up to ethnic and other kinds of heritages. Some are
voluntary. Take a certain job, move to a certain area, and you more or less automatically acquire a set of well-defined links to others. You may join political
or religious organizations. You may also leave them. But other communities
you are simply born into, and leaving is not an option: ethnic communities,
for instance, or a religious heritage, even if you decide to give it up or change
later; and of course the current global "community"—for as co-inhabitants
of this fragile ecosphere we are also and inescapably linked with every other
human on the planet.

Such communities literally make us who we are. The educator Janie
Ward writes of African Americans:

> Throughout our history, from plantation proverbs to freedom songs, we
> have grappled with questions about who we are as an African people and
> where we are headed. The moral lessons we've learned and passed on have
> had to be culturally specific, responsive to the effects of injustice that have
> circumscribed our lives, and respectful of the care, connectedness, and in-
> terdependence that assured our survival through the best and the worst of
> times.

Such relationships are "culturally specific," she says—distinct from (though
surely overlapping with) the legacies of other peoples—but still, crucial to the
identities of individual African Americans.

In fact, identity is *always* communal in essential ways. We cannot even
imagine being without a specific history, without family or a civic community in a broader sense, or even without a place. For most of human history,
people lived in groups and communities so small that everyone's name and
personal history were known to almost everyone they might encounter. In
modern times, most of us typically have much more anonymous encounters,

but we still share communal identities such as ethnicity or politics or even allegiances to certain soccer or hockey teams.

Even speaking a particular language is a form of community. A language is an automatic link with any other speaker of the same tongue. Halfway around the world, maybe, think of running into someone who speaks your language, when maybe you haven't heard it out of anyone else's mouth for months. A language is also a rather amazing link with everyone in the past—literally millions and millions of people—who made that tongue what it is today, so that it could be passed on to you as such a supple and live cultural legacy. This kind of community is so basic as to often be invisible, but it is no less essential for all that.

IMPLICATIONS

Gratefulness follows, for starters. What precious and immense legacies we all inherit! Countless people over long stretches of time have helped make me what I am—what a gift.

Second, right away, in consequence, a commitment also follows to do our part to respect and sustain our communities and their core values. Ward, for example, speaks immediately and emphatically of the need to be "respectful of the care, connectedness, and interdependence that assured our survival through the best and the worst of times."

It's not that community values are necessarily trump. Here as in many places, some kind of balance is required. To take the example of African-American community ethics once again, listen to the words of Vanessa Siddle Walker and John R. Snarey in their book *Race-ing Moral Formation*:

> [T]hose who follow African American ethics refuse to starkly dichotomize self and community. To care for the self is to care for the group, and to care for the group is to care for the self.... [This is a] moral legacy of the West African heritage of most African Americans. The successful realization of a balanced community-and-individual ethic produces the fruit of *uplift*—the enhancement of the community and the valuing of the individual's diverse gifts.... [T]he weakness that would result from a large imbalance is either *one-sided selfishness*, acting according to one's needs and interests without any balanced regard for the larger community; or *one-sided self-sacrifice*, the obliteration or denial of one's own interests, needs, or selfhood for the sake of "more worthy" community or cause.

Notice also the parallels to Gilligan's model of moral development here: again, on another level now, the struggle of moral maturation is to find a balanced way between and beyond both self-seeking and self-sacrifice. It also sounds rather like Aristotle's doctrine of the Mean!

Finally, beyond both gratefulness and respect, it is our challenge to *contribute* in turn to the communities that form and sustain us. Ethnic or religious heritages are ours to carry on. The work of a profession; sustaining, adjusting, or improving a form of government or a style of art; rebuilding a landscape or a place: all of these may call to us, and among them, somewhere, we will find our life's tasks.

Once again it's not that the current or the most visible or insistent community values are necessarily trump. One kind of contribution can even be loving resistance. If there are wrongs, it is our responsibility to right the wrongs. Still, this is *our* tradition, our country, our community. We are responsible for it even if we would rather sometimes walk away.

From "The Moral Foundations of an African Culture"

KWASI WIREDU

Community is always particular. We are linked with *these* specific others in thus-and-such a way. Even in making the very general and introductory points just above, I have needed to draw on a specific relationship, in this case African-American ethnic identity. To carry the point further we must get still more specific. These passages by Kwasi Wiredu (b. 1931), a widely read contemporary Ghanaian philosopher who teaches in the United States, paint a rich picture of an ethical life deeply constituted by family and communal relations, in his own people, the Akan of West Africa. Wiredu both shows us an explicitly communal ethics from the inside, so to speak, and shows us a few of the deep historical and cultural roots of African-*American* ethical practice in turn.

Akan society is of a type in which the greatest value is attached to communal belonging. And the way in which a sense of communal belonging is fostered in the individual is through the concentrated stress on kinship identity.... Thus conceived, a human person is essentially the centre of a thick set of concentric circles of obligations and responsibilities matched by rights and privileges revolving round levels of relationships irradiating from the consanguinity of household kith and kin, through the "blood" ties of lineage and clan, to the wider circumference of human familyhood based on the common possession of the divine spark....

From Kwasi Wiredu, "The Moral Foundations of an African Culture," *Person and Community: Ghanaian Philosophical Studies* I (Center for Research in Values Philosophy, 1992), pages 193–206.

...[T]he Akan philosophy of life...is made explicit in the maxim, *Onipa hia moa,* meaning, by way of first approximation, "A human being needs help." The intent of the maxim, however, is not just to observe a fact, but also to prescribe a line of conduct. The imperative here is carried by the word *hia,* which in this context also has a connotation of entitlement: a human being deserves, ought, to be helped.

This imperative is born of an acute sense of the essential dependency of the human condition. The idea of dependency may even be taken as a component of the Akan conception of a person. "A human being," says a noted Akan proverb, "is not a palm tree so as to be self-sufficient" (*Onipa nye abe na ne ho ahyia ne ho*). Indeed, at birth a human being is not only not self-sufficient but also radically self-insufficient, if one may be permitted the expression: he/she is totally dependent on others. In due course, through growth and acculturation, acquired skills and abilities will reduce this dependency but will never eliminate it completely. Self-reliance is, of course, understood and recommended by the Akans, but its very possibility is predicated upon this ineliminable residue of human dependency. Human beings, therefore, at all times, in one way or another, directly or indirectly, need the help of their kind.

One very standard situation in Akan life in which this truth was continually illustrated was in traditional agriculture. As hinted earlier, this was generally based on smallholdings worked by individual farmers and their households. In such a mode of production recurrent stages were easily foreseeable where the resources of any one farmer would be insufficient to accomplish a necessary task efficiently—be it the initial clearing of the ground or the scooping out of, say, cocoa beans from great heaps of pods. At such moments, all that was necessary was for one to send word to one's neighbours indicating the time, place, and the nature of the help needed. Very much as day follows night, the people would assemble at the right time at the indicated place with their own implements of work and together help get the job done speedily and with almost festive enthusiasm, in full and warranted conviction that when their turn came the same gesture would be returned in exactly the same spirit. Anybody who availed himself of the benefits of this system and yet dragged his feet when the call came from others was liable to be convicted, at the bar of public opinion, of such fathomless degeneracy as to be branded a social outcast. The type of mutual aid here discussed probably occurs in varying intensities in rural communities all over the world, but in traditional Akan society it was so much and so palpably a part of working experience that the Akans actually came to think of life (*obra*) as one continuous drama of mutual aid (*nnoboa*). *Obra ye nnoboa:* "Life is mutual aid," according to an Akan saying....

...[K]inship support...is of the highest importance in the Akan communal set-up, for it is the basis of the sense of belonging which gives the individual much of his/her psychological stability (this, incidentally, is why a traveller bereft of it strikes the Akan so forcefully as a sad case). It is also, conversely, the basis of a good proportion of the obligations in terms of which the individual's moral standing is assessed. The smallest and most intimate Akan kinship unit is the matrilineal household. This includes a person's mother and his/her mother's children, his/her mother's sisters and brothers, the children of the mother's sisters, and, at the top, the grandmother. It is instructive to observe that the English words aunt and cousin fail to capture the depth of kinship feelings corresponding to the relations of mother's sister and mother's sister's children respectively, in spite of their mechanical correctness as translations. In the Akan language the words for mother and mother's children are the same as for mother's sister and mother's sister's children. Since the relationships noted already comprehend quite a sizeable community, especially if the grandmother concerned has been even averagely fertile, this guarantees that in a traditional setting an Akan child begins life with quite a large sense of belonging and a broad sweep of sympathies.

The next extension of the circle of the kinship relations just described brings us to the level of the lineage. Here the *basic unit* consists of a person's grandmother and her children and grandchildren, together with the grandmother's brothers and sisters and the children and grandchildren of her sisters. This unit quickly swells with the culturally legitimate addition of a grandmother's maternal "cousins" and their descendants. From the point of view of a person's civic existence, this is the most significant circle of relations, for it was through the head of the lineage that, in traditional times, a person had his/her political representation. The lineage, as can easily be imagined, is a quite considerable group of people, but it is small in comparison with the maximal limit of kinship grouping, which is the set of all the people descending from one woman. The latter is the clan. For a quick idea of magnitude, consider that the Akans, now numbering in the region of seven million, trace their collective ancestry to seven women. Patently, individual Akans will never know all their relatives, but they can rest assured that they have a million of them.

THE EXPANDING CIRCLE

Finally, we are invited also to recognize how deeply we are related to the rest of the Earth and Earth's creatures. Until now this chapter has spoken of "community" in a wholly human sense, and we've been acting like this is the most natural thing in the world. But in fact it is not natural at all. We are also inescapably linked with the Earth: with other living creatures and with the all-encompassing ecosphere. Any ethics of relationship must recognize the *Earth* community as well.

We know that *egocentrism* is a spectacularly narrow-minded way of living. But what about our still-easy assumption that ethics goes only as far as the human—as if the entire world apart from us were simply a means to our ends, merely a collection of resources, morally irrelevant? Call this *anthropocentrism:* a kind of human-centeredness exactly parallel to self-centeredness. It's species-egoism, as it were. It's also a kind of blindness:

> When you narrow down...and act on the premise "What interests me is me, or my organization, or my species," you chop off consideration of other loops of the loop structure [that includes your loop]. You decide that you want to get rid of the by-products of human life and that Lake Erie will be a good place to put them. You forget that the...system called Lake Erie is a part of *your* wider...system—and that if Lake Erie is driven insane, its insanity is incorporated in the larger system of *your* thought and experience.

Contrariwise, to try to live in harmony with larger natural systems is not to serve narrow ends. "Sanity" means being in relation, indeed what Buddhists call "right relation": it's sane, it's right, and it's *rich:* the natural world becomes more like a companion and less like a resource or adversary or stage scenery.

The Lakota people have a phrase used to begin and close many ceremonies. It has been translated into English as "all my relations," and its point is to highlight the interrelatedness of all life on Earth—not only in the sense of global interdependency, but also in the specific sense that each species is a relative, a member of our family, quite genuinely and literally a *relation.* We're in *community* with them (too).

Animals, for instance. In Chapter 6 you read Alice Walker's story of her relation to one animal—a relation that prompted her to rethink her (and our) relations with many other animals, as well as with oppressed groups and peoples. Animals surround us, work with us, sing in the trees all around us or swim in the same seas, romp through our dreams and stories and myths and often enough through our houses and daily lives too. The human ecologist Paul Shepard even wrote a book subtitled *How Animals Made Us Human.* Just as with our other relations, life in the community of other beings shapes our own identities as well.

And of course we are animals too! The whole point is that we have many of the same feelings, experiences, and needs as other creatures. Utilitarians argue that therefore animal suffering counts morally just as the same suffering in us would count; but here suffering is not the whole story, either. Just like suffering in any other of our relations, it is morally bad partly because these are our *kin.*

And it's not just animals that "make us human." Truly, it's nature as a whole. This is, after all, the world we are built for. Its climates shaped our skins, its terrains shaped our bodies, its sounds and sights and textures shaped our senses, its mysteries shaped our minds. And all of this shaping continues. The magician-philosopher David Abram writes beautifully of the Pacific Northwest:

> Oak, madrone, Douglas fir, red-tailed hawk, serpentine in the sandstone, a certain scale to the topography, drenching rains in the winter, fog off-shore in the summer, salmon surging in the streams—all of these together make up a particular state of mind, a place-specific intelligence shared by all the humans that dwell therein, but also by the coyotes yapping in those valleys, by the bobcats and the ferns and the spiders, by all beings who live and make their way in that zone. Each place its own psyche. Each sky its own blue.

IMPLICATIONS

Again, gratefulness surely follows, for starters. Respect too, as toward those human communities that also nurture us. A commitment to attend to the world's needs and to respond. As the Swiss doctor and humanitarian Albert Schweitzer wrote:

> The great fault of all ethics hitherto has been that they believed themselves to have to deal only with the relations of man to man. In reality, however, the question is what is his attitude to the world and all life that comes within his reach. A man is ethical only when life, as such, is sacred to him, and when he devotes himself helpfully to all life that is in need of help.

Schweitzer acknowledges human ethics too—as a special case of the larger *life* ethic. "The ethic of the relation of man to man is not something apart by itself; it is only a particular relation which results from the universal one."

These are in fact huge questions. Philosophers have been asking them seriously for several decades now, and only the barest outlines of answers are emerging. Some, like Schweitzer, want to extend ethics to all of life—not only ourselves and all other animals but also trees and plants. Usually the argument is that all living things, even if not "aware," at least strive toward something, have a "good of their own," which can also be taken as a good by others.

Then again, we may need to go further. It's interesting that the Lakota, like many native peoples, do not divide living from nonliving forms as insistently as we do. They consider everything "living" to some extent. In any case, it may well be that rivers and mountains must also have a direct voice in our ethics: they too are "relations." Families of animals or plants—species—may also count in their own right.

For that matter, what about whole ecosystems, systems that include many different kinds of creatures and elements? Ecology is supposed to be a holistic science—surely moral value should attach to whole natural systems too, and not just to certain of their parts.

The ethical circle, in short, is expanding. Our survey of the ethics of relationship comes to rest, perhaps, with a maximally expansive understanding of relationship. And why not? "All our relations"!

From "The Land Ethic"

ALDO LEOPOLD

Aldo Leopold (1887–1948)—forester, educator, philosopher, farmer—is widely considered the father of the contemporary American environmental movement. In this famous essay from the end of his book *Sand County Almanac,* he arrives at an explicit environmental ethics.

Notice how Leopold roots human communities in the character of the land they inhabit. Note also, near the end, Leopold's famous criterion for right action: "A thing is right when it tends to preserve the integrity, stability, and beauty of the biotic community. It is wrong when it tends otherwise."

When god-like Odysseus returned from the wars in Troy, he hanged all on one rope a dozen slave-girls of his household whom he suspected of misbehavior during his absence. This hanging involved no question of propriety. The girls were property. The disposal of property was then, as now, a matter of expediency, not of right and wrong.

Concepts of right and wrong were not lacking from Odysseus' Greece: witness the fidelity of his wife through the long years before at last his black-prowed galleys clove the wine-dark seas for home. The ethical structure of that day covered wives, but had not yet been extended to human chattels. During the three thousand years which have since elapsed, ethical criteria have been extended to many fields of conduct, with corresponding shrinkages in those judged by expediency only.

THE ETHICAL SEQUENCE

This extension of ethics, so far studied only by philosophers, is actually a process in ecological evolution. Its sequences may be described in ecological as well as in philosophical terms. An ethic, ecologically, is a limitation on freedom of action in the struggle for existence. An ethic, philosophically, is a differentiation of social from anti-social conduct. These are two definitions of one thing. The thing has its origin in the tendency of

---

By permission of Oxford University Press.

interdependent individuals or groups to evolve modes of co-operation. The ecologist calls these symbioses. Politics and economics are advanced symbioses in which the original free-for-all competition has been replaced, in part, by co-operative mechanisms with an ethical content....

The first ethics dealt with the relation between individuals; the Mosaic Decalogue is an example. Later accretions dealt with the relation between the individual and society. The Golden Rule tries to integrate the individual to society; democracy to integrate social organization to the individual.

There is as yet no ethic dealing with man's relation to land and to the animals and plants which grow upon it. Land, like Odysseus' slave-girls, is still property. The land-relation is still strictly economic, entailing privileges but not obligations.

The extension of ethics to this third element in human environment is, if I read the evidence correctly, an evolutionary possibility and an ecological necessity. It is the third step in a sequence. The first two have already been taken. Individual thinkers since the days of Ezekiel and Isaiah have asserted that the despoliation of land is not only inexpedient but wrong. Society, however, has not yet affirmed their belief. I regard the present conservation movement as the embryo of such an affirmation.

An ethic may be regarded as a mode of guidance for meeting ecological situations so new or intricate, or involving such deferred reactions, that the path of social expediency is not discernible to the average individual. Animal instincts are modes of guidance for the individual in meeting such situations. Ethics are possibly a kind of community instinct in-the-making.

THE COMMUNITY CONCEPT

All ethics so far evolved rest upon a single premise that the individual is a member of a community of interdependent parts. His instincts prompt him to compete for his place in that community, but his ethics prompt him also to co-operate (perhaps in order that there may be a place to compete for).

The land ethic simply enlarges the boundaries of the community to include soils, waters, plants, and animals, or collectively: the land.

This sounds simple: do we not already sing our love for and obligation to the land of the free and the home of the brave? Yes, but just what and whom do we love? Certainly not the soil, which we are sending helter-skelter down river. Certainly not the waters, which we assume have no function except to turn turbines, float barges, and carry off sewage. Certainly not the plants, of which we exterminate whole communities without batting an eye. Certainly not the animals, of which we have already extirpated many of the largest and most beautiful species. A land ethic of course cannot prevent the alteration, management, and use of these "resources," but it does affirm their right to continued existence, and, at least in spots, their continued existence in a natural state.

In short, a land ethic changes the role of Homo sapiens from conqueror of the land-community to plain member and citizen of it. It implies respect for his fellow-members, and also respect for the community as such.

In human history, we have learned (I hope) that the conqueror role is eventually self-defeating. Why? Because it is implicit in such a role that the conqueror knows, ex cathedra, just what makes the community clock tick, and just what and who is valuable, and what and who is worthless, in community life. It always turns out that he knows neither, and this is why his conquests eventually defeat themselves....

That man is, in fact, only a member of a biotic team is shown by an ecological interpretation of history. Many historical events, hitherto explained solely in terms of human enterprise, were actually biotic, interactions between people and land. The characteristics of the land determined the facts quite as potently as the characteristics of the men who lived on it.

Consider, for example, the settlement of the Mississippi valley. In the years following the Revolution, three groups were contending for its control: the native Indian, the French and English traders, and the American settlers. Historians wonder what would have happened if the English at Detroit had thrown a little more weight into the Indian side of those tipsy scales which decided the outcome of the colonial migration into the cane-lands of Kentucky. It is time now to ponder the fact that the cane-lands, when subjected to the particular mixture of forces represented by the cow, plow, fire, and axe of the pioneer, became bluegrass. What if the plant succession inherent in this dark and bloody ground had, under the impact of these forces, given us some worthless sedge, shrub, or weed? Would Boone and Kenton have held out? Would there have been any overflow into Ohio, Indiana, Illinois, and Missouri? Any Louisiana Purchase? Any transcontinental union of new states? Any Civil War?

Kentucky was one sentence in the drama of history. We are commonly told what the human actors in this drama tried to do, but we are seldom told that their success, or the lack of it, hung in large degree on the reaction of particular soils to the impact of the particular forces exerted by their occupancy. In the case of Kentucky, we do not even know where the bluegrass came from—whether it is a native species, or a stowaway from Europe.

Contrast the cane-lands with what hindsight tells us about the Southwest, where the pioneers were equally brave, resourceful, and persevering. The impact of occupancy here brought no bluegrass, or other plant fitted to withstand the bumps and buffetings of hard use. This region, when grazed by livestock, reverted through a series of more and more worthless grasses, shrubs, and weeds to a condition of unstable equilibrium. Each recession of plant types bred erosion; each increment to erosion bred a further recession of plants. The result today is a progressive and mutual deterioration, not only of plants and soils, but of the animal community subsisting thereon....

In short, the plant succession steered the course of history; the pioneer simply demonstrated, for good or ill, what successions inhered in the land. Is history taught in this spirit? It will be, once the concept of land as a community really penetrates our intellectual life.

THE LAND PYRAMID

...In the beginning, the pyramid of life was low and squat; the food chains short and simple. Evolution has added layer after layer, link after link. Man is one of thousands of accretions to the height and complexity of the pyramid. Science has given us many doubts, but it has given us at least one certainty: the trend of evolution is to elaborate and diversify the biota.

Land, then, is not merely soil; it is a fountain of energy flowing through a circuit of soils, plants, and animals. Food chains are the living channels which conduct energy upward; death and decay return it to the soil. The circuit is not closed; some energy is dissipated in decay, some is added by absorption from the air, some is stored in soils, peats, and long-lived forests; but it is a sustained circuit, like a slowly augmented revolving fund of life. There is always a net loss by downhill wash, but this is normally small and offset by the decay of rocks. It is deposited in the ocean and, in the course of geological time, raised to form new lands and new pyramids.

The velocity and character of the upward flow of energy depend on the complex structure of the plant and animal community, much as the upward flow of sap in a tree depends on its complex cellular organization. Without this complexity, normal circulation would presumably not occur. Structure means the characteristic numbers, as well as the characteristic kinds and functions, of the component species. This interdependence between the complex structure of the land and its smooth functioning as an energy unit is one of its basic attributes.

When a change occurs in one part of the circuit, many other parts must adjust themselves to it. Change does not necessarily obstruct or divert the flow of energy; evolution is a long series of self-induced changes, the net result of which has been to elaborate the flow mechanism and to lengthen the circuit. Evolutionary changes, however, are usually slow and local. Man's invention of tools has enabled him to make changes of unprecedented violence, rapidity, and scope....

THE OUTLOOK

It is inconceivable to me that an ethical relation to land can exist without love, respect, and admiration for land, and a high regard for its value. By value, of course, I mean something far broader than mere economic value; I mean value in the philosophical sense....

The "key-log" which must be moved to release the evolutionary process for an ethic is simply this: quit thinking about decent land-use as solely an economic problem. Examine each question in terms of what is ethically and esthetically right, as well as what is economically expedient. A thing is right when it tends to preserve the integrity, stability, and beauty of the biotic community. It is wrong when it tends otherwise.

It of course goes without saying that economic feasibility limits the tether of what can or cannot be done for land. It always has and it always will. The fallacy the economic determinists have tied around our collective neck, and which we now need to cast off, is the belief that economics determines all land use. This is simply not true. An innumerable host of actions and attitudes, comprising perhaps the bulk of all land relations, is determined by the land-users' tastes and predilections, rather than by his purse. The bulk of all land relations hinges on investments of time, forethought, skill, and faith rather than on investments of cash. As a land-user thinketh, so is he.

 **FOR REVIEW**

1. What is Care Ethics?
2. Contrast Kohlberg's and Gilligan's views of moral development.
3. According to Nel Noddings, what are some of the implications of an ethics of care?
4. What is a "community"?
5. What ethical difference does community make?
6. How does kinship shape morality for the Akan people?
7. What is "anthropocentrism"?
8. What is the "expanding circle"?
9. What do the Lakota mean by "all my relations"?
10. What is Aldo Leopold's criterion for the ultimate standard of right and wrong?

EXERCISES AND NOTES

SELF-REFLECTIONS

Think about the communities that are most present in your own life. Family, a team or other group perhaps, maybe a religious community. Maybe something as simple as your dormitory, which for many students is the first real experience of community, anyway with biologically unrelated people: the first time living so interdependently with a large number of people to whom there are responsibilities and with whom there is accountability as sharers of a common place. In dormitories, the entire residence hall may be affected by the actions of one member—what kind of ethics then follows?

Imagine actually being without any of these relationships. Can you picture it at all? Remember that it is not simply a matter of being a "loner," say: for loners still live in society, among other creatures, and so on (in fact to some degree they may consciously live *against* others, which paradoxically enough is a very strong form of relationship). Can you even begin to conceive yourself without a history or a people or a language? And again: if not, what follows?

Would you want to be a member of Akan society? Why or why not? Also: in what ways are our own societies more similar to the Akan than at first it may seem? And again: if there are specific ways in which you do think you'd like a community more like theirs, what are some ways within our own traditions to bring it about?

CARE ETHICS

Noddings calls care ethics a "feminine" approach and the "ethics of the mother." Hers is a gendered approach, in short, even though she is careful to say that care is available to men and fathers as well. She's even willing to speak of appropriately caring men as "mothers," which I guess is either remarkably gender-free or else even more insistently gendered. But this is an issue of contention among many feminists. Gilligan argues that both Care Ethics and the more traditional "Justice Ethics" are represented by *both* males and females: that is, that a full ethical toolbox needs to recognize both sets of values (and more) and that both care and justice are capacities we *all* have and use. To the extent that women are more associated with the care approach—and the empirical evidence is actually complex and unclear on this—it may be more due to social training and stereotype than, somehow, to "nature." What do you think?

ANIMALS ONE MORE TIME

Can we be in genuine community with animals and still eat them? Put this way, a "yes" answer may not seem promising, but it's also true that most traditional human cultures, all of whom ate at least some animals, believed that they did live in community with even those animals they hunted for food. Ted Kerasote, again, suggests a similar view in Chapter 6. So look at the question seriously. What could such a community look like? Is there a danger here of self-serving human "projection," or could there be good reason to think that the animals see it in something like the same way? Would elementary fairness also require that under certain conditions we allow ourselves to be food for *them*?

OLAM, 2274 CE

Imagine you are the crew of a starship, crash-landed on an unknown planet called Olam. You have no way to leave for a *long* time. You quickly discover that most of Olam is quite temperate and there are many suitable places for human habitation or other use (mining, agriculture, etc.) though of course all of them are currently occupied by Olamian ecosystems and species.

Olam has an enormous number of species. The exact number or even its order of magnitude cannot be guessed even by your best scientists. Tiny single-celled beings make up the bulk of its inhabitants, as measured by biomass. These beings live just about everywhere, from high in the atmosphere to the intestines of some of the animals to deep in some rocks. Next most common are the beetlelike species, of which there are several million different species at least. Other species range from the microscopic (one mm or less, like the single-celled beings just mentioned) through the enormous (there are several huge four-legged land species, up to three m high and seven m long, and sea creatures up to 30 m).

There are intelligent species on Olam too. Among them are sea organisms of different sorts, like a tenacled blobby creature with complex feelings (it changes colors with different emotions) and a seemingly high capacity for problem-solving. Some of our scientists have established contact with several species of large finned sea creatures with brains up to six times the size of human brains. They produce complex sound patterns, and it appears that some of these "songs" (100 million "bytes" in length—about like *The Odyessy*—sung in half an hour) are transmitted all the way around the planet through the oceans. Your scientists have held "jam sessions" with these animals using electric guitars and microphones lowered into the Olamian oceans. However, you have not been able to master their language, nor they yours—if indeed there *is* any way you might translate their "songs" at all.

There are two- and four-legged social species that show advanced social behaviors (fidelity, care, complex interaction patterns). Some of your crew members, perhaps out of homesickness, have adopted them as pets. (Actually, many of your survey crews have adopted Olamian "pets," everything from some flying and swimming creatures to large predators to snaky reptilelike tubular creatures. It all seems to work out quite well.) There are some vaguely humanoid animals that have a rudimentary language and also very tight social groupings. These creatures seem to be too disturbingly similar to humans to be made into pets, or perhaps they wouldn't tolerate it, but they have been fairly friendly and are certainly smart.

There are also vast communities of smaller organisms, sometimes containing millions of individual members, which appear to work together as a single unit. Indeed your scientists disagree about which is the real "organism": the individual insectlike creatures or their whole "hives." At any rate, it appears that on Olam intelligence can exist on several levels at once. Some scientists even speculate that *all* life on Olam works together as a single unit, maintaining the optimal atmospheric and other conditions for life itself.

Again, this is only a small sampling of Olamian species. Some of these species consume each other for food. Many other species eat the plants, trees, or even the rocks. Humans could survive and thrive on a diet of either Olamian plants, animals, or both. Certain Olamian animals could also live on humans.

As you take stock of your situation, ask yourselves how you should relate to Olam. Are there moral limits to what you should do here? Should you take into account only your own good, or do the goods of some of Olam's species or ecosystems or perhaps the planet itself also have a claim on you? As you continue to talk, suppose you find yourselves divided into five basic views:

A: Might makes right. We should take and use anything and everything on Olam. No moral considerations apply. Tough luck to the other species; lucky for us they're here to use. God probably planned it this way from the start so they'd all be here when we crash-landed.

B: Only we humans count morally—morality only came to Olam with us, as it were—but we need to take a little care not to ruin the planet for ourselves and our children. So we need to keep our consumption and exploitation somewhat within bounds, but of course only where necessary to serve our own future happiness. It also wouldn't hurt to try to understand Olam a little better. If it's anything like Earth, it's an incredibly complex place with a lot of hidden surprises.

C: We do need to take some care for Olam and its species in their own right. Maybe we're the most important species here but the other species have some valid claims too. They are ancient, beautiful, mysterious: this planet is bigger than us, even though—now that we're here—we're at the moral center.

D: We are only one species among all the others. Rightly understood, all species are at their own "centers." Nothing special about us—or rather, something special about *all*. Thus, we should seek to become part of Olam's larger community of life. We should seek to establish only limited colonies, and only where we will cause the least harm. We should also try harder to make contact with the intelligent life-forms on Olam.

E: We have no right to be here at all. We are alien invaders in a world that is complete without us and does not want us. We should write a statement explaining what we are doing, in case anyone ever finds the wreckage of our starship, and then commit mass suicide (of course in an ecologically responsible way).

Which view strikes you as the most reasonable? Why? How would you defend your view against the others?

NOTES

Carol Gilligan is quoted from *In a Different Voice* (Harvard University Press, 1982, 1993), pages 30–31. The quote in the text about Gilligan's findings is from Eve Browning Cole's *Philosophy and Feminist Criticism: An Introduction* (Paragon House, 1993), pages 105–106. Against Kant's dismissal of the emotions, see Lawrence Blum, *Friendship, Altruism, and Morality* (Routledge, 1982). A fine collection on Gilligan's work is Eva Feder Kittay and Diana Meyers, eds., *Women and Moral Theory* (Rowman and Littlefield, 1987). For a variety of feminist views of ethics (not all of them "care" ethics, either), see Virginia Held, *Justice and Care: Essential Readings in Feminist Ethics* (Westview, 1995).

Janie Ward is quoted from Gilligan and Ward, "Foreword," *Race-ing Moral Formation: African American Perspectives on Care and Justice* (Teacher's College Press, 2004), page xi. Vanessa Siddle Walker and John R. Snarey are cited from the same book's "Introduction: Race Matters in Moral Formation," pages 10–11, and "Conclusion: Primary Values and Developing Virtues of African American Ethics," pages 136–137. In the same book, see also Walker's essay with Renarta Tompkins, "Caring in the Past: The Case of a Southern Segregated African American School," pages 77–92. Classic in this area is Patricia Hill Collins, *Black Feminist Thought* (Routledge, revised 10th anniversary edition, 2000).

In the last section, the first quote is from Gregory Bateson, "Pathologies of Epistemology," in *Steps to an Ecology of Mind* (Chandler Publishing Company, 1972), page 484. David Abram is cited from his book *The Spell of the Sensuous* (Pantheon, 1996), page 262. Albert Schweitzer is cited from his *Out of My Life and Thought* (Holt, Rinehart, and Winston, 1949), pages 158–159. Aldo Leopold's essay "The Land Ethic" can be found at the very end of *A Sand County Almanac* (Oxford University Press, 1949, 1968)—the whole book is well worth the read—or online at http://www.luminary.us./leopold/almanac .html. For a general "next step" into environmental ethics, see my collection *An Invitation to Environmental Philosophy* (Oxford University Press, 1999); don't overlook its extensive annotated bibliography, "Going On."

Many thanks to Beth Raps for the early conceptualization and drafts of parts of this chapter.

III

ETHICAL PRACTICE

CHAPTER 11

Critical Thinking

Critical-thinking skills include the ability to generalize accurately and carefully, to look past vivid but possibly misleading examples and analogies, to use words carefully, and to be fair-minded and especially careful when our own favorite beliefs are under the microscope. All of these skills are as essential in ethics as in other realms of life. Let us begin our survey of skills for everyday ethical practice here.

FACTS AND SOURCES

Moral disagreements are much more than differences about values. Sometimes, indeed, we differ about values hardly at all. Many disagreements are about *facts:* about how to produce certain desired effects, for instance; or about what the causes of a current problem really are; or even just about simple and specific information that you could look up in ten minutes on the Web or in the library.

On some issues even a few simple facts can change everything. Discovering that there is still slavery in the world today—does that not make a difference for all of us? Facts about pollution, facts about who is actually "on welfare" and what kind of support they get, facts about the recovery prospects of comatose patients on life support, the actual history of the institution of marriage: all of these facts may transform our understanding of an issue and our ethical views about it.

And if even a few facts can change everything, then it is part of our responsibility to *seek out* the facts—honestly and persistently. We need to do more than simply assert what we think is "obvious" or cherry-pick a few facts to support what we already think. The real challenge is to find out more, to understand better, even if what we think may have to change as a result.

WHAT IS AT STAKE?

The first step is to get clear yourself just what is at stake. Clarify the underlying factual questions in pressing moral issues. Do children raised by gay couples grow up sexually confused (any more than the average adolescent)? Specifically what differences do the new sweatshop standards actually make? Is "restorative justice"—reconciliation rather than retribution—possible? How much do animals suffer in laboratories and slaughterhouses?

These questions are factual. That is, actual *evidence* is available. Many children have been raised by gay couples, for instance: no one is entitled to make assumptions about them without actually checking them out. Or again: specifically what differences *do* the new sweatshop standards actually make? It's not that hard to find out.

Check out even those claims you think are obvious. If they're central to serious moral disagreements, then they're pretty likely *not* obvious to others. In any case, you need actual evidence. Don't just appeal to what "everybody knows." Case in point: though American fear of crime is at an all-time high, and everyone seems to "know" that crime is skyrocketing, in fact it isn't. What's really increased dramatically is crime *coverage* on TV. The specific stories are no doubt true, but overall they create a false impression. Think, think, think!

GET THE FACTS

Two of my students disagreed vocally in class about the possibilities for radically more efficient and less polluting cars. One student argued that cars could easily be ten times more efficient than they are now. The other acknowledged that some hybrids now get two or three times the mileage of the average car, but argued that these are specialty cars—small, expensive, hard to get—and that still higher efficiency is just wishful thinking.

Well, I said, why don't you find out? No point in having a debate as if this were just a matter of opinion. There are facts of the matter, actual data: go find them.

They did. The next class we had actual facts before us. The average U.S. car, it turns out, gets around 27 miles per gallon right now. This figure drops to around 22 when you include SUVs and vans. It also turns out that there are indeed cars, right now, that get over 100 miles per gallon—adaptations of currently available hybrids, with a (separately developed) plug-in device for recharging the car batteries overnight from line current. The same vehicles *can* average over 200 mpg under the right conditions. On the other hand, the plug-in device is hard to get and expensive, so far, and not marketed with the original cars, which also must be driven just right to get the really high mileage.

So both students were right in a sense. *Nearly* ten times better mileage (200+ mpg) is possible, at least going by the overall passenger fleet average

(22 or so), *but* right now at least, it is a stretch. Even more importantly, though, when these students came back with what they'd learned (I assigned it as a joint project), the issue itself was transformed. It was no longer a contest of loud off-the-cuff opinions. They were no longer even disagreeing, for one thing. And with a few facts on hand, the ensuing discussion was far more productive. Why are the averages (and for that matter, federal standards) still so low, we asked. How might it be possible to make plug-in hybrids less costly and more widely available? What's likely to develop in the next few years? Carmakers wildly underestimated the demand for hybrids in the first place—should we believe them now, that most drivers won't be willing to plug in their cars at night? What if we took the opposite tack and tried to make plug-in cars more chic?

Some people defend the death penalty by arguing that it deters would-be murderers from committing murders. This is regularly said to be "obvious." But is it? How would you get *evidence* for or against a deterrence effect? You could compare states with the death penalty to states without it. You could compare U.S. murder rates when the death penalty was widely used to the murder rates when it was barred. These kinds of studies have been done. What do they say? You need to know before you can weigh in on this question.

One widely publicized study from the 1970s correlated the decline in capital punishment in the United States between 1933 and 1969 with a rise in murders, and therefore concluded that the death penalty does indeed deter murderers. On the other hand, most contemporary studies show the opposite. It's hard to know what to make of this. Mightn't other changes (that is, besides the decline in executions) between 1933 to 1969 better account for the increase in murder rates in that period? Another remarkable statistic is that states with the death penalty on average have *higher* murder rates than states that don't. Is it possible that the death penalty actually encourages some would-be murderers? Or is the murder rate now higher in death penalty states for reasons unrelated to the death penalty? (Or perhaps such states have enacted the death penalty *because* the murder rate is felt to be unacceptably high?)

So this question, in turns out, can't be answered with an emphatic yes or no. But we nonetheless learn something very useful: that the actual effects of the death penalty are uncertain. It's just *not* "obvious," either way. That's a fact too—and it makes a difference. For example, uncertainties about deterrence have pushed some defenders of the death penalty away from utilitarian arguments and toward arguments about justice. They have also prompted some utilitarians to come out against the death penalty.

The point is: it's possible to think intelligently about such issues in the face of complex or surprising evidence. But it's *not* possible to think intelligently about such issues if we don't look for the evidence at all. So look for it!

WHICH FACTS ARE RELEVANT?

by VANCE RICKS

With some difficult moral issues, it is pretty clear what the underlying factual questions are, even if we may not know where to find answers to them. Some of the examples so far in this chapter are like that: moral debates about how to control pollution, or about the deterrent effects of capital punishment, are ones where we know—or can easily figure out—what the main related factual debates are.

With other difficult moral issues, it may not be so easy to see what the main underlying factual questions are. For example, what factual questions are relevant to a dispute about the moral permissibility of same-sex marriages? Or the opening of adoption files? Or assisted suicide? If you find yourself struggling to figure out what the main "relevant" facts are, keep some of these tips in mind.

1. *Read and listen widely.* Sometimes the best way to see what facts are relevant to a particular moral issue is by reading or listening to a variety of people who are discussing that issue. What are some of the facts that those people bring up? What are some of the facts about which they agree or disagree?

In the case of same-sex marriage, for example, there are many types of facts that people on all sides of the question consider relevant. Many of those facts fall into one or more of these interrelated categories:

- Definitions: What does "marriage" mean? The definition of "marriage" is complicated by the fact that marriage can be a civil institution, a religious sacrament, or both. For example, it is possible for two (or more) people to be married as part of a religious ceremony, without having that marriage recognized by civil authorities. (The Conservative branch of Judaism, for example, recently voted to allow its congregations to sanction same-sex marriages. "Fundamentalist Mormon" churches allow polygynous (more than one wife) marriage. However, almost no US states recognize same-sex marriages, and no US state recognizes polygynous ones.) The converse—civilly sanctioned marriages that are not recognized by religious authorities—is also possible. (The Roman Catholic Church forbids divorce, and it considers a divorced person who remarries to be an adulterer.)

- Histories: What is the history of marriage, as an ideal and in practice, in this society and in other societies? Is it true that most human marriages throughout history have consisted of only one man and only one woman? Have most societies viewed marriage as an exclusive, lifelong partnership for the raising of children?

- Contemporary Law and Society: What percentage of people in our society live in a companionate but non-marital relationship? What sorts of tangible benefits—tax exemptions; health insurance; inheritance rights; and so on—are granted to married people and not to unmarried ones? What sorts of restrictions—by age, race, blood ties, mental disability—have been (or continue to be) placed on those seeking to get married?
- Consequences of Change: What will happen to marriage rates among opposite-sex couples if same-sex marriages are allowed? What will happen to rates of out-of-wedlock childbirth? What will happen to divorce rates?

2. *Approach the topic from the perspective of the different families of values.* Each family of values brings some features to the foreground and puts others into the background. The facts that are most relevant, from the perspective of someone holding one set of values, might not seem as relevant from the perspective of someone who is using a different "lens" of values.

Take capital punishment as an example. From a utilitarian point of view, the most relevant factual questions include: how do the violent crime rates in places without capital punishment compare to those with it? How much (in attorneys' fees, court costs, utilities, medical expenses) does capital punishment cost when compared to alternatives? How many people are actually sentenced to death, and for which crimes? How are executions actually carried out?

A virtue-centered ethics, by contrast, asks questions more like: What percentage of people convicted of serious crimes express remorse and offer to make amends? What psychological effects are reported by officials who conduct executions? What psychological effects are reported by the victims' loved ones when the criminal is executed—or when the criminal is imprisoned for life?

Likewise, a person-centered ethics might be most interested in how the courts have interpreted and balanced the rights of accused and convicted murderers, and whether sentencing guidelines require (or at least allow) consideration of impairments such as mental retardation, a childhood history of abuse, or psychological disturbances.

From the point of view of an ethics of relationship, finally, a vital question is: are there workable methods of punishment that also help restore community—that speak to the needs and possibilities of everyone involved?

3. *Be wary of "research by opinion poll."* When I ask my students which facts might be relevant to a given moral issue, often some reply that "what people's opinions are" is a relevant fact. And, they suggest, we can look for opinion polls or other statistical instruments to see what people's opinions actually are.

The question of people's opinions can indeed be approached as a question of fact. Polls (if well-conducted!) will give you some answers. And of course, as we consider whether to change or keep various social structures and institutions, or how to implement changes, it is important to take people's strongly held feelings and opinions into account. However, the real question is how well people's opinions are based upon the actual facts of the case. Mere opinion is not the end of the matter—only the beginning.

In other words, the real question is: What *should* we think? What information do people need—in particular, do *we* need—in order to have an *informed* opinion? Asking around, listening to others, and using the different families of moral values to guide your factual inquiries are vital to that outcome. This is a good point at which to reiterate central themes from Chapters 1 and 2 of this book: Careful, informed thinking is central to ethical deliberation and action!

SOURCES

Go to the source when you can. A useful all-around source is the *Statistical Abstract of the United States.* There are similar volumes for other countries. Federal budget data and automotive fuel economies are all easily accessible public information. You may need to search for books or articles on the topic that concerns you. Library catalogs and online databases have keyword-search systems: using them you can spotlight helpful sources very quickly. Ask for help when you need it.

Look for thorough and careful coverage of the issues in books or journal articles by well-informed people. Check to see who the authors are, and where they get *their* information. What are their qualifications? Are they relatively impartial? On global warming, for example, neither oil-industry publications nor environmental magazines are likely to give you the full story. The best sources are scientific journals, whose articles are carefully reviewed by other experts and where the norm is supposed to be scrupulous neutrality. (They will mostly tell you that global warming is quite real, though the causes and timetables are less clear.) Books published by academic presses or large trade presses are more reputable (more carefully and critically reviewed) than books from presses that only publish books promoting a specific point of view.

Cross-check sources, too, to see if other, independent sources agree. Are the experts sharply divided, or pretty much in agreement? If they're pretty much in agreement, theirs is the safe view to take. (At the very least, if you propose to take a different view, you have some serious explaining to do.) Where even the experts disagree, it is best to reserve judgment yourself too. Don't jump in with two feet where truly informed people tread with care. See if you can argue on some other grounds—or change your conclusions.

Watch the tone of your sources. Sources that make extreme or simplistic claims, or spend most of their time attacking and demeaning the other side, weaken their own claims. On most issues, reasonable disagreement is possible. Seek out sources that responsibly and thoroughly engage the arguments and evidence on the other side.

THE WEB

Used carefully, the Web is a great resource—the world at your fingertips. Many sites are very informative—I cite them myself repeatedly in this book. However, other sites are pure fabrication. Academic libraries and even most public libraries have at least some checks on the reliability of the books and other materials they collect, but there are very few (in fact, usually, there are *absolutely no*) checks on Internet sites. Any site can announce all it wants that it is objective or unbiased, but that hardly makes it so.

Even the flimsiest opinion site can dress itself up to look professional. Without a critical eye, then, the Web can seem just a mass of conflicting viewpoints and claims, and you are left adrift or misled. Sometimes the results can be lethal. I regularly run across hate sites disguised as "information," or deliberately misleading sites designed to snare unsuspecting and perhaps desperate people looking for the facts: sites on abortion, for example, that look sympathetic and objective but are designed to frighten pregnant young women away from even thinking about it. Sometimes these sites are downright lies, other times they merely cherry-pick their facts, which may be true enough, but they also leave aside others, so that they paint a false picture without telling an actual lie.

Do not rely on the Internet alone, then, unless you are dealing with an identifiable and independently reputable source—and don't rely on a website *at all* unless you have some idea of what its source is. Ask some questions of any site: who created this site? Why did they create it? What are their qualifications? What does it mean if they don't tell you? Again, cross-check sources, look for the most thorough and impartial sources you can, and never stop thinking!

INFERENCES

We make *inferences* when we move from certain facts to further conclusions. We may generalize from a few cases to many, or use a similar case to draw conclusions about a case that interests us, or notice the correlation of two events and conclude that one causes the other. Each kind of inference can be tricky.

GENERALIZATIONS

You or I will never know all sweatshop workers or women in the army or gay couples or rich people or poor people or drug users or businesspeople or environmental activists and so on and on—yet we may need to draw conclusions about them if we are to form an intelligent opinion about certain moral issues. So we have to *generalize:* we take a small sample—limited data, a few examples—to stand for the whole.

But we may generalize well, or poorly. A good generalization:

1. Rests on *specific* and *clear* examples.
2. Rests on *many* examples.
3. Rests on *representative* examples—that is, not all of one type—and offers enough *background information* to allow us to evaluate for ourselves how significant and representative the examples are.

We generalize, for example, about the conditions and nature of happiness. What does it take to be happy? There are striking examples of spectacularly rich people who have been spectacularly unhappy. Shall we therefore conclude that money cannot make you happy? (Or even, that it makes you unhappy?) People do:

> The misery of the rich is legendary. The late oil billionaire J. Paul Getty was notoriously unhappy and lonely for much of his life. Entrepreneur and socialite Howard Hughes became reclusive and paranoid, while multimillionaire pop star George Michael revealed in a recent documentary how his wealth and fame had never made him happy.... The tales of many lottery winners are replete with envy, spite, and family break-up.

So that's it, eh? If you want to be happy, give away your money if you have any, and never enter lotteries. Well, slow down a little.... First it might be wise to ask how this argument fares on our criteria.

Requirement 1 asks for specific and clear examples. But the ones offered here are sketchy and anecdotal, almost one-liners. Those cited need more detail and support: citations (how do we find out whether the claims about these billionaires are true?), biographies, careful scientific surveys of lottery winners. None of that is offered here.

Requirement 2 asks for many examples—more than a few, at least if the class being generalized over is large. Here, conclusions are being suggested about all people, a pretty large group! More examples are needed than three rich people and a few lottery winners.

Requirement 3 is the key here, and helps justify requirement 2. Without a range of examples, we have no way of judging whether a few miserable rich people are representative or not. Surely there are *some* people who will be unhappy regardless of how much money they have—just as there are surely some who will be happy regardless. Or maybe something else, quite unrelated to money, leads to unhappiness in their case. The question remains whether *most* richer people tend to be happier. Maybe, maybe not—but a large number of examples, fairly detailed and as representative and varied as possible, rather than a few striking cases, are necessary before we can say anything with confidence.

This is a poor argument, then, as it stands. But don't overgeneralize from that fact either. A failed generalization does not prove its opposite. This argument, so far, fails to prove that wealth makes you miserable, but its failure does *not* prove that wealth makes you happy. A failed generalization proves nothing at all. Until you can get more information, the question remains open.

COMPARISONS

Sometimes we make inferences by comparing one kind of situation with another seemingly similar situation about which more is known. A good comparison:

1. Cites as a comparison a *clear* case about which *true* claims are made.
2. Cites as a comparison a *relevantly similar* case. That is, the cases compared must be as similar as possible in ways that matter to the conclusion— though they can be very different in other, less relevant ways.

In the Netherlands, people are allowed to have small amounts of marijuana for personal use and "coffeehouses" sell small amounts openly for use on the premises. The results of this policy are reasonably positive. People therefore argue that legal marijuana should be manageable in America. This is an argument by comparison. Is it a good one?

To meet requirement 1 we need to know more about the Dutch policy and its results. Technically all drugs are illegal there, but in practice only harder drugs are prosecuted. The coffeehouse system is meant to make it difficult to buy large amounts. Documented marijuana use has increased significantly among Dutch young people, but hard drug use has actually declined. The law still prohibits unsafe driving and public nuisances created by any intoxicant, legal or not: rates have not increased. Some political arguments continue—the current policy seems hypocritical to some, and the issue of supply has not been addressed (some argue that the Dutch state should grow its own marijuana so there are legal sources for the coffeehouses!)—but on the whole, it seems fair enough to conclude that the results are indeed "reasonably positive."

Requirement 2 requires a *relevantly similar* comparison. Can we infer that a social policy that works in the Netherlands will therefore also work in America? How similar are the two?

The Netherlands is a small, densely populated, homogeneous nation, whose people tend to be more socially minded than many Americans. These are major relevant differences. Drug abuse is therefore less likely (in fact, it turns out that the bulk of the customers in the coffeehouses are foreigners, including many American college students) and much harder to hide if it does occur. On the other hand, the Netherlands is a modern, developed, democratic state, like the United States, and it gives its citizens a wide range of freedoms. These are major relevant similarities.

This comparison, then, is only partly successful on the second require-ment. It seems likely that the potential for abuse is higher in the United States (at least, the comparison doesn't persuade me that it isn't). On the other hand, the Dutch system does suggest that some creative forms of con-trolled availability could be workable here too as well. We could even take it as an incentive to do some creative thinking about other possible systems here. To that extent, the comparison is useful and revealing.

INFERRING CAUSE FROM CORRELATION

Happiness may not correlate with money, but it does correlate with things like good health, a loving marriage, and lots of friends. Therefore it might be concluded that good health, a loving marriage, and lots of friends *lead to* or *cause* happiness. This is an argument from correlation to cause.

A good argument from correlation to cause:

1. Cites *accurate* correlations.

2. *Explains* how the (proposed) cause leads to the (proposed) effect.

3. Argues that the proposed cause-effect relationship is the *best explana-tion* of the correlation.

To meet requirement 1, you'd need to consult social-scientific research for reliable statistics to show that married people, say, are more likely than unmarried people to report being happy.

The proposed cause-effect connection then needs to be spelled out—that is the point of requirement 2. How marriage is supposed to lead to happi-ness, psychologically, is pretty clear: having a spouse can be a pleasurable and supportive thing. Filling in such links is crucial: it's what turns a mere cooccurrence into a plausible *connection*.

Requirement 3, however, is still hard to meet. The problem is a general philosophical one: *any correlation can be explained in a variety of ways*.

A and B, let's say, are correlated. It could well be that A causes B. It could *also* be that B causes A (instead, or in addition), or that both A and B have a common cause, or that A and B are not causally related at all.

It is true that a strong correlate of happiness is marriage. The proposed conclusion is that marriage tends to cause happiness. But the evidence only really says that the two tend to occur together. Other conclusions remain pos-sible. It could also be that happy people are better at forming and sustaining marriages—so that happiness leads to marriage, not necessarily vice versa. That is, the connection could be the other way around, and the evidence—the correlation—would be exactly the same!

Or perhaps a certain sort of character—say, cheerful and kind—leads *both* to better marriages *and* to happiness. That is, marriage and happiness may have a common cause, rather than being directly connected.

Yet again, each could affect the other, in a kind of feedback loop. Maybe happy people have better marriages, which in turn make them happier, which in turn...The story might well be complex.

Clearly it makes a big difference which of these stories is true. But it certainly isn't easy to tell which. This is why a good argument about causes must explain how the proposed cause could lead to the proposed effect (requirement 2 again) *and* must try to show that the proposed explanation is the *best* or most *likely* explanation of the observed correlation—requirement 3.

Many other issues involve similar questions. To return to the drug question, for example, here's another statistic. It turns out that a significant proportion of the homeless are drug users. We might conclude from this that drug use leads to homelessness. It's a plausible inference, and it suggests in turn that to address homelessness we need to crack down on drug use. On the other hand, the very same correlation could equally well suggest that homelessness leads people to use drugs, suggesting that we need to address homelessness directly, in part to reduce drug use. Probably both are true to some extent, but which is the *main* effect is a crucial question for social policy.

Or again, as I mentioned earlier, though a decline in capital punishment in the United States from 1933 to 1969 corresponds to a rise in murders, it's hard to know what to make of this. There have been vast changes in American life in this period. Cities have become crowded, weapons have become readily available, drugs and gangs are widespread. Any of these factors could explain the rise in murders at least as readily as the decline in executions. And why do states with the death penalty on average have higher murder rates than states that don't? Inferring from correlation to cause here is tricky at best.

DEFINITIONS

Another critical-thinking task is to clarify the very words we use in framing ethical issues. Again the task may take a variety of forms—and usually takes work.

WHEN TERMS ARE UNCLEAR

Even some fairly basic categories are unclear in popular ethical debates. People who oppose "assisted suicide," for example, often use the term in a very different and much broader way than people who favor legalizing it. Both sides get emotional. Proponents' definitions sound positively lovely and tend to be narrowly framed. Opponents' definitions sound horrible and prominently feature disturbing cases. The proposed definitions on both sides also tend to be rhetorical, not carefully thought through.

These are solvable problems. First, when a new or specialized term is at issue, misunderstanding can be cleared away just by proposing or agreeing upon a definition. In the case of "assisted suicide," for example, the intended definition is: allowing doctors to help aware and rational people to arrange and carry out their own dying. It does *not* include allowing doctors to "unplug" people without their consent (that would be some form of "involuntary euthanasia"—another issue). There may be good reasons to object to assisted suicide so defined, but at least the parties to the argument can ensure that they are talking about the same thing.

Be precise. Don't just replace the problematic word with a synonym—it will be just as confused as the original word. Get technical if you have to.

Keep the dictionary handy—often it is a model of precision and impartiality. Just don't expect that it will resolve all your questions when issues get difficult. Dictionary definitions often just use synonyms. Dictionaries also usually give multiple definitions, so that you still have to pick and choose between them.

For some words, you just have to make the term more precise yourself. Again: explain *carefully;* use neutral, not loaded terms; and use concrete, definite terms rather than vague ones.

WHEN TERMS ARE CONTESTED

Sometimes the term in question is not merely unclear but actually is *contested*. That is, people are arguing over the term, not just confused about what it means. In this case, you cannot simply stipulate a meaning—for people are disagreeing over what the term *ought* to mean—and the dictionary, wisely staying out of moral issues, seldom does more than suggest equally inconclusive synonyms.

In this case, you must work out a careful definition yourself. The rule is: *work from the clear cases.* Here is what I mean.

Whenever a term is contested, you can distinguish three relevant sets of things. One will be those things to which the term clearly applies. Second will be those things to which the term clearly does *not* apply. In the middle will be those things whose status is unclear—including but not restricted to the things being argued over. Your job is to formulate a definition that:

1. *Includes* all the things that the term clearly fits.
2. *Excludes* all the things that the term clearly does not fit.
3. Draws the *plainest possible line* in between.
4. *Explains* why the line belongs there and not somewhere else.

In discussing the "drug" issue, for instance, we could certainly use a clear definition of the term "drug" itself. But what *is* a drug?

Drugs are substances, clearly (as opposed to institutions or actions or animals...), and substances that we ingest (eat, breathe in, snort, or apply to various body parts). But we ingest many different substances. Which ones are "drugs"?

Clear cases of "drugs," in the current moral sense, include heroin, cocaine in its various forms, and marijuana.

Clear cases of substances that are *not* drugs include air, water, most foods, sunscreen lotions, and shampoos—though all of these substances are clearly chemicals, in a broad sense of "chemical," and all are ingested or applied to our body parts.

Unclear cases include tobacco and alcohol. Here is where the debate swirls. Is it fair, for example, to ban marijuana but allow the sale of alcohol, both of which may work on the body in similar ways and which may have at least as bad effects? Should the Food and Drug Administration be able to regulate cigarettes, on the grounds that nicotine is a drug?

Unclear in another way are substances such as aspirin, antibiotics, and vitamins and psychiatric medicines such as antidepressants and stimulants—the kinds of things we buy in "drug stores" and call "drugs" in a pharmaceutical sense. But these are *medicines,* let's say. In moral contexts the word "drug" is used more narrowly.

Is there a definition that meets the four requirements outlined here?

A "drug" has been defined—by a Presidential Commission, no less—as a substance that affects mind or body in some way. This definition meets requirement 1: it includes all the clear cases of drugs. But it is far too broad to meet requirement 2. It also includes all the clear cases of substances that are *not* drugs. (And naturally enough it does not meet the third either, since it effectively draws no line at all.) We need a more limited definition.

We also can't define a "drug" as an *illegal* substance that affects mind or body in some way. This definition might cover more or less the right set of substances, but it does not meet requirement 4. It does not explain why the line belongs where it is. After all, part of the point of trying to define "drug" in the first place might well be to decide which substances *should* be legal and which should not. Defining a "drug" as an illegal substance short-circuits this project. (Besides, if marijuana were legalized tomorrow, would it stop being a drug overnight?)

Try this:

> *A drug is a substance used primarily to alter the state of the mind in some specific way.*

Heroin and the like obviously count. Food, air, and water don't—because even though they may have effects on the mind, the effects are not specific and are not the primary reason why we ingest them. Unclear cases we then approach with the question: is the *primary* effect *specific* and on the *mind?* Perception-distorting and mood-altering effects do seem to be what we are concerned about in the current debate about "drugs," so arguably this definition captures the kind of distinction that people really want to make.

Should we add that "drugs" are addictive? Maybe, maybe not. There are some substances that are addictive but not drugs—certain foods, perhaps. And what if a substance that alters the state of the mind in some specific way turns out to be *nonaddictive* (as some have claimed about marijuana, for example)? Is it therefore not a drug? I think it is better to take addiction to define drug *abuse* rather than "drug" as such.

CRITICAL THINKING WITH DEFINITIONS

Definitions help us to organize our thoughts, to group like things with like, to pick out key similarities and differences. By themselves, though, they seldom settle ethical questions.

We may look to a definition of "drug," for example, for guidance about what sorts of substances we should use or avoid and what should be legally allowed or banned. My proposed definition certainly may redraw some lines in ways that surprise or unsettle us. My proposed definition, for instance, includes antidepressants and stimulants as well as alcohol and even coffee. It doesn't follow, however, that all of these are morally problematic or should be banned as well. We'd need an *argument* to go that far.

The argument could be made—certainly for alcohol.

> Alcohol is the most widely-used drug; over 100 million Americans drink. Alcohol may cause more harm than all illegal drugs put together. One in ten drinkers—some 10 million Americans—becomes an alcoholic. (By contrast, there are fewer than 500,000 heroin addicts.) In addition, about half of all fatal car collisions, accidental drownings, and violent crimes are alcohol-related. One of the most common severe birth defects, fetal alcohol syndrome, is caused by women who drink while pregnant. And alcohol costs our economy $120 billion yearly in work, property, and medical costs.... We would not legalize any currently illegal drug that caused even a fraction of these problems.

This is an argument for restricting alcohol, but notice that it does not depend on alcohol's being a drug. This argument would be damning even if alcohol did *not* count as a "drug." The definition cannot do that work by itself.

On the other hand, coffee has specific effects on the mind too, may be harmful, and is clearly addictive. Still, it has nothing like the social effects of alcohol, so perhaps we would stop there. And many antidepressants and stimulants, while clearly and appropriately called "drugs" under the proposed definition, are also legal, under prescription, and have clear benefits as such.

Again, then: that a substance is a "drug" is not, by itself, a sufficient reason to object to or ban it—for otherwise we would have to object to and ban coffee and psychiatric medicines as well. The drug in question must also cause a certain degree of personal and social harm—like alcohol or cocaine.

By the same token, just because marijuana, say, *is* a drug, it doesn't follow automatically that it should be banned. Some people would argue that coffee is a better comparison to marijuana than alcohol—both have relatively mild effects, though both can be misused—and (someone might argue) the best approach might be like the Netherlands', making it available in coffeehouse-like settings where the amount used can be carefully controlled. (So perhaps the same restrictions should be extended to coffee?)

Of course, if marijuana is much more addictive than coffee, or if it really is a "gateway" to other and harder drugs, then there may be a good case for prohibition after all. It would take some good data to know better. (And by the way: is coffee a "gateway" to other stimulants? Didn't many stimulant-takers start out as coffee-drinkers?) Or perhaps marijuana is most akin to certain antidepressants and stimulants—the drugstore sorts of "drugs"—medicines that are "drugs" on the proposed definition too, but call not for bans but for *control*. The point once again is just that none of these conclusions follow just from the fact that marijuana is a drug.

Nor of course are we entitled to object to or ban *only* substances that are "drugs." Tobacco, for example, may *not* be a drug according to the proposed definition (it's not clear, at least to me, whether the primary intended effect is on the mind), but it still is addictive and massively destructive (350,000 Americans die every year from it). Here we just come to recognize once again that the question of the morality or legality of substance use is more complex than the question of which substances are "drugs." Definitions contribute to clarity, but don't expect them to get you all the way home by themselves.

FOR REVIEW

1. Pick a moral debate and give an example of a specific fact that could help resolve it.

2. How would you locate a reliable source for such a fact?

3. Pick a moral debate and give an example of a factual generalization that is relevant to it.

4. What three requirements does such a generalization face?

5. Pick a moral debate and give an example of a factual comparison that is relevant to it.

6. What two requirements does such a comparison face?

7. Pick a moral debate and give an example of a cause-and-effect inference that is relevant to it.

8. What three requirements does such a cause-and-effect inference face?

9. Pick a moral debate and give an example of a definition that is relevant to it.

10. What requirements does such a definition face?

QUICK REFERENCE: CRITICAL-THINKING BASICS

WHEN FACTS ARE AT ISSUE

- Clarify *what* facts are at issue.
- Do your research.
- Seek out the best sources.

WHEN INFERENCES ARE AT ISSUE

A good *generalization*:

1. Cites *specific* and *clear* examples.
2. Cites *many* examples.
3. Cites *representative* examples and gives enough *background information* to allow us to evaluate for ourselves how significant and representative the examples are.

A good *comparison*:

1. Cites as a comparison a *clear* case about which *true* claims are made.
2. Cites as a comparison a *relevantly similar* case.

A good *argument from correlation to cause*:

1. Cites *accurate* correlations.
2. *Explains* how the (proposed) cause leads to the (proposed) effect.
3. Argues that the proposed cause-effect relationship is the *best explanation* of the correlation.

WHEN DEFINITIONS ARE AT ISSUE

A good definition:

1. *Includes* all the things that the term clearly fits.
2. *Excludes* all the things that the term clearly does not fit.
3. Draws the *plainest possible line* somewhere in between.
4. *Explains* why the line belongs there and not somewhere else.

EXERCISES AND NOTES

IDENTIFYING FACTS AT ISSUE

Identify two or three factual questions that are central to the following ethical debates as you understand them. That is, ask: what sorts of factual claims tend to be made, or presupposed, in this debate? What facts could we find out, through the appropriate kinds of research, that would make a difference? Be specific!

• Should states run lotteries to help fund state budgets (e.g., for education or other good causes)?
• Should tax money pay for private-school vouchers?
• Should gay marriage be legalized?
• Should tax money be used for welfare payments to provide food stamps to poor people and aid to poor families with dependent children?
• Should adoption files be opened so that people separated by at-birth adoptions can later find each other?
• Should marijuana be legalized?
• Should genetic engineering be banned?
• Should assisted suicide be permitted?
• Should a parent be encouraged or expected to stay home with preschool children?
• Should throw-away consumer goods be banned in the name of environmental protection and the needs of future generations?
• Should you stop eating meat?

Add your own favorite issues as well.

PURSUING THE FACTS

The next step is to consider how you could begin to resolve these factual questions. What sources can you find? For what questions can you find reliable and reasonably objective information on the Web? Where? Will answering some of these questions require inferences? What sorts of inferences (generalization, comparison, reasoning from correlation to cause, others?) might you have to use? Which is likely to be the most successful?

    Please note again that the challenge is not to construct an argument for your favored conclusion about the whole issue. It remains much more specific: it is to consider what kinds of exploration or research it would take to resolve (or, anyway, advance) the particular factual issue you've identified.

Vegetarianism, for example. You might have said that one central factual question in this debate is how readily people can live without meat. Is a vegetarian diet healthy? If this is your question, a way to find out is to consult nutritionists or nutrition textbooks. (While you're at it, you could also ask: is a *meat* diet healthy? and: what sort of diet is health*iest*?) There may be some disagreement, but with some persistence you still should be able to find a reasonably well-informed and neutral answer. Of course this is not the same as answering the whole question. Suppose you find out that a vegetarian diet can be as healthy as or healthier than a meat diet. It would not necessarily follow that you must become a vegetarian. After all, there are other relevant values besides health. The point here is simply to ask how we might resolve the specific factual questions you've identified—not how we might resolve the whole issue. One thing at a time!

TAKE UP SOME ISSUES IN DETAIL

For a further step, take up some specific issues with all of the tools in this chapter. Go into them in depth. This would make a good research paper: take a very controversial moral issue and simply research its factual basis critically and open-mindedly. Make your moral conclusions secondary, if you draw any at all.

For example: welfare. The debate, very roughly, is over whether tax money should be used for monetary support for poor people—help with housing and food costs—and aid to poor families with dependent children. As you probably know, it's intensely emotional, on both (all) sides, and also (not coincidently) is shaped by many second- or third-hand beliefs. You can do better, using the skills in this chapter.

Start with definitions. Most people in national polls oppose something called "welfare," but when asked whether they favor most of the individual programs that make it up, they overwhelmingly say yes. Opponents reduce it, sometimes, to just one or two out of several dozen major social-support programs, especially food stamps. Among others are Unemployment Compensation, Medicaid, Supplemental Social Security for the disabled and elderly poor, housing assistance, and infant supply and nutrition programs, which are all "means-tested" (i.e., to receive benefits a person must demonstrate a certain level of financial and other need), as well as entitlement programs that are not means-tested, like the more familiar kind of Social Security, military and civil service retirement funds, Veteran's Administration medical care, Low-Income Home Energy Assistance, student loan programs (yup, you're "on welfare" too), and still others. So how would *you* define "welfare"? What is the most useful way to understand that term?

Now get some facts. How much money are we talking about here? (And for which programs?) Are the critics right that special corporate tax breaks ("corporate welfare," they call it) cost more money than all means-tested welfare programs put together? How have welfare laws and provisions changed recently?

Who's *on* welfare (on, let's say, the more controversial means-tested type)? How long do they tend to stay? *Why* are people on welfare? (Best not to follow the stereotypes here, eh? Talk to people to really find out.) How do poverty and homelessness relate to violence against women? To veteran status? To the impoverishment of central cities?

What social-support programs are available, and to whom, in your area? When cash is involved, how much is paid? Is it liveable? Do benefits increase with the recipients' number of children? If so, find out how much more money a parent gets per month for a second, third, or fourth child. How does it compare with the additional monthly costs of diapers, baby food, medical care, and so on? How do you get *disqualified*?

Look for the most up-to-date information. Local social-service workers, administrators of soup kitchens and shelters for the homeless, and human-services departments at your school should be good sources of information. For current U.S. government data, try www.census.gov/hhes/www/poverty. And finally, hardest and most important: talk to poor people themselves. Work in a homeless shelter or soup kitchen. I have found that many nonpoor people with the strongest views about welfare (both pro *and* con) have little or no experience of the life of the poor. This is easy to remedy, though, and you can help out while you learn besides.

I hope you see that even these quick questions both invite you to look more deeply into a variety of factual questions—there is real information, not just opinion, about most of these issues—and open up some unexpected ways of thinking and even possible creative solutions (a point to which we return in Chapters 15 and 16). But of course welfare is only one issue. Pick one or two that concern you and begin to explore them in the same way.

CLARIFYING UNCLEAR TERMS

Not all terms need clarifying—lucky for us. Still, some do. Look around at the ethical debates that currently occupy us. Ask which of them could benefit from careful attention to definition. Where is the meaning of a word or words central to the debate? What word or words are these? How could you begin to define them?

Specify a definition for *assisted suicide*. What do you think of the definition proposed in the text? Can you do better? You may need to do a little research.

Here's another example: *affirmative action*. This is a fairly specific term, and it would seem that it could be easily defined. Perhaps it can be. But we seem confused most of the time about what we mean by it. Can you formulate a good definition—or a useful set of distinctions? Try it, and then check out others' definitions. Are some that you find more reliable and usable than others?

The following terms play major roles in some current moral debates. Try to define each term. You'll need to work from the clear cases, so start by specifying what they are. Look out for possible ambiguities. Keep open the possibility that for some of these terms there are simply not enough agreed-upon clear cases to define the term successfully at all (and if not, are there other useful ways to clarify and focus the debates of which they are a part?). If you think an explicit and clear definition is possible, work it out. Sketch some sort of argument in support, and explore some of its implications in the case(s) in question as well as others.

Here are the terms.

• *Selfish,* as in the perpetual debate over whether humans are "basically just selfish" or have other motives as well. (Recall also our discussion in Chapter 2.) Can you define "selfish" in some way that doesn't automatically include all human behavior (for surely we mean *something* when we say of someone that they're selfish—it must be possible for someone *not* to be selfish) and on the other hand also does not make selfishness automatically horrible? Once you've defined it in such a way, can you use your definition to actually *investigate* how "selfish" people really are?

• *Adultery,* as in this question recently faced by the New Hampshire Supreme Court: if a married woman has sex with another woman, is that adultery (and therefore grounds for her husband to sue for divorce)? Many dictionary definitions tend either to assume heterosexuality (that is, to define adultery for a married man, say, as sex with a woman other than his wife) or to leave the matter ambiguous (one dictionary I found even uses the phrase "sex with another" without saying another *what*). Does it matter that gay marriages are not legal in most places?

I will not tell you what the court decided, but you might want to decide the matter yourself—argue it carefully and well—and then look up the answer the court gave.

• In the same ballpark: *sex,* as in the famous question of whether Bill Clinton did or did not lie when he said that he did not have "sex" or a "sexual relationship" with Monica Lewinsky, with whom he later admitted doing various sexual things that did not include penile-vaginal intercourse. Though his accusers claimed that this was an obvious lie, some interesting survey research published at the time suggested that many Americans—interestingly, both older traditional people and college students—would not call Clinton's relationship with Lewinsky a "sexual relationship." So what do *you* think? How would you define "sex" or "sexual relationship"? How could you back up your definition?

• *Fairness,* as in, for example, the question of affirmative action again. What is fair? Treating people equally? Maybe, but this is a vague phrase too. In a famous simile of Abraham Lincoln's, it's hardly fair to make a runner run a footrace hobbled by a chain and ball while others run unencumbered. Yet in some sense they are being treated "equally." No one blocks their way. They get a lane in the track just like everyone else. If this strikes you as unfair all the same, how would you specify what fairness is? An equal chance at winning? But that can't be right either, since some people do run faster than others, and that's the whole point of the race...

• *Natural,* in the context of environmental debates. Sometimes people argue that air and water pollution and the pollution of the land with nonbiodegradable wastes (plastics, etc.) is "natural" in a larger sense because the raw materials after all came from nature ("Where else could they come from?") as did we ourselves. Others want to argue that despoiling the earth is wrong because the materials and maybe the acts themselves are "unnatural." Is there a useful way to define "natural" in this context?

Related is the question of what constitutes "natural" foods. Since all foods come from "nature" in some ultimate sense, what makes some foods "natural" and some not natural? The absence or presence of "artificial" ingredients, maybe? OK, but what makes an ingredient "artificial"?

The last questions may sound skeptical, but they may well have answers. In any case, don't just dismiss the whole question. After all, people are trying to make some sort of distinction with this word. What distinction are they trying to make? If the word "natural" is too ambiguous to carry this kind of weight, what terms would you suggest instead?

• And finally: *person*, especially as we try to arrive at some consistent position connecting our views on, say, abortion on the one hand and the treatment of animals on the other. Very roughly, the problem is that if you define "person" broadly enough to include fetuses, then many other animals count too, which is not a welcome conclusion for many moral positions that oppose abortion but also oppose animal rights. On the other hand, to turn the very same point inside out, if you define "person" broadly enough to include other animals, then fetuses count too, which is not a welcome conclusion for many moralists who favor animal rights but tend to be pro-choice. There's also the problem that a more restrictive standard for personhood tends to exclude newborns as well as fetuses and most (though perhaps not all) other animals. And while tying personhood to being human may help draw something like the desired line, it has problems on requirement 4: why should mere species membership make such a huge difference? Surely it's not that hard to imagine nonhuman persons, even if we don't know any at present. Hmm... this one takes a lot of thinking!

NOTES

Fact-finding, inference, and definition are enormous topics. Even brief guidebooks can run to hundreds of pages, and there is a wide range of texts and courses available in "informal logic" and persuasion, rhetoric, and argumentative writing. One I especially like is Lewis Vaughn's *The Power of Critical Thinking* (Oxford, 2005). A well-presented classical approach is David Kelley's *The Art of Reasoning* (Norton, many editions). A very brief introduction is my own book *A Rulebook for Arguments* (Hackett Publishing Company, many editions)—a fine little book indeed, if I may say so myself (note that I am certainly well-informed on the subject, but not exactly unbiased!).

Information on hybrid cars is cited from http://www.motherearthnews.com/Alternative_Energy/2005_October_and_November/Pay-Less-at-the-Gas-Pump-Hybrid-Revolution, accessed 10/23/06. The argument about miserable rich people comes from Nick Louth, "Wealth and Happiness Are Not the Same Thing," http://money.uk.msn.com/Investing/Insight/Special_Features/Active_Investor/article.aspx?cp-documentid=143226, accessed 10/23/06.

For an introduction to reasoning about causes, see the Vaughn book just cited or other critical-thinking texts. More difficult but also richly rewarding and provocative is Richard Nisbet and Lee Ross, *Human Inference: Strategies and Shortcomings of Social Judgment* (Prentice-Hall, 1980). Correlations between intimacy, health, and happiness are cited from Dayana Yochim, "Money=Happiness," http://www.fool.com/news/commentary/2004/commentary040120dy.htm, accessed 10/23/06.

Colin McGinn's *Moral Literacy* (Hackett/Duckworth, 1992) offers a vigorous and provocative discussion of drugs, beginning with a proposed definition: see his Chapter 6. The quote at the end of the last section comes from Mike Martin, *Everyday Morality* (Wadsworth Publishing Company, 1995), page 149.

GUEST AUTHOR

Vance Ricks teaches in the Department of Philosophy at Guilford College in Greensboro, North Carolina, where he has also been interim director of the First Year Program, director of the Honors Program and Department Chair. He received the Ed Lowe Teaching Excellence Award in 2000. His box in this chapter, "Which Facts Are Relevant?" speaks to student questions based on his long-time use of the first edition of this book.

CHAPTER 12

Judging Like Cases Alike

Kant argues that it is the essence of a moral judgment to generalize to other cases. For my act or decision or position to be *moral,* it must be one that I would accept and support anyone else holding in similar cases—and one that I hold myself in similar cases.

In practice, though, we often make judgments about one kind of case without thinking a great deal—or thinking at all—about what our judgments imply for similar kinds of cases not before us right now. If we did think about those other cases, though, we might end up thinking differently about the one before us. This too is our responsibility. There *are* implications for similar kinds of cases, and like cases must be judged alike.

CONSISTENCY IS A CHALLENGE

Suppose I am prepared to misrepresent my car in order to sell it. It's expected, I say. Besides, the buyer can get the car checked herself. The moral question is: would I consider it equally justified for someone else to misrepresent *their* car in the same way and for the same reasons in order to sell it (say, just per-chance, to *me*)? If not, then I am not judging like cases alike. As Kant would put it, I really am just "making an exception for myself"—treating others as mere means to my ends, acting like somehow I am fundamentally different from them.

In the same spirit, the psychologist Lawrence Kohlberg—you'll remem-ber him from our brief discussion in Chapter 10—spoke of "moral musical chairs." If I judge a moral situation one way from the position we occupy in it, I need to be willing to judge it the same way from the other positions too—say, in particular, from a position in which I am *dis*advantaged. "Moral musical chairs" is an imaginative method, then: a way of considering each of the different people affected and looking at the situation from their points of view. It's the Golden Rule in practice. Sit in their chair for a while. A true moral act must be judgeable the same way from every position.

Would I consider it equally justified if someone else did the same thing to me? The honest answer *could* be "yes." After all—back to the car—maybe I too would recognize that misrepresentation *is* expected, and of course it's true that I *could* get the car checked myself. In that I case I do judge like cases alike, and I have done my ethical homework (or some of it, though there may be other moral objections to misrepresenting cars). But this is probably not the norm. Normally we either don't think about it at all or would judge other people quite differently than ourselves. Here the Golden Rule has some bite!

"EXECUTION STOPS A BEATING HEART"

You may have seen a bumpersticker that says EXECUTION STOPS A BEATING HEART. What does this mean?

Literally, it's just a simple true statement. Execution—capital punishment— stops a beating heart. Since stopping a beating heart—that is, killing someone— is usually a bad thing, it's a fair guess the person who put on this bumpersticker is opposed to the death penalty. But there is more going on than this.

This bumpersticker is an *argument*—in fact a specific challenge. It's an ironic response to the anti-abortion bumpersticker ABORTION STOPS A BEATING HEART. Essentially it argues: if you are opposed to abortion on the grounds that it's an act of killing, then you also ought to be opposed to the death penalty too, since it too is an act of killing. Many people who are pro-life on the abortion issue, however, tend to favor the death penalty. The question is: how can this be a consistent position? The implication is: perhaps you ought to reexamine your reasons for opposing abortion—or for favoring the death penalty.

This is a challenge to "judge like cases alike." It might be met in various ways, as we will see in a few pages. The first point, however, is that it must be met somehow. You may even have to rethink your views!

Note that the challenge arises the other way around too. Many people who oppose the death penalty tend to be pro-*choice* on the abortion issue. But if "stopping a beating heart" is an objection to execution, why isn't it an objection to abortion?

RESPECTING INNOCENT LIFE

Here is another example—a related bumpersticker.

WE BRAKE FOR ANIMALS.
WE SAVE THE WHALES AND THE BABY SEALS.
WHY DO WE STILL TOLERATE ABORTION?

Good question. To spell it out: one common case for legal abortion rests on the claim that fetal human life is less important not only than nonfetal (born) human life but also less important than many other human needs, for example, the need to have a manageable family size or a chance at a career. But people who accept the case for legal abortion also often are committed to saving the whales, protecting animals, and so on. And that commitment seems to come from a very different place: from an unwillingness to subordinate other lives to human needs, at least needs such as fur coats, meat, and new drugs or household chemicals that won't harm us.

In the one case innocent life seems to be a prime value; in the other it does not. The challenge is: how can these two commitments be consistent? Doesn't something have to give somewhere?

Nobody gets off easy here, though—this challenge too works in reverse. People who *oppose* abortion but *tolerate* the mistreatment of animals must

---

RATIONALIZATION ALERT!

Challenges to "judge like cases alike" can be irritating. Downright annoying, in fact. It's no fun having our consistency challenged, and it takes work to figure out just what the relevant distinctions are. And of course there's always the danger that we will not be able to find a relevant difference, so that we may even be required to change our minds!

The temptation is to dismiss the challenge—to brush it off as irrelevant or invent some excuse off the top of our heads for treating two apparently like cases in different ways—a form of rationalization, or what Chapter 2 calls "offhand self-justification."

Don't do it. An honest and careful attempt to meet the challenge of consistency—acknowledging that it *is* a real challenge, and that it must be met—is what critical thinking in ethics is all about. Moral principles *are* general in nature. They do apply to other cases besides those that may be in the front of our minds. And if our reasons really are the reasons we are giving, we must be prepared either to draw similar conclusions about those other cases or to change our conclusions in the first case.

You're not obliged to change your mind instantly. It may not even be clear how to answer some of these challenges. The main thing is to keep thinking about the issues. Come back to them when you can. Raise them with others who share (and maybe others who don't share) your judgments of the cases in question. (And don't assume that *they're* so consistent either.) Some philosophers say that it's a lifelong task to work out a set of practical reasons that really do consistently apply to all "like cases." Any such reasons are going to be in constant flux as new cases come along and as we grow and learn. And that's probably a good thing too.

also consider how their commitments might be consistent. Once again, in the one case innocent life seems to be a prime value; in the other it does not. I once had a neighbor whose truck was plastered with pro-life slogans but who was also an avid deer hunter "for fun," as he put it. It didn't sound too "pro-life" to me. What gives?

HOW TO RESTORE CONSISTENCY

Suppose someone argues that your judgment about one case is not consistent with your judgment about another seemingly "like case." There are three possible ways in which you might respond.

- You can argue that the alleged "like cases" are not really alike. In that case you need to figure out the *morally relevant difference* between the cases and explain what difference that difference makes.
- You can change your judgment about the "like case" or cases.
- You can change your judgment about the original case or cases.

In short, you can either try to show that your judgments aren't inconsistent or change one of them.

Take again the question of abortion and capital punishment raised by the EXECUTION STOPS A BEATING HEART bumpersticker. Suppose you oppose abortion but favor capital punishment. Consider your options:

- You could try to establish a difference between the two cases and explain what difference it makes. For example, a natural response is: fetuses are "innocent" but murderers are not. And innocence makes a difference because the innocent have a right to all the protection we can afford as a society. Those who have killed, however, forfeit the right to that protection (or some of it, anyway: they still have a right to a fair trial and humane treatment in prison). Arguably, those who kill forfeit their own right to life, a right which all the rest of us, including fetuses on the pro-life view, still have.

Of course, this response might be debated in turn. Many people believe that it may be acceptable to kill innocents in wartime, for example, while others argue that even those who are not "innocent" still have the right to life. So there are further cases to consider. Still, probably some distinction can be maintained. Maybe the two alleged "like cases" are fairly far apart in the end.

- You could decide that, all things considered, you should change your mind and oppose capital punishment too. This is an argument made by some modern Catholic moralists who argue for a "consistent ethic of life": that if we are to be "pro-life" on some issues we need to be "pro-life" across the board.

• You could decide that, all things considered, you should change your mind and become pro-choice about abortion. The comparison of cases might show you that, in your mind, life is actually not the only or the most important value. You might conclude that your pro-life views about abortion do not reflect your most considered thinking.

There is no automatic way to decide which way to go. Trying to make the most sense of our many moral beliefs and commitments is an ongoing and hard job! You may want to try out all of the possibilities before deciding, and take some time too. Again, though, going in one of these three directions is ultimately necessary. There's nowhere else to go.

MORE EXAMPLES

We've already noted that the abortion/death penalty challenge also holds the other way around. Many people who oppose the death penalty tend to be pro-*choice* on the abortion issue. But, again, if "stopping a beating heart" is an objection to execution, why isn't it an objection to abortion?

Can *this* challenge be met? Logically there are the same three options. Perhaps pro-choice people would argue that the cases are not truly "like." Many would argue that fetuses are not fully human beings, for example— while murderers *are* fully human beings (though maybe bad ones). Or: some might conclude that capital punishment is morally acceptable too. Or: some might decide that they really ought to become pro-life on the abortion issue.

Again, there is no automatic way to decide—but thinking the question through is essential.

Another bumpersticker, remember, asks how some people can reconcile great concern for other animals with a seeming lack of concern for human fetuses, which also have a kind of life and awareness but are at risk if abortion is legal. How can there be "animal rights," say, and not fetal rights?

Once again, there may be answers. Maybe there is a relevant distinction between the two cases. Maybe it's that other animals are actually born, unlike a fetus of whatever species (in fact, most animals used for food or testing are full-grown adults) and are conscious of what is happening. Or maybe you'll want to say that abortion is *not* justified when the reasons are mainly utilitarian—if solely for reasons of cost, for example—just as you might also hold that it's no excuse for testing drugs on animals merely that other forms of testing would be more expensive.

This challenge too (like most, you may be noticing) also works the other way around. Can there be fetal rights but not animal rights? If you're pro-life but not a vegetarian, I leave that question for you.

INVENTED CASES

Not all "like cases" need be *real* cases, either. The logic of invented cases is perhaps a little harder to see, but it also opens up some intriguing new possibilities.

THE LOGIC OF INVENTED CASES

Consider the "Golden Rule" case again. The argument, remember, was that I cannot morally misrepresent my car in order to sell it if I would object to anyone else doing the same to me.

Now notice that it does not matter whether I am actually buying a car or not. It is enough that *if* I were buying a car I would have such objections. Here, then, you have a "like case" that is not exactly real (suppose I'm not really buying a car right now)—yet it does the work that's needed. A space opens here—indeed the necessity emerges here—for what we could call "moral imagination."

Sometimes we have to go further.

G: Protests caused McDonald's restaurants to pull out of many cities in India. I guess the Hindus didn't take too happily to the idea of eating sacred cows. I wonder why McDonald's didn't think of that...

N: I think it's outrageous. McDonald's has the right to offer a legal good for sale. People don't have to buy it if they don't want to.

G: Well, if you were a Hindu you'd probably see it a little differently.

N: I'm not a Hindu! I have no sacred cows.

G: You have certain beliefs that a restaurant could offend, don't you? What if some cannibals started a fast-food chain and opened a take-out place down the street from you. Would you have a problem with that? After all, you don't have to buy it if you don't want to.

N: Outrageous! I'd go down and picket the place myself.

G: Maybe you *do* have a scared cow!

It seems to be hard for N to put himself into the Hindus' shoes—at least by imagining himself a Hindu. So G tries something else. G invents a scenario in which someone *else* does to N what McDonald's did to the Hindus—so that N can stay in his own shoes, as it were, and still imagine himself in a situation *like* theirs.

Here the imagination stretches further, but the logic stays the same. You essentially *invent* a "like case." The point is that it is still relevantly similar (you claim) to the real-life case you are thinking about. Inconsistency can still arise, even if the allegedly "like case" may be entirely unreal. And the same options arise in response: deny the likeness, or change one of the inconsistent judgments.

THE RIGHT TO LIFE AND THE UNCONSCIOUS VIOLINIST

Here is a famous example of an argument from an invented case. On both sides of the abortion debate it is usually assumed that if the fetus has a right to life, then choosing abortion violates that right and is wrong. The philosopher Judith Thomson argued in a famous essay that this conclusion doesn't follow. Imagine, she says, that

> You wake up in the morning and find yourself back-to-back in bed with an unconscious violinist. A famous unconscious violinist. He has been found to have a fatal kidney ailment, and the Society of Music Lovers has canvassed all the available medical records and found that you alone have the right blood type to help. They have therefore kidnapped you, and last night the violinist's circulatory system was plugged into yours, so that your kidneys can be used to extract poisons from his blood as well as your own.

If you unplug yourself now, the Music Lovers point out, the violinist will die, and after all the violinist does have a right to life... Yet surely, Thomson argues, you have the *right* to unplug yourself, even so. It might be *nice* to donate nine months' use of your kidneys to the violinist, but you cannot be compelled to do so.

Suppose you agree—that is, suppose you think that you have the right to unplug yourself in this case. Therefore, even if another being is dependent upon you for life support (and in Thomson's case a being who is clearly and uncontroversially a human being—and "innocent," too), and even if that being has a right to life, you believe that you may still, morally, pull the plug. It's still within your rights to refuse to go through with it.

Thomson argues that abortion in some cases, especially if you are pregnant unintentionally or against your will, is exactly parallel to pulling the plug on the violinist. By analogy, then, in the case of abortion, Thomson concludes that the fetus's right to life (even if it has such a right) does not necessarily make abortion a violation of that right. You did not ask for this other life to be hooked to yours; you are being asked to make an enormous sacrifice of your time and your body's very energies; you acknowledge that there will be a loss if you "unplug"—the dependent being will die—but your right to your own body must take precedence. You must be allowed the choice.

SO...?

This is a pretty wild analogy. It's not something that is actually likely to happen. But that it is a completely imaginary case, once again, does not affect the problem of inconsistency. *If* you would object to being hooked up to the violinist, real or not, then you ought to support abortion rights in at least some cases—so the argument goes. Indeed, precisely the fact that it is not likely to happen helps make Thomson's point. We would never stand for pulling people off the streets to provide life support for dying musicians—so, if outlawing abortion would really be analogous to that, we should not outlaw abortion either.

One nice feature of this analogy is that it puts males into a situation that Thomson thinks is *like* being unintentionally pregnant. (Notice that only an imaginary case is likely to do this—surely an advantage of the imaginary.) She suspects that few men, even those who are strongly anti-abortion, would agree that they have no right to unplug themselves from the violinist. But then the challenge is acute: can they then consistently be anti-abortion? What's the difference between this case and unintentional pregnancy?

Some deny that being tied to the violinist really is like being unwillingly pregnant. Conservatives argue that a relevant difference between pregnancy and Thomson's case is that pregnancy is a known risk of having sex, even with contraception. In Thomson's case you're simply kidnapped off the street and involuntarily plugged to the violinist, but in the case of having sex, even with contraception, you are quite aware that pregnancy is at least possible. It's not quite so involuntary. You need to take some responsibility.

This is a fair point. Maybe the two cases aren't so "like," and we can consistently judge them differently.

On the other hand, this difference does not always hold. In some cases, at least, pregnancy *is* that involuntary. Think of pregnancy caused by rape. Though many pro-life advocates make an exception in this case, not all do. Some still insist that the fetus's right to life has priority. There, at least, Thomson's analogy has real bite (unless, of course, those pro-life advocates agree that they must stay hooked up to the violinist for nine months too—restoring consistency in a more extreme, and frankly unlikely, way).

Thomson or her defenders might also recast the analogy to acknowledge the conservative response. Suppose it was known, for example, that the Society of Music Lovers was looking for someone to hook up to the violinist, and you went out for a walk of your own free will even knowing that there was a small probability that you might be kidnapped for this purpose off the street. Maybe you even took an escort. This might be like using contraception—taking reasonable precautions—even knowing that there is a small probability that it won't work. Don't you still have a right to unplug?

Thomson would say so. After all, people can't really be obliged to stay inside all the time just because there is a small chance they might find themselves kidnapped and hooked up to the violinist if they go out. You're not responsible, even a little, as long as you take reasonable precautions. It would not be fair to ask more. This might be like saying: women can't really be obliged to refrain from sex totally until they are ready to carry through with an unintended pregnancy. Again, you're *not* responsible, even a little, as long as you take reasonable precautions—it would not be fair to ask more.

Thomson's analogy, and others she proposes like it, have set off a continuing debate among philosophers, much larger than we can review here. You see the point, though: working through "like cases"—even imaginary ones like hers—is an essential part of moral thinking. It is a complicated business (no surprise), but it can also be intriguing and revealing. And sometimes necessary.

"Speciesism"

COLIN McGINN

Philosopher Colin McGinn uses two thought-experiments—extended analogies like Thomson's—to raise questions about the offhand ways we treat other animals. Often we look at animals as mere objects to be consumed or entertained by or experimented upon, and we justify this practice without considering what our reasons imply about "like cases."

But suppose we were the *victims* of this kind of treatment rather than its perpetrators? It's not likely that we'd judge it the same way then. Or suppose the victims of it were just a little more like ourselves than other animals are now—what then? At least there would be some uneasiness about it. We'd pay some serious attention and give the victims' side a little closer look.

McGinn makes these suppositions a bit more vivid: he tells a couple of stories. Of course, these stories are made up, and so once again it may be tempting to dismiss them without thinking them through. But take care—there is a serious challenge here. Are we guilty of "speciesism"—a preference for humans over nonhumans merely on the basis of our *being* human, a difference that, according to McGinn, is not a relevant difference when issues of pain and abuse are at stake? If you are passionately convinced (in your guts, let's say) that it would be wrong for McGinn's vampires to suck *you* dry, why are you eating that hamburger without a second thought? Are the cases relevantly different? How?

We have all seen those vampire films, creepy tales of powerful pale predators who live on human blood. Well, let me tell you a story about a particularly successful vampire species. This species is unusual among the run of vampires in that it can live equally well off human blood or orange juice.

It is also more in control of its food supply than your average vampire. In addition to producing ample supplies of orange juice, it keeps throngs of humans locked up in huge prisons so that it can get to their necks with minimum effort. The vampires raise human infants in these prisons for the sole purpose of drinking their blood at maturity (and they have been known to do it at tenderer ages too). There is a bit of a snag, though, from the vampires' point of view, namely that you can't drink blood from the same human more than three times without that human's dying, so they are continually needing to replenish their stocks as thrice-bitten humans die off. The humans are powerless to resist because of the superhuman capacities of the vampires. When the vampires aren't dining on human blood (and the occasional glass of orange juice) they do the usual civilised things: go to the movies and the opera, make love, get married, play tennis, whatever.

They also have strict laws governing conduct within their species and are generally law-abiding and polite. They are actually not such a bad lot, generally considered, apart from this human blood business. But they don't see much of a problem about that because, after all; we humans belong to a different species from them and look and act differently; anyway they have been doing it for millennia. They sometimes think it is a pity about the pain and fear the humans feel while their necks are being punctured and drained, not to mention all the death that results, but there is no point in being squeamish and sentimental about your farm animals, is there? And yes, they could live just as well on orange juice—which they actually rather enjoy at breakfast time—but it would be a little monotonous to have only that to drink: they like some variety in their diet. True, also, it would be healthier to give up human blood, as some of them are always tediously insisting, but they relish their pint of blood at dinner time and feel that life would be poorer without it. So they don't take much notice of the "juicetarians" among them, a small minority anyhow, who fitfully campaign for humane treatment for humans—and even go so far as to call for complete human liberation! Why, what would become of all the humans if they were set free to roam the land? No, it is inconceivable.

I don't know about you but I find this vampire species a pretty selfish, blinkered and cruel bunch. They have got their values all wrong. If I were a powerful Martian visiting earth and found it dominated by these bloodsuckers, with the human species reduced to the status of mere blood vats, I would insist that they damn well stick to orange juice. Variety, freedom, tradition—don't give me that! Just look what you are doing to these poor humans, the pain and misery and confinement you cause them—and all because you don't fancy orange juice all the time. I mean, honestly, are you really telling me that it is morally acceptable to put that child to a slow and painful death rather than squeeze a couple of oranges? Can the difference of taste be that important to you? Human liberation! That is what I would say; and if I were one of the unlucky human victims I would plead the same case, hoping to appeal to the vampires' moral sense—of which they seem to have plenty when it comes to the welfare of their *own* species.

Here is another example, in which the human role is reversed. Imagine that there are two humanlike species, not one, either naturally evolved or created by God, rather as there are a number of monkey species. We are in the dominant position relative to the other humanlike species—call it the "shuman" species. Shumans like humans, are intelligent, sensitive, social, civilised—in fact very much on a par with humans in their level of development. However, their warlike prowess is much inferior to ours, and as a result they have been conquered and tyrannised by the "superior" species. Not content merely with enslaving them to do our dirty work, we also use them for food, as subjects of vivisection experiments and in blood-sports. Our exploitation of them gives us a higher standard of living than we would have otherwise. Their flesh is excellent when barbecued; medical science has progressed rapidly by using them instead of lower species which are biologically less like us; and it is jolly amusing to watch them running away from, and being caught by, the starved dogs we let loose on them on Saturday afternoons. Of course, the shumans complain all the time about what we humans do to them, always petitioning the government from their special reservations, trying to work up some emotional sympathy, causing trouble in the streets. We are not impressed, though, because they belong to another species from ours: we can't interbreed with them, they are completely hairless with pointy ears, and the mothers carry the babies for twelve months not nine. Admittedly we don't need to use them in this way—we already have plenty of other species to depend on, as well as the vegetable kingdom—but it can't be denied that we derive pleasure from them that we wouldn't enjoy without exploiting them as we do. So you see it is all right to ignore their interests in order to cater to ours. We don't need to *balance* their interests with ours, treating similar interests equally, since the shumans belong to a different biological group from us. The biological distinction cancels the moral commitments we would have with respect to the interests of members of our own species.

Again, I maintain that this isn't right. We are doing to them what the vampires were doing to us—trampling over the legitimate interests of another group. In essence, we are refusing to take their welfare seriously simply because they belong to a different biological species from us—*and this difference does not warrant that refusal*. There is a word for this attitude, coined about twenty years ago, namely "speciesism." It was coined on analogy with the concept of racism and sexism, and is intended to suggest that what is morally irrelevant or insignificant—species or race or sex—is being treated as if it carried decisive moral weight. The point of my two imaginary examples is to demonstrate that speciesism *as such* is a form of unacceptable discrimination. There is no good moral defence of what the vampires do to us or what we do to the shumans, and to try to base one on a mere difference of species is transparent special pleading. It is simply quite unconvincing as a justification for what looks on the surface like a naked exercise of power designed to benefit one group at the ruthless expense of another. Cruelty is cruelty is cruelty—and a mere difference of species doesn't make it right. Ditto for murder, imprisonment, and so on.

The question we must then ask, returning now to the real world, is whether our actual treatment of animals is founded on a tacit speciesism—that is, whether we would rationally condone it if it weren't for mere species differences. Do we, in other words, accord mere zoological distinctions too much weight in deciding what to do and not do to animals? Is the speciesist attitude the only thing that sustains our exploitative treatment of other species? Could we defend this treatment without reliance upon *naked species bias*?

Once this question is clearly raised, it is very hard to avoid the answer that we do rely, unacceptably, on speciesist assumptions. What tends to obscure this fact is that animals differ from us not *only* in point of what species they belong to: they differ, also, mentally, in terms of their cognitive abilities. They don't have our intellects, our brain power, our moral sense. Their minds are just not as rich and complicated as ours.

But it is easy to see that *this* difference cannot make the moral difference we tend to take for granted—unless, that is, we are prepared to set up a new and pernicious form of social discrimination: intelligenceism. Surely we don't think that mere inferiority of intelligence (by some possibly arbitrary standard) is enough to justify, say, slaughtering the intellectually inferior for food or electrically shocking them for scientific purposes. If we did believe that, we would have the freedom to do these things to human children, mentally backward adults, and senile old people. Indeed, there would be no moral objection to intentionally raising genetically engineered "simple" humans for such purposes. But being intelligent is not what gives you the right not to be abused. The reason it is wrong to cause pain to people is not that they are intelligent or members of the human species. It is that pain hurts, it is bad to suffer it, people don't like to be in pain. If you want to know whether an action is wrong, you have to look at its actual effects and ask if they are bad for the thing being acted on—not ask what *else* happens to be true of the thing. If forced confinement, say, is bad *for* an animal, then it is bad to do this *to* an animal, unless you can think of a reason why this badness is justifiable in the light of a greater good. It isn't a question of the animal's ability to do mathematics or appreciate chamber music—still less of its species per se. It is a matter of sentience, the ability to suffer.

And here we reach the nub of the issue about our moral treatment of animals. *Is* there a greater good that justifies what, considered in itself, appears to be bad? Can we argue that what is bad for the animals is over-ridden by what is good for us? Is it possible to defend something bad in itself by claiming that the ends justify the means? Note, now, that we are assuming that our treatment of animals would be morally wrong if it were *not* for some supposed greater good.

A clear-eyed look at the facts quickly reveals that there is no such means-end justification, at least in the vast majority of cases. The test to use here is whether you would condone a given form of treatment if it were practised on humans, thus eliminating the speciesist bias from your deliberations. You may also consider "simple" humans in order to eliminate intelligenceist bias. That is, you have to ask whether you would do to intellectually comparable humans what we regularly do to animals. I won't bother to run through the whole gamut of things we do to animals, leaving this as an exercise for the reader; once the principle has been grasped this is fairly mechanical work. But it must be clear enough already that you would not condone killing humans for food in the way we now do animals, or experimenting on humans as we now do on animals, or using them in sports as we do now, or using their skins for clothes as we do now, and so on. You wouldn't even do these things to humans who were mentally *inferior* to the animals in question. The pain, the fear, the frustration, the loss of life—these would be quite enough to deter you. And the reason for these sound moral judgments is simply that the ends do *not* justify the means. A life lost for a pleasant taste gained? Mutilation for some possibly trivial increase in knowledge? Dismemberment in the jaws of dogs for the "thrill of the chase"? Trapped and skinned for an expensive fur coat? We would never accept these cal-culations if humans constituted the means, so why should we suddenly change our standards when we move outside the human species? Only, it seems, because of the prejudice that declares our species sacred and other species just so much exploitable stuff. Unfair discrimination, in other words.

So what should be done, now that we have seen our treatment of other species for what it is—immorally benefiting ourselves at the expense of other animals? (Actually, it is more that we *think* we are benefiting our-selves, since a lot of what we get from them is bad for us.) We should, at the very least, do everything we can to minimise our dependence on ani-mals, treating their interests as comparable to the interests of fellow hu-mans in the respects relevant to the case at hand. This will mean, just for starters, stopping eating meat if you live in one of the societies in which it is perfectly possible to find other sources of food, i.e. almost everywhere on earth. Don't even think about owning a fur coat. Very few animal ex-periments, if any. Bloodsports—give me a break. In sum, we have to cease doing to animals what we would not in good conscience do to humans. We must make our morality consistent.

You ask: if it is so wrong, why do people do it? Good question. To answer it, a glance back at history helps. It is a sad fact about human affairs that power tends to rule, and this includes our relation to the animal world. Nor is power always, or indeed often, on the same side as justice. If A is more powerful than B, and A can get something off B which B may not want to give to A, then A is apt to take that something from B by brute force—unless A is a just and moral individual, which he very often isn't. People all too often do what they have the power to do, and to hell with morality. Whenever you have imbalances of power, and a relation of domination that serves one party not the other, then be on the look-out for the kinds of prejudice and ideology that sustain basically immoral arrangements.

Historically, two areas of intense and terrible exploitation stand out, both of which were "justified" by all manner of strange doctrines at the time: slavery and child labour. I need not review these familiar stories of human brutality and moral blindness, since they are now accepted as such, though it is easily forgotten how recently young children were put through unspeakable miseries in supposedly civilised countries like England and slavery was legally permitted in America. My point is that at the time, and for hundreds of years before, these forms of subjugation were widely taken for granted and not regarded as morally dubious. Only now, in enlightened retrospect, do we wag the finger of condemnation at our forebears and marvel at their moral insensitivity. But which of us alive now can be sure that we would have been on the side of the angels had we lived in those benighted days? The pressures of conformity and self-interest and sheer inertia are very strong. May it not now be the case that our treatment of animals, so redolent of the barbarities of slavery and child exploitation, is just one more example of brute power holding sway over natural justice—of self-interest stifling moral decency? But, as with those other cases, it is not always easy to see this when it is all around you. You tend to think it must have *some* justification, even if you can't produce one. But maybe it just doesn't.

FOR REVIEW

1. Explain "judging like cases alike."

2. How is the bumpersticker EXECUTION STOPS A BEATING HEART an *argument?*

3. When our moral stances seem inconsistent, what are the three ways in which we can logically respond?

4. Explain the first possible response with an example.

5. Explain the second possible response with an example.

6. Explain the third possible response with an example.

7. How could a purely invented case be relevant to "judging like cases alike"?

8. What is the point of Judith Thomson's violinist analogy?

9. What are Colin McGinn's two analogies to the human treatment of other animals?

10. What does McGinn conclude from his analogies?

QUICK REFERENCE: JUDGING LIKE CASES ALIKE

PAY ATTENTION

Systematically and honestly extend your moral reasons in one kind of case to other "like cases." (Example: if you oppose abortion in order to protect "innocent life," then consider other cases where other kinds of innocent life are at stake. Is there a real difference?)

WHEN INCONSISTENCY ARISES

When your judgments vary between these cases, consider your options.
- You could argue that the alleged "like cases" are not really alike. In that case you need to figure out the *morally relevant difference* between the cases and explain what difference that difference makes.
- You could change your judgment about the "like case" or cases.
- You could change your judgment about the original case or cases.

CONSIDER "LIKE CASES" FOR FURTHER CHECKING

Consider hypothetical cases to sharpen and test your thinking further. (Case in point: McGinn's thought-experiment.)

RECHECK

Rethink your views, re-articulate your reasons, and try again. Remember, consistency takes time and work!

EXERCISES AND NOTES

GROUNDING THE GOLDEN RULE

Review the reasons why the Golden Rule applies to our moral thinking. This should take you back to Chapter 7. When we violate the Golden Rule, are we making a mistake of some kind? What kind of mistake?

TAKING UP THE CHALLENGE

Working through "like cases" is a way of *thinking*. It is a way of clarifying what's morally at stake in a specific situation by comparing it with other seemingly similar cases to see what the relevant differences are—and aren't. And it is a way of working toward greater consistency and clarity in your moral views generally by comparing them with each other so as to bring out your general moral commitments.

Colin McGinn's analogies may give you much to think about: you might want to look at more of the chapter on animals in his book *Moral Literacy* (Hackett/Duckworth, 1992). Judith Thomson's violinist analogy comes from her essay "A Defense of Abortion," widely available in recent ethics collections (a citation follows in the Notes); she also proposes a number of other striking analogies to other kinds of unintentional and involuntary pregnancy. On the question of our responsibility to respond to world poverty and hunger, a provocative article using some invented cases is "The Singer Solution to World Poverty" by the utilitarian philosopher Peter Singer, available on the Web at http://www.utilitarian.net/singer/by/19990905.htm. Consider his conclusions as well as his methods in light of the tools in this chapter.

Go on to invent some analogies of your own to test your own or other people's moral generalizations. Consider some issues such as responses to international terrorism, high-technology medical interventions or genetic engineering, and sexual orientation issues. Remember, of course, that your supposed "like cases" actually have to be fair analogies. The challenge is not rhetorical: instead, once again, it is to think carefully and see further than we might without the analogies.

Or again, as Chapter 7 also points out, modern Catholic moral theologians are not merely "pro-life" when it comes to fetuses, but argue for what they call a "seamless garment" of respect for life in *all* cases, which to them means being not only anti-abortion but also anti-war, anti-assisted suicide, and anti-capital punishment and pro-environment, pro-welfare, and pro-animal. In this they differ from many Protestant pro-life activists, who tend to be pro-life on abortion but conservative on most of these other issues. If we're going to be pro-life, these moralists argue, we have to be pro-life *across the board*. Thus Catholic moral theology challenges those who wish to be pro-life on some issues but not on others to "judge like cases alike"—to ask if there really is a difference between those issues, and if not to "get consistent."

Of course, there are other possible responses. Perhaps some of those issues *are* relevantly different from abortion, so that defending the fetus's right to life does not necessarily imply defending, for example, a poor person's right to food stamps. It's also possible to "get consistent" by giving up one's pro-life views on abortion (perhaps one could still be anti-abortion for other reasons), rather than embracing a pro-life view in other similar cases.

Once again, though, meeting the challenge takes some work. What do *you* say to it, at bottom? How many of us really *are* "pro-life" across the board? Must we be? Should we be? Most of us are probably "pro-life" on *some* issue. But if on some issues, why not *all*?

NOTES

Judith Jarvis Thomson's "A Defense of Abortion" is one of the most widely reprinted articles in recent philosophical ethics. It appears in Joel Feinberg's collection *The Problem of Abortion* (Wadsworth, 1984), where my citation can be found on page 153. Thomson also proposes a number of other striking analogies to other kinds of unintentional and involuntary pregnancy. For commentary, see Rosalind Hursthouse, *Beginning Lives* (Blackwell, 1987), pages 181–194.

For contemporary Catholic literature on the "seamless garment" or "consistent ethic of life," see Joseph Cardinal Bernardin, *A Moral Vision of America* (Georgetown University Press, 1998). A good introduction can be found at http://www.priestsforlife.org/magisterium/bernardinwade.html. For an evangelical version of a similar argument, see Ronald Sider, *Completely Pro-Life* (InterVarsity Press, 1997)—revealingly subtitled "Building a Consistent Stance."

CHAPTER 13

Mindful Speech

SPOMA JOVANOVIC

Because speaking involves far more than stringing together a series of words, it is essential to cultivate an awareness and appreciation of our communication with other people. Mindful speech is a way of speaking and listening with careful attention to what is being said, in what ways, and with what impact or consequence.

In other words, speaking is an *ethical act* that entails verbalizing our values, feelings, thoughts, and passions. We communicate through words, tone, and action not only our thoughts or ideas but also our ethical relationship to others. Our speech communicates our personal obligations, position of power, interest in fairness, displays of care, and ongoing expectations.

In addition, when we speak, we are speaking to *someone,* not just anyone. For instance, when you speak to someone whom you have known personally for many years, the talk likely sounds different than how you address someone you have only just met. Familiarity may be conveyed in more relaxed language, references to past events that do not need explicit explanation, joy in talking to an old friend, and more. Further, talking to your best friend who knows your deepest fears and hopes will also be different than talking to your next door neighbor whom you may have known for an equally long time but without developing the same bonds of closeness. In these situations, most of us can see that *what* we talk about will be different, but also *how* we talk will reflect the distinctive quality of the relationships.

As we focus on mindful speech and notice and observe the details and nuances that flow between people in conversation, we experience a full appreciation of the rapport that emerges among speakers. Being mindful causes us to consider the degree of sensitivity with which we construct our words, the attitude with which we enter a conversation, the responsibility we assume for the quality of our interactions, and the actions that arise from our talk.

WORDS MATTER!

We learn early on in our lives that words represent something—an object, a perception, a viewpoint, a judgment, or a concern. Drawing from what is estimated to be one million words in the English vocabulary, we have choices to make about which word or words best reflect what we wish to communicate.

But our words do more than describe; they actually *create and define.* Our words have meanings that shape how we understand our world. For instance, someone who has been raised in a loving and safe neighborhood would help others as a natural expression of what it means to be a good neighbor. Thus, the word "community" might be selected to define the situation at the same time that it actually constructs a sense of belonging and helpfulness. For someone else who grew up in a part of town absent close relationships, perhaps riddled with crime and fear of others occupying nearby residences, other words would likely be used to name the living situation—"district," "quarter," "south side"—in ways that define with little more than a reference to a geographic location. So our word choices are important to name, create, and define our own and others' understanding.

In this way, words are powerful—they can change the way we think. Our words can be used constructively to invite others into conversation, they can be used to effectively shut down the possibility of talk, they can be used to evoke feelings, they can be used to exploit others, they can be used as instruments of care, and they can be used as weapons to discredit—to name but a few possibilities.

Take for example the many ways in which we use words to describe and define someone who is living on the streets. "Bum," "vagrant," and "transient" are terms that generally signify contempt for a person who chooses not to work, instead taking advantage of hard-working others to get money. Other words or labels communicate a more neutral or even strong-felt compassion, such as "unfortunate soul," "impoverished," or "homeless person." Some terms point toward the person's financial condition, while other words suggest that being homeless may be the by-product of failing mental health, emotional instability, and severed social interactions.

LINGUISTIC SHADING

Substituting one word with a near equivalent, *linguistic shading,* allows us to change our understanding of someone or something. One word can pin blame on the homeless person, while another can recognize that the prevailing economic conditions make it difficult for some people to move up the social class ladder.

Talking about "bums" prompts us to discuss how many of us feel "used" by panhandlers. Talking about "homeless veterans"—who account for one-third of the homeless in America, according to the National Coalition for Homeless Veterans—can evoke feelings of responsibility or guilt for how we have treated men and women who have served our country. In doing so, our discussion may shift away from the character flaws we see in "bums" toward the resources we collectively think are necessary for substance abuse recovery programs, affordable housing, psychiatric evaluation, and job training. When we talk about the homeless condition as a reflection of a person's lack of initiative or personal short-coming, our words are more harsh and our actions less caring. When we talk about the homeless condition as an unfortunate consequence of any number of factors, our words convey concern with actions that move toward finding solutions for the unfortunate in our communities.

Maybe you have seen a group of people holding up signs in opposition to war. You may have called the people "protestors," "activists," "troublemakers," "traitors," or "patriots," depending on what views you hold about the war, our country's involvement in it, the role of citizens in a democracy, and the possibilities or liabilities of protest action. If you choose to describe the people and their protest action as patriotic, you will create and define the situation as a noble act and, more importantly, your conversation will be focused on the ways in which citizens express their views in our civil society. This is far different than the conversation that might ensue if you proclaim that protestors are "traitors" for holding views different from your own or ones that challenge the prevailing foreign policy.

Or think about how we describe older people in our community. "Old," "elderly," "senior," and "mature" are considered synonyms. Yet, each of these words may be interpreted in slightly different ways. The descriptive word, "old," may generate or reinforce views that older people are frail, likely to soon die, and a burden for family members. More positive attitudes about "older adults" or "retired professionals" communicate a respect for the wisdom and wealth of experiences acquired over a lifetime. Common core values and beliefs in Asian and Native American societies translate into a deep respect for "elders" who keep culture alive, teach young people through stories, and reinforce strong family and community structures. Elders are viewed as the ones who not only know the facts surrounding traditions but also demonstrate deep and thoughtful judgment that comes from the study and practice of those traditions.

It is worth noting here that our word choices are more than choosing "politically correct" language, which has acquired the connotation that "regular" people somehow have to walk on eggshells so as not to offend others. What we are discussing here is the recognition that our words indeed impact others, but also shape our feelings and thoughts. In being mindful of the power of speech, and its naturally ethical nature, we will make choices to reflect our care for others.

When we decide to substitute one word for another, a new meaning emerges and with it opportunities for creative conversation and practical options for future action. With some linguistic shading, we generate a fresh look at a situation. This is especially helpful when you find yourself in "conflict with someone" (or, we could say, when you are confronted by "someone you hate" because of their views, but that particular shading would close off conversation possibilities rather than opening them up). The choices we make in the words we use reveal what we know, see, hear, feel, and desire. To resolve the conflict and restore the relationship in the example here, we need to recognize the conflict as an opportunity to learn something new through conversation.

Ethical communication requires that we strive for collective understanding and that we appreciate the views others hold. Thus, the practical benefit of linguistic shading is the potential to enrich your understanding of an issue, or affect another's understanding of an issue, in order to generate new conversation possibilities.

To put the ideas of linguistic shading to work, brainstorm vivid words and features to describe a person, situation, or idea. Then, consider how each option points to a different characterization of the person, thing, or idea. Note how each option expresses a different set of values and beliefs, even if the difference is small. Finally, ask how each option might, on the one hand, open up conversational possibilities and practical action, or, on the other hand, close down any such desire.

LOADED LANGUAGE

While selecting one word to substitute for another can lead to greater empathy and understanding, the same process—substituting one word for another—can create something altogether different if the ethical posture is forsaken. When language is used strategically to manipulate our feelings and response, it is called *loaded language*. The language tends to exaggerate and depersonalize people and issues in an attempt to persuade us to think a certain way.

For example, "tree huggers" is a caricature of environmentalists that all but eliminates the desire or need to engage in the substantive issues surrounding reforestation. Beyond that, the term "tree huggers" is generalized and sometimes used in disparaging ways to describe all people who are concerned with any environmental issue, from recycling to water conservation to global warming.

Using the generally pejorative term "tree huggers" does little to deepen the conversation possibilities and understanding of ecological matters. Instead, it becomes the term to symbolize that the person and the issues at stake are insignificant or not worth engaging. The loaded language here is highly charged, both conveying strong negative emotions and creating equally negative responses that certainly don't encourage us to think about the finer points of the need of loggers to use trees for the production of paper products, homes, and a variety of other sources and the desire by environmentalists to ensure our natural resources are protected.

Labels and phrases used to describe people who are African American, Latina/o, Polish, Jewish, Italian, or Asian, just to name a few ethnic groups, often contain loaded language to depict stereotypes of the kind referenced in jokes and the media. In these cases, the humorous or insensitive communicators (depending on the meaning you assign to their words) are sometimes charged with being "racist," a term itself that is loaded. Contemporary conversations in newspaper columns, on television, in comedy clubs, and in college classrooms, for instance, question if "nigger," "kike," and "spic," though clearly loaded terms, are also "racist." What does the loaded language accomplish and at whose expense? Does the race of the person using the word matter in determining whether the use reflects racist attitudes? These are difficult questions that raise our awareness of our ethical sensitivities.

On the international scene, a recent debate surrounds the term "torture." According to some who would defend current military strategies to solicit information from the enemy, "torture" is simply a case of loaded language used to inflame public opinion. For them, using the term is an exaggeration of appropriate wartime interrogation methods. For others, the term "torture" is not loaded, but an accurate, descriptive term to define unethical practices that sacrifice standards of decency necessary in our world, even in times of war. The disagreement points out that while we may indeed hold conflicting perspectives, by being conscious and careful about our language, we can talk about the issues constructively.

In the public arena, loaded language reveals itself also as "spin," "euphemisms," and "doublespeak." These forms of language are used to lull citizens into a false sense of comfort, or alarm, depending on the intentions about the state of things.

Spin and *euphemisms* forsake the complete truth in order to boost an image, soften pain, or redefine what is often consider unpleasant. Social critic Noam Chomsky points out, for instance, that the U.S. Department of Defense is not devoted to defense at all, but in fact is financed for the purpose of entering into wars. Before 1947, what is now the Department of Defense was named the Department of War. The trouble with using spin or euphemisms comes when they are used to dilute or conceal the harsh reality of a situation, as when "collateral damage" in war is used to refer not just to property damage but also to people killed as a result of bombings or other assaults. Closer to home, when someone dies, we may say instead that "he passed away" or that an animal was "put to sleep." When you say someone "let the cat out of the bag," it may sound less harsh than saying that she revealed a secret or broke a confidence. Spin and euphemisms attempt to alter how we understand things by subtly or not so subtly appealing to an alternate set of values.

Doublespeak entails using words to specifically confuse and obscure the truth. During the civil rights struggle, it was a common practice for (some) white politicians desperately attempting to maintain their power and privilege to describe black activists and their supporters as communists. In doing so, the point was to deflect the focus away from the struggle for equality by causing confusion in the minds of citizens about the purpose of civil rights actions. These politicians used their words to instill fear into the minds of citizens that our democratic way of life was being threatened, instead of addressing the injustices perpetuated by Jim Crow laws.

DEEPENING ETHICAL DIALOGUE

Speech is a move to extend ourselves to another human being, and in doing so our talk becomes a way to *put a voice to ethics*. Put another way, we often think of speech as just an individual behavior that translates our thoughts into words. But upon closer reflection it becomes clear that because our speech is directed at another person, it is inherently value laden.

ACKNOWLEDGMENT

In fact, even to speak to another person at all is an important form of acknowledgment that we live among others who are deserving of our attention and care—as we are of theirs. Communication philosopher Michael Hyde poses a most interesting question, "What would life be like if no one acknowledged your existence?" You can imagine the isolation, fear, and anger that might mount under such conditions. Indeed, acknowledgment creates the space for others to enter our lives, and in doing so welcomes others to continue the conversation we start. As such, acknowledgment is an ethical move that oftentimes begins with a simple but earnest, "How are you?" or "Here I am!" in response to another's call.

Acknowledgment is powerful. When it is offered in positive ways, a more caring relationship between people develops. When it is offered with negative intent in some forms as sarcasm, insults, or disrespect, it has the effect of making people feel bad, unloved, and unworthy. Because we have a choice to make as we encounter friends and strangers, acknowledgment is a way to communicate our ethical posture.

FROM MONOLOGUE TO DIALOGUE

Speech is ethical when it appreciates the value of another, is spoken in a way to create new meaning, and is genuine in its expression. This special form of speech is what philosophers and communication experts refer to as *dialogue*. Following the ideas offered by Martin Buber and Emmanuel Levinas in Chapter 7, as well as the concepts taken from philosophers Mikhail Bakhtin and Hans Georg Gadamer, the theme of dialogue has over time achieved a mark of distinction in the study of communication. This is because dialogue engages another fully with a spirit of support, as contrasted to argument, which tends to encourage competitive behavior with the goal of beating the other in a reasoning game. Dialogue invites a sense of community by speaking to the other person where he or she is, as distinguished from monologue, which tends to create distance among people who are primarily concerned with their own individual agendas. Dialogue targets honest, heart-felt communication with another, with unconditional regard for his or her well-being.

Have you ever been in a classroom, for instance, when someone started talking about a difficult subject from a very personal perspective in an attempt to educate and inform others? When this happens, dialogue can follow.

Euthanasia, for instance, is a topic on which many people have a pre-determined position either for or against. In a classroom discussion years ago, a student revealed that her family chose "passive euthanasia" for a loved one by not administering any more life-saving drugs. She detailed the decision-making process and the pain that accompanied both the decision and the eventual death of her father. She revealed the initial questions they considered—would it be what he wanted, would the neighbors and other relatives understand, would we be able to do it—and she detailed the lingering questions—did we do the right thing? The student offered an honest portrait of her family's situation by detailing the research they did and the tears they shared. The result was that her classmates were driven to ask more questions and eventually understand that textbook and media discussions on the subject often miss the important human dimensions of care, agony, uncertainty, and hope that are woven into the fabric of the subject. The dialogue in the room that day transformed how many understood the controversial practice of euthanasia.

Classroom discussion in no way guarantees dialogue, however. Have you ever been in a situation when someone started talking about abortion, for instance, and soon the talking turned into heated conversation and then forceful argument? The speaker likely never even considered that there might be people in the room who had an abortion, or counseled someone not to have one, or had been close to someone who had to make a decision about keeping or terminating a pregnancy.

What typically follows when the topic of abortion becomes a depersonalized yet heated monologue is that many of the other students simply tune out what the speaker is saying. Or, if someone does respond, and the reply comes out just as forcefully as the first speaker's words, the interaction quickly becomes a competition to "win" the argument or at least to have the last say. This sets up a negative spiral of communication that disregards the possibility of deep understanding or the transformation of our views or even taking some time to think. Rather, people get locked into their positions as they experience agitation toward the others who hold different views. This kind of *polarized communication* is best recognized as the "I am right, you are wrong" form of talk, which you've visited already in Chapter 3 of this book.

DON'T POLARIZE—CONNECT!

The corrective to polarized communication is to encourage dialogue, often with the first move involving a question or a proposition that is open-ended. For example, someone who wanted to honestly confront the complexities of abortion might offer this opening to the conversation. "I have never known anyone who had an abortion and I know that those on both sides of the issue hold strong views. I, myself, am against it because I love children so much. Still, I know most people love children so I wonder how people who are in favor of abortion see the issue?"

Discussions of ethically controversial issues can take place with or without dialogue, but when dialogue is absent, the conversation is often full of technical arguments or settled/insistent/self-righteous moral judgments. One of the most widely witnessed case of euthanasia involved the 41-year-old Terri Schiavo of St. Petersburg, Florida. When she was 26, Terri collapsed at home, and with oxygen cut off to her brain, she fell unconscious and ten days later lapsed into a coma. Three years later she was diagnosed as being in a "persistent vegetative state." The public debate surrounding the issue came to a head in 2005 after years of legal struggles between husband Michael Schiavo and Terri's parents, Robert and Mary Schindler.

The communication in the public arena generally lined up behind either the husband or the parents. For the husband and his supporters, keeping Terri in a "vegetative state" was, just as the words suggest, cruel and not in keeping with her wishes. The parents and those who supported them proclaimed that no medical professional or other human had the moral or legal authority to take away Terri's "right to life." The way in which people took sides and labeled the situation left little room to have *any* conversation about important end-of-life definitions and issues. Instead of seeking understanding, the focus of the talk shifted to defending a position by trashing the other position, name-calling, and blaming. On March 31, 2005, Terri Schiavo was pronounced dead after her gastric feeding tube was removed in accordance with the last legal verdict.

Euthanasia is not an easy subject to discuss. And there are no guarantees that people will want to engage in a dialogue about it. However, when the euthanasia debate takes the turn toward dialogue, as it did in the classroom example described earlier, the conversation will generally surface the deep struggle we as individuals experience in wanting to preserve a loved one's dignity and at the same time exhaust all possibilities that a medical cure will be discovered to save a life that still has a beating heart. When that happens, euthanasia moves out of declarations of moral righteousness. When someone speaks from their experience to explain how and why an end-of-life decision was made or not for a family member, even listeners who have not had to face the same decision are invited to imagine something real through the words, tone, and invitation of another. The result is rarely to cast judgment. Instead, an empathetic hand is extended outward.

Sometimes that hand can be extended quite literally. Ethics is communicated not only through our words, but also in simple gestures like a celebratory pat on the back, or the enthusiastic grasp of another's hand in support, or the comfort of a touch on the shoulder. The ways we physically approach another, stand close to her, or demonstrate a recognition and appreciation of another through our head nods and eye contact convey our ethical posture. This desire to build relationships underscores the ethical imperative to put ourselves in the company of others. Philosopher Alphonso Lingis reminds us that in the end, communication is foremost an expression of this longing to be with other people. What we say in our interactions is sometimes less important than just being there, next to someone, saying something, anything.

PUBLIC DIALOGUE

Differences among people are vast, deep, and surely inevitable. Those differences can become reasons for separating ourselves from one another or resources for working together. When we appreciate the differences, the variations among us reveal the myriad experiences, stories, successes, and failures that contribute to a rich understanding of our communal life. When people are willing to struggle together in honest, open dialogue, a collective compassion can emerge that moves conversation toward inclusion of varied views, respect for one another, and trust that our common fate in a common world will be good for all. To get there, however, requires a desire to see the value offered in another's comments.

Despite the potential for transformative outcomes that dialogue promises, experience shows that we are not always willing to struggle together through talk in cooperative ways. Sometimes, we want to hold on to our beliefs or position tightly, leaving no room for another's views. Sometimes, we feel so certain that "our" way is the best that we fiercely work to persuade others to believe the same. That can work, sometimes, when our approach is fueled by a compassionate desire that reaches the other's heart and mind. However, when the strategies we use end up backing other people into the proverbial corner—it's my way or no way—the creative spark is extinguished and along with it, any hope for meaningful dialogue. Instead, we find ourselves locked into competing positions and wondering what's wrong with those who disagree with us.

A number of models exist for encouraging dialogue about public issues. The National Issues Forum, Study Circles, Public Conversations Project, The

Democracy Project, Let's Talk America, Public Dialogue Consortium, and the Search for Common Ground projects are just some of the organizations working to bring people with differing views together in order to learn from one another and make decisions about their collective future. From small groups to large gatherings, citizens generally meet to discuss a relevant topic, listen to the stories others tell about their understanding and experiences, consider options, explore choices, pursue consensus and/or public judgment, and discuss the values inherent in each position. Participants are encouraged to share their opinions, concerns, and knowledge as they listen to what others also have to say before analyzing possible next steps and taking public action. In these dialogue groups, people discuss campaign issues, the environment, religion, community planning visions, educational reform measures, health issues, domestic and foreign policy, and even democratic cornerstones for public participation.

Whether in a group, or through one-on-one conversations, each of us has the capacity to open ourselves up to dialogue about world issues—ask questions, listen intently, contribute ideas, and learn from others. You might even want to take a lesson from someone like Fran Peavey, who traveled the world with a sign saying "American Willing to Listen," hoping to learn what mattered to people in different countries by asking broad, open-ended questions and then just earnestly listening. The effect was that the experience changed her life, broadened her perspectives, and sharpened her desire to do more to help the world.

DIALOGUE AND RECONCILIATION

It is vital to talk about our past and our hopes for the future within a context of current conditions so that we can bear witness to the suffering that exists in the world. Many people would rather not see the pain and misery that occur in virtually every community alongside the joy and success that are evident as well. But to be able to work toward a more just world, we need to see, hear, and feel the anguish that some people experience. We need to ask why they are not benefiting from a community's resources. Doing so allows us to assess how we can contribute to a collective solution. When we choose to see the injustices in the world, talk to people who have been wronged, and stand with those who fight for fairness and equality, we put our ethics into action through speech and deed.

In addition to being an ally to someone or some group who could benefit from your voice, it is vital to recognize the importance of reconciliatory gestures to help move us through our conflicts and pain. When Amish children in a one-room schoolhouse in Pennsylvania were taken hostage and killed by a gunman, Charles Roberts, who then committed suicide, grief-stricken Amish families also reached out to console Roberts's wife and children. They immediately organized a charitable fund for the family. Dozens even attended

Roberts's funeral. As we turn our passion and compassion into action, it is helpful to now and again take a step back to survey the situation. Are there people who need to be acknowledged for their work? Does someone deserve your apology? Can forgiving others, or ourselves, help us to repair our relationships and our community?

From individual action to collective response, many countries around the world and cities in the United States have had to confront difficult histories. Task forces, commissions, and state-sponsored panels have researched horrific acts of violence or tragedies with enduring effects.

In Greensboro, North Carolina, a Truth and Reconciliation Commission was established in 2004 to examine the context, causes, sequence, and consequence of the events of November 3, 1979, when five anti-Klan demonstrators were killed and ten wounded by Ku Klux Klan and Nazi party members. In the absence of any police, a nine-car caravan of white supremacists drove into town to disrupt a "Death to the Klan" march in a black public housing community. Despite film footage captured by four television crews on the scene, the Klan and Nazis involved were twice found not guilty of criminal charges by all-white juries. A third, civil trial eventually found members of the Greensboro Police Department jointly liable with Klan and Nazi members for the wrongful death of one of the victims.

Many in the Greensboro community felt that justice had not been served, and so they initiated the Greensboro Truth and Community Reconciliation Project, a democratic process to investigate and assess trial evidence, records from law enforcement departments, media coverage, and hundreds of interviews and personal statements. Seven truth commissioners, their staff, and volunteers spent two years reviewing and weighing the evidence to prepare a 529-page final report.

The commission's findings, conclusions, and recommendations were made public to prompt dialogue that could lead to much needed reconciliation among various sectors of the community. Part of that process, the commissioners hoped, would include citizens becoming more aware of the signs that problems exist in the community surrounding labor, race, poverty, oppression, privilege, and justice. Nearly one hundred religious, civic, neighborhood, and educational groups agreed to read portions of or the entire report in order to have conversations about the content. It is through those conversations that the truth commissioners expected positive changes to occur in city policies, community governance, and citizen initiatives.

Hope for a better future resides in episodes of talk and displays of action infused with an ethical sensibility to care for and understand others. This work, of taking the time to sit with another, engaging in conversation, being mindful of our speech, and sometimes even working through difficult dialogues, is not always pleasant. It is work, however, that is important and necessary to reach understanding, appreciation, and respect in a world we occupy with diverse others.

From "Speaking from the Bedrock of Ethics"

SPOMA JOVANOVIC AND ROY V. WOOD

Spoma Jovanovic is assistant professor of communication studies at the University of North Carolina, Greensboro, and Roy V. Wood is professor of human communication studies at the University of Denver. In this essay they explore what they call "the bedrock of ethics in speech" by drawing on remarkable examples of care, rescue, and sacrifice during the events of September 11, 2001, and the days that followed. "Scores of eyewitnesses," they say, "gave accounts of the ways that people responded to the needs of others. We argue that the ethical imperative to respond conditions every rhetorical situation, and that this is no more clearly seen than in times of crisis."

Emmanuel Levinas places the other, not the self, at the bedrock of human sociality. It is the face of the other that interrupts the interiority of the self's consciousness, pulling us into the relationality of the world and to the imperative to speak....The ethical relation with the face of the other commands response not with force, but with invitation and hands wide open....Levinas describes sociality of the kind we are discussing as a "moral summons."

The "summons" in accounts of the World Trade Center often centered on movements. There was only one sensible place to move—out! But many people chose otherwise. Harry Ramos helped fellow employees down the stairwell. At the 53rd floor, he found Victor, a large stranger who was exhausted. Victor kept moving at Harry's urging until they reached the 36th floor when Victor proclaimed his energy was spent. A firefighter rushing by urged Harry to leave Victor and run, but Harry chose instead to stay *with* Victor. Moments later the building collapsed with Victor and Harry trapped inside.

Eric Jones was driving safely past the Pentagon just when it was hit but instead of driving on, he left his car to run *to* the Pentagon to rescue a rescuer whose clothes had caught on fire. Tyree Bacon, an employee of the New York courts who worked several blocks away, was one of four men from his office who ran *to* the World Trade Center and *up* the stairs to help people. Tyree's third trip was to the seventy-eighth floor where he retrieved a woman who was burned on 48 percent of her body. Tyree's three friends died. He lived. Mike Kehoe became the symbol of firefighters' sacrifice when a survivor snapped his picture running *up* the stairs in full gear. And another kind of ethical movement is signified in Todd Beamer's exhortation

From Spoma Jovanovic and Roy V. Wood, "Speaking from the Bedrock of Ethics," *Philosophy and Rhetoric* 37, no. 4 (2004): 317–334.

to his fellow passengers to roll to the front of Flight 93 in an apparent move to scuttle the plane before it could be crashed in Washington, D.C.

Each of these moves is a graphic example of the approach, the move to the other.... For [Emmanuel] Levinas, there is a call from a place "otherwise than being" that demands response. Eric Jones was asked why he had done what he did and he said, "I think everybody was afraid a little bit, but when you hear people yelling out to you for help, you...put that [fear] on the back burner." The move to the other is not calculated, it happens because it must as a responsibility of one for the other....

For Levinas, speaking begins with the imperative issued by the presence or "face" of the other. He calls that issuance the "saying"...a commitment of an approach to the other, the move to response.... The saying exists in the gasp or the suspended word, clinging to the lips unable to be voiced. The saying, as ethics, is always subject to the threat of betrayal by the said that operates as a system of nouns to name and constitute things. Nevertheless, Levinas suggests that the saying is powerful enough to remain as a "trace" even if the deeds of the said point in another direction....

The reports of 9/11 underline that in this crisis, the massive call of conscience was answered over and over again. David Frank worked his way down 40 flights with a blind salesperson, Michael Hingson. "The people in the stairwell were incredibly gracious," said Frank. The days that followed were filled with stories of people's rush to rescue whoever they could from the burning, smoldering rubble.

> Dr. James J. Moore, a professor of anthropology at the University of California at San Diego, said he had studied many species, including many different primates. "We are the nicest species I know," he said, "To see those guys risking their lives, climbing over rubble on the chance of finding one person alive, well you wouldn't see a baboon doing that." The horrors of last week notwithstanding, he said, "the overall picture to come out about human nature is wonderful."

Or, more to the point of what goes through people's minds in the moment of the actual crisis, it seems clear that people acted without "thinking" or they set aside "thought" to do what they must....

These moments of crisis exist in the world of life, not in the world of talk about life. Whatever a person might have hypothesized about what he or she would do in a situation like this, the situation happened and the person acted. The crisis interrupted the world of the said and the person acted. Eric Jones moved his foot from the accelerator to the brake, and opened the door, and put his foot out to begin to run toward a burning firefighter. Tyree Bacon climbed to the seventy-eighth floor of the World

Trade Center to rescue a woman who until that moment was a complete stranger to him. And Harry Ramos simply stopped and opened his mouth to say to Victor, in a tone we can only imagine, that he would wait there with him....

To get to the heart of ethics, the saying, and communication...[we can] look to tone, to voice, to body, and to other unarticulated traces of answerability that signal the responsibility of the self to the other. There we might detect the residue of the saying that carries forward from the place of ethics.

One of our favorite bits of tracework from 9/11 is carried to us in an account by biologist Stephen J. Gould. Gould, his wife, and daughter had volunteered to deliver asbestos shoe pads and food to the rescue workers. As they left a restaurant with some meals, the cook gave them a dozen apple brown bettys, his best dessert, fresh from the oven. Gould was moved to write about the reception those brown bettys received. "We gave the last one to a firefighter, an older man in a young crowd, sitting alone in utter exhaustion as he inserted one of our shoe pads. And he said, with a twinkle and a smile restored to his face, 'Thank you. This is the most lovely thing I've seen in four days—and still warm!'" Surely that warmth was the living trace of human care from a cook to a firefighter he would never even meet. For Levinas, the face of the other holds the trace but as the Gould story shows it extends far beyond that. "And the whole body—a hand or a curve of the shoulder—can express as face."

More than anything else, it may be the voice that extends the body with the trace of the saying. [Eric King] Watts has urged that we explore the power of voice in ethics and rhetoric.

> The important point here is that "voice" is not detachable from a body (singular or collective). Similarly, it is always in excess of the body presumed to contain it. I have proposed a notion of "voice" that concerns itself with the material or symbolic conditions of "speaking" or "hearing." Constitutive of an ethical or emotional event, "voice" needs rhetoricians to explore the social commitments that speech entails.

Ethics is...revealed in the approach and the voice, inspired by the trace that signals our obligation to respond to the other.

If the saying is the initial dialogic move, [it is important to remember that]...the said can overwrite the saying and consequently the dialogic tone....Following the attacks on the World Trade Center, President Bush visited a mosque in Washington, D.C. and many Americans reached out to their Islamic neighbors. Still, we witnessed diatribes about "towel heads" and worse that showed how hate speech trumps the impulse to approach the other in care.

That is why Levinas is distrustful of the word alone. Ethics in communication is the safeguard to make sure words do not limit what the other can be or do. Ethics in communication reaffirms the other. Taken together, the saying and the said are forever in steadfast relation. For the saying cannot achieve all that it reaches for without the said in which it is embedded. Again, we note the incredible alignment between Harry Ramos' move to stay with Victor and the words he chose, "I'm with you."

NOTES

For more information on the heroes mentioned in the reading, see:

Candy Crowley, "In Depth Special: America Remembers," www.cnn.com/SPECIALS/2002.

Sgt. Michael A. Ward, "Air Force Nearly Sweeps DOD Firefighter Awards," *Fire Chief*, September 18, 2002, News & Trends.

Jodie Morse, "Glory in the Glare," *Time*, 158, December 31, 2001, 96.

Dean E. Murphy and Clifford J. Levy, "The Evacuation That Kept a Horrible Toll from Climbing Higher," *New York Times*, September 21, 2001, B10.

Natalie Angier, "Of Altruism, Heroism and Evolution's Gifts," *New York Times*, September 18, 2001, F1.

Stephen Jay Gould, "A Time of Gifts," *New York Times*, September 26, 2001, A19.

FOR REVIEW

1. How is speaking an ethical act?
2. Illustrate the ethical power of two specific word choices.
3. What is linguistic shading?
4. What is loaded language?
5. Give examples of morally questionable euphemisms and double-speak.
6. What are the moral presuppositions of dialogue?
7. Contrast a monologue to a dialogue about a contentious issue such as abortion or euthanasia.
8. How can public dialogue lead to reconciliation?
9. According to the reading, what is the "bedrock of ethics"?
10. What are some ways in which ethical "speech" can move beyond words entirely?

QUICK REFERENCE: BASICS OF MINDFUL SPEECH

WORDS

The way we communicate and the words we choose can reflect an ethical commitment to others and society. Choose words that are not inflated or inappropriately shaded; seek mutual understanding rather than obstructing the discussion or obscuring the values at stake; work to open up conversational possibilities rather than close them down.

DIALOGUE

1. *Acknowledge the person(s) with whom you are speaking.*

   • Speak calmly and respectfully. Your voice is to welcome and reassure, not to overpower. *Listen* more than you talk.

   • Show that you know that you are speaking with people who may have strong feelings (pains, hopes, fears) on the subject. Show that you know that you are speaking with people who may have more knowledge, or other knowledge, than you on the subject.

   • Ask open questions, and mean them. You may also wish to respond to others' questions as if they were open-ended questions, even if they were not originally meant that way.

2. *Sustain true dialogue.*

   • Avoid monologue and polarization. Avoid automatic responses (quick comebacks; "Yeah, but…"; slogans, sound bites…). Always be *for* something and not just *against* something. Seek areas of common understanding. Disagreement isn't *necessarily* the point: how about trying to get somewhere together?

   • Expect the key questions to remain open. Resolving the question may or may not be possible right now, but dialogue itself is a means of sustaining connection—and that is the most fundamental thing.

GESTURE

Remember that how you stand and walk and physically reach out to people also is "speech" and has moral content. Before someone even hears your words, for instance, they note where you're standing, the direction of your gaze, and your interest (or lack of it) to initiate interaction.

Give your full attention to another. Look into his or her eyes, give a firm handshake, and avoid standing or sitting at too great a distance.

Moderate your tone in response to what the other needs—a joke with a belly laugh, a nod of the head, or a smile of approval, for instance. Stay close when someone needs support, even if you don't say a word.

EXERCISES AND NOTES

FOR REFLECTION

Reflect on your own style of choosing words and engaging in dialogue (or monologue). What are your strengths in this area? Where do you need to make some improvements?

In the Jewish tradition there is a time set aside each year—Yom Kippur—to ask forgiveness of people you may have wronged, either intentionally or unintentionally. Think back over the recent past and see if you can identify moments when your speech was too harsh, or your declarations of a point of view too rigid, and then seek out the people to whom you can extend a reconciliatory gesture.

The Jewish and other traditions also tell us that the true sign of repentance for an unethical or hurtful act is that we do not repeat the act given the same circumstances again. How can you make it more likely that you will turn a different way next time? What new habits of speech might it be useful to develop?

RETHINKING WORDS

Think of how you might describe someone who is physically or mentally handicapped. What words cast the handicap as a kind of fragility of mind and body? What words cast it as a challenge and occasion for developing strength of character? Notice how even a slightly different linguistic shading can transform how we view and treat others.

As blended families become more common, we need to find the right words to describe our new relationships. A new "stepmother" may not appreciate a term that conjures up Cinderella images of a strict old woman making her stepchildren do hard labor. "Stepbrothers" or "half-sisters" are words that define some sibling relationships, yet they also may fail to convey loving relationships that often result as two families come together as one. Consider what words and terms of endearment can best describe a blended family you know. Maybe you'll have to come up with altogether new words in order to communicate the quality of relationships that exist in that family.

The abortion debate is filled with loaded language that has the ability to sidetrack conversation before it even begins. What happens when we use the term "unborn child" instead of "fetus," "product of conception," "embryo," or "baby"? What feelings do these words evoke, and how do the words condition the conversation to follow? The use of clinical or scientific terms may deflect the moral concerns, while the use of family terms will surely evoke feelings of protectiveness. Think about how our talk is affected by using words like "mother" rather than "pregnant woman." When we talk about abortion as a "procedure" we will likely focus on the medical aspects. When we talk about abortion as "murder" we evoke a very different set of values and judgments.

Whether you are "pro-life" (against abortion) or "pro-choice" (for a woman's right to choose), draft a statement of how you feel and what you would like to know more about on this issue, using terms that do not condemn positions different than your own. Find someone else willing to do the same and then read each other's statements. Note what conversation follows. What words triggered negative emotions for you or the other person? What words or terms invited you to ask more questions?

DIALOGUE PROJECTS

Chapter 4 offers some dialogue skills primarily keyed to classroom discussions. This chapter has framed the challenges and possibilities of dialogue much more broadly. Here are some projects that may help you carry your dialogue skills further.

- You and your friends probably agree on a lot of things—best kinds of music, important issues in society, and even ways of talking to one another. To expand your horizons, actively seek out someone who has a vastly different orientation to yours and listen to what he/she has to say on these subjects. Does that change, in any way, how you feel? Do you better see (really *feel,* not just "know" in some abstract sense) that your perspective is not necessarily the "best" but only one of the possible ways of understanding?

- Spend time at a homeless shelter or assisted living facility so that you can get to know some of the people there. As you gain their trust, listen for the stories of their lives and see what values emerge in the telling. As you tell others about your experiences, notice what information you highlight and how that carries with it certain values as well. Do the two sets of values coincide? What differences emerge?

- Identify someone with whom you have a relationship who would benefit from your heartfelt listening and set up time to do just that. It may be helpful to set aside thirty minutes for the other person to do most, if not all, of the talking. At the end, consider what you learned about this person you didn't know before, and examine your own feelings at stepping back into the role of listener.

- Identify a situation where you have a different perspective than the one being discussed, and, staying true to ethical speech that considers fully the other person (or people), put forth your best attempt at explaining your position and understanding the other position. What happens? Analyze what you might do differently next time.

- Attend a public meeting (city council, county commissioners, school board) and pay attention to the ways in which the elected or appointed officials listen (or don't) to one another and the public. Notice, too, if you can tell what values are being communicated in the words, tone, and focus of their talk. What recommendations could you make to improve the quality of ethical discussion?

NOTES

For more on communication ethics and dialogue, see William Neher and Paul Sandin's introductory textbook, *Communicating Ethically* (Allyn and Bacon, 2007), and Josina Makau and Ronald Arnett's *Communication Ethics in an Age of Diversity* (University of Illinois, 1997). Sharon Bracci and Clifford Christians's *Moral Engagement in Public Life: Theorists for Contemporary Ethics* (Peter Lang, 2002) details the assumptions and prescriptions of twelve philosophers on moral reflection and practice from a uniquely communicative perspective.

To read the Greensboro Truth and Reconciliation Commission's Final Report or Executive Summary, see www.greensbororc.org. For more information on the project that initiated the commission, see www.gtcrp.org. A practical account of twenty-one truth commissions from all over the world is offered in *Unspeakable Truths: Facing the Challenge of Truth Commissions* (Routledge, 2002) by Priscilla B. Hayner.

To access the many free guides and reference materials available about community dialogue projects, see the websites for the organizations listed in this chapter:

- The National Issues Forum, www.nifi.org
- Study Circles, www.studycircles.org
- Public Conversations Project, www.publicconversations.org
- The Democracy Project, www.aascu.org/programs/adp
- Let's Talk America, www.letstalkamerica.org
- Public Dialogue Consortium, www.publicdialogue.org
- Search for Common Ground, www.sfcg.org
- National Coalition Building Institute, www.ncbi.org

GUEST AUTHOR

Spoma Jovanovic is associate professor in the Department of Communication Studies at the University of North Carolina, Greensboro. Through teaching, research, and advocacy, she examines ways that communal life is enriched by ethical dialogue that has, at its heart, a commitment to social justice. She facilitates workshops, consults on communication programs, and researches critical community questions. Her research on ethics and dialogue has appeared in book chapters and journals including the *Journal of Applied Communication Research, Philosophy & Rhetoric, Communication Quarterly, Academic Exchange Quarterly,* and *Business Ethics Quarterly.*

CHAPTER 14

When Values Clash

One of the aims of ethics is to help us make progress when values clash. Mindful dialogue can help, and you can take more care with facts and inferences and look for "like cases" and carefully spell out the values at stake. Still, even so, deep conflicts will arise. What then?

BOTH SIDES COULD BE RIGHT

Here is a starting point. In nearly every serious moral conflict, both sides have a point. Both (or all) sides speak for something worth considering. *Each side is right about something.*

This statement may seem totally obvious. Indeed, it *is* totally obvious. In fact, it is why we have such deep-seated conflicts in the first place. Like the proverbial blind men and the elephant, we each come to the debate tightly grasping our one small part of the beast, certain that we have the truth—and of course it *is* true enough, just not the only truth.

In popular moral debate, though, the loudest advocates almost always act as if only one side can be right, that only one side—their own, of course—has a monopoly on truth and the other side is just misguided or blind. On most major moral issues, there are usually supposed to be just two, clearly distinct and opposite, positions. "Pro-life" sets itself up against "pro-choice" and vice versa. On animal rights, assisted suicide, abortion, and a host of other issues, it's always just "yes or no." Almost no other options even get discussed. No ambiguity, no gray areas, no middle ground.

Yet the minute we step back from the heat of debate, we can readily see that both sides could be right in their ways. Most moral conflicts are real, not just mistakes by one side or the other about what really matters. There is genuine good (and/or right and/or virtue and/or care) on *both* sides—on *all* sides. There are compelling reasons to promote assisted suicide and affirmative action and abortion rights and animal rights—*and* there are other compelling reasons to resist them. That's life. "Only dogmatism," wrote the pragmatic social philosopher John Dewey,

> can suppose that serious moral conflict is between something clearly bad and something known to be good, and that uncertainty lies wholly in the will of the one choosing. Most conflicts of importance are conflicts between things which are or have been satisfying, not between good and evil.

Again—they are choices between one good thing and another. Not "right versus wrong" but "right versus *right*." We need to start by honoring that fact.

WHAT IS EACH SIDE RIGHT ABOUT?

If moral conflicts pose choices between one good thing and another, then instead of approaching the opposing views looking for their weak points (according to us), we can and should start the other way around. Look for their strong points. Ask not which side is right, but what *each* side is right *about*. Even moral arguments that make absolutely no sense to you do make sense to others who are every bit as intelligent and well-intentioned as you. There's got to be *something* in them. Figure out what it is.

Yes, the question of "wrong" can also be raised. Each side, including our own, is likely wrong about something too. Still, the first and vital step is to seek out the positive on the other side. In fact, our side and the other side are often two ways of looking at the same thing. What's weak or incomplete (in that sense "wrong") about our own views is often a strong point of (something "right" about) others'—and vice versa. We might as well look at it constructively!

Take for example the debate about assisted suicide. Should doctors be able to assist certain people to enable their own dying—at least, people who are approaching death or total disability, and probably in great pain? One side says yes: suicide may be the only way in which some people can finally escape their unrelenting pain; and besides, we are free individuals entitled to make that choice. Others say no: allowing and perhaps encouraging doctors to kill, or even just to assist in death, takes a step toward devaluing life, and who knows where it will lead. Life is precious even in pain.

This is a difficult matter, for sure. But it is difficult precisely because both sides have valid points. Freedom from pain matters, and autonomy matters, and also respect for life matters. We do have a problem here. But the problem is not really that we disagree about basic values. We agree all too well, about *many*!

The same goes for ethical theories. Utilitarians are surely right to stress that one good reason in favor of assisted suicide is the relief of pain. The prevention or relief of pointless suffering is a good thing. Listen to the stories of some of the people who want and need help to die, and your heart goes out to them. They have little to look forward to but unrelenting and debilitating pain. Let them go!

But there are other values in play too. Kant, for example, proposes a striking way to think about suicide. "If [we] kill [ourselves] in order to escape from painful circumstances," he wrote, "we use a person [ourselves] merely as a means to maintain a tolerable condition to the conclusion of life." Once life offers us no more pleasure we conclude that our life has no more value. But this move, so very natural if you think just in terms of pleasures and pains, is for Kant to overlook a whole dimension of value. Our lives, he argues, matter *in themselves,* not just as a means to something else, even of our own. We must respect our *own* lives just as we must respect the lives of others around us.

Character matters too in the face of suffering and death. We can respond with courage, humility, resoluteness—virtues. We are called to care and responsiveness in the face of others' suffering as well. When we begin to realize that people sometimes choose suicide out of a pain that is not so much physical as emotional (from bereavement, abandonment, sense of uselessness), we realize that other and more life-affirming responses are also possible.

In short, each family of values has a contribution to make. We're not necessarily stalemated if we can't choose between them—that's only if you assume that we must finally go with just one. But we don't. Each highlights certain values left to the side by the others. They're *all* right in their ways. Each has at least some pieces of the puzzle.

Naturally, this does not make the problem easier. Still, we end up with a complex situation—many sorts of values that we are trying to live up to together—which is already very different than a *fight*. Not a collision between polarized points of view, but instead a shared challenge to take up together.

IS CONFLICT THE NORM?

For some people ethics seems to be *only* about the conflict of values. Mention the word "ethics" itself and we may immediately think of moral controversies: abortion, affirmative action, animals, assisted suicide...and that's just the A's.

But conflict stands out partly because we expect and look for it. We are told constantly that we live in a conflictual society. The media thrive on opposition and anger. Adversarial argument is the foundation of our court system. Even the TV news now features opinionated and loud arguments.

Even so, I would argue that conflict is really more like a special case, not the whole story of ethics or even the main story most of the time. Many moral values have very friendly relations. Think of the four main families of moral values. Each is a big tent. Aristotle and Confucius endorse very similar virtues. Kant and the pope find themselves on the same page, more or less literally, when it comes to the values of persons. Each family may be viewed as an inclusive group—an extended family, we might say, with room for relations from many times and places.

Of course, the families themselves differ, at least in theory. In practice, though, many times the different families agree on practical conclusions. It's not surprising that what serves happiness, for example, also tends to be considered virtuous, caring, and so on. Even when the families do not entirely agree, you could read the differences not so much as oppositional as *complementary*: that is, they simply speak for different but important aspects of problematic situations.

Specific moral values differ all over the map, actually. Just think of how differently various cultures have treated sex, or our obligations to the poor, or who raises the children. But again, difference about these things does not automatically equal *conflict*. Sometimes our differences are just fascinating. They may even be a kind of cultural resource: looking at other cultures' ways may give us more new angles on our own. And often, even when we do feel dissonance between specific values, we can at least treat it as an invitation to keep thinking and exploring, not somehow as a demand to immediately nail down "our" single answer.

Of course there are, sometimes, clashes of values: direct oppositions, either within ourselves and/or between ourselves and others, that seem to require immediate attention. But how many must really be settled, once and for all, right now? What if we looked for complementarity or common ground even then—and also took our time?

INTEGRATING VALUES

Probably the chief reason we hesitate to acknowledge that "Both (or, all) sides are right" is that we're afraid that then we'll be unable to do or decide anything. If both sides are right, what can we *do*? How can we possibly resolve the question and move ahead? Wouldn't we just be stuck?

In fact, there are many ways of going on from the acknowledgment that both (or all) sides have a point. People who deal regularly with conflict resolution usually insist that only such an acknowledgment makes it *possible* to go on constructively. Moreover, most of the conflict resolvers' methods are familiar. All of them are so eminently sensible that nothing in this section will be a surprise—though I hope it will be an inspiration. The task is to put them to use in ethics.

METHODS

Specifically, the task is to *integrate* the values at stake. We need to try to answer to all of the important values at stake, to try to honor what is right in each of them, rather than just one or a few.

This is a lot less mysterious than it may sound. In fact, we do something of the sort constantly in nonmoral matters. One simple method is *compromise*. Suppose that for a trip my partner wants to go to the beach and I want to go to the mountains. We could just battle it out, or flip a coin, and end up doing one or the other. That's how it usually goes—a "win/lose" battle. Better would be to at least split the difference. Maybe this trip the beach, next trip the mountains. Or maybe we could do a little of each this time. Though compromising is sometimes treated as disgraceful or weak-willed, here it seems to be quite the opposite: a clear-headed acknowledgment of the diversity of values at stake, no big deal, and an attempt to answer at least partly to both of them.

Another method, better still, is to work from *compatible values*. Suppose that my partner and I try to figure out *why* we want to go to the beach or the mountains. Maybe it turns out that she wants to be able to swim and sunbathe and I want to be able to hike. These goals are not incompatible at all. There are some great lakes in the mountains and some great hiking trails at the beach. Both of us could have exactly what we want, at the same time. Why are we arguing?

Or suppose tonight my daughter and I are at home and she wants quiet and I want to listen to music. It would be a little crazy for us both to insist that only our desire is "right" and fight it out until one of us gets just what we want, putting down the other in the process. Why not just have music for a while and then quiet? Some of both. Or we can just work in different rooms. Or I could get a pair of earphones, in which case we could both have exactly what we want. Here we move beyond mere compromise to a truly "win/win" solution. It may turn out that our competing desires aren't incompatible at all.

Finally, sometimes when we really look into the values on the "other" side, it turns out that some of them are not merely compatible but are in fact the very same values we hold ourselves. Though we tend to focus on our disagreements, our background agreements may be far more important. For example, in the trip question, my partner and I agree from the start that we want to spend our free time outside—in nature. It may be that the exact location matters much less than simply being outside together, and being physically active. Suppose that we started our negotiation there: on *common ground*. Basically, we're on the same page. We're in it together. Only the details need to be worked out.

ASSISTED SUICIDE REVISITED

It may be hard to imagine how to apply integrative methods in ethics. In fact, however, it's easy. These strategies are no more than common sense in ethics too.

Take the assisted suicide debate again. As soon as we shift focus and look for integrative possibilities, the "conflict" looks very different. For one thing, there is extensive shared moral ground. Though it is almost completely invisible if we view it as a battle, one of the most obvious things about the whole issue is that both sides agree that it is a very bad thing to suffer such pain that death seems appealing by comparison.

Well then, we need to ask: what can be done about *that*? What about developing super-powerful painkillers? What about removing the barriers that still block some dying people from using massive amounts of morphine or other painkillers that would be addictive or otherwise harmful if used by healthy people? Right away we have some common strategies.

And what about those people whose pain is so intense, even with medical help, and hope so remote, that it seems hard to deny that death can be a considered and humane choice? Your heart goes out to them, and I for one know that in their situation I might well wish the same thing. My experience in many discussions of this issue over the years is that many people on both sides would be willing to accept a policy that allowed assisted suicide in such cases, but under tightly controlled conditions—that is, a compromise. Several independent doctors would have to concur; waiting periods could be required; double- and triple-checks would be necessary to be sure patients were not just temporarily depressed; communities and governments would need to be sure that people in pain always have alternatives—but *then,* given all this, if a person resolutely seeks to die, it is time to respect their wishes.

It may be possible, in short, to legalize assisted suicide in a limited way that both acknowledges the seriousness of taking life and its social dangers while also recognizing that, sometimes at least, it can be a humane and proper choice. You might be interested to know that just this kind of solution has been adopted in the state of Oregon (and reaffirmed by the voters), with results that, while still controversial, at least aren't an epidemic of suicides. About forty to fifty people per year have secured permission to request assisted suicide in recent years.

More exploration might help us see other possibilities and overlooked complexities. Actually, for example, pain isn't always the main issue. Surveys suggest that people who seek assisted suicide often feel helpless, useless, and abandoned. Some of my students found a website that included biographies of the people that Dr. Jack Kevorkian—the famous (some say infamous) freelance crusader for assisted suicide—had helped to die. Though it was a pro-Kevorkian website, in reading people's stories we began to realize that Kevorkian became a last resort for many people because they were not only in pain but also lacked any kind of family or social support. In some cases their spouses or children were driven away by their very condition—and in at least one case this very absence meant in turn that the affected person could not take strong painkillers, since he had no one to look after him when he was partly "knocked out."

Neither side would say that in this kind of case the right "answer" is death. The real answer is to create communities of care such that people are not abandoned in this way. Relationship-centered values come to the fore. That's a challenge to all of *us*, too, not just to stand by and judge the morality of certain kinds of suicide, but to keep people from the kinds of losses that drive them to such desperation in the first place. Once again a constructive and *shared* response.

SAME-SEX MARRIAGE

Here is a second example. The debate over same-sex marriage is wide-ranging and touches deep nerves. Some same-sex couples and their supporters absolutely insist on the right to share in marriage. Some conservatives cannot even begin to imagine such a thing.

All the same, once again, the debate is framed by some striking but seldom noticed agreements. This, for instance: *both sides believe in marriage.* This debate is not about whether marriage itself is a good thing. It is only because many same-sex advocates care so much about marriage that they argue, so passionately and persistently, that same-sex couples ought to be able to share it.

So is this glass half-empty—or half-full? You can focus on the areas of disagreement and say "half-empty." But you could as readily focus on both sides' broad background agreement and say "half-full." The rather amazing fact, right in front of us and yet totally invisible if we concentrate just on the areas of conflict, is that the "opposed" sides have common ground. The issue is only joined in the first place because they both care deeply about the same thing.

I don't mean that the minute you find some common ground you have somehow resolved the issue. No. What you *do* find, again, is a basis for shared problem-solving. As Roger Fisher and William Ury put it in their influential book *Getting to Yes*, it's not the other side that's really the problem, it's the *problem* that's the problem. Rather than fighting each other, you can now stand on the same side, even with your differences, and take up the shared challenge together.

For instance: maybe what we need is a legal structure allowing for different kinds of marriage. This would at least be a useful compromise, but maybe much more. Countries like France and South Africa, along with some U.S. states, have established or are establishing "civil contracts" and/or "domestic partnerships" as alternative legal frameworks for marriagelike commitments, for both same-sex and opposite-sex couples. It is not necessarily a second-rate status. Often the takers turn out to be *straight* people. They're looking for alternatives too: something different than traditional marriage, but not lesser.

Meanwhile, some conservatives are promoting a sort of super-marriage, called "covenant marriage." So marriage itself—even, oddly enough, "traditional" marriage—is already diversifying. Others—mostly conservatives too—have argued that the government should get out of the business of making marriage law entirely and allow religious and other communities to unite people however they see fit.

So maybe there are ways to improve committed relationships, of all sorts, for *everyone*. Wouldn't that be a worthy and absolutely shareable goal? It does seem that we have some room to move on this issue after all.

"FOCUS ON INTERESTS, NOT POSITIONS"

You've seen fine wood furniture whose pieces are fitted together with interlocked wedge-shaped cuts, like a dove's tail, that fit together to form a tight joint. Carpenters call this "dovetailing." Fisher and Ury invite us to take dovetailing as a metaphor for another integrative possibility when values conflict. We may be able to fit different values—even seemingly opposite values—together in an analogous way.

The key, they say, is to separate what they call "positions" from "interests." Your position is what you say you want—which is often, truth be told, a rhetorical or political exaggeration, quite separate from your actual *interests*, which are your carefully considered needs. Fisher and Ury observe that although our positions often conflict head-on, our underlying interests may be much more compatible. Enter the integrative thinker...

Here is a classic political example. From the Six-Day War of 1967 until Israel and Egypt sat down to negotiate after their next war in 1977, the Sinai Peninsula was a central and seemingly irresolvable issue between them. Egyptian territory, it had been captured by Israel and occupied as a buffer zone. Egyptian tanks right on the border had put hostilities on a hair-trigger in 1967, and Israel did not want to be so vulnerable again. Egypt, for its part, naturally wanted its territory back. Both sides insisted on their firmly opposed positions and the fundamental and quite legitimate principles (self-defense, historical right) behind them.

Their *interests*, however, were not so opposite. Neither side wanted another war, for one thing. On that point even these (then) deeply antagonistic states had something fundamental in common. Moreover, even about Sinai their goals were rather different. Egypt wanted sovereignty: they wanted the land back. Israel wanted security: some kind of buffer zone. Do you see any way forward?

The eventual solution: Sinai was returned to Egypt, but *demilitarized*. Egypt got the land back *and* Israel got security. And the solution has held. Egypt and Israel have been at peace ever since.

In ethics too, we know that "positions" often collide head-on. For decades, for example, moral and political pressure mounted to stop whale hunting, while whalers, from the shipowners to the crews, resisted. No surprise—their livelihood was at stake. Others were resolutely opposed to the whalers. Members of Greenpeace began to motor out in small boats in the open ocean to place themselves between the harpooners and the whales. Radical moral challenges were being raised, animals were dying, species were threatened. Things were intense.

Yet about a decade ago a transformation occurred. Shipowners began to realize that they could make far more money taking people out to *watch* whales than they could by killing them. Things started to look rather different. The very people who were the industry's resolute enemies could become, well, *customers* of a successor industry, and an industry that did not endanger its own resource, to boot. Sea-people's livelihoods turned out to be compatible, after all, with a new attitude toward the great sea mammals. It was not long before the old whaling ports were becoming whale-watching ports, and we were discovering that even the most hostile whales (and why wouldn't they be hostile after three centuries of being hunted without mercy?) can be affectionate and curious. People are even out there making music with them. A benign (and from the industry's point of view, profitable) fascination with whales is blossoming all around the world.

Did the whalers change their minds about whales too? Some did, I'm sure, once they were freed to look at whales another way. But some did not. They may still look at whales as a source of jobs and income. Yet even so, there turns out to be a better way than killing them—and a way that makes peace with the whales' defenders as well. Former whalers themselves now campaign against the whale-killing that continues. It's bad for business! And a variety of different interests are served—including the whales' own.

WHEN TO HOLD FIRM

Integrative methods do have their limits. "Each side is right about something," I have claimed. But there are surely exceptions. Mightn't some issues really come down to "right versus wrong"? And don't we want to hold firm to the "right" there?

How to Tell?

Sometimes it is easy to tell when a viewpoint really can't claim any validity. Seething hatred, needless injury, random violence—these things have no defense.

In real, deep moral disagreements, things are not so clear. How can we tell whether we face another view that does speak for something important, even if at the moment we can't see it—or a view that really *is* just plain wrong?

There are some ways. In the first place, keep in mind the basic families of values: the rights of the person, the happiness of society, the essential virtues, care and community. If major violations of these *central* values are proposed without a genuine reason of equal seriousness proposed in justification, warning flags should go up. This may not be a situation for compromise or any other kind of accommodation.

Of course, basic values can conflict—that is what creates the toughest moral problems in the first place. To serve fairness, the general happiness sometimes may need to be curtailed, and vice versa. But these are conflicts *between* basic values, not between basic values and less basic ones. To violate rights for the sake of appearances, or to abandon caring obligations because they got a little more expensive than we expected, is not a valid compromise but more like a betrayal.

Also: listen to the people. Normally there are serious people of good will on the other side, people who are reasonable and well-intentioned, informed and careful. If you can find such people, you have a good sign that they do indeed speak for something important. If you can't, more warning flags.

Of course, to do this you really have to *listen*. Remember that merely disagreeing with you does not make a viewpoint invalid or a person "uninformed" or "unreasonable." (That would argue in a tight little circle, wouldn't it: I'm right—because anyone who disagrees with me is uninformed and unreasonable—and I know they're uninformed and unreasonable because they disagree with me!) It's hard but not impossible: it just takes some honesty and humility on your part. Take your time.

In fact, even when we really are confronted with an evil viewpoint, it is still essential to listen to its advocates. Not because we agree with them, but in order to ask why the evil is so attractive. For example, fanaticism may sometimes arise out of a profound sense of insecurity. Hatred against "outside" groups may arise out of a deep sense of exclusion and disempowerment. And this too, before it settles on some scapegoat, could be a perfectly valid feeling. Just repressing the advocates of such evils leaves the attraction of the evil itself untouched. It may even become more attractive. Even here, then—even when we can genuinely speak of right versus wrong—we need to try to listen, to try to figure out the other side rather than just condemning it outright. That's ethical too!

Drawing the Line in Real Life

Knowing where to draw the line is probably easier in practice than it sounds in theory. Many of the most difficult moral conflicts occur within groups or between people who are in other ways in regular contact and already respectful of each other. Here the other side's intelligence and good intentions are not in question. And, of course, it's easier to listen to them.

For example, many politically liberal secular groups make common cause with Catholics in a wide range of "pro-life" issues, from welfare and children's rights to environmental causes. The same sides tend to divide sharply over a few issues, especially abortion. Here, though, channels of respect and communication have been easier to keep open. Neither side can demonize the other—they know each other too well!

Day to day, meanwhile, the people we argue and negotiate with—constantly—are our family and friends and colleagues, whose intelligence and good intentions are not in question either. Here especially the polarized language of "right" and "wrong" is not helpful. Keep a more open mind. There are certainly times to refuse any kind of integrative thinking, but they are the exception—not the rule.

BIG DECISIONS

Sometimes conflicting values go to the core of a community's very identity. A religious congregation may be trying to decide whether or not to bless same-sex marriages. A town or city may be trying to decide how to defend its shrinking open space while being fair to landowners and keeping housing affordable. Are we willing to use extreme measures—what many would call torture—on suspected terrorists? And could we *please* work out some sort of settlement, finally, on abortion, and avoid a similar thirty-year battle over stem-cell research?

These are big decisions. The stakes are high, everyone in the community or nation or maybe even the world is potentially affected, and the consequences are lasting. Thus the stakes are high also for integrative decision-making. In everyday integrative thinking, a certain amount of horse-trading is fine: that is how legislatures pass budgets and co-workers in an office get along. But for larger and community-shaping decisions, integrative thinking must *draw explicitly and centrally on basic and broadly shared values.* It takes more time—and patience.

TAKING DEMOCRACY SERIOUSLY

Democracy is one of our key values. But democracy means much more than making decisions by majority vote. It means working by persuasion, open discussion, and consensus-building around basic shared values. Again: *broad* majorities must be *settled* in their direction, not only to make a "big" ethical decision stick, but also to make such a decision ethical in the first place.

True, a temporarily ascendant side may suppress the opposition and force a decision. Prohibition is one example. Temperance moralizing had always had a place in America, especially on the frontiers, right alongside a lot of hard drinking. Activists would enter saloons, singing, praying, and urging saloon-keepers to stop selling alcohol—a striking precursor to modern sit-ins and other protests on both ends of the political spectrum. But all of this remained on the moral fringes. With World War I, though, the government needed to divert grain from alcohol production to ethanol, saving gas for the war effort, and it became possible, just for a moment, for the Anti-Saloon League to play on anti-German sentiment (German immigrants were the stereotypical beer-drinkers) and push the 18th Amendment through state legislatures.

Prohibition actually succeeded, in the sense that it reduced alcohol consumption sharply in many areas. The problem was that it had no roots in broadly shared and durable values. Its moment passed almost immediately. Already by the mid-1920s, normalcy returned. Prohibition was widely mocked, then ignored, and soon repealed—but not before it helped fuel the rise of the Mob and undercut the moral authority of future prohibitions that might be better founded.

Likewise, some commentators suggest that the *Roe v. Wade* decision short-circuited a larger discussion that was moving toward a more sustainable resolution on the abortion issue. It's hard to imagine now, but in the early 1970s momentum was building for liberalizing the then very strict abortion laws. Conservatives actually tended to favor legalizing abortion as a means of population control. Many churches were acknowledging that abortion could be a moral choice under some circumstances. The law was lagging behind, yes, but it was still a shock when the 1973 Supreme Court declared abortion a constitutionally protected privacy right in the first trimester of pregnancy.

Roe has been controversial ever since, both as an exercise of state power and as an assertion of the priority of privacy rights over other rights and/or other relevant values. But what might have been? What if we had been able to work the abortion question out in a less polarized and gradual way? The last thirty-odd years might have been different. Even now some such movements are happening. The Supreme Court spent much of the 1980s and 1990s hedging: a variety of restrictions, such as waiting periods, parental notification, and so on, have been allowed by the Court, while others have been rejected. Middle ground may be reemerging, but it is such slow and difficult work!

By contrast, consider the way in which the nation moved in response to the civil rights movement. It too evoked intense opposition at first. But here the appeal to shared values, basic human rights, was also evident and clear. It was the genius of the civil rights movement's leadership to put the challenge in just those terms. Think of Martin Luther King Jr.'s constant appeals to the Declaration of Independence and the Bill of Rights and the Bible. Demonstrations also galvanized moral responses. When people were harassed, beaten, even murdered for trying to *vote*—when the whole world saw fire hoses turned on black children peacefully demonstrating for basic rights—we knew what we had to do. In five years we had a Voting Rights Act and an end to de facto school segregation. Although racial equity remains a difficult and ongoing struggle, there is no question about the basic commitments. Now we can't even imagine that basic civil rights were ever controversial.

"SHAREABLE TERMS" AGAIN

In response to sectarian religious dogmatism, Chapter 3 insisted on *finding shareable terms*. The point here is the same, only broader. Common values do exist—they are in fact the norm. They can be drawn upon strategically for integrative decision-making at many levels, from family trip destinations to demilitarizing the Sinai. But in the big decisions, they need to be especially clear and settled and drawn upon explicitly and repeatedly.

And contrariwise, if you *can't* draw on such basic shared values, then maybe you haven't got such a good argument. Certainly no group should try to make the community as a whole take on its particular or unique moral stances—even if that group strongly believes that its stance is the only right one—without a real give-and-take, in which their views too are open to question, and without a broad consensus emerging as a result. Maybe it will, maybe it won't...but in any case the shared values must come first.

Even dogmatists might see the wisdom of this if they consider how many other dogmatists are out there who have just as fervent beliefs as they do but in different or even opposite directions. Each side likes to demonize the extremists of the other—"Do you want *them* making the law?" No. But most of us don't want *you* making the law either. You are welcome to try to persuade the rest of us—using good arguments, of course—but you need to listen too, and then we decide together. If we are ready! Otherwise, let's honor democracy—let's celebrate our shared communities whatever they are—and, well, keep talking.

From "How to End the Abortion War"

ROGER ROSENBLATT

When I introduce integrative thinking, someone always soon says: well, integrating values might be a fine idea in general, but what about abortion?

What about abortion? The fear is that our divide over abortion, at least, is utterly unbridgeable. Here, at least, there is no way to say "each side is right about something"—no way to split the difference (or no excuse for it: after all, the other side is dead wrong, even evil) or, God forbid, find common ground or shareable answers. We are hesitant to even talk about abortion as a result.

Yet integrative methods *can* be applied to the abortion debate. This short suggestion about "How to End the Abortion War" is a first look at how. Social commentator Roger Rosenblatt gives the debate some context, cites poll data showing that there is indeed substantial common ground on abortion (and it persists: more later), and briefly outlines some practical next steps to dovetail values and build on our shared, though conflicted, feelings on abortion. This is just a start too; the next few chapters will add details as we develop more tools for creative problem-solving and reframing problems. We return to abortion specifically at the end of Chapter 16.

The veins in his forehead bulged so prominently they might have been blue worms that had worked their way under the surface of his skin. His eyes bulged, too, capillaries zigzagging from the pupils in all directions. His face was pulled tight about the jaw, which thrust forward like a snowplow attachment on the grille of a truck. From the flattened O of his mouth, the word "murderer" erupted in a regular rhythm, the repetition of the r's giving the word the sound of an outboard motor that failed to catch.

She, for her part, paced up and down directly in front of him, saying nothing. Instead, she held high a large cardboard sign on a stick, showing the cartoonish drawing of a bloody coat hanger over the caption, "Never again." Like his, her face was taut with fury, her lips pressed together so tightly they folded under and vanished. Whenever she drew close to him, she would deliberately lower the sign and turn it toward him, so that he would be yelling his "murderer" at the picture of the coat hanger.

For nearly twenty years these two have been at each other with all the hatred they can unearth. Sometimes the man is a woman, sometimes the woman a man. They are black, white, Hispanic, Asian; they make their homes in Missouri or New Jersey; they are teenagers and pharmacists and college professors; Catholic, Baptist, Jew. They have exploded at each other on the steps of the Capitol in Washington, in front of abortion clinics, hospitals, and politicians' homes, on village greens and the avenues of cities. Their rage is tireless; at every decision of the United States Supreme Court or of the President or of the state legislatures, it rises like a missile seeking only the heat of its counterpart.

This is where America is these days on the matter of abortion, or where it seems to be. In fact, it is very hard to tell how the country really feels about abortion, because those feelings are almost always displayed in political arenas. Most ordinary people do not speak of abortion. Friends who gladly debate other volatile issues—political philosophy, war, race—shy away from the subject. It is too private, too personal, too bound up with one's faith or spiritual identity. Give abortion five seconds of thought, and it quickly spirals down in the mind to the most basic questions about human life, to the mysteries of birth and our relationship with our souls....

The oddity in this unnatural silence is that most of us actually know what we feel about abortion....

Seventy-three percent of Americans polled in 1990 were in favor of abortion rights. Seventy-seven percent polled also regard abortion as a kind of killing. (Forty-nine percent see abortion as outright murder, 28 percent solely as the taking of human life.) These figures represent the findings of the Harris and Gallup polls, respectively, and contain certain nuances of opinion within both attitudes. But the general conclusions are widely considered valid. In other words, most Americans are both for the choice of abortion as a principle and against abortion for themselves....

The fact that abortion entails conflict, however, does not mean that the country is bound to be locked in combat forever. In other contexts, living with conflict is not only normal to America, it is often the only way to function honestly. We are for both Federal assistance and states' autonomy; we are for both the First Amendment and normal standards of propriety; we are for both the rights of privacy and the needs of public health. Our most productive thinking usually contains an inner confession of mixed feelings....

Yet acknowledging and living with ambivalence is, in a way, what America was invented to do. To create a society in which abortion is permitted and its gravity appreciated is to create but another of the many useful frictions of a democratic society. Such a society does not devalue life by allowing abortion; it takes life with utmost seriousness and is, by the depth of its conflicts and by the richness of its difficulties, a reflection of life itself....

...Since the end of the Second World War, American society, not unlike modern Western societies in general, has shifted intellectually from a humanistic to a social science culture; that is, from a culture used to dealing with contrarieties to one that demands definite, provable answers. The nature of social science is that it tends not only to identify, but to create issues that must be solved. Often these issues are the most significant to the country's future—civil rights, for example.

What social science thinking does not encourage is human sympathy. By that I do not mean the sentimental feeling that acknowledges another's pain or discomfort; I mean the intellectual sympathy that accepts another's views as both interesting and potentially valid, that deliberately goes to the heart of the thinking of the opposition and spends some time there. That sort of humanistic thinking may or may not be humane, but it does offer the opportunity to arrive at a humane understanding outside the realm and rules of politics. In a way, it is a literary sort of thinking, gone now from a post-literary age, a "reading" of events to determine layers of depth, complication, and confusion and to learn to live with them.

Everything that has happened in the abortion debate has been within the polarities that social science thinking creates. The quest to determine when life begins is a typical exercise of social science—the attempt to impose objective precision on a subjective area of speculation. Arguments over the mother's rights versus the rights of the unborn child are social science arguments, too. The social sciences are far more interested in rights than in how one arrives at what is right—that is both their strength and weakness. Thus the abortion debate has been political from the start.

A good many pro-choice advocates, in fact, came to lament the political character of the abortion debate when it first began in the 60's. At that time, political thinking in America was largely and conventionally liberal. The liberals had the numbers; therefore, they felt that they could set the national agenda without taking into account the valid feelings or objections of the conservative opposition. When, in the Presidential election of 1980, it became glaringly apparent that the feelings of the conservative opposition were not only valid but were politically ascendant, many liberals reconsidered the idea that abortion was purely a rights issue. They expressed appreciation of a more emotionally complicated attitude, one they realized that they shared themselves, however they might vote.

If the abortion debate had risen in a humanistic environment, it might never have achieved the definition and clarity of the *Roe v. Wade* decision, yet it might have moved toward a greater public consensus. One has to guess at such things through hindsight, of course. But in a world in which humanistic thought predominated, abortion might have been taken up more in its human terms and the debate might have focused more on such unscientific and apolitical components as human guilt, human choice and human mystery.

If we could find the way to retrieve this kind of conflicted thinking, and find a way to apply it to the country's needs, we might be on our way toward a common understanding on abortion, and perhaps toward a common good. . . .

…For the ordinary private citizen, the elements of a reasonably satisfying resolution are already in place. I return to the fact that the great majority of Americans both favor abortion rights and disapprove of abortion.…What most Americans want to do with abortion is to permit but discourage it. Even those with the most pronounced political stands on the subject reveal this duality in the things they say; while making strong defenses of their positions, they nonetheless, if given time to work out their thoughts, allow for opposing views. I discovered this in a great many interviews over the past three years.

Pro-choice advocates are often surprised to hear themselves speak of the immorality of taking a life. Pro-life people are surprised to hear themselves defend individual rights, especially women's rights. And both sides might be surprised to learn how similar are their visions of a society that makes abortion less necessary through sex education, help for unwanted babies, programs to shore up disintegrating families and moral values, and other forms of constructive community action.…

Taking a stand against abortion while allowing for its existence can turn out to be a progressive philosophy. It both speaks for moral seriousness and moves in the direction of ameliorating conditions of ignorance, poverty, the social self-destruction of fragmented families, and the loss of spiritual values in general. What started as a debate as to when life begins might lead to making life better.…The permit-but-discourage formula on abortion offers the chance to test our national soul by appealing to its basic impulse. Were we once again to work actively toward creating a country where everyone had the same health care, the same sex eduation, the same opportunity for economic survival, the same sense of personal dignity and worth, we would see both fewer abortions and a more respectable America.

FOR REVIEW

1. How does John Dewey characterize most moral conflicts?
2. Instead of asking which side is right, this chapter advocates asking what?
3. How could both sides be right in the assisted suicide debate?
4. According to this chapter, are conflicting values the norm? Explain.
5. What is "integrating values"?
6. What are three specific methods for integrating values?
7. What is "dovetailing" values? Give an example.
8. Those "big decisions"—what special standards come into play?

QUICK REFERENCE: WHEN VALUES CLASH

WHEN TRULY OPPOSITE VALUES CONFLICT, AT LEAST SPLIT
THE DIFFERENCE

Both (all) sides can be, and often are, partly right. Even when we have trouble seeing what the other side is about, splitting the difference affirms and sustains the shared moral community. Here each side gets half, anyway, of what it wants.

FOCUS ON INTERESTS, NOT POSITIONS

Different values may still be compatible. Look beyond contending positions to try to *dovetail* the underlying interests: the core values. Often there are ways to satisfy both at the same time. Here each side can get more than half of what it wants—and again, shared community is served too.

WORK FROM COMMON GROUND

When disagreements are framed by deeper shared values, work from those shared values toward jointly agreeable resolutions. Each side might even get *all* of what it *really* wants. Shifting figure and ground is useful here. Rather than defining ourselves by our disagreements, let us highlight our commonalities.

BIG DECISIONS

When the ethical decision involved has especially high stakes and major consequences, take special care to act only from broadly shared and carefully articulated values.

---

9. According to the text, why did Prohibition fail? What's the relevance of that failure now?
10. How does Roger Rosenblatt suggest that we can end the abortion "war"?

 **EXERCISES AND NOTES**

FOR DISCUSSION

Why are we so ready to think that moral issues must be matters of "right versus wrong"? Why do we polarize values? Take some time with this question: there are many levels to the answer.

Here is another way into these questions. Many differences of moral values don't bother us at all—or at least, most of us. We're more apt to just find them fascinating, like differences in speech or sexual customs. Still, very serious values may be involved here. We don't generally announce that the work ethic, say, is "right" and any other way is wrong—yet work is one of the central projects of our lives. Chivalry is an ethic too—rooted in the medieval practices that also give us romantic love—but again we are not prone to moralize. A certain chivalry may be nice in a lover, but people may as well prefer to do without. Why do we seldom worry or argue about "conflicts" of values in cases like these? Why do we not insist that these differences be morally sorted out too?

Quite apart from what you may think about the morality of abortion, do you think that a Supreme Court decision such as *Roe v. Wade* was the best procedure for resolving the question? What would have been a better one? Apply your answer to emerging contemporary issues.

"EACH SIDE IS RIGHT ABOUT SOMETHING"

Integrative thinking begins with the acknowledgment that all sides speak for something worth considering. Given our usual habits, though, it is a hard message to get. We're too used to debating polarized issues. Just the mere acknowledgment that the other side has some points needs a lot of *practice*. Here is one way.

First, identify your position on some hot-button issues, such as:

- Capital punishment
- Meat-eating
- Drugs (hint: take some time to define your terms here)
- Affirmative action (ditto)
- Welfare (ditto)
- Gay marriage

Now here's the challenge: consider the opposite position—the other side or sides. Ask yourself what the other side(s) are right about—not wrong, but *right*. Where do you actually agree with them? What are their strongest and most important points?

Of course you don't agree with their conclusions—or most of them—but it's almost certain that you can still find common ground or at least compatible interests. In fact, probably you even share *most* of the other side's values, though you may give them somewhat different weights or rankings. So: what *are* those shared or compatible values? Take your time, be careful, try to put them in a fair way.

Suppose you are thinking about capital punishment. Shared or compatible values might include:

- *Life* (both sides insist that life is precious, which is why murder is considered by both so heinous a crime, why the pro side thinks murderers deserve death, and also why the anti side thinks that execution only doubles the crime)
- *Appropriate punishment* (since both sides condemn murder, both propose "ultimate punishments": execution or life in prison)
- *Deterrence* (preventing future murders)
- *Fairness* (convictions must be fair; the execution of innocent people and racially tainted verdicts are wrong)

Please note: The task is not just to describe the other side's view. It's tempting to answer by just summarizing what you think they think. "They think this; they think that." That's helpful too, but the task here is to go much further. What do they think that *you think too*? What do you actually think they're right about? Go beyond "I think..." and "They think..." to "*We* think..."

If you're in a group setting, a variation of this exercise is to make a list together of all of the relevant values that *both* (all) sides in some debate share. Usually you can come up with a very long list! That in itself should be surprising—and inspiring.

PRACTICE INTEGRATIVE THINKING

To learn how to actually put integrative tools into practice, it is useful to start with nonethical issues, or at least issues that are not so hotly debated. Here are some examples:

- Should medical insurance pay for alternative medicine (e.g., massage, acupuncture)?
- Should 15-year-olds (or: 85-year-olds) be allowed to drive?
- Should children's TV-watching be limited?
- Should elections be held on Saturdays rather than on Tuesdays, so it would be easier for people to vote?
- Should tax money pay for private-school vouchers?
- Should we build more roads to relieve traffic congestion?

In each case, ask first: what are the values that are competing here? What is each side speaking for that is important? Take some time with these questions—don't just name one value on each side. You know from Chapter 6 that the real story is likely to be more complex.

Now bring your integrative methods to bear. Are there ways to "split the difference" in these debates? What ways? Can the relevant values be dovetailed? Is there common ground to be found? What new options then open up?

Now pose the same kinds of questions about moral issues. If you think you're ready, try the issues in the previous exercise or some of these (somewhat) less controversial ones:

- Should political campaigns be publicly financed?
- Should there be mandatory drug testing?
- Should employees be encouraged to "blow the whistle" on business or organizational misdeeds or corruption?
- How should gay people be treated in the military?
- Should we allow the testing of new drugs and other products on animals?

INTEGRATIVE BUMPERSTICKERS

Visit some parking lots and write down the bumperstickers on ethical issues you see. Look for a wide range, including the ones that infuriate you.

Pay attention to the ways in which positions are misrepresented and common ground—shared values—is obscured. Look at the manipulative language, the appeals to authority, the air of finality. Of course, there is a limit to what can be said in a bumpersticker. But how often do we fall into "bumpersticker thinking" even when we could actually say something constructive?

Now take some of the issues that turn up in your survey and try to write integrative alternative bumperstickers. Is there a way to say something pithy that brings us together rather than divides us, that clarifies or connects rather than misrepresents and polarizes?

You will discover a great deal of pro-choice and pro-life sloganizing, for example. GOD HATES ABORTION, they say. ABORTION STOPS A BEATING HEART. On the other side, IF YOU'RE AGAINST ABORTION, DON'T HAVE ONE. So it was an inspiration one day to see EVERY CHILD A WANTED CHILD. Think of that: instead of trashing the other side for the evils of their ways, here is an appeal to the kind of value that unites us. It doesn't insist on one "side" over the other; it reminds us of what we should all aim for in the end. Every child a wanted child—which means: women have both the right and the responsibility to regulate pregnancy. Every child a wanted child—which means: when pregnancy occurs, we need to do everything we can to be sure the potential child is "wanted"—that is, that the family can sustain the pregnancy and the child. The whole issue appears in a different light—and as a collective responsibility, an invitation to try to better the world.

Another one I'd like to see: instead of the current IT'S A CHILD, NOT A CHOICE, how about IT'S A CHILD *AND* A CHOICE? Here's one I actually saw recently: PRO-CHOICE BEFORE CONCEPTION, PRO-LIFE AFTER. I realize that this is meant to be pro-life, the way the debate is now framed, and even a little nasty. But doesn't it have bigger possibilities?

NOTES

John Dewey is quoted from "The Construction of Good," Chapter 10 of his book *The Quest for Certainty,* widely reprinted, for example in James Gouinlock, *The Moral Writings of John Dewey* (Hafner-Macmillan, 1976), Chapter 5, where the quotation can be found on page 154. The general theme of integrating values is thoroughly Deweyan, as Gouinlock's collection makes clear. A previous and (somewhat) more theoretical work of my own on this theme is *Toward Better Problems* (Temple University Press, 1992).

Roger Fisher and William Ury's book *Getting to Yes* (Penguin, many editions) is essential practical reading on integrating values: see especially Chapters 2 and 3. On compromise, a careful philosophical treatment is Martin Benjamin's *Splitting the Difference* (University Press of Kansas, 1990). Benjamin systematically contests the various arguments that ethical philosophers have offered (or might offer—the arguments are seldom fully spelled out) against taking compromise seriously as an ethical method.

Roger Rosenblatt's article "How to End the Abortion War" appeared in the *New York Times Magazine* on January 19, 1992, and is reprinted from Rosenblatt's book *Life Itself* (Vintage).

CHAPTER 15

Creative Problem-Solving

Many times, confronting an ethical problem, we feel stuck. Only a few options come to mind, and none of them are very appealing. Indeed, one of our most immediate associations with the word "moral" seems to be the word "dilemma." Moral *dilemmas*. We are supposed to have two and only two choices—or anyway only a few—and often neither choice is much good. We can only pick the "lesser of two evils." But, hey, that's life. Or so we're told.

Is it? In all seriousness: is it? How many alleged "dilemmas" are actually only what logicians call *"false* dilemmas"? How many times, when we seem stuck, do we just need a little more imagination? For one thing, mightn't there be some ready ways of multiplying options: of simply thinking up other possibilities, options we might not have considered?

THE NEED FOR INVENTIVENESS IN ETHICS

The psychologist Lawrence Kohlberg, briefly introduced in Chapter 10, conducted his research on moral reasoning by confronting children with a series of moral dilemmas such as this one, famously known as the "Heinz Dilemma":

> A woman was near death from cancer. One drug might save her, a form of radium that a druggist in the same town had discovered. The druggist was charging $2000, ten times what the drug cost him to make. The sick woman's husband, Heinz, went to everyone he knew to borrow the money, but he could only get together about half of what it cost. He told the druggist that his wife was dying and asked him to sell it cheaper or let him pay later. But the druggist said "no." The husband got desperate and broke into the man's store to steal the drug for his wife. Should the husband have done that? Why?

It is all too easy to agree with Kohlberg's assumption that Heinz really has but two choices: either to steal the drug or to watch his wife die. But mightn't there be other options too? If we look at such problems with fresh eyes, might we even see possibilities in them that we can barely imagine now—maybe even new ways of approaching ethics itself? How far might a few creative problem-solving skills take us?

I ask my students to re-approach the Heinz dilemma with the problem-solving tools you will pick up in this chapter. Can they imagine any other options for Heinz? Yes they can...

Maybe Heinz could offer the druggist something besides money. Maybe he's a good piano tuner or a skilled gardener or a chemist himself. Why not trade his skills for the drug?

Or again: is this drug actually scientifically tested? Apparently not yet. In that case, maybe the druggist should pay "Ms. Heinz" for, in effect, volunteering in a drug test.

Why is the druggist so inflexible, anyway? Possibly he needs the money to promote or keep on developing his drug. But in that case Heinz could argue that a spectacular cure would be the best promotion of all. Maybe his wife should get it free! Or Heinz could buy half the drug with the money he can raise, and then—if it works—ask for the rest to complete the demonstration.

Also, Heinz and his wife don't live in a vacuum. What about public aid? Where are their family, friends, community? Think of the appeals you see in hardware stores and community groceries, complete with photos, a town rallying to buy an afflicted kid a bone marrow transplant, another chance at life. Just this summer my little hometown on the Wisconsin prairie raised $35,000 to buy a young man an artificial leg. Two thousand dollars is not exactly a lot of money anymore.

So Heinz—and his wife, and the rest of us—*do* have a few more options, don't we? And how many other problems might be similar? How will we know, without re-approaching them with some creative skills in our toolbox?

Notice too: many of these suggestions do much more than merely bring forward some dramatic and unexpected practical options for Heinz and his wife—which is already a lot. They also invite us to think very differently about ethics itself. Just asking what Heinz should do overlooks the question of what *we* can do—and sometimes that is a lot more. Suppose our job, in the end, is not so much to judge this alleged dilemma as to figure out how we can help?

A full-scale ethical resolution, for one thing, also challenges us to think about how we can prevent such dilemmas from even coming up in the first place. Forty-five million Americans, right now, have no health insurance—a problem that both political parties sporadically address, but surely something that needs much more attention, however you think it might be resolved. Here too we can and must take some responsibility for making the world a better place—not just judging someone else's (say, Heinz's) response to the world as it is. Myself, I can't imagine a more constructive or a more, finally, *ethical* approach than that!

CREATIVE EXPLORATION

We now begin a survey of specific methods for creative problem-solving in ethics. First up are a number of modest types of *exploratory* thinking. Modest, yes—but don't underestimate them on that account. Slowly but surely they can open up unsuspected new ethical possibilities, and meantime they help prepare the ground for the more dramatic methods to come.

GET A FULLER PICTURE

First: find out as much as you can about the specific situation that presents itself as an ethical problem.

Suppose someone put this question to you:

> *Terri Schiavo was on life support for fifteen years, diagnosed as in a "persistent vegetative state" by most doctors. Was it ethical to remove her feeding tube and allow her to die?*

You should answer: "Isn't there more to the story?" This too-brief sketch gives us no idea of Schiavo's actual situation: how she ended up on life support with such brain damage, what her family situation is, if there is any hope of recovery, and what her own wishes might have been in this situation. It is a bit like the Heinz case and other Kohlberg dilemmas: a short and starkly presented description, stripped down, with details resolutely left out. In fact in the original Kohlberg research, respondents were specifically discouraged from asking for more information, and their moral rankings were downgraded if they persisted. Yet it is precisely in the details that we may find unsuspected possibilities in such problems that on the surface just seem "stuck."

You'll remember that Chapter 13 offered more detail on this case. Spelling it out further, we begin to get enough detail to get a sense of where there might be room to move.

> Terri Schiavo suffered severe brain damage from oxygen deprivation after cardiac arrest, leaving her on life support for 15 years in a condition diagnosed as an irreversible "persistent vegetative state" (PVS) by most doctors. Her husband, Michael, began efforts to remove her feeding tube and let her die, reporting that Terri had said several times that she would not want to be kept alive in such a state. Terri had made no formal declaration of her end-of-life wishes, though, and her parents disputed her husband's report.

> The diagnosis of PVS was also disputed by her parents and a few doctors, and became the center of court battles and political debates. In the meantime Michael became engaged to another woman, fathering two children with her, but was unable or unwilling to end his marriage to Terri. He also won a large malpractice award, partly to be devoted to continuing to take care of Terri, but soon afterwards seems to have lost all hope for her. Her parents, suing to recover custody, declared in court that they would go to almost any lengths to keep her alive, including heart surgery and removal of her limbs....

The added detail makes the case stickier, yes—even gruesome. On the other hand, the very same detail opens up new possibilities that would not even have been on the horizon before. There's the point: we can already get much more creative than we could with just the first bare description.

If Schiavo had been kept alive, for example, various new therapies for PVS or near-PVS conditions might have been tried on her. If she recovered, wonderful, but even if not, testing new therapies might still "serve the cause of life," as some of her defenders were so eager to do. There would have been a better reason to keep her going.

The fuller description brings husband and parents into the picture too, which complicates things but again opens up new angles. My students insist, for instance, that Michael Schiavo needed to be able to move on. Fifteen years wedded to someone who cannot respond to you in any way is enough.

Terri's parents, though, seem to have taken a pretty extreme position too. So maybe what Terri really needed was a freshly appointed, and hopefully somewhat impartial, legal guardian. We have worked out ways of appointing relatively impartial mediators, even in very contentious cases: why not extend them?

Finally, the fuller description also tells us that the case really turned on lack of clarity about Terri Schiavo's end-of-life wishes. Surely, then, we should promote living wills: ways that people can declare their end-of-life wishes while still in full possession of their faculties. Apparently many people did fill out living wills after the Schiavo controversy hit the news—but we'd do well to make it an expected thing. An ounce of prevention...well, you know.

WATCH FOR SUGGESTIVE FACTS

Suggestive facts are those that open up whole new ways of approaching a problem. Keep an eye peeled especially for them.

It turns out that air conditioning is necessary in cars mainly because roads heat up so much in the summer sun. How unfortunate, we might say! How badly planned! Reframe such little facts as suggestive, however, and you could be off and running. Couldn't we make roads that are less heat-absorbent?

Why not use different, less absorbent materials? Paint the roads white to make them more reflective (and more visible at night). Or: couldn't we figure out something else to do with the heat besides just letting it radiate back into cars? Install pipes in the roads and pipe through water to warm it up for home heating or wash water? Generate electricity?

A few years ago I looked up the number of deaths caused by guns every year in America. The answer is about thirty thousand. This is a vastly disheartening number, in my view, but I already knew it was something like that. What surprised me was another figure that showed up along the way. Nearly half of these deaths are *suicides*. (Did you know that?)

This one number put the whole debate in a different light for me. True, the old argument is still there: the availability of guns makes impulsive killing easier, whether you kill yourself or someone else. But impulsive suicide is less likely than impulsive homicide: the inhibitions are greater, or maybe it's that we are just less likely to get murderously angry with ourselves.

I'm still leery about guns. But the fact that fifteen thousand people a year deliberately kill themselves with guns surely suggests a need not so much for gun control as for suicide-prevention programs. And since suicide prevention must ultimately mean giving people compelling reasons to live, what it really means is finding ways to make life more exciting and rewarding for everyone. I was led to a very new way of thinking about the whole issue. Notice also that *this* project, unlike the continuing debates about gun control, both works from common ground (Chapter 14) and starts from a compelling moral vision (Chapter 17).

GET HELP

Other people naturally have different perspectives and different experiences than you do. They can also help bounce ideas around, sparking a new one or making a rough idea better. Seek out friends who are willing to think in an exploratory spirit with you—and be such a friend to others.

Here is a short creative dialogue about the Heinz Dilemma.

A: It's funny that we aren't told what "Ms. Heinz" herself wants her husband to do in this dilemma. I wonder what she thinks.

B: I don't—I have enough trouble figuring out what *I* think.

C: She could be quite ready to die. Heinz could be the one grasping for straws, desperate to do something, anything, like stealing the drug.

A: And landing himself in jail, where he's not going to do her much good either. She'd be better off trying to steal it herself!

C: You know, what if "Ms. Heinz" *did* steal the drug? She has less to lose, that's for sure.

B: Yeah, jail will do wonders for her health.

A: Actually it just might! Did you know that jails have to provide medical care for inmates? That might just be her ticket to the drug!

This is a quick but productive exchange. We catch sight of several new ideas. And it works for a very specific reason. A and C are consciously exploring, working toward some new possibilities together. Their sentences start with phrases like "I wonder..." and "What if...?" They bring in new knowledge. They prompt each other's thinking along. Even in this very short exchange we get three or four new ideas and perspectives, ending with a really unique one: that "Ms. Heinz" could deliberately get herself arrested so that she'd have a legal right to the drug. Now there's some real creativity!

But B is a foot-dragger. He seems to think that his job is only to judge or to react to the others' ideas, rather than add to them or develop or deepen them or even to offer an alternative. Reactions like B's could derail such a conversation. But notice the spirit in which the others take them here. They keep right on thinking in a more open-ended way, while making a few bows

---

BRAINSTORMING

Though we speak loosely of "brainstorming" for any attempt at creative thinking, the idea has a specific origin. Advertising executive Alex Osborne invented it (in 1939!) as a deliberate process to facilitate creativity in groups. The key rule is to *defer criticism*. Welcome all new ideas without immediately focusing on the likely difficulties and problems. Give new ideas, still barely hatched, enough space to develop and link up with others, to pass around the room, to provoke other ideas in turn.

The other guidelines for formal brainstorming work are:

- *Hitch-hike on others' ideas.* Improve the last idea; or spark off it.

- *Wild ideas are OK.* No taboos; let the creative "juice" flow.

- *State ideas briefly, like telegrams.* This keeps the process flowing. You can always come back to expand the best ideas later.

- *Aim for quantity, not quality.* If you stop to try to develop the first good idea you have, you'll miss even better ideas that may come along after you've really gotten going.

toward B along the way, and even take his last remark in an unintendedly suggestive light. B helped out in spite of himself!

COMPARE AND CONTRAST

Do you know that there are some societies that will not tolerate leaving even a single person homeless? That many countries have both fewer restrictions on alcohol and dramatically fewer drunk-driving deaths? That for certain tribal peoples in North America no decision was settled until the people had heard from the animals?

Even the wildest (to us) arrangements have probably been normal for some group of people somewhere and sometime. Probably even now. Did they learn anything from this? Couldn't we—from them?

Well, of course. We are not the only people to think long and hard about life-and-death decisions, or marriage, or punishment, or justice. All sorts of people have been thinking about ethical problems for a long time. All sorts of answers have been tried.

Another method for creative problem-solving in ethics, then, is simply to explore some of those other answers: that is, to explore other approaches to the same problems, at other times and places. Find out how quite different people and societies have dealt with these issues. You do not have to agree with them. Nor is the point to instantly produce workable solutions. The point *is* to free up our thinking: to look at our problems from new directions, once again; to widen our sense of possibility.

You may discover that certain problems that seem utterly stuck to us may not be problems at all for other people or at other times. Abortion, for example, one of America's most divisive and painful and seemingly fundamental social conflicts over the past thirty years, is barely an issue in many other countries (though now we're exporting it), and historically was not much of an issue even here. (It may feel that the abortion debate has been going on forever, but that is only because most of us aren't that old—and because we haven't really gotten anywhere.) Just by itself this background may not suggest any solutions, of course, but it does give us a sense of possibility and movement. Things aren't necessarily as stuck as they look.

Or take the much-fought-over issue of marriage. In Australia many couples live together in so-called "de facto" marriages: they seem to do about as well as the more official kind. The French have created civil contracts for same-sex couples, as the last chapter mentioned, with the unexpected result that many opposite-sex couples also opted for them. Some conservatives are now promoting a new and stricter kind of marriage themselves. Different arrangements are possible. Instead of struggling over the definition of one kind of marriage, maybe we should, well—diversify?

Comparing and contrasting may take some research. You need to look for contrasting views and approaches: that is, contrasting both to our own and to each other. Find the practical details, too. How do the French civil contracts work? How *do* other countries handle alcohol? How do native peoples manage to listen to the wolves and even the rivers and stones? How can it be that very potent hallucinogens are widely used but not addictive in intact indigenous cultures? Really, *how*? The detail alone is often fascinating; the practical lessons are sometimes vital; and above all we may come back to our own problems with an entirely new set of ideas.

CREATIVE PROVOCATIONS

Creative ethical thinkers also attempt some rather more dramatic kinds of exploration—methods of mental *provocation* as well. These are also, as it happens, the favorites of most creativity experts. Maybe they'll be yours as well.

INVITE EXOTIC ASSOCIATIONS

For better or worse, we are creatures of habit. If we always had to think things through from the beginning, we'd barely be able to get out of bed in the morning. But mental habits can also become mental ruts. We can get so stuck in certain ways of thinking that we barely are aware of them at all—so it's especially hard to realize that there may be entirely new possibilities right next door, so to speak, but invisible to us still. And therefore the task of creative thinking is to wake us up to them—even abruptly, as sometimes it may have to be.

Already in the last section you have been watching for suggestive facts and drawing on your friends for their different experiences and ideas. They can be sources of unfiltered and unfamiliar ideas. By way of a full-scale method, you can now take the same process much further.

Try this: generate a set of prompts or "provocations" in a random way, and then free-associate from there. That is, invite—even force—*exotic associations*.

For such "provocations" your source can literally be anything: a dictionary, an overheard conversation, some images from your house or a book, a mystery, a magazine. If you're using words, it's best to have a source with a varied and rich vocabulary—a good classic writer, maybe—but in a pinch you can even take words or images from billboards along the freeway, or by turning on the car radio for two seconds, as I sometimes do if I am using this method while driving. Or look around the room you are in, right now (or out the window, or try to remember last night's dreams…).

The aim is simply to produce as truly different and varied a set of new ideas as you can. Now you really have a new, unfiltered stimulus for your thinking—from outside whatever "box" you are currently in. Right away something fresh. Then put it together with the problem you are thinking about. Don't censor, edit, judge. Give each association, however crazy it may seem, some time. What new possibilities, what new ways of thinking, might it suggest?

Take the problem of litter—of thrown-out cans and bottles for instance. We're used to hearing all about our responsibility to use trashcans, to recycle. Well, it's true, we should. But is that it? Nothing more to say? Could we think further and more creatively about this problem that is so familiar it's boring?

Let us try some exotic associations. Looking around, just past my desk, I see my houseplants. Alright then: could the image of a houseplant (that's random, eh?) suggest some new associations, different ways of thinking about discarded cans and bottles?

Now I free-associate...hmm...Well, houseplants do make the room more beautiful. So maybe...we could start making cans and bottles that are the same? Art made with "junk" can be wonderful; but we could imagine something more systematic, like juice containers made of different-colored plastic that can be joined Lego-style into kids' play structures, or (who knows?) stained-glass windows. Paper wrappers that could be used for origami?

Plants are also food—one way or another nearly everything we eat comes from plants. Well then: what if we associate edibility with can and bottle litter? Any usable ideas there?

How about...um, edible cans and bottles?

It sounds crazy at first—new ideas quite likely will. Some of them no doubt *are* crazy. But this one has some promise. Picture it: you could eat your food, then eat the wrapper to top it off. Drink your coffee and then down the cup too. Actually, we do this very thing already with some foods: think of tacos, or pita-wraps, or, for Heaven's sake, ice cream cones. So edible food "wraps" are not even that unfamiliar. Couldn't we extend the idea?

Maybe there's something to this exotic-association method after all?

Plants...gardens? Bottles and cans in the garden...? This may provoke yet another idea: bottles and cans as *fertilizer*? At least we could make cans and bottles so that they biodegrade really fast, couldn't we?

Keep going...Suppose we add some fertilizer and grass seeds or wildflower seeds or something and then, rather than discouraging "litter," encourage it instead. Don't stick those cans and bottles in the boring old bins; just throw them onto some bare ground, thank you. Or into your garden. Cans of tomato juice could have tomato seeds in them, apple juice bottles could contain apple seeds...

We could go further with this, but you see the point. Even with a couple of seemingly unpromising associations, we are now thinking *way* out of the box about the litter issue. No more guilt-tripping about recycling—just eat the stuff. There's creativity for you!

NO FILTERS

How to pick useful provocations? The key point is: you can't select them in advance according to your hunches about what would be most relevant or helpful. That is exactly what you are trying to *find out* in the first place. No—just try some different prompts and see what comes of them.

A good rule is: stick with any prompt, no matter how unpromising it seems, for at least three minutes (and use a timer: three minutes may be longer than you think). You won't know what you can get from it until you try.

Trust the process. Don't try to edit or filter or prejudge it—just give yourself over to it. Free-associating on the Heinz dilemma, for instance, I turned to the dictionary for random words, and the first word I found was "oboe." "Oboe?" I said to myself. "You've got to be kidding!" Then I thought: Well, an oboe is a musical instrument; an oboe-like instrument is used to charm cobras in India; maybe Heinz could somehow charm the druggist?

How? Well, I'm not sure, but it seems worthwhile for Heinz at least to talk to the druggist some more. We shouldn't assume the druggist is a completely boxed-in automaton, any more than Heinz is, or you or me.

Or again: People play oboes—it is a skill—people have skills—Heinz has skills...From here it might occur to us that Heinz could barter other things besides money for the drug.

The next word I found was "leaf." Leaf: "turn over a new leaf"? "Read leaves"? (Hmm—foretelling the future, as people used to do with tea leaves? How do we know that this drug is any good...?) Use leaves instead of drugs? (Are there herbal remedies...?)

If you absolutely must shape your prompts, seek out the wildest ones you can find. Oboes, leaves, OK, but what about *really* wild provocations, like going to the Moon, or lassoing a dinosaur, or the year 5000 CE. Sky-diving? The circus? (Try them.)

REVERSALS AND EXAGGERATIONS

Another way to provoke your thinking out of the usual boxes is to deliberately *reverse* certain features of the problem. Take for example the issue of animal dissection in schools: should students with objections be excused from animal dissection? Should animals be used in this way in the first place? Now think of the elements of this possibly problematic situation: students, curriculum, teachers, the specimen animal, and so on. Perhaps these could be interestingly switched around. What if...I don't know...maybe students dissect the teacher? Come to think of it (which is really what we're doing, isn't it—helping ourselves to come to think of new things?), what if the specimen animal dissects *you?*

The moralist in you may be shocked, and you may want to quickly disavow any morally questionable or otherwise gross sorts of options. But again, don't.

Obviously we are not going to actually dissect a teacher or ourselves—but couldn't this thought, taken as a provocation, open up some other interesting ideas, just around the corner?

One interesting new question is: how much can we learn from looking carefully at our own or each others' bodies—maybe about blood flow, or muscles and leverage? Think of how exercise machines are designed to isolate muscle groups. Truly, we could learn anatomy by paying attention to our own living bodies. And notice: studying our own bodies, live, would mean that we wouldn't need to use animals at all. Or we could study animals themselves *live,* rather than dead. Now there's a practical and fresh idea!

Yet another way to go to extremes is to *exaggerate* some aspect of the problem before you. Take some feature of it and make it as extreme, as overdone as you can. Then stand back and see what new ideas or perspectives it might provoke.

How do you exaggerate dissection? What I visualize is somehow literally going inside the animal. Not merely by methodically disassembling its remains with a knife in a lab, but actually jumping inside its body.

Wild, eh? Impossible, of course. But hold on…couldn't we once again move from this "crazy" idea to something more workable? How about computer simulation? In fact, doesn't the computer open up all sorts of nifty possibilities, like shrinking yourself down to the size of a cell and touring a living body through the veins (or lymphatic system or bile ducts or…) or tracking changes in the body over time or in different activities (sleep, exercise, sex, alarm…)?

Along these lines, here's my suggestive fact for the day: already in use are jellybean-sized "camera pills" that can pass through the stomach and intestines scanning for tumors or infections. Next up are even smaller and remote-controlled versions that can also collect cell samples and administer medication. Soon enough we should be able to send them through the blood as well.

So really, in the long run, we might not even need computer simulations: we can tour our own bodies *in fact*. We need only expand the use of "camera pills" from diagnosis into the schools. We can explore our very own bodies as living laboratories. Classes can explore each other's stomachs, bad knees, you name it, from the inside. Kids will love this! And who would need dissection then?

THE "INTERMEDIATE IMPOSSIBLE"

Finally, here is my own favorite method: what the problem-solving guru Edward DeBono calls the "intermediate impossible." Imagine what would be an *ideal* solution to your problem. Then, once you've imagined such an outcome, however "unrealistic" it might be (or seem), you can work your way back to a more realistic idea. In short, make your very first imaginative step a really big one. It's easier to tone it down later than to ramp up a timid little half-step idea into something bigger.

Take for example the question of assisted suicide. Usually we just ask: should it be legalized or not? Neither way is very "ideal." But now try the intermediate impossible. What would be a *radically better* solution to the underlying problem? Immortality wouldn't hurt, of course. Apart from that, though, a radically better solution might be for people to be able to choose death in some way that is not so secretive, passive, and (at least in some people's eyes) shameful. So one "perfect" solution might be a *heroic* death, like carrying out some sort of "suicide mission"—in space, underseas, in places where those who want to survive can't go—or (more likely) volunteering to test a new drug or medical procedure. Not that this could be made a requirement: but the idea does, immediately, give us something dramatic and new to work with. Ideas begin to flow.

Once you practice the intermediate impossible you will quickly discover that in many cases we do not really know what a "perfect" solution to our problem would be. We complain a great deal, we believe things are bad, yet often we have not really begun to imagine—to consider carefully—what we want instead. Maybe when we actually arrive at an idea of what we want, we'll discover that it is not so different from what "the other side" wants. Or not so different from what we've got already.

Do we really want to say, for example, that no one should ever want to die—that no one *could* ever want to die so much that they should be helped to do so? Is that really the "ideal" answer? Contrariwise, if we agree that some people could justly choose death, then what counts as an "ideal" death? These are not easy questions, and it is natural to wonder whether we are so confused about assisted suicide in general partly because we are so confused about them.

"WHAT IF . . . ?" MORAL THINKING

Creative thinking can provoke us to stretch and rearrange ideas and even values in search of new perspectives and possibilities. It may not only open up new practical options but also give our moral thinking itself more depth and resiliency. Ultimately our moral views may be stronger for having really considered them from a wide range of different points of view and "what ifs." Besides, who knows, sometimes we may even change our minds!

Take the question of meat-eating. Vegetarians question whether we should eat meat at all. By way of self-provocation, perhaps we could *exaggerate* in the other direction.

What if...we eat nothing *but meat?*

Some native peoples do: traditional Inuit, for example (Eskimo), who live so far north that nothing really grows. Fish, seals, and whales form their entire diet. What shall we say of them? Should they move? But moving would destroy their culture—other values would suffer more. Importing nonmeat foods would also damage the culture, making them economically dependent. It may be better to conclude that for them, at least, eating meat is acceptable. They have no real alternatives.

The other side of this thought, though, is that meat may be much more questionable when there *are* alternatives. And almost all of the rest of us do have alternatives. So perhaps "ethical eating" is different depending on where one lives?

Reversal? Meat as we know it comes from animals. So:

What if... meat does not *come from animals?*

At first the idea seems crazy. But keep thinking... Scientists can now take a single cell from an animal body and create tissue cultures—test tubes of animal tissue, but without bodies or brains—on which to test drugs. Might they do the same for meat—that is, to grow animal muscle tissue without body or brain? Certain science fiction writers have imagined this already: it is a way of having meat without animals, and therefore without animal suffering.

This may or may not be a good idea. (If it strikes you as ghoulish, a good question would be: why does it *not* strike you as ghoulish to eat the flesh of an actual animal?) In any case, the point is: it's an idea. We're out of the box now for sure!

Another reversal. Here some "normal" feature of a situation is turned exactly on its head. We eat animals, so...

What if... animals eat us?

A few animals do eat us—or would if they could. It seems to strike some people as "only fair" that therefore we eat them. The problem is that the animals who eat us are not the animals we eat, like cows and chickens, who tend to be friendly and who in nature mostly eat plants or insects. We don't even favor animals who typically eat each other (except for fish). So maybe it is acceptable to eat animals, but not the ones we currently eat? Crocodile, anyone? Vulture?

Or maybe the idea is that if we are to eat animals, we need to allow ourselves to be eaten in return in some way? After death, many of the Plains

Indians tribes put out corpses in special places where the wolves and the vultures would pick the bones clean. Is that the idea—some appropriate ceremonial return of our own flesh to the flesh of the living world? How might we do something of the sort now?

Vegetarians sometimes complain that the lives and deaths of the animals we eat are normally completely out of view. Children often are shocked to discover what meat actually is when they finally put two and two together. So...

> *What if... the lives and deaths of the animals we eat were completely* in *view?*

That is, what if the "facts of meat" were not hidden? What if we did not try to disguise the costs to animals with cute ads about fish leaping into tuna cans and chickens living it up in factory farms? Perhaps people might even be expected to kill some of the animals they themselves eat. This is not impossible: hunters for example do it all the time. But it does change the picture. It makes us think about meat-eating in another way—and that, once again, is the point.

QUICK REFERENCE: CREATIVE PROBLEM-SOLVING IN ETHICS

In dealing with any moral problem or issue, use creative methods to widen the range of options you consider and to deepen your sense of the issue and the values involved.

- Get a fuller picture. Find out as much as you can about the specific situation; look to the details to suggest new ideas.
- Watch for suggestive facts.
- Get help. Find people to brainstorm difficult issues with you.
- Compare and contrast. Explore how the same problem is treated in other places and times.
- Invite exotic associations. Seek unfiltered "provocations" in random words, analogies, or images; free-associate from there.
- Reverse or exaggerate key features of the problem.
- The intermediate impossible: start with "ideal" solutions and work toward realism.

FOR REVIEW

1. What are some creative options in the "Heinz Dilemma"?
2. What is the point of seeking a fuller picture of an ethical problem? Who needs more details?
3. What is an example of a "suggestive fact"?
4. What is the key rule for brainstorming? Why?
5. "Compare and contrast"—what could be creative about that?
6. How can you "invite exotic associations"?
7. Illustrate "reversal."
8. Illustrate "exaggeration."
9. Illustrate the "intermediate impossible."
10. Illustrate "What if?" moral thinking.

EXERCISES AND NOTES

PROBLEM-SOLVING WARM-UPS

The methods introduced here are useful across the board, not just in ethics. Though the aim is to use them in ethics, you might begin by practicing more broadly. Try some "novel function practice," for example. Most of us have been asked, in some game or quiz-book, how many new and different uses we can think of for some everyday object, like a brick. What can you do with a brick, besides build houses? Well, a brick can be a paperweight or a doorstop. You can make bookcases out of bricks and wood. Are there more creative uses? Suppose you tape on a return-postage-guaranteed junk mail reply form and drop it in a mailbox—a good way to protest junk mail. Suppose you leave it in your yard until you want to go fishing, and then lift it up to collect the worms underneath. (This suggestion is courtesy of one of my students. Brick as "worm-generator," he called it.)

So find some other everyday object and practice. What can you do with a...cheap ballpoint pen (besides write)? ...a piece of paper? ...a rotten apple?...a bad joke? Can you think of ten ways (or if that's easy, twenty) to get water out of a glass without moving the glass or damaging it? (Evaporate it? Soak paper towels or sponges in the water? Suck it out with a straw? And where do you get a straw, right now? How about the casing of that cheap ballpoint pen?) Or: suppose an elephant (or python, or pack of cats, or…) has escaped in your neighborhood. Figure out five (or ten, or…) ways it can be recaptured.

Now pick some specific practical problems around your school or area and challenge yourself to add to (let's say, double or triple) the number of options usually considered. Don't evaluate them yet—just aim to diversify options. Here are some sample problems.

- Waste (styrofoam cups, lights left on all the time, newspaper, etc.)
- Alcoholism and other addictions
- Too much television
- Lack of affordable childcare for working families with young children
- Lack of inexpensive travel options
- Alternatives to on-the-air fundraising for public radio
- Not enough parking at school or elsewhere
- Difficulties maintaining nuclear test bans
- Low voter turnout

Now consider some social issues—just don't take the biggest ones right away. Any new ideas about pornography? For slowing down speeders? What about, say, five original ways for improving teen-parent relations? Keeping politicians honest?

CREATIVE PROBLEM-SOLVING IN ETHICS

Now consider more familiar moral issues, and treat them exactly the same way. Use the option-multiplying methods just as you did with the practical problems in the last exercise. Again, don't evaluate them yet—just aim to diversify options. Challenge yourself to double or triple the number of options usually considered. Here are some possible issues.

- Gun control
- Marriage—it's not working very well in general…
- Drug use
- Blowing the whistle on business or administrative corruption
- The treatment of gay people in the military
- Political campaign finance abuse
- Medical testing on animals
- Rainforest destruction

Here are some more detailed challenges.

- Our children's, maybe even our own, moral and personal role models, tend to be movie stars, athletes, political leaders (?). Who might be more suitable? More specifically: what more suitable role models might also have the allure and the visibility of the movie star or athlete? Might we have to create them? How?

- What might the elderly do with their time? How could society be restructured to respond to their needs and to better enable them to speak to ours? How about a system of adoptive grandparents, as some of my students have suggested? And what other opportunities might aging represent? Must even selective memory loss necessarily be viewed as a mental failing? Could it even be regarded as an *advantage*? How?

- We're told that there is a dilemma between birth mothers' rights to privacy and adoptees' rights to "know where they came from." Maybe so, maybe not. We won't really know until we look at actual evidence. Some states, for example, allow adoptees to find out who their birth mothers are. Others have established a registry so that those birth mothers and adoptees who wish to be found can be. What might be some useful further experiments?

- Some standard objections to welfare programs are fairly specific and not so hard to fix once you seriously try to multiply options. For example, many people are offended by the use of food stamps to buy morally disapproved items like cigarettes and alcohol. Supposing that this *is* a widespread problem (which is not so clear, as data are hard to come by and it is especially tempting to fly by the stereotypes on this issue), is it so hard to resolve?

- We say that drugs offer an escape from school or work or just life itself. But this leads to other questions. Why do so many people need such an escape in the first place? And what can we do about school or work or life itself, so that such an escape is less tempting? Aren't there less lethal ways to make life more joyful and interesting?

- What happens when personal ethics conflict with organizational practices: say, in business or the military or government? How could such conflicts be better handled? Are there new and creative ways to deal with the problem of "whistle-blowing"—and the kinds of problems that lead to the need for whistle-blowing in the first place?

- Rich countries try to help less well-off countries when natural disasters strike (earthquakes, hurricanes...). What about also helping to overcome the underlying causes of poverty itself? Meanwhile, aren't there some ways in which *we* need *their* help? What would a system of truly *mutual* aid look like?

- We are consuming food, energy, and other natural resources at unsustainable rates, and what kind of world we will pass on to our descendants is becoming increasingly uncertain as a result. What to do?

ANOTHER FAMOUS DILEMMA

This chapter began with the Heinz Dilemma, a case that philosophers have found so difficult that it became a classic example of an ethical dilemma. Here is another—we could probably even say *the* other—famous modern moral dilemma. The French philosopher Jean-Paul Sartre described a young man in occupied Paris during World War II who came to him for advice.

> His father was on bad terms with his mother, and, moreover, was inclined to be a collaborationist [that is, he cooperated with the Nazis]; his older brother had been killed in the German offensive of 1940, and the young man, with somewhat immature but generous feelings, wanted to avenge him. His mother lived alone with him, very much upset by the half-treason of her husband and the death of her elder son; the boy was her only consolation.
>
> The boy was faced with the choice of leaving for England and joining the Free French forces—that is, leaving his mother behind—or remaining with his mother and helping her to carry on. He was fully aware that the woman lived only for him and that his going off—and perhaps his death—would plunge her into despair. He was also aware that every act that he did for his mother's sake was a sure thing, in the sense that it was helping her to carry on, whereas every effort he made toward going off and fighting was an uncertain move which might run aground and prove completely useless.... He was faced with two very different kinds of action: one concrete, immediate, but concerning only one individual; the other concerned an incomparably vaster group, a national collectivity, but for that very reason was dubious, and might be interrupted en route.

Imagine that this young man came to you for some help in this situation. Do you see any options for him? Take your time, and use the methods in this chapter.

NOTES

"False dilemma" is a classic fallacy in informal logic that is usefully discussed and illustrated in many informal logic textbooks, such as Howard Kahane's *Logic and Contemporary Rhetoric* (Wadsworth Publishing Company, many editions). Moral philosophers who might want a bit more about my treatment of the "Heinz Dilemma" as a false dilemma should consult the Teacher's Appendix at the end of this book.

There is a huge literature in creative problem-solving, but most of it addresses nonmoral issues and contexts, such as management and design.

For a range of approaches to problem-solving broadly conceived, see Edward DeBono, *Serious Creativity* (HarperCollins, 1992) and *Lateral Thinking* (Harper, 1970); Barry Nalebuff and Ian Ayres, *Why Not? How to Use Everyday Ingenuity to Solve Problems Big and Small* (Harvard Business School Press, 2003); Charlie and Maria Girsch, *Inventivity* (Creativity Central, 1999); and Marvin Levine, *Effective Problem-Solving* (Prentice-Hall, 2nd edition, 1993). On proactive thinking, Stephen Covey's *The Seven Habits of Highly Effective People* (Simon and Schuster, 1990) is classic. Two books of my own specifically on the subject are *Creative Problem-Solving in Ethics* (Oxford, 2006), which mostly covers the same ground as this and the next chapter, and its sister, *Creativity for Critical Thinkers* (also Oxford, 2006), which you might find a helpful complement.

For an introduction to "What if...?" thinking (DeBono calls it PO thinking, for POssible or hyPOthesis) and the specific methods outlined here, see his *Serious Creativity* (HarperCollins, 1992), especially pages 163–176. On the origins of brainstorming, see Alex Osborne's *Applied Imagination: Principles and Procedures of Creative Problem-Solving* (Creative Education Foundation, 1993).

The extended description of the Schiavo case is my abridgement and adaptation of an entry from Wikipedia at http://en.wikipedia.org/wiki/Schiavo, accessed 7/7/05.

Jean-Paul Sartre is cited from his *Existentialism and Human Emotions* (Philosophical Library, 1957), pages 24–25.

CHAPTER 16

Reframing Problems

We come next to a set of creative strategies that work at a deeper level. It's one thing to solve a problem more or less in the terms in which it presented. A wider-ranging kind of creativity invites us to rethink and possibly to transform the problem itself in fundamental ways.

OPENING UP A PROBLEM

Just back from study in Bolivia, a student told me one day that the practice among the young Bolivian males he knew was to go to a prostitute for their sexual initiation. He was disturbed by this, and since he knew that I write ethics books, he wanted my opinion.

I suppose he expected moral outrage. And I'm sure that moral outrage is appropriate, especially from the point of view of a society struggling to value women as full partners and equals. The problem, once again, is that the insistence on making such judgments pretty much closes down the discussion. Nothing else is explored; we think we've said everything that needs to be said.

In fact we'd only begun. My student and I ended up in a long conversation. It turned out that when he had expressed his surprise and confusion to his Bolivian friends, they became curious about how sexual initiation works in America. Do *we* have a better way? My student was not at all sure. How do we teach young people about sex, anyway? Locker-room conversations? Movies? Pornography? How ethical is that?

Notice how the question shifts here. We don't have much say over Bolivian men, but we can make a difference to what we ourselves do. So how might *we* do better? Seriously: this is a real question. Never mind the Bolivians—right here at home is where we might be able to make some creative moral progress. That is a complex question, an ongoing struggle, a much more open but also vital question.

ATTENTION SHIFTS

Ethical problems can be pressing and painful. They may compel our full attention. Often some kind of crisis brings them to us. But crisis management is not the only mode in which we can or should engage them. At some point we also need to step back far enough to be able to ask how we got into this crisis in the first place, and what can be done about *that*. We can begin to *reframe problems*.

We debate whether doctors should be able or obliged to help people die. But how did doctors—and now increasingly hospitals and their lawyers—get in this position of power? Is this arrangement a good idea? What might some better alternatives look like?

The Heinz problem likewise poses a compelling question that seems to require a yes-or-no, one-or-the-other sort of answer—while all around and before and beside it are a number of other, more intriguing and also more unsettling questions to ask, and other directions our thinking might go in. Answering "the" original question is important, for sure, but that's only a beginning. Oughtn't we be asking about the design of the whole health-care payment system as well? For why does the sick woman have no insurance? Why can't public assistance help her? If either insurance or public assistance were real options, Heinz's dilemma would not even come up.

And what are the causes of this illness, anyway? The American Cancer Society estimates that 80 percent of all cancers are environmentally caused. So perhaps we have here a workplace issue or a diet issue, or polluted air or water? How could we leave all of this alone, as if the whole problem were just Heinz's, or rather his wife's?

Indeed this may be the best response of all to the original Heinz problem: that there is *no* good solution to the problem as it stands—and therefore the best thing we can do is to try to prevent such dilemmas from even coming up at all. The best strategy is to "look upstream," to head it off next time, or to try to transform it into something more easily manageable. These in turn may well require structural change, rethinking and trying to reconstruct and indeed reframe larger social arrangements: insurance, public provision, how medicine itself is organized, workplace safety or environmental protection. No simple answers—but good work to do.

It is true that large families of moral values also seem to come into conflict here. This is why the Heinz Dilemma is widely used by moral theorists to focus the difference between a consequence-oriented moral theory like utilitarianism, which might support stealing the drug, and a theory of personal rights, which is often supposed to favor the druggist. But this needn't be the end of the matter either. If we care so deeply about both consequences and rights, oughtn't we try to redesign our institutions *in general* so that these two families of values conflict less often or less viciously? How hard would that be? Reconciling rights and utility is arguably one of the aims of modern systems of public provision. So perhaps it is time to begin to work out new ways as well...

"Strategic Questioning"

FRAN PEAVEY

"Fran Peavey is an inventive, resolute and funny woman whose life is an adventure in progressive social change," reads the first line of Fran's biography on the back of her third book, from which this excerpt is taken. She has worked to clean up the Ganges, done stand-up comedy on nuclear weapons as a member of the Atomic Comics, and developed Strategic Questioning as a major part of the social change work she does in the world. Her newest work is *Strategic Questioning: An Experiment in Communication of the Second Kind,* which is available from her through her website at www.crabgrass.org, along with Crabgrass newsletters and information about her other projects.

Strategic questioning is the skill of asking the questions that will make a difference.* It is a powerful and exciting tool for social and personal change. I have found it a significant service to any issue because it helps local strategies for change emerge.

Strategic questioning involves a special type of question and a special type of listening. Anyone can use strategic questions in their work and in their personal lives to liberate friends, coworkers, and political allies and adversaries to create a path for change.

Strategic questioning is a process that may change the listener as well as the person being questioned. When we open ourselves to another point of view, our own ideas will have to shift to take into account new information, new possibilities, and new strategies for resolving problems.

What would our world be like if every time we were listening to a gripe session, someone would ask, "I wonder what we can do to change that situation?" then listened carefully for the answers to emerge, and then

---

* I didn't invent the words "strategic questioning," although I thought I did. I had been using the term for four years when a few years ago, while doing some research, I came upon a small book about teaching called *Strategic Questioning* written by Ronald T. Hyman, a close friend of a college professor of mine. So I must have heard the words twenty-five years ago and the word seeds got planted way back there in my mind; then when I needed them they came blossoming up. Thank you, Ronald T. Hyman.

From Fran Peavey, *By Life's Grace* (New Society Publishers, 1993), pages 87–93.

helped that group to begin to work for change? What would it be like for you to do that in your work, family, or social context? Your attention and context might shift from a passive to an active one. You could become a creator, rather than a receiver, of solutions. This shift in perspective is one of the key things that people need in our world just now. And the skill of asking strategic questions is a powerful contribution to making such a shift.

Were you ever taught how to ask questions? Were you ever encouraged to ask questions where the answers are not already known? Have you ever been taught about asking questions that will really make a difference? Most of us who were brought up in traditional families or in a traditional education system were not. Traditional schooling was based on asking questions to which the answers were already known: How many wives did Henry VIII have? What color is that car? What is four times five? We learned that questions have finite and "correct" answers, and that there is usually one answer for each question. The wrong answer is punished with a bad grade. The landscape of learning was divided into "right" and "wrong."

This may be a convenient way of running schools and testing people's capacity for memory in examinations but it has not been a very empowering learning process for students, or a good preparation for the questions that come up in life.

Shaping a strategic question involves seven key features:

1. A STRATEGIC QUESTION CREATES MOTION

Most of the traditional questions that we've been taught to ask are static. Strategic questions ask, How can we move? They create movement. They are dynamic rather than allowing a situation to stay stuck.

Often the way a conversation is structured creates resistance to movement. The martial art t'ai chi teaches a lot of wisdom about meeting resistance. It says that when you meet an obstacle, you only make it more firm by pushing directly on it. If you meet an object coming at you with resistance, it is not very useful at all. T'ai chi says that if you meet and move with the energy of the obstacle coming at you, taking the energy from the other, then motion in a new direction emerges. Both parties end up in a different place than where they started, and the relationship between them is changed.

This same shift in a new direction happens when you ask a strategic question. As an example, suppose Sally is working on where she will live, and perhaps she has heard of some good real estate bargains in Sydney, and she's a bit stuck on what she should do next. I could say to her, "Why don't you just move to Sydney?" This question might be provocative, but is not very helpful. Really it's a suggestion pretending to be a question. For my own reasons I think she should move to Sydney. Perhaps I am projecting into the question my own wish to move to Sydney. Whatever my reasons I'm leading her because I am asking a manipulative question, and it is likely that the more I pressure Sally, the less likely she is to consider the Sydney option.

A more strategic question would be to ask Sally, "What type of place would you like to move to?" or "What places come to mind when you think of living happily?" or "What is the meaning of this move in your life?" Sally is then encouraged to talk about the qualities she wants from her new home, to set new goals. You can then work with her to achieve these goals.

Asking questions that are *dynamic* can help people explore how they can move on an issue. On my first working trip to India with the Friends of the Ganges project, I asked the local people, "What would you like to do to help clean up the river?" Now, you might ask, "How did I know they wanted to clean up the river?" Well, I wanted to ask a question that assumed motion on this issue. I assumed that people are always wanting to do more appropriate behavior. I further assumed that they wanted to move from their state of powerlessness regarding what to do about the pollution in the Ganges. Many interesting ideas emerged when I used that question—some of which we have implemented.

When we are stuck on a problem, what keeps us from acting for change is either a lack of information, or that we have been wounded in our sense of personal power on an issue, or that no system is in place that enables us to move the issue forward. In our stuckness, we don't see how to make the motion. When I ask a question like, "What would you like to do to help clean up the river?" I open up a door for the local people to move beyond their grief, guilt, and powerlessness about the pollution to active dreaming and creating of their own contributions.

2. A STRATEGIC QUESTION CREATES OPTIONS

If I asked Sally, "Why don't you move to Sydney?" I have asked a question that is dynamic only in one direction (Sydney). It very much limits the options she is challenged to think about. A more powerful strategic question opens the options up. "Where would you like to live?" or "What are the three or four places that you feel connected to?" These are much more helpful questions to ask her at this time. Sally might have been so busy thinking about the real estate bargains in Sydney that she has lost a sense of all the other possibilities and her real goals.

A strategic questioner would help Sally look at the many options equally. Supposing Sally says she could move to Byron Bay or Sydney. It's not up to me to say to myself, "I think Sydney is the best, and I should encourage her down that path." If you're being ethical about it, then you could best help Sally sort out her own direction by questioning all the options evenhandedly, with the same enthusiasm and interest in discussing both Sydney and Byron Bay. Not only that, but you could help by asking if any more options occur to her during the questioning time (Twin Falls, Idaho...or New Plymouth, New Zealand). Out of these questions, a new option may emerge.

It is particularly important for a strategic questioner not to focus on only two options. We are so accustomed to binary thinking, whether it's either Sydney or Byron Bay...that Brisbane cannot emerge as a viable alternative. Usually when someone is only considering two options, they simply have not done the creative thinking to look at all the possibilities. People are usually comfortable when they have two options and think they can make a choice at that level. This "choice" is part of the delusion of control. And since two alternatives are already more complex than one, people stop thinking. Though the world is far more complex and exciting than any two options would indicate, having two options creates the idea that a choice, however limited, is being made.

I have a friend whose daughter got into some trouble and ran away. My friend was fortunate in that she knew which train her daughter was probably leaving on in a few hours' time. She was trying to decide whether to just let the daughter get on the train and run away, or to go to the train and insist that she come home. I talked it over with her, and we worked on these options for a while, and then I asked, "What else could you do to help your daughter with her conflicts?" She thought and then a new idea came up. She could run away *with* her daughter, and take the twelve hours on the train to help her sort things out. Now, because my friend was scared and afraid for her daughter, she had been unable to think of this fine option until the door was opened through the question. It was the kind of option that she might have thought of when all her anxious feelings had subsided.

3. A STRATEGIC QUESTION DIGS DEEPER

Questions can be like a lever you use to pry open the stuck lid on a paint can. And there are long-lever questions and short-lever questions. If I have just a short lever, we can only just crack open that lid on the can. But if we have a longer lever, or a more dynamic question, we can open that can up much wider and really stir things up.

Some people approach problems with their heads just like a closed paint can. If the right question is applied, and it digs deep enough, then we can stir up all the creative solutions to that problem. We can chip away a lot of the crusty sediment that is trapping the lid on that person's head. A question can be a stirrer. It can lead to synthesis, motion, and energy.

4. A STRATEGIC QUESTION AVOIDS "WHY"

When I asked Sally, "Why don't you move to Sydney?" it was a question that focused on why she doesn't do it, rather than creating a more active and forward motion on the issue. Most "why" questions are like that. They force you to defend an existing decision or rationalize the present. "Why" questions also have the effect of creating resistance to change.

The openness of a particular question is obvious at the gross extremes, but becomes far more subtle and subjective as you deepen your understanding of the skills of strategic questioning. For example, can you feel the difference between asking, "Why don't you work on poverty?" and, "What keeps you from working on poverty?" Sometimes a "Why" question is very powerful as you focus on values, and meaning. But in general it is a short-lever question.

5. A STRATEGIC QUESTION AVOIDS "YES OR NO" ANSWERS

Again, these type of questions ("Have you considered...") don't really encourage people to dig deeper into their issues. A question answered with a "yes" or "no" reply almost always leaves the person being asked in an uncreative and passive state. A strategic questioner rephrases their queries to avoid the dead end of a "yes" or "no" reply. It can make a huge difference to the communication taking place.

I heard of a student who was very intrigued by the ideas behind strategic questioning. He realized that he hardly ever spoke a question to his wife without getting simply a "yes" or "no" in reply. A week after the class on strategic questioning, he reported that the technique had completely changed his home life! He had gone home and told his wife about these special types of questions, and they agreed to avoid asking a question that had a "yes" or "no" answer for a week. He reported they had never talked so much in their lives!

6. A STRATEGIC QUESTION IS EMPOWERING

A strategic question creates the confidence that motion can actually happen, and this is certainly empowering. When I asked people in India, "What would you like to do to clean your river?" it assumes that they have a part in that picture of healing. It even expresses a confidence in the person being questioned that they have a contribution to designing the cleaning-up process.

One of my favorite questions is, "What would it take for you to change on this issue?" This question lets the other person create the path for change. Imagine an environmental protester going to a lumber mill owner and asking, "What would it take for you to stop cutting down the old-growth trees?" This question is an invitation to the mill owner to cocreate options for the future of his business *with* the community. The owner might tell the questioner the obstacles he faces in making changes to his business, and maybe they can work together to satisfy some of their mutual needs so that the old-growth trees can be preserved. The planning that comes out of asking such a strategic question may not exactly resemble what either party wanted in the beginning, but a new reality is born out of the dialogue and could well work to achieve both the protester's and the mill owner's goals.

Empowerment is the opposite of manipulation. When you use strategic questioning, rather than putting ideas into a person's head, you are actually allowing that person to take what's already in their head and work with it.

7. A STRATEGIC QUESTION ASKS THE UNASKABLE QUESTIONS

For every individual, group, or society, some questions are taboo. And because those questions are taboo they wield tremendous power. A strategic question is often one of these "unaskable" questions. And it usually is unaskable because it challenges the values and assumptions that the whole issue rests upon.

I like the fairy tale about the emperor who walked in a parade without any clothes on because he had been tricked by some unscrupulous weavers into thinking he was wearing a magnificent costume. It was a child that asked the unaskable question, "Why doesn't the emperor have any clothes on?" If that child had been a political activist, she might have asked other unaskable questions, such as, "Why do we need an emperor?" or "How can we get a wiser government?"

In the early 1980s, one of the unaskable questions for me was, "What shall we do if a nuclear bomb is dropped?" You couldn't answer that without facing our overwhelming capacity for destruction, and the senselessness of it. That question allowed many of us to move beyond terror and denial, and work politically to keep that destruction from happening.

Some other unaskable questions might be: for the seriously ill person, "Do you want to live or die?" For those involved in sexual politics: "Is gender a myth?" For the workaholic: "What do you do for joy?" For the tree activist: "How should we make building materials?" Or for the politician: "What do you like about the other party's platform?" or "How could both parties work together more closely?"

Questioning values is a strategic task of our times. This questioning is important because it is the values behind highly politicized issues that have usually gotten us into the trouble in the first place. We need to look at a value, a habit, an institutional pattern, and ask, "How is this value functioning in my own life?" "In what ways do these values work for and against the common good?" "Are these values pro-survival (pro-life) or anti-life?" If you can ask the unaskable in a nonpartisan way, not to embarrass someone but to probe for more suitable answers for the future, then it can be a tremendous service to anyone with an issue on which she or he is "stuck."

THREE METHODS

THINK PREVENTION

We understand the logic of prevention when it comes to health. Everyone knows that it's better to take vitamins and exercise than to wait until you get sick and then have to deal with the illness. We don't always act on this knowledge, for a variety of reasons, but we do know it.

In ethics the strategy could be the same: look before or behind a problem as it is usually presented. Don't just take "the" problem for granted. Instead, consider whether it even needs to come up in the first place. Ask whether a few changes a few steps back can change everything about "the" problem here and now, or perhaps even keep it from coming up at all.

We are consumed by the question of whether killing murderers is right or wrong. But the best answer may lie in a different direction entirely. Why not refocus at least part of our energies toward reducing the number of murders in the first place? After all, we do understand something about what drives people to kill other people. Everything from emotional and social stresses (unemployment, for example) to the easy availability of weapons makes a difference. And not just to murder, of course. A great many other goods would also be served if weapons were less readily available, if unemployment were lower, and if people were enabled to deal with conflicts and anger in more constructive ways.

Of course, reframing the problem in this way doesn't answer the moral question of capital punishment itself. The point is that problems like this may not *have* "solutions"—at any rate, no solutions a tenth as good as trying to head the problem off, so to speak, at the pass. Sometimes prevention is not only the best medicine, it is the *only* medicine. Of course we will not eliminate all murders, and therefore we will still have a moral question about capital punishment. But we do not need to spend so much energy on that question and so very little energy where it could do so much more good.

Or take "the drug problem." It's a large and puzzling issue. By way of response, though, we are usually invited to consider only tougher law enforcement or drug resistance training. Sometimes "the" drug problem is even reduced to the question of how to get dealers off the streets. Longer jail terms, mandatory sentencing, more police.

Once again, we need to ask: what is the bigger challenge? Are there ways to rethink and shift "the" problem itself? Why, in particular, are so many people tempted by drugs in the first place? What combination of social pressures, hopelessness, the wish to experiment, and so on, are at play, perhaps on the part of different people and with respect to different drugs?

Surely part of the allure of drugs is that they offer some excitement in the midst of an otherwise uninteresting life. Then one bottom-line reconstructive question is: are there less lethal ways to make life interesting? Yes, obviously. Well, what ways? What can we do to make life so interesting that people are no longer tempted to escape through drugs?

Now *there's* a fine question—what Fran Peavey would call an empowering strategic question: no longer punitive, widely engaging, open-ended, more promising for all of us. Here too, of course, the old questions remain—but they are no longer the only questions. A new sense of freedom opens up, and maybe of hope as well.

PAPER OR PLASTIC?

The quandary of the modern grocery check-out: "paper or plastic?" It *is*, in part, an ethical question: a question of our impact on the Earth and on future human generations. It's also a debatable question. Even some ecologists advise using plastic bags because they can be used longer and take less and cleaner energy to produce. Plastic bags save trees. On the other hand, thousands of tons of nonbiodegradable plastic wastes are an environmental disaster too. Which is the lesser of two evils?

We could get creative with that question, for sure. Maybe we could invent lighter bags, or perfect biodegradable ones, or...

But why must we pick one or the other "evil"? Suppose that we step back a little and reframe the problem itself. Why do we need to use disposable bags, of *either* kind, in the first place? Surely the best answer is to *reuse* bags: cloth bags, super-strong paper bags, backpacks, and so on. We do not need to choose the lesser of two evils. Pick *no* evils. Try to change the problem instead.

The best answer to the littering question, in short, is to avoid creating the potential litter in the first place. My Chinese students tell me that it is common in China for people to carry around their own chopsticks, rather than requiring new ones every time they eat out. Japanese carry around their own cups. Why couldn't we?

The story goes that when Henry Ford was setting up the first assembly lines to build the Model T, his suppliers got very specific requests about how to build the boxes in which they sent their bolts or cushions. A certain kind of wood had to be used, cut to certain sizes, with holes drilled just in certain places. Puzzled, but anxious for Ford's business, they complied. It turned out that once the boxes were unpacked at the assembly line, they were taken apart and used for the Model T's floorboards. They were already cut and drilled in just the right ways!

In short, Ford took two problems—getting rid of unwanted boxes and procuring floorboards—and turned them into one solution. Reuse was planned into the very design of things. We could do the same. Rather than raising the question of recycling only after a thing has been used, we ought to raise it before the thing is even made. Imagine selling food in containers that you could then use as plates and glasses (or just *eat* too), or milk or juice containers that you could refill at the store, or automotive frames that can be updated in pieces rather than junked as a whole. Or...? Some thinkers now call this "precycling": it is still, sadly enough, a cutting-edge idea.

Environmentalists argue that there are good alternatives to *most* of our environmentally destructive practices. Air conditioners are massive energy hogs—but there are other ways to beat the heat, like building houses open to the breezes, or partly buried and thus insulated and cooled by the Earth itself. The supposed problem might also be reframed. Maybe we should just get used to the heat again? How about just taking siestas rather than insisting on working all day in wool suits? Once again the results might be better all around.

REVISIT OUTLYING PARTS OF THE PROBLEM

In a well-known riddle, a truck stands before a highway overpass, half an inch too high to get under. How to get through? Most people focus on somehow raising the bridge. But the answer is not to raise the bridge. It is to lower the truck—readily done just by letting some air out of the tires.

Confronting an obstacle, we're tempted to charge right into it, tackle it head on. If there are major hurdles, we prepare to jump them. But a straight line is not always the best way between two points. What about running *around* the hurdles, using a side door, finding another way? This is what

Edward DeBono calls "lateral thinking." I prefer a more descriptive label: *revisiting outlying parts of the problem.*

The method is this. Systematically survey all the parts of a problem, not just the one or two that currently fill the screen. Highlight and reconsider each part of the problem. Each can be deliberately varied and questioned. New possibilities will come up. It may well be that some other aspect of a problematic situation, pushed into the background at the moment, offers us a way to go forward while the current routes seem blocked.

Emmanuel Evans ran a department store during the 1940s and 1950s in my city, Durham, North Carolina. The store had an attached sit-down cafeteria. Segregation-era laws forbade the seating of black people in such eating establishments. Black people had to stand, get their food, and go outside to eat. Evans was unwilling to treat his black customers in this way. But what to do? The direct approach—seating black people in defiance of the law—would quickly end with fines and jail (remember, this was before the civil rights movement and the era of mass civil disobedience). Closing the cafeteria served no one's interests either.

So the direct approach was blocked. What about an indirect approach? Mightn't the problem yield to an approach from another angle? Think about it...

Naturally we first imagine changing things for the black customers. But suppose things could be changed for the *white* customers instead? Couldn't white people (also) *stand?* Evans finally realized that he could just remove *all* the tables, so that no one was seated. Which is what he did. No law was broken, but a powerful statement was made. His cafeteria became the first desegregated eating place in town. And Evans, by the way, later became one of Durham's best-loved mayors.

Environmentally too there are many examples of "lowering the truck," shifting the action to readily solved problems rather than beating our heads against immovable obstacles. Rather than building ever more electrical generating capacity, for example, it is usually far easier and quicker, as well as far less expensive, for power companies to promote conservation. Some even give away high-efficiency lightbulbs. Instead of building more reservoirs and sewage systems, cities can promote water conservation. Low-flush toilets reduce water usage and sewage flow by an astonishing 80 percent. Native plants that don't require watering at all reduce lawn water needs by, well, 100 percent...

LOOK FOR OPPORTUNITIES IN THE PROBLEM

A third and still more dramatic way of reframing problems is to take the problem before us not as a difficulty to be overcome or gotten rid of but as an actual *opportunity* to be welcomed. Believe it or not: instead of trying to get rid of "the problem," we can ask instead how we can make *use* of it—and not, or not just, as a "problem," but as a resource, as a solution already, if we can just find the right problem for it or reframe the one in front of us.

The method itself is, once again, very simple. Take any problem. Seek out the very core of the difficulty. Identify it, state it clearly. Then ask yourself: can I think of any way in which this "problem" might actually be *welcomed?* Are there opportunities in it? For what?

Power plants produce, among other things, heat. Big plants build huge cooling towers and/or locate where they can discharge large volumes of hot water. The heat, in short, is considered a problem—a waste. And so it becomes. But then again...isn't heat often just what we want? Why consider it "waste" at all? Couldn't it be used for something? Suppose for instance that we piped the hot water or steam into homes for heat. In fact this is already done in Scandinavia, where they speak of "co-generation." The power plant becomes a heating plant as well. Viewed ecologically, the co-generated heat is not an inconvenience and a burden, to be dumped as cheaply as possible into the environment, but a *resource*.

Go to any old-age home and you will find people desperate for something constructive to do. There are some organized games and other activities, but the feeling is simply that time is being filled. Professionals are even trained and hired to find ways to keep the occupants busy—disguising what we normally assume to be the simple fact that really there *is* "nothing for them to do."

I am sure, after the last chapter, that you can readily think of some creative responses in the usual problem-solving mode. Adapting computer games for older people? (A rather large market, you'd think.) Or how about more crafts? And these are fine ideas. They are also still entirely in the mode of solving the problem as it stands: filling up old people's time. A seriously creative approach would be to ask what their unfilled time is an opportunity for. Is it really a problem, at all, we'd want to ask—or, once again, more like a *resource?*

Ask the question in this way, as radical as it may sound, and everything looks different. *Of course* it is a resource! Obviously most older folks aren't going to be blazing wilderness trails or hanging telephone lines or sheet rock or something. Surely, though, there are many ways that they can contribute. Here we have skilled, experienced, patient people, anxious for some constructive work...why should it be hard to hook their abilities up with community needs?

Nursing homes could be connected with public libraries, and the occupants take over cataloging and book care. It's good, careful, and quiet work—plus they'd have all the books and videos they want close at hand. Older people could take over or create community historical museums. In almost all tribal and traditional communities, the elders are the custodians of the community's history. They carry the memories and instruct the young. Why are we letting both the elders and the history slip away?

Even better: we know that many young parents are desperate for good-quality daycare. Once again buildings are built, sometimes right next to the nursing home, where staff are once again trained and hired, this time to find ways to keep the children busy and maybe even teach them something. Hopefully not just watching TV. But why not bring the very young and the very old *together* in a setting in which both can help each other? The old can tell their stories to the very people who above all love stories. And the young can help tend to the needs of the old, learning something of life cycles and of service in the process.

In traditional societies, the older generations are also the natural custodians not just of the past but also of the *future*. Freed from the immediate pressures of survival, reproduction, and work, having lived long enough to glimpse the grander flow of time, older people can take a longer view of things. Perhaps a little forgetfulness also helps. (Could memory loss even be an *advantage* in certain ways?) The old are the ones, freed up precisely by the changes that age brings, who can become society's greatest visionaries! A colleague of mine is already hard at work creating councils of elders who take visionary thinking as their project, indeed their responsibility. He's creating a new kind of retirement community as well—as natural homes for such councils. A core group of elders would live in such places and regularly host wider groups, of all ages, for facilitated visioning. Elder communities as creative incubators of the future—a beautiful and unexpected vision.

Reframing problems in this way does take some imaginative work. Usually it will not be obvious at first what the seeming problem could possibly be an opportunity for (except for pulling your hair out). Often it will seem silly even to ask. Patience, patience... Just ask anyway: "Even so, even so, what *could* it be an opportunity for?" Use the tools from previous chapters to help generate some concrete ideas. Stick with it. Don't be blinded just because a situation is *labeled* a "problem" (or "dilemma"). There will still be possibilities in it. The essential step is your willingness to look for them—your expectation that maybe, just maybe, there might be something to be found.

REFRAMING THE ABORTION DEBATE

Let us now use these tools for reframing problems to re-approach the most painful and seemingly "stuck" debate we have: the abortion debate. We've already started, with the reading from Roger Rosenblatt in Chapter 14, "How to End the Abortion War." But now we can go much further.

THE SPACE FOR INTEGRATING VALUES

Sometimes I divide my students into pro-life and pro-choice groups. Each group looks at case studies of unintended pregnancy and is asked to guess what they *and the other group* will say about them. Pro-life groups assume that the pro-choice side will more or less automatically opt for abortion when the going gets tough. They are surprised to discover that the pro-choice groups consider abortion only a last resort. Similarly, pro-choice groups assume that the pro-life group will be against abortion no matter what. But they're not: they make exceptions too. Rosenblatt reports something similar:

> Pro-choice advocates are often surprised to hear themselves speak of the immorality of taking a life. Pro-life people are surprised to hear themselves defend individual rights, especially women's rights.

In truth, every one of us is pro-life. Life is what makes love and community and beauty and everything else possible. Those acts associated with creating and preserving and honoring life—sex, childbirth, nurturing a baby, caring for the sick, mourning the dead—are among the deepest and most profound of life's experiences.

Every one of us is *also* pro-choice. Freedom, self-determination, the right to control what happens in and to our own bodies—these are basic values too. In politics, in the stores, in "lifestyle"—choice is everything. Some people even think that seat belts and speed limits are unjustified limits on physical freedom, but these are trivial restrictions compared to pregnancy and childbirth.

Rosenblatt goes on to say that there is therefore a broad and persistent middle ground on the question: something like "permit but discourage." For the last twenty-five years, while the abortion debate raged all around us, the U.S. population consistently has divided into about a fifth strongly anti-abortion, a quarter strongly in favor of abortion rights, and the remaining 55 percent or so against abortion personally, most of the time, but also in favor of allowing it as a limited legal right. Almost 60 percent continue to support the *Roe v. Wade* framework.

Likewise, the most common view I find among my students, too, is that "I probably wouldn't choose abortion myself, but I think the choice should be there for others." This would probably be classified as a "pro-choice" view, as the usual categories go—but those categories may hide more than they reveal. There's middle ground here—*between* the usual views. *Both* sides acknowledge that abortion can be a painful and tragic but also (sometimes) necessary choice.

In fact, then, despite the painful and persistent debate between two single-minded sides, most people recognize that abortion choices pit two genuine values against each other in a case where both of them count. Both of them are right in their way. How to put them together is still a (hard) question, but at least we can find here a kind of shared starting point. It might help to remember that there already is a large network of people devoted to working from common ground, or at least compatible values, in this very debate: The Common Ground Network for Life and Choice—again: Life *and* Choice—devoted to dialogue and working from a common agenda. You've seen some of their materials in Chapter 4. They were not much in the news, but they worked away for ten years, and their umbrella organization—Search for Common Ground—has expanded to other conflicts too.

STRATEGIC QUESTIONS: PREVENTION

Common agenda? Did I say that? Anyone immersed in the current debate may have trouble even beginning to imagine what such a thing might look like. But in fact common concerns emerge immediately and even obviously once we reframe the problem in the way just suggested. Remember what Rosenblatt says:

> Both sides might be surprised to learn how similar are their visions of a society that makes abortion less necessary through sex education, help for unwanted babies, programs to shore up disintegrating families and moral values, and other forms of constructive community action.

No one thinks that abortion, by itself, is a good thing. This is why the term "pro-abortion" is unfair for the pro-choice side: there the view is really only that it is sometimes the least bad option. The natural next questions are how we can prevent situations with such bad options from even arising. As Julie Polter writes in *Sojourners,* a liberal Catholic journal, "If pro-life people know that one abortion is too many and many pro-choice people can at least agree that there surely shouldn't be as many abortions as there are, shouldn't we do what we can in the scope of that common territory?"

We could start by asking how to reduce the demand for abortions themselves. Is there any realistic way to reduce the number of unwanted pregnancies and/or to keep those unintended pregnancies that do occur from being unwanted?

More than half of all women who seek abortion were not using contraception when they got pregnant. Why? We need to find out. Lack of access? Lack of education? Violence? These things can be changed. Changing them might not even be controversial.

And what about the other half, women who used contraception and still got pregnant? Again we need to find out why. Poor or difficult-to-use methods? Resistance from spouses and lovers? These things too can be changed. With a fraction of the energy and intensity put into the present abortion debate, they *could* be changed.

When the welfare laws were up for revision in 1996, conservatives proposed to deny assistance to children born of mothers under 18, or currently on welfare, or whose paternity hadn't been established. Many of these limits are now law. But a remarkable thing happened along the way. Nearly all major organizations on *both sides* of the abortion issue campaigned against the bill—including the National Right to Life Committee, Planned Parenthood, the U.S. Catholic Conference, and the National Organization for Women (NOW). Both sides feared that the results would be to coerce abortions among poor women. Both sides made the connections back to economic conditions. Pro-choice and pro-life organizations even *jointly designed* a comprehensive child-support reform plan. Common ground emerged in the face of a common threat. Maybe next time we shouldn't wait.

STRATEGIC QUESTIONS: SURPRISES

But of course there will still, sometimes, be unintended pregnancies. What about when prevention fails? Why does abortion sometimes become so desperate a need? Why does a child, or another child, or a child at the "wrong" time, sometimes promise only disaster for a mother or family?

Some on the pro-life side answer: the real problem is that we think we can have everything. We want to control every aspect of our lives. Maybe we ought to be more humble in the face of life's mysteries. When we speak of "unintended" pregnancy, for example, we set it up from the start as a failure of control and therefore a problem, a potential disaster. Some people propose to speak of "surprise" pregnancy instead. A "surprise" is not necessarily a disaster—it can also be a kind of gift, an opportunity.

But *still:* "surprises" can be unpleasant. More must be said. Why is the surprise sometimes unwelcome? A "strategic question" might be: How can we make these particular surprises more welcome, more bearable?

Part of the problem is that women still confront inflexible expectations about career tracks, work schedules, and schooling, coupled with lower pay in general, poor or super-expensive childcare, distant extended families (not much help), and all the rest. Though a few in the pro-life movement may believe that women should not aspire to careers, most pro-lifers agree with nearly everyone else that careers ought at least to be one option for women. Women have a right to seek that kind of life—and to have a sex life too. But then the trap closes. How to have a baby when it would mean two or three years out of school or part-time at work, long-term financial costs, and permanent emotional commitments elsewhere?

This is a fixable problem. We need more flexible expectations and alternative work and schooling patterns that do not punish or impede women (and men) who also choose major family responsibilities. Most European countries are far ahead of the United States in this area. It's not so hard to work out the details.

Equal pay for women is, or ought to be, one goal. Shared child-raising has everything to recommend it. At the very least, fathers should be expected to support their children financially (at present, even with greatly expanded enforcement, only a third contribute anything at all). Paid parental leaves are the norm in Europe. My students, working on this problem in a creative mode, have suggested still other ideas, such as a system of "adoptive grandparents." What do you think?

The same goes for schools. One of my ethics classes was discussing the abortion issue with our college chaplain. He remarked that in his decade or so at the college he had seen only three or four students carry pregnancies to term and stay in school too. A (male) student then said:

> I'm pro-life, but I can't blame a fellow student for getting an abortion when the choice is between the abortion and finishing college. Your whole future

is at stake. I think the real question is: why should she be put in that position?

Why indeed. So the question to us is: what can *we* change—teachers,
students, chaplains—so that fewer women are put in this position in the
future? Class schedules, assignments, how financial aid is calculated? How
hard would that be?

And adoption? Far more could be done to make it more workable, from
settling the vexed question of adoptees' access to biological-parent records
to supporting genuinely women who choose to go through pregnancy and
then choose adoption: economically, emotionally, and especially socially.
Deep-seated sexual norms and expectations have regularly been stood on
their heads in the last half-century: the "shame" of bearing and "giving
up" an unintended child would hardly be the biggest. How much would it
really take?

ACKNOWLEDGMENT AND RECONCILIATION

Sometimes, though, *still*, there will be losses, indeed tragic losses, no matter what is chosen or how you look at it. Different lives and life-choices are
at stake, all of them precious, and they cannot all be lived out. Most people,
even most pro-lifers, for instance, accept abortion in cases of rape or when
the mother's own life is at stake: though the fetus and potential baby is no
less innocent for all that.

The most obvious loss, of course, is the physical life of the fetus, the child-
to-be. The loss of a pregnancy to miscarriage is acknowledged all around as a
serious loss. Why not the same in abortion? The usual response is that sometimes the other stakes—the life prospects of the pregnant woman and/or
also those around her—are also great, though less visible. Often, surely, this
is true. In practice, though, we have trouble holding both kinds of stakes, or
potential losses, in mind at the same time. Tragic choices trouble us—we do
like to see the world in blacks and whites—and so there is a tendency (on *both*
sides) to discount or even deny the losses on the "other" side.

But why? Mightn't this kind of denial even be part of the problem? Trying
another tack, suppose that we consider how to make the loss of the fetus—
the loss of a potential life—both more visible and at the same time possibly
more bearable.

Japanese Buddhists have developed a kind of memorial ritual, even sometimes a kind of apology, for aborted as well as miscarried fetuses (also,
strikingly, for animals deliberately killed in the course of drug experiments).
Mizuko Kuyo, it is called. It is a way of facing rather than denying the
consequences—underscoring the seriousness of the choice, which is surely
good from the point of view of all sides—but also reaching some kind of closure, making it possible to go on. Loss can be acknowledged without shutting

---

QUICK REFERENCE: WAYS TO REFRAME PROBLEMS

Open up the question. Ask open-ended or "strategic" questions—of others and also of yourself. How did we get into a situation in which this sort of thing (whatever it is) emerges as a problem? Are there other ways it could be viewed? How can we dig deeper and create more options? What keeps us from moving toward effective solutions?

Specific reframing methods are:

- Think prevention. How can this problem be headed off before it even comes up?
- Revisit outlying aspects of the problem. Mentally vary *all* the changeable aspects of a problematic situation, not just the ones right now in the spotlight. See what new ideas are provoked.
- Look for the opportunities in the problem. Could the very situation that seems to be such an ethical problem actually be an ethical opportunity if viewed in the right way? An opportunity for what?

---

down the hard choices required. Those facing such a choice can have a better way to get a grip on just what is at stake. Those who have made such choices can have a better way to make peace with them.

It seems wise to me. What could similar rituals look like with us? Wouldn't it be a worthwhile project to develop our own forms of remembrance and reconciliation, while also acknowledging that sometimes, at least, the choice must remain with the pregnant woman and those close to her? A delicate task, yes, especially in the present atmosphere of intense moralism and blame, private tragedies made public, and wounds again and again rubbed raw. But there is also a glimmer of an unexpected possibility of healing here. Another place for some good reframing and reconstruction!

FOR REVIEW

1. What is the aim of opening up a problem?
2. What further ways does this chapter suggest to rethink the Heinz problem?
3. What is "strategic questioning"?
4. Give two examples of strategic questions.

5. Illustrate preventive thinking.

6. How can we think preventively about the drug problem?

7. "Revisit outlying parts of the problem"—what does this mean?

8. How can an ethical problem be taken as an opportunity?

9. How can preventive thinking help us reframe the abortion debate?

10. What might Japanese Buddhist practice have to offer the abortion debate?

EXERCISES AND NOTES

PRACTICE REFRAMING PROBLEMS

Consider again a list of practical problems around your school and area—you'll remember the list from the last chapter. There you practiced multiplying options, finding creative ways to solve these problems more or less as they are usually understood. Now try to *reframe* these problems. Use Peavey's "strategic questioning." What things need to be changed so that the present problem does not come up, or comes up in a more manageable way than it does now? Would changing the problem in some of these ways be preferable to leaving the problem as it stands and trying to solve it as such?

Here is the list again:

- Waste (styrofoam cups, lights left on all the time, newspaper, etc.)
- Alcoholism and other addictions
- Too much television
- Lack of affordable childcare for working families with young children
- Lack of inexpensive travel options
- Alternatives to on-the-air fundraising for public radio
- Not enough parking at school or elsewhere
- Difficulties maintaining nuclear test bans
- Low voter turnout

Preventive options might sometimes seem easy. If the problem is crowded roads, we could prevent it by building more roads. But again, think more creatively. Look deeper. We can't keep building roads forever: they have massive social and economic costs, and they tend to create even more demand. Are there deeper ways to reframe the whole problem? Maybe this: is there a way we could reduce the amount of required travel itself? For example, could we not begin to relocate work and shopping closer to home, so people need to drive less in the first place? *There's* a preventive strategy that is also creative, and it offers a vision of a better life for all of us.

Use your other tools from this chapter as well. Revisit outlying aspects of the problems. Look for opportunities even in what seem to be irresolvable disasters...

PRACTICE REFRAMING MORAL PROBLEMS

Now pose the same kinds of questions about moral problems. Again the list from the last chapter might be useful:

- Gun control
- Marriage
- Drug use
- Blowing the whistle on business or administrative corruption
- The treatment of gay people in the military
- Political campaign finance abuse
- Medical testing on animals
- Rainforest destruction

Or again, pick your own. The key question remains: How can these problems be prevented from even arising? Can they be "solved" by being *changed*— or perhaps eliminated entirely? What would it take to achieve this? Revisit outlying parts of the problem. Ask in what ways this problem itself may be an opportunity. Can we see it in a more positive and constructive light? What would we have to do differently?

NEW CHALLENGES

Here are several further moral problems on which to use your full set of creativity methods.

- Defenders of the death penalty say that murderers forfeit their own right to life, that execution is the only really "proportionate" penalty for murder, and that the threat of execution deters would-be murderers from committing the act. Opponents argue that if cold-blooded killing is wrong, it is wrong when the state does it too; that life in prison is at least as appropriate a penalty; and that the threat of execution does not deter real murderers. American states that use the death penalty do not, on average, have lower murder rates than states that don't; some actually have higher rates, though it could be argued that they would have had higher rates anyway. Hard to know. How else could you think of this whole issue?

• The average age of first sexual intercourse is under 16 years for American teens, the lowest age of any major industrialized countries. It seems a bit young. (Is it? Why?) Meanwhile the United States also has a much higher teen pregnancy rate than most other industrialized nations and a vastly higher STD rate—in part because we do such a bad job at sex education. (Sure, you can teach abstinence, but the majority of young people who nonetheless choose to be "sexually active" consequently don't get decent information on contraception, STD prevention, or, for that matter, sexual relationships in general.) Any ways to change our angle here? (Hint: Why does "sexually active" have to mean exactly *one* form of sexual activity? Isn't that just a bit, well, unimaginative?)

• Another drug issue: the "performance-enhancing drugs" used, and abused, by some athletes. High school and even younger athletes risk their health for an unnatural edge; meanwhile on a global scale, the World Anti-Doping Agency (great name, huh?) polices competitions such as the Olympics. Other competitors want to stay drug-free but to compete on a level playing field. Any other ways to approach all of this?

• People who disagree profoundly with important political and social decisions need some way to visibly register their disagreement and attempt to sway others to their point of view—in short, to protest. But what is the best form for such protest? Too many of the current forms of protest are so obviously pushed into invisibility or irrelevance that the protestors become embittered and cynical—or turn to violence. (Witness the fringes of the anti-abortion and anti-logging movements, just for two examples.) See if you can imagine healthier and more productive forms of protest. What would be two steps toward making them workable?

• Especially in rough economic times, large numbers of people fall into poverty and need some kind of help, at least for a short time. On the other hand, dependency and abuse are worries in the welfare system as we have known it. How else might welfare systems be organized? Hint: Compare welfare systems around the world. One thing we might learn from Norway is that what's really important is not the sheer amount of money spent on social welfare, but *what* it's spent on. It's not spent on so-called "handouts" to people who have already fallen into poverty. Norway spends it on social-support measures that are intended to prevent poverty (as exclusion, disempowerment) from even arising in the first place. Good medical care for all, good education, good transportation and housing. As one writer describes the system: the approach "is not an individualistic, Band-Aid approach but rather a universal, preventive one, a policy consistent with a value system based on care and absolute security." Notice that such a system has immense advantages not just for those who would otherwise be poor, but for everyone. Medical care for *all*; education...

• We also struggle with how to respond, person to person, to people asking for money in the streets. We want to help, we say, but have also learned to wonder what the money is really going for. Some of us give a dollar anyway—how can you turn away? Others make it a policy to refuse. Couldn't there be some rather different ways of meeting the situation? (Hint: what if what's given isn't money?)

WHY WAIT FOR PROBLEMS?

A further step. Look around for institutions or practices that are *not* currently ethical problems, and consider how you might creatively improve them in ethical directions. For example: we have Mother's Day, Father's Day, and increasingly Grandparents' Day, but mostly as occasions for sending a card or maybe a shopping trip. Why not ask: How can we better celebrate each other—more fully, more meaningfully, more consistently? (Fun question, eh? Also, by the way, what about *Children's* Day? Cat Day? School or State Day? Who/what else are we not celebrating enough?)

Or again: Might we soon need to develop a new kind of etiquette for e-mail, cell-phones, and so on, so that we are not constantly "on call," expected to respond just as fast as the messages arrive, and also, too often, only half attentive to wherever we actually are and whomever we are actually with? Better start now... (And a hint: must an "etiquette" of this sort be merely a set of *constraints?*)

Variation: Look for places where ethics has been notably successful, and then ask whether the same successes can be generalized to other areas. Find solutions first, so to speak, and then search for suitable problems. Chapter 1 spoke of solidarity, for example, as when families or neighborhoods shave their own heads to support someone who has lost their hair to chemotherapy. We have the general idea. But are there other and still more powerful ways, both practical and symbolic, to show solidarity with those fighting cancer or similar diseases? With the dying? With children, with soldiers? With each other, day to day? With the Earth?

While you're at it, why not invent some new ethical practices out of the blue? Create something completely new!

NOTES

Parts of this chapter closely follow Chapter 4 of my book *Creative Problem-Solving in Ethics* (Oxford, 2007).

For general background on reframing problems, see the works of Edward DeBono cited in Chapter 15. Also widely discussed is the idea of "proactive thinking": looking ahead to potential problems and working now to head them off later—as opposed to "*reactive thinking*," which waits until they arrive as full-blown problems and then struggles to find some response. See Stephen Covey, *The Seven Habits of Highly Effective People* (Simon and Schuster, 1990), Habit 1. Covey subtitles his book *Restoring the Character Ethic*. Proactive thinking for him is a moral *virtue*!

Philosophers who want more argument for the importance of reframing problems might consult my book *Toward Better Problems* (Temple University Press, 1992), where it is mostly called "reconstructive thinking," using John Dewey's term. The classical source is Dewey's *Reconstruction in Philosophy* (Beacon Press, 1948). See also Caroline Whitbeck's article "Ethics as Design: Doing Justice to Moral Problems," *Hastings Center Report* 26 (1996): 9–16.

For updated data on abortion attitudes I draw on an online article, "Many Americans Support Roe v. Wade Decision," *Angus Reid Global Monitor: Polls & Research,* July 29, 2005: see http://www.angus-reid.com/polls/index.cfm/ fuseaction/viewItem/itemID/8287, accessed 9/30/06. Julie Polter is quoted from her article "Women and Children First: Developing a Common Agenda to Make Abortion Rare," *Sojourners,* May–June 1995. On Mizuko Kuyo, see William R. LaFleur, *Liquid Life: Abortion and Buddhism in Japan* (Princeton University Press, 1992) and the Ethics Updates website at http://ethics .sandiego.edu/Applied/Abortion/index.asp.

Moral Vision

Making a moral contribution is not merely a matter of issuing moral judgments or just reacting to moral problems that come along. It may ask for more than creatively resolving or even reframing problems as well. *Vision* is vital in ethics too.

WORKING FROM A VISION

August 28, 1963. Under a nearly cloudless sky, more than a quarter of a million people gathered near the Lincoln Memorial in Washington for a rally to forward the cause of civil rights, and in particular to insist that the Kennedy administration's civil rights bill, bottled up in congressional committees by Southern opponents, be brought out of committee and passed.

The idea of such a march was itself visionary. By far the largest march on Washington ever held (more than ten times larger than the next largest, which turns out to have been a Ku Klux Klan rally in 1925), it brought together a wide range of previously unconnected groups, both black and white—a fifth of the marchers were white—and a range of black groups that were often at odds. Though the police and the administration feared that violence might occur, all was peaceful. There were speakers from nearly every segment of society—labor leaders like Walter Reuther, clergy, actors, folksingers like Bob Dylan and Joan Baez. It was a watershed day for many more who listened on the radio, or perhaps were not even born in 1963 but who still look back to that day as a turning point. And chiefly what we remember is one speech: Martin Luther King Jr.'s "I Have a Dream."

WE NEED DREAMS

Now here is a remarkable thing. When King walked up to the microphone at the Lincoln Memorial, he did not have that whole speech prepared. Only the first part was written (in fact, it was handed out in advance), a some-what formal recitation of Negro injustice and suffering and an exhortation to carry on the struggle for equal rights with "dignity and discipline." He intended that to be the whole speech—it was all that fit within his allotted time.

He finished the prepared speech. He was about to sit down. But the story goes that then the gospel singer Mahalia Jackson called out, "Tell them about your dream, Martin! Tell them about the dream!" Other listeners shouted encouragement too. And so King launched into an impassioned improvisation that made an already good speech into one of the most moving and powerful speeches of the 20th century.

Obviously King was an extraordinarily adaptable speaker. He was a preacher, of course, experienced in the cadences that make the end of his speech so memorable. He knew how to weave the Bible into his preaching, holding many verses in memory. Likewise he could draw upon the great rhetoric of America's founding documents. He began by echoing Lincoln's Gettysburg Address and ended by citing the Declaration of Independence.

Yet for our purposes another point stands out. It is what Mahalia Jackson asked for: the Dream. King had only barely mentioned it, but she wanted more. The reaction to the speech afterward—continuing to this day—shows that she was not alone in wanting more. What she asked for was a *positive moral vision*: a vision framed not simply as a set of complaints but in terms of ideals and hopes. An explicit and open invitation to a wary nation to join in the spirit that the march had already embodied. And that is what King then—on the spot—offered:

> I have a dream that one day on the red hills of Georgia the sons of former slaves and the sons of former slave owners will be able to sit down together at the table of brotherhood.
>
> I have a dream that one day even the state of Mississippi, a state sweltering with the heat of injustice, sweltering with the heat of oppression, will be transformed into an oasis of freedom and justice.
>
> I have a dream that my four little children will one day live in a nation where they will not be judged by the color of their skin but by the content of their character. I have a dream today.
>
> I have a dream that one day, down in Alabama, with its vicious racists, with its governor having his lips dripping with the words of interposition and nullification; one day right there in Alabama, little black boys and black girls will be able to join hands with little white boys and white girls as sisters and brothers. I have a dream today.

Now that King's speech is so famous, this imagery of a "dream" has gotten rather, well, dreamy, and people invoke it for any kind of unrealistic fantasy. But King's dream is much more focused and modest. In fact it is only a vivid description of what morality itself asks of us. Community with all others without prejudice. Children, and everyone, judged by who they are and not by external characteristics. King just paints the picture in a way that brings tears to our eyes and makes us all want it too.

"VISION" DEFINED

Sometimes moral values operate by *pushing* us, somewhat unwillingly or at least unexpectedly, toward some sort of moral minimum, morally getting by. But pushes are generally not so welcome or so motivating. No one likes to be nagged or constantly to be reminded of their failings, however necessary it sometimes is.

A *pull* is also possible. It captivates us, it rouses the heart and the mind: we move not wearily or out of accommodation but out of real inspiration. This is what I mean by *moral vision*: the capacity to do just what King did—paint a picture of a morally better world in a way that deeply engages and attracts us. It is to draw us toward something grand and lovely.

Of course the civil rights movement was against things: discrimination, disenfranchisement, the routine terrorization of whole populations. It took on deeply entrenched, hateful, often violent resistance. But it never defined itself in predominantly negative terms. What it opposed was not the fundamental point. Always the language, the imagery, even the demonstrations and legal briefs and political platforms, were framed in terms of ideals and hopes. And this is why King's speech is the iconic speech.

It could have been argued—in fact it *was* argued, all the time, by the "realists"—that dreaming was a luxury. But who would remember King's great speech today if he had put all the same points negatively? Suppose he'd said it this way:

> I have a *nightmare* that one day on the red hills of Georgia the sons of former slaves and the sons of former slave owners will *never* be able to sit down together at the table of brotherhood.
> I have a *nightmare* that...the state of Mississippi, a state sweltering with the heat of injustice, sweltering with the heat of oppression, will be *never* transformed into an oasis of freedom and justice....

You get the picture. These are exactly the same points, in a way, only the moral tone is reversed. Here racial equality is presented only as a way to stay slightly ahead of moral disaster. The feeling is aversive, unwelcome. We may go forward, but unhappily, always looking backward in fear and pain. King, by contrast, invites us to something wonderful. That is the vision, and that is what compelled people and spoke so powerfully to the moment. King showed us a future that we want to run forward to greet.

SHAREABLE TERMS

Notice also how consistently King appeals to shared terms and common values. At the time, the civil rights movement was regarded by many conservatives as anti-American, and therefore, in the Cold War categories of the time, "communist." Indeed King was called a communist many times, was harassed and constantly watched by J. Edgar Hoover's FBI, and was constantly criticized by mainstream politicians and clergymen for moving too fast and asking too much. Yet his appeals are always to the most fundamental American values, and beyond them to biblical values and precepts that will be recognizable and compelling to nearly all his hearers. He's asking for very little, and for what we all recognize to be every American's birthright.

The march itself came at a moment of great tension and uncertainty. King makes this point early on:

> It would be fatal for the nation to overlook the urgency of the moment. This sweltering summer of the Negro's legitimate discontent will not pass until there is an invigorating autumn of freedom and equality.... Those who hope that the Negro needed to blow off steam and will now be content will have a rude awakening if the nation returns to business as usual.

These are strong words. They could even be taken as a threat. Yet King's aim was very different. He wanted to call black people and their white allies to continue the struggle with "dignity and discipline" and indeed peace and love. It was an invitation for more allies. Literally in the very shadow of Lincoln, King spoke of the Emancipation Proclamation as a kind of "promissory note" that the nation had not yet paid. Yet he fully expects that it *will* be paid, and freely and gladly too, once Americans recognize the moral need. That is the Dream, and that is what people so needed to hear: a dream of genuine equality, a better way for everyone.

> Five score years ago, a great American...signed the Emancipation Proclamation. This momentous decree came as a great beacon light of hope to millions of Negro slaves who had been seared in the flames of withering injustice. It came as a joyous daybreak to end the long night of their captivity.
>
> But one hundred years later, the Negro still is not free.... One hundred years later, the Negro is still languishing in the corners of American society and finds himself an exile in his own land.
>
> In a sense we have come to our nation's capital to cash a check. When the architects of our republic wrote the magnificent words of the Constitution and the Declaration of Independence, they were signing a promissory note to which every American was to fall heir. This note was a promise that all men, yes, black men as well as white men, would be guaranteed the unalienable rights of life, liberty, and the pursuit of happiness.

…Instead of honoring this sacred obligation, America has given the Negro people a bad check, a check which has come back marked "insufficient funds." But we refuse to believe that the bank of justice is bankrupt.…We have…come to this hallowed spot to remind America of the fierce urgency of now.…Now is the time to make real the promises of democracy. Now is the time to rise from the dark and desolate valley of segregation to the sunlit path of racial justice.…Now is the time to make justice a reality for all of God's children.

King's whole strategy was to call America to recognize in this struggle its own deepest ideals. Here in Washington he speaks from a "hallowed spot," he says. Justice appeals to all of us as equally "God's children." The founding documents of this country, still loved by her black citizens despite her manifold injustices, offer everyone basic and unalienable rights. The dream of racial equality itself, King says,

is deeply rooted in the American dream. I have a dream that one day this nation will rise up and live out the true meaning of its creed: 'We hold these truths to be self-evident: that all men are created equal.'

And so his appeal is to *all* of us, together. Racial equality is not simply about black people: it is about what sort of society we create and sustain together.

The marvelous new militancy which has engulfed the Negro community must not lead us to distrust of all white people, for many of our white brothers, as evidenced by their presence here today, have come to realize that their destiny is tied up with our destiny and their freedom is inextricably bound to our freedom. We cannot walk alone.

In fact, then, contrary to the accusations, it was King and not his accusers who was quintessentially American—and that was the very source of the civil rights movement's power.

KEEP THE VISION INCLUSIVE

Vision looks ahead to an ideal state or possibility. In order to be realistic, though—to really make a difference—that ideal must be in some way attainable. It is not enough to imagine changing one feature of the world, or making a specific moral choice, as if it were independent of everything else. Nothing is independent of everything else! And thus our visions of better moral choices need to be imagined *inclusively*: they must speak to multiple values and to our practical situation as a whole.

Our vision must be a *whole* vision. The task is to integrate one set of moral values and moral actions with a larger encompassing set of values and actions so that the whole is compelling and lovely and grand. People must be able to see a way to realize them in their own lives and society. And our visions in turn become stronger by being linked to other values and families of values.

Maybe you are very concerned about animal rights. It is certainly important to argue with people about how much animals feel and understand and how our basic families of values—say, the value of persons and/or utilitarianism—might have to be extended to at least some of them.

Fair enough, so far. But it's not far enough. We need something more: a sense for how these arguments relate to others. For one thing, it may be hard to see how animal rights can apply in our own lives. Many people think that they literally cannot live without meat. They need some idea of how to cook and eat differently. Meanwhile, we may also have a sense—quite justified too—that the animal question opens the door to many others: that taking animals seriously will soon require us to rethink all sorts of other things, not just our attitudes toward food but also our attitudes toward ourselves, toward the natural world as a whole, and maybe even some of our religious beliefs. So...open up some of these other questions too. Shall we after all rethink that supposedly sharp line between humans and the rest of the world? How *do* our values and even perceptions and maybe even our theology change when we do so?

It's not necessarily that we are averse to looking at these other questions too. We know that there is much to learn! The point is just that we need some help. "Dreaming" a different relation to animals is not enough. Now comes the work of giving it substance, looking at the bigger picture. Make the connections!

ENVIRONMENTAL VISIONS

In the popular impression, environmentalists are the very model of naysayers. Opposed to this, worried sick over that, ill-disposed by reflex to almost any human impact on nature. The Voice of Doom. We may listen and adjust, yes, but unhappily and with a constant sense of worry. Mightn't we conclude that what environmentalism really needs is—a vision?

THE VISION

Certainly there is much to worry about. Yet worry is not at all the whole story. The story is really, at bottom, about *love:* love for the Earth, love for Creation, love for the more-than-human wonders that surround us.

And dreams? We know very well what the dreams are. The eco-theologian Thomas Berry even wrote a book explicitly in this key: he called it *The Dream of the Earth.* So cannot we take our cue from Martin Luther King and highlight our dreams more brightly than our fears? Why are we so hesitant about this love?

Try it:

> We have a dream that our own children and our children's children will again be able to freely drink the waters of rushing streams and breathe deep in the morning air and see the glittering stars at night.
>
> We have a dream that we will at last learn to treasure the purple mountain majesties and the great wild creatures of this land—and give them the space that they require to flourish in their own ways.
>
> We have a dream that the children of loggers and the children of tree-huggers will one day work together in a vibrant forest from which they can take what they need without taking its vibrancy.

This is not just stating the obvious: it is *changing the key*. Here, finally, environmentalism clearly and emphatically is presented as *for* something, not just *against* things. Just as King did, it *pulls* us toward something and doesn't just push. Again: what truly motivates and inspires is a picture of what the world might be instead.

A WHOLE VISION

Once again we must go further. One of the persistent difficulties with environmentalism is that it has not always been so visibly integrated with other values. Critics continue to argue that nature is a "special interest": that it doesn't really fit with our other values, or with most people's values, and indeed that it is at odds with more central values that most of us hold, such as a good standard of living and a healthy economy. Some years back a memorable newsmagazine headline—it happened to be about the standoff between timber interests and defenders of the endangered spotted owls in the Pacific Northwest—read "Owl Versus Man." That stark image of opposing interests struck a nerve. We need to know how environmental values *fit in*.

For one thing, we need a vision of a healthy nature that is not only compatible with a healthy economy but also crucial to it. Even in purely economic terms, most environmental measures are actually more profitable in the long run than one-shot exploitation, which enriches a few investors but leaves the community poorer, indeed often wrecked and displaced. (Think of clear-cutting forests, or rainforest burning: what remains is *nothing*.) Economies further into solar and wind power turn out to have fuller employment and healthier populations than those more invested in oil and nuclear power.

Of course we need to cut and use some trees. But what we really need is a *sustainable* timber industry, using wood in a more intensive, craft-based way, rather than shipping massive amounts of raw wood abroad and/or pulping it for plywood, as the timber corporations do at present. Imagine forest communities once again developing furniture shops and speciality woodcrafts—living *with* the forests rather than "off" the forests until they're gone. The wood stays at home, and every tree, every log, invites a great deal more labor than it takes merely to cut it down and ship it out. That kind of logging, unlike the present practice, would have a future: better for loggers *and* the forests.

Besides, environmental ethics argues here that we are working with far too narrow a picture of human values. We do value comfortable living, of course, but we also value many other things, like keeping awe and respect alive in response to nature—say, endangered owls and the old-growth forests that are their only homes—or just having natural and wild places to go to see the stars and rediscover the tanagers and the turtles. These are genuine values too. Indeed, we are speaking of the whole encompassing Earth, the air and the water and the living communities of land and sea which all of us, *and* all of our children and our children's children, *and* all of the other creatures depend upon. These are hardly "special" interests—they are universal, common, basic interests, which literally ground all others. Here a whole vision brings us back to basics—the "big picture" indeed!

In that sense, titles like "Owl Versus Man" sell "Man"—humans—terribly short. Our interests, our values, are not just economic. The unifying vision is one that is better for us *and* nature—for us as *part* of nature. Tensions no doubt remain—as in any family, short-term interests sometimes pull apart—but the idea that "we" live irrevocably at odds with "nature" is really part of the problem. It's time to look first for the commonalities—the ways in which the "web of life" is *one*.

TOWARD A CELEBRATORY ENVIRONMENTALISM

Now about those creativity skills . . . they too may have a role to play as we both paint the visionary "big picture" and also push it further.

Creative environmental thinking is bubbling up already. As established religions are coming to the forefront of environmentalism, for example, they bring new and unexpected associations to the table. People are actually founding "eco-stories" on the model of the medieval world's monasteries, places where nature is honored and preserved "for the long haul" and for its own sake. Meanwhile, NASA is experimenting with "Living Arks," realizing that entire living communities must go into space if long missions are to be possible at all. While philosophers labor over an ethic of respect for other animals, other people are developing new forms of life that actively embody such a respect—some of them absolutely new and fascinating, like musicians creating new musical forms with orcas. They actually go out and *jam*. What next?

To truly establish a visionary turn in environmentalism, we might add our own forms of environmental creativity. Here's one: suppose that we imagine a *celebratory* environmentalism? Suppose, for instance, that we begin to create new environmental holidays. Festivals, maybe, for bird migrations and eclipses. Already at New Year's many people all across the country venture out, before dawn, to count birds for the Audubon Society. Why not take this much further? Imagine weeks of preparation by eager schoolchildren learning to identify birds. Imagine the hopefulness of the observers that a rare bird might come their way, like amateur astronomers hoping to discover a comet. Imagine "Star Nights" on which all lights everywhere are turned out, even in the blazing cities, timed to coincide with meteor showers, eclipses, occlusions. Ralph Waldo Emerson once said, "If the stars came out only one night in a thousand years, how people would believe and adore, and preserve from generation to generation, remembrance of the miracle they'd been shown." For us the miracle is there every dark and clear night—we just need a little help to see it.

The word "holiday" itself, by the way, comes from "holy day," a time when we remember what really matters. Who wouldn't want a few new ones? And when we come to the Earth as a holy place, in love and joy rather than in fear and ignorance, treasuring and preserving it isn't even a question.

We can take a new look at the old holidays too. Many of these are rooted in natural cycles as well. Winter Solstice, the moment when the long descent of the cold and the dark finally ends, the days stop shortening, the sun begins its ascent anew. It is the rebirth of the year: and of course at the moment of greatest darkness we celebrate with lights, on Christmas trees and in menorahs (Hanukah) and kinaras (Kwaanza). Spring brings the Vernal Equinox: Earth itself is, well, resurrected, bursting into new life. Ancient "Samhain," midway between Fall Equinox and Winter Solstice, became All Saints Day—its eve, All Hallows Eve, which we now call Halloween: the death festival, as the leaves fall and the darkness descends. No light without dark, no life without death. Why not? Really, why not?

"May's Lion"

URSULA K. LE GUIN

The deepest lesson of moral vision is that *things do not need to be the way they are.* The world could be different: worse, better, but, for sure, emphatically and systematically different.

It is the imagination that makes this leap. It is imagination that enables us to look at the world as it is and ask how else it might be. And this sort of imagination can itself be examined in action, and trained. Here is a little story that shows the imagination at work in a beautiful and sparkling clear way. Read it several times—once just for the story; then once to be sure you've gotten the details. Then start asking about Le Guin's *method*. How is she able to turn things so deftly? Are her methods ones that you and I could also use? (Hint: yes!)

Jim remembers it as a bobcat, and he was May's nephew, and ought to know. It probably was a bobcat. I don't think May would have changed her story, though you can't trust a good story-teller not to make the story suit herself, or get the facts to fit the story better. Anyhow she told it to us more than once, because my mother and I would ask for it; and the way I remember it, it was a mountain lion. And the way I remember May telling it is sitting on the edge of the irrigation tank we used to swim in, cement rough as a lava flow and hot in the sun, the long cracks tarred over. She was an old lady then with a long Irish upper lip, kind and wary and balky. She liked to come sit and talk with my mother while I swam; she didn't have all that many people to talk to. She always had chickens, in the chickenhouse very near the back door of the farmhouse, so the whole place smelled pretty strong of chickens, and as long as she could she kept a cow or two down in the old barn by the creek. The first of May's cows I remember was Pearl, a big, handsome Holstein who gave fourteen or twenty-four or forty gallons or quarts of milk at a milking, whichever is right for a prize milker. Pearl was beautiful in my eyes when I was four or five years old; I loved and admired her. I remember how excited I was, how I reached upward to them, when Pearl or the workhorse Prince, for whom my love amounted to worship, would put an immense and sensitive muzzle through the three-strand fence to whisk a cornhusk from my fearful hand; and then the munching; and the sweet breath and the big nose would be at the barbed wire again: the offering is acceptable....After Pearl there was Rosie, a purebred Jersey. May got her either cheap or free because she was a runt calf, so tiny that May brought her home on her lap in the back of the car, like a fawn. And Rosie always looked like she had some deer in her. She was a lovely, clever little cow and even more willful than old May. She often chose not to come in to be milked. We would hear May calling and then see her trudging across our lower pasture with the bucket, going to find Rosie wherever Rosie had decided to be milked today on the wild hills she had to roam in, a hundred acres of our and Old Jim's land. Then May had a fox terrier named Pinky, who yipped and nipped and turned me against fox terriers for life, but he was long gone when the mountain lion came; and the black cats who lived in the barn kept discreetly out of the story. As a matter of fact now I think of it the chickens weren't in it either. It might have been quite different if they had been. May had quit keeping chickens after old Mrs. Walter died. It was just her all alone there, and Rosie and the cats down in the barn, and nobody else within sight or sound of the old farm. We were in our house up the hill only in the summer, and Jim lived in town, those years. What time of year it was I don't know, but I imagine the grass still green or just turning gold.

And May was in the house, in the kitchen, where she lived entirely unless she was asleep or outdoors, when she heard this noise.

Now you need May herself, sitting skinny on the edge of the irrigation tank, seventy or eighty or ninety years old, nobody knew how old May was and she had made sure they couldn't find out, opening her pleated lips and letting out this noise—a huge, awful yowl, starting soft with a nasal hum and rising slowly into a snarling gargle that sank away into a sobbing purr....It got better every time she told the story.

"It was some meow," she said.

So she went to the kitchen door, opened it, and looked out. Then she shut the kitchen door and went to the kitchen window to look out, because there was a mountain lion under the fig tree.

Puma, cougar, catamount, *Felis concolor*; the shy, secret, shadowy lion of the New World, four or five feet long plus a yard of black-tipped tail, weighs about what a woman weighs, lives where the deer live from Canada to Chile, but always shyer, always fewer; the color of dry leaves, dry grass.

There were plenty of deer in the Valley in the forties, but no mountain lion had been seen for decades anywhere near where people lived. Maybe way back up in the canyons; but Jim, who hunted, and knew every deer-trail in the hills, had never seen a lion. Nobody had, except May, now, alone in her kitchen.

"I thought maybe it was sick," she told us. "It wasn't acting right. I don't think a lion would walk right into the yard like that if it was feeling well. If I'd still had the chickens it'd be a different story maybe! But it just walked around some, and then it lay down there," and she points between the fig tree and the decrepit garage. "And then after a while it kind of meowed again, and got up and come into the shade right there." The fig tree, planted when the house was built, about the time May was born, makes a great, green, sweet-smelling shade. "It just laid there looking around. It wasn't well," says May.

She had lived with and looked after animals all her life; she had also earned her living for years as a nurse.

"Well, I didn't know exactly what to do for it. So I put out some water for it. It didn't even get up when I come out the door. I put the water down there, not so close to it that we'd scare each other, see, and it kept watching me, but it didn't move. After I went back in it did get up and tried to drink some water. Then it made that kind of meowowow. I do believe it come here because it was looking for help. Or just for company, maybe."

The afternoon went on, May in the kitchen, the lion under the fig tree.

But down in the barnyard by the creek was Rosie the cow. Fortunately the gate was shut, so she could not come wandering up to the house and meet the lion; but she would be needing to be milked, come six or seven o'clock, and that got to worrying May. She also worried how long a sick mountain lion might hang around, keeping her shut in the house. May didn't like being shut in.

"I went out a time or two, and went shoo!"

Eyes shining amidst fine wrinkles, she flaps her thin arms at the lion. "Shoo! Go on home now!"

But the silent wild creature watches her with yellow eyes and does not stir.

"So when I was talking to Miss Macy on the telephone, she said it might have rabies, and I ought to call the sheriff. I was uneasy then. So finally I did that, and they come out, those county police, you know. Two carloads."

Her voice is dry and quiet.

"I guess there was nothing else they knew how to do. So they shot it."

She looks off across the field Old Jim, her brother, used to plow with Prince the horse and irrigate with the water from this tank. Now wild oats and blackberry grow there. In another thirty years it will be a rich man's vineyard, a tax write-off.

"He was seven feet long, all stretched out, before they took him off. And so thin! They all said, 'Well, Aunt May, I guess you were scared there! I guess you were some scared!' But I wasn't. I didn't want him shot. But I didn't know what to do for him. And I did need to get to Rosie."

I have told this true story which May gave to us as truly as I could, and now I want to tell it as fiction, yet without taking it from her: rather to give it back to her, if I can do so. It is a tiny part of the history of the Valley, and I want to make it part of the Valley outside history. Now the field that the poor man plowed and the rich man harvested lies on the edge of a little town, houses and workshops of timber and fieldstone standing among almond, oak, and eucalyptus trees; and now May is an old woman with a name that means the month of May: Rains End. An old woman with a long, wrinkled-pleated upper lip, she is living alone for the summer in her summer place, a meadow a mile or so up in the hills above the little town, Sinshan. She took her cow Rose with her, and since Rose tends to wander she keeps her on a long tether down by the tiny creek, and moves her into fresh grass now and then. The summerhouse is what they call a ninepole house, a mere frame of poles stuck in the ground—one of them is a live digger-pine sapling—with stick and matting walls, and mat roof and floors. It doesn't rain in the dry season, and the roof is just for shade. But the house and its little front yard where Rains End has her camp stove and clay oven and matting loom are well shaded by a fig tree that was planted there a hundred years or so ago by her grandmother.

Rains End herself has no grandchildren; she never bore a child, and her one or two marriages were brief and very long ago. She has a nephew and two grandnieces, and feels herself an aunt to all children, even when they are afraid of her and rude to her because she has got so ugly with old age, smelling as musty as a chickenhouse. She considers it natural for children to shrink away from somebody part way dead, and knows that when they're a little older and have got used to her they'll ask her for stories. She was for sixty years a member of the Doctors Lodge, and though she doesn't do curing any more people still ask her to help with nursing sick children, and the children come to long for the kind, authoritative touch of her hands when she bathes them to bring a fever down, or changes a dressing, or combs out bed-tangled hair with witch hazel and great patience.

So Rains End was just waking up from an early afternoon nap in the heat of the day, under the matting roof, when she heard a noise, a huge awful yowl that started soft with a nasal hum and rose slowly into a snarling gargle that sank away into a sobbing purr....And she got up and looked out from the open side of the house of sticks and matting, and saw a mountain lion under the fig tree. She looked at him from her house; he looked at her from his.

And this part of the story is much the same: the old woman; the lion; and, down by the creek the cow.

It was hot. Crickets sang shrill in the yellow grass on all the hills and canyons, in all the chaparral. Rains End filled a bowl with water from an unglazed jug and came slowly out of the house. Halfway between the house and the lion she set the bowl down on the dirt. She turned and went back to the house.

The lion got up after a while and came and sniffed at the water. He lay down again with a soft, querulous groan, almost like a sick child, and looked at Rains End with the yellow eyes that saw her in a different way than she had ever been seen before.

She sat on the matting in the shade of the open part of her house and did some mending. When she looked up at the lion she sang under her breath, tunelessly; she wanted to remember the Puma Dance Song but could only remember bits of it, so she made a song for the occasion:

You are there, lion.

You are there, lion....

As the afternoon wore on she began to worry about going down to milk Rose. Unmilked, the cow would start tugging at her tether and making a commotion. That was likely to upset the lion. He lay so close to the house now that if she came out that too might upset him, and she did not want to frighten him or to become frightened of him. He had evidently come for some reason, and it behoved her to find out what the reason was. Probably he was sick; his coming so close to a human person was strange, and people who behave strangely are usually sick or in some kind of pain. Sometimes, though, they are spiritually moved to act strangely. The lion might be a messenger, or might have some message of his own for her or her townspeople. She was more used to seeing birds as messengers; the fourfooted people go about their own business. But the lion, dweller in the Seventh House, comes from the place dreams come from. Maybe she did not understand. Maybe someone else would understand. She could go over and tell Valiant and her family, whose summerhouse was in Gah-heya meadow, farther up the creek, or she could go over to Buck's, on Baldy Knoll. But there were four or five adolescents there, and one of them might come and shoot the lion, to boast that he'd saved old Rains End from getting clawed to bits and eaten.

Moooooo! said Rose, down by the creek, reproachfully.

The sun was still above the southwest ridge, but the branches of pines were across it and the heavy heat was out of it, and shadows were welling up in the low fields of wild oats and blackberry.

Moooooo! Said Rose again, louder.

The lion lifted up his square, heavy head, the color of dry wild oats, and gazed down across the pastures. Rains End knew from that weary movement that he was very ill. He had come for company in dying, that was all.

"I'll come back, lion," Rains End sang tunelessly. "Lie still. Be quiet. I'll come back soon." Moving softly and easily, as she would move in a room with a sick child, she got her milking pail and stool, slung the stool on her back with a woven strap so as to leave a hand free, and came out of the house. The lion watched her at first very tense, the yellow eyes firing up for a moment, but then put his head down again with that little grudging, groaning sound. "I'll come back, lion," Rains End said. She went down to the creekside and milked a nervous and indignant cow. Rose could smell lion, and demanded in several ways, all eloquent, just what Rains End intended to *do*? Rains End ignored her questions and sang milking songs to her: "Su bonny, su bonny, be still my grand cow..." Once she had to slap her hard on the hip. "Quit that, you old fool! Get over! I am *not* going to untie you and have you walking into trouble! I won't let him come down this way."

She did not say how she planned to stop him.

She retethered Rose where she could stand down in the creek if she liked. When she came back up the rise with the pail of milk in hand, the lion had not moved. The sun was down, the air above the ridges turning clear gold. The yellow eyes watched her, no light in them. She came to pour milk into the lion's bowl. As she did so, he all at once half rose up. Rains End started, and spilled some of the milk she was pouring. "Shoo! Stop that!" she whispered fiercely, waving her skinny arm at the lion. "Lie down now! I'm afraid of you when you get up, can't you see that, stupid? Lie down now, lion. There you are. Here I am. It's all right. You know what you're doing." Talking softly as she went, she returned to her house of stick and matting. There she sat down as before, in the open porch, on the grass mats.

The mountain lion made the grumbling sound, ending with a long sigh, and let his head sink back down on his paws.

Rains End got some cornbread and a tomato from the pantry box while there was still day light left to see by, and ate slowly and neatly. She did not offer the lion food. He had not touched the milk, and she thought he would eat no more in the House of Earth.

From time to time as the quiet evening darkened and stars gathered thicker overhead she sang to the lion. She sang the five songs of *Going Westward to the Sunrise,* which are sung to human beings dying. She did not know if it was proper and appropriate to sing these songs to a dying mountain lion, but she did not know his songs.

Twice he also sang: once a quavering moan, like a housecat challenging another tom to battle, and once a long, sighing purr.

Before the Scorpion had swung clear of Sinshan Mountain, Rains End had pulled her heavy shawl around herself in case the fog came in, and had gone sound asleep in the porch of her house.

She woke with the grey light before sunrise. The lion was a motionless shadow, a little farther from the trunk of the fig tree than he had been the night before. As the light grew, she saw that he had stretched himself out full length. She knew he had finished his dying, and sang the fifth song, the last song, in a whisper, for him:

> The doors of the Four Houses
> are open.
> Surely they are open.

Near sunrise she went to milk Rose, and to wash in the creek. When she came back up to the house she went closer to the lion, though not so close as to crowd him, and stood for a long time looking at him stretched out in the long, tawny, delicate light. "As thin as I am!" She said to Valiant, when she went up to Gahheya later in the morning to tell the story and to ask help carrying the body of the lion off where the buzzards and coyotes could clean it.

It's still your story, Aunt May; it was your lion. He came to you. He brought his death to you, a gift; but the men with the guns won't take gifts, they think they own death already. And so they took from you the honor he did you, and you felt that loss. I wanted to restore it. But you don't need it. You followed the lion where he went, years ago now.

RADICAL IMAGINATION IN "MAY'S LION"

Le Guin is reimagining May's story. She retells it as it might have happened instead. This is already an act of radical imagination, and inspiring too. In not so very long, on this very land and with the same creatures that live in it now, we may develop a culture that treats aging (in this case May's) and death (in this case the lion's) in a much more welcoming and rich way. Old women will know how to sing to the animals, and death may not be given over to those who "think they own it already."

But Le Guin also does more than this. By intertwining the stories in this way, she begins to show us that that other world, that other culture, is already present, at least in part, right here and now. The distance between what "actually happened" (already interestingly embellished and adjusted by May's own retellings) and what the story *might* have been is not actually so great.

All of the same elements are there, for one thing: the lion, the long afternoon, the cow, the death, and May herself. In both cases the arrival of the lion is enigmatic: an offering, but we are not sure of what; and a solicitation, also uncertain at first, but then, more clearly, to share a death. It is not nothing to be freely solicited to share the dying of such a creature. And in both cases May recognizes the solicitation and responds within the range of her powers, which are much greater than others give her credit for.

I think the story tells us, in part, that what she needs are *more* powers: specifically, a culture that gives her songs and rituals for the purpose. Even in the second story she still needs songs for animal dying, not just for humans. More broadly, it would have to be a culture that *attends* to the animals, a culture that sees the more-than-human world as itself communicative, that understands and seeks meanings in everything, if only we attend to them, and knows how to communicate back in the same spirit.

None of this is unattainable for us. For many indigenous cultures it was and is the norm. Le Guin also gives us some very concrete tools and hints about what it might take in our case. Certain rituals, for one thing: songs for dying, again, and songs (we infer) for all of life's transitions. A way of naming that better attends to nature ("May" becomes "Rain's End"...). Summer living in pole houses in mountain meadows—or something in the same spirit for other sorts of climates and terrain. A place for older people as healers, wise ones, mediators between human and larger worlds. And again—why not?

 **FOR REVIEW**

1. What is moral vision?
2. How is Martin Luther King Jr.'s "I Have a Dream" speech an example of moral vision?
3. In what ways does King's vision draw upon "shareable terms"?
4. What is a "whole vision"?

QUICK REFERENCE: WORKING FROM A VISION

WORK FROM A VISION

Aim for more than a collection of criticisms and negative moral judgments. What truly motivates and inspires is a picture of what the world might be instead. Paint a picture of a morally better world in a way that deeply engages and attracts. Speak the dream.

WORK FROM A WHOLE VISION

Paint the big picture. Make the dream practical—show "how to get there from here." Integrate it with other values and even other dreams. Make the whole hang together!

PRACTICE RADICAL IMAGINATION

Things do not have to be the way they are right now. Even basic things can change, sometimes quite fast. Ask *how* (not whether) they could be different. Push yourself to find a path. Imagine not just two steps down that path, but all the way. Why not?

---

5. Why is whole vision necessary?
6. Does environmentalism need a vision? What vision?
7. Does environmentalism need a *whole* vision? What whole vision?
8. What is "celebratory environmentalism"?
9. How does Ursula Le Guin exercise moral imagination in her story "May's Lion"?
10. How specifically does the second telling of May's story differ from the first?

 **EXERCISES AND NOTES**

REFRAMING MORAL POSITIONS AS VISIONS

We do not always put moral positions as visions. Environmentalism was the text's case in point, but there are many others. But, as the text argues, things may look very different if we did.

Take this as a challenge. Take prominent moral positions on issues that interest you, and reframe them as visions. Do this for your own positions, for sure—and just as importantly, try to do it for moral positions to which you are indifferent or opposed. Remember, it's not just a matter of stating the position or of stating it fairly and accurately. These are important skills in their own right, but you've already practiced them in previous chapters. The challenge here is to find the vision, the "Dream." Do a little research if you need to. Are some of these dreams already articulated? Why don't we hear more of them?

Can you do this for both sides (all sides) in the abortion debate, for example? Look also at the different positions on capital punishment, sexuality, gay marriage, business ethics, welfare, and any other issue that interests and engages you.

REFRAMING VISIONS AS WHOLE VISIONS

Use this exercise as a follow-up to the last one. You have now laid out some of the visions that lie behind current moral contentions. Now try to develop them as *whole* visions. That is, don't leave them just "dreamy." Make them as integrated with other values and as practical as you can.

Abortion, for example. Here again both sides' positions can be better expressed as visions, in fact as complex whole visions. Again, I leave it to you to spell out the "dreams"—just notice that they are *big* dreams. They are not simply about abortion. Passionate defenders of "life," say, would hardly rest content if *Roe v. Wade* were merely overturned. There are a host of other things to do: strengthen the family, enhance prenatal and postnatal care, speak to the hypersexualization of everything teenaged. Work it out.

Use your other ethical tools as well. For example, as you become more detailed, be alert for ways in which different dreams intersect and overlap. Passionate *defenders* of abortion rights, for example, would hardly rest content if *Roe* were merely secured either. Once again there are a host of other things to do, such as, um, strengthening the family, enabling adequate prenatal and postnatal care, and speaking to the hypersexualization of everything teenaged, as well as equal access to childcare, family leave policies, and rethinking the relations between the sexes in general. Common ground here looks extensive. Of course disagreements remain, even fundamental ones. But again: the "big pictures" are not pure and simple opposites. Whole visions complexify, overlap, draw us back into connection and interdependence, make it possible for us to go forward together.

Your challenge, then, is to take up this same sort of *whole* visioning for some of the other issues that interest and engage you. Gay rights? Business ethics? What about that slogan: "If you want peace, work for justice"? What about the work ethic? Chapter 9 hints that perhaps the work ethic is evolving into something new. But what? What is the vision? How much further might the vision go?

PRACTICING RADICAL IMAGINATION

If things really do not have to be the way they are at the moment, then whenever we confront something morally problematic or even just morally neutral, we can always ask: How else could this be? What seems to be a "given" can be reapproached as a *question*—and, often, a fairly radical question. Quite seriously and practically, we can ask: Why? And the natural follow-up is: How could it be different?

Consider aging. Must it be a disaster, a decline and fading away? What if it were instead deeply treasured and revered? The coming of wisdom, even blurring of the lines between ancestors and the living as one moves close to ancestorhood oneself…mightn't such a thing even be eagerly anticipated? Another "strategic question": What would it take to create a culture that honored age in this way? For one thing, rather than build itself so wholly around the young and their demands and needs, it would have to be a culture that asked first how to accommodate the needs of older people, starting with technologies more user-friendly for them; living places at the centers rather than exiled to the irrelevant peripheries; *pro*-tirement rather than re-tirement, that is, the graduation to greater rather than lesser tasks—maybe you couldn't even *begin* certain kinds of work until you were, say, seventy-five…

Your challenge is to practice this same sort of radical reimagination with regard to other issues: the same you have been considering in the previous exercises, and others as well. Le Guin shows us a way to do this. We can reclaim a story of ethical failure or incompleteness by retelling it in a way that shows us that a better outcome is possible, and (but) also shows us what additional skills or cultural resources a better outcome would take. There are surely many stories—many events, many encounters, many actions—that we might wish to reclaim in this way. Events in your own life, maybe. Encounters you have had personally, or seen first-hand. Violent public events, such as the response to the Rodney King verdicts in Los Angeles. How we respond to terrorism in general and responded to September 11 in particular. The run-ups to wars. How Europeans first came to North America. Or again, moral or other issues that engage and interest you right now. Describe some of them and retell them in the way Le Guin suggests.

NOTES

Martin Luther King Jr.'s "I Have a Dream" speech is widely available on the Web and in historical collections. On the end of the speech as an inspired improvisation, see http://usinfo.state.gov/usa/infousa/facts/democrac/38.htm.

Thomas Berry's *The Dream of the Earth* is now out in a second edition from Sierra Club Books, 2006. *Time*'s "Owl Versus Man" cover appeared on June 25, 1990. A thorough study concluding that environmentalism and economic welfare are *not* at odds—that, in fact, they go together—is Stephen

Meyer, *Environmentalism and Economic Prosperity* (MIT Project on Environmental Politics and Policy, 1992).

Ursula Le Guin's story "May's Lion" appears in her collection *Buffalo Gals* (Penguin, 1990), pages 214–225. In a brief introduction in that volume, Le Guin tells us that this story was an experiment in connecting, as she puts it, "the factual and the fictional," to get us from the world of the present to the world that *could* be. It worked: this story showed her the way that eventually is represented in her long novel *Always Coming Home* (University of California Press, 2001).

For more on radical imagination, see my little book *How to Re-Imagine the World* (New Society Publishers, 2007).

IV

MAKING A DIFFERENCE

CHAPTER 18

You Can Change Your Life

"Realists" will tell you that ethics is nice for classrooms or Sunday mornings, but not practical in the world as it is. And as for actually changing the world—"get over it!" But this book tells a different story. Ethics as pictured here is *essentially* practical, and possibilities for making ethical change, even dramatic ethical change, lie all around us. Recognizing those possibilities and effectively taking them up is also an ethical skill. Methods for change-making—and concepts, inspirations, stories—must be part of your ethical toolbox as well.

We can start right at home: with the question of changing *ourselves*. Rethinking and perhaps remaking our own habits and practices. Here is a kind of change you very definitely *can* make—never mind the rest of the world for a moment—with an excellent chance of real success. Changing yourself may even be a precondition for being able to make changes in the larger world beyond.

SELF-POSSESSION

Self-possession means the capacity to choose for yourself who you will be and what you will do. And *truly* choosing: that is, thinking and choosing in a way that is relatively free from the familiar social pressures that are questionably ethical, such as the pressure to conform, and from old habits that may seem the most natural things in the world but still need rethinking. John Sullivan, remember, speaks of self-possession as "response-ability": the capacity to choose one's responses, or, more specifically, the capacity to observe one's own habits of responsiveness, and then to rethink them and change them as necessary.

Sullivan points out that response-ability must be *cultivated*. It is not a natural thing. Too many forces push the other way. People are often afraid to step even a quarter inch out of line, even when no one else would notice. Unhelpful habits can be immensely restricting too. We try to force ourselves into impossible body types or take up habits we know are self-destructive, because, well, others around us are doing so. TV ad campaigns create overnight fads, and ads in general fuel the persistent craving for more *stuff*. Two years later we wonder what got into us. The same is sometimes true for political passions, going to war, seizing on a career, even getting married. Sometimes we are very far from freedom.

Experiments even suggest that people will readily accept a completely mad system just because someone in authority expects it of them. You may have heard of experiments conducted by social psychologist Stanley Milgram in the early 1960s. Prompted by the trial of Nazi war criminals, Milgram wrote,

> I set up a simple experiment...to test how much pain an ordinary citizen would inflict on another person simply because he was ordered to by an experimental scientist. Stark authority was pitted against the subjects' [participants'] strongest moral imperatives against hurting others, and, with the subjects' [participants'] ears ringing with the screams of the victims, authority won more often than not.

What Milgram described as the "extreme willingness of adults to go to almost any lengths on the command of an authority"—in this case, simply an actor wearing a white lab coat—is deeply disturbing. Some subjects woke up as a result of the experience—a few even wrote to Milgram later to thank him for showing them the need for moral backbone—but most apparently did not, and of course, even when people had regrets later, their original acts still stood.

The problem is not merely that lacking response-ability makes us susceptible to bad influences. After all, in the same way we're also susceptible, presumably, to good influences. Lack of response-ability can also make of our selves a resentful wasteland. Spending our lives feeling (and *being*) manipulated and weak does not make for self-respect or creativity or joy. It leads to anger that can easily be manipulated back against others, or even against ourselves. We need another way!

CULTIVATING RESPONSE-ABILITY

So how do you make your thoughts—your *self*—a little more your own, and therefore also make your acts more self-possessed and free?

Of course it is partly a matter of willpower, determination, even of a kind of courage. Commitment and persistence are essential. You have to be willing to take on self-possession as a project, stop simply "going along," and sometimes take a harder path.

But will by itself is not enough. In fact, it's hardly even a start. What we really need are *methods,* strategies: ways of creating an alternative momentum for ourselves. Some of these methods may seem obvious—some *are* obvious, but need to be pointed out anyway—while others may surprise you. Try them all!

First: Give yourself some space to think. Literally. Regularly seek out quiet places to be safe and alone, set aside time that is not rushed or distracted. It is for good reason that the world's religious traditions embrace the practice of spiritual retreat. Give yourself the chance to catch your breath, to get a little distance, to take stock of things on your own terms.

Second: Rearrange your inputs. Carefully list the pressures that tend to pull you in the way you really want to go, and then consider how you might rearrange your life so that more of these pressures are present, and/or fewer counterpressures. To use your school time productively, hang around productive places like libraries and studios and gyms. If you want to reduce your alcohol use, don't spend your time in bars or with drinkers. Find yourself attractive alternative activities and friends. In general, don't set up your life so you constantly have to battle temptations and swim against the current. Find yourself a different river! Avoid manipulators: the incessant and insistent voice of the commercial media, for example, and ads or films that are regularly using ever more extreme imagery to catch your attention.

Keep at it. You will not free your mind overnight. Also, take manageable steps. This may mean starting small. It may take time to find your moral voice and the courage of your convictions. One thing will lead to the next. Get in the habit of going your own way about small but important things to you—avoiding sexist or racist humor might be one good place to start—so that when bigger things come along, you have had some practice. You may also find, once you step out on your own in any way, that people will begin to look to you for leadership. Even small things make a difference!

Get informed. Identify the facts and resources you will need, and go find them. I have seen many students decide to go meat-free, for instance, with the best of intentions and goodwill, only to discover after a month that they cannot, so to speak, live on bread alone. Of course not! Yet an *informed* vegetarian diet can be easy and extremely healthy, and fellow vegetarians (and cookbooks, grocery stores, restaurants, clubs, etc.) can now be found nearly everywhere.

Remember your critical thinking skills. The point is not to embrace some new dogma and thereafter define yourself by it. Ultimately that isn't response-able either: you make yourself unable to respond in any way but one. Thinking more deeply means recognizing complexity and ambiguity and the changing face of many issues. Expect—and invite and celebrate—growth and change.

And finally: Enjoy yourself. Love what you are doing—or rather, wholeheartedly do what you love. You are not going your own way to prove something to yourself or your mother or to impress or offend or guilt-trip other people. You are doing it because it is right by your lights. Fulfilment without pride.

SEXUAL CHOICES

Sexual self-possession is a case in point. Sex is an unmatched source of pleasure and celebration, an essential element of happiness for many people. As such it is already, also, of central moral value. Though the term "sexual ethics" seems to suggest to some people a kind of kill-joy fuddy-duddyism, ethics has a few more notes to play than that.

SEX AND MORAL VALUES

We get crude, maybe, if we reduce sex to nothing but the immediate pleasure or release of tension. But there is much more to sex than this, even in purely hedonistic terms. Sex involves the many pleasures of companionship and mutual appreciation, of touching and simple physical togetherness, of wonder and gracefulness and humor too. The needs it fulfills are not just passing and physical but go to the very core of our beings. Nothing crude about that.

Other families of moral values also immediately come into play. Sex can be seen as the desire to unite with another person, to go beyond the limits of our own being and solitude. In this way we can view sex as a fitting completion of our natures, both as animals and as social and spiritual beings. Sex is part of what brings us into caring and community. It transmutes physical desire into loyalty, sharing, family, love.

Cautions and limits therefore arise against this very background of moral complexity—out of the very nature of sex itself. They aren't arbitrary moral impositions from somewhere else. One familiar guideline comes straight from the first family of values: sexual love should respond to a *whole person*— body *and* soul, as it were, together. Sexual acts are physical, in part, usually: but sex is nonetheless a relation between persons, and thus has the power to put us and keep us deeply in touch with the reality of another person, inexhaustible and "infinite," as Levinas would say; an end in themselves, as Kant puts it, not as a mere means to pleasure.

Sex also offers a radical kind of trust, which calls for trustworthiness in return. We give of our bodies, which can be treasured and honored or hurt or infected or unwillingly impregnated; and of our feelings, which can be shared and deepened or betrayed or manipulated. Thus we are called to take care with the gift of another's trust. In a situation of such profound vulnerability, irresponsibility—carelessness, deception, coercion—is the complementary vice.

A second guideline, then, is that sexual love should sustain connection, relationship, and trust. It is no accident that we speak of "making love." Questions of attachment and love are unavoidable. Sex so understood is part of the central dynamics of our lives: part of marriages and families and communities, part of the joint work of a household and child-raising, part of life partnerships that go far beyond what happens in bed. And so, our moral traditions suggest, moral sex—or "good sex," if you like—needs to attend to the whole network of relationships that come to be at stake. It should sustain and deepen them, not undermine or weaken or pull them apart.

Younger people may have a more exploratory sexual attitude. Though moralists take varied views of this, a basic and common-ground imperative is this: at least, *communicate*. Sex itself, the very acts, are deeply communicative— far beyond words. But ethics would also have us attend to "communication" on the more ordinary sense, even to just plain talking. Generally speaking, young lovers and especially first-time lovers can *not* assume that there is just one sort of thing that sex could be or that what's happening is understood the same way by both parties. *Ask,* talk, keep talking... you will find yourself with a deeper and more fulfilling sex life as well as a deeper and more ethical relationship generally.

"PERVERSION"

To "pervert" something, according to *Webster's,* is to "turn it aside from its proper use or nature." We can pervert justice; we can pervert sport—what about sex? "Can you deflect sexual desire," philosopher Colin McGinn asks, "from its true or proper course?" His answer is *yes*.

"To make sense of this," he begins, "we obviously need some concept of what the 'proper use or nature' of human sexual desire is." Here is his proposal.

> From a purely biological perspective, the human sex drive has as its primary object sexual activity of a kind that would lead to conception if it occurred in the right circumstances.... But of course there is more to sexual desire than this purely biological function; it also has an emotional or personal side. Sex makes us relate in certain ways to other persons *as persons;* it is connected in all sorts of respects to our nature as social beings. I would like to suggest that the proper nature of sex, from a psychological point of view, involves a desire for another person as a sentient and physical entity: it is a complex passion aimed at another person conceived as possessing a sensual nature.

Think the object of sex in this way and it turns out that we can readily define what "perversion" could mean:

> That sensual nature is the proper object of sexual attraction—a living body capable of sexual feelings and desires. If sexual desire becomes detached from such an object, it can be said to have been perverted from its proper course.

So sex with objects is perverse, obviously, because they are not living and have no "sensual nature" of their own at all. Sex with animals is another example, where responding to and being responded to as a "whole sensual nature" is not possible.

Sex with other humans can be perverted too, by this definition. Here too, sexual desires can be "detached from the whole sensual nature" of the other person.

> I think we generally appreciate that certain elements in [the structure of our sexual desires] shouldn't be allowed to take on a life of their own, squeezing out the rest. The focus must remain on the other person as a complete sensual being, and not shift to something that lies to the side of the person, or is a mere part of him, or is quite impersonal.

"Sexual tunnel-vision," then, is the essence of sexual "perversion" according to McGinn. Perversion is a failure (or inability?) to respond to another person as a *person*—thus a failure of respect as well.

The term "pervert" these days is often thrown—not necessarily in polite company—at people whose sexual orientation is bisexual or homosexual. Even as studies suggest that up to 10 percent or more of the population may be primarily homosexual (and more bisexual), there is a vast well of uneasiness, condemnation, and hostility toward anyone perceived to be "perverse" in this way.

But notice that, on McGinn's analysis, the term does not apply. Homosexual desire can respond to the "whole sensual nature" of a person just as can heterosexual desire. Likewise, and even more important for our purposes here, both homosexual *and* heterosexual desire may *fail* to respond in this way—may become "tunnel-visioned," fixated, or objectified. There is nothing in homosexual love *as such* that makes it necessarily objectified, any more than heterosexual love. Neither orientation has a monopoly on objectification.

Sexual "tunnel-vision," in short, is "perverse" wherever it occurs. Addiction to pornography, or hitting on someone only to "score" are perverse whether gay or straight. In McGinn's account, sexual perversion simply has nothing to do with sexual orientation. It has everything to do with sexual *ethics*.

SEXUAL RESPONSE-ABILITY

Another moral guideline for sex arises directly out of the discussion of response-ability in the first part of this chapter. *Sexual choices should be response-able.*

Of course you have heard all too often about sexual responsibility: keeping yourself safe from unwanted pregnancy and STDs, and so on. Note well: the theme here is different. To be response-*able*, remember, means that you come to recognize that we can choose how we respond to anything— and that there is always more than one way to respond. Response-*ability* means embracing the freedom to choose: the real, deep freedom to shape the world you will live in. Freedom of mind is as vital in sexual choices as anywhere else.

I do not have to remind you that sexual pressure in our society is intense. Young children, especially girls, are molded by social ideals of beauty—that is, more or less, sexual attractiveness—practically from birth. Teen anorexia and other kinds of self-starvation to fit the current hyperthin ideal body types; all-consuming attention to the details of clothing and makeup, for females, and rigid gender roles for males; and much more—you know the story. As sexual maturity arrives, the dance around sexual acts themselves begins. Your whole life may seem to turn on whether a certain person likes you this afternoon, and what you do with him or her. And all of this can continue, in one form or another, practically throughout a life.

Sexual pressures arise in relationships as well. My students, especially women, report regularly feeling pressured into having sex. Others feel pressure from a more subtle source: their own past acts. Having had a sexual relationship that they later regret, they may feel permanently marked by it, as if, to use the religious metaphor, they have "fallen" in a way that can't be redeemed, and they may as well continue to follow the same path.

Sullivan's ethic of response-ability invites you to another way of thinking. All of these pressures are just that: pressures. They are not necessities. You are not on an irresistibly slippery slope with only one place to end up— at the bottom. There are always other ways to respond, whatever other people expect and whatever your past responses have been.

Build the personal strength, then, not necessarily to say no, but to find out and then express what you really want to say yes to. Or maybe you will find yourself in the end saying neither no *or* yes but something that is truer and more specific to you, now. Why reduce sexual communication to monosyllables?

From Being Sexual … and Celibate

KEITH CLARK

How we engage in sexual activity is a choice, or rather an ongoing series of choices, but it is not the only kind of sexual response-ability to which we are called. Prior to these choices in turn is the choice to engage in sexual activity itself in the first place.

Other choices are possible. Abstinence—anyway, from sexual intercourse until marriage—is widely promoted by many religious conservatives. A more radical choice is to abstain from sexual activity entirely: a life of *celibacy*, a choice that, however radical it may seem, has always been expected of its priests by the Catholic

From Keith Clark, *Being Sexual … and Celibate* (Ave Maria Press, 1986), Chapters 2 and 3.

Church. In this selection, Father Keith Clark, a Capuchin Franciscan monk, semi-
nary administrator, and author, portrays the celibate life from the inside. "Part of
the reason celibacy seems so irrelevant to many people," he writes, is that "the
connection between celibacy and sexuality is almost completely ignored." Read on
as he connects them.

Much of the discussion of human sexuality seems to center around the
biological and bio-psychological level, and comparisons are made between what humans experience and what is true of the higher forms of
animals. A lot of what I have heard and read relegates consideration of the
personal/spiritual level to the domain of philosophers and theologians.
The implication seems to be that anything said about sexuality beyond the
biological and bio-psychological cannot be verified by empirical research,
and has little value. Sociology claims to add to the discussion of human
sexuality by researching human sexual behavior and the verifiable consequences of behavioral patterns in a given culture. Anthropology compares
the sexual practices of various cultures. But human sexuality, like that of
the higher forms of animal life, is thought by many to have been completely covered in its objective aspects when the biological and bio-psychological levels are studied.

I think I have experienced something sexual which is not merely biological or bio-psychological and which does not stem from the fact that
I am a Christian and a Catholic. I am spiritual even if I have no interest in
religion. I have experienced connecting with other human beings in ways
which I cannot explain solely by my biological urges and bio-psychological
drives.

Even the sexuality of the higher forms of animals is not totally explained by their biology and bio-psychology. There is something else op-
erative in their sexual lives: the level of need. And the meaning of animal
sexuality is determined by the need which is met by the animals' instinctively moderated sexual activity. Meeting the need is achieved, not through
the having and the operation of the animal biology and bio-psychology, but
by the instinctively moderated behavior.

In human sexuality there is also a third level of need which gives meaning to human sexual activity. But that need cannot be ascertained simply by
observing human sexual behavior, because human sexual behavior, while
instinctively motivated, is not *regulated* by instinct. It is regulated by the
spiritual and personal capacities of insight and freedom.

With insight we human beings can see that the species needs more
human beings. The need for the species to continue gives meaning to
human sexuality.

But there is another human need which gives meaning to human
sexuality. It is the need for intimacy with other human beings. It is the

deepest personal need we have, and it is a spiritual need. We long to come together with other human beings so that our spirits touch and our personalities fuse without being lost in each other. In intimacy the expanse which separates us from every other human being is bridged, and the separateness, the insufficiency, the neediness which we inherit from our birth is temporarily alleviated. . . .

Some people accept the gratification of urges and drives as sufficient meaning. I do not. Even animals are instinctively directed in their sexual activity to achieve more than that. My interpretation of what I have heard from married couples suggests that human sexual activity achieves its highest meaning when both the need for the species to be propagated and the need for intimacy are intended and pursued. Sexual activity which intends and pursues neither need ranks among humanity's most disappointing and devastating experiences.

I don't believe that married couples who love each other are supposed to enter into sexual activity encumbered with weighty thoughts and lofty ambitions. I presume sex is fun! It's a way for people who are permanently committed to each other to play, to enjoy each other, and to further their intimate relationship. Such play and fun has meaning, not because the partners' heads are full of ideas about "meaning" and "communication" and "self-disclosure," but because they have an intimate, committed relationship.

Sexual activity which is not more than the gratification of urges and drives is frequently portrayed as fun and fulfilling. But conversations I have had over the years with those who engaged in sexual activity in such a way have convinced me that genital sexual activity and romantic behavior of themselves will eventually disappoint, not because they are bad, but because they are not enough.

I have chosen a celibate life for myself, and my intent in my own sexuality does not include having a child of my own. I must find other ways to be generative. But my need for intimacy is as great as anyone else's. And intimacy is just as much a part of my sexuality as it is part of a married person's. Having decided not to marry and have children does not make my view of human sexuality that of an outsider.

"Human sexuality is about intimacy, period!" Jerry said one night. I told him I thought he had a point, but that he was overstating it. We argued and discussed the matter for several hours that night and on many other evenings. Eventually he convinced me. Human sexuality IS about intimacy. Not only about intimacy, but always about intimacy. Intimacy is possible for me because I was born a *sexual person*. Both words are important—"sexual" and "person." . . .

In the presence of those with whom I have an intimate relationship, I feel invited to *be* myself and to *reveal* myself. I have a sense that they feel the same with me. When we can be ourselves and reveal ourselves to each other, something grows between us.…

For me, romantic pursuits are those activities which stimulate our sexual emotions for another and are designed—consciously or unconsciously—to evoke a similar emotional response from another. Although romance can distort our perception of one another, it can also lead us to a sense of safety and relatedness with one another which will allow us to eventually be ourselves and reveal ourselves to one another. If we do, intimacy can arise from the romantic pursuits. Romance is not intimacy, but it can lead us to behave in ways which will allow intimacy to arise. What is important is that we recognize with our insight and pursue with our free choice those behaviors which will bring us together without anyone being dominated, manipulated, mutilated or changed.

A good friend, a perpetually professed woman religious for about ten years, told me very matter-of-factly one evening that she was quite sure that she would be seeking a dispensation from her religious vows. I was shocked. In fact, I said to her, "You're kidding!" and took another bite of the Chinese food we were sharing. Then I looked at her expression, set my fork on the plate, and said to myself more than to her, "No, you're not kidding."

She told me of a man who had been instantly able to invite her out of herself like no one else had ever been able to do. She was both popular and respected within her community, a potential leader because she was intelligent, witty, personable and sympathetic. As the evening together continued, she told me of her own sense of isolation within her community. She was becoming very aware of her great need for intimacy, for connectedness. Randy entered her life and invited from her a response no other person had ever invited; and she responded. She found she could be open with him—completely open. "He loves all of me," she said with feeling too great and too real to be dismissed.

Within three months she had taken a leave of absence from her community and had moved in with Randy. During the course of those three months we spoke several times, and she appeared to me to be completely infatuated with Randy. Over those months she had told several of her sisters in the community of her decision, and saw the pain and sadness in each of their faces. But she regarded leaving as something she had to do. Being with Randy had awakened in her feelings and responses which she had never had before. She attributed to Randy the ability to make her feel what she felt. And she therefore attributed to him the response she gave him. "He makes me feel so free, so loveable, so able to be myself."

She cried with almost every one of her sisters whom she told about her decision to leave. At first, with real pain and disappointment and eventually with some deep anger, she asked why it was only when she was leaving that her sisters seemed to reach out to her. "Now that it's too late they are willing to get close," she said to herself in my hearing.

I tried arguing with the stories she told herself. But I lost every argument. I remain convinced that she found Randy "the right one," the one who stimulated her romantic sexual emotions and she became fascinated and then infatuated with him. These emotions led her to behave in ways which allowed intimacy to begin to arise in her life. She told her sisters one by one, and the revelation of herself to them and their response gave her the first taste of intimacy she had experienced with them. And she resented them for being too late.

By the time she left, she was in fact experiencing intimacy with a lot of people. She chose behaviors with Randy which were romantic as well as intimate; romance had awakened in her the inclination for behaviors which allowed intimacy to arise. Intimacy had come into her life on the wings of romance, and she really couldn't imagine that she could experience intimacy without romance.

Randy is a Catholic who was free to marry my friend. My friend said he loved all of her. But he didn't love her commitment to a way of life which precluded her marrying him. In their coming together a very significant part of my friend was obliterated. That having taken place, I imagine that their life together will be as happy as any other life. I assume that genuine intimacy will continue to grow between them. I don't know what happens to the realization in my friend that part of her is gone. She chose to have it be gone; I can't argue with her for that. But she did so by telling herself the story: "He loves all of me." I do argue with that.

The stories I tell myself about romance and intimacy come from my experience of being in love. I too have been loved by a woman who felt as romantically inclined toward me as I did toward her. I too told my brothers in the Order of my feelings for her. And they marvelled, feared, laughed and cried with me. I too thought seriously about romantically pursuing this woman. I didn't think at first of marrying her, just behaving toward her in ways which would continue the stimulation of my romantic feelings and perhaps encourage her romantic feelings for me. Ten years later she is still the woman I would want to marry. Her romantic feelings for me were never acted out. I never received from her any "mixed messages" which suggested that she wanted me to leave the Order and marry her. Nor did I give her any such messages. Today we talk about our relationship over the years, and she says to those who occasionally ask her why she never married me, "I love him too much to try to take him away from his commitment." She loves all of me. The intimacy we share is as great as any I have experienced in my life. It is an intimacy arrived at without romantic activity. Her love is one of the greatest gifts of my life.

From Real Live Nude Girl

CAROL QUEEN

Writer and organizer Carol Queen tells us on her website that

> [m]y focus, whether writing, speaking, consulting, or providing erotic entertainment, is to empower and inspire others to discover their own unique sexual profile—we have to remove the stigma from sex before we can make it fabulous. I have had to struggle to find the place and permission to express my own sexuality, and I am committed to facilitating others as they do the same. Until we honor the full spectrum of consensual erotic desire, none of us will be truly free to pursue our own.

You can read Queen's essay as the polar opposite of Clark's, and in many ways her vision is indeed far from his celibate ideal. But then again...Queen celebrates sexual expression in many forms, yes, but she too questions what is "normal" sexually, as if one form of sexual expression were really the only form possible, and in speaking frankly of sexual experience she is also morally specific and demanding. Do not *both* writers actually put sexual expression in the mode of response-ability?

Consider how you might (re?)read Queen's title, too: as the insistence that there is after all a *real live person* in the sexual picture.

I believe that most of us want enough sexual knowledge to let us feel comfortable and competent. (If we don't want this for ourselves, it is a quality we want in our partners.) I believe most people want sex to be good, not problematic, dangerous, or bad. They want (though often they are nowhere near able to articulate wanting) a sex-positive world: a world in which sex enhances human connection and sexual possibilities can be explored without shame.

Hearing the words "sex-positive" made me realize I'd grown up in a fundamentally sex-negative world. Even the so-called sexual revolution hadn't knocked out the old guns: religious morality, legal sanctions, threadbare sex education or none at all, the "war between the sexes." Erotophobia fed on itself, generation after generation, continually reproducing conditions of fear, shame, and danger. This has not truly changed. Even the generation which fought for sexual liberation has mostly retrenched, refusing to stand up and fight for good sex education for its own children.

From Carol Queen, *Real Live Nude Girl* (Cleis Press, 2002), pp. ix–xxiv.

It may sound odd to make the claim that U.S. culture is erotophobic. We live, after all, in a society that splices sex into practically everything: music, movies, commercials, the Internet, cable TV.... But sexual variety is not in fact so mainstreamed, and neither is the notion that everyone deserves the sex life that is the expression of their own unique set of desires, as long as it can be had consensually. The people bouncing up and down on adult cable are not fat, old, or in any way ordinary-looking. They're not queer—at least, the script doesn't portray them that way. They're not disabled. And on the info and opinion shows, most sexual discussion is not especially deep. Eroticized images are great for keeping us distracted, and they're pretty good at getting us to spend money. But shows that risk exploring sexual subjects are preceded by a warning: "May be offensive to some viewers." Instead of the message that sex is of very nearly universal interest and deserves the best efforts of our culture-makers, we get spam.

We're sexually schizophrenic. We don't want kids to have good, clear, pleasure-based information. We want, if we're grown-ups, to have access to sexual materials, but we won't fight for them, and often we can't tell if they're any good when we get them. We won't insist our elected representatives stand up for this material, so for the most part they don't, even when they're big consumers of it themselves. Sex drives us, and it is cannily marketed to do so, and most of us get enough sexual titillation and entertainment that we can easily ignore the question of sexual rights. Anyway, why would we involve ourselves in someone else's personal issues? Sex is supposed to be private....

...[T]he culture is lousy with sexual secrets and people who have been punished for them. My parents lived their pain around sex in airless silence, though their pain around everything else was easy enough to see. I was eighteen before my mother admitted to me she had been married twice (imagine that as a source of shame!), twenty-seven before she told me she had a history of incest. She had only told my father a few years before he died. He lived for thirty years with a woman who took no pleasure in sex; for most of those years he had no way of knowing why. I knew, before I knew what sex was, that something was wrong with them, very wrong. Today I know what was broken, and I know it never had half a chance to heal.

Gays and lesbians are incorrect when they say straight people have it easy. Sometimes straight people lack the very language to name the pain they feel when the culture thwarts their desires, even cuts off their access to desire itself. Did it ever occur to my parents to try to get help with their broken sex life? Did it seem "normal" to them—men wanting sex, women resisting? Did they even understand they each had a sexuality, much less that they had choices around how they would manage their sexualities over the course of their lives? My friend Will Roscoe once told me his theory of homophobia: Straight people, he said, are jealous of us, because we have a sexual orientation and they don't. In our sexual otherness, we have to learn to talk about sex; it defines us in a way it doesn't define heterosexuals, and in the process of becoming a community, we learn comfort with the language.

Many of us do, anyway. Not all of us escape the closet, the self-hatred, the too-tight clothes of Normalcy that fit us so poorly. But no one can tell me that the life of a hidden queer is unhappier than the pain I saw in my father. No one can tell me that heterosexual privilege did my mother a damned bit of good.

I saw in my parents' example, and I learned from the gay movement, how crucial to happiness sexual honesty is. When I realized that my fantasies hid a sexual profile much more complicated than I admitted to, I knew I hadn't yet done justice to Harvey Milk's directive to "Come out!" I started by moving to San Francisco, where every kind of queer has fled to escape restrictive homes.

There my world no longer seemed split so neatly into Us and Them. I learned in the gay and lesbian communities a way to understand and politicize sexual identity: The idea of "sexual minority" lends itself to looking at other secret or embattled or oppressed ways of living in the desire-and-gender-coded body. But when gayness proved unable to contain all my desire, I learned to translate "Gay Is Good" to "Sex Is Good," and that is a badge virtually all of us could learn to wear.

It is clear to me today that the pain and failure at the heart of my parents' sexual relationship does not mean less—or more—than the pain and oppression the gay-rights movement works to alleviate; that even below the hatred and small-mindedness that power homophobic and all manner of censorious impulses, there is distress and pain about sex that, were it healed, might wither the roots of the poisonous tree. Erotophobia and xenophobia work together to empower every sort of despisal, including many of those at the heart of the "war between the sexes." Given this, I wish to speak to a vast and varied audience.

More than any academic credential that provides both an overview and a screen of depersonalizing ivory-tower smoke, my experience living in many different sexual realms sources my qualification to speak up now. Too often we hear talk about sex that never seems to come from anyone's first-person experience; how much easier to discuss *other people's* real and imagined sexual experiences and shortcomings. We lack, more than any other things, an atmosphere in which each of us might tell the stories of her or his experience and be heard by an audience who did not presume it appropriate to immediately hit the switch of excoriation or analysis. While we lack this in any sort of public arena, too many of us also lack it in private, in the silent circles of our marriages and significant-otherhoods, which should be the first places adults practice the skill of tolerance. And in our families, within which most of us failed to learn that our desires are our own, failed to have our growth in them respected, too many of us find our sexuality undermined and learn from this the habits of secrecy and blame....

For a while I believed what others told me: that men and women were erotically incompatible; that males got what they wanted out of sex while women did not; that it was my partners' incompetence that kept me from having orgasms during sex with them. Men and women were seemingly separate species, and only gradually did it dawn on me that the legacy of my parents' and my culture's sexual silence resided in my own body, not just in mismatched sexual couplings: I did not know how I could be pleased, and so how could anyone be expected to know how to please me? By now it seems that I can trust my own experience more than anyone else's version of love and sex, but in those days I had practically no experience on which to draw. Most of the sex I had had was not very impressive. It seemed as likely that clumsy, selfish male sexuality was to blame for this state as any other thing.

But in retrospect I realize I didn't have enough information. I couldn't even make myself have an orgasm until I snitched my parents' vibrator (and, bless them, they never asked for it back—it must not have been missed). It shouldn't have been surprising that my partners couldn't "make" me have an orgasm, either. When my lovers asked me what I wanted in bed, I said, "Oh, everything you do feels wonderful," even when it didn't. I failed them as thoroughly as they failed me—partly because, as a young woman, I'd gotten too little access to good sex information and even less access to anything that would encourage me to take my own sexual needs seriously. Of course, my adolescent male partners hadn't had much access to useful information, either.

I think now that much of the sexual resentment I see troubling women and men derives directly from our having been hormone-ridden, largely ignorant teenaged animals struggling to learn to make love while burdened with the weight of acculturated shame and crippling gender roles. My prescription for change—that children and adolescents be freely given permission and correct, wide-ranging sex information—seems farther away in this decade than it did when I was a teen. Child abuse is heinous—but why do I hear no outcry about the abuse that lies at the heart of sexual silence, of inculcated shame?

...Each of us can stop cowering at the notion that we might be different. Of course we are—we all are....While there's more of life than sex (I guess), sex is a good place to start this project of listening to our own voices. *Sex-positive,* a term that's coming into cultural awareness, isn't a dippy love-child celebration of orgone—it's a simple yet radical affirmation that we each grow our own passions on a different medium, that instead of having two or three or even half a dozen sexual orientations, we should be thinking in terms of millions. "Sex-positive" respects each of our unique sexual profiles, even as we acknowledge that some of us have been damaged by a culture that tries to eradicate sexual difference and possibility....

...Once I decided most of what my culture had told me about sex was wrong, I set out on a prolonged walk on the wild side, and by now I've walked into more secret places than I ever knew existed.

They are wild and spirit-filled gardens, indeed.

EATING

Food is certainly a less sexy topic than, well, sex. But choices we make about food are at least as significant for ourselves, for others, and even more for the world. Eating is a practice that also begs for ethical thinking.

MORAL VEGETARIANISM

First of all, unavoidably, there is the question of animals. All through Part II of this book, you'll remember, the exercises and sometimes the text raised the question of animals and suggested that at the very least our use of animals for food, however habitual and traditional, needs serious thinking. Our diets are literally full of the bodies of other living creatures. But animals *suffer*, massively, in the run-up to our plates. Many are tightly confined, against all of their natural instincts, often for their entire short lives. Every element of their environment is manipulated to produce the most meat (or eggs, or milk...) in the shortest time. And they come to their deaths knowing what is happening—in slaughterhouses with hundreds of others, the smell of death always in the air, often with other animals killed right in front of their eyes.

You may know how veal is produced. At birth, male calves are immediately separated from their mothers. They are tightly penned to prevent them from developing their muscles (it toughens the meat). They are restricted to a liquid diet when all their urges tell them to begin chewing grass. That diet among other things deprives them of iron (which would also develop muscle and color the meat) so that they become so desperate for it that they may spend hours gnawing on the bars of their pens or any nails in sight. Then they are slaughtered, at four months or less—unless they have died already, as 10–15 percent regularly do, from the sheer stress and frustration of their lives.

Many people have given up veal out of outrage at this way of treating calves. Yet animal advocates argue that veal production is only slightly more horrible than what is done routinely with all the familiar meat animals. Commercially raised chickens may spend their whole lives in cages too small for them even to turn around, much less spread their wings or fly, or in huge sheds holding tens of thousands of birds, so large that all social structure breaks down and the birds have to be "debeaked" (have their beaks cut off) so that they do not kill each other in their fury and confusion. When egg production in a multiple-thousand bird unit falls off too much, the whole bunch is just shipped off for killing. Americans currently consume about five *billion* chickens per year.

Utilitarians, not surprisingly, have therefore taken the lead in arguing for moral vegetarianism. Pain is pain, suffering is suffering, and if animal suffering counts at all, then even the roughest calculus requires major changes. But the other families of moral values have their say too. Some animals suffer knowingly, as "subjects of a life," and so the values and rights of persons arguably also apply. When we don't live in relations of community and care with other animals, or when we cut ourselves off from them emotionally in order to avoid recognizing their suffering, we also do violence to ourselves and deepen the oppression of all life, as Alice Walker suggests. A caring community must make some bows toward other creatures, even though it may not follow that they have as strong a claim as we do.

The arguments on the other side have a harder time of it, frankly, at least in my view. It's no longer very plausible to argue that animals don't suffer at all. More common is the claim that they don't suffer as much, or suffer differently. But these admissions already have ethical implications. Surely we should still reduce what suffering we can. Making such tradeoffs, even if they are often in our own favor, is very different from dismissing the whole subject from the beginning.

Likewise, though rights arguments may not apply to all animals, they may apply to some: pigs, cows, maybe chickens, maybe not fish. But few non-vegetarians make these kinds of distinctions. What I usually hear is the argument that vegetarianism is simply not healthy or not practical. Even standard grocery stores carry a wide range of meat-free options, though, and if anything it's meat that isn't healthy: the two leading killers in America, cancer and heart disease, are both linked directly to high-meat diets. Vegans—people who eat neither meat nor dairy products—have the highest life expectancy of any Americans. And, vegetarians report, their meals taste just as delightful and varied—if not more—than the traditional meat meals.

Meat or not, then—it is a *choice*. When it comes to food we need to have some idea of what we are doing, morally speaking, and why. And there are compelling reasons to at least reconsider a kind of diet most people still take for granted.

VEGETARIANISM 101

I am a vegetarian myself, but I am not arguing here that you should become one too. My point, again, is only that whatever we eat is a choice, and that there are moral reasons as well as other kinds of reasons, to think it through seriously. If you do make the choice to give up meat, though, you need to know what you are doing! Here is the briefest of guides to a nonmeat diet.

For one thing, a vegetarian is not someone who simply eats vegetables. Actually, the term "vegetarian" does not refer to vegetables at all: it traces back to the Latin word *vegetus,* meaning "whole, sound, fresh, lively." Vegetarians do not eat the flesh of other creatures, but we certainly enjoy food in all of its fabulous variety! Good eating for us is vital to a "whole, sound, fresh, and lively" way of life. But like any healthy and enjoyable diet, it takes planning.

I can't say this strongly enough: *don't just drop meat out of your diet and expect that everything else can stay the same.* Instead, replace the usual meat entrée with a nonmeat entrée—or do away with the "entrée" format entirely and prepare a different *kind* of meal. In any case, carefully plan to include adequate proteins. Here are some specific meal-planning suggestions.

Pasta and sauces: There are many interesting and even exotic varieties of pasta available. In the sauce, replace any meat with marinated artichokes or olives. Add a little tofu or textured vegetable protein (TVP) to the sauce for more texture and protein. Vegans can use a soy cheese. Variations: tomato, pesto, or cheese sauces (e.g., rarebit, fondue) over bread or baked potatoes; pizza of all sorts; spinach lasagna.

Beans and rice: Beans and rice are a full-protein combination, which is why so many different cuisines are built upon them. Think Mexican here. In many Cajun-spiced dishes the beans can mainly carry the dish. My own household is big on bean/rice soups (nice thick hot soups for cold winter evenings; add a loaf of fresh bread and a salad and you have an unmatchable meal).

Ethnic foods: Middle Eastern food is great for vegetarians: falafel, hummus (chickpeas and tahini), baba ganouj (eggplant sauce), tabbouli (wheat bulghur salad), stuffed grape leaves, and so on. All of this can be served cold: wonderful summer fare. For an oriental meal, stir-fry vegetables (broccoli, onions, bamboo shoots, etc.) with soy or teriyaki sauces, and serve over brown or wild rice. Nuts or tofu give you protein. From India come great meatless curries and dals (lentil soups). From Mexico, try quesadillas: refried beans (you can buy great dried refried bean mixes in natural foods stores: just add hot water and wait), salsa, cilantro, tomatoes, cheese perhaps, and anything else you want (my children like okra, a friend includes sweet potatoes), all layered together inside a tortilla shell and pan-fried five minutes or so each side.

Also consider nutloafs, tofu/tempeh products (there are many varieties of tofu and tempeh burgers, as well as beanburgers, for cookouts), vegetable soups (e.g., gazpacho), and all the other delightful things you might do, like garnishing salads with flowers or making fresh bread. Our household Thanksgiving tradition is nutmeat brioche (an egg bread with a spicy nut/wine/cheese filling), sweet-potato soup, artichoke salad, fresh rosemary bread, and lots of pies (and singing).

For some cookbooks and other resources, see the Notes for this chapter.

THE ECOLOGY OF FOOD

The strongest arguments *for* eating meat may come from another direction—and invite other forms of mindfulness (too). Though meat production is typically an ecological disaster, the typical vegetarian diet is not so ecologically benign either. As Ted Kerasote argues (remember Chapter 6), many small animals of the fields die when grains are harvested. Vegetables and fruit are sensitive to growing season and are often shipped cross-country in trucks, which pollutes and increases the demand for fossil fuels—the same fuels that are often used to produce fertilizers and power the farmers' tractors. Kerasote therefore argues that shooting and eating a local elk is more ecological than eating vegetarian. Hunting and eating wild animals, he argues, is part of living close to the land, and ecologically it is most efficient.

Of course, this is no defense of eating hamburger that may also have been shipped halfway across the continent from a slaughterhouse that pollutes the local rivers and brings you meat from cows that were fed grain produced in the same harvests just mentioned. Wild fare will also vary depending on where you live. Around where I live, it probably means eating squirrels. Or maybe roadkill...

Kerasote also reminds us of the Buddhist argument that all food suffers—not just animals. All things have souls, they say, and life pretty much *is* a round of suffering. But Buddhists certainly do not go on to conclude from this jolly thought that we should therefore be completely heedless of our effects upon animals—as if, since suffering is inevitable, it doesn't really matter how much suffering we cause. Their view, by contrast, is that since suffering is inevitable, we must be as careful as we can be *all the time.*

So vegetarianism is not the only ethical option. The whole question is too complex for that. The key thing, I believe, is not necessarily to follow Kerasote's conclusions—you'll remember that he himself struggles with the question and has eaten differently at different times and places—but rather to take on a similar mindfulness. To pay attention, or, again, to think responseably. We have obligations to ourselves and other people, *and* to the animals, *and* to the Earth; and how all of these balance out, case to case, isn't so clear. Nonetheless our task is to try.

More religiously, we might view eating as a form of communion with the Earth. It's the literal truth: we eat the very Earth itself—its plants, its other beings, and its water, air, soil, even rocks (salt). We must not continue to act as if our food were just another industrial product like flyswatters or something (not that even flyswatters don't come from the Earth too, in the end, but...), or plastic food is what we'll end up with. In some ways we're close already.

Many writers and activists argue for renewed attention to the sources of our foods, as much as possible staying with organic, local, and seasonal foods. *Organic* foods mean foods raised without chemical pesticides and herbicides and fertilizers. Instead the health of the soil is maintained by recycling food and animal wastes and by good maintenance. The soil, earth, is regarded as a living thing itself, and treated with respect and love.

Local foods are those grown as close to you as possible: in any case not shipped across the whole continent or even flown around the world as is so often the case now (tomatoes from California, kiwis from New Zealand—the energy costs and pollution consequences of getting them to us are spectacular, and they are often of much poorer quality because they must be picked unripe). Our local farmers' market only admits growers who farm within fifty miles of the market. Know where your food comes from, support those in your own community who love not just any land but *this* land, your place too.

Seasonal eating is one consequence: when you eat what the local farmers are harvesting at the time, it varies over the year. It's one way of coming back into tune with the land, and natural food advocates argue in addition that it's simply healthier too. Local foods at each season give you what you need to deal with the seasonal changes: high-starch root vegetables in late fall and winter, for example, as we pull back a bit into ourselves; exuberant light greens in the spring, as both we and the world burst back into life. "Health" means, in part, being in tune with the world. Why wouldn't the daily "communion" of food be *essential* to that process?

SLOW FOOD AND NO FOOD

At the other extreme from a response-able sort of thoughtfulness about eating is, I'm sorry to say, *fast food*. Even the name gives it away. Completely homogenized, completely disconnected from anything local or seasonal, replete with styrofoam or other immensely wasteful and usually nonbiodegradable packaging—well, let's just say it might be something you want to reconsider.

There's a final point too: the *fast* part. Food slapped together and then gulped at the same speed. It's not even pleasurable, really; it's just a way of keeping fuelled, like a fast gas station. Well, if we were just cars, it might make sense; but . . .

There are choices. In particular, a growing "slow food" movement already claims tens of thousands of members in one hundred countries, devoted to biodiversity issues, new types of food-growing, and recovering the sheer pleasures of eating—by consciously eating *slow*. And how about you? Worth a try?

The sheer amount of eating is also an issue. We seem to train ourselves, courtesy of the ads and the restaurants, to eat vastly more than we need, which is one reason why weight is such a problem in this country. Worldwide there are now more overweight people than there are people starving, an astonishing enough fact in itself before we even add that there are huge numbers of both. Some vast proportion of American children are overweight, a product of couch potatoism, TV and computer games, poor food choices, and sheer overeating. Binge eating and binge self-starvation are both epidemic. Indeed, it is possible to be both overweight *and* malnourished (in the sense of lacking vital nutrients)—and increasing numbers of Americans are both.

Once again, the point is simply that there are other choices—choices that ethics surely asks us to think about. *What* we eat, *how* we eat, *when* we eat, how *much* we eat—all of these may need more response-ability.

In fact, even *whether* to eat is a choice. Many people, both traditionally and today, periodically fast: that is, stop eating entirely for some period. And they don't do this out of some kind of masochism. The point is not to take pleasure out of life. It's more getting the pleasure, and/or the mindfulness, back *into* life: to sharpen the senses, to cleanse both body and mind, to make us appreciate food when we do eat it.

Once again, fasting is not something to undertake without knowing what you are doing! There are long traditions and practices for fasting, many of them originally rooted in the great religions. Here in this chapter, it's at least a useful reminder about response-ability. Once you realize that fasting is an option—that even eating when we are truly hungry is a *choice,* and not a choice that everyone always makes—you have opened up some space for freedom. Feeling a strong desire for anything (say food or, for that matter, sex) is not somehow the end of the matter. Desire only poses a *question.* How you answer it always remains up to you.

FOR REVIEW

1. What is self-possession?
2. Why does response-ability need cultivating?
3. What are some ways to cultivate it?
4. Why is ethics relevant to sexual matters?
5. According to Colin McGinn, what is sexual "perversion"? Why?
6. What does sexual response-ability imply?
7. According to Keith Clark, how is it possible to be both sexual and celibate?
8. According to Carol Queen, what does a "sex-positive" world require?
9. What is the utilitarian argument against eating meat?
10. What are some other questions of response-ability in regard to eating?

EXERCISES AND NOTES

RECLAIMING YOUR SELF

From the Buddhist sociologist Inge Bell comes a lovely book called *This Book Is Not Required,* in which, among other things, she proposes what she calls "adventures in de-socialization." Socialization, she explains, is the process of inculcating children with the beliefs and habits of their culture. Generally it works so well that we're only vaguely aware that it ever happened. This is why we can think of ourselves as completely free when in fact, on the sociological view, we are completely creatures of our culture.

Correspondingly, sociologists also believe that it is possible to *re*-socialize ourselves by changing our environments. But is it possible to *de*-socialize ourselves without just creating new social norms and pressures? Bell thinks so. Buddhists think so, too, she points out—and tell us that this kind of self-freeing is in fact the path to enlightenment. In our terms, it may at least suggest some interesting practices to help improve our response-ability.

Start by identifying, say, three specific forces that limit some aspect of your response-ability now. Maybe for one person it is parents' or friends' expectations and norms—as if there is only one way, their way, that things can be in the world. For another it may be the seduction of TV advertisements to buy new things. Yet another may feel swept away by the rush-rush-rush in which we all live. And you? Lift your head periodically from what you are doing and ask why you are doing it. What led you here? Is it what you in your heart of hearts want to be doing? If not, why *are* you doing it?

Now consider what you might do to gain a little more freedom from these forces. To give yourself a sense of "room to move," for instance, seek out other points of view and practices. Visit some alternative religions. Study abroad. Join an organization of people very different from yourself. Try giving up TV for a week or two weeks or a month. Don't just cut back a little—eliminate it altogether. And don't replace it with films or Web-surfing or anything involving sitting still and looking at a screen. Go outside, read, run, meditate, talk to people, get enough sleep. How does your life change? My students often report feeling far freer, mentally clearer, more self-possessed, less rushed. What about you?

Take something you normally do quickly and without thinking, and do it at half or one-quarter your normal speed. Do this with a supportive friend or group if possible. Walking is good for this purpose. Eating is wonderful. (Driving is not good!) Writing is good. Writing with the hand you *don't* normally write with is good, as is brushing your teeth or doing other activities you can do consciously and safely. These all may help bring you to the "beginner's mind" relished by Zen practitioners—"ready for anything, open to everything."

MORE RESPONSE-ABILITY

This chapter promotes response-ability in sexual behavior and in eating. Ethics has more to say about both of them than we sometimes think, and the space for choice is also much greater than we are usually told. Now ask: are there other areas where similar ethical questions come up for you—that is, specific questions of personal response-ability and freedom?

One often identified by my students is racist or sexist humor. Prejudiced joking can become habitual for individuals or in groups. It sometimes gets further and persists longer than more overt prejudice because it can excuse itself as "just in fun"—not exactly an honest excuse, though, since the jokers know very well not to share the "fun" with those who are being mocked. But you do not have to play this game, and you can do more than abstain from it yourself. *Visibly* abstain from it, first of all—change the subject in a deliberately awkward way, maybe; or explicitly discuss it with your group; or find more deft ways to make change, maybe by making fun of the prejudiced joking itself. And/or find different friends.

Are there other kinds or expressions of prejudice you might also work on? You might find Peggy McIntosh's classic short essay on "white privilege" useful here: it is available on the Web in several places, such as http://seamonkey .ed.asu.edu/~mcisaac/emc598ge/Unpacking.html.

Health is an issue: building healthy habits, from eating decently to getting enough exercise to avoiding substance abuse. Again, if you are tempted to unhealthy behaviors, analyze causes and try some changes. Though the major effect of most bad health habits is on yourself, others are most definitely involved too, and when it comes to substance abuse issues in particular, the effects on others—on those you love and on those who love you, as well as on random unlucky strangers who deserve better—can be just as lethal as to you.

Finally: one of the ways in which my students are very definitely not free is that they feel compelled to get a standard job and start their career right after college. They know they're supposed to "use their degree" (and get a degree that they can "use"), settle down, have a nice place to live and a nice car and maybe get married and start a family...Meanwhile, so much more is possible! Nothing is stopping them—or you—from building Habitat for Humanity houses in New Orleans or trails in the High Sierras or bumming around Europe or the South Pacific or joining the Peace Corps or starting a downtown artist collective and making free art or music festivals or you name it.

Imagine that your college education has been offered to you free, on one condition: that afterward, for five years, say, you are required to find an imaginative and adventurous way to better the world. You are expressly *forbidden* to get a standard job or "settle down." Work out some ideas about what your alternative work/life could be. Then find three actual, existing job openings or programs that are actually hiring or looking for people to do such work—conceivably someone just like you. Make contact with at least one. *Now* you have some options, eh?

SEX AT ANTIOCH COLLEGE

Sexual pressure and coercion, up to and including date rape, is widespread on college campuses. Most colleges now offer some warnings about sexual miscommunication and coercion at least as part of standard orientation presentations. Some administrations have formalized policies for dealing with allegations of sexual coercion.

A few have gone further. At Antioch College, in Yellow Springs, Ohio, the entire community—students, faculty, administration, and staff—has formulated and tested a policy meant to deal with—and prevent—"sexual offenses" such as this.

The statement begins with values:

> Antioch College has made a strong commitment to the issue of respect, including respect for each individual's personal and sexual boundaries. Sexual offenses are dehumanizing. They are not just a violation of the individual, but of the Antioch community.

Sex must be *consensual*, the policy insists. That is, participants must "willingly and verbally agree to engage in specific sexual behavior." Participants need to share enough common understanding to be able to request consent and to clearly consent or not, and also must not be so intoxicated or threatened that consent or the request for it is meaningless. Moreover, and crucially, "silence and/or non-communication *must never be interpreted as consent.*"

Consent, moreover, is understood to be an *ongoing process* in any sexual interaction. The most controversial part of the policy is this:

> Verbal consent should be obtained with each new level of physical and/or sexual behavior in any given interaction, regardless of who initiates it. Asking "Do you want to have sex with me?" is not enough. The request for consent must be specific to each act.

Certainly Antioch's is not the only way that a college community might address issues of sexual communication. It may seem awkward and stiff—but is it better to leave all the crucial things unsaid? And it raises useful questions. Does sex at Antioch sound exciting? If fully mutual sex with explicit consent at each stage does *not* sound "sexy," why not? What does it say about *us* (about what we assume sex *must* be like) if we can't imagine sex like that?

Is there even a way to make the requirement of consent at each stage into a kind of *opportunity* (remembering Chapter 16)? One of my students wrote, in response to these questions: "Actually, I think whispering to someone, communicating, and asking permission to do fun things is pretty cool."

Consider the pros and cons of such a policy for your own school. How would it change or not change sexual interactions for you and your fellow students? How would you write such a policy for your own school? Should your class try it? Can men and women in your very own class actually communicate about these things? Why or why not? If communication breaks down, where do you think it breaks down, and why?

NOTES

Stanley Milgram is cited from his article "Obedience," an article abridged and adapted from his book *Obedience to Authority* and posted online at http://home.swbell.net/revscat/perilsOfObedience.html. On the aftermaths of the experiment, see the provocative discussion on Wikipedia under "Milgram Experiment," http://en.wikipedia.org/wiki/Milgram_experiment.

On the inner work of freedom and self-possession, two useful and accessible works are Inge Bell's *This Book Is Not Required* (Pine Forge Press, 2005), cited in the exercises, and John Sullivan's *Living Large,* of which you got a taste in Chapter 9.

On "perversion," Colin McGinn is cited from his essay "Sex," in *Moral Literacy* (Duckworth/Hackett, 1992), pages 60–64. For a sampling of what philosophers say about sex, see Robert Baker, Kathleen Winninger, and Frederick Elliston's collection *Philosophy and Sex* (Prometheus, 3rd edition, 1998) and Sallie Tisdale's personal and deeply philosophical *Talk Dirty to Me: An Intimate Philosophy of Sex* (Anchor, 1995). You can find a current version of Antioch's "Sexual Offense Prevention Policy" at http://www.antioch-college .edu/Campus/sopp/index.html. *Philosophy and Sex* includes a discussion of the (early) debate over Antioch's policy by Matthew Silliman. An intense book on male identity and the devaluation of the female is John Stoltenberg's collection of essays, *Refusing to Be a Man* (Routledge, 2000). One especially relevant essay invites men to consider a range of erotic possibilities available beyond, as he puts it, "a macho definition of maleness."

Almost any current introductory textbook/collection of articles in philosophical ethics will include some articles on ethics and animals. For an overview of the discussion, try the Ethics Updates site, http://ethics.sandiego.edu, under "Animal Rights." For more information on meat-free menu planning, vitamins, and vegetarianism and children, start with the Vegetarian Resource Group's website at http://www.vrg.org. For vegan resources (eating no animal products at all, i.e., no dairy either), see http://www.americanvegan.org. On other food issues, see Eric Schlosser, *Fast Food Nation* (Harper Perennial, 2002); http://www.slowfoodusa.org on the "slow food" movement; Norman Wirzba, ed., *The Essential Agrarian Reader: The Future of Culture, Community, and the Land* (Shoemaker and Hoard, 2004); and Wendell Berry's classic, *The Unsettling of America* (Sierra Club, 1996).

CHAPTER 19

You Can Change the World

THE POWER OF ONE

The Nobel Peace Prize for 2004 went to Kenyan Wangari Maathai for promoting sustainable economic and cultural development in Kenya and in Africa. The "Green Belt Movement" that she founded thirty years ago has mobilized tens of thousands of poor women to plant more than thirty million trees. She has been violently assaulted—once beaten unconscious by the police, served years in jail for demanding fair elections and equal rights for women, almost single-handedly saved a major Nairobi park from pillage by cronies of the corrupt former president, run for Kenyan president, was later elected to Parliament (with 98 percent of the vote), and has been assistant minister in the Ministry of Environment, Natural Resources and Wildlife ever since. She's also, by all accounts, a lovely and generous person.

Nelson Mandela was awarded the Nobel Peace Prize in 1993 along with F. W. De Klerk, the South African president who set in motion the end of apartheid in that country. Mandela spent his life fighting apartheid and the governments that enforced it; spent twenty-seven years in prison, often in solitary confinement or at hard labor, for that fight; and came out of prison not seething with hatred for the lost years but just as anxious as when he was imprisoned to create—in his famous words from the dock as his imprisonment was about to begin—"a democratic and free society in which all persons live together in harmony and with equal opportunities." In 1994, as blacks attained the right to vote for the first time, the previously banned African National Congress swept to power and Mandela became the first black president of South Africa. He too, by all accounts, has an almost saintly way.

Chapter 3 has already spoken of Mandela's colleague the Anglican bishop Desmond Tutu, himself the winner of the Nobel Peace Prize in 1984, while still in the midst of the struggle against apartheid. Everything still teetered on the brink. Descent into civil war and the bloodiest of revenge-taking were universally expected. Tutu became the prime mover behind the Truth and Reconciliation process that, astonishingly, brought former killers together with

395

victims all over the country. Mandela managed to make his own person and story, known to every South African, into a kind of parable of reconciliation and co-existence. South Africa's transformation, inspired by these remarkable figures, remains one of the most amazing moral success stories of the 20th century.

MUHAMMAD YUNUS: "THE GOOD BANKER"

The Nobel Peace Prize for 2006 went to Muhammad Yunus, a Bangladeshi banker, inventor, and tireless promoter of "micro-credit" through the now-famous Grameen Bank. Beginning by lending small amounts of money out of his own pocket to destitute village craftspeople, mostly women, Yunus discovered that such loans were enough to free the craftspeople from middlemen and make them canny and effective entrepreneurs. Scaffolded by support groups but with no collateral requirement and no repayment date, his loans are still repaid at a higher rate than many banks can boast—out of, basically, *gratitude*.

Yunus started out as a professional, U.S.-trained economist, teaching "elegant theories of economics" (as he puts it) in the newly independent Bangladesh while massive numbers of people were dying of hunger in the streets. The famine of 1974, which killed a million and a half Bangladeshis, changed his life. "Why did people who worked twelve hours a day, seven days a week, not have enough food to eat? I decided that the poor themselves would be my teachers. I began to study them and question them on their lives."

He began to work with farmers and set up farmers' cooperatives. But it soon became apparent that the truly destitute, the landless rural poor, needed some more dramatic kind of help. Alan Jolis's article "The Good Banker" explains:

> One day, interviewing a woman who made bamboo stools, [Yunus] learnt that, because she had no capital of her own, she had to borrow the equivalent of [30 cents] to buy raw bamboo for each stool made. After repaying the middleman, she kept only a [2 cent] profit margin. With the help of his graduate students, he discovered 42 other villagers in the same predicament.
>
> "Their poverty was not a personal problem due to laziness or lack of intelligence, but a structural one: lack of capital. The existing system made it certain that the poor could not save a penny and could not invest in bettering themselves. Some money-lenders set interest rates as high as 10 per cent a month, some 10 per cent a week. So, no matter how hard these people worked, they would never raise themselves above subsistence level. What was needed was to link their work to capital to allow them to amass an economic cushion and earn a ready income."

And so the idea of credit for the landless was born. Yunus's first approach was to reach into his pocket and lend each of the 42 women the equivalent of [about $40]. He set no interest rate and no repayment date: "I didn't think of myself as a banker, but as the liberator of 42 families."

Immediately, Yunus saw the impracticality of carrying on in this way, and tried to interest banks in institutionalising his gesture by lending to the poorest, with no collateral. Bankers laughed at him, insisting that the poor are not "creditworthy." Yunus answered, "How do you know they are not creditworthy, if you've never tried? Perhaps it is the banks that are not people-worthy?"

He went on to create his own lending system, at first run by his own students; he then finally convinced the central bank to take it on and later incorporated Grameen to go it alone. Grameen Bank is now the largest rural bank in Bangladesh, with millions of borrowers. It also has spinoffs the world over, including more than five hundred community banks in the United States alone.

ORDINARY PEOPLE

The list of Nobel Peace Prize winners is an inspiring list all around. Martin Luther King Jr.; Lech Walesa, the Polish dockworker who became central to the Solidarity movement in Poland under the last years of communism and eventually became president of Poland. The Dalai Lama; Mother Theresa. Betty Williams and Mairead Corrigan, cofounders of the Northern Ireland Peace Movement.

Of course these world-changers are now highly honored. Some are household names around the world. They serve in governments, run organizations. People listen when they speak.

But they did not start that way. Most of them started in ordinary places. Maathai just planted a few trees in her backyard, and got to thinking. No one supported or believed her in the early years—not even her then-husband (who in fact quickly divorced her). Walesa was a shipyard worker, a common electrician: fired for organizing a memorial to some assassinated workers, he scaled a wall to rejoin the next strike...and one thing led to the next. Williams and Corrigan met when an Irish Republican Army getaway car was hit by British gunfire and veered out of control, killing three children. Corrigan, a Catholic, was the children's aunt; Williams, also Catholic but with Protestant and Jewish roots, just happened to be walking by. One a secretary, the other a receptionist; both ordinary mothers with small children themselves. Two days later, they led ten thousand Protestant and Catholic women, marching together, at the dead children's funeral. That march was disrupted by Catholic hardliners for being "dupes of the British." So they held another, and this time thirty-five thousand people came. A peace movement was born.

These people didn't make change alone, of course. Walesa cofounded an organization literally called "Solidarity"—the very name announced that change only comes when many people stand together. Sometimes, recognizing the crucial role of organizations, the Nobel Peace Prize is actually awarded to organizations directly. Yet more common is that, even when an organization is honored, so are the individuals who created and sustained it in turn. In 1997 the prize was co-awarded to Jody Williams and the organization she helped create, the International Campaign to Ban Landmines, for their work banning and clearing anti-personnel mines. The 2006 prize went jointly to Muhammad Yunus and his Grameen Bank.

Right in my community and among people I know personally, there are artists who use "Art Walks" to revitalize their neighborhoods, both economically and personally; specialists in socially responsible investments; schoolteachers who spend their own money to buy poor students textbooks or take them on trips when neither the school nor the parents can pay; and the creator of a new organization to promote long-term adaptive thinking about climate change.

At my university, colleagues are helping to rebuild New Orleans and take students to Central America over spring break to build homes with Habitat for Humanity. They advise and staff local social services and health organizations and prison ministries. Students organize for Sexual Assault Awareness and to bring locally grown and organic food into the university cafeterias, supporting local growers and introducing fellow students to totally new ways to eat. The chaplain's office invites students every year to nominate people from their hometowns who have made a difference. "Hometown Heroes," they're called. The winners, five a year, are invited to campus, speak to classes, and are honored at a convocation. Regularly the winners are family members—father, grandmother, sibling—reminding us among other things that among "the powers of one" is *inspiration*. This year one of the winners was the nominator's father, a police officer who has run the torch for Special Olympics for twenty years and has become chair of the eighty five thousand–member International Torch Run Council. Another student's mother is a breast cancer survivor who made herself into an advocate for other cancer sufferers and for more research, earlier detection, and better treatments. Several created local projects to support people in some of the poorest countries on the planet, such as Haiti. Another was among the liberators of the Woebbelin concentration camp at the end of World War II who has, ever since, annually revisited the spot and has dedicated his life to understanding the genocide and to the theme of "Never Again."

Again: these are ordinary people, ordinary friends and family and neighbors. In fact, I am sure that most readers of this book have already taken part in the kind of work just outlined, or at least know someone who is doing it, right here and now. The challenge and invitation now, maybe, is to step up to more of a leadership role. But the opportunity and the role models are already here—often enough, right there in front of us.

BECOMING A CHANGE-MAKER

How can we follow in their footsteps? Here are some guidelines.

First: Find your own way. There is no one single way to make ethical change. Very varied people are change-makers: housewives and office workers, tribal elders, dockyard electricians, yoga students, college professors. Even bankers, of all things, like Muhammad Yunus.

There are *many* ways—probably as many ways as there are different individuals. Play to your strengths. You may not be witness to a society-changing event, or arrive on the scene just as some new need opens up that you might fill. But don't assume you haven't, either—for *noticing* the need, noticing the possibilities opening up, is part of the creative and perceptive challenge. Again, find ways that work for you.

Second: Keep at it. Persistence pays off. Few substantial ethical changes come easily or quickly. Many of the changes cited here—in fact, nearly all of them—are still being contested, still being achieved. Some Nobel Peace Prize winners spent years or even decades in jail, endured risks, struggled against prejudice and ill-will and just plain inertia for much of their lives. They found joy in it still—and it was the right thing to do, in their view—but there is no denying the difficulty and the danger. Be ready.

Don't expect that you will always know what difference you are making or have made. The ways of the world can be subtle and circuitous. Have some faith. Here is one instructive story, described by Paul Rogat Loeb in his collection *The Impossible Will Take a Little While.*

> In the early 1960s, a friend of mine named Lisa took two of her kids to a Washington, DC vigil in front of the White House protesting nuclear testing. The demonstration was small, a hundred women at most. Rain poured down. The women felt frustrated and powerless. A few years later, the movement against testing had grown dramatically, and Lisa attended a major march. Benjamin Spock, the famous baby doctor, spoke. He described how he'd come to take a stand, which because of his stature had already influenced thousands, and would reach far more when he challenged the Vietnam War. Spock talked briefly about the issues, then mentioned that when he was in DC a few years earlier he saw a small group of women huddled, with their kids, in the rain. It was Lisa's group.

"I thought if those women were out there," he said, "their cause must be really important."

And that was enough to set him down the path. Lisa might never have known that she and a few others helped change the course of history, yet she did.

We honor Rosa Parks for sparking the fateful bus boycott in Montgomery, Alabama that helped bring down the segregated South. She refused to leave her seat when it was demanded by a white man. It doesn't detract from her courage and her accomplishment to know that her arrest, and the boycott that followed, was carefully planned and prepared. And who, Loeb asks, got *her* started? It turns out that she was prompted to attend her first NAACP meeting by her husband, who was already involved. And who got *him* involved? Loeb concludes: "Even in a seemingly losing cause, one person may unknowingly inspire another, and that person yet a third, who could go on to change the world."

So be careful not to judge yourself or someone else a failure, or ineffective, just because you, or they, maybe did not have the immediate effect intended. Be careful not to suppose that the only worthwhile ends of action are quick and clear "results." Do what is right and don't worry too much about it. You never know what pathways you may be starting for yourself or someone else.

"Not Deterred"

PAXUS CALTA-STAR

Paxus Calta is the chosen name of a writer, activist, and former software designer born Earl Schuyler ("Sky") Flansburgh. He studied engineering and economics at Cornell University. In the 1990s, invited by the Czech anti-nuclear movement, he moved to Czechoslovakia and lived there throughout most of the 1990s. He's the author of several "fingerbooks" (small handbooks) on topics including alternative relationship forms (polyamory), how to make revolutionary change, and activist self-empowerment. He teaches the latter, fundraises for local literacy programs, and works on heritage seed-saving with the Thomas Jefferson Center in Monticello, not far from the well-known intentional community where Calta resides, Twin Oaks in Louisa, Virginia.

The time is the winter of 1996; the place is the Bulgarian capital city of Sofia. Polina is a student who has recently gotten involved in activism. She is eighteen years old.

Unlike most of the rest of Eastern Europe, Bulgaria did not throw out its Communist rulers in the revolutions of 1989 or 1991. Instead, some minor reforms were enacted, including some freeing of the media. In the late 1990s, the Bulgarian government is widely distrusted, disliked, and recognized as deeply corrupt. Bulgaria's class structure resembles that of the United States in the 1950s, where old gray-haired men with many initials after their names dominate discussion and policy making. These figures are well represented in our story.

The Belene nuclear power plant is an unfinished reactor complex in the eastern part of the country, near the Ukrainian border. It was designed and partially built by the Russians during the Cold War and was stopped by popular protest in 1990. In December 1996 the government put together a deal with the Russians, the United States, and the European Union to complete these reactors. After a number of serious accidents, the other Bulgarian reactor complex had been identified by the U.S. Department of Energy as one of the ten most dangerous in the world. Mostly the same people will be building and running Belene.

Polina is part of an ecological organization called For the Earth, which is fighting against the completion of Belene. They convene a national conference to discuss how to stop this reactor complex from being finished. At this conference, Professor Uzinov from the Technical University of Sofia says, "We need to promote renewable energy sources so that nuclear power will not be necessary. We can do this effectively by pursuing energy credits from the European Union."

Dr. Svetlana from the National Academy of Sciences counters with a conservation-based strategy. "We have one of the least energy-efficient countries in the world. We should rather turn our attention to the U.S. alternative model for funding and technology to generate megawatts."

Finally Polina is recognized. "If you want to stop the construction of the Belene reactors, you need to overthrow the government," says the eighteen-year-old student. Participants smile politely as if thinking, "What a nice thing for this child to say." They continue talking about return on investment and various energy aid schemes being offered worldwide.

But Polina is not deterred. She goes with twenty friends to the steps of the Parliament and starts a daily protest against the government. The media thinks it is charming and puts them on TV. This is December 1996.

Three months later, in March 1997, there are 20,000 people on the steps every day. Bowing to popular pressure, the government resigns. Shortly thereafter, the first democratic reform government is elected. A couple of months after that, they release their energy policy—canceling the Belene project.

BEYOND "REALISM"

A third guideline: Always remember that much more is possible than we usually imagine. People and situations always have hidden possibilities. Beware of the self-satisfied "realism" that looks at the world as it is (or anyway *seems,* on some interpretations) and imagines that the world as it is is the only world possible. Remember your vision!

Muhammad Yunus again:

> Poverty covers people in a thick crust and makes the poor appear stupid and without initiative. Yet if you give them credit, they will slowly come back to life. Even those who seemingly have no conceptual thought, no ability to think of yesterday or tomorrow, are in fact quite intelligent and expert at the art of survival. Credit is the key that unlocks their humanity.

In short, he imagines that everyone has the ingenuity to lift themselves out of poverty. We just aren't going to *see* that ingenuity until it is given the chance to show itself.

Likewise, Mandela and Tutu actually imagined that South Africans could forgive the apartheid regime for the decades of oppression it fostered, and go on together. It certainly didn't look that way at the time—yet they were right. Vaclav Havel and Lech Walesa actually imagined that a few playwrights or ordinary workers, standing up in their lonely way for the right thing, could bring down authoritarian governments that had the whole might of the Soviet Union behind them. These were not exactly "realistic" hopes. Nonetheless, these things came to pass. Maybe what's "realistic" is a little more fluid than we think.

What's "realistic" becomes still more open if you add to its fundamental uncertainty another fact: just committing ourselves to working for change itself makes a difference. Imagine, like Polina, that an entire government can be changed, take even a few steps in that direction, and then maybe others will take a few steps too. Then a few more. What seemed impossible, out of the question, yesterday suddenly begins to look entirely feasible. Considering how far we've already come toward questioning our use of animals for food, it is entirely possible that in twenty years most people will no longer eat meat at all. Perhaps instead of executing anyone, we will expect those sentenced to death to choose self-sacrifices of some sort (drug tests? suicide missions?) that offer a kind of redemption or restitution for the life they have taken. Perhaps...who knows?

So don't be deterred by the "realists" who look at the present situation and see no hope. "Realism" may only be an excuse for resignation or lack of imagination. They may actually be right: maybe there really isn't any hope in the present situation. Your response might be that therefore we need to *change the situation.*

From On the Rez

IAN FRAZIER

Ian Frazier's *On the Rez* chronicles of the modern life of the Plains Indians, especially the Oglala Sioux. This excerpt describes a deed of SuAnne Big Crow, the most admired Oglala basketball player of all time, which Frazier calls "one of the coolest and bravest deeds I have ever heard of."

The setting is a racially charged 1988 high school basketball game in Lead, South Dakota, where SuAnne's team from the Pine Ridge reservation are the visitors. The host gym, as often happens, "is dense with hostility..."

SuAnne was a full member of the team by then. She was a freshman, fourteen years old. Getting ready in the locker room, the Pine Ridge girls could hear the din from the fans. They were yelling fake-Indian war cries, a "woo-woo-woo" sound. The usual plan for the pre-game warm-up was for the visiting team to run onto the court in a line, take a lap or two around the floor, shoot some baskets, and then go to their bench at courtside. After that, the home team would come out and do the same, and then the game would begin. Usually the Thorpes lined up for their entry more or less according to height, which meant that senior Doni De Cory, one of the tallest, went first. As the team waited in the hallway leading from the locker room, the heckling got louder. The Lead fans were yelling epithets like "squaw" and "gut-eater." Some were waving food stamps, a reference to the reservation's receiving federal aid. Others yelled, "Where's the cheese?"—the joke being that if Indians were lining up, it must be to get commodity cheese. The Lead high school band had joined in, with fake-Indian drumming and a fake-Indian tune. Doni De Cory looked out the door and told her teammates. "I can't handle this." SuAnne quickly offered to go first in her place. She was so eager that Doni became suspicious. "Don't embarrass us," Doni told her. SuAnne said "I won't. I won't embarrass you." Doni gave her the ball, and SuAnne stood first in line.

She came running onto the court dribbling the basketball, with her teammates running behind. On the court, the noise was deafeningly loud. SuAnne went right down the middle; but instead of running a full lap, she suddenly stopped when she got to center court. Her teammates were taken by surprise, and some bumped into one another. Coach Zimiga at the rear of the line did not know why they had stopped. SuAnne turned to Doni De Cory and tossed her the ball. Then she stepped into the jump-ball circle at center court, in front of the Lead fans. She unbuttoned her warm-up jacket, took it off, draped it over her shoulders, and began to do the Lakota shawl

From Ian Frazier, *On the Rez* (Farrar, Straus, and Giroux, 2000), pp. 208–213. Used by permission of Farrar, Straus, and Giroux.

dance. SuAnne knew all the traditional dances—she had competed in many powwows as a little girl—and the dance she chose is a young woman's dance, graceful and modest and show-offy all at the same time. "I couldn't believe it—she was powwowin', like, 'get down!'" Doni De Cory recalled. "And then she started to sing." SuAnne began to sing in Lakota, swaying back and forth in the jump-ball circle, doing the shawl dance, using her warm-up jacket for a shawl. The crowd went completely silent. "All that stuff the Lead fans were yelling—it was like she *reversed* it somehow," a teammate said. In the sudden quiet, all you could hear was her Lakota song. SuAnne stood up, dropped her jacket, took the ball from Doni De Cory, and ran a lap around the court dribbling expertly and fast. The fans began to cheer and applaud. She sprinted to the basket, went up in the air, and laid the ball through the hoop, with the fans cheering loudly now. Of course, Pine Ridge went on to win the game.

[Frazier inserts here a short history of Lead. The name, it turns out, refers not to lead, the metal, but rather to the miners' term for a gold-bearing deposit, in this case what became a $10 billion gold mine in land that was dispossessed from the Sioux in the midst of the Indian wars of the 1870s. It took a hundred years for the U.S. Supreme Court to affirm the Sioux (Lakota) people's right to at least minimal compensation for the theft of their land—a tiny fraction of what the land yielded in gold, which now sits in a bank account unused, because the Sioux no longer want minimal compensation for the land but want back at least some small portion of the actual land itself. Everyone on the reservation, and in Lead, knows this story.]

Inescapably, this history is present when an Oglala team goes to Lead to play a basketball game. It may even explain why the fans in Lead were so mean: fear that you might perhaps be in the wrong can make you ornerier sometimes. In all the accounts of this land grab and its aftermath, and among the many greedy and driven men who had a part, I cannot find evidence of a single act as elegant, as generous, or as transcendent as SuAnne's dance at center court in the gym at Lead.

For the Oglala, what SuAnne did that day almost immediately took on the stature of myth. People from Pine Ridge who witnessed it still describe it in terms of awe and disbelief. Amazement swept through the younger kids when they heard. "I was, like, '*What* did she just do?'" recalled her cousin Angie Big Crow, an eighth-grader at the time. All over the reservation, people told and retold the story of SuAnne at Lead. Any time the subject of SuAnne came up when I was talking to people on Pine Ridge, I would always ask if they had heard about what she did at Lead, and always the answer was a smile and a nod—"Yeah, I was there," or "Yeah, I heard about that." To the unnumbered big and small slights of local racism which the Oglala have known all their lives, SuAnne's exploit made an emphatic reply.

Back in the days when Lakota war parties still fought battles against other tribes and the Army, no deed of war was more honored than the act of counting coup. To count coup means to touch an armed enemy in full possession of his powers with a special stick called a coup stick, or with the hand. The touch is not a blow, and only serves to indicate how close to the enemy you came. As an act of bravery, counting coup was regarded as greater than killing an enemy in single combat, greater than taking a scalp or horses or any prize. Counting coup was an act of almost abstract courage, of pure playfulness taken to the most daring extreme. Very likely, to do it and survive brought an exhilaration to which nothing could compare. In an ancient sense which her Oglala kin could recognize, SuAnne counted coup on the fans of Lead.

And yet this coup was an act not of war but of peace. SuAnne's coup strike was an offering, an invitation. It took the hecklers at the best interpretation, as if their silly mocking chants were meant only in goodwill. It showed that their fake Indian songs were just that—fake—and that the real thing was better, as real things usually are. We Lakota have been dancing like this for centuries, the dance said; we've been doing the shawl dance since long before you came, before you had gotten on the boat in Glasgow or Bremerhaven, before you stole this land, and we're still doing it today; and isn't it pretty, when you see how it's supposed to be done? Because finally what SuAnne proposed was to invite us—us onlookers in the stands, which is the non-Lakota rest of this country—to dance, too. She was in the Lead gym to play, and she invited us all to play. The symbol she used to include us was the warm-up jacket. Everyone in America has a warm-up jacket. I've got one, probably so do you, so did (no doubt) many of the fans at Lead. By using the warm-up jacket as a shawl in her impromptu shawl dance, she made Lakota relatives of us all.

"It was funny," Doni De Cory said, "but after that game the relationship between Lead and us was tremendous. When we played Lead again, the games were really good, and we got to know some of the girls on the team. Later, when we went to a tournament and Lead was there, we were hanging out with the Lead girls and eating pizza with them. We got to know some of their parents, too. What SuAnne did made a lasting impression and changed the whole situation with us and Lead. We found out there are some really good people in Lead."

CREATIVITY

A fourth guideline: Use your creativity. General thinking skills can get pushed to the side when we think of ethics primarily as a mode of personal response. Yes, ethics is in part an affair of the heart. But other skills come into play as well—and sometimes creativity is the most crucial.

Bo Lozoff, cofounder along with his wife Sita of the Human Kindness Foundation, was living in a yoga ashram—a secluded and intensive religious community—when he noticed with a certain shock (as it happened, visiting a relative in jail) that their life was not so different from the life of a prisoner. Both are very highly constrained and lack many worldly comforts. But their life was *liberating*. How interesting, he thought. And just possibly a creative provocation... He went on to create the "Prison-Ashram Project" to enable prisoners to treat their prisons as ashrams: that is, to make use of the very isolation and "deprivation" and silence that can make prison so awful as, instead, occasions for spiritual growth. He reframed the entire experience and institution of prison.

Among the many recognitions Lozoff has received for this work is an award for "Creative Altruism" from the Institute for Noetic Sciences. Creative. Altruism. Those two words are not often put together. But why not? As we've seen already in Chapters 15 and 16, creativity has as much to offer ethics as it has to offer anywhere else—maybe even more.

"Stories from the Cha Cha Cha"

VERN HUFFMAN

Here is a little story of ethics in action with both creativity and humor—sometimes an irresistible combination. Vern Huffman is an artist and peace activist who works for Boeing Commercial Aviation in Everett, Washington. His wife, Majori Funka, was a member of the Zambian National Dance Troupe and taught at the University of Zambia.

Simon Kapwepwe didn't approve of the racist law in Rhodesia requiring black Africans to do all their shopping through the windows of stores. Never allowed to step inside, they were to present their money at the window and have goods passed out through the window. Simon devised a way to challenge the law, saving enough money to buy a car. He went to the window of the Land Rover dealer and waved his cash at a salesman. He pointed out the vehicle he wanted and asked them to pass it through the window, as the law required. The salesman offered to bring the vehicle to the gate, but Simon was adamant that the law be followed. A crowd gathered and, in the ensuring fracas, Simon went in and got his car, driving it out through the window and bringing down the entire wall. This was the beginning of the nonviolent uprising known as the Cha Cha Cha.

In Northern Rhodesia, which would become Zambia, the rebels were organized but not armed. Though many were followers of the teachings of Mahatma Gandhi, there were episodes of stone throwing and destruction of government property. But the key element was noncooperation with the colonial infrastructure. The people of this region had survived for a thousand years without the colonists and were not interested in buying into a system that did not respect them. And the colonists were not prepared to face living in Africa without the support of native inhabitants.

After several months of this insurrection, the British chose a new administrator for the colony. With his stiff upper lip and strong sense of discipline, this man would soon whip those unruly natives into line! But Julia Chikamonenga organized a welcome party at the Lusaka airport. She gathered together the biggest women she could find to explain her plan. When the new administrator stepped from his plane, he looked across a sea of huge Zambian women, all naked, singing songs of greeting. When he got his mouth closed, he stepped back onto the airplane and ordered the pilot to return him to London.

Within weeks, Zambia was an independent nation, and Simon Kapwepwe later become its vice president.

NO SELF-RIGHTEOUSNESS

Guideline five: Stay open to complexity. It can be tempting to picture ethical change-makers as single-minded, even fanatical, and to think that we must make ourselves the same in order to succeed. When I say that you need to find your own way, persist, and have confidence that dramatic change is possible, it may seem that these guidelines too suggest a kind of dogged self-confidence or even moral self-righteousness.

But the stories we have told actually have a different moral. The change-makers we have featured are firm in certain ways, but not in a narrow-minded or self-righteous way. Muhammad Yunus is devoted to eradicating poverty (completely!), but his means are maximally flexible and creative. SuAnne Big Crow made change by dancing and singing, inviting a hostile crowd to look again. Nelson Mandela was always committed to equality for black South Africans but never to suppression of white South Africans. Mandela's long imprisonment, in fact, actually made him *more* open and tolerant.

If anyone in these stories is morally self-righteous or dogmatic, it is the defenders of the status quo. They're the ones a little too comfortable with how things are—too threatened, maybe, by the thought of change to see the change-makers clearly. They're the ones who will not understand your motives and will make all sorts of stereotypical assumptions—such as, most basically, that you're the fanatic. Don't fall into that stereotype! Part of your strength, in fact, is that you are (can be) much more flexible. You're more apt to build alliances, find an unexpectedly innovative alternative, to bring together a variety of values into some more balanced picture.

On the other hand, advocating for ethical change can put you out in edgy and controversial territory. Many of those we celebrate—even many of those Nobel winners, for example—worked for changes that at the time seemed politically and even ethically questionable to most people: civil rights, artistic and political freedom under communism, tree-hugging, religious diversity.

So again: in ongoing and unsettled struggles, avoid stereotyping any of the advocates involved as fanatics, even the ones you don't like. And avoid sliding toward narrow- and single-mindedness yourself. Think one more time of our debates over guns, or abortion, or the ethical claims of other animals. Sometimes, I am sure, some of the people involved really are fanatics. But that is no reason to make ourselves fanatical in response, or to respond to others only in a dismissive or single-minded way. Expect to find common ground; stay open to complexity in your own stance and to complementarity in others'.

"Questioning the Media's View of Women"

FRAN PEAVEY

We met Fran Peavey in Chapter 16, where she laid out the method of "strategic questioning." Here is a striking short illustration of how strategic questioning opened up entirely unexpected possibilities.

A couple of weeks after attending a strategic questioning workshop in Auckland, New Zealand, a woman saw a television show about violence against women. The show did not adequately condemn such violence and it carried a commercial that she thought was also anti-women. The women's community in Auckland was upset about this show and the commercial. They put out the message that women should call the manager of the station and give him a piece of their minds.

This particular woman decided to see what would happen if she tried strategic questioning. She called the manager but instead of lecturing him about what she thought, she started off with some questions: "How does a show get on the air?" "What review policies do you have about combining commercials and the content of your shows?" "How could the women's community work with the television station to create better programming around this issue?" Notice here the "how could..." nature of the question. If she had phrased the question, "Is there a way we could work together..." she might have received the answer, "No, there is no way." This success story exemplifies why you should avoid questions that set up a "yes or no" answer.

Finally the manager said, "Say, you seem to be quite knowledgeable about this matter. Would you like to be on a advisory board that screens each show and commercial and decides what should go on the air?" No others who had called with their opinion were invited into this powerful board. Her questioning opened valuable doors to cooperation and common ground.

From Fran Peavey, *By Life's Grace* (New Society Publishers, 1993), pp 109–110.

THERE IS NO WAY TO ETHICS; ETHICS *IS* THE WAY

Our last guideline is a Gandhian saying you may have heard: "There is no way to peace; peace is the way." This puzzles people. Isn't peace a goal that we are struggling for, someday to achieve down the road? Not exactly, says Gandhi. We certainly work for a world in which everyone has well-developed and nonviolent habits of living with and working out conflicts. Yes. Right here and now, though, *we* at least can develop our own nonviolent habits of living with and working out conflicts, including our conflicts with those who themselves are prone to violence. Peace is how we relate to each other right now.

Exactly the same is true in ethics proper. There is no way to ethics; ethics *is* the way. We can certainly work for a world in which everyone has well-developed ethical habits and a full ethical toolbox. Yes. But right here and now *we*, at least, can develop our own ethical habits, including ways to deal ethically with those who themselves have only a few ethical tools, or none at all. Ethics is how we relate to each other right now.

Here's another of Gandhi's sayings you may have heard or seen on a bumpersticker:

YOU MUST BE THE CHANGE YOU WISH TO SEE IN THE WORLD

In the first place, this means: actually *do* something. Promote the change you wish to see in the world. Advocate a serious environmental ethic, for example, in part by actually living it.

But this much is obvious. The deeper meaning is more intriguing and difficult. Acting in the name of ethics, even as we strive to bring that ideal into reality, we cannot and must not act in ways that are unethical or violate that ideal. Do not imagine that you can achieve peace with your neighbors by killing some of them. You may attain the façade of peace, but hatred and pain will be at its foundation still, and will poison the so-called peace in time. Do not imagine that legally imposing your ethics on other people somehow makes the world right. Maybe sometimes we will conclude that it is necessary, but the true ethical change only follows when you, or they, bring others around by force of example, by word and deed, by *being* a full-fleshed ethics in action.

An environmentalist friend of mine says: People will not live in harmony with nature until we also come to live in harmony with *each other*. Therefore it does not effectively promote long-term environmentalist goals to create sustained conflict among people: politically, in local communities, wherever. No: our way of moving toward an ecological future must itself be ecological. It must seek connection, mutuality, interdependence, synergy—right now, and in every move we make toward a more ecological world. Even when we must set ourselves into opposition to others, do not let it become total opposition. Hug trees *and* hug people! she concludes. Let us live our own lives in ways that so manifest a love for Creation in all its forms that other people, feeling themselves already included in that love, are drawn to change their lives too.

Maybe this sounds way too sentimental or idealistic for us? Gandhi, though, would not regard it as sentimental or idealistic at all. It's just *practical* ...

THIS MEANS YOU!

Most users of this book will be students and probably young. People like you, you might be thinking, seldom have the connections or the power to make major ethical changes.

Sometimes it's true. Sometimes making change does take powers you don't yet have. But only sometimes. Remember that some of the change-makers featured in this very chapter are just like you. Polina, in Paxus Calta-Star's account, was eighteen years old, also a student. SuAnne Big Crow was fourteen, a high school freshman.

Moreover, sometimes it's precisely the fact that you *are* young people or students that gives you a kind of power that other, older people don't have. For one thing, simply being a student gives you a natural solidarity with other students everywhere. You can organize *as students* across campuses, across the country, even across the world. This is especially true when the ethical issues around which you organize show up on campus—and across campuses—in distinctive ways. Students around the country stand in the forefront of organizing against sweatshops, for example, because their universities are among the prime customers for products made in sweatshops: clothes stamped with university logos. Students have a good bit of leverage at their own institutions, and universities, being large single-order customers, have a good bit of leverage over suppliers. Very specific changes can therefore be demanded. This is why national organizations like Students Against Sweatshops are naturals, and have been very effective in recent years.

In Eastern Europe in the 1990s, hundreds of thousands of students and young people like Polina took to the streets to protest, and soon enough to replace, authoritarian governments no longer propped up by the Soviet Union: in Czechoslovakia and East Germany and Bulgaria and Romania, and in the former Yugoslavia and then again in the separate republics into which Yugoslavia dissolved, especially Serbia, where students resisted the authoritarian Milosovic regime and eventually helped oust him as well. Not that it was easy. Whole universities were closed down. Activists were harassed and sometimes "disappeared." The entrenched political leadership stalled or sympathized (without changing anything) or just lied through their teeth. But the students persisted. They took their universities back, or started "Free Universities" of their own. They continued to take to the streets—and increasingly to the airwaves and the Internet. Older people had all the power, or so it seemed—but the young had the chutzpah and the computer savvy to catch the attention of the world.

Nearly all of this was accomplished peacefully. Here too the students' powerlessness—in the usual terms—was actually crucial to their success. You've seen the famous photo of the unknown young man in China's Tiananmen Square, during the mass protests of the summer of 1989, single-handedly holding off a line of tanks simply by standing in front of them. Those tanks could have crushed him in seconds. But he had—and used—a moral power rooted precisely in his extreme vulnerability. And he didn't stop there, either. Apparently he also yelled at them, "Why are you here? You have caused nothing but misery!" and later climbed up onto the turret of the lead tank to speak to the soldiers—young people, after all, like himself—inside.

Hundreds of students at Tiananmen went on a hunger strike to advance their demands, prompting the national leadership itself to come to the Square and plead with them not to starve themselves to death. ("We were young once too," they said.) The students also invoked a long-standing Chinese archetype of the selfless intellectual who speaks truth to power. And although the Tiananmen protests ultimately were suppressed, the after-effects continue even now, both in Chinese and world politics and in the imaginations of change-makers everywhere. *Time* magazine subsequently named that anonymous young tank-stopper one of the one hundred most influential people of the 20th century.

Young people stand among the most prominent ethical change-makers in the United States as well. The Freedom Riders, for example, young black and white people together, rode interstate buses into the segregated South in the summer of 1961 to test a Supreme Court decision outlawing racial segregation in interstate transportation facilities—and to visibly model a new respect and cooperation across racial lines. They were imprisoned, beaten, harassed. But when one group could no longer take the violence, student organizers brought in others. They kept coming. By the end of that summer the Interstate Commerce Commission was enforcing and extending the Supreme Court decision, and the civil rights movement had been galvanized. Campaigns for voter registration and desegregation of restaurants, hotels, and workplaces were underway as well—again often spearheaded by young people. One of the many leaders of this action was John Lewis, soon to chair the Student Non-Violent Coordinating Committee and later a long-time U.S. congressperson from Atlanta and one of the leaders of the Congressional Black Caucus.

Young people continue to take the lead in certain areas—again drawing precisely on their youthfulness, inventiveness, and natural open-heartedness and solidarity. Sweeping the campuses as I write is "Invisible Children," an MTV-ish film by three students from the University of Southern California

who went to Africa with a camera bought on e-Bay to see what was happening and ended up encountering the massively displaced and orphaned
children of Northern Uganda. It's a film, a website—and a movement to help
rebuild schools and create teacher exchanges and volunteer opportunities
for everyone to help. Twenty-somethings have started get-out-the-vote campaigns based on music, like Rock the Vote, and even general disaffection, like
the League of Young Voters (also known as the League of Pissed-Off Voters),
founded by William Upski Wimsatt—a college dropout and phenomenal
journalist and organizer.

Students are taking a huge lead in environmental action. Every school
has its student Sierra Clubs and environmental coalitions. Look on the web
(e.g., www.broweryouthawards.org) for biographies of young people who
have stood up and stood out for environmental action: organizing to promote
green buildings on their campuses or loggerhead turtle preservation or campaigns to reduce campus paper use to help save old growth forests or creating relay races thirty-six miles up salmon streams, paralleling the run of the
salmon themselves. Many are still in high school—in fact, some started still
earlier. Shadia Wood began at the age of *seven* to lobby New York State lawmakers to fund toxic waste site cleanups, doing everything from appointing
herself national spokesperson on the issue to setting up a lemonade stand on
the steps of the Capitol and donating her $16 in earnings to the cause. The
media loved it—and Shadia stood by the governor's side five years later when
he signed the Superfund reauthorization.

I'd like to leave you with one more especially inspiring example. At
age 23, Julia Butterfly Hill spent two years living mostly alone 200 feet up in
an ancient redwood tree, Luna, trying to keep it from being cut down. Her
book *The Story of Luna* is an account of how she ended up in Luna and how it
felt, day to day, often enough full of despair and doubt as she worked the cell
phone, weathered storms of all sorts, and tried to make a human connection
with the loggers and the lumber company executives.

It was not exactly what she planned to do with her life. Starting as what
she describes as a "somewhat aimless regular teenager," she suffered a traffic accident that forced a slow recovery and eventually led her to a cross-
country road trip with friends. Almost by chance, along the California coast,
she encountered a grove of magnificent and ancient redwood trees—and fell
in love.

> At first [the trees] seemed like normal trees, but as I leaned my head back as far
> as I could, I looked far up into the air. I couldn't even see their crowns. . . . Their
> trunks were so large that ten individuals holding hands would barely wrap
> around them. Some of the trees were hollow, scorched away by lightning
> strikes, yet they still stood. These trees' ancestors witnessed the dinosaur
> days. Wrapped in the fog and the moisture they need to grow, these ancient
> giants stood primordial, eternal. My feet sank into rich earth with each step.
> I knew I was walking on years and years of compounded history.

She soon learned that groves like these were rapidly being destroyed by lumber company clear-cutting. She resolved to help stop the cutting. But the defenders of the trees were desperate. Everything had been tried and had failed. Tree-sitting was their last resort. If a tree-sitter's tree is cut, the sitter dies with it. It has happened—though, supposedly, by accident. Like the Chinese tank-stopper, they put their own lives on the line:

> "I have no other way to stop what is happening" is basically what a tree-sitter is saying. "I have no other way to make people aware of what is at stake. I've followed the rules, but everything I've been told to do is failing. So it is my responsibility to give this one last shot, to put my body where my beliefs are."

So up she went, for what she thought would be a two- or three-week stint. It turned out to be more than two years, on a tiny, leaky, rickety platform, before her feet touched the ground again. She endured two winters, weeklong El Niño storms, helicopter harassment, sieges by company security guards, repeated close calls as the loggers took down the trees around her, and the tremendous sorrow it all brought. Yet there was unassailable joy too, as she finds an unexpected and deep intimacy with Luna and with the whole ridge where she stands. She climbs to the very top—250 feet high, in her bare feet.

> I made it to her lightning-hardened pinnacle, the most magical spot I'd ever visited. Luna is the tallest tree at the top of the ridge. Perched above everything and peering down, I felt as if I were standing on nothing at all, even though this massive, solid tree rose underneath me. I held on with my legs and reached my hands into the heavens. My feet could feel the power of the Earth coming through Luna, while my hands felt the power of the sky....
> No way could I allow Luna to be cut! Ever!

Speaking of famous photos, there is also a picture of that moment, with Julia at the very top of the tree, exultant—and a banner she unfurled, far below, saying "Respect Your Elders!", meaning Luna herself.

And she succeeded in the end. After long negotiation, she was able to save Luna and at least a small surrounding grove (and Luna still stands, though damaged by an unknown chainsaw attacker in 2000). Through an almost equally long and sometimes comical struggle, she also succeeded in being recognized as an actual person by at least some of the loggers. Through her Circle of Life Foundation, Julia Butterfly Hill serves now as a spokesperson for the interdependence of all life and for the power of every individual as well as every community to make a real difference in the world. "The question," she says, "is not 'Can you make a difference?' You already do make a difference. It's just a matter of what kind of difference you want to make."

FOR REVIEW

1. For what was Muhammad Yunus awarded the Nobel Peace Prize?
2. What is a "hometown hero"? Do you have one?
3. What are the guidelines this chapter offers for changing the world?
4. What led Dr. Benjamin Spock to his anti-war stance?
5. "People and situations always have hidden possibilities." Such as?
6. In what sense did SuAnne Big Crow "count coup"?
7. Why do single-minded and fanatical people often make less effective ethical change-makers?
8. Explain: "There is no way to ethics; ethics *is* the way."
9. How can powerlessness, for example in young people, also sometimes be a source of strength?
10. Who is Julia Butterfly Hill?

EXERCISES AND NOTES

FOR REFLECTION

Recently I learned that philosophers are among those people entitled to nominate a person for the Nobel Peace Prize. In fact I learned this from a colleague who says that it is one of his life's ambitions to come to know and work with a suitable nominee. He's still young. But put yourself in his position. Who would you nominate? (You don't actually have to know the person.) Why? What traits would you look for?

Why do you think we are sometimes so pessimistic about the possibility of making real change? It's not as though real change hasn't happened. In fact it is happening all around us right now. Twenty years ago communism ruled the East and South Africa was on the brink of a massive racial bloodbath. We could not have imagined even something now as basic as recycling bins in everyone's basement or the rise of environmental consciousness in general.

Radical change happens. But suddenly then the new status quo seems to define the limits of possibility in turn, and we can't imagine even the same degree of change happening *again,* in the same or some other direction. Why not? Can you figure out the psychology of this rather limiting kind of "realism"? Do you see any useful ways to help ourselves and others avoid it?

SEEK CHANGE-MAKERS

Find people in your community or among your circle of friends and connections who are ethical change-makers. Again, they needn't be high-profile. A lot of moral action goes on way below the radar, by people who don't think of themselves as special. Think again of my university's "Hometown Heroes," for example. Who are *your* change-making heroes? Perhaps there are even some in your class, right now.

Cast your nets widely. People who are energetic and visible advocates for certain moral positions are good candidates, but they are by no means the only ones. Look also for people who are making a creative difference, or bringing more people into moral action, or are in any of a hundred ways "being the change they wish to see in the world." Once you've identified some ethical change-makers, invite them to speak to your class or group. Talk with them. What are they doing? Why and how do they do it? What motivates them? It will be an honor for them and an earful, I hope, for you.

BECOME A CHANGE-MAKER

Ultimately, of course, the task is to become an ethical change-maker yourself. Commit yourself as an individual or a group (your class? why not?) to some project of ethical change. Use your work with this book to frame your project. Expect it to be a learning experience, about basic values as well as the nitty-gritty of getting action moving. Work toward and work *at* dialogue. Get your facts straight. Speak and act mindfully. Use your creativity and vision. There is no lack of possibilities right around you. Identify a doable project—something you can at least initiate—and get to work.

Note that this work is somewhat different than "service" or "service-learning" as usually conceived and as discussed in Chapter 5 of this book. Service is *helping:* dealing with immediate need by offering aid and succor. Change-making more likely addresses the causes of need themselves and/or promotes changes that offer all of us opportunities for ethical transformation and better understanding.

Defining these projects is hard, and finding some that get seriously underway in the space of an academic term is even harder. This is itself usefully educational. Maybe consider a multiterm project that a teacher's classes (or school or department) could sustain over a number of years. A single class could at least get the ball rolling. My own students, lately, have initiated such projects as making our own school more connected and responsive on issues of race—both working to make race issues more prominent and consistent in the curriculum and forging links between the university and communities of color right in our own region. Another group instituted biweekly meals at all of the university's cafeterias with all locally grown, seasonal, and organic food, educating students, staff, and food service personnel about alternative agriculture and diets and creating ongoing connections between the university and local suppliers. A colleague's class is partnering with students at other and very different institutions to jointly further the work of Greensboro's Truth and Reconciliation Commission (introduced in Chapter 13) from the student side. Another group has just constructed a website for local teens to get them sex-education information they were being denied in their own schools, along with local resources and help designed to promote sexual response-ability, up to and including abstinence. Now they are handing the site off to local high-schoolers themselves.

So many possibilities. More projects are afoot. I would be honored to hear about yours. Good luck!

NOTES

At http://almaz.com/nobel/peace/peace.html you can find a listing of all the recipients of the Nobel Peace Prize, along with short biographies and useful links. I might add to the discussion in the text that it is sometimes the intention of the Nobel Peace Prize committee to lift up certain people or organizations precisely so that they can be heard, or even to protect them, to make them too visible for governments to suppress or others to hurt. Again, then: however extraordinary the work they may be doing, often they are ordinary people who have simply stepped up to a need or a responsibility. Here the prize serves the struggle.

Alan Jolis's essay on Muhammad Yunus, "The Good Banker," comes from *The Independent on Sunday Supplement* (London), May 5, 1996, and can be found online, along with much other useful information, at http://www.grameen-info.org.

Paul Rogat Loeb is cited from the introduction to his fine collection *The Impossible Will Take a Little While* (Basic Books, 2004), pages 6–7. I have heard another version of this story in which Spock was actually at a meeting *in* the White House when he saw the women's demonstration in the rain. Spock, by the way, was also the person who revolutionized child-raising in the 1950s. Parents had been told by the experts not to kiss or hug or even comfort their children. Spock's book, by contrast, encouraged parental warmth. It subsequently sold more copies than any other book except the Bible. Spock was later blamed by some conservatives for creating too "permissive" a culture leading to the 1960s. He also became a prominent opponent of the Vietnam War, was regularly jailed (on one occasion ending up in a cell with the poet

Allen Ginsburg, where he learned to meditate), and even ran for president in 1972 on a minor party ticket.

Paxus Calta-Star's "Not Deterred" comes from Loeb's collection, pages 196–197, as does Vern Huffman's "Stories from the Cha Cha Cha," pages 161–162. On Bo Lozoff's work, see http://humankindness.org.

Julia Butterfly Hill's book *The Legacy of Luna* (Harper San Francisco, 2000) is excerpted from pages 7, 24, and 123. For updates on Luna and on Julia Hill's current work, see http://www.circleoflife.org.

CHAPTER 20

Making Change Together

COMMUNITIES MAKING CHANGE

A *community* is a group of people united by common interests and concerns. People who live in the same neighborhood or city or even region form one kind of community. Other times the people involved may live widely spread around a region or even the world, as when we speak of "the business community," "the community of scholars," "the black community," and so on. Communities of all sorts can be essential agents of ethical change.

LOCALITIES

First of all, we are inevitably in community with those right around us. We share schools and roads, political and cultural life, and of course the air and water and the land. Much community action is local in this sense. We have marches to raise money to aid soup kitchens or preserve open space. Local "preservation communities" try to protect local heritage, from buildings to watersheds. There's downtown revitalization work: for when inner cities are cut off and impoverished, the whole community is affected, and the walls of fear and denial begin to rise. "Communities in the Schools" programs aim to keep kids in school through adult mentoring. Recent graduates, also part of the school "community," stick with their schools to bring younger kids along. The Community-Supported Agriculture movement aims to preserve rural open space, water quality, small farms and the culture that goes with them: people buy the produce directly, know where it comes from, sometimes work the farms themselves—it's not called *Community*-Supported Agriculture for nothing.

Specific localities bring with them specific issues. Progressive communities in New Orleans are trying to rebuild an entire city in an ecologically sustainable and just way. Community organizations right in the West Virginia coal fields have risen up to demand an end to the coal companies' practice of creating huge toxic sludge ponds near or even right above town, infiltrating ground water and threatening floods, challenging as well the massive dyna-miting of whole mountaintops that creates such toxic by-products in the first place. Individuals help: recently the grandfather of a child attending elemen-tary school directly below a three-billion-ton sludge pond walked hundreds of miles from the capital of West Virginia, near the coalfields, to Washington, DC, holding press conferences and others events all along his walk. Once upon a time, he was a sludge pond builder. One purpose of his walk was spe-cifically to move his own town's school. But never far from the surface was the crying need to organize his community and all such communities—often poorly educated, disempowered, discouraged people, traditionally beholden to the coal companies and with no sense of any real options—to take control of their lives and communities and find new ways.

One night last spring three crosses were burned in several parks in my city. This was perceived, immediately and widely, as an assault on all of us: on everyone committed to even the most minimal ideal of racial justice and respectful coexistence. And I am proud to say that the community responded. Hundreds of people came the very same night at the burning sites to "re-ject the hate." A week later a mass meeting drew thousands from the city to condemn the burnings and to build better ways to go on together. Musical groups, religious leaders, mayors and state representatives and police chiefs and even the state attorney general turned out.

Of course the hate still exists—no one is so naïve as to think that it doesn't. But the actual effect of the burnings, thanks to immediate and effective com-munity response, was to reinvite serious commitments from across the com-munity to continuing to improve race relations. And in Greensboro, North Carolina, just down the road, as Spoma Jovanovic describes in Chapter 13 of this book, a citizens' commission has just finished a three-year project of hearing testimony and drawing conclusions about a 1979 incident, modeling their work after the Truth and Reconciliation Commissions set up in South Africa at the end of apartheid. Communities are in action!

ORGANIZATIONS

Churches and synagogues and mosques can also be ethical change-making communities. They are organized primarily around religious commitments and beliefs, of course, but many of these commitments and beliefs are in turn ethical. They are meant to be acted upon in the world. Historically it was the black churches that nurtured the civil rights movement. Lately nearly all of the established religions, from the most liberal to the most fundamental-ist, are getting into environmental issues.

Businesses also support ethical causes and make ethical changes them-selves. When the world finals for the Special Olympics—sporting events for mentally handicapped people—came to my area a few years back, local busi-nesses moved quickly from just giving money to the Olympics to (also) hiring mentally handicapped people in special programs. That is, they not only gave charity but also made long-term changes in their own practices to expand opportunity and justice for mentally handicapped people. Other businesses are moving from just donating money to environmental causes to (also) reducing their own pollution. Some offset their pollution by investing in an equivalent amount of clean energy production or in mitigation projects such as tree plantings to absorb the CO_2 produced. Whole Foods Corporation, for example, already buys enough wind-power credits to offset all of its electricity use.

Then there are voluntary organizations of so many sorts that a quick Web search turns up over three hundred such organizations just in my own city. Some of these are more service-oriented than change-making—Hospice, the Humane Society, Meals on Wheels—but some of these are change-makers too, and meantime there are many others primarily about change. Just a bare sampling: Boat People SOS (action for the Vietnamese expatriate community); the Empowerment Project (democratizing access to media); Child Abuse and Family Violence Prevention; Fair Housing Advocacy; Fighting Blindness; Guardian Ad Litem programs (advocacy and human rights work); Mothers Against Drunk Driving; Justice for Animals; groups to limit kids' exposure to TV; Peace Action; the Hunger Network; StandUp for Kids (helping homeless and street kids); Americorps Youth Mentoring; Student Action with Farmworkers; Student Literacy Coalition; Stop Hunger Now; the Rails-to-Trails Conservancy; Keep America Beautiful; urban gardening organizations ("working together to create green areas of neighborhood pride and enjoyment"); the Center for Economic Justice; the World Library Partnership ("advocates for sustainable, community-based libraries in developing areas of the world"); the World Wildlife Fund...and finally the alphabet runs out. There are still other change-oriented organizations that didn't make the list, for whatever reason: political organizations, neighborhood-specific organizations, the co-ops, less formal groups....

TWO ORGANIZATIONS FOR DIRECT ACTION

You may have heard of the group Doctors Without Borders.

> Doctors Without Borders/Médecins Sans Frontières (MSF) is an independent international medical humanitarian organization that delivers emergency aid to people affected by armed conflict, epidemics, natural or man-made disasters, or exclusion from health care in more than 70 countries....In emergencies and their aftermath, MSF provides health care, rehabilitates and runs hospitals and clinics, performs surgery, battles epidemics, carries

out vaccination campaigns, operates feeding centers for malnourished children, and offers mental health care.

A line featured on their website is simple and eloquent: "There is so little care available that the only ethical position is to take action" (Jean Hevre Bradol). They too have been awarded a Nobel Peace Prize—as a whole organization.

MSF also is committed to what they call "witness." They do not simply deal with the medical need and suffering they see on the ground. They also aim to make it visible to others as a way of making change.

> MSF unites direct medical care with a commitment to speaking out against the causes of suffering and the obstacles to providing effective assistance. MSF volunteers raise the concerns of their patients with governments, the United Nations, other international bodies, the general public, and the media. In a wide range of circumstances, MSF volunteers have spoken out against violations of international humanitarian law they have witnessed— from Chechnya to Sudan.

This tradition of "witness" is carried on by other change-oriented organizations, such as the environmental direct-action group Greenpeace. Rex Wyler, cofounder of Greenpeace International, was interviewed on this theme in 2006:

> The Quaker idea of bearing witness is that when we witness an event, especially when we witness injustice, we become an agent of change. If you see injustice and you understand it as injustice, you almost can't help but become an agent of change—even if all you do is talk about it or point it out or shine the light of day on it.

So "shine the light of day" is part of what Greenpeace did:

> One of our innovations was to actively engage the electronic media and produce images that we knew and felt strongly would move through that media. For example, most people—when they thought of whaling at that time in the late '60s, early '70s—would have had a 19th-century version in their mind's eye: little men going up against Leviathan, throwing spears out of boats. That was the image that people had of whaling from all the woodcuts and artwork of the *Moby-Dick* era. No one had ever seen a whale being dragged up on the stern of a factory ship, making it look like a little fish.

Greenpeace began sending dramatic and gruesome images around the world of what an industrialized whale hunt actually looks like. Everyone became a witness, and it was no longer possible just to turn away. Activists also began putting themselves in small boats on the high seas between harpooners' guns and whales, as well as chaining themselves to chemical discharge pipes to protect rivers and sailing or hiking into nuclear test zones to put their own bodies in the way of bomb tests.

There is also a deeper aspect of "witness": making unethical acts visible in a new way to the perpetrators themselves. Often we think that in the face of unethical actions our only or best response must be force: actually stopping the actions. Quakers and others committed to nonviolence, by contrast, argue that simply stopping such an action does nothing to address the ethical failures that brought it about in the first place. In fact it may worsen some of them, locking the perpetrators into a new self-perception as victims. Ultimately the perpetrators themselves must be changed, and (the idea goes) this change can be set off if the perpetrators are made to see themselves through someone else's eyes. They cannot any longer act so anonymously or habitually, or respond automatically as they would if they were physically or otherwise threatened or attacked.

In this respect Rex Wyler isn't quite right to say, "No one had ever seen a whale being dragged up on the stern of a factory ship." The *whalers* saw it all the time. On the Quaker theory, though, they hadn't quite *seen* it—that is, fully looked at it, understood it, rather than simply accepting it or not thinking about it—until they had to see it through someone else's eyes. Just watching, then—just "witness"—can be a powerful force for ethical change.

Both groups lobby in the traditional way too. Greenpeace advocates much stronger environmental protection, permanent weapons test bans, and of course an end to whaling and other assaults on the seas and sea creatures. And MSF again:

> Based on its field experience, MSF is addressing obstacles preventing people in the developing world from obtaining affordable, effective treatments for diseases such as HIV/AIDS, malaria, and tuberculosis....MSF is advocating to lower drug prices, stimulate research and development of new treatments, and overcome trade and other barriers to accessing treatments...

GOVERNMENT

Communities also make change through the basic functions of local governments, school boards, planning commissions, and the like. Vital matters are decided here: how well your community preserves open space, how fairly it deals with different neighborhoods or different groups' concerns, what is taught in the schools, what kind of public transportation is supported, whether you will act as a community on pressing issues of the day, from problems with voting machines to global warming—all of these issues are decided in local meetings in which any citizen can take part.

When zoning changes are requested or new building proposals are being advanced, my city has open hearings, at first specific to different parts of the city, where anyone can come, hear, and discuss the proposals. Eventually there is also a vote—of whoever happens to show up. The results go to the City Planning Commission—on a nonbinding basis, but they do make a difference. I have seen one or two knowledgeable and concerned citizens stop an ill-conceived project in its tracks—and I have also seen the lawyers for that project publicly thank the community gadflies, by name, at a later meeting, for making them improve or rethink their projects.

Likewise, school boards struggle with curricular issues: sex education, evolution and creation, and the like. Of course these can be frustrating struggles on all sides. The deeper point, though, is that community discussion of such questions is entirely appropriate in a democratic society, and school board meetings are a good place for it. We ought to be glad we live in a society in which there are places for such discussions. Maybe we even ought to join them!

Cities and other localities even act on the global stage. In the absence of U.S. federal action on global warming, for example, state governors and even mayors of cities publicly committed their states or cities to meeting international greenhouse-gas emission standards. In the political arena, there are many national and international political discussions and communities as well: the political parties, both the old standards and small and/or new ones; human rights action groups such as Amnesty International; and national lobbying groups on a vast range of issues. Just enter the phrase "National Coalition for…" as a Web search, and in the blank you get everything from "Literacy" and "Anti-Deportation Campaigns" to Cancer Survivors, Haitian Health, the Promotion of History, Marine Conservation, Homeless Veterans, Life, Sexual Freedom, Dialogue and Deliberation…and on and on and on.

JOINING A CHANGE-MAKING COMMUNITY

The last chapters offered guidelines for trying to jump-start change on your own. When organizations or communities or movements are involved, the task may be easier. You're in it with others, and the organization or movement already exists and is (let's hope!) in motion. Your job is to *get involved*.

FIND A PLACE

First: explore what is actually happening. It might be helpful to start by asking what change-making communities are you already part of, though perhaps you have not yet thought of them quite that way. Where is change already underway in your neighborhood or city or business or work? If you belong to a religious congregation, for example, what kinds of social or community work is it already involved with? Is more help needed? Is there potential to broaden the work (perhaps, as your special contribution)?

In general, think about what issue or issues you should take up, and who is doing the kind of work you want to join. Obviously the answer will vary with your interests and abilities and location. You'll want to explore specific issues: look for organizations working on those issues in particular. You'll also want to explore what's happening in your communities in general. This is often a larger and less well-defined realm. Your first question might well be: what *are* the issues that most deeply affect this community? Then find out who is pursuing them. Who is doing things? What things? Where are the openings?

We've just looked at a wide range of communities that are making change. You might just note in addition that a wide range of approaches are involved. Some kinds of change are immediate and direct, like responding to an emergency or making a drastic change in policy. Others are slower and work more in the background, like trying to keep more kids in school (preventing a whole range of more difficult problems down the road) or preserving locally owned media (enabling more diverse and locally empowered discussion of *other* issues). Likewise different kinds of change may call for very different strategies, sometimes even on the same issue. Direct-action strategies coexist readily with longer-term structural change goals. Again, your task is to find a good fit for you: for your resources, your skills, and what you see as the most pressing demands of the moment. Others will do other things, and there is no lack of things to do. Find a place!

SHOW UP

Next, show up. Meet the people, join the organization or recommit yourself to it if you're already a member, start going to meetings. See what needs to be done. This may take some time. Go and listen for a bit to see what is happening: then commit yourself to some part of the work, maybe small at first. See what grows on you.

If your interests run toward local governance, show up for public meetings: City Council, School Board, community responses to crises or opportunities that arise. If you are a student, check out your student government, and also committees and other institutional planning and organizing that involves students along with faculty and administrators. Do you know when and where your local student government association meets? The meetings must be open to all, so you do not have to ask to come, or be invited, though you may have to ask ahead of time to be on the agenda. In order to speak persuasively when you seek to get on the agenda, of course, you also must have something to say. Seek something within the student government association's power to grant, and something that will be good for at least a number of your fellow students. Refine your understanding of the issues, and of what can be done at the point where you are intervening.

The same is true for local government meetings. They are usually held "in the sunshine," which means they are required by law to be open to the public, although again, you usually have to request in advance to be on the agenda to speak. In addition to usual, regular meetings of government entities, most cities and towns in the United States are required to hold hearings on important decisions to be made by that entity.

Make yourself visible at these meetings—and then make yourself heard. In most organizations, new people with ideas and energy are always very welcome. Speak up! In the case of local governmental decision-making, the actual deciders are your elected officials, but a great deal of influence is still simply a matter of ordinary people showing up. Sometimes that's literally all it takes: officials often judge public opinion on a matter by how many people come to the relevant meetings. (A great line from Woody Allen: "Eighty percent of success is just showing up.") Actually say something besides, and you magnify the effect. Not only come and speak, but speak *well*, and you'll pretty quickly be approached to run for office yourself. And why not?

Also, watch who else shows up. You will probably encounter the same cross-section of civic-minded people at a variety of public and organizational venues. Introduce yourself, see what is happening, who they represent and who stands behind them. Make yourself one of them!

BRING YOUR WHOLE TOOLBOX

Once you've jumped in, the key thing is to *bring along your ethical toolbox*—all of it. If this book has served you well, you have some special skills that you now can draw upon. To make yourself a voice for ethics within your organization or community, as well as articulating its ethical commitments to others, draw on Part II of this book. To "think out of the box" on issues where other people might not even realize that there *is* a "box," reframe problems and ask strategic questions, bring in your critical thinking skills, mindful speech, moral vision—all skills from Part III. Dialogue skills will be essential (Chapter 3). And so on. Keep all your skills sharp and ready for use.

Be strategic. Some situations call for pressure on elected officials; others call for independent organizing. And some of course for both. To help the homeless, for example, we need better municipal provision of shelters (work for local governments, ideally partly backed by state and federal support), as well as enhanced private shelters (here in North Carolina, anyway, mostly sponsored by religious coalitions), *and* more serious public efforts to address the causes of homelessness in turn (economic squeezes, mental health issues…). As with many issues, this suggests work on a variety of fronts.

Ask yourself (and others) where real movement is possible, and where you can make the most change with the most efficient effort. On campus, for example, directly battling students' addiction to fast foods and throw-away containers, say, by offering more classes on nutrition or by multiplying recycling bins, may be a difficult task. Suppose instead you work with the food service to change the cafeteria offerings, or with local take-out restaurants to use only biodegradable containers? Here you could have a big and quick impact. Trying to change state-wide Department of Education policy on sex education, say, can take enormous energy to gain mere inches, if that. While such efforts are important as a way of keeping up public dialogue on the basic issues, it might be more helpful, especially to the young people actually affected, to create new independent resources for and with the community, such as some of my own students have done by launching websites for local teens both to help them toward sexual "response-ability" and also to connect them with local resources for information, birth control, and counseling. Or again, on national or international issues, Greenpeace's strategy of "witnessing" and exposing whaling to the world did not directly address lawmakers or the International Whaling Commission, yet the impact on policy was very powerful. Multiple strategies can easily coexist too, of course.

Get creative. Alongside the familiar kinds of work on homelessness, for example, there are truly amazing initiatives underway. The Homeless World Cup organizes annual international street soccer tournaments with teams made up of homeless people. Another project facilitates and trains homeless people to mount *opera,* of all things—no kidding—and places them in arts organizations and as performers. ("With Streetwise Opera I not only exist, I *live,*" says one formerly homeless participant.) Why not?

Always look to the next step. One of the beautiful things about the very idea of Doctors Without Borders, for example, is the underlying imperative of, basically, *Ethics* Without Borders. After all, why stop with medicine? Already there is also a group called Students Without Borders, linking students around the world to promote travel, cross-cultural understanding, and academic freedom. Now how about, say, Librarians Without Borders, or Musicians, or democrats (small-d), or, who knows, Elders or Builders or even Ethics Students Without Borders? (That's you...)

DON'T POLARIZE—CONNECT!

One danger in making change in community is that communities can exclude others, or indeed, all too often, set themselves up in opposition to others. You have tools in your toolbox to avoid this kind of polarization too: dialogic, collaborative, and integrative approaches. Use them!

As Chapters 13 and 14 suggest, deep and long-lasting change requires us to hear everyone's voice, especially those often left out or made invisible. So ask: is everyone included? What other people or groups or institutions in your (local, geographical) community may have a stake in addressing and resolving the problem or issue? Work for collective solutions, and nurture the process of framing them together.

It's true, local disagreements are one reason we often seek nonlocal communities in the first place. In almost any geographic community of any size, we find important differences in people's values and concerns. We find disagreement, disparity, inequality, and different life experiences, all of which result in people who are all members of the same (local) "community" who may take very different positions on community issues. And they are probably people who not only don't think like us, but who also don't look, eat, sound, play, or work like us either.

So prejudice rears its head... Still, we need to notice these kinds of prejudices and work to end them. Deliberately meet and form friendships with people who are different from you. Figure out what are their issues of concern and embrace them. Remember that there are very likely common interests underlying even seemingly directly opposed "positions." Expect to find them, then; welcome them; work to dig them out. We have already noted some surprising confluences of interests: pro-life and pro-choice movements, for instance, joining forces to promote better economic support for unexpectedly pregnant women; evangelical and conservative church groups joining the environmental movement in the name of "Creation Care"; and so on. Not only do we not have to live in a world of opposition and polarization: we'll get much further together.

Remember also that the boundaries of "community" are more fluid than we sometimes think. This chapter has spoken of "community" solely in human terms. Often, though, more-than-human communities may also be at stake. On most environmental issues, as Aldo Leopold urges, the "community" includes also other animals, the plants and trees, and the land itself. Global threats require a response on behalf of the whole community of life, with the interests of all living things in mind. Australian environmental activists have created "Councils of All Beings," one framework in which we can begin to find our way back to dialogue beyond the realm of the merely human. Plains Indians peoples, in tribal council, would appoint spokespeople for the wolves and the buffalo and even the mountains and rivers—sometimes, the shamans said, they even consulted them directly. Remember that Lakota saying: they too are "our relations."

"The Restorative Justice Movement"

MARTIN FOWLER

Martin Fowler is a lecturer in philosophy at Elon University who is deeply interested in community-based social justice and new possibilities in our judicial system. Here he introduces the ideas and the practice of restorative justice, a community-based response to crime that speaks to the needs and better possibilities of everyone involved: victim, offender, and the larger community. On a restorative view, "justice" becomes much more than a transaction between civic authority and an individual offender.

Crime on all scales—from genocide to individual acts of violence—degrades whole communities. Ultimately, then, the most ethical response is an attempt to restore what has been lost—to knit back together the fractured relationships that, yes, include the offenders themselves, and to build social peace and alternative skills for dealing with tension and conflict so that community relationships are less likely to fracture so badly again.

As a volunteer in the St. Philip's Episcopal Church Jail Ministry, I meet with jail inmates on Saturday mornings for an hour to offer them greeting cards, Bibles, and prayer. It's strictly voluntary. I'm not the person they offended, but I am a member of the community. What do you assume about all these inmates in orange jumpsuits? Actually, a jail is not a prison. People in jails are either serving short term confinement or are waiting for a trial. For the most part, they haven't yet been convicted of anything yet. They're typically too poor to pay bail. Many are from minority groups in the community. They range in age from 18 to 60. We pray together for what their concerns are. Once you get past your discomfort and false assumptions, you can identify with how they must feel: How would you feel if you were locked away from most contact with school, family, work, and friends for an indefinite period of time? How would you deal with the shame? That doesn't make them any less innocent or guilty of whatever they're charged with. It just means that they remain human beings.

I also train people who assist family members who have lost loved ones to homicide. They go through more than just a death in the family. It is traumatic, public, and involves fear, litigation, and incredible loss. Victims have more rights in the litigation of such crimes than in the past, but, as you can imagine, there are compelling reasons why victim (or survivor) and offender wouldn't want to look at each other right after the crime. The justice system keeps them apart from each other. The offender might not want to face those he hurt. The victim may be frightened of the offender or only want the criminal to be locked away. But at times…there is a need felt by both to meet to deal with what happened.

Let's take an example in which you are the victim of a robbery or vandalism. The police find the criminal and impose sanctions. You may or may not get your property recovered or prepared. BUT suppose also that police, or a community agency, or a church group told you that you may have an opportunity to MEET the person who had robbed you or vandalized your property. Stunned? What's left to talk about?

Well, if you're like many people who must deal with the shock, anger, and disorientation of having this violence upset your life, no matter how many well-meaning people tell you it's time to "get on with your life" and to "put this behind you," you have deep questions. You might want to know: why did this happen to me? What could I have done to prevent it? Why did I act as I did at the time? What if it happens again? Why have I acted as I have since that time? What does this mean for me and for my outlook? You might want to tell the offender face-to-face exactly how much it hurt and how it hurt you. You might want the offender to apologize to you and make up for the damage he caused if that's possible. You probably wouldn't want to face the offender alone—you'd want a trained facilitator in the meeting to keep things on a civil basis, however emotional it may be for both parties. Here's where the community contributes by providing the place, the facilitator(s), and the preparation for the encounter. You don't usually have a legal opportunity to ask these questions of the offender or talk together in such a way, but what if you did have that opportunity?

Hopefully we're not so scared, apathetic, or passive about acts of violence in our community that we take no action at all. Community members and the community together suffer when violent crime happens amongst us. Do communities have ethical obligations, possibilities, and responsibilities to secure and maintain justice, or would assuming those burdens amount to stealing the job of the sheriff or other lawful authority? Just whose proper business is crime in a community?

We often assume that the local communities to which we belong, such as schools, neighborhoods, and community clubs, have no business dealing with crime. We consign that job to the State. Our communities might assist law enforcement, but we expect federal, state, and local law enforcement agencies to define crimes, apprehend those suspected of committing crimes, determine their guilt or innocence, and perhaps lock them up. We're not vigilantes. What other role would the community have in dealing with crime?

All the same, the community is not merely a passive bystander to crime nor a neutral and detached site where crimes are committed. If someone commits a violent crime against a neighbor (e.g., an assault or a rape in your dormitory), it makes the rest of the community feel more vulnerable and unsafe. The fact that your own individual room happened to be untouched and uninvaded doesn't help your peace of mind much.

In fact, reports of that crime in your community may make the community look unsafe in the eyes of outsiders. The impact of a violent crime ripples outward to affect how people in a community view their neighbors and their own present and future well-being. That's such a hard part of being interconnected, that we may try hard to unplug and isolate ourselves from this violence. We may seek to disconnect ourselves when we hear or read about a crime in our community. Should we talk about it a lot? That might be cruel to the victim and give the wrong impression that such violence is common in our community. Should we keep it as quiet as possible? That would keep the community silent about something it cares about and needs to address. We can tell ourselves that the crime victim was someone who was someplace doing something with which we couldn't *possibly* be involved (perhaps a "drug-related" or "gang-related" shooting). When we're scared, we want our own personal fortress. But, when we're less self-centered and more honest about how crime affects us and our neighbors, we can't deny that crime affects the entire community, and our own sense of well-being, no matter how many locks we install, no matter how the courts, law enforcement, and the local media deal with the crime. We want to feel safe.

Leaving communities out of the issue of crime has another drawback. Jailing criminals has mushroomed in the United States over the past twenty years. As of 2003, more than 5.6 million Americans were in prison or had served time there. That's 1 in 37 Americans—the highest incarceration level in the world. It's expensive and difficult to sustain. Although every community wants the moral reputation of having dealt ethically or at least decisively with crime, it has a long community aftermath. Most convicts must eventually re-enter and attempt to become productive community members.

Unfortunately, our communities can look like passive open venues for violence where we draw chalk lines around victims and don't know or care how to really make ex-convicts our neighbors again. Not only do we not do a good community job making the ex-convicts part of our community; we don't even know how to extend our full moral and financial support to the victims themselves. Being mixed up in a crime—even as an innocent victim—brands the victim with a negative stigma in our culture. When we read or hear of a crime in our community, it's very human, though not charitable or fair, for us to first shrink back from the trauma of crime to protect our own sense of well-being and safety. It's practically a superstitious sense that being a violent crime victim makes one contagious or unlucky, as though we might "catch" violence by getting too close. We don't spontaneously plan moral and effective responses which the community might make to victims or to ex-offenders. We need constructive alternatives between the extremes of expecting the State to deal exclusively with crime, and expecting the community to deal with crime single-handedly, like vigilantes. How can communities work with judicial authorities, and with each other, to legitimately and wisely "restore justice" for everyone affected by crime?

One genuinely community-empowering way of dealing with crime has emerged within and alongside the criminal justice system over the past twenty years. It is called "Restorative Justice," and was championed by early reformers in the 1970s such as Howard Zehr in his text, *Changing Lenses*. The restorative justice movement argues that while the State is charged with maintaining public order, doing justice and building peace is the appropriate but largely neglected business of communities.

In starting to build restorative justice, members of the community may create *victim-offender mediation programs*. Victim and offender meet with a community facilitator. The mediation process is not about determining guilt and punishment. Usually the offender has already confessed or been found guilty by the court. Instead, the aim is to try to restore the losses suffered by victims and hold offenders accountable for the harm they have caused, through direct encounter between victim and offender, resulting in some sort of restitution agreement and building greater peace in the community.

Such an encounter between victim and offender takes a facilitator who invests patience, compassion, and considerable preparation with both the criminal and the victim (or survivor). It may take much more time in the aftermath of violence for the guilty and the offended to both affirm a need to meet each other. Here is a general description of how victim-offender mediation works.

The process begins by giving voice and witness to determine what the experience and impact of the crime were for all persons affected by the crime. Offenders must listen to others' experiences first, so that they have reflected upon the full consequences of what they have done and its meaning for the victim. It's vital that they understand what the crime felt like and meant to those who suffered from it, especially if the offender is to offer a sincere apology to the victim. That kind of empathy also underlines what it means to truly belong to a community.

The offenders then speak about how it was for them to do what they did, perhaps to apologize as well. Victims often want to know "why me?" and want to receive an apology from the one who hurt them. Since that doesn't necessarily happen in a courtroom, a restorative justice meeting may be the best place. Perhaps the victim will eventually decide to forgive the offender. That takes time and patience.

A plan is made to prevent future occurrences, and for the offender to heal the damage caused. All must agree to the plan. Of course, some damage, such as a rape or murder, cannot be "fixed" by the victim, the offender, or the community. Still, reparation, even if symbolic, might matter very much to the victim and those who care about the victim, even after such violent crimes. Finally, the community holds the offender accountable for adherence to the plan.

If the restorative mediation process is a court sentencing option, then the offender might face judicial sanctions for not abiding by the plan. However, there is often no court sanction available. So what enforces accountability? First, the voluntary dialogue between victim and offender requires that the offender actually face the person who has been harmed. This is a key element of accountability. Further, although the offender bears the responsibility for compliance, as in any effective mediation, all sides need to have "ownership" of the agreement as a satisfactory restorative response to the crime. The offender won't feel accountable if the agreement has simply been imposed upon him. The community facilitator may check to see if there has been follow-through and whether further restitution mediation is needed. If the meeting involved family members or friends, there is also social pressure for accountability. Communities can organize themselves specifically for this. For instance, there is the Native American tradition of "sentencing circles," particularly for juvenile crimes, in which the community participants gather in a circle which includes friends, family, and other members of the support groups for the victim and the offender. Everyone takes responsibility for reaching an agreement and making it work.

After twenty years of development and many thousands of cases (primarily property crimes and minor assaults) in more than 1,000 communities throughout North America (more than 300) and Europe (more than 700), victim-offender mediation is finally beginning to move toward the center of criminal and juvenile justice systems. Some programs are still small, with a very limited number of case referrals. Many other programs are receiving several hundred referrals per year. A few programs have recently been asked to divert 1,000 or more cases each year from the court system, and county governments have provided hundreds of thousands of dollars to fund these programs. The Texas State Department of Corrections has done over 200 mediations for victims and offenders when the crime has been violent.

"The Environmental Justice Movement"

LUKE COLE AND SHEILA FOSTER

Here is another emerging ethical movement, specifically a movement that brings environmental and social justice concerns together: the environmental justice movement. In this set of excerpts from their book *From the Ground Up: Environmental Racism and the Rise of the Environmental Justice Movement*, Luke Cole and Sheila Foster tell the story of an early struggle to overcome "environmental racism" and the

From Luke Cole and Sheila Foster, *From the Ground Up: Environmental Racism and the Rise of the Environmental Justice Movement* (NYU Press, 2001), pages 1–7, 152–153, and 164–165. See also http://www.ejrc.cau.edu/ejinthe21century.htm.

transformative effects of such struggles on disempowered communities. Cole is director of the California Rural Legal Assistance Foundation's Center on Race, Poverty, and the Environment. Foster is a professor at Rutgers University School of Law.

Kettleman City is a tiny farm-worker community of 1,100 residents in Kings County, in California's San Joaquin Valley.[1] Ninety-five percent of Kettleman residents are Latino, 70 percent of the residents speak Spanish at home, and roughly 40 percent are monolingual Spanish speakers. They are primarily farm-workers who work in the fields that spread out in three directions from Kettleman City. Kettleman City is much like many other rural communities in the Southwest, and few people would know about it were it not for the fact that Kettleman City is also host to the largest toxic waste dump west of Alabama, a landfill that is owned and run by Chemical Waste Management, Inc., about three and a half miles from town, hidden behind some low hills. The dump was created in the late 1970s without the community's knowledge or consent.

People marvel that a gigantic toxic waste site can be placed just miles from a community without the community's knowledge. In California, under state environmental law, government agencies are required to provide public notice in three ways: (1) through notices printed in a newspaper of general circulation, which in Kettleman City means a small box in the classified ads in the Hanford *Sentinel,* published forty miles away; (2) by posting signs on and off the site, which means on a fence post three and a half miles from Kettleman City; and (3) by sending notices through the mail to adjacent landowners.[2] The adjacent landowners to the Chem Waste facility are large agribusiness and oil companies such as Chevron....

Things changed in 1988, when Chem Waste proposed to build a toxic waste incinerator at the dump site. Residents in Kettleman City heard about this proposal not from Chem Waste, not from Kings County or state officials, but from a phone call from a Greenpeace organizer in San Francisco. Bradley Angel, Southwest campaigner for Greenpeace's toxics campaign, had received a phone call from the Kings County sheriff one afternoon in January 1988, asking him whether Greenpeace planned to demonstrate at the hearing, in Kettleman City that night. After finding out about the hearing, Angel called one of the few people he knew in Kettleman City at the time, Esperanza Maya, and said, "Espy, did you know that there's a hearing tonight in your community about a toxic waste incinerator?" She said, "I haven't heard a thing about it."

Maya grabbed a few of her neighbors and went to the hearing. They were shocked to find out that Chem Waste was proposing to build an incinerator that would burn up to 108,000 tons—216,000,000 pounds—of toxic waste every year. That translates to about 5,000 truckloads of toxic waste that would pass through the Kettleman area each year, in addition to the hundreds of daily truckloads bound for the existing toxic dump.

After the hearing, many Kettleman City residents began to do their homework about the dump, the incinerator, and the company, Chemical Waste Management. They formed a community group, El Pueblo para el Aire y Agua Limpio (People for Clean Air and Water). The group found out that the air in the San Joaquin Valley was already contaminated, that the Valley is considered the second-worst polluted air basin in the United States, ranking behind only Los Angeles. And, whereas Los Angeles has ocean breezes to cleanse it, the San Joaquin Valley, because of its unique bathtub shape, is a closed system, so pollutants stay put and fill the Valley.

Members of El Pueblo also found out about a 1984 report done for the California Waste Management Board. That report, known popularly as the Cerrell Report, and paid for by California taxpayers' dollars, suggested to companies and localities that were seeking to site garbage incinerators that the communities that would offer the least resistance to such incinerators were rural communities, poor communities, communities whose residents had low educational levels, communities that were highly Catholic, communities with fewer than 25,000 residents, and communities whose residents were employed in resource-extractive jobs like mining, timber, or agriculture.[3] When members of El Pueblo looked around Kettleman City, they were startled. "The Cerrell report fit us to a T," says Mary Lou Mares, one of the leaders of El Pueblo....

..."Our initial reaction was outrage," says Maricela Alatorre, a student leader during El Pueblo's struggle who has lived in Kettleman City her entire life. "We felt we were being targeted, that Chem Waste as a corporation was targeting these communities on purpose because their ethnic make-up would make people least likely to protest." Every single community where Chem Waste operated its toxic waste incinerators is a community of color, and substantially so: 79 percent in Chicago and Port Arthur, in the 90s in Sauget, and 95 percent in Kettleman City. They found out later that Chem Waste had planned to build an incinerator in Tijuana, Mexico, thereby hitting the 100 percent mark.[4]

The residents of Kettleman City then turned to Chem Waste's compliance record. At the Kettleman City facility, Chem Waste had been fined $3.2 million for more than 1,500 incidents of dumping too much waste into its evaporation ponds.[5] Chem Waste's incinerator in Chicago had blown up and been shut down by the Illinois EPA.[6] Illinois State Representative Clem Balanoff came to Kettleman City and told residents about Chem Waste's overfilling of the Chicago incinerator, which then spewed black smoke plumes, and about the fine Chem Waste faced for having turned off the incinerator's air monitoring equipment so that nobody would know what was coming out. And it did so once, not twice, but many times over a period of months.[7] In Vickery, Ohio, Chem Waste took in PCB-contaminated oil for disposal and then turned around and resold it to a company that used it to repave streets and as fuel oil in nearby communities.[8] The residents took note of Chem Waste's actions in Louisiana, where the company was caught storing toxic waste in one of those store-yourself rental locker.[9]

The public hearing on the incinerator was scheduled not in Kettleman City but forty miles away, in the county seat of Hanford. It was held in the largest venue in Kings County, the County Fairground building, which is about the size of a football field. The hearing room was set up with a raised dais in the front, with a table at which sat the Planning Commission, looking down on the room. Then there was an open space; beyond that, two microphones set up for the public. Behind the microphones were about fifty rows of seats, and there were some bleacher seats at the back of the room. Behind the bleachers was empty concrete floor back to the very rear of the auditorium, about 300 feet from the Planning Commission.

Kettleman City residents showed up at the meeting in force. About 200 people came by bus and carpool from Kettleman City, and, as one of their leaders made clear, "We're here, we want to testify on this project, and we brought our own translator." The chair of the Kings County Planning Commission looked down on the crowd and said, "The request has been denied. The translation is taking place in the back of the room and it won't happen up here."[10] Residents looked at where the Planning Commissioner was pointing: they looked from the Planning Commission up on their dais, they looked at the open space and the microphones, they looked at all the rows of chairs, and they looked at the bleachers. And they looked way back behind the bleachers, nearly at the rear of the room, where there was one forlorn man sitting surrounded by a little circle of about twenty-five empty chairs. The Planning Commission chair said again, "Why don't you go back there? There are monitors back there. We are all in the same room." The 200 people from Kettleman City looked around, and they looked at the back of the room at those twenty-five chairs, and they looked at the empty chairs up front, and they said, "Adelante, adelante" ("forward, forward"), and they moved up to the front of the room. Residents testified in Spanish, from the front of the room, that the last time they had heard about people being sent to the back of the room was when African Americans were sent to the back of the bus—a policy dumped in the dustbin of history a generation ago. They said they weren't going to stand for that.[11] "The incident summed up what the County felt for the people out here in Kettleman City," notes Maricela Alatorre. "Our rights were second to this huge corporation."

[*The struggle continues for five years. After the all-white King's County Board of Supervisors votes 3–1 for the incinerator—it will have huge tax benefits to the county, though little will trickle down to Kettleman City—the residents sue. They win, both for lack of adequate environmental impact analysis and the community's exclusion from the permitting process. Chem Waste appeals. El Pueblo and Greenpeace take the campaign national, telling the story anywhere they can. Finally at the end of 1993, Chem Waste withdraws its permit application.*]

Many people who become involved in community struggles for environmental justice have never been active in their communities before and do not have, or perceive themselves as not having, the courage and skill it takes to be a community leader.... However, through the process of the struggle—becoming aware of environmental threats in the community and then becoming involved in ameliorating those threats—countless individuals have come to realize that they can speak out and take action, perhaps even become leaders.

There comes a moment in many activists' lives when the feeling "I could never do that" is replaced with the realization—called by some the "aha! Moment"—that "I can do that!" In the Buttonwillow struggle...community leader Rosa Solorio-Garcia came to this realization at a large rally in a neighboring town. At the rally, a woman from the community was exhorting the crowd, shouting from the stage. Solorio-Garcia turned to Lupe Martinez, the community organizer, and said, "God, how can you do that? I'm never going to do that. Don't you expect me to ever do that." Martinez responded by putting Solorio-Garcia next on the agenda to speak to the crowd. "Just like that. And here I was at the rally yelling at everybody and telling them about all the stuff in Buttonwillow. It's made me a totally different person. More outgoing, more positive about a lot of things."

> I would take something on because it had to be done, and then you learn how to do that.... I think that some of those were empowerment pieces along the way—you accomplish something you never thought you could do. It gives you something inside that says—when a new challenge comes on—"confidence." It gives you the confidence to say, "I don't know how it will be, but I'll give it my best shot," and then you get through that, you overcome that and you have the confidence again to go on.
> —Jackie Warledo, Indigenous Environmental Network

Achieving confidence is an often intangible outcome of taking part in an environmental justice struggle. On a more tangible level, participants in local struggles acquire skills and information that increase their capacity, or "personal efficacy,"[12] to become active in crucial decisions that affect their lives. Many individuals, through environmental justice struggles, gain expertise on several levels. One a skills-building level, for example, they may learn how to hold a press conference or speak in public. On a substantive level, they often become sophisticated about the process or industry they are challenging, emerging as "citizen experts" on hazardous waste incineration, sludge dumping, or pesticide spraying, for example.

...[An] important power building...is occurring between the Environmental Justice Movement and other social justice activism, what we call "movement fusion": the coming together of two (or more) different social movements in a way that expands the base of support for both movements by developing a common agenda. As we explained in chapter 1, environmental justice advocates, like their predecessors in the civil rights and the anti-toxics movements, understand that environmental problems are a manifestation of other, larger problems endemic to our social and economic structure. In addition to the fusion of civil rights and anti-toxics concepts and strategies that are evident in the Environmental Justice Movement, other examples of movement fusion offer a glimpse of the transformative possibilities of this fusion.

In the San Francisco Bay Area, the women's organization Breast Cancer Action has shifted from focusing on a *cure* for breast cancer to focusing on *prevention* of the disease. Its members are women who have had breast cancer, and they recognize that the cure can be as devastating as the disease for many women. In a fusion that has national implications, the group is linking up with environmental justice activists to challenge the use of endocrine-disrupting chemicals by industry. Breast Cancer Action has worked with Bay Area environmental justice groups like Greenaction and Communities for a Better Environment to sponsor an annual "Cancer Industry Tour" of downtown San Francisco, including stops at Chevron (accused of dumping dioxin, a carcinogen, into San Francisco Bay), Bechtel (accused of constructing polluting nuclear reactors), and the EPA (accused of not stopping pollution).

This movement fusion is bringing together other (perhaps unlikely) allies. Members of the Environmental Justice Movement and the immigrants' rights movement formed a coalition to beat back an attempt by right-wing environmentalists to have the Sierra Club oppose immigration on environmental grounds. The United Farm Workers has fused the two issues of labor rights and environmental toxicity for the past three decades, calling attention to the effects of pesticides on workers. The recently formed Just Transition movement, bringing together the Oil, Chemical and Atomic Workers Union and environmental justice networks like IEN [Indigenous Environmental Network] and the Southwest Network for Environmental and Economic Justice, continues this fusion. Workers and environmental justice activists recognize that steps taken to protect workers also protect the communities that surround industrial facilities or fields. Workers want sustainable, clean, and safe jobs; residents want safe neighborhoods, and neighbors.

NOTES

1. This story is drawn from one of the authors' work, over a period of many years, with the community group El Pueblo para el Aire y Agua Limpio. The author, Luke Cole, began work as the group's attorney in October 1989 and continues to represent the group today.

2. CALIFORNIA CODE REGS, Title 14, §15072(a).

3. Cerrell Associates, POLITICAL DIFFICULTIES FACING WASTE-TO-ENERGY CONVERSION PLANT SITING 17–30 (1984) (commissioned by the California Waste Management Board).

4. The Tijuana incinerator was denied a permit by the Mexican government after long community opposition, including a meeting between Kettleman City activists and Mexican environmentalists. Joel Simon, *U.S. and Mexican Activists Stop Incinerator Project*, CALIFORNIA LAWYER 89 (February 1993); see also Mark Grossi, *Tijuana Activists to Visit Waste Site in Kettleman City*, FRESNO BEE (March 7, 1992).

5. California Assembly Office of Research, TODAY'S TOXIC DUMP SITES: TOMORROW'S TOXIC CLEANUP SITES 19, 24 (1986) ("In 1985, the EPA fined CWM Kettleman $7 million for improper groundwater monitoring, dumping incompatible wastes into ponds, keeping inadequate records, and more than 1,500 incidents of over-filling ponds. CWM settled by agreeing to pay EPA $2.1 million and DHS $1.1 million."). See also County of Ventura, Department of Sheriff, WASTE MANAGEMENT, INC. (1991), Attachment 6; Edwin L. Miller, Jr., District Attorney, FINAL REPORT: WASTE MANAGEMENT, INC. (San Diego District Attorney's Office. March 1992).

6. See Casey Bukro, *A $587,900 Lesson on Whistle-blowing: Incinerator Staffer's Retaliatory-Firing Suit Zaps Chemical Waste*, CHICAGO TRIBUTE (October 24, 1994); David Young, *Waste Firm Agrees to Pay $4.3 Million More*, CHICAGO TRIBUNE (December 24, 1991).

7. Cyndee Fontana, *Kettleman Incinerator Draws Fire: Firm's Poor Record in Illinois Cited*, FRESNO BEE (January 17, 1990). Balanoff told the people of Kettleman City that Chem Waste is "not a company that can be trusted at all." Id. See also Ron Nielsen, *Illinois Politician Denigrates Burner*, HANFORD SENTINEL (January 17, 1990), at 1.

8. Jeff Bailey, *Tough Target: Waste Disposal Giant, Often under Attack, Seems to Gain from It; Waste Management's Jousts with Environmentalists Deter Rivals from Field; How It Sanitizes Its Image*, WALL STREET JOURNAL (May 1, 1991), at A1.

9. Memorandum from John D. Dingell, Chair, Subcommittee on Oversight and Investigations of the Committee on Energy and Commerce, to members of the subcommittee (dated September 9, 1992), at 4–5, 24–30 (detailing storage of dioxin contaminated material at David's Mini-U-Storage in a residential neighborhood of Baton Rouge) (reproduced in Subcommittee on Oversight and Investigations of the Committee on Energy and Commerce, U.S. House of Representatives, EPA's CRIMINAL ENFORCEMENT PROGRAM, Serial No. 102–163 [September 1992], at 13–14, 32–39). According to Rep. Dingell,

> Rather than immediately alerting the EPA, Chem Waste initiated a cover-up effort, designed to protect the reputation and interests of Chem Waste at the expense of the public....The dioxin-contaminated drums were falsely manifested as an "unknown" and delivered by night to Chem Waste's facility at Emelle, Alabama. Emelle had no permit to receive dioxin-contaminated waste.

Id. at 14. A criminal prosecution ensued and a trial in Lousiana resulted in felony convictions of several individuals in 1991. Id.

10. Remarks of Chair Mike Wheatley, Kings County Planning Commission, in Reporter's Transcript, Kings Country Planning Commission Special Meeting, Public Hearing for Conditional Use Permit No. 1480, November 14–15, 1990, at 172.

11. Testimony of Mary Lou Mares, in Reporter's Transcript, Kings County Planning Commission Special Meeting, Public Hearing for Conditional Use Permit No. 1480, November 14–15, 1990, p. 257; testimony of Ephrain Camacho, id. at 180; testimony of Allen Brent, id. at 149.

12. Robert D. Bullard, DUMPING IN DIXIE: RACE, CLASS, AND ENVIRONMENTAL QUALITY 2 (2d ed., 1990), at 2.

FOR REVIEW

1. What is a "community"?
2. Give examples of two different kinds of communities making ethical change.
3. What are two ways that "witness" can lead to ethical change?
4. In change-work, when is "80 percent of success just showing up"?
5. What are three good uses of your ethical toolbox when making change in communities?
6. According to the text, what is one prime danger in making change in communities? How do we resist it?
7. What is restorative justice?
8. What is the role of the community in restorative justice?
9. What is environmental justice?
10. How has the environmental justice movement created and transformed communities?

EXERCISES AND NOTES

THINKING COMMUNITY

What are *your* communities? Make a list. Start with the communities in which you live: local and not so local. Add the various communities you have joined by choice: religious, maybe, or political, or professional.

What about your ethnic communities? We all have ethnic identities, though we are more apt to embrace them when they are more self-conscious because they are in the minority (as when people speak of "the black community" or "the Korean community," etc.). Still, even if you don't embrace them now, couldn't you imagine occasions, both positive and not so positive, when you would? What would they be? How might they be agents of ethical change? Are they perhaps agents of ethical change already?

Many readers of this book will be students. So do you consider yourself to belong to a community of students? (And: on what scale? How big?) If you did, what would change, as far as your loyalties and perhaps actions? Do you identify with your college or university community—which includes not only current students but alumni, faculty and staff, and perhaps local residents as well? Again, would embracing such a community more explicitly change things for you? What about the community of students worldwide—as in the idea of "Students Without Borders" mentioned in the text? (Actually, "students without borders" is not a single official organization but a whole set of them: Google the term and see what comes up.)

This chapter ends with a look at two current justice movements that centrally involve community: restorative justice and environmental justice. Once again you can look around your own area and ask what local communities are doing, or might do, in response to crime and in regard to environmental threats, especially as both intersect with race issues and poverty. If you don't know, work on finding out. How does your sense of your own communities change as a result?

EXTENDING RESTORATIVE JUSTICE?

Here are two questions about restorative justice from Martin Fowler.

• Terrorists kill innocents, sometimes out of religious zealotry. Can we find any community even with these groups to restore justice, peace, and safety in our communities? If that sounds far-fetched, think of moderates within religious traditions trying to dialogue with extremists. Hatred runs deep, but our need for justice runs deeper. What if we had a "restorative" form of justice in which communities in conflict could, step by step, grow into a larger community to work out constructive long-term fairness? What would this look like in practice? When people deny that they have any community with each other, taking steps towards restorative justice is also taking steps towards building or restoring that larger community which has been lost—or forgotten. How can you find a restorative solution when the hatred on both sides is intense and is long-standing? What buried and unmet shared needs could provide a beginning towards "making things right"?

• Can restorative justice be extended? We know that human beings have done great harm to our biospheric community. Though humans are victims, the most massive and voiceless victims are plants and animals. Entire species are becoming extinct due to human activity. It's not easy to see how they might speak for themselves in something like victim-offender mediation [though there might be ways, such as the Councils of All Beings—AW]. How could we extend our apologies to a biosphere? Still, it's a community project and a community need. How would we begin to say "we're sorry" sincerely—and to make reparations and repair? In other words, in what specific and visible ways do we need to acknowledge that humans live in community with the rest of life in order to deal with this "crime" against nature's well-being and survival? And then: how do we deal with it?

GET INVOLVED

This entire chapter is a guide and an invitation to get involved with ethical change-making communities. A range of options now lies before you, along with some advice and encouragement and a reminder that this book as a whole—your ethical toolbox—can and should go with you. So, go to it!

NOTES

I cite the Doctors Without Borders website at http://www.doctorswithoutbor ders.org, accessed 11/12/06. Greenpeacer Rex Wyler is interviewed by Micah Toub in "Man Overboard," accessed 11/12/06 at http://www.thismagazine .ca/issues/2005/07/qa_manoverboard.php. You can check out the Homeless World Cup ("Kick Off Poverty") at http://www.homelessworldcup.org. On opera with the homeless ("Giving the Homeless a Voice"), see http://www .streetwiseopera.org.

On change-making in communities, two inspiring sources are Frances Moore Lappe, *Democracy's Edge: Choosing to Save Our Country by Bringing Democracy to Life* (Jossey-Bass, 2005) and Laurent Parks Daloz et al., *Common Fire: Leading Lives of Commitment in a Complex World* (Beacon, 1996). For an introduction to the Councils of All Beings, see http://www.rainforestinfo.org.au/deep-eco/coab.htm.

There are large literatures on restorative justice and environmental justice. For detailed links, go to the Ethics Updates site (again, http://ethics.sandiego.edu) and follow the links within "Environmental Ethics" to "Environmental Justice" or within "Justice" to "Restorative Justice." On restorative justice, see also http:// www.beyondintractability.org/essay/restorative_justice and www.restorativejus tice.org, along with the extraordinary stories of reconciliation and restoration at www.theforgivenessproject.com and (for one specific instance) www.tkf.org.

I am grateful to Martin Fowler both for his contributions to this chapter and for his persistent and unassuming commitment to make restorative justice real in the community we share. Beth Raps was instrumental in shaping this chapter's themes and approaches, based upon her many years' experience in community organizing and change-work, and many of her words are here as well.

Notes for Teachers
The Toolbox in the Classroom

The notes to follow are for teachers planning to use this book as the primary text in an ethics course. At the beginning, and occasionally throughout, there is some commentary speaking to general philosophical issues—concerns addressed here because they are much more likely to come up for fellow teachers than students—but for the most part I simply describe my own uses of this material and offer some pedagogically oriented notes. Let me add that I would very much appreciate hearing any of *your* suggestions and exercises or projects that prove useful with this text, or any other reactions that you or your students may have—please e-mail me at weston@elon.edu.

GENERAL ISSUES

PRAGMATISM

Philosophers and others trained in ethics will recognize how sharply some of the starting points of this book vary from those standard in the field. It's been clear since the beginning of this book that I see ethics as a reconstructive and practical enterprise, open-ended and evolving, rather than a contest of theories or an attempt to discover at last the real truth about how we should live.

Many philosophers prefer to concentrate on ethics' unique intellectual challenges—on theory-building and conceptual analysis—following a model of ethics essentially laid down by the English philosopher Henry Sidgwick in the late 19th century. And this professional model of ethics, as it were, may be entirely appropriate in upper-level classes, in courses mostly for majors or minors or where some specialization is useful and appropriate. But for lower-level, introductory, general-curriculum ethics courses, in which very few if any students intend to become specialists in ethics, it seems to me that we are missing an opportunity to do them much more good.

Students in such classes, like most people, come to ethics to learn how to *live*. This is a far broader matter—not merely an intellectual challenge, but a challenge to the imagination and to the heart too, and to ourselves as effective moral citizens. It may be that by concentrating on certain intellectual challenges unique to ethics, we have slighted the practical skills that are vital to ethics but *not* unique to it. So part of the aim of this book is to rejoin ethics to life skills—to put ethics into what I see as its rightful place.

This approach to ethics traces back to the American pragmatists, John Dewey in particular, and has affinities as well with a number of pragmatist, feminist, and other critical views of ethics that are now developing rapidly in the midst of the current and vast philosophical debate about the very foundations of ethics. But I don't defend my starting points in this book itself—though it's been difficult to resist!—nor critique the usual ones. A textbook is not the place for methodological debates (and of course it's not exactly as though traditional textbooks spend their time laying out and defending *their* presuppositions either, do they?). Interested or provoked readers might consult my book *Toward Better Problems* (Temple University Press, 1992) for a development and defense of some of my assumptions. A useful overview of Dewey's approach can be found in James Gouinlock's collection *The Moral Writings of John Dewey* (Prometheus, 1994).

It's a striking thing, though, that despite the current challenges to "ethics as usual," it remains virtually impossible to teach *practical* ethics without plowing the same old theoretical furrows, simply because there are very few textbooks that present ethics primarily in another key. My main aim, then, has just been to write such a book—to make it possible to *teach* ethics on the view laid out in this book's Preface: as a collection of practical skills that enable us to make a constructive difference in problematic ethical situations. Practical pragmatism, so to speak. No other book, as far as I know, takes on this task. So it is struggle enough—quite enough for one book.

Finally, though, I do admit that I hope *A 21st Century Ethical Toolbox* will be read as a contribution—albeit oblique—to the philosophical debate about the foundations of ethics too. Every approach to ethics must be judged partly by how it looks in action: by what kinds of tools it brings back to practice; by how constructively and invitingly it enables us to contribute to improving our common life. Could not each then be judged partly by what kinds of introductory texts and courses it makes possible—by what an introduction to ethics *that* way leaves students able to *do*? Proof is partly in the pudding. I am proud to offer this book as one relevant kind of pudding.

COURSE DESIGN USING THIS BOOK

The book is designed to serve as the chief or even sole textbook in an ethics course, though it can be supplemented in a variety of ways too, and could well serve as a supplement itself. Some may wish to supplement it with a standard text, like a collection of readings from traditional ethical theories, or a collection of more professional articles on "applied" themes, or a text that combines both. Others may supplement it in quite different ways: say, with books that go into depth on a single issue raised here more briefly. Some colleagues have used it successfully with Peter Singer's *Animal Liberation,* for example; others have used Ram Dass and Paul Gorman's *How Can I Help?* or Colin McGinn's brisk little essay *Moral Literacy,* which takes provocative positions on a number of the issues discussed here. (I draw upon McGinn several times myself, you'll recall.) Others couple it with popular and provocative books such as Daniel Quinn's *Ishmael.*

I usually assign one chapter per class (I have 100-minute classes twice a week). This schedule presupposes, of course, that students read and understand the chapters mostly on their own. In class I may spend five or ten minutes reviewing the readings, just to remind people of the main points, but I rely on the students to raise questions or issues if there are sticking points in the chapters. (A useful way to do this, by the way, is to pass out 3x5 cards at the beginning of class each day and ask for questions or points of unclarity in the day's reading. Organize these at a later short break and respond to them right away.)

I don't lecture. I've already shot my bolt in the book, as it were. Class is almost entirely application and practice. Suggestions for in-class applications and practice, chapter-by-chapter, follow below—they are the main part of these notes.

Please note that there are sometimes substantive new points in the "Exercises and Notes" sections. I suggest assigning them right along with the text sections, even if the exercises aren't always used as writing projects or classwork.

The first edition's reviewers reported that they taught through the chapters of the first edition in a wide variety of different orders. I have changed the order myself for the second edition, moving the chapters on dialogue and service up to Part I, partly to help set general ground rules for the class early on, and in order to encourage ethics classes to launch service work early on. Some subsections do unfold in order—Chapters 6 through 10, for instance, and 15 through 17. Still, for the most part, the chapters remain largely independent and nonsequential. You can use them in a variety of orders. I should report that in my own current teaching I actually use them entirely out of order too. My class begins with a skeleton of skills and topics—Chapters 1, 2, 6, 11, 15, 16, 17, 19, 20—in order to help student groups frame and launch their own ethical-change projects; then we return to the rest as the projects get underway.

GRADING

Over the years I have graded my course in a variety of ways. Half of the grade has sometimes depended on journals—student notebooks with notes *and their own thoughts* (that's a crucial part) on all the chapters and class discussions. Group work, attendance, and service work made up the rest. Other times I have graded mainly on short weekly papers, mostly assignments directly from the "Exercises" that conclude each chapter. I say more about paper assignments in the next section.

Currently I keep tabs on students' reading with short weekly quizzes. One change from the first edition, accordingly, is the addition of review questions at the end of each chapter. I use these as quiz questions at the beginning of each class day. For some variation and challenge, recycle some questions from earlier chapters as you move through the book, and/or add some bonus questions that can only be answered by a student who has gone above and beyond the reading to, say, look up some references. Couple quiz grades with attendance and participation grades, regular short writing assignments or options, service requirements, and maybe a term paper, and you have a workable and familiar grading plan.

PAPER ASSIGNMENTS USING THIS BOOK

You might draw paper topics directly from the "Exercises" that conclude each chapter. Some of these ask for self-reflection; some call for critiques or extensions of the ideas in the text; some propose other and quite different projects. All should give students a strong start and some good support, drawing on the material in the chapter in focused ways.

For my part, I am no longer much inclined to assign free-standing writing of any length, like the usual term paper. It's certainly true that writing such papers may be one way in which students can display the skills they are (hopefully) learning. But papers are not the only way, and often may well not be the best way. I'm more inclined toward practical projects, actually trying to make a difference. As the Preface indicates, my classes have sponsored workshops on conflict mediation and creativity, conducted a "Council of All Beings" to conclude our discussion of environmental ethics, put up websites for local teens to get sex-education information, and many other similar projects. This kind of work can be *coupled* with writing—one of my requirements with all of these projects, in fact, is that students produce an explicit and detailed ethical rationale, posting it on line for example if they put up a website. But these pieces are not academic papers in the usual sense. They are usually written by groups rather than individuals; they are public rather than addressed solely to me, part of larger projects with multiple stake holders who will also weigh in; and the usual academic voice is often out of place, if not downright inappropriate.

If you do assign longer academic papers, emphasize that a wide variety of writing styles are possible. Too often we, and correspondingly our students, assume that only papers in an argumentative style are appropriate in philosophy. Once again, certainly it is an important thing to train students to write in this style. It asks a vital kind of rigor and clear thinking, and is one style of contributing to public debate. Yet just as certainly it is not the *only* kind of effective and appropriate writing.

For example, much of the writing in this book—to take models close at hand—is in very different styles. The two student papers, both first-place winners of the prestigious Elie Wiesel Prize for Undergraduate Writing in Ethics, differ both from each other and from the usual academic model. Sarah Stillman's "Made by Us" (Chapter 1) offers gripping reportage. Courtney Martin's "The Ethics of Transformation" (Chapter 5) is a very personal reflection on her own transformation. Again, these are *student* essays. You and your students might find it useful to look at more winning student papers at the Wiesel Foundation's website, http://www.eliewieselfoundation.org/EthicsPrize. More than a decade of winning papers can be found there, three to five a year, all extraordinary work in a mix of voices that your students may want to emulate.

Other good models of short pieces of writing in this book include Alice Walker's "Am I Blue?" (Chapter 6); Bertrand Russell's "The Harm That Good Men Do," despite or maybe because of its irony (Chapter 8); Aldo Leopold's "The Land Ethic" (Chapter 10); Colin McGinn's "Speciesism" (Chapter 12); and Ursula Le Guin's "May's Lion" (Chapter 17). Note again: these are all short pieces of writing in ethics, genuine contributions, indeed offerings from some of the best writers in the English language in the 20th century, yet few of them go in for the usual kinds of arguments. Again, you and your students might find it useful to compare and contrast some of these essays specifically with attention to their aims and writing strategies: then you are in an excellent position to articulate expectations for the writing they will be doing themselves.

Finally, there are the mechanics—especially but not exclusively for the usual sorts of academic papers. Some of my other books offer a guide to paper-writing: *A Rulebook for Arguments* includes rules for any argumentative papers; *A Practical Companion to Ethics* ends with an Appendix on writing papers in ethics, specifically asking students to start planning the paper by asking what is their *aim* with it. Explore an issue? Get some problem "unstuck"? Make a case? Take a stand? Each aim suggests a quite different kind of paper. Know where you are going! There are also many other fine resources for paper-writing in philosophy generally, such as Anthony Graybosch et al., *The Philosophy Student Writer's Manual* (Prentice-Hall, 2nd edition, 2003). "Ethics Updates" (http://ethics.sandiego.edu) also offers a useful (though very traditional) guide to writing ethics papers.

TOOLBOX CHAPTER BY CHAPTER

Here are a few classroom ideas for each chapter, with running commentary and other suggestions.

CHAPTER 1: ETHICS AS A LEARNING EXPERIENCE

My strategy in most of the chapters is to focus on one or a few practical topics, so that the "applications" stay somewhat consistent through the chapter. I suggest doing this in each day's class as well. Thus, for Chapter 1, following Sarah Stillman's theme, you might take up the question of fair trade. Students will have heard of it but may not know much about the underlying politics and issues. You may wish to invite in speakers—for information's sake, though, not necessarily to make a one-sided argument, or indeed any argument at all. You may also want to have students do a little research to see if they can determine the origins of everyday consumer items in their own lives. Who made these? Under what conditions? What are our responsibilities to those people? What are the responsibilities of the manufacturers and the importers?

Remember, though, that the aim here is not to close down the question, as if there is only one simple right answer. It is to wake up to the *questions*. If you bring in guest speakers, this would be a useful point to review with them beforehand.

CHAPTER 2: ETHICS-AVOIDANCE DISORDERS

As soon as my class gets underway, I assign one or a few students each day to bring in a short article or something else we can look at together that involves some sort of ethical issue. These have ranged from on-campus debates to current Supreme Court cases to surprising or disturbing international political or technological developments, and occasionally a piece of litter or an art object. We begin class by looking at these—a kind of warm-up. Right away I stress that our aim is not to judge the issue or in any other way close it down. Instead, our aim is to *explore* it in as open-ended and intelligent a way as we can: to see it more deeply, to see possibilities in it that might not have been evident at first or to participants, even to consider if there is some useful intervention or contribution we might make.

This procedure continues through the term, but I like to introduce it in conjunction with Chapter 2. Dogmatism, dismissal, "flip" relativism—none of them work in the face of this kind of exploration. Yet this exploration is *fascinating*, inviting, and a way of talking and thinking about ethics that students will rarely have encountered before. Ultimately, I believe, this is the best pedagogical answer to the various ethics-avoidance "disorders": to exemplify, together, an alternative—to begin to experience real, intelligent, constructive ethical thinking.

Generally I do not tackle any of the "disorders" head-on. The text is enough already. We don't want to drive people into defensiveness. And we don't need to. It is striking, for example, that although the spectre of relativism seems to loom extremely large for some ethics instructors—and most textbook writers—it simply doesn't comes up the minute a real issue or a real person comes on the scene. (Nobody says: "Oh well, maybe exploiting child workers is right for Nike.") Despite the veneer of relativism, most of us come with strong moral opinions. Dogmatism is the much more real danger.

Sure, students express relativistic sentiments from time to time (like "Who am I to say?"). Still, I think that philosophers read too much of a theory—Relativism with a capital-R—into them. Maybe when students say things like "Who am I to say?" they are just trying to give others some space—and asking for space themselves, in a context where they are unsure of themselves. After all, college is a time of radical change and experiment for many people: things are in flux; they justly want room to move. Maybe they want some freedom from the moral deliverances of others, time to work things out for themselves. This is not unreasonable—and it has nothing to do with the philosophical debate about relativism. I don't think it's wise to take a few relativistic-sounding expressions as on the way to relativism, as it were, and then try to lay out the whole capital-R theory and defeat it. It may actually *make* them relativists, for one thing—if they're persuaded by this that philosophical relativism is the only way to defend the personal space they genuinely do need—and then it *will* be a problem.

Besides, even if they really are (philosophical) relativists from the beginning, it strikes me as unwise pedagogy to think that we must begin a course by "defeating" something students are supposed to believe so strongly. Wiser and more effective would be to take them where they are and build from there. How inviting is ethics likely to be if it sets itself up from the start as an assault upon their convictions?

So my advice is to just tolerate the occasional "Who is to say?" rhetoric without wheeling out the heavy artillery. Just point out that we do in fact have more to think about and say. Send the harder-core relativists to the box at the end of this chapter. You'll have a lot more space for the real work of ethics.

CHAPTER 3: ETHICS AND RELIGION

Modern philosophical ethics tends to avoid religious themes and terms. However wise this may be as an expression of secular pluralism, it does make it harder to speak to many of our students, whose ethical frames of reference are often insistently religious and sometimes sectarian. I think we need to take them more seriously. The aim of this chapter is to suggest a path toward the sort of ethics familiar to philosophers that lies *through* religion rather than opposed to it.

Invite in your college chaplain for a dialogue on these matters with you and the class. Most college chaplains deal with a religiously diverse community: they *have* to be at least somewhat ecumenical. In most places they also have to make their peace with the prevailing secularism.

   Actually reading the Bible can be a fascinating project in an open college classroom. A few examples are suggested in the text. Another I find useful is the story of Judah and Tamar in Genesis 38. Sometimes I hand out a copy of that chapter and we read it right in class. It is a wild tale of sudden unexplained death, betrayal, seduction and adultery, which concludes with the pardon and full acceptance of the female adulterer (Tamar) and no question even being raised about the male adulterer (Judah). In fact, Tamar is specifically listed as one of the ancestors of King David and therefore of Jesus Himself. Judah founds one of the twelve tribes of Israel and later gives his name to Judaism itself. So the story seems to go rather light on adultery and seduction, to say the least. It is also complicated by certain sexual customs practiced by the Hebrews of the time, in particular the expectation that if a husband dies, it is the obligation of his next youngest brother to impregnate his widow—in particular, to sire a son—who counts as the dead man's son for the sake of inheritance. (Recently I learned that something like this "levirate marriage" is still practiced in Iraq. There are a lot of widows.)

   In this story, Onan, the second son, does in fact follow his dead brother (killed by God for an unspecified reason) to the widow's bed, but deliberately does not get her pregnant. God kills him too, for a reason that seems unclear. Was it that he disobeyed his father? Was it his selfishness—for if his dead brother had no heirs then the father's property would pass to Onan and *his* descendants? Or something else? It is not so clear. Yet this story, like the story of Sodom, was made the basis for a very strong prohibition in the Christian tradition. Challenge the students to figure out what exactly, on this view, was the sin of Onan (hint: they'll find this most intriguing) and then to ask whether the actual story can be made to bear such weight.

CHAPTER 4: ETHICAL TALK

Chapter 13 goes much more deeply into the ethics of dialogue. The aim of Chapter 4, and the reason for its new placement in Part I, is mainly to help you and your class set ethical ground rules for constructive dialogue as you work through the issues in this book.

   Again, practice is key. In class, work through the dysfunctional dialogues in the exercises. Be especially alert to missed opportunities in these little exchanges: to questions that could be taken as real questions, for example, and not just as mere rhetorical questions. Highlight any movement toward creative thinking.

   Don't allow students simply to rewrite the disagreements in these dialogues in a way that preserves the disagreement but merely makes it "nice." It's not enough if people just don't insult each other any more. My students, at least, are sometimes too easily satisfied if tensions are kept submerged or merely politely sidestepped. No: they need to *confront* those tensions, but in a constructive way. For more dialogues to work on, videotape some talk shows on current issues, and pick some excerpts short enough to view a number of times and then rework.

CHAPTER 5: SERVICE AND SERVICE-LEARNING

I strongly suggest setting up a class service project, starting as soon as you can in the term. My students almost always report that working in the homeless shelter was among the most significant aspects of the course for them—some say it changes their lives. This kind of service is not hard to arrange—quite the contrary, most service organizations are dying for help, are more than happy to help coordinate a hefty group of volunteers, and often take public education to be part of their mission. Make the phone call!

I've tried to highlight some pitfalls in this, though: chiefly that service can easily become a sort of unilateral do-goodism. It can be too easy to put into familiar categories, and therefore never becomes as unsettling and reciprocal as it can be at its best. Lately, therefore, I have been pushing my classes into less unilateral situations, such as studying *jointly* (versus tutoring) with students at disadvantaged schools. If you do go into shelters or other more familiar helping situations, try to arrange to have the students go individually or in very small groups (as long as they don't feel unsafe). Without someone familiar to fall back upon, they attend better and more readily take the steps to connect with people very different from themselves.

CHAPTER 6: TAKING VALUES SERIOUSLY

Take current issues out of newspapers, take children's story books, bring the Bible back, invite in people who practice tae kwon do or weekly fasts or Civil War reenactments (there also may be some in your class) or you name it. Whatever you put in front of them, ask your students to try to understand and uncover the values at stake and spell them out just as the chapter does. Be specific! For example, if a value like "responsibility" comes up, ask *whose* responsibility and *for what?*

This is probably a good time to add that whenever you invite guest speakers to your class, be sure your guests understand what you are asking of them: an exploration of values, not a conversion!

I organize this kind of work by dividing the class or group into small groups, each of which is asked to identify *one* value at stake in the situation (practice, issue, or whatever) and write a description of it, in a few words, on the board (use one section of the board for each issue) or on a flipchart—in, say, three minutes (the first one is easy).

Then each issue passes to the next group (number the groups and issues: issue 1 now goes to group 2, etc.), with the same assignment and, say, five minutes. Repeat for as much time as you have, allowing a few more minutes each time around if needed.

My students generally do not believe that more than two or three values can be drawn out of such issues. They are surprised when the groups are still going strong on the fourth or fifth round. Sometimes in later rounds a number of values of the same general sort come out together: it's striking to see connections between quite different issues emerge. By the end, you have a board full of different values all drawn out of situations that we usually just quickly pass over. Next time we ask more of ourselves.

You may wish to take the occasion to delve much further into the issue of ethics and animals, since this is the theme of Walker's and Kerasote's pieces. There is a vast literature here, of course: for a start, make use of the Ethics Updates website, http://ethics.sandiego.edu, under "Animal Rights."

CHAPTERS 7–10: GENERAL COMMENTS

For these chapters I usually arrange for brief classroom visits by some of the figures we read: Kant, Russell, Lao Tzu, or others (they can be contacted at your local costume store or theater department). A student or a colleague can usually be induced to interview them (i.e., you) talk-show style. *Personify* them, in short—that way their thought becomes far more vivid.

Compared to the usual treatment of theory in ethics texts, these chapters go light. A *family* is much broader than a *theory*: families are much more loosely related, more like a style of thinking and certain characteristic preoccupations than anything tight or systematic. This treatment reflects my own and my department's teaching practice, in which the traditional ethical theories and the usual forms of contention about them are introduced, at least in the usual elaborate ways, only in the *second* ethics course. For instructors who wish to do more theory in the first course, though, supplementation is natural and easy. There are dozens of theory-oriented collections to choose from. Theodore Denise et al., *Great Traditions in Ethics* (Wadsworth, many editions), presents a number of traditional theorists, along with some less traditional contemporary and ancient figures, in their own words with helpful arrangement and commentary. Wanda Torres Gregory and Donna Giancola's *World Ethics* (Wadsworth, 2003) is another helpful and wider-ranging collection.

I suggest picking two or three specific issues that you can explore from the point of view of each of these families of values: whatever issues are pressing or intriguing for you and your students. Address them first perhaps as you take up Chapter 6; then revisit them with each ensuing chapter. (Another way to do more theory: assign, or compile, a little anthology just on the ethics of that issue.) Issues around race and racial prejudice work well for this purpose; animal issues are excellent and provocative; try also the question of drugs; or of course any others you and your students are concerned with.

The families of values are first introduced in Chapter 6 and then elaborated in 7–10. Sharon Hartline's essay, following these notes, suggests an exercise to invite students to really inhabit these distinctions—use it when you come to the end of Part II.

CHAPTER 7: THE ETHICS OF THE PERSON

For an in-class exercise, try the following simulation. Try to design a welfare system under which you can all live. Appoint certain groups (by random lot, say, to make it fair) to represent rich people, poor people, middle-class taxpayers, and social-service administrators. Each group should try to speak for its interests, but each group should be realistic too. They can't have everything they want. They should seek a system to which they all can agree.

Now deepen and vary this exercise in various ways. A Rawlsian variant: instead of assigning people to known interest groups, ask the students to imagine that they have entered a special kind of moral space in which they *don't know* whether they are rich or poor—they don't know whether they will be supporting the system they are designing, or supported by it. What kind of system will they design then?

You could add another level of impartiality too—also a Rawlsian point. After all, even if the simulators do not know whether they are rich or poor, they still come to this choice knowing "who they are" in the sense that they know their age, gender, race, general level of motivation and ability, hopes and fears, and so on. So a young well-educated white male, for example, might feel confident that he could easily work his way out of poverty, and therefore might be tempted to opt for a minimal welfare system that expected people to go out and make it on their own. He might not feel the same way, however, if he could just as easily find "himself" an older person or a minority group member or someone who has never had the opportunity of good schools or family support. More systematic barriers and prejudices might have to be recognized.

So make a list of various people (gender, race, education levels, family support, life situation), representing a good cross-section of the population, and then ask students to imagine that they are designing a welfare system in which they will potentially play any one of these roles. They might be a billionaire or a sports superstar or a rich right-wing heiress, but they might also be a middle-aged single mother of three young children or a survivor of an abusive childhood or a physically challenged war veteran or...? What kind of system will they design then?

You can make this more vivid by ending this exercise by actually assigning roles (I use numbered playing cards) and figuring out how each person will fare under the system they designed.

This simulation is my variation of an exercise developed by Peter Williams of Stony Brook University. For several other ways of modeling the Rawlsian "Original Position" in the classroom, see James Moulder, "Playing with Justice," *Teaching Philosophy* 10 (1987): 339–344, and Ronald Green, "The

Rawls Game," *Teaching Philosophy* 9 (1986): 51–60. I am grateful to my colleague Nim Batchelor for these references.

CHAPTER 8: THE ETHICS OF HAPPINESS

Utilitarianism has many intriguing ins and outs, especially if you try to nail down an explicit and complete standard for moral action. Some of these are broached in the exercises, such as the infamous "Experience Machine" (if pleasure is really the sole good, then is it not equally good whether the causes are real or not?), and possibly radical implications for our treatment of other animals. Peter Singer's little book *Practical Ethics*, as my Notes indicate, is an excellent source on a variety of questions here: his views are much more subtle than the public debate over them might suggest. There are also well-known questions about rule– versus act–utilitarianism, and less well-known questions, most sharply raised by Derek Parfit, about utilitarianism's sometimes bizarre implications for population policy and the future. Anyway, this is your best opportunity to give students a taste of how theory might work in ethics: you may wish to make use of it.

CHAPTER 9: THE ETHICS OF VIRTUE

Invite students in groups of two or three to choose one virtue they especially admire, and draw a poster for it, illustrating and advocating it. Post the results and discuss them. At Elon, many classrooms have virtue-oriented posters already, usually short quotations; so we sometimes ask whether our posters would be good additions or substitutes, or anyway what kinds of posters would. For a next step, find, copy, and display the *Harper's* posters for the Seven Deadly Sins mentioned in the exercises (in the November 1987 issue: I have not been able to find them online). How do these posters compare with your own? Do they make you rethink what you drew, or even the virtues you picked? Send students back to rework their original posters, and consider going public with the results. You might also conduct the whole exercise for *vices* as well.

CHAPTER 10: THE ETHICS OF RELATIONSHIP

One of the key questions in this chapter is what the true boundaries of the moral community are. It is worth remembering that for most of human history, not even all human beings were included in the moral community. As Leopold points out, for Odysseus the slave girls in his own household were just property, to be disposed of as he saw fit. Even in the Greek Golden Age, the city-states enslaved captured soldiers from other Greek cities and considered everyone else barbarians without any moral standing at all. The European conquerors of the Americas saw the native people as animals, sexual objects, circus attractions, slaves, and finally just impediments—certainly not as fellow human beings. Only slowly did the moral categories develop that enabled people to see all other humans as part of a moral community—and we are certainly not all the way there even yet. So are we entitled to be so sure that now we've finally gotten it right? What *about* other animals—some or all? What about even artificial intelligence? What about even mountains and rivers, or the encompassing Earth itself?

"Olam" (the box at the end of the chapter) offers a simulation exercise that is a provocative follow-up. Have students divide themselves into groups corresponding to the five possible responses outlined. Each group should prepare to present its case, after which you can try in discussion to reach some sort of consensus. My classes often end up roughly in the middle. When they're done, ask them how their proposed Olamian ethic compares to the way we've treated our own Earth. Likely it will be much more ecologically minded and respectful. This is an interesting result already. It's a little as if (as one of my students put it) Olam offers us a "second chance"—a chance to do right what we did so wrong on Earth. But then: why couldn't we begin to do better *now*?

There is a further twist. Olam actually *is* Earth! Every animal on or feature of Olam is actually an animal on or feature of Earth (whales, octopi, bacteria, the "Gaia Hypothesis"…). Sometimes when I have my students do this exercise I play whale-songs in the background—they sound truly alien indeed—so at this point in the discussion I reveal what they really are. Even the abruptness of our own arrival on Olam is mirrored, more or less, by our very short tenure on Earth.

Now ask: what does it mean that the class has (probably!) settled on an ethic for Olam that is so radically out of joint with the kind of ethic we have lived by on our own planet, which actually *is* Olam except for a few details? Does the question of our relation to Earth now seem a little different?

CHAPTER 11: CRITICAL THINKING

These are familiar themes, though not so often considered in ethics courses. Obviously there is time only to touch on a few main points: chiefly, that taking some care to identify and seek out the relevant facts is a key to intelligent ethical thinking. A handout of sample ethical arguments, drawn from the newspaper or widely available critical-thinking texts, is useful to analyze inferences. Any of the exercises can easily take up a whole class period: sometimes I allow several days for this practice. If students work in groups, some of this work can be initiated in the first session, carried on in between, and presented to start off the next.

CHAPTER 12: JUDGING LIKE CASES ALIKE

Most ethical philosophers agree that we must "judge like cases alike," but this requirement may be cashed out in different ways. For many contemporary philosophers, it means arriving at universal principles that can be tested by application and defended against or adapted in the face of possible counter-examples (allegedly "like cases" where the proposed principle seems to yield the "wrong" result). This Sidgwickian approach still so dominates ethics in England and America that many philosophers simply identify it with moral reasoning as such.

Lately there has been criticism, most markedly from philosophers who want to recover a case-based approach, which starts with those cases about which there are clear and accepted conclusions and then explores their analogies—similarities or differences—with confusing or contested cases. On this way of thinking, universal principles seldom come up or get us very far. This is a far older approach, called "casuistry," long a strength of Catholic moral theology, with Jewish and Islamic parallels too. For a fascinating history and defense of casuistry, see Albert Jonsen and Stephen Toulmin's *The Abuse of Casuistry: A History of Moral Reasoning* (University of California Press, 1988). In this chapter I have tried to present the requirement to "judge like cases alike" in a way that is compatible with both approaches.

Physically playing something like "moral musical chairs" is a revealing and fun exercise. Create scenarios in which students actually, visibly, switch roles (that is, move between chairs), or set it up in a Rawlsian way, as suggested in the notes for Chapter 7, so that they don't know until the dust settles which role they will actually occupy.

In the reading, Colin McGinn asks us to imagine a species of vampire doing to us essentially what we do to other animals we use for food. You could elaborate this into a sort of simulation. Suppose that vampires or some other species of alien have taken over the Earth and are preparing to factory-farm humans for meat and use us to test drugs and other products. Could we—and *how* could we—persuade them to stop? Just such a scenario has been the premise of science-fiction movies from time to time: for example, "Z," a TV miniseries from the 1980s. In all of the science-fiction versions of which I am aware, though, the aliens lose in the end, usually through some fluke, as in "War of the Worlds," the original of this theme, where they are killed off by the common cold. Beware of the Hollywod cliché that humans will somehow win out in the end—and of the Wild West version in which we finally just fight them off. No: for us only moral arguments will do.

Suppose that the human race has one last appeal before their plan is put into effect. As it turns out, *this class* must convince them to stop. Teams of students should prepare arguments that can be presented to the aliens (also role-played by students from the class) in a grand hearing. This exercise works especially well if animals also show up. (Perhaps as a surprise: you can have a group or two prepare outside the classroom and swear them to secrecy.) The animals need not be anti-human—though you can understand why they might be—but they should make sure that humans judge like cases alike. If the humans really want the aliens to take human suffering seriously as a moral counterargument to their plan, for example, humans need to clean up their own act as well. Or is there some way to show that humans are distinct from the other animals in ways that make them more akin to the aliens—so that, maybe, the aliens really should eat animals too, or instead? Sides may shift…

CHAPTER 13: MINDFUL SPEECH

Practice identifying loaded language in various statements, perhaps first in statements students disagree with, and then in more congenial statements, including their own (videotape some discussions on controversial topics for this and other purposes). Most textbooks in informal logic cover "loaded language" and offer exercises to practice identifying and avoiding it. The habit of analyzing ethical arguments on their merits and putting them fairly, even if we don't agree with them, comes as a shock to many students, but for precisely that reason it is crucial.

Then extend the same kind of care to dialogue. For Chapter 4 students have already begun to practice this skill. Now go further: use more difficult and real dialogues as starting points for discussion and/or reenactment. For one example of an intense, often angry or despairing but also constructive dialogue on an enormously difficult problem—race relations—look at Lee Mun Wah's film "The Color of Fear" (Stir Fry Productions, www.stirfryseminars.com). You may find the topic itself a useful one to raise with your students, but the film also appeals as a model of dialogue under the most trying conditions.

Early on in my class I make it an assignment for every student to learn every other student's name (me too, obviously). Sharon Hartline offers a concrete way to do this in her essay to follow. My colleague John Sullivan asks his students *bow* to each other, after a look right into their eyes, in silence. These practices sometimes subtly or dramatically change how we then relate. Is this not ethics too?

The box at the end of Chapter 4 speaks about "silencing." Ask students to recall some occasions in their own experience when dialogue failed. Consider *why* it failed. Recall the various kinds of nonparticipation, resistance, advantage, and disadvantage outlined in that box. Were any of these factors at play? What could have been done about them? What could be done about them next time? If you're very brave, consider your own class or group in this regard. Who typically speaks and who doesn't? Why? Consider having a day when only certain people can speak: only people who have not spoken before; or only women (say, on the subject of abortion); or only those who admit to being confused about the whole topic; or…? What changes? Or try a "talking stick." Again: what changes?

CHAPTER 14: WHEN VALUES CLASH

In presenting ethical theories in Part II, I try to leave space for many nontheoretical approaches to conflicts of values as well. Regardless of what you think of the usefulness of theories, sometimes an entirely different approach is needed.

Integrative methods will be less familiar to many ethical philosophers, at least in the context of ethical debates. They're quite familiar, though, in our everyday lives. I used to feel some temptation to spend some class time justifying them. I don't anymore, and I don't recommend it. The justifications were more for myself, I finally concluded—or colleagues I imagined looking over my shoulder. Few students have this kind of resistance. Indeed it's the other way around: they resist *theory*.

Since the culture does not support them, though, at least in ethics, integrative skills may be hard to put into practice. They *need* practice. Spend some time on the exercises. Take the first one—better yet, assign it in advance. Though it sounds easy, in my experience it is very hard for most students to pull off. Typically they end up, despite the instructions, describing moral debates in an "I think..."/"They think..." kind of way. It takes some work to get to "*We* think...". Then move to the second exercise.

Note that many of these strategies are useful on the practical level even if you wholeheartedly subscribe to a theoretical approach too. A fuller toolbox of conflict-resolution skills is still helpful. Fisher and Ury, for example, make no claims about the disutility of theory: they only elaborate another and very powerful—but often overlooked—set of tools in addition.

On the next page is a survey on abortion attitudes used by the Common Ground Network for Life and Choice. If you use it, have the class fill it out *before* you assign this chapter, since (I hope) reading this chapter might affect how they answer it. Use an op-scan type answer sheet (just leave off the names) so that the results can be automatically tabulated and graphed.

To tabulate the results, divide the answer sheets into three groups: Pro-Life, Pro-Choice, and Uncertain (use question 26). Then calculate the *average* answer for each question for each group.

Now compare the averages (it helps to have them displayed graphically, and juxtaposed with each other). Take it that differences of 1.0 or less between the averages are not significant differences. Differences of more than 1.0 show some serious divergence. Ask how many of the twenty-five questions show a significant difference between Pro-Life and Pro-Choice groups.

Network organizers find that there is generally much less difference than we are led to believe—and that's among *activists* on the issue. Using this survey over a number of years, I have seldom had a class differ significantly on more than five or six questions, usually the same ones. So what about your class, or whatever group you surveyed? Where are the disagreements? How do they compare with the agreements? Go through the questions one by one. They'll be surprised.

Now continue: it is not merely that our agreements are more numerous than our disagreements. We can also use those agreements as starting points for "common ground" problem-solving: that is, for integrating values. Look at

ABORTION ATTITUDES: SURVEY

Please answer each of the following questions on a scale of 1–5, where 1 means *strongly agree* and 5 means *strongly disagree*.

1. Economic constraints make it very difficult for some women to carry their pregnancies to term, or to imagine being able to raise their children.
2. Adoption can be a positive choice for structuring family life.
3. Reducing the number of abortions is a worthwhile goal.
4. Abortion is an appropriate method of birth control.
5. To preserve their independence and freedom women sometimes need to have abortions.
6. There are acceptable alternatives to abortion currently available.
7. Alternatives to abortion should be encouraged.
8. In order to reduce the number of abortions, it is important to improve the economic status of women.
9. It is inevitable that some of society's problems can only be solved by using violent means.
10. Recreational sex without relational commitment is acceptable.
11. Women and men are equal in rights, value, and human dignity.
12. Motherhood is one desirable full-time career for women.
13. The future of children ought to be a major concern of US public and private policy.
14. Women and men are equally capable and both should be encouraged to take part in public decision-making roles.
15. Spirituality is an important dimension of being human.
16. Abortion is an acceptable option for terminating a pregnancy.
17. The natural order of things dictates that males are the dominant gender in societal structures.
18. Belonging to an organized religious group is an important aspect of full human development.
19. In most circumstances a collaborative decision-making process is preferable to having one clearly-designated authority figure.
20. We cannot always live up to our ideals, because the world of everyday circumstances makes this impossible.
21. Fidelity to one sexual partner is preferable to multiple sexual relationships.
22. Abortion is a violent procedure for terminating a pregnancy.
23. I feel certain about when human life begins.
24. It is very difficult to establish a law or rule that can be applied universally and justly in all circumstances.
25. Marriage is the proper context for sexual intercourse.
26. Are you: 1 Pro-Life, 2 Pro-Choice, 3 Uncertain

the questions on which your class or group agrees. Number 3, perhaps: that reducing the number of abortions is a worthwhile goal? Or: number 2? What would that suggest? Number 7? Then start working on alternatives! Number 8? Once again you have an agenda—quite likely a *shared* agenda.

Network organizers sometimes use this survey to open their dialogue sessions and ask people to answer it twice: once for themselves, and once giving the answers they think the "other side" would give. It emerges that both sides think the other side is much more extreme than they really are. Once again it's a useful basis for reframing the problem in the way proposed in this chapter. This usually leads to quite a bit of surprise and discussion too.

CHAPTERS 15 AND 16: CREATIVE THINKING IN ETHICS

Creative-thinking tools are less familiar to many ethical philosophers, but I hope the text makes their usefulness clear. In nearly every user's experience, too, these tools are among the most engaging to students. Once again the exercises give you a lot to work with: once again it is tempting to expand the time you spend here.

If there is time, begin by organizing into three- to five-person problem-solving teams. Make each team's first challenge to devise a team name or slogan ("Brainstormers"; "We eat problems for breakfast"; etc.). This is fun, it builds group spirit, and it opens up the kind of mutual appreciation and whimsy helpful to creative thinking generally. Then on to "novel function practice" and other warm-ups. The first exercise in both chapters starts on purpose with nonethical problems. You might spend half a class or more on this before shifting to moral problems. Note that exactly the same tools apply in exactly the same way—then move into the second exercise. A follow-up writing exercise is to ask students to come up on their own with a completely new idea on one of these or other ethical topics.

Make sure the students actually use the techniques. Sometimes they can be only half-hearted, and thus never get the full effect. Require them when reporting their results to also report what method they used—what was their specific random prompt, for example—and how it worked.

On the level of commentary, I want to add a bit more about my treatment of the Heinz Dilemma in these chapters, as this goes to the very heart of how creativity relates to ethics as traditionally conceived.

Ethical philosophers typically consider the Kohlberg dilemmas illustrations of the divergences and conflicts between major ethical theories, especially between utilitarian and deontological theories. And of course if that is your interest in the dilemmas, you can alter them in various ways to close off the possibility of other alternatives. I have even seen ethics textbooks in which students aren't considered to have understood an issue until they identify "the" dilemma that is supposed to lie at the root of it.

The problem, of course, is that this essentially makes ethical problems dilemmas by fiat. It simply *builds in* the assumption that dilemmas are, after all, what we typically face. But are they? How can we know, without creatively seeking alternatives? This requires different attitudes from the start, as I have tried to show; and I hope it is also evident from these chapters that many alleged dilemmas actually can be resolved or at least constructively reframed. The supposed dilemma between utilitarianism and deontological ethics itself has come in for some question, even theoretically; but even if these theories do conflict, one *could* construe their conflict too as another practical creative challenge—to so design social institutions that these different sets of values seldom or only harmlessly conflict in practice. That an entire approach to ethics should instead be built around the supposedly fundamental conflict is not obviously the best response. Surely, at the *very* least, such an approach is not entitled to claim with no further ado that it alone constitutes "ethics" itself.

Sometimes my students try to cook up dilemmas that really do allow no other options. That's a useful discussion too, I guess, but for the most part it is worth trying to set up the dynamics in the opposite direction. See if they can cook up situations that *look* like complete traps but really have dramatic new options. I offer some exercises to this effect in my book *Creative Problem-Solving in Ethics,* Chapter 3.

CHAPTER 17: MORAL VISION

Spend good time on all the exercises, especially the last one. They will not be easy, but they will also be very welcome, changing the key from so much moral debate and discussion now. You might also ask your students to try rewriting selected morally problematic stories in the style Ursula Le Guin adopts for "May's Lion." This is harder than it may look to them at first. The essential thing is to consider what kinds of different but imaginable cultural resources and practices would be necessary to transform our responses to a problem. For May, it seems to be a culture more at peace with other animals—and with aging and death—than ours, in general, and specifically it is a set of songs for dying. I say more about this in the notes to her story. Point out to students that it's not just a matter of new attitudes: that is only part of the story. How to reconstruct the practices that *create* and *sustain* and *enable* new attitudes—there's where the real work is.

CHAPTER 18: YOU CAN CHANGE YOUR LIFE

Students know about sexual "responsibility": it means using contraception and protecting themselves from STDs, right? The more dramatic themes in this chapter are more apt to get them thinking: the possibility of choosing not to have sex at all, ever (Clark's position); the possibility that gender itself is significantly a social construction (Queen's suggestion); the sharp but intriguing contrast between the two (Queen calls herself "sex-positive": does this mean that Clark is "sex-negative"?). Practitioners of celibacy make intriguing class speakers (hint: try for people close to your students' age); or anyway advocates of abstinence (hint: try to look at it as a spiritual issue but not one of religious dogma—it's too easy to dismiss if seen as only a sectarian position).

On the food question, bring in some vegetarian food (sometimes we cook right in class) or draw on vegetarians in the class. Sometimes my college's health program sponsors a vegetarian cafeteria in conjunction with health classes—maybe yours will cook for you. Look more into fasting—food abstinence, as it were. (And by the way, what's the connection between the food and the sex topics?).

These themes are very concrete, but the larger point of the chapter is the general way in which our responses to the world are up to us: once again, response-ability. Don't lose sight of that in the energy that naturally comes up around the food and sex topics. The exercises take the same theme in some other directions: keep it in focus.

CHAPTERS 19 AND 20: CHANGING THE WORLD

These chapters are meant as segues to actual action. Their chief aim is inspiration, advice, and empowerment. Supplement them, if you wish, by following up some of the references, looking at the biographies or websites of people and communities and organizations making a difference—especially in unexpected ways, and ideally close to home. Bring in some change-makers as speakers.

To go all the way, invite your class in turn to collectively undertake some kind of change project of their own. They'll need all their tools from this book. They'll also need time to frame it and put it into action, which creates a bit of a bind at the beginning of the class: it's as if you need to do everything at once. As I have mentioned, I myself start with only a skeleton of the book—Chapters 1, 2, 6, 11, 15, 16, 17, and 19—to help students frame and launch their own projects. We work through the rest as the projects get underway. Larger classes may need to launch several projects, ideally closely related, side by side. Teachers need to be constantly attentive to community needs, national or international possibilities (just check out, for one example, the variety of "students without borders" sites mentioned in Chapter 20), and ideally should build a network of contacts, so that the circles of change-making readily widen outward.

This work, I find, is always a bit of a whirlwind ride, but it is also always immensely invigorating, and the projects become great learning experiences for me as well as the students. And of course the students end up with the most vital message of all: that they *can* change the world! Best of luck to you and to them, and once again, I would love to hear of the work that you and they undertake.

Experiential Teaching in Ethics

SHARON HARTLINE

On my office door at Radford University hangs a poster that I received from an art major last year. This poster was his response to an assignment that involves advertising an ethics class to the students at our university. I asked students, "How do you sell ethics?" In this poster, the student drew two pundits who are literally "taking sides." Their faces are strained because they are yelling at each other across the paper. Between them appears the face of a young man. His chin is on his fist, the corners of his mouth are drawn down, and he looks out at the audience with a bored expression on his face. The caption reads, "Ethics: Where do you stand?"

What I love about this poster is that it is NOT an advertisement for ethics. It does not sell ethics, but rather it is a striking representation about what is wrong with ethics. It addresses the way in which ethical issues are often discussed in our society. It visually represents how ethics boils down to what Weston calls "polarized debates" where pundits line up on opposite sides of a page about abortion or stem-cell research and attempt to outdo their opponent or rehash the same debate we heard about last year. Quite frankly, it can get tedious and boring.

Similar limitations continue in many ethics classrooms. Many university courses focus on the Western philosophical tradition and show how these theories can be applied to ethical issues. Often, the rights theorists position themselves on one side of the page and the virtue theorists line up on the other; the Kantians locate themselves on the right side of the page and utilitarians stand on the left.

Is it important to cover different theoretical frameworks in class? I think so. Theories help us understand the social discourse about ethical issues and provide students with the tools to organize and evaluate personal and social issues. What becomes problematic is when this approach serves as the main (or only!) focus of the classroom. This focus can conceal the fact that there may be other ways to consider ethical issues that do not result in polarization.

Another problem lies in the methods that are used to teach in this fashion. If ethics is construed as debate, then how do teachers transmit knowledge and teach other constructive skills? Some of my students have studied ethics in high school or at community colleges before they enroll in my class. When I ask them about how those classes were taught, they tell me that their teachers lectured. Sometimes, teachers set up debates—the "Pro's" on one side of the room and the "Con's" on the other. Some teachers required students to pick a position with which they disagreed and then argue for that viewpoint.

There is a lot to be said for these techniques. Lecturing is a straightforward method of transferring information to students. Sometimes, it may even be necessary! Who really understands Kant's ethical philosophy when they read the original text for the first time? It's very useful to know how to think critically and be able to debate ideas. But is that it? Is this the best we can do? Are there other topics that are required for people to become ethically competent? Do we need other teaching methods? Can we improve our ethics classrooms? I think we can.

THE ACTIVE CLASSROOM: CONTENT AND METHOD

Weston's text makes it very clear that we can alter the content of ethics classes. We can incorporate material that attempts to move beyond the polarization that characterizes so many ethical debates and, for example, discuss how we can change ethical problems themselves. The focus is on "us" because ethical issues seldom arise in isolation from other people, and therefore, one person can seldom solve such issues by herself. Weston's text incorporates creative thinking, problem shifting, prevention, and opportunism in order to help students, individually and collectively, think and act beyond polarization.

Weston's text not only suggests changes to the content of ethics classes, but also implies a radical departure from traditional teaching methods used in ethics classrooms. His work shifts our attention to the kinds of skills one needs to enact ethics when they leave the classroom. No longer is ethical competency about retaining knowledge and acquiring rhetorical skills, but now morally mature people must actually know how to have fruitful discussion with people who hold differing viewpoints, how to resolve real conflicts and issues they will face in the workplace and community, how to uncover and critique the assumptions that inform social institutions, and how to unleash their creativity when they really need it.

Suddenly the classroom looks a lot different. Students practice skills and discover their capabilities as well as make mistakes. Teachers employ student-centered learning techniques like experiential learning techniques. These changes don't only come from teachers, for students are also responsible for the operations of the classroom. Students can request activities or develop their own to use for presentation materials.

So how does one go about developing techniques that give students (and teachers!) the opportunity to learn by practicing together and learning through group activities in the classroom? Now you may be thinking, "Oh no! She's going to talk about group work." Teachers may also be thinking, "I've tried group work, but students don't really do that much with it." Students may also be thinking "It's such a waste of time! And I always end up doing the work for everyone else in the group." Both of these outcomes can occur when group activities are used in the classroom. But there are also ways to structure group work, as well as quite different kinds of engaged classrooms, that sustain and even intensify everyone's focus on the real content.

THE EXPERIENTIAL LEARNING CYCLE: A TOOL FOR TEACHERS AND STUDENT PRESENTERS

While lecturing is useful, not everyone learns best by sitting and listening to someone else speak. We are multidimensional beings who inhabit bodies, rely on senses, recall memories, and make associations that help us process information. We learn through discussions, through visual cues, and through physical activities and personal experiences. People learn in all sorts of ways.

So how can we address these various modes of learning and still teach the content of courses? I've used the experiential learning cycle (ELC) to help me incorporate a variety of activities into the classroom. The ELC outlines the learning process and presents a structure for setting up activities in the classroom so that the learning process can take place. It relies on the idea that in order to learn we have to have an experience and then reflect on it. There are different models of the ELC. I use a four-stage method, presented in David Kolb's *Experiential Learning* (Prentice Hall, 1984). This model allows me to focus on different cognitive processes that help to clarify the concepts in my classes. But there are other models out there. See Kolb's *Experiential Learning Theory Bibliography 1971–2001* (McBer and Co., 2001). Find one that works for you.

As one would expect, the first stage of the ELC begins with the *experience or activity*. The trick is that the activities or experiences have to be carefully planned. Below I share with you a couple of the activities that I use. But you can use readings, labs, videos, games, puzzles, and meditation—just to name a few.

The second stage of the experiential learning cycle involves *reflection*. Here reflection usually means individual reflection upon the experience or activity. This is the stage where I hold individual students accountable for their learning by requiring them to write down their reflections about the material or relate their response to an activity. For part of their grade, students have to convince me that they REALLY participated in the exercise by at least sharing their reflections on the activity.

The third stage of the experiential learning process involves *generalization* whereby participants are asked to abstract from their concrete experience. One can do this as an individual exercise, but I often do this in groups. I find that because students have written something down from the reflection phase, they are more likely to participate in the group discussion and contribute to the process of generalizing.

The fourth stage of the experiential learning process involves *transfer or application*. At this stage I try to begin with issues that students really care about and interest them. Then I may move on to other issues that I think are important for them to consider.

Here's what I've learned by using the ELC to plan my classes. If I am going to use an activity, the goal has to be clear and specific. I also have to make sure we apply what students learned during the activity and reflection, preferably to something they cared about or find interesting. This isn't easy. It takes time and effort. Sometimes, even I consider just lecturing—it's actually much easier. Yet, it doesn't meet all my goals in the classroom. Something else I've learned is that I have to require verbal and/or written feedback from the individual and groups. Inertia is a fact of human life; we all feel it sometime during our life. So I have to find ways to respond to it in the classroom. A student once said to me, "I couldn't fall asleep in here if I wanted to!" I took it as a compliment.

The last thing I learned was that I can use experiential learning IN my classroom. In many universities "experiential learning" is the label that covers activities that take place beyond the bounds of the classroom through programs like internships and service learning projects. But you don't have to leave the classroom to participate in experiential learning.

EXPERIENTIAL LEARNING IN THE CLASSROOM

So how does one put this cycle into practice? The best way for me to answer that question is to elaborate several exercises that I have developed while using this text. The first activity, the Ethics Advertisement, is fairly simple and relies mainly on facilitation skills and a few leading questions on the part of the presenter. The second activity, the Moral Values Exercise, is a rather complex exercise. You need to bring different materials with you, and there are many parts to the exercise.

ETHICS ADVERTISEMENT

The first exercise is called the "Ethics Advertisement." This is a wonderful exercise to do the first week of class. Also, with a few minor changes this exercise can be used in any class. I use it when I teach other philosophy courses as well.

Experience/Activity

At the end of a class, I give students a sheet of newsprint and tell them that they have to advertise the class to the students at our university. They can use any medium—collage, drawing, painting, etc....I suggest that in order to do this exercise they have to figure out two things. First, they have to answer the question, "What is ethics?" Second, they have to figure out how to sell it! "How do you sell ethics?"

When they arrive for the next class, I ask them to hang their posters at eye-level on the walls and remind them to put their names on the front. I then ask students to participate in an "art show." I tell them that one can view art in two different ways. One can view art like the person who trots through a museum, quickly glancing from side to side with a puzzled expression on his/her face. Or one can view art like a student who has the audio-tour in hand, holds a pencil and pad in the other, and misses a lunch date because she or he is engrossed in the artwork. I ask them to approximate the latter person's mode of viewing. I ask them to take notes on topics, verbs, names, and other ideas that they learn from the posters.

Reflection

When they are finished viewing, I ask them to get into groups. Once in groups, the students pick a scribe to take notes on the information they gleaned about topics, verbs, and names as well as their individual reflections about the posters. (I collect the "scribes' report" at the end of class.) I ask them to come together as a class, and we put the groups' ideas up on the board.

Generalization

After we've listed their responses on the scribes' report I ask them "What is ethics?" At this point, someone inevitably states a standard definition of ethics—the study of moral standards/principles or the study of the standards or principles of moral conduct. (A few posters always include such a definition.) Then we explore that definition. What is a standard? What is a principle? What terms on the board refer to standards? What does one do with standards? If we move beyond that definition, what else can we say about ethics generally? Here are some of the ideas we often discuss:

1. Why study ethics? How does this "study" of ethics help us in our day-to-day lives? Ethics allows us to explore moral problems that we have to deal with on a daily basis. Here I talk about the distinction between ethical theory

and applied ethics. Theory can help us make sense of complicated issues like the issues presented on the posters.

2. People often point out that this definition is abstract. The real goal of ethics is to help us live our lives well. We usually talk about happiness at this point. Also, we discuss the ways we are already always in relationships that presuppose ethics—from the respect we grant a waiter to the trust we have of the drivers on the other side of the road. Someone inevitably brings up the fact that if we didn't have this trust we would never leave our homes! I read Judith Boss's quote, "Ethics is like air; it is pretty much invisible. In fact, for many centuries, people did not realize that such a substance as air even existed. So too we often fail to recognize the existence of ethics or morality until someone fails to heed it." [See *Ethics for Life: An Interdisciplinary and Multicultural Introduction* (Mayfield Publishing, 1998).]

3. "There are only two answers to ethical issues." I use this comment and talk about the polarization of ethical issues presented as decisions about right and wrong, pro and con, good and bad, or appropriate and inappropriate. We talk about whether this is the only way to discuss ethical issues. Sometimes we will get into discussions of compromise or prevention as other viable approaches. I ask the students if these problems can be viewed as opportunities for learning or development. Many are skeptical or reject the idea that one can approach polarized issues in any other way.

Transfer/Application

Next we take some of the ideas we discussed and apply them to topics that are presented on the posters—abortion, death penalty, premarital sex, underage drinking, and discrimination, among others. We discuss how standards are used to make moral judgments about these topics. I guide the discussion in order to bring out the point that people's convictions about standards are what create polarization with respect to the issues at hand. I also suggest that ethics isn't just about those polarized issues. I ask them for ethical issues that don't have to do with these polarized topics. They talk about relationships with partners, raising children, and even caring for pets. We talk about what it means to live one's life well and what it means to be a good person. Students often say that moral standards aren't enough. Emotions and kindness count. At this point, I talk about the Good Life and the unit on Greek philosophy, and we are ready to move into a closer study of ethics.

THE MORAL VALUES EXERCISE

I specifically call the Moral Values Exercise an "exercise." I used to call it a game, but eyes rolled when I said that. So now it is an "exercise." Remember delivery is important in gaining the attention of your audience.

Experience/Activity

When students enter the room, I put a card on each person's back with a specific moral value printed on it (e.g., responsibility, right to life, well-being, etc.). I also hand them a 3 × 5 index card. When everyone is assembled, I tell them that we'll be doing an exercise called the Moral Values Exercise, and that during the exercise they will receive clues regarding their moral value. I tell them that by the end of class each student will have to guess what moral value is on his or her back and what kind of value it is.

Then we review the operating definition of a moral value (that which gives voice to our needs and legitimate expectations that we have of ourselves and others) and we revisit the families of values and their definitions (the boxes in Chapter 6 and at the head of each chapter in the rest of Part II). Note that the structure of this exercise is flexible. You can highlight different categories of values. For example, you may wish to highlight the values of justice as a separate category.

Next, I describe the rules of the exercise. Here are the rules:

1. Find a partner.
2. Each person looks at the card on his or her partner's back and gives the other person clues regarding their moral value. "Good clues" tell what needs or legitimate expectations that moral value gives voice to. "Good clues" should not state the moral value or what kind of value it is.
3. Write down the clues on the 3 × 5 card. You will need them later.
4. When you are cued, find a new partner and repeat the process.

I have students do three or four rounds with different partners. I give each pair about one to two minutes to give each other a clue. I check in with them and if many of them still need a clue, we do one or two more rounds. At this point, students sometimes ask me what they should do if they know what their value is. I ask them to continue to collect clues.

Reflection

Next I ask students to work by themselves and fill out a worksheet with some reflection questions. I ask them to do four things: write down their three best clues, guess what their moral value is, tell what family (kind) of moral value it is, and explain what they learned about their individual moral value through this exercise. On the walls around the classroom I put up cards with the titles of the families of moral values written on them. After students have completed the worksheet, I ask each student to go to the area by the card that indicates the type of moral value on his or her back. After groups form around each of these cards, I have each group stand up and show their backs to the class. Many students are in the correct group. If a student has not identified their type of moral value correctly, I ask a student to direct them to the correct family and then explain why that value belongs to that family. This is one way to incorporate "student teaching" into the exercise.

Generalization

This stage, in which students are asked to abstract from their concrete experience, relies heavily on the facilitation skills of the teacher. When I facilitate during this stage, I start with getting them to verbalize their responses to the last question on the handout—what did you learn about your moral value? Then through questions and discussion, I get them to generalize further. Here are some examples of their statements and ideas for facilitation of the subsequent discussion.

> *a. "Our moral values were in the rights category, and they were easy ones."*
> *"We use this language all the time."*

[Facilitation questions: Is that the case in all cultures? Are there other values that take precedence in our culture?]

> *b. "Our parents use virtue language, and we resist it!"*

[Facilitation questions and responses: Do certain groups rely on certain kinds of language and use certain types of values? We discuss which people tend to use which kinds of values. For example, economists/teens often discuss goods; religious leaders/parents often address virtues; lawyers/disenfranchised groups often speak of rights.]

> *c. "Everyone gave me the same clue." "People have very different expectations regarding this moral value."*

[Facilitation questions or responses: Why do we agree (or disagree) on the meaning of this value? Is this a group phenomenon, e.g., parents, children, professionals? Is this true of our culture? Is it true of other cultures?]

> *d. "I didn't know what I was because people don't know what this value means."*

This comment was actually made about nonmaleficence in a nursing class.
[Facilitation questions or responses: What does the principle of no harm mean, and will it mean the same thing to your clients/patients? Will you have to explain your intentions as you hurt them? I remind them that all healthcare professionals cause pain to their patients sometime. In addition,

we discuss the difference between knowing terminology and understanding an ethical principle.]

I also used this comment as a "teachable moment" about accountability. (Nonmaleficence was discussed in their reading the week before we did this exercise.) Students recognize that in our classroom if they aren't prepared they let their classmates down. In addition, I use this as a bridge to the next stage because it brings us to the issue of recognizing and using principles. This is related to application, the final stage.

Transfer/Application

For this stage of the Moral Values Exercise, I use case studies or scenarios. When I use this with nursing students, I give them cases in medical or professional ethics. I ask students to identify the major moral values that define the case. I also ask them to explain what they would do if they were the professional in the case, and why they would choose that approach. Students get to practice identification, definition, and application of values to a specific situation that they care about. After all, they may find themselves in a similar situation one day.

Here is what I observe: Most students are very good at identifying the moral values of the persons with whom they identify. But many have difficulty identifying moral values of people with whom they do not identify or about whom they have negative judgments. One of the major tasks that I have is getting them to be objective, that is, to see the perspectives of all parties involved in the situation. They also bring up concerns about the conflicts of the values that they see operating in case studies. These concerns propel us toward Chapters 7–10 about different families of values, Chapter 13 about ethical dialogue, and Chapter 14 about how we can resolve conflicts between moral values.

These are, of course, only two examples of how one can use the ELC to develop a class that requires student preparation and participation and allows students to learn thinking and communication skills by using these skills. Remember that there are many types of materials already available to use. For example, you can show a short film, design meaningful questions for reflection and generalization, and find a text or scenario to which students can apply their conclusions. The possibilities are endless and the outcomes rewarding!

CREATING A TEMPORARY COMMUNITY

I want to leave you with a few suggestions for creating an active classroom in which experiential learning techniques can succeed. I have found that experiential learning exercises work best in classes that become *temporary communities.* Respect and beneficence are two main components of communities, for they create an atmosphere in which people feel valued and are willing to participate. When people respect each other, they take each other seriously. They listen to each other's ideas. In addition, beneficence motivates people to help each other so that they provide constructive criticism and nurture initial thoughts of their classmates. In turn, students facilitate discussion by tracking the implications of others' ideas. So how can we promote these values and activities in the classroom?

1. NAMES, NAMES, NAMES!

I find it quite ironic that in ethics classes where we discuss respect for individuals, a student can remain "The Woman in the Second Row, Third Seat" or "You there" for the entire semester! Teachers and students don't always know the names of other people in the classroom. Knowing these names fosters respect, assists with discussion, and helps to create the Active Classroom.

I often start my semester with a name game. I ask students to rise and get into a circle. I then give these directions. The first person, whoever begins the exercise, says his or her name. The second person says the first person's name and his or her own name. The third person states the first person's name, the second person's name, and his or her own name. The game continues until each person in the circle has had his or her turn. I always go last and say everyone's names. This game often requires that students ask for other students' help (some forget the names) and that students offer this help. At the very beginning of class, it sets up the kind of reciprocity that is required in communities and in the Active Classroom.

2. EVERYONE'S RESPONSIBLE

It's everyone's responsibility to create an Active Classroom. Traditionally, students are not responsible for how the class operates, except when they are required to make presentations. In the Active Classroom, everyone contributes to the pace, flow, and content of the class to some extent. One problem is overcoming inertia. Inertia is a fact of life with which we all struggle. We're all busy and we get tired. I try to find ways to make all the members of the class accountable for the class. I often require students to hand in individual or group writing to account for their reflections during the class period. In addition, I know my students' names and they know it. I can call on them at any moment. Students don't always find that a comfortable position, but they tell me that it keeps them on their toes.

In order for students to be responsible and effect change in the classroom, they must be given the opportunity. Thus, I use a variety of feedback mechanisms. One is called the "minute card" that was suggested to me by

Bethany Bodo. It's no surprise that she is the director of Academic Assessment at Radford University! At the end of class I give students a slip of paper with the following items printed on it.

1. What concept do you feel is the most important one you learned regarding this topic?
2. What one concept is unclear to you?
3. What is one question you have about this topic that you would like to have answered?
4. Think of one real-world situation in which a concept from this topic is demonstrated.

I collect these papers, and I use them to review and to inquire about what we need to revisit and how we should do that. I use another feedback form on which I ask students to evaluate their performance and my performance. I ask them to give suggestions for changes and improvements of the course. I also ask them to explain how these changes will assist their learning process. This last item requires that they reflect on learning and how they learn. There are many ways to collect feedback, but all of them require students to take responsibility to some degree for their learning and how the class operates.

3. DIALOGUE!

Presenters need to remember that the attention span of a person can only be pushed so far. If you use lecture, break it up with shorter activities. I often begin with a summary of ideas and then have students break into groups and then finish the class with discussion and lecture. I also have students write questions down during class and we work our way through the material. Inevitably, if I address a question in writing, verbal questions follow and before you know it we're talking about the material. If all else fails I ask students to think of a concrete experience in their lives. People can usually talk about themselves and these experiences can be used to illuminate the material.

4. MAKE MISTAKES, PLEASE!

Very few people get anything "right" the first time. It takes time to experiment with and perfect new methods. If a teacher or presenter is comfortable making mistakes as he or she tries new techniques, it gives other people permission to express themselves and take risks. If you're not making any mistakes, you're not challenging yourself and you're not learning.

Patricia Ryan Madson, founder of the Stanford Improvisors, discusses how she requires her acting students to make "at least one ego-crushing mistake per class to get used to the experience." In her chapter, "Make Mistakes, Please!" she describes the "Circus Bow."

> This is how circus clowns deal with a slip in their routines. Instead of shrinking and berating himself silently with "Oh, no, I really blew it!" the clown turns to the crowd on one side and takes a magnificent bow with his hands extended and his arms high in the air, proclaiming "Ta-dah!" as if he had just pulled off a master stunt. [See Madson's *Improv Wisdom: Don't Prepare, Just Show Up* (Bell Tower, 2005).]

I have started doing the Clown Bow in my classes when I stumble over words or get confused on a point. I find that it helps to create an atmosphere in which it is acceptable to make mistakes. This doesn't mean that one does not prepare or pay attention to details. This does mean that if an exercise does not go according to plan, it is all right to admit that and try another avenue. I find that this atmosphere helps students feel comfortable sharing their views.

CONCLUSION

I invite you to experiment with experiential learning techniques and wish you much success. If you would like to share or discuss an experiential exercise that you use in your ethics classes, I would enjoy hearing from you. Contact me at shartlin@radford.edu.

GUEST AUTHOR

Sharon E. Hartline is Professor in the Department of Philosophy and Religious Studies at Radford University, where she has also chaired the Peace Studies program. Her research interests include ethics, professional ethics, and Buddhism. She works extensively with health and human service programs at Radford University and serves on ethics committees in the New River Valley area in Virginia. She is actively working to promote responsible development in Blacksburg, Virginia, where she currently resides.

Index

Page ranges in boldface indicate readings by indexed named authors, or the indexed named works from which the readings are selected.